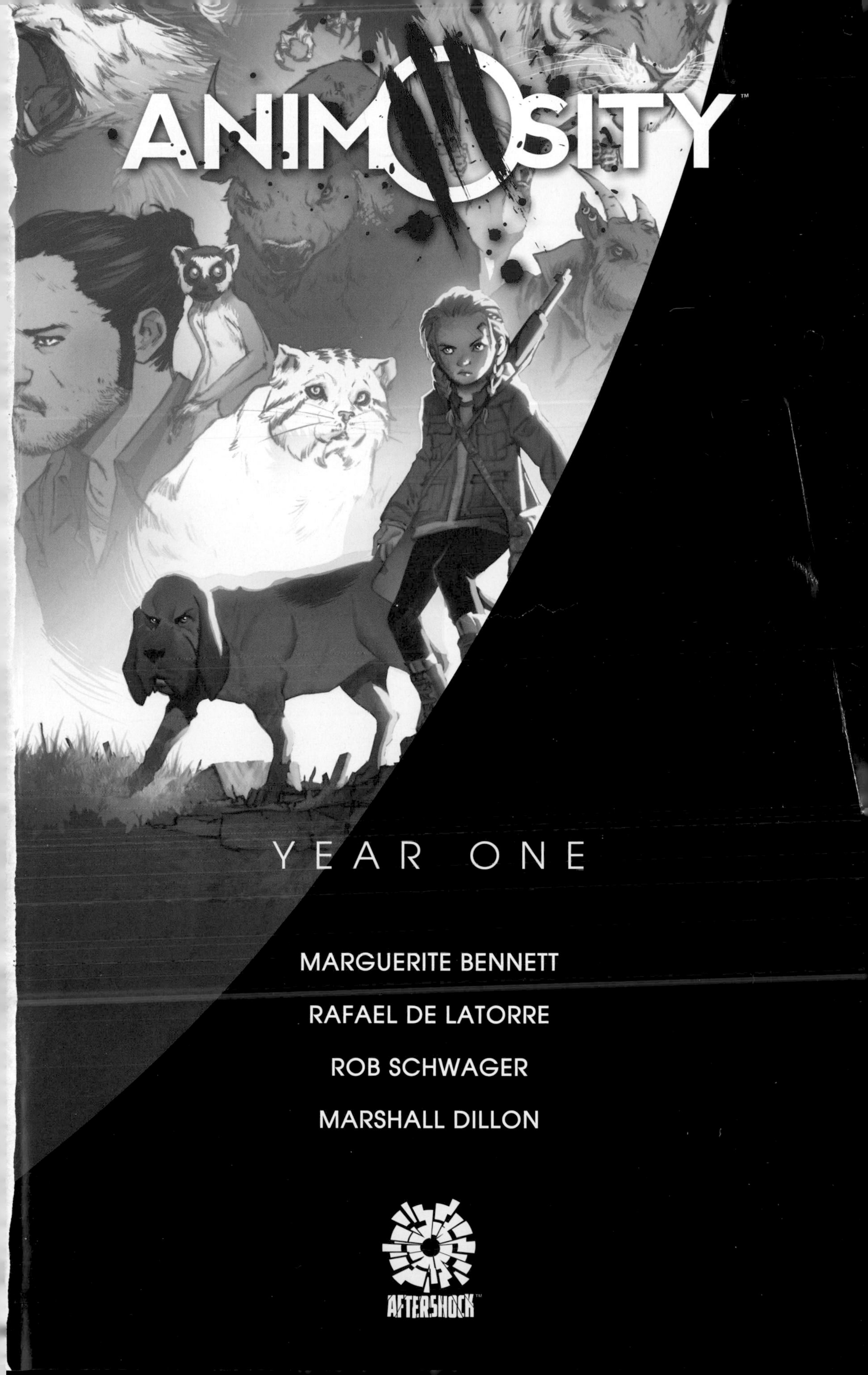

ANIMOSITY™

YEAR ONE

MARGUERITE BENNETT

RAFAEL DE LATORRE

ROB SCHWAGER

MARSHALL DILLON

AFTERSHOCK™

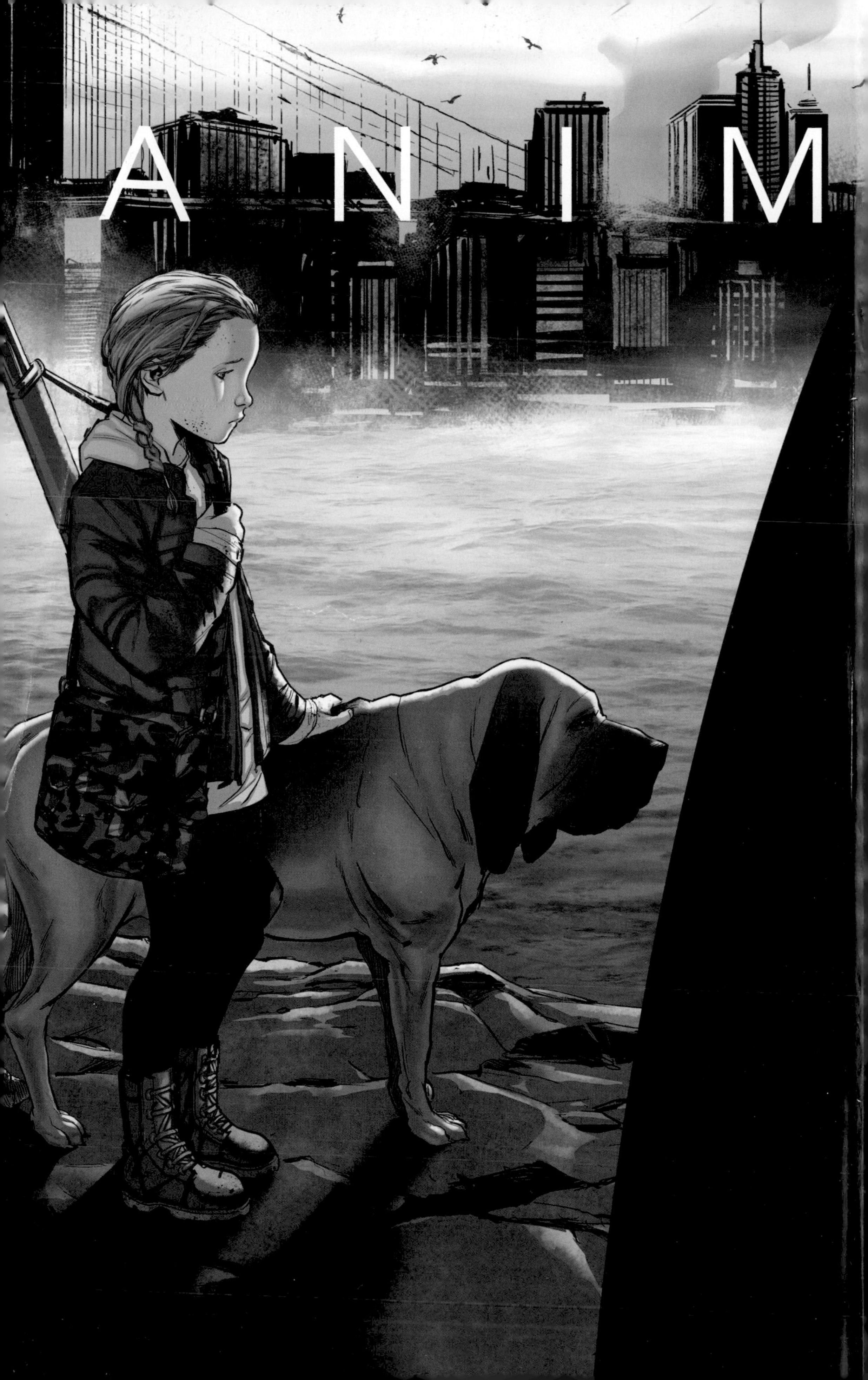
A N I M

O S I T Y

Y E A R O N E

MARGUERITE BENNETT creator & writer

RAFAEL DE LATORRE artist

ROB SCHWAGER colorist

MARSHALL DILLON letterer

RAFAEL DE LATORRE w/ **MARCELO MAIOLO** front & original series covers

KARL WALLER, ANDRE SZYMANOWICZ & **COREY BREEN**
WORLD OF ANIMOSITY art & design

COREY BREEN book designer

JOHN J. HILL logo designer

MIKE MARTS editor

AFTERSHOCK

MIKE MARTS - Editor-in-Chief • JOE PRUETT - Publisher/ Chief Creative Officer • LEE KRAMER - President
JAWAD QURESHI - SVP, Investor Relations • JON KRAMER - Chief Executive Officer • MIKE ZAGARI - SVP, Brand
JAY BEHLING - Chief Financial Officer • STEPHAN NILSON - Publishing Operations Manager
LISA Y. WU - Retailer/Fan Relations Manager • ASHLEY WYATT - Publishing Assistant

AfterShock Trade Dress and Interior Design by JOHN J. HILL • AfterShock Logo Design by COMICRAFT
Original series production (issues 1-8) by CHARLES PRITCHETT • Proofreading by DOCTOR Z.
Publicity: contact AARON MARION (aaron@publichausagency.com) & RYAN CROY (ryan@publichausagency.com)
Special thanks to CHRIS LA TORRE, SVEN LARSEN, TEDDY LEO, LISA MOODY & KIM PAGNOTTA

AFTERSHOCKCOMICS.COM Follow us on social media

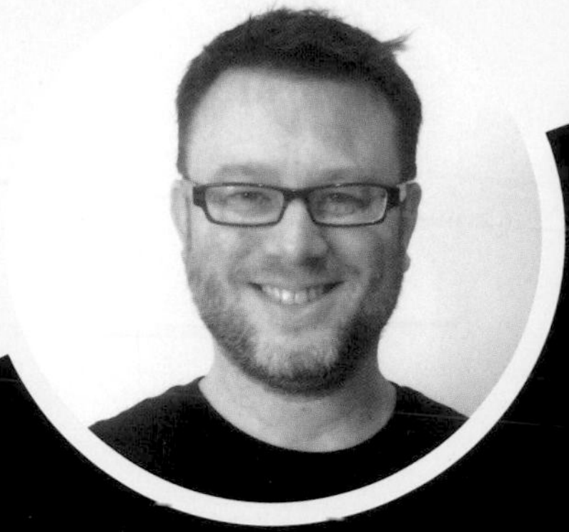

INTRODUCTION

"Greenlighting a project."

It's a term we've all heard used, especially in regards to TV shows, films and comic books.

Maybe some of you reading this know exactly what the greenlight process entails, maybe some of you don't. For the unenlightened, greenlighting means, *"collectively agreeing upon a project under consideration and deciding to move forward with it."* At least that's my definition of it.

Greenlighting usually comes about only after hours of listening to pitches, pouring over countless script revisions and agreeing upon the high concept, genre, target audience, tone, visuals, etc. etc. It generally involves more than one cook in the kitchen. It often means at least one or more people compromising their views to bend towards the general opinion of the majority...just to get the project moving. There are many, many factors at play in greenlighting: artists' availability, budget, schedule, consumer needs, the direction of the wind...and so on.

Greenlighting is a process. A process that takes TIME.

And then a project like ANIMOSITY comes along and breaks all rules.

Every few months, the AfterShock crew gets together for a summit to discuss everything from projects to strategy to branding to budget. One of the first summits we had took place in late 2015, just a month before our first launch titles hit the stands. Since a few of our crew live in Los Angeles, we usually conduct the ASC summits in their town. And since we have several creators that live in the Los Angeles area, it's customary for us to invite a few of them out to those famous AfterShock meals.

For this specific summit, we invited INSEXTS writer Marguerite Bennett out for some Mexican food in Santa Monica. We had a great time dining, all of us excited about the AfterShock launch looming just several weeks away. Shortly after dinner, we asked Marguerite if she had any ideas for down the road, possibly after INSEXTS ran its course.

"Well, I do have one idea," she said. So we all turned our heads and gave her our attention.

"One day, for no reason, the Animals woke up. They started thinking. They started talking. They started taking REVENGE."

And that was it. We were hooked. A high concept so pure, so engaging, that there wasn't any need for endless hours reviewing the pitch. No need for debating. No need for discussions. Unanimously, and without ever conferring to one another privately, we accepted it on the spot, at that table.

And not surprisingly, ten months later, ANIMOSITY became AfterShock's first breakout hit and without question, our flagship title.

I envy those of you reading this story for the first time. In this special YEAR ONE hardcover, we have the first two complete story arcs, the WORLD OF ANIMOSITY one-shot, plus dozens of behind-the-scenes extras like concept sketches, interviews and a cover gallery.

Enjoy this series that broke all the rules, that bucked all trends. Enjoy ANIMOSITY.

1

"THE WAKE"

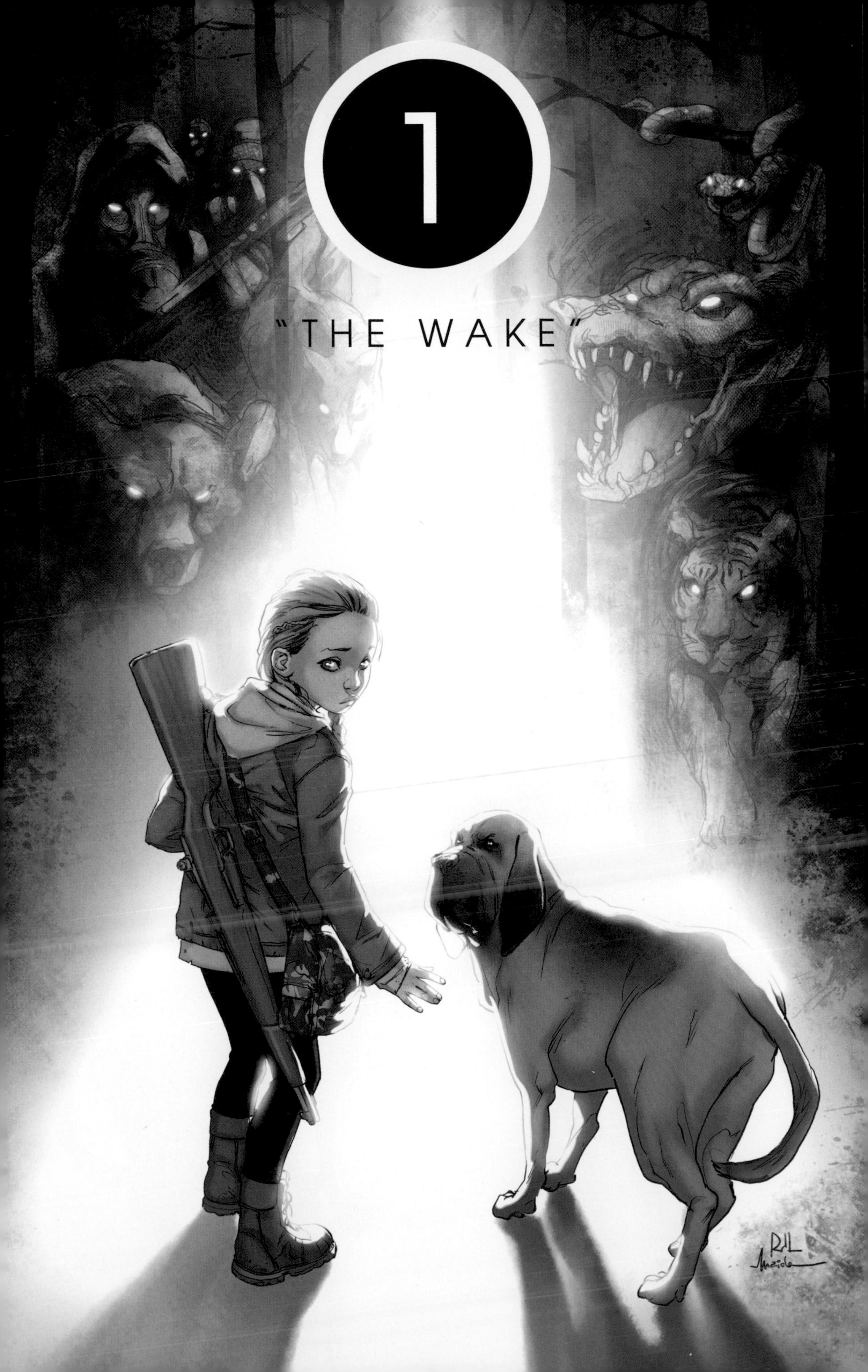

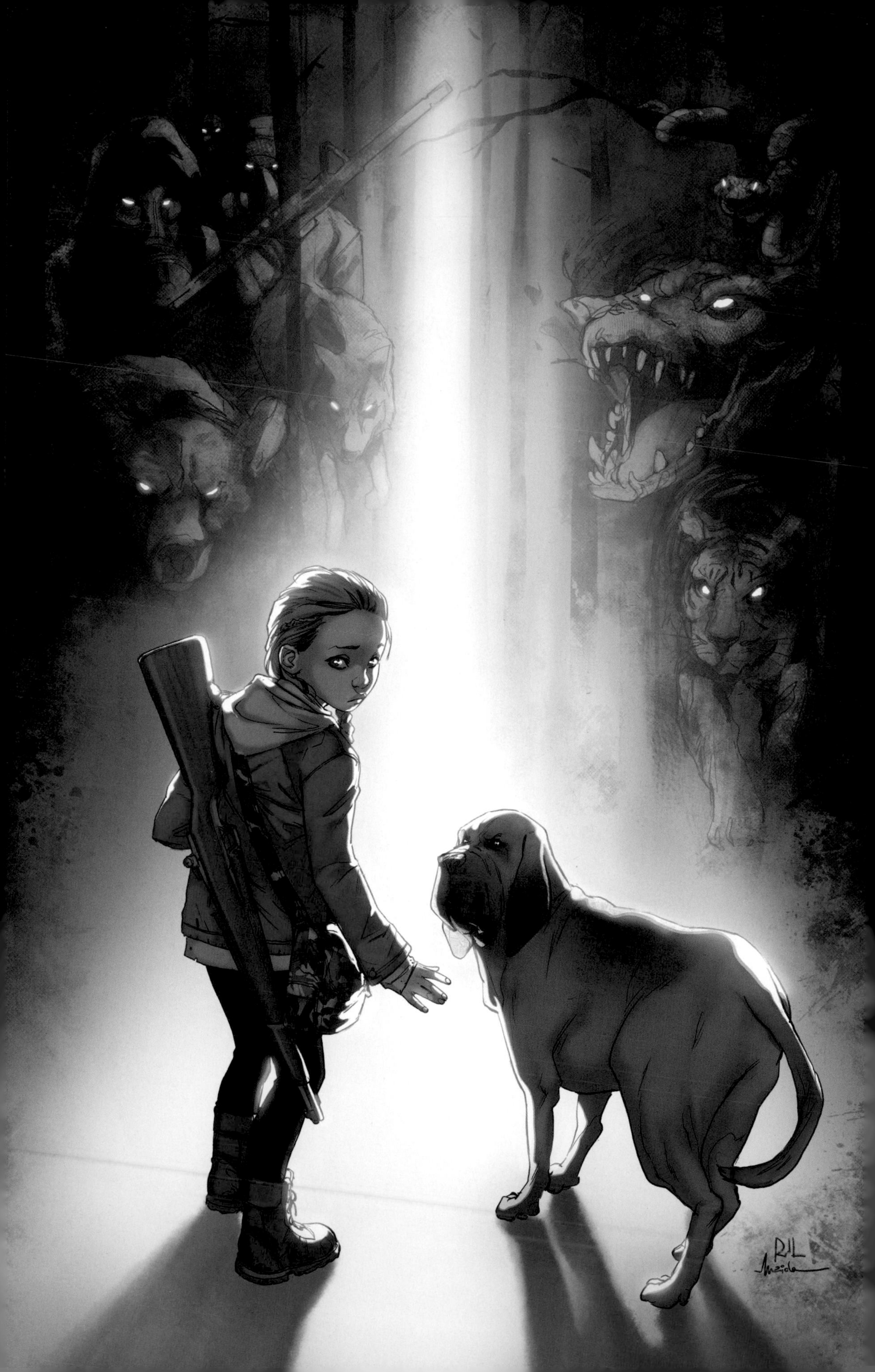

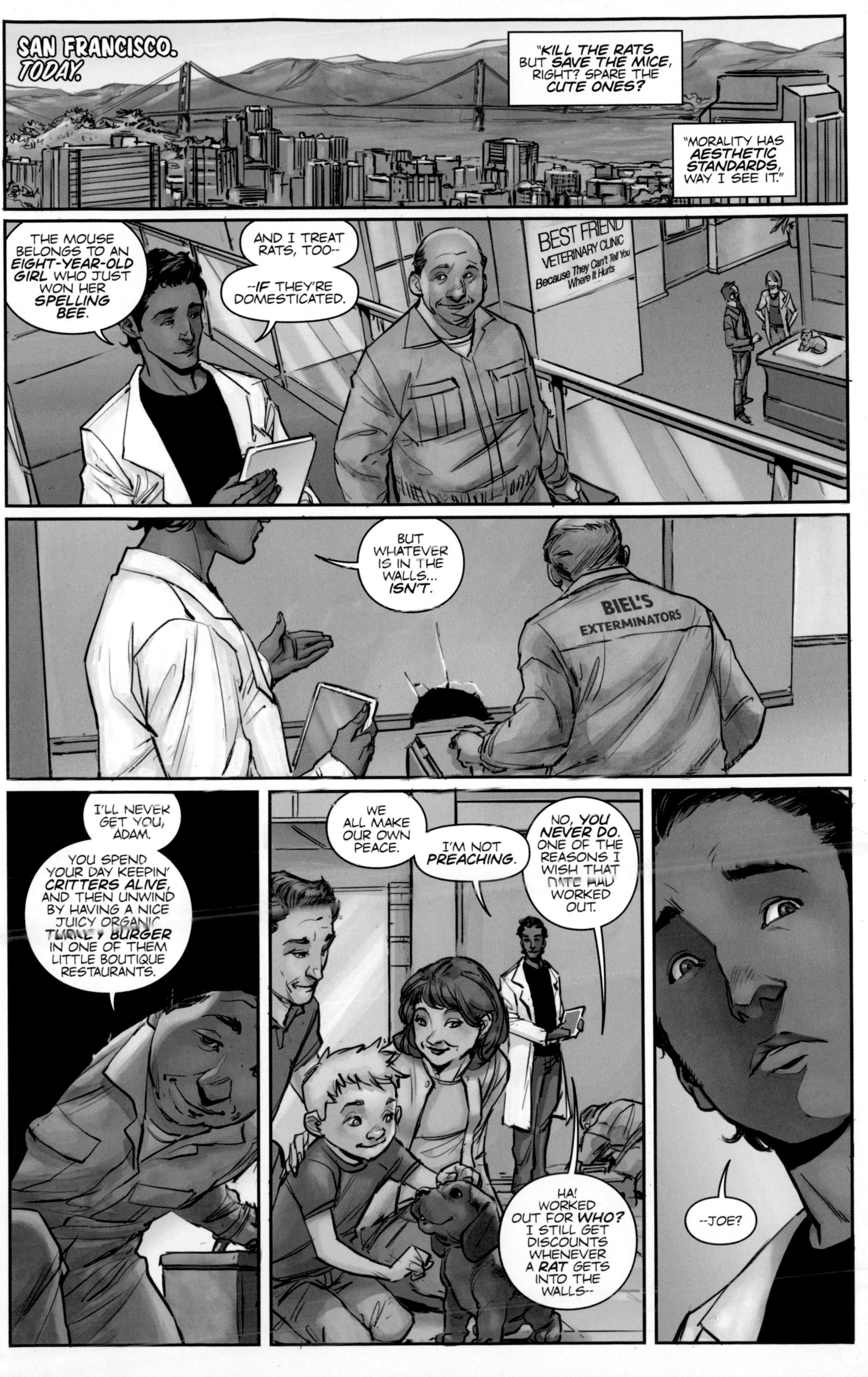
SAN FRANCISCO. TODAY.
"KILL THE RATS BUT SAVE THE MICE, RIGHT? SPARE THE CUTE ONES?
"MORALITY HAS AESTHETIC STANDARDS, WAY I SEE IT."
THE MOUSE BELONGS TO AN EIGHT-YEAR-OLD GIRL WHO JUST WON HER SPELLING BEE.
AND I TREAT RATS, TOO--
--IF THEY'RE DOMESTICATED.
BEST FRIEND VETERINARY CLINIC
Because They Can't Tell You Where It Hurts
BUT WHATEVER IS IN THE WALLS... ISN'T.
BIEL'S EXTERMINATORS
I'LL NEVER GET YOU, ADAM.
YOU SPEND YOUR DAY KEEPIN' CRITTERS ALIVE, AND THEN UNWIND BY HAVING A NICE JUICY ORGANIC TURKEY BURGER IN ONE OF THEM LITTLE BOUTIQUE RESTAURANTS.
WE ALL MAKE OUR OWN PEACE.
I'M NOT PREACHING.
NO, YOU NEVER DO. ONE OF THE REASONS I WISH THAT DATE HAD WORKED OUT.
HA! WORKED OUT FOR WHO? I STILL GET DISCOUNTS WHENEVER A RAT GETS INTO THE WALLS--
--JOE?

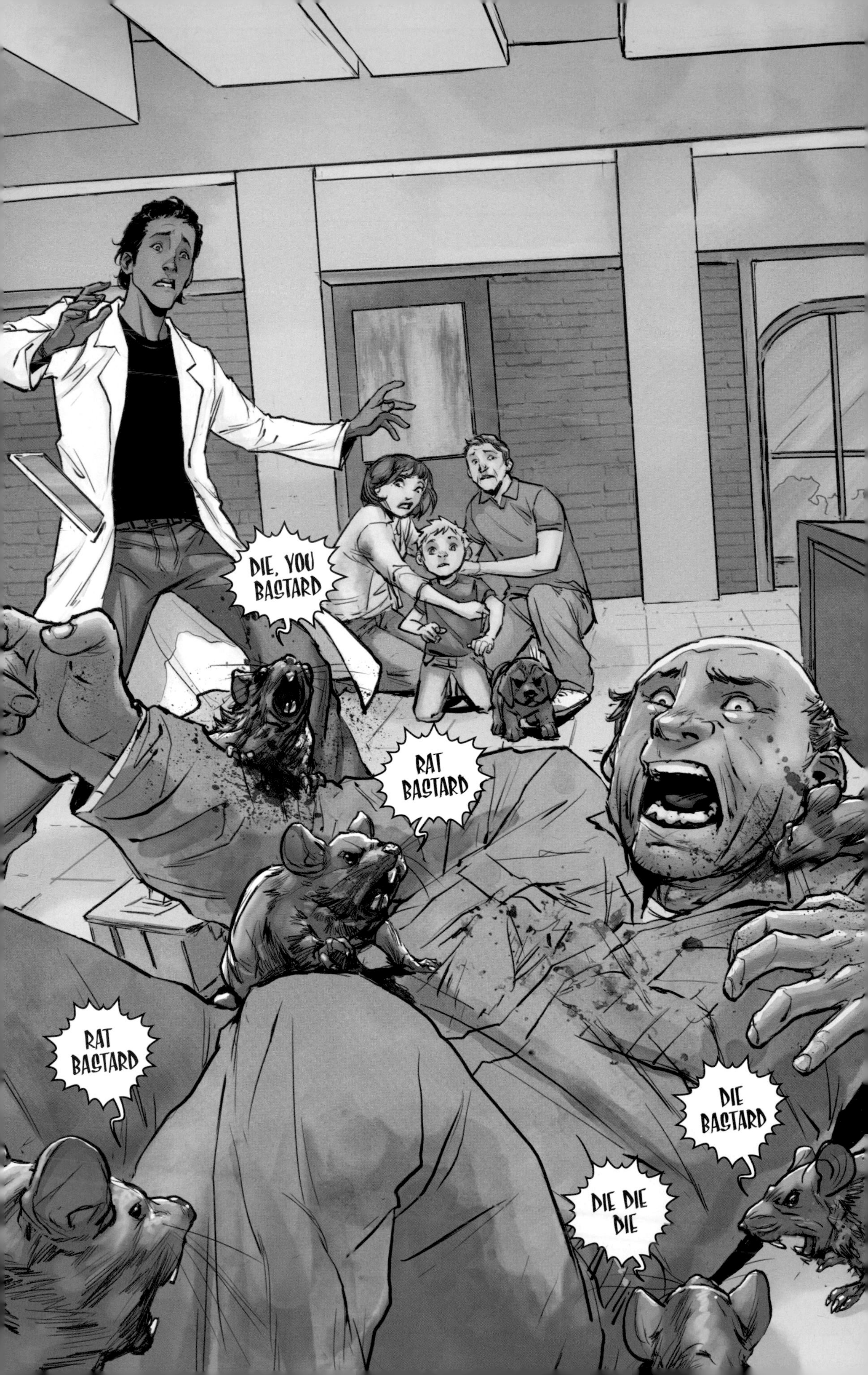
DIE, YOU BASTARD
RAT BASTARD
RAT BASTARD
DIE BASTARD
DIE DIE DIE

Then the Lord God said,
"Behold, I have given thee every plant yielding seed that is on the surface
of all the Earth, and every tree which has fruit yielding seed;
it shall be food for you;
and to every beast of the Earth and to every bird of the sky and
to every thing that creepeth upon the Earth,
I have given every green plant for food";
and it was so.

God saw all that He had made, and behold,
it was very good.

And there was evening and there was morning, and that was the sixth day.
—Genesis 1:29-31

Yesterday, God was in His Heaven,
the average American consumed 38lbs of meat per year,
and there were roughly 20,000,121,091,000,000,000 animals on planet Earth.

This number can be expressed as 20 quintillion,
or the equivalent of 20 billion billions,
and includes 500 trillion krill, 50 billion chickens, 1 billion cattle, 1 billion swine,
1 billion domestic sheep, 850 million goats, 600 million cats, 400 million dogs, 60 million horses,
40 million donkeys, 3 million whales, 500,000 elephants, 200,000 chimpanzees,
30,000 American bison, 20,000 polar bears, 8,000 cheetahs, 4,000 Komodo dragons, 1,500 pandas,
500 Siberian tigers, 100 red wolves, 45 amur leopards, 5 two-horned rhinos, two billion tons of fish,
and 10 quintillion insects.

There are also 7,250,000,000 humans, but who's counting.

As of 2016, there were over 1,203,375 species of animals,
and one species of human,
but as more than 10,000 new species are identified and categorized each year,
these statics are nebulous.

And since we got the data from the Animals, who knows?
Maybe they're fucking liars.

Mostly, what we know is this:

One day, for no goddamn reason, the Animals woke up.
They started thinking.
They started talking.
They started taking revenge.

We call it the Wake.

It's less dramatic than the Funeral.

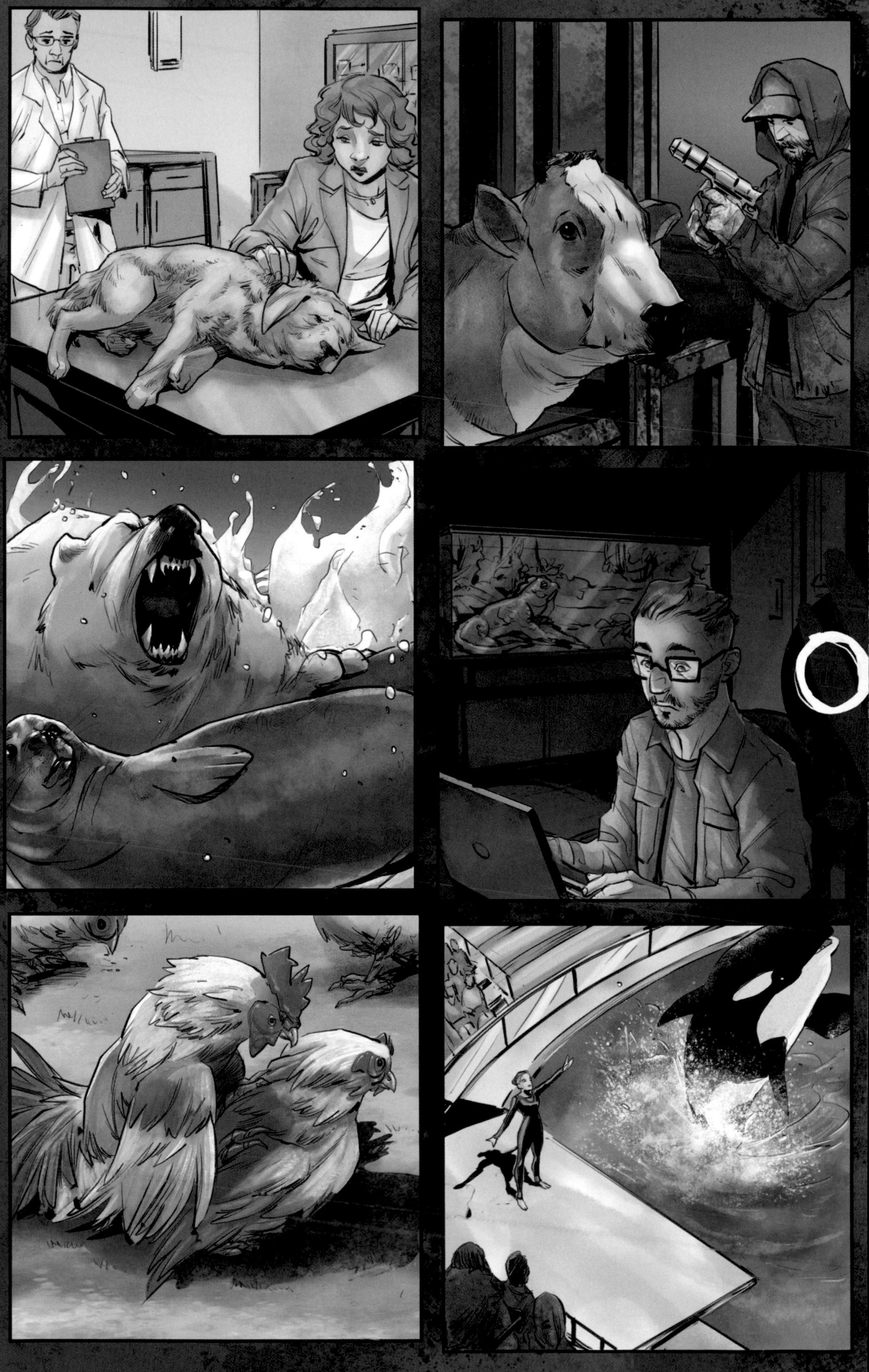

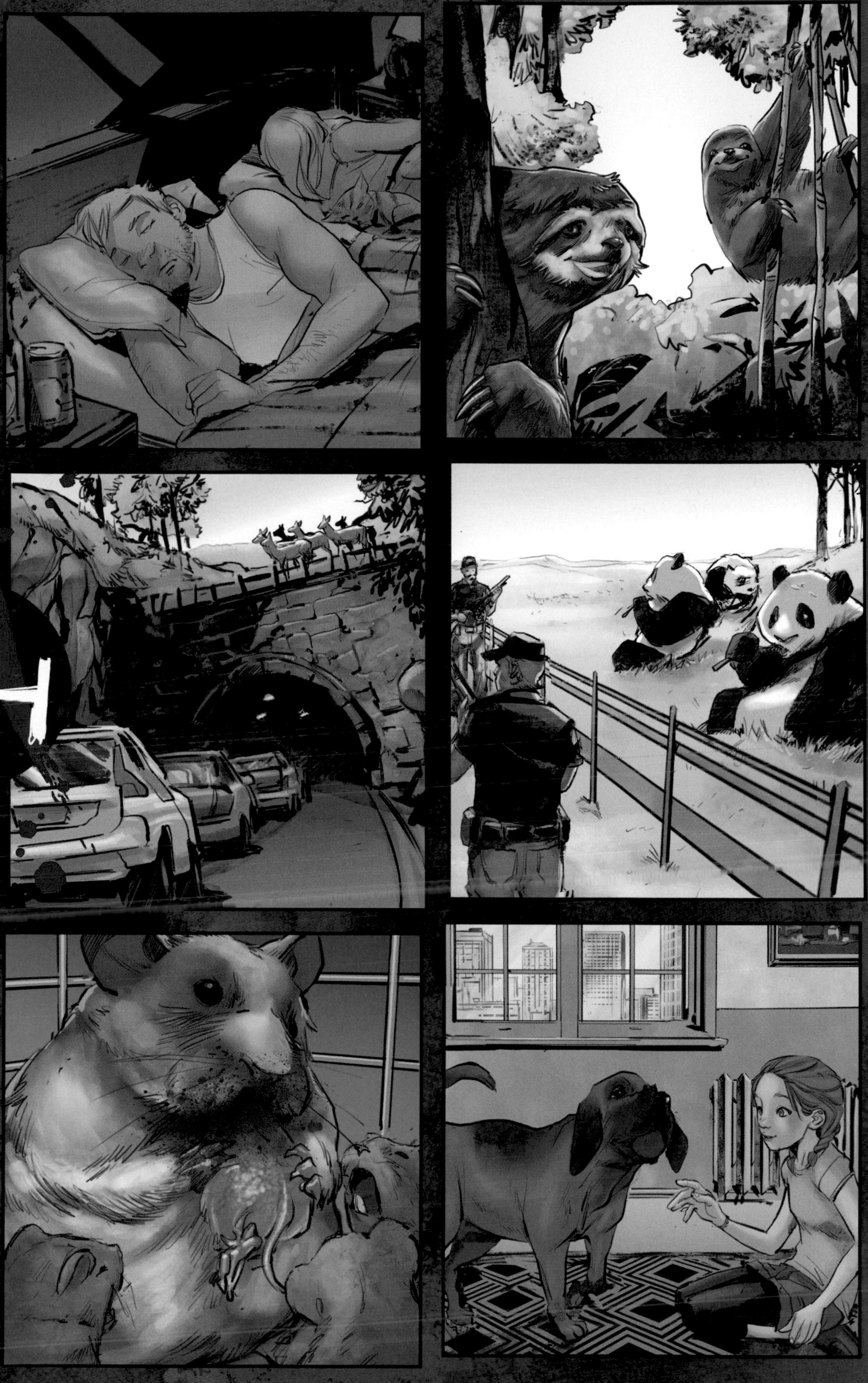

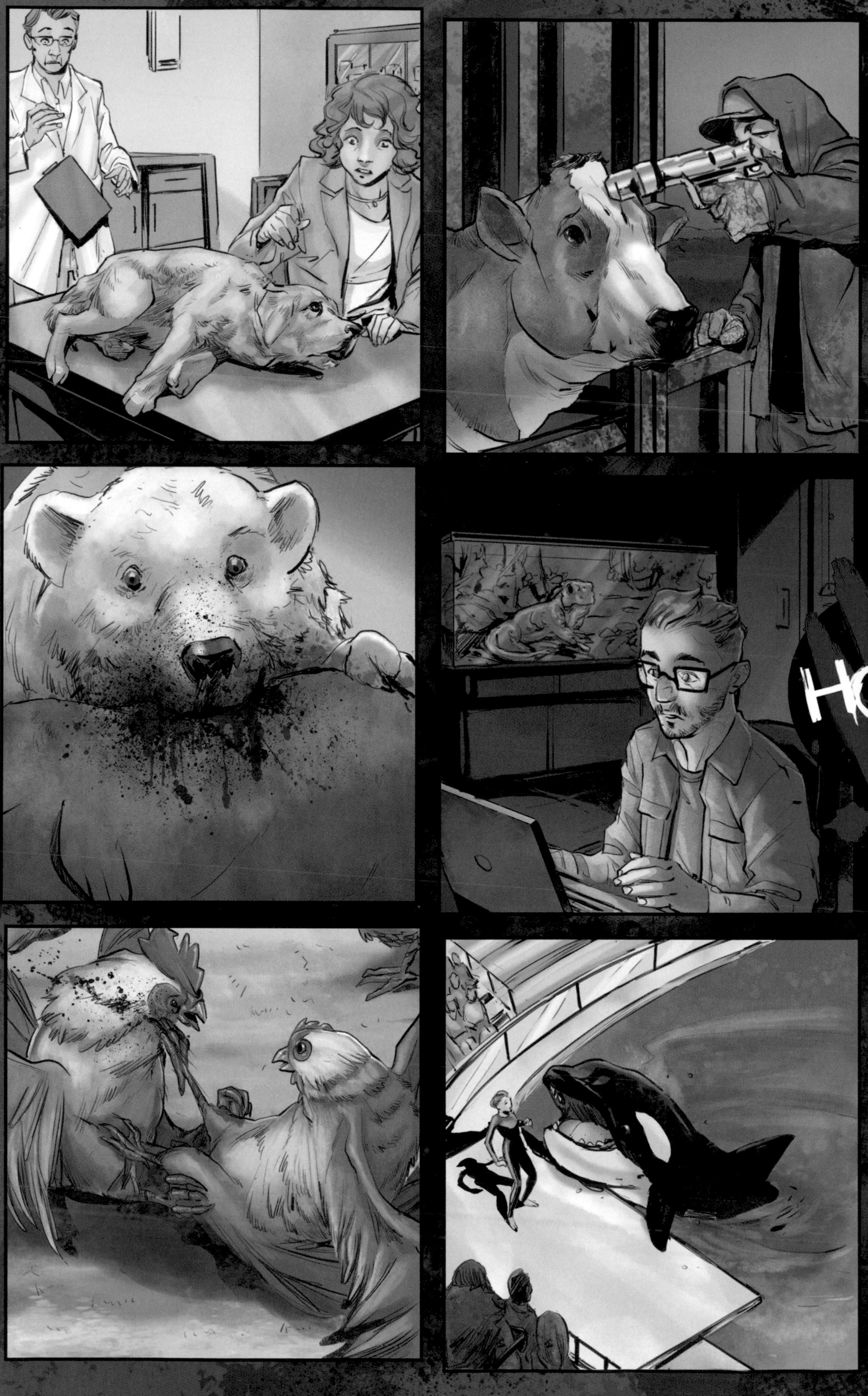
HO

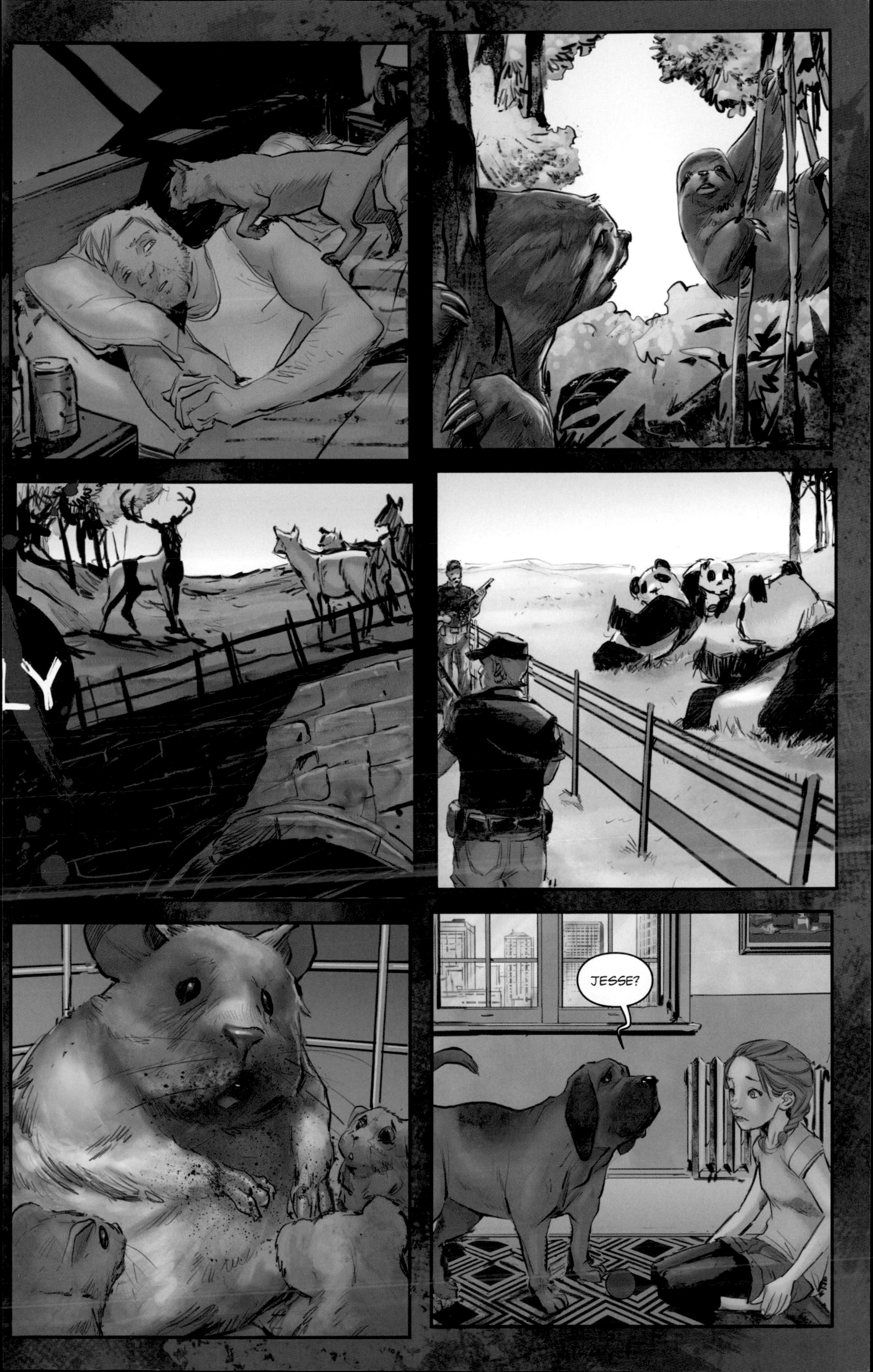
LY
JESSE?

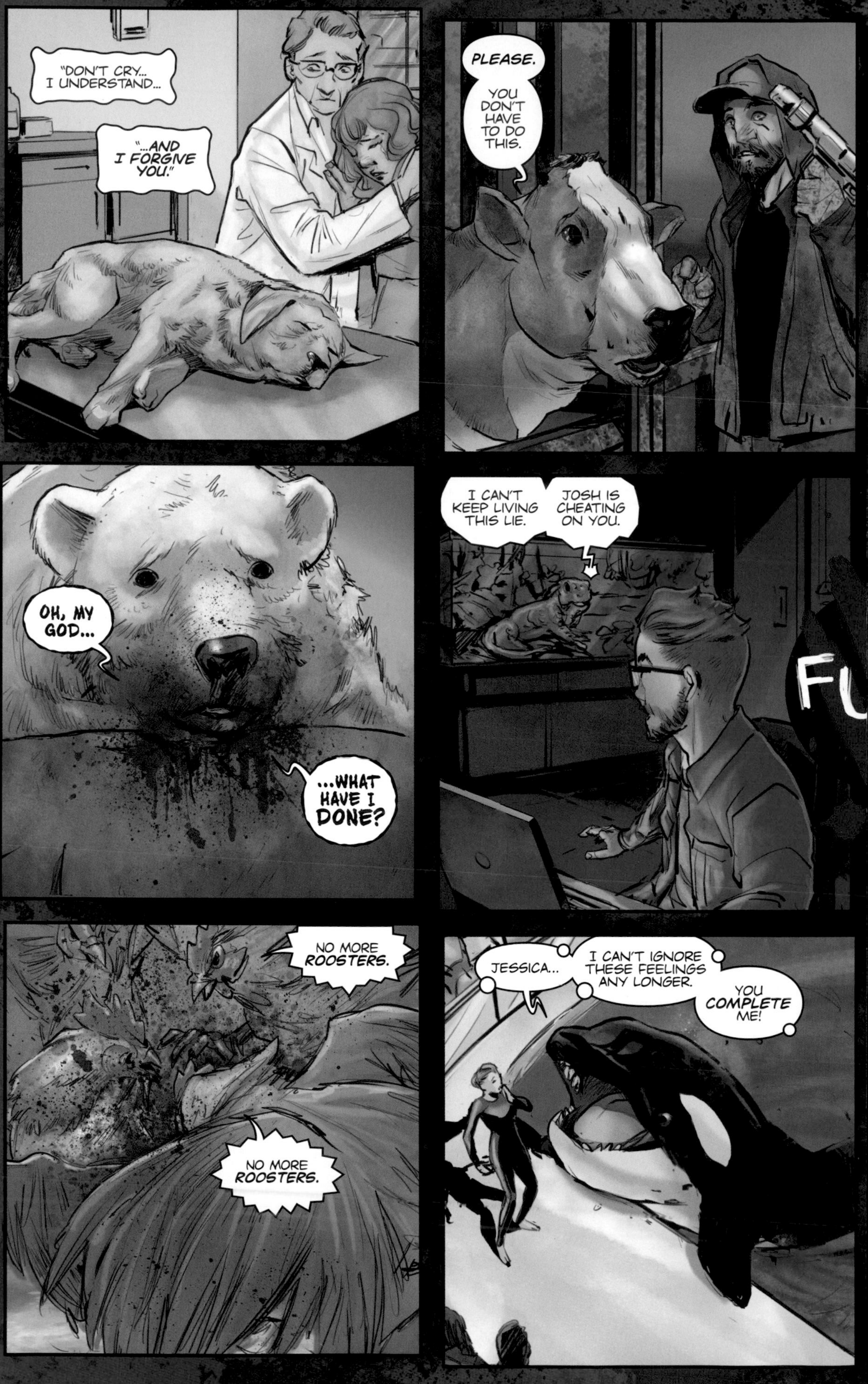

"DON'T CRY... I UNDERSTAND...
"...AND I FORGIVE YOU."
PLEASE.
YOU DON'T HAVE TO DO THIS.
OH, MY GOD...
...WHAT HAVE I DONE?
I CAN'T KEEP LIVING THIS LIE.
JOSH IS CHEATING ON YOU.
FU
NO MORE ROOSTERS.
NO MORE ROOSTERS.
JESSICA...
I CAN'T IGNORE THESE FEELINGS ANY LONGER.
YOU COMPLETE ME!

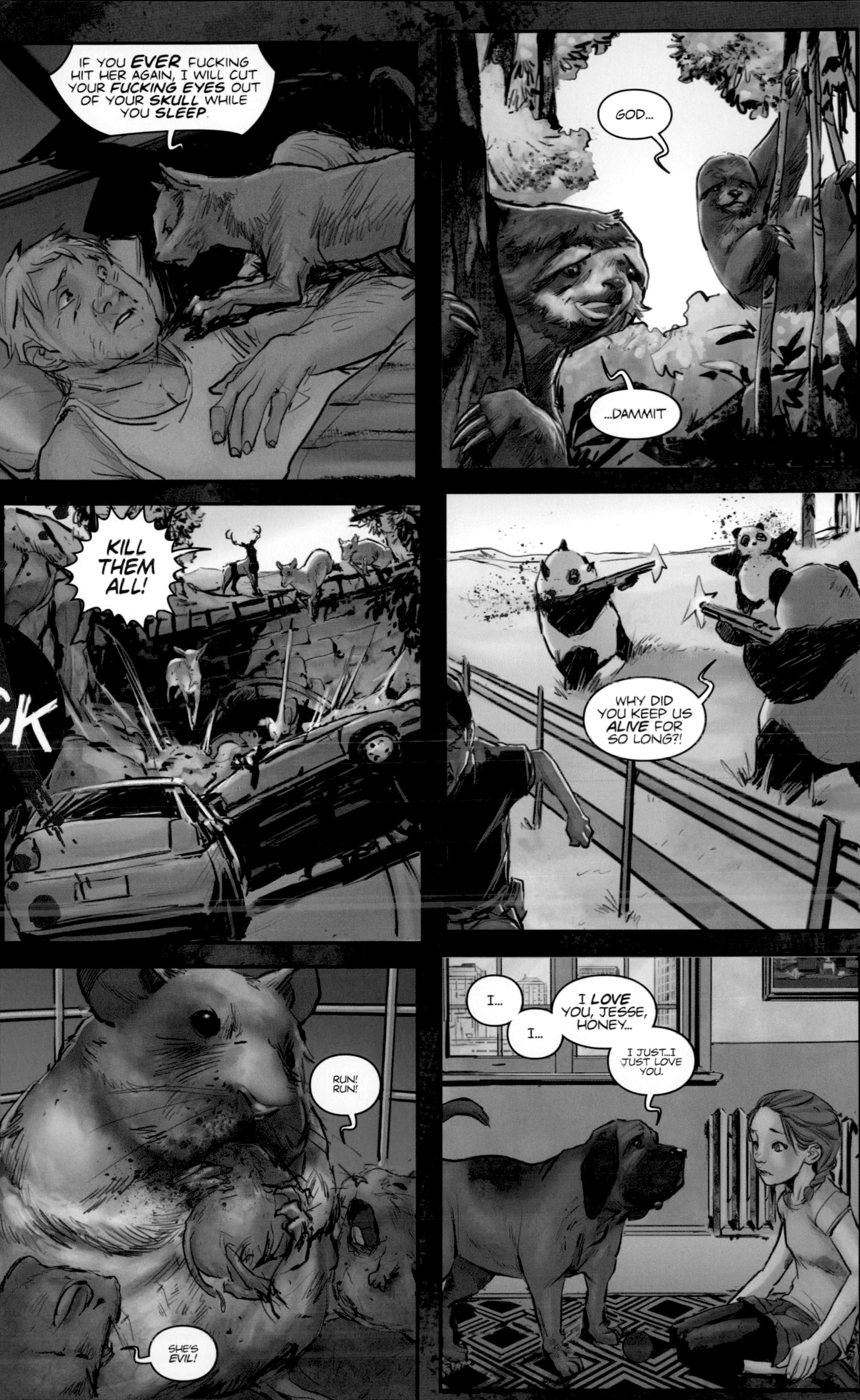

IF YOU EVER FUCKING HIT HER AGAIN, I WILL CUT YOUR FUCKING EYES OUT OF YOUR SKULL WHILE YOU SLEEP.
GOD...
...DAMMIT
KILL THEM ALL!
CK
WHY DID YOU KEEP US ALIVE FOR SO LONG?!
RUN! RUN!
SHE'S EVIL!
I...
I...
I LOVE YOU, JESSE, HONEY...
I JUST...I JUST LOVE YOU.

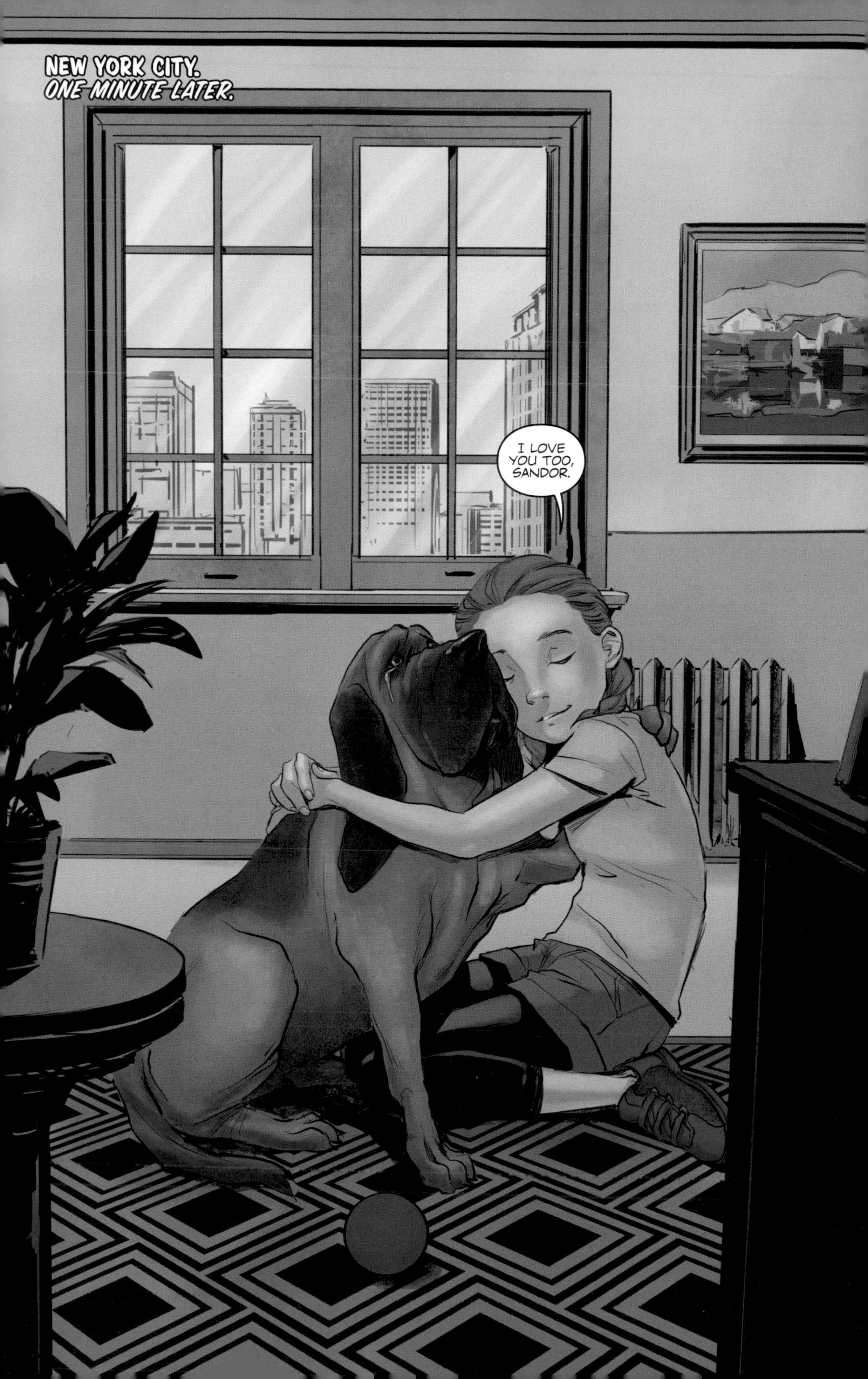
NEW YORK CITY.
ONE MINUTE LATER.
I LOVE YOU TOO, SANDOR.

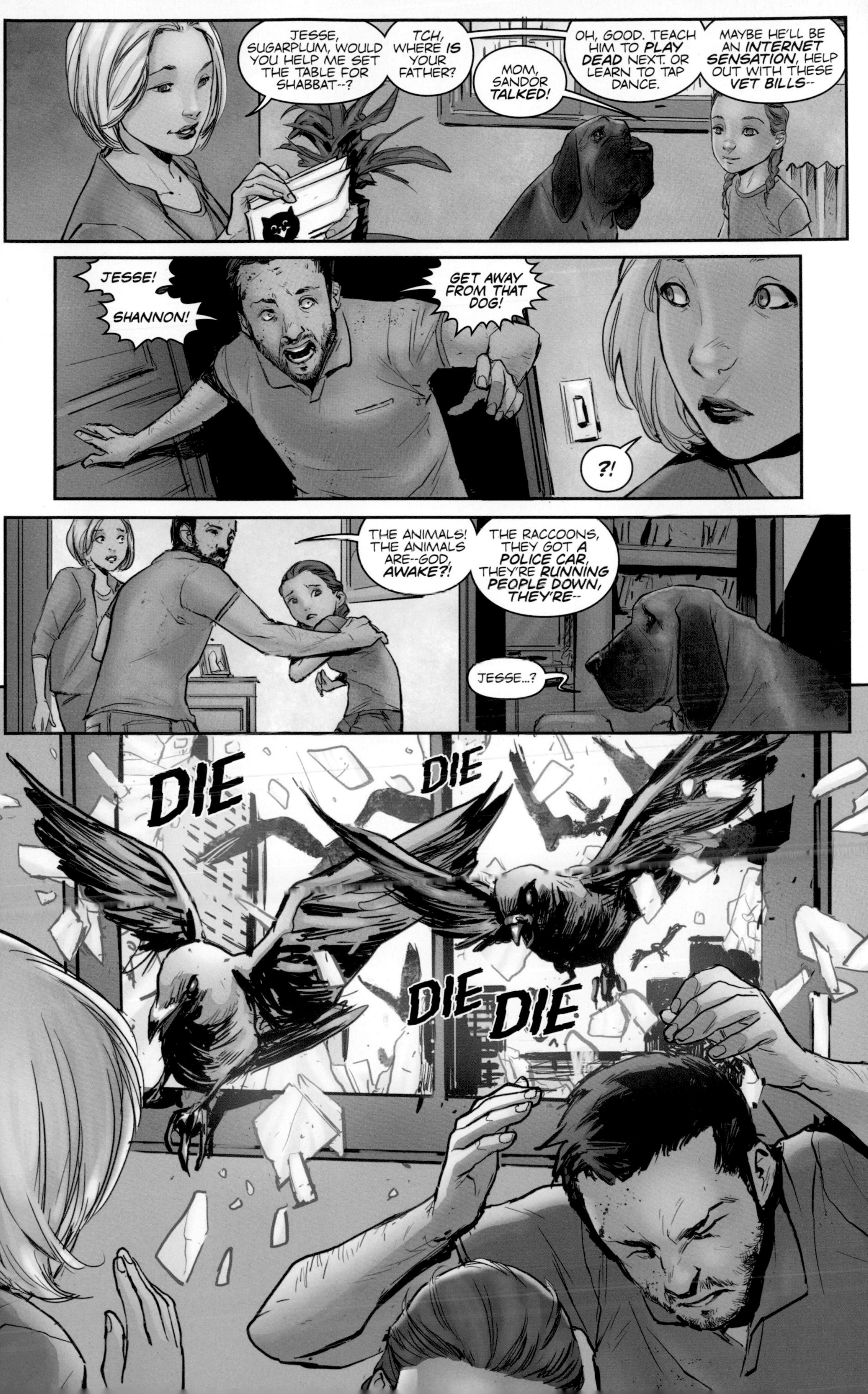
JESSE, SUGARPLUM, WOULD YOU HELP ME SET THE TABLE FOR SHABBAT--?
TCH, WHERE IS YOUR FATHER?
MOM, SANDOR TALKED!
OH, GOOD. TEACH HIM TO PLAY DEAD NEXT. OR LEARN TO TAP DANCE.
MAYBE HE'LL BE AN INTERNET SENSATION, HELP OUT WITH THESE VET BILLS--
JESSE!
SHANNON!
GET AWAY FROM THAT DOG!
?!
THE ANIMALS! THE ANIMALS ARE--GOD, AWAKE?!
THE RACCOONS, THEY GOT A POLICE CAR, THEY'RE RUNNING PEOPLE DOWN, THEY'RE--
JESSE...?
DIE
DIE
DIE
DIE

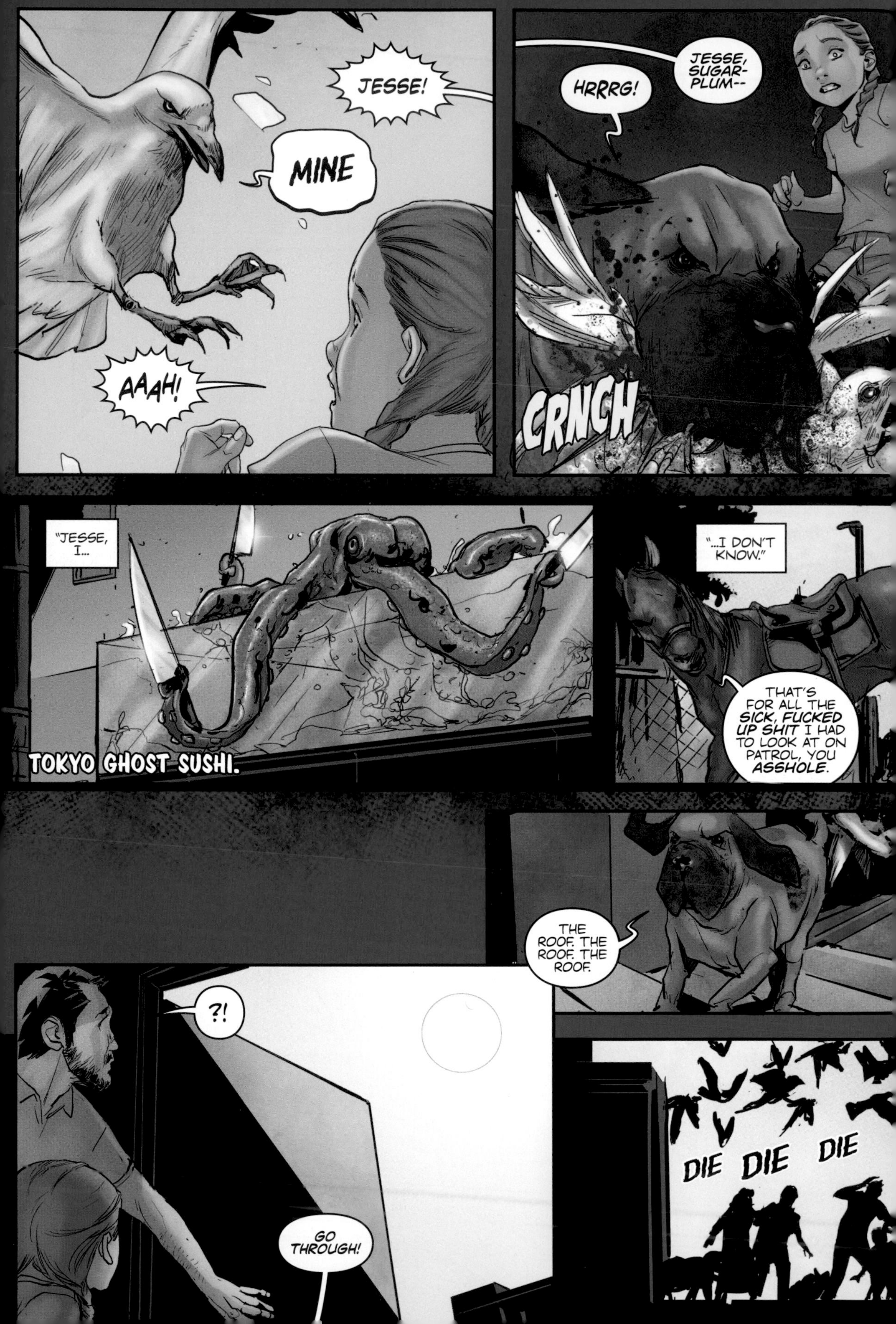
JESSE!
MINE
AAAH!
JESSE, SUGAR-PLUM--
HRRRG!
CRNCH
"JESSE, I...
TOKYO GHOST SUSHI.
"...I DON'T KNOW."
THAT'S FOR ALL THE SICK, FUCKED UP SHIT I HAD TO LOOK AT ON PATROL, YOU ASSHOLE.
THE ROOF. THE ROOF. THE ROOF.
?!
GO THROUGH!
DIE DIE DIE

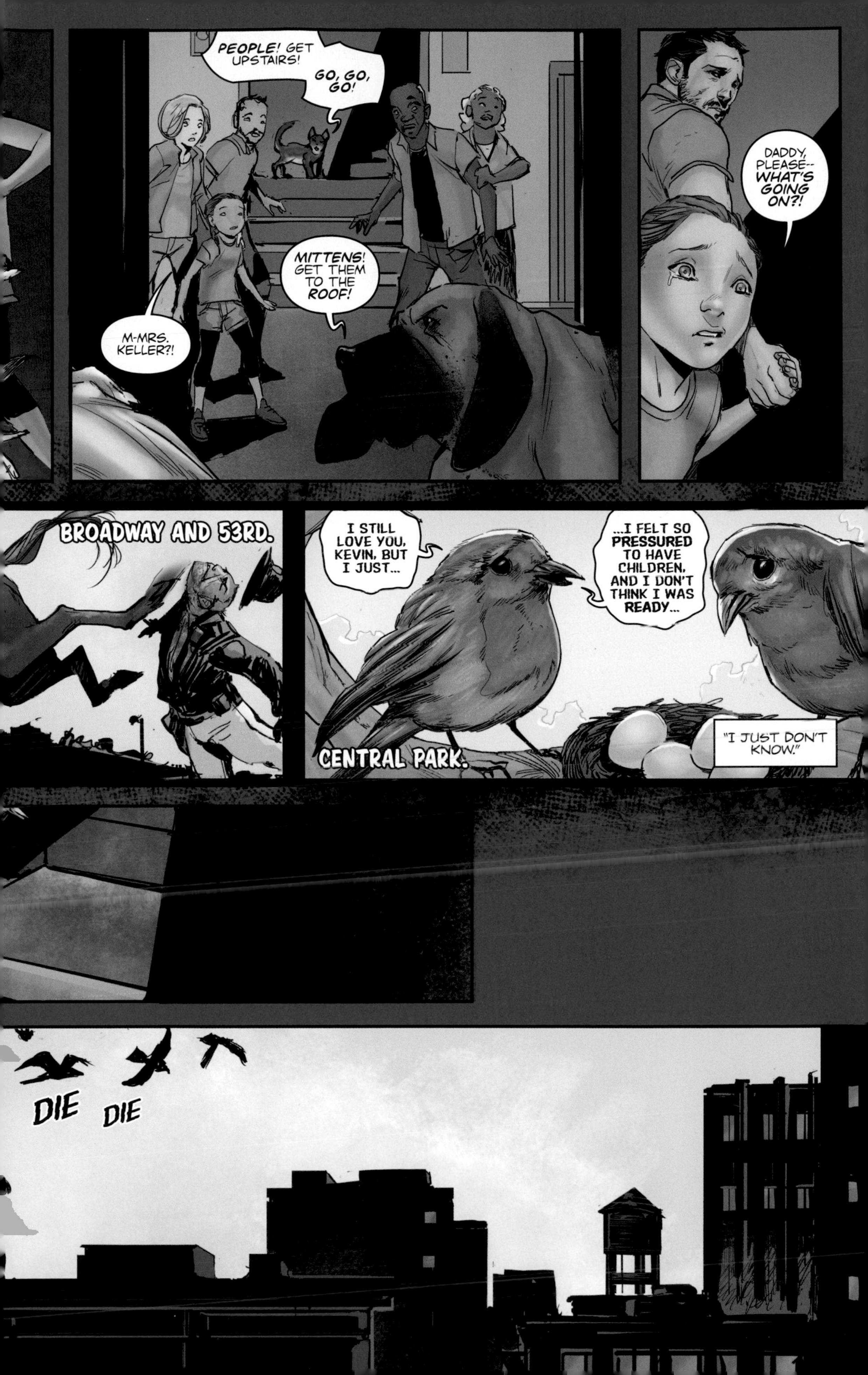
PEOPLE! GET UPSTAIRS!
GO, GO, GO!
MITTENS! GET THEM TO THE ROOF!
M-MRS. KELLER?!
DADDY, PLEASE-- WHAT'S GOING ON?!
BROADWAY AND 53RD.
I STILL LOVE YOU, KEVIN, BUT I JUST...
...I FELT SO PRESSURED TO HAVE CHILDREN, AND I DON'T THINK I WAS READY...
CENTRAL PARK.
"I JUST DON'T KNOW."
DIE
DIE

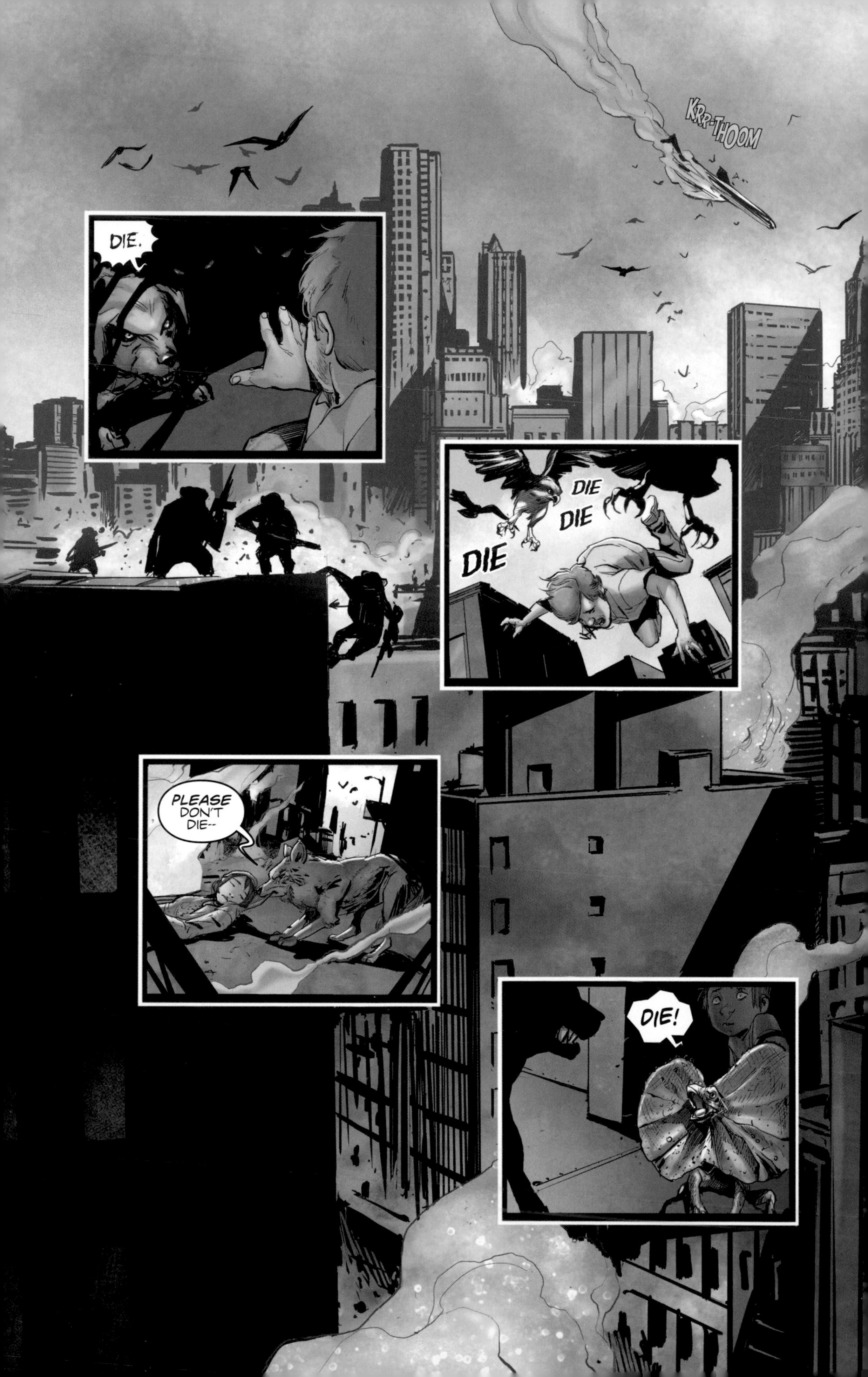
KRR-THOOM
DIE.
DIE
DIE
DIE
PLEASE DON'T DIE--
DIE!

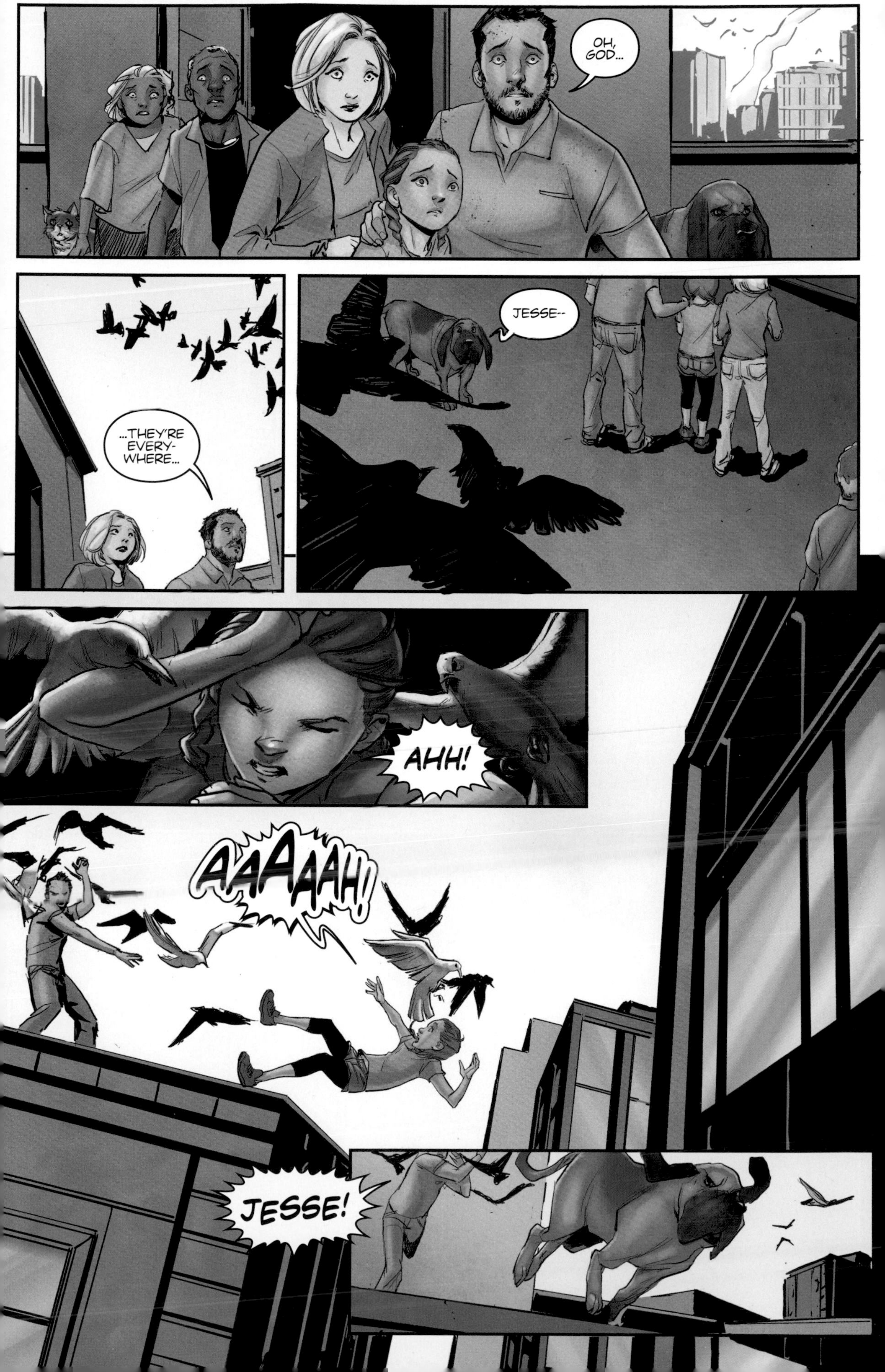

OH, GOD...
...THEY'RE EVERY- WHERE...
JESSE--
AHH!
AAAAAH!
JESSE!

I'VE GOT YOU.
CRSSSSH
J-JESSE?!
JESSE, ARE YOU--
KOFF
I'M OKAY, I'M... I'M...
S-SANDOR...

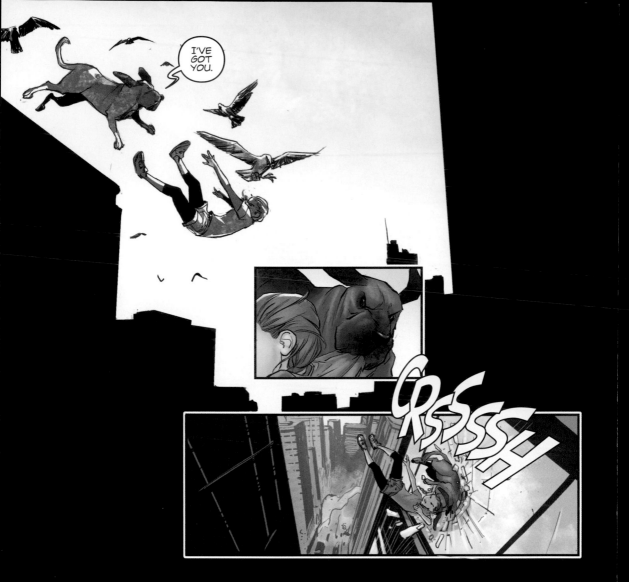

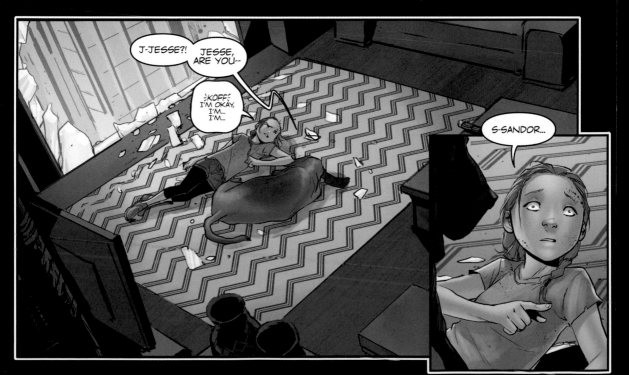

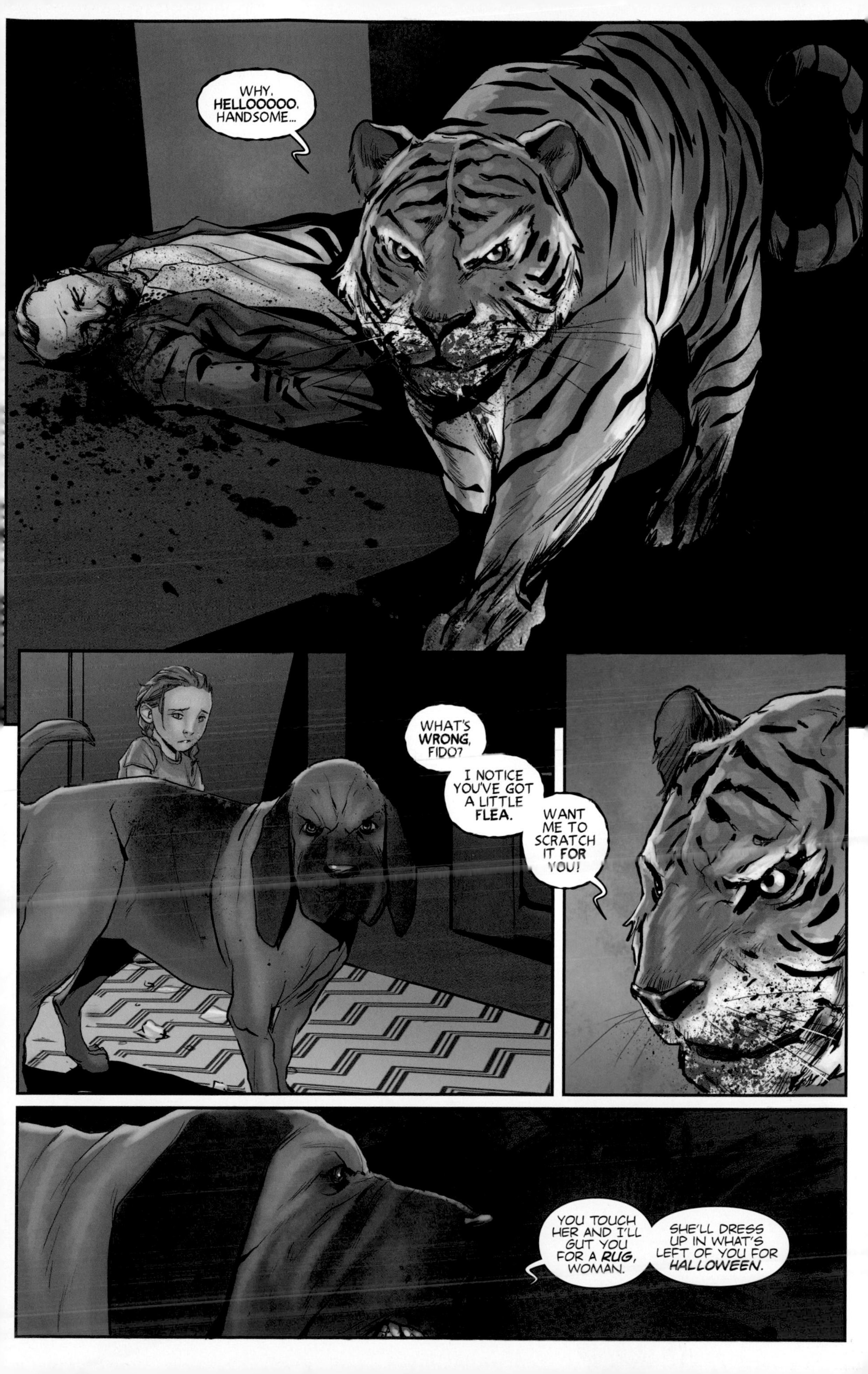

WHY, HELLOOOOO, HANDSOME...
WHAT'S WRONG, FIDO?
I NOTICE YOU'VE GOT A LITTLE FLEA.
WANT ME TO SCRATCH IT FOR YOU!
YOU TOUCH HER AND I'LL GUT YOU FOR A RUG, WOMAN.
SHE'LL DRESS UP IN WHAT'S LEFT OF YOU FOR HALLOWEEN.

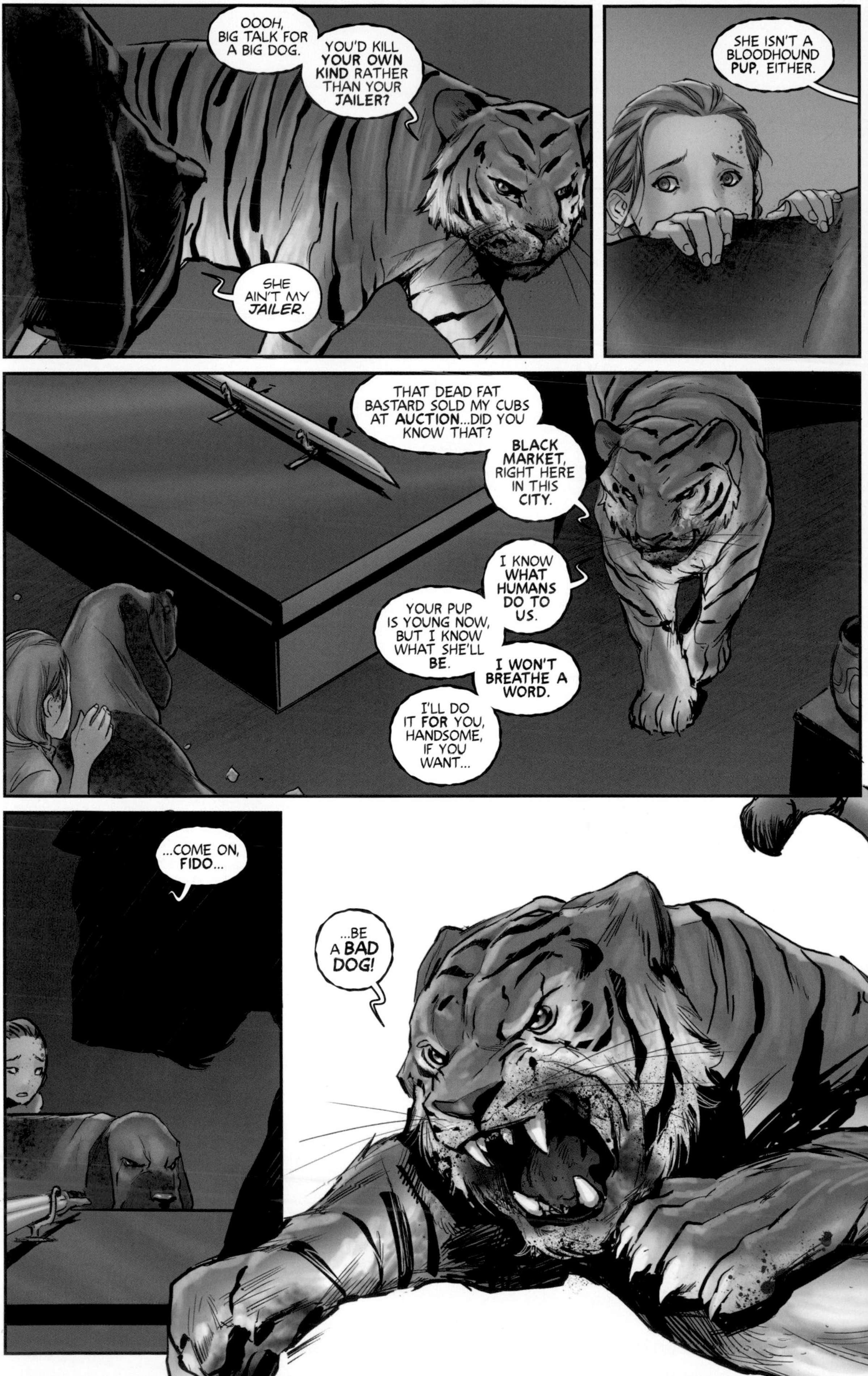
OOOH, BIG TALK FOR A BIG DOG.
YOU'D KILL YOUR OWN KIND RATHER THAN YOUR JAILER?
SHE AIN'T MY JAILER.
SHE ISN'T A BLOODHOUND PUP, EITHER.
THAT DEAD FAT BASTARD SOLD MY CUBS AT AUCTION...DID YOU KNOW THAT?
BLACK MARKET, RIGHT HERE IN THIS CITY.
I KNOW WHAT HUMANS DO TO US.
YOUR PUP IS YOUNG NOW, BUT I KNOW WHAT SHE'LL BE.
I WON'T BREATHE A WORD.
I'LL DO IT FOR YOU, HANDSOME, IF YOU WANT...
...COME ON, FIDO...
...BE A BAD DOG!

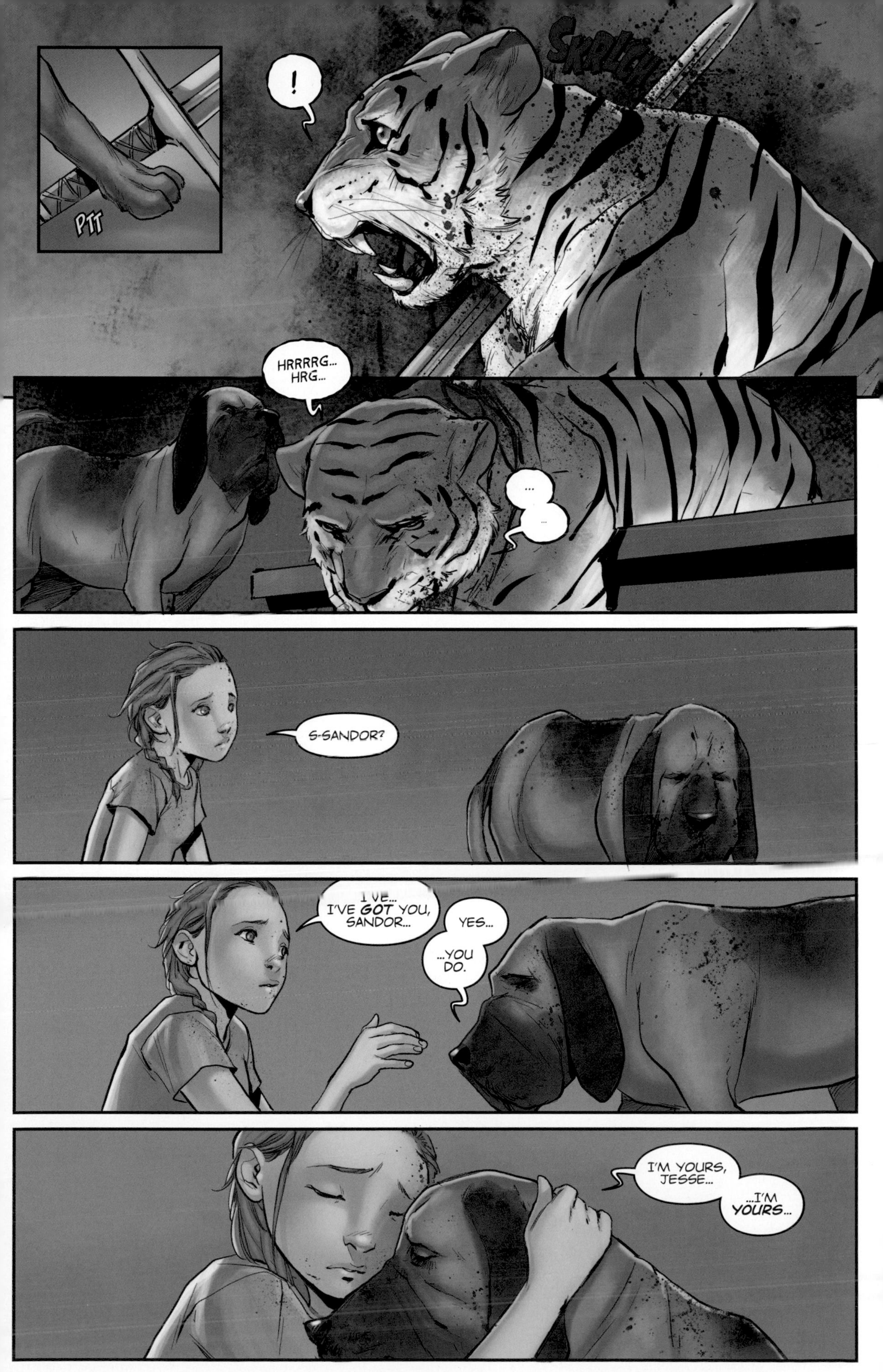
PTT
!
SKRUCH
HRRRRG... HRG...
...
...
S-SANDOR?
I'VE... I'VE GOT YOU, SANDOR...
YES...
...YOU DO.
I'M YOURS, JESSE...
...I'M YOURS...

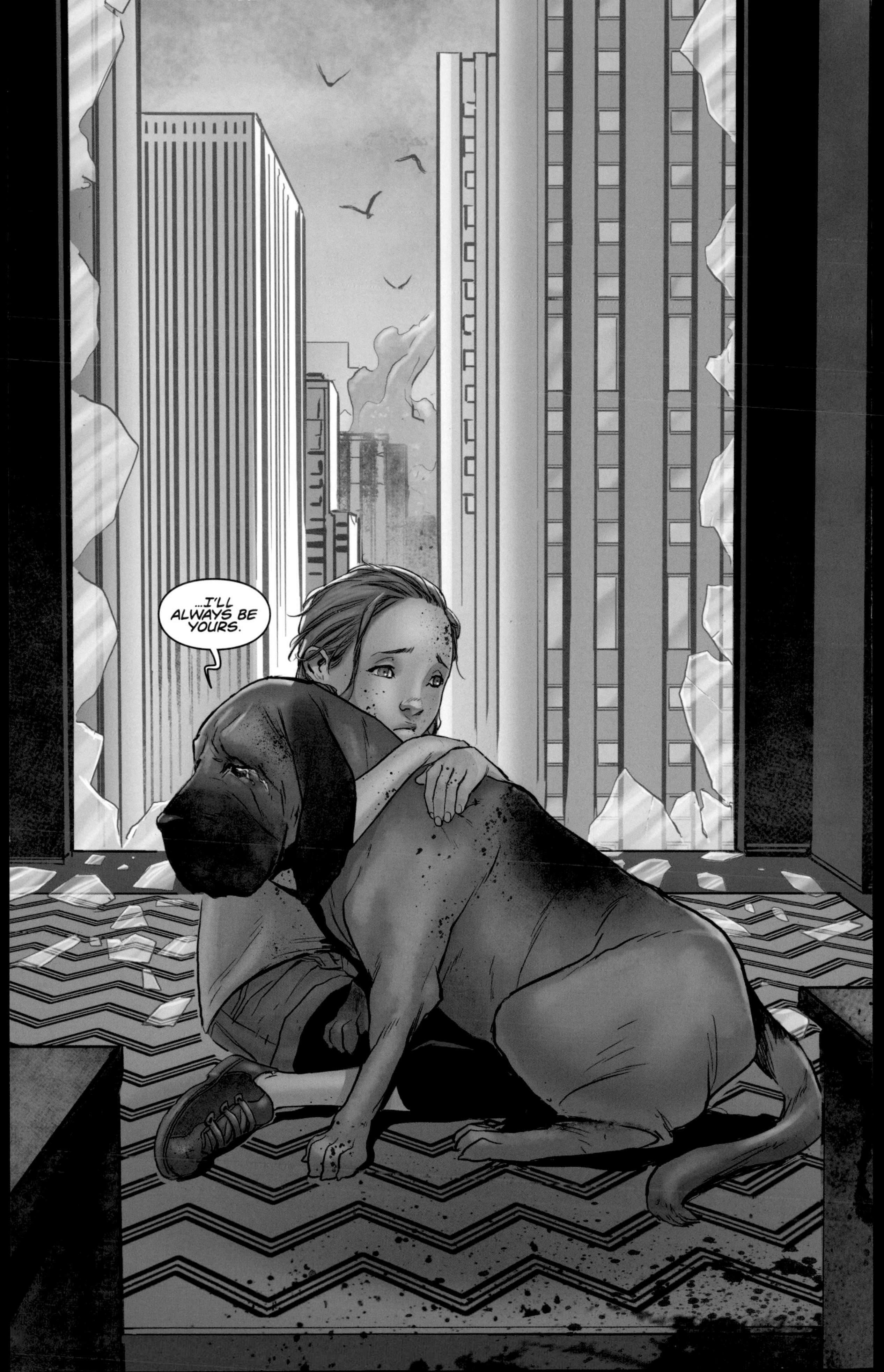
...I'LL ALWAYS BE YOURS.

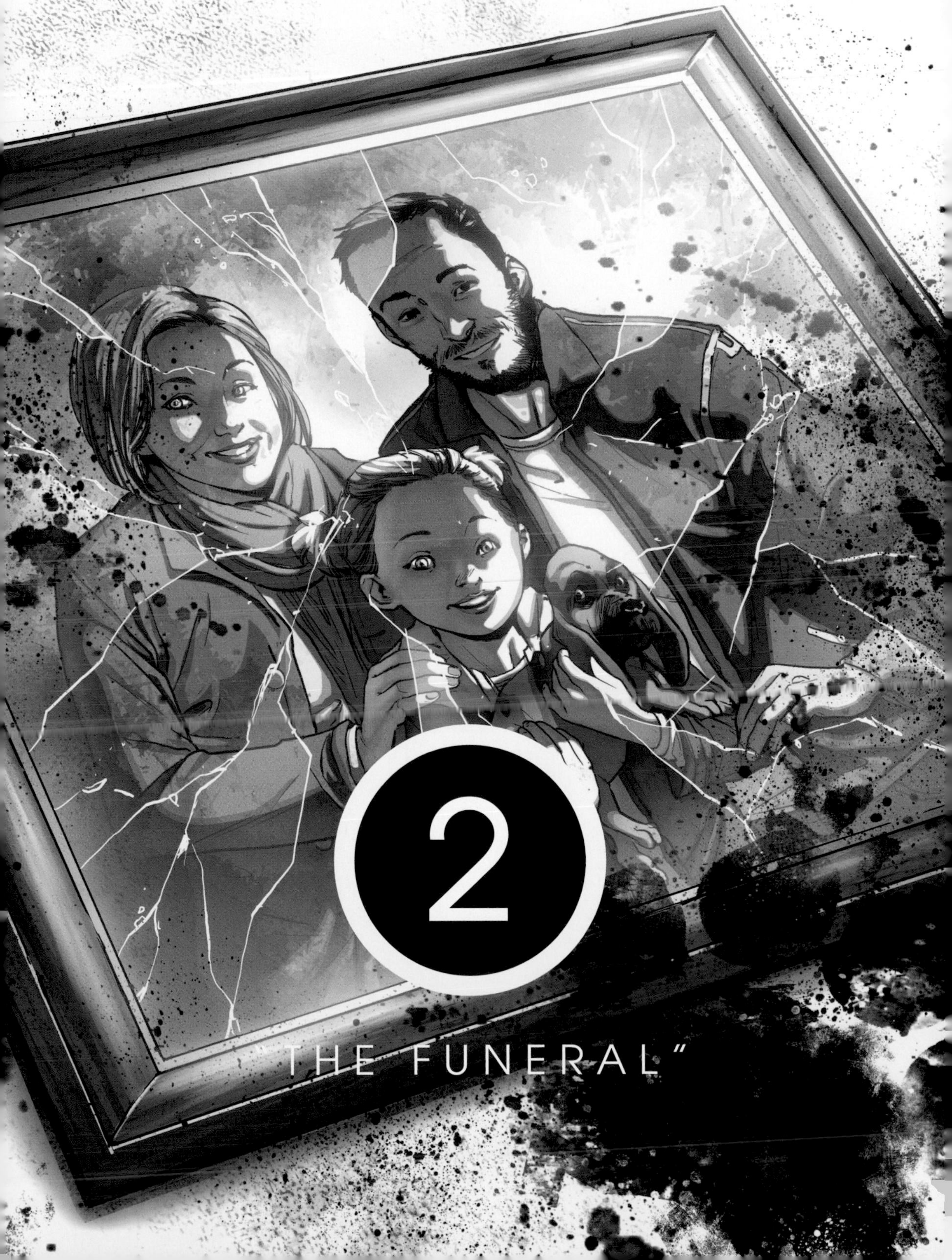
2
“THE FUNERAL”

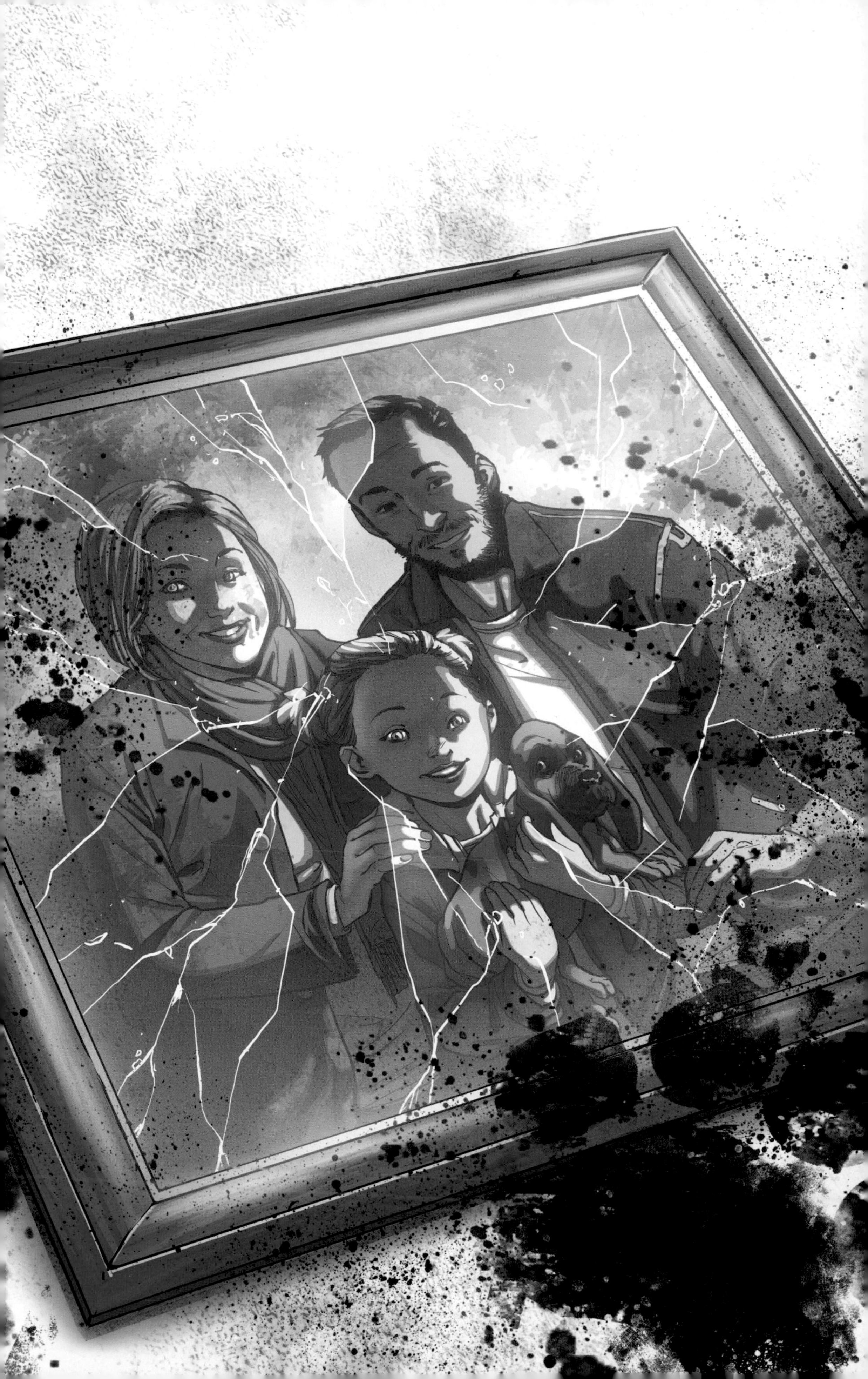

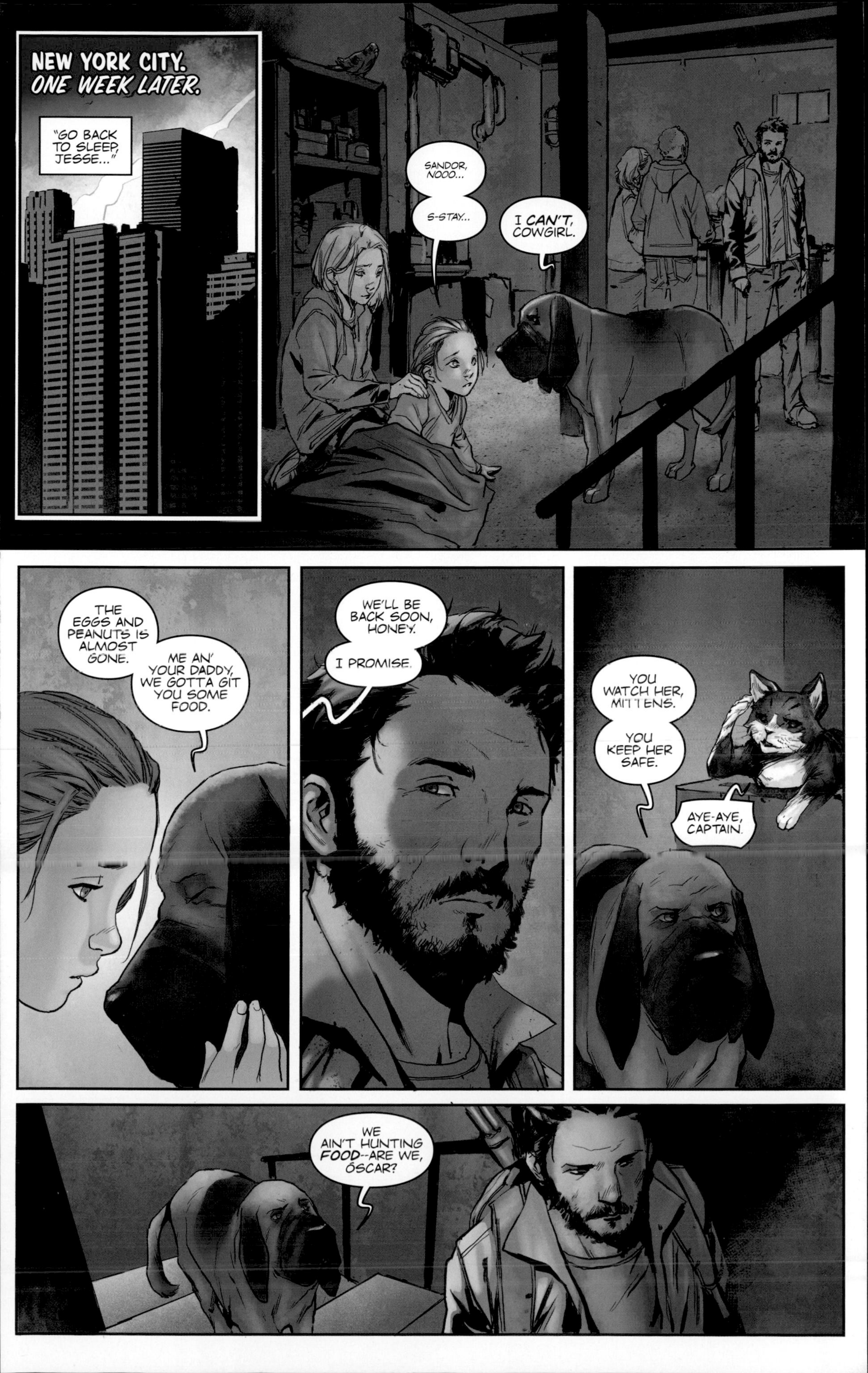
NEW YORK CITY.
ONE WEEK LATER.
"GO BACK TO SLEEP, JESSE..."
SANDOR, NOOO...
S-STAY...
I CAN'T, COWGIRL.
THE EGGS AND PEANUTS IS ALMOST GONE.
ME AN' YOUR DADDY, WE GOTTA GIT YOU SOME FOOD.
WE'LL BE BACK SOON, HONEY.
I PROMISE.
YOU WATCH HER, MITTENS.
YOU KEEP HER SAFE.
AYE-AYE, CAPTAIN.
WE AIN'T HUNTING FOOD--ARE WE, ÓSCAR?

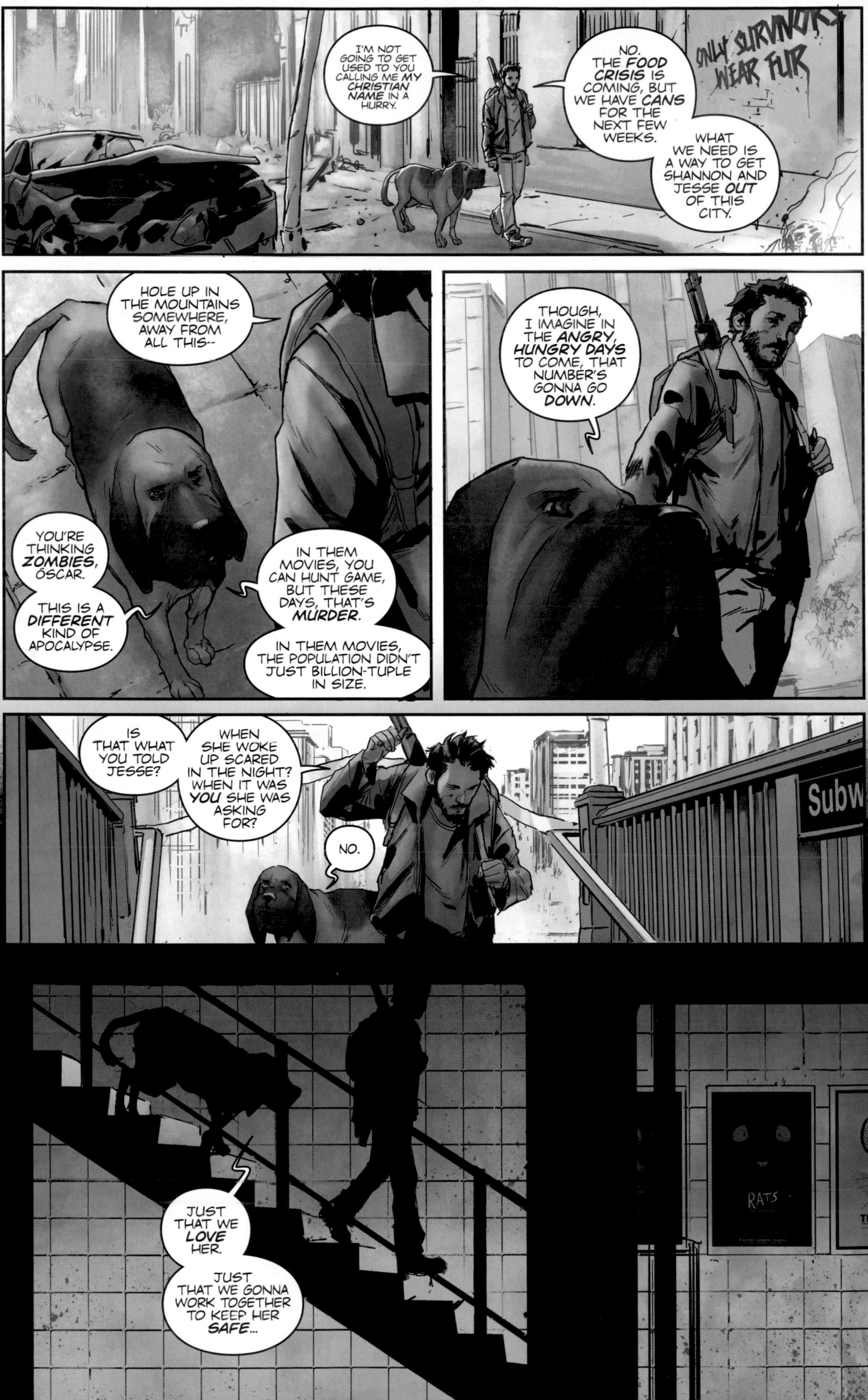
ONLY SURVIVORS WEAR FUR
I'M NOT GOING TO GET USED TO YOU CALLING ME MY CHRISTIAN NAME IN A HURRY.
NO. THE FOOD CRISIS IS COMING, BUT WE HAVE CANS FOR THE NEXT FEW WEEKS.
WHAT WE NEED IS A WAY TO GET SHANNON AND JESSE OUT OF THIS CITY.
HOLE UP IN THE MOUNTAINS SOMEWHERE, AWAY FROM ALL THIS--
YOU'RE THINKING ZOMBIES, ÓSCAR.
THIS IS A DIFFERENT KIND OF APOCALYPSE.
IN THEM MOVIES, YOU CAN HUNT GAME, BUT THESE DAYS, THAT'S MURDER.
IN THEM MOVIES, THE POPULATION DIDN'T JUST BILLION-TUPLE IN SIZE.
THOUGH, I IMAGINE IN THE ANGRY, HUNGRY DAYS TO COME, THAT NUMBER'S GONNA GO DOWN.
IS THAT WHAT YOU TOLD JESSE?
WHEN SHE WOKE UP SCARED IN THE NIGHT? WHEN IT WAS YOU SHE WAS ASKING FOR?
Subw
NO.
RATS
JUST THAT WE LOVE HER.
JUST THAT WE GONNA WORK TOGETHER TO KEEP HER SAFE...

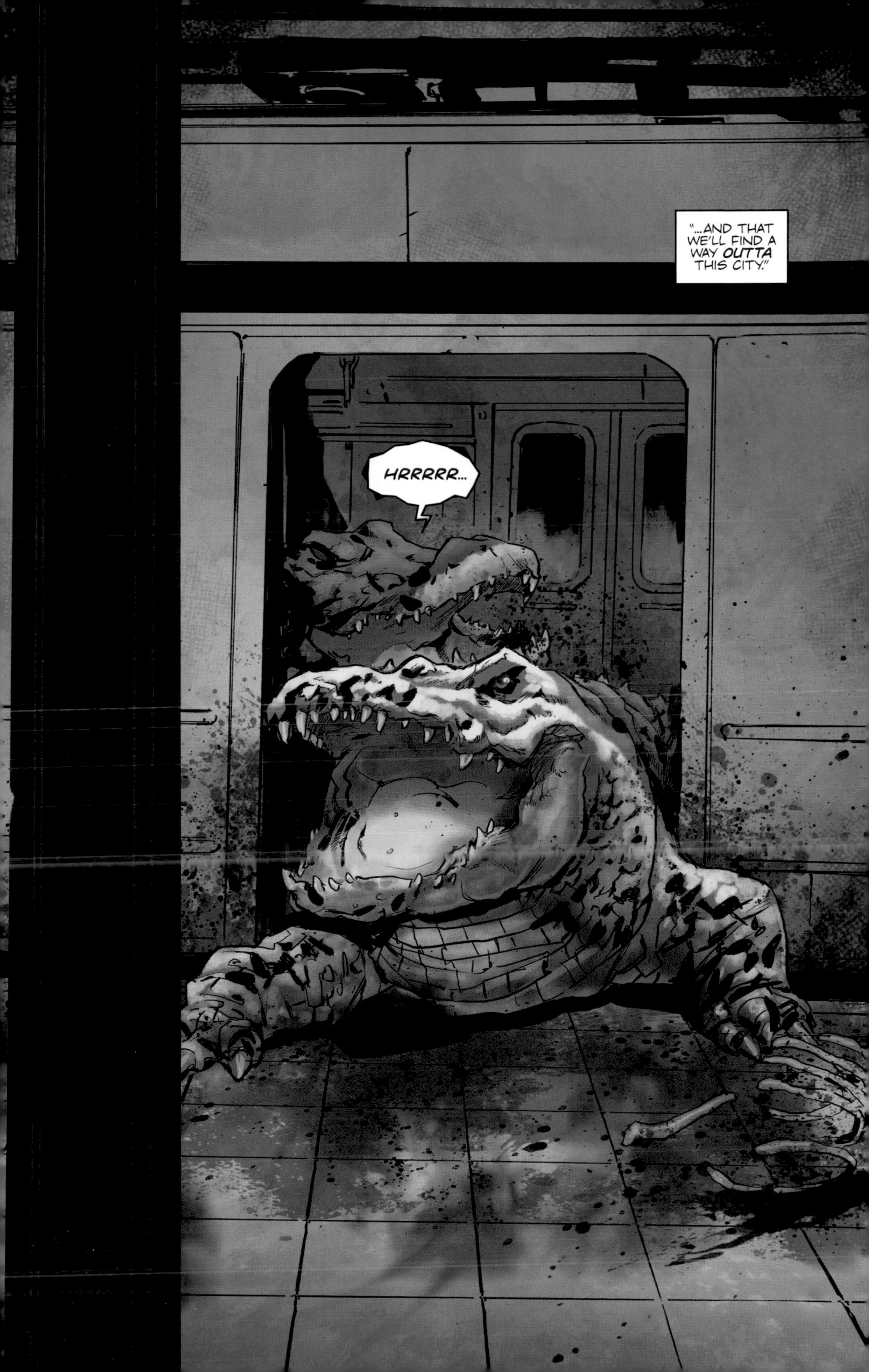
"...AND THAT WE'LL FIND A WAY *OUTTA* THIS CITY."
HRRRRR...

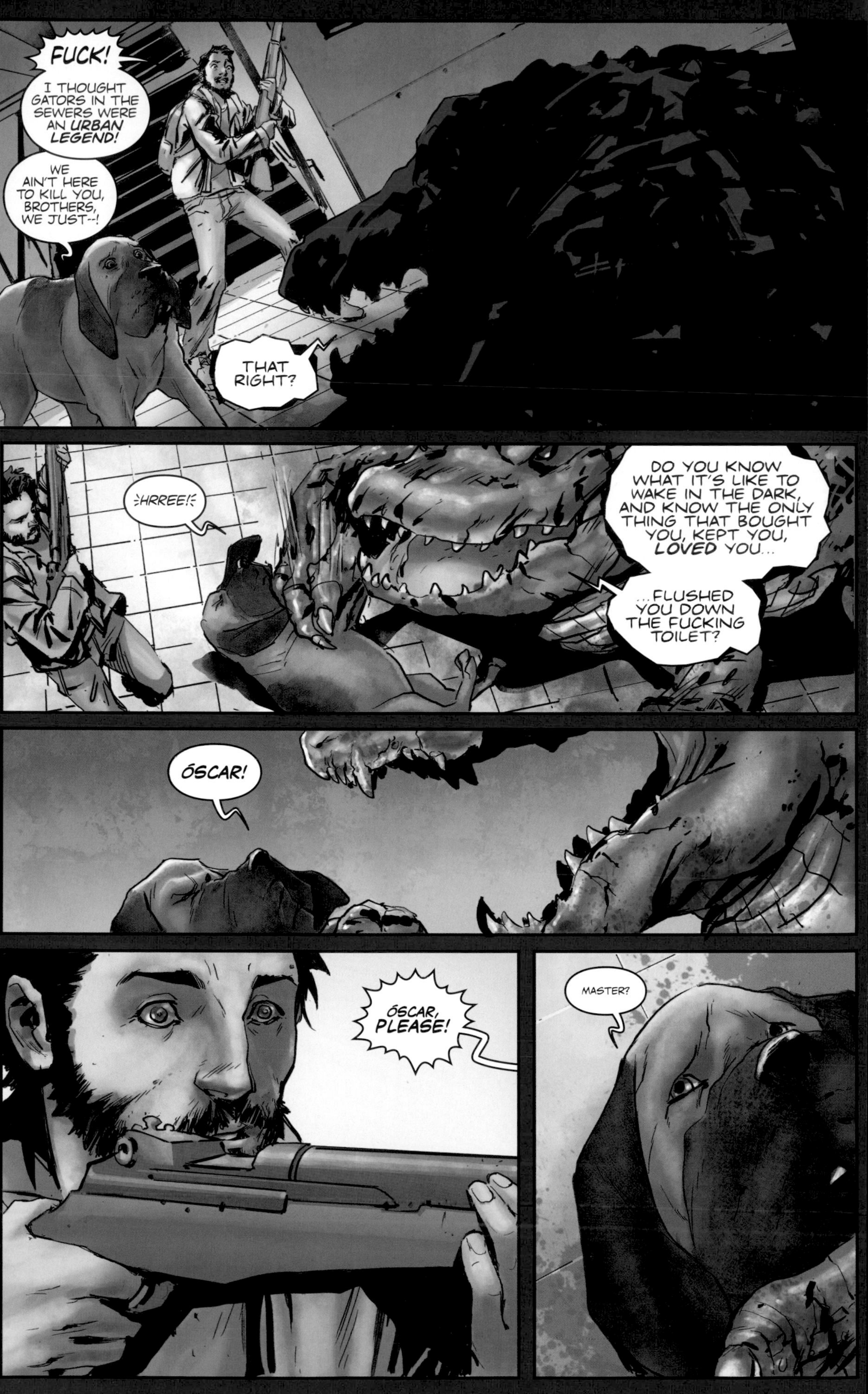
FUCK!
I THOUGHT GATORS IN THE SEWERS WERE AN URBAN LEGEND!
WE AIN'T HERE TO KILL YOU, BROTHERS, WE JUST--!
THAT RIGHT?
HRREE!
DO YOU KNOW WHAT IT'S LIKE TO WAKE IN THE DARK, AND KNOW THE ONLY THING THAT BOUGHT YOU, KEPT YOU, LOVED YOU...
...FLUSHED YOU DOWN THE FUCKING TOILET?
ÓSCAR!
ÓSCAR, PLEASE!
MASTER?

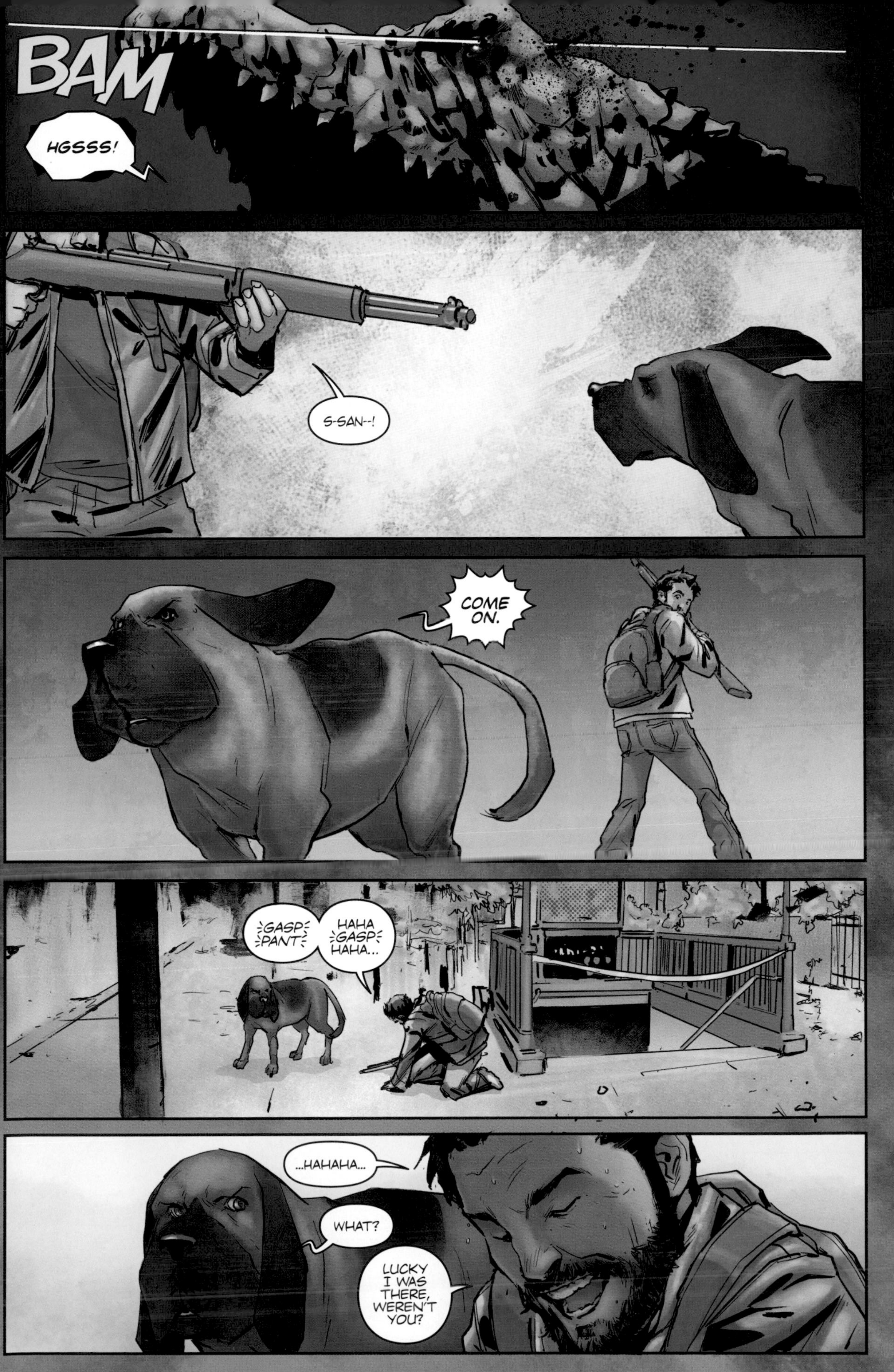
BAM
HGSSS!
S-SAN--!
COME ON.
GASP PANT
HAHA GASP HAHA...
...HAHAHA...
WHAT?
LUCKY I WAS THERE, WEREN'T YOU?

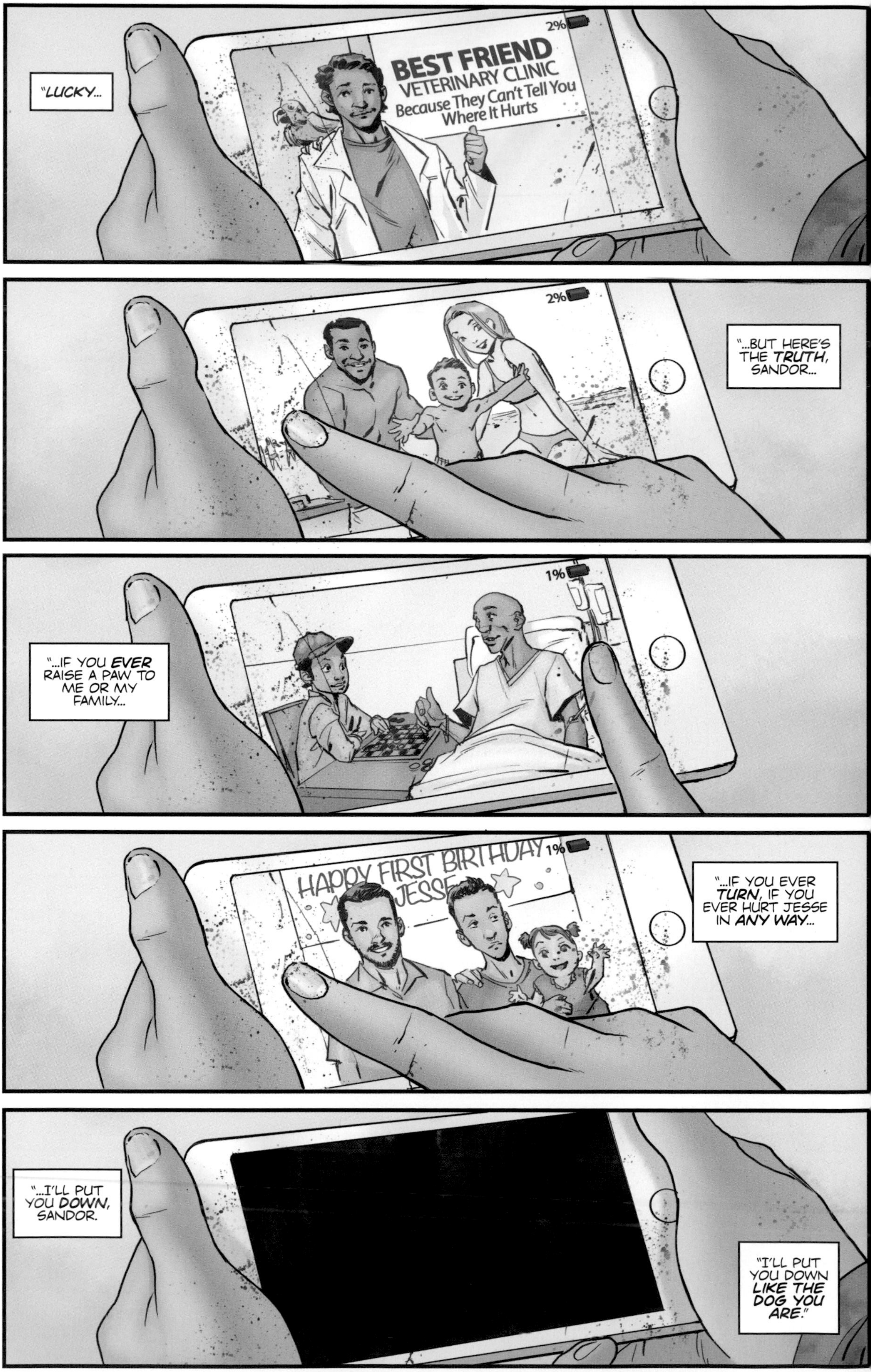

2%
BEST FRIEND
VETERINARY CLINIC
Because They Can't Tell You Where It Hurts
"LUCKY...
2%
"...BUT HERE'S THE TRUTH, SANDOR...
1%
"...IF YOU EVER RAISE A PAW TO ME OR MY FAMILY...
HAPPY FIRST BIRTHDAY JESSE
1%
"...IF YOU EVER TURN, IF YOU EVER HURT JESSE IN ANY WAY...
"...I'LL PUT YOU DOWN, SANDOR.
"I'LL PUT YOU DOWN LIKE THE DOG YOU ARE."

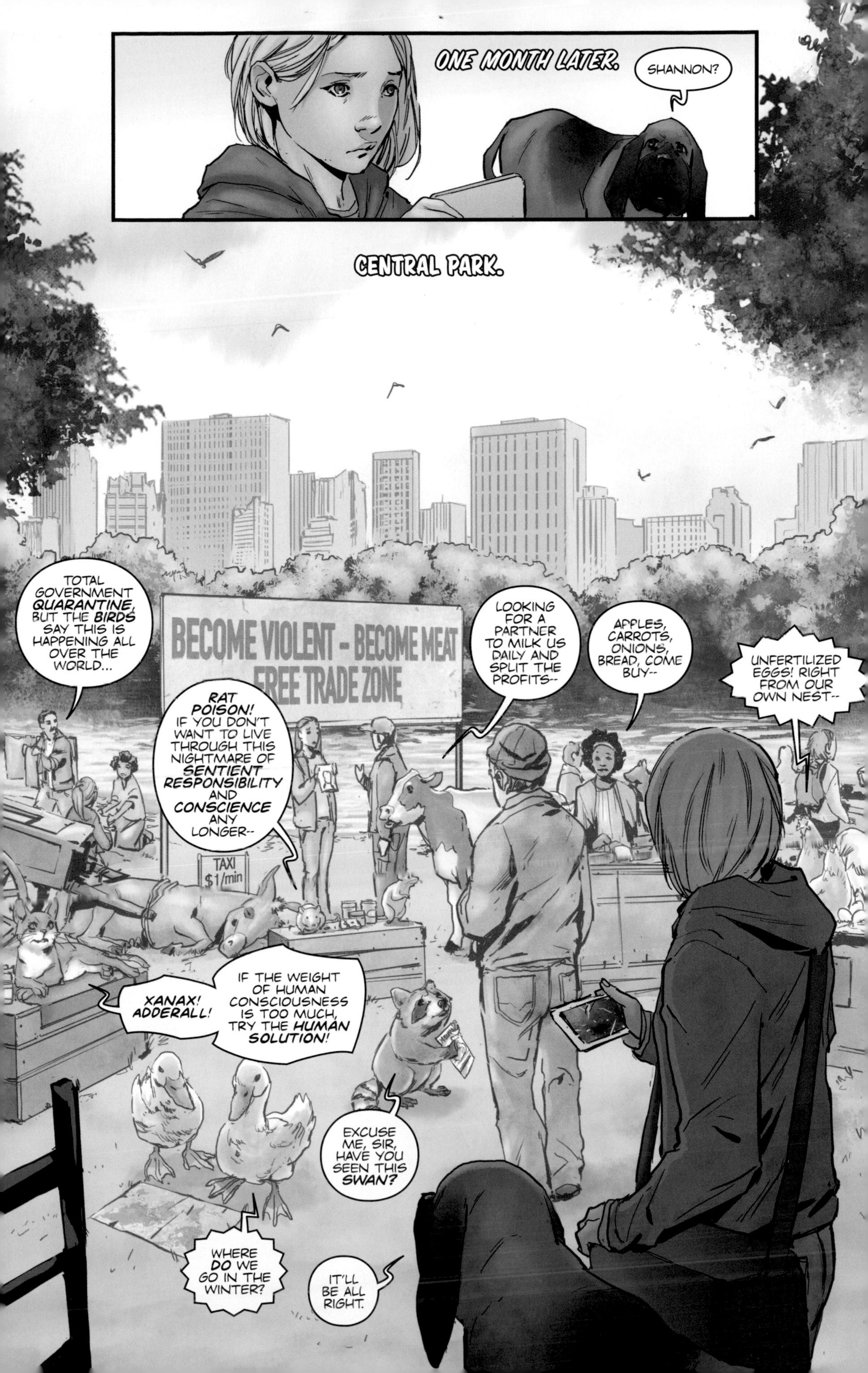
ONE MONTH LATER.
SHANNON?
CENTRAL PARK.
BECOME VIOLENT - BECOME MEAT
FREE TRADE ZONE
TOTAL GOVERNMENT QUARANTINE, BUT THE BIRDS SAY THIS IS HAPPENING ALL OVER THE WORLD...
RAT POISON! IF YOU DON'T WANT TO LIVE THROUGH THIS NIGHTMARE OF SENTIENT RESPONSIBILITY AND CONSCIENCE ANY LONGER--
LOOKING FOR A PARTNER TO MILK US DAILY AND SPLIT THE PROFITS--
APPLES, CARROTS, ONIONS, BREAD, COME BUY--
UNFERTILIZED EGGS! RIGHT FROM OUR OWN NEST--
TAXI $1/min
XANAX! ADDERALL!
IF THE WEIGHT OF HUMAN CONSCIOUSNESS IS TOO MUCH, TRY THE HUMAN SOLUTION!
EXCUSE ME, SIR, HAVE YOU SEEN THIS SWAN?
WHERE DO WE GO IN THE WINTER?
IT'LL BE ALL RIGHT.

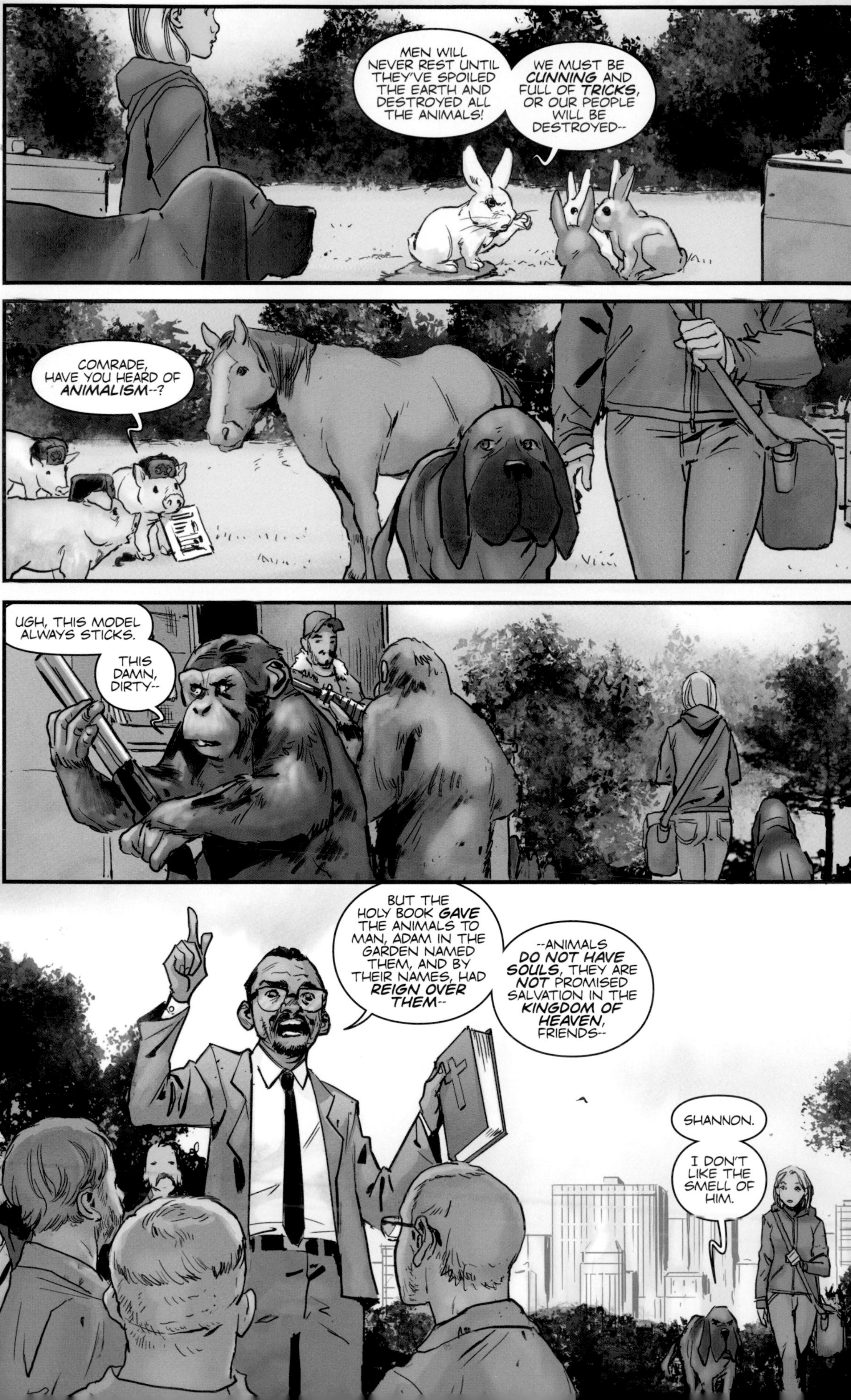
MEN WILL NEVER REST UNTIL THEY'VE SPOILED THE EARTH AND DESTROYED ALL THE ANIMALS!
WE MUST BE CUNNING AND FULL OF TRICKS, OR OUR PEOPLE WILL BE DESTROYED--
COMRADE, HAVE YOU HEARD OF ANIMALISM--?
UGH, THIS MODEL ALWAYS STICKS.
THIS DAMN, DIRTY--
BUT THE HOLY BOOK GAVE THE ANIMALS TO MAN, ADAM IN THE GARDEN NAMED THEM, AND BY THEIR NAMES, HAD REIGN OVER THEM--
--ANIMALS DO NOT HAVE SOULS, THEY ARE NOT PROMISED SALVATION IN THE KINGDOM OF HEAVEN, FRIENDS--
SHANNON.
I DON'T LIKE THE SMELL OF HIM.

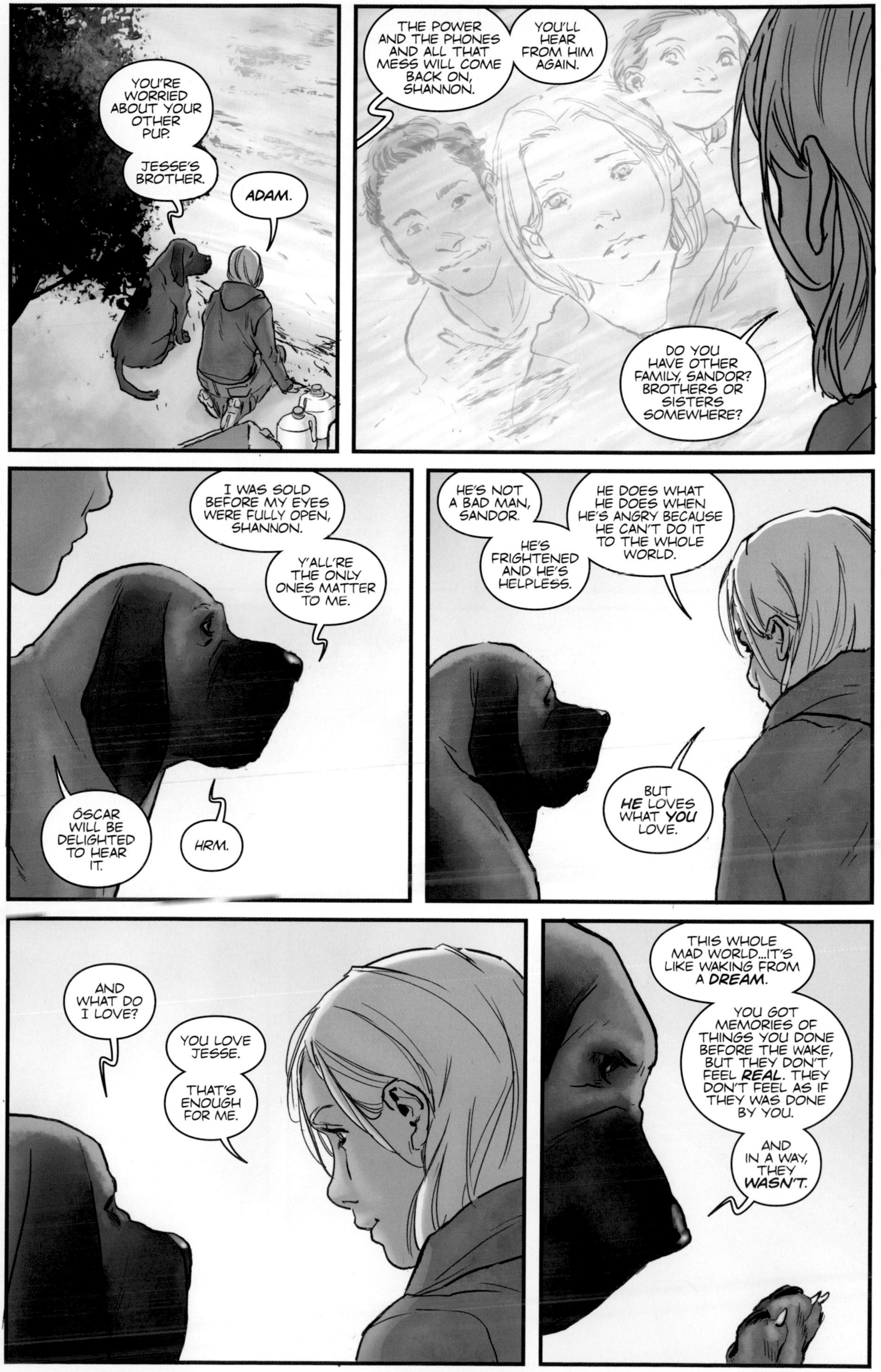
YOU'RE WORRIED ABOUT YOUR OTHER PUP.
JESSE'S BROTHER.
ADAM.
THE POWER AND THE PHONES AND ALL THAT MESS WILL COME BACK ON, SHANNON.
YOU'LL HEAR FROM HIM AGAIN.
DO YOU HAVE OTHER FAMILY, SANDOR? BROTHERS OR SISTERS SOMEWHERE?
I WAS SOLD BEFORE MY EYES WERE FULLY OPEN, SHANNON.
Y'ALL'RE THE ONLY ONES MATTER TO ME.
ÓSCAR WILL BE DELIGHTED TO HEAR IT.
HRM.
HE'S NOT A BAD MAN, SANDOR.
HE'S FRIGHTENED AND HE'S HELPLESS.
HE DOES WHAT HE DOES WHEN HE'S ANGRY BECAUSE HE CAN'T DO IT TO THE WHOLE WORLD.
BUT HE LOVES WHAT YOU LOVE.
AND WHAT DO I LOVE?
YOU LOVE JESSE.
THAT'S ENOUGH FOR ME.
THIS WHOLE MAD WORLD...IT'S LIKE WAKING FROM A DREAM.
YOU GOT MEMORIES OF THINGS YOU DONE BEFORE THE WAKE, BUT THEY DON'T FEEL REAL. THEY DON'T FEEL AS IF THEY WAS DONE BY YOU.
AND IN A WAY, THEY WASN'T.

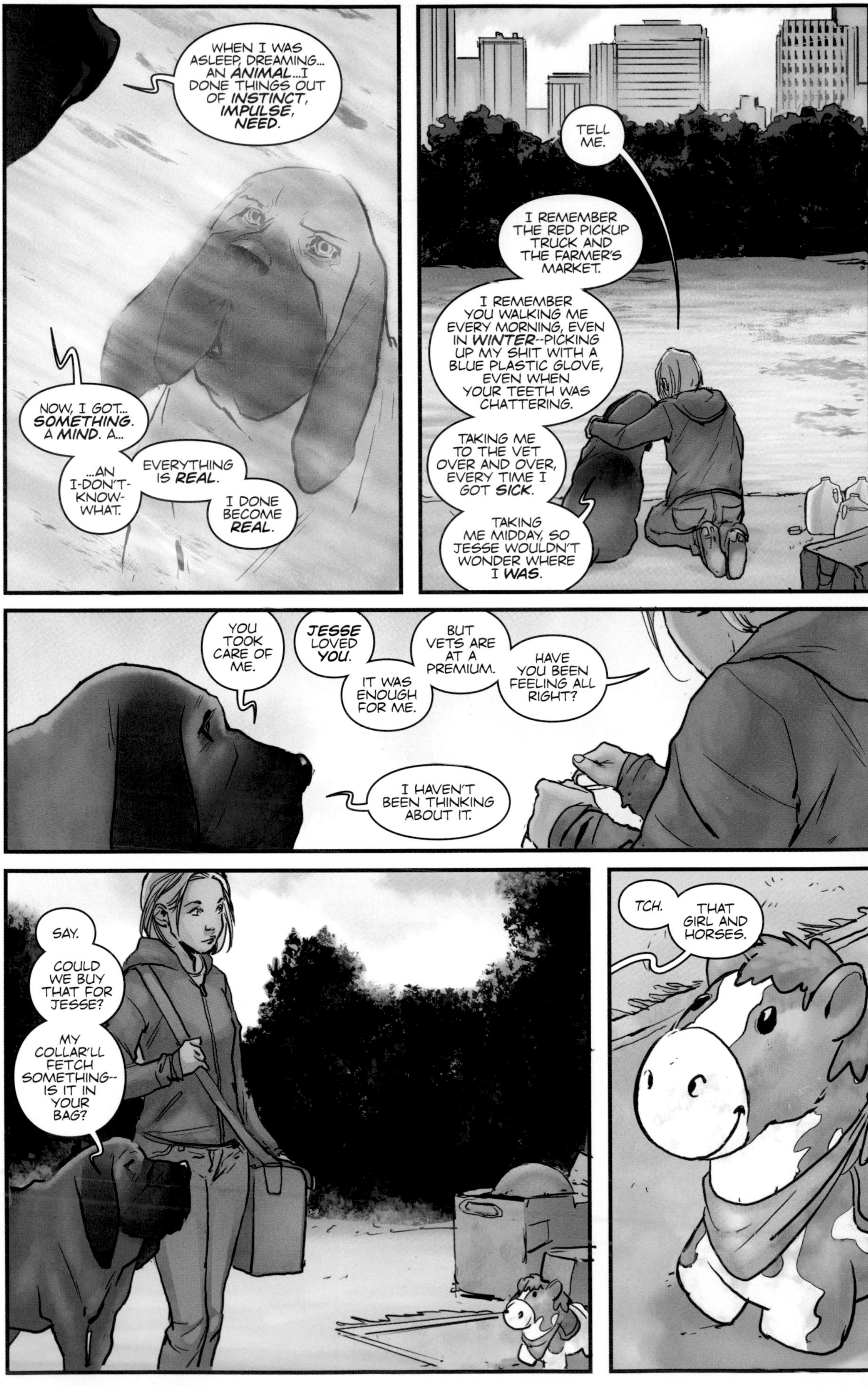
WHEN I WAS ASLEEP, DREAMING... AN ANIMAL...I DONE THINGS OUT OF INSTINCT, IMPULSE, NEED.
NOW, I GOT... SOMETHING. A MIND. A...
...AN I-DON'T-KNOW-WHAT.
EVERYTHING IS REAL.
I DONE BECOME REAL.
TELL ME.
I REMEMBER THE RED PICKUP TRUCK AND THE FARMER'S MARKET.
I REMEMBER YOU WALKING ME EVERY MORNING, EVEN IN WINTER--PICKING UP MY SHIT WITH A BLUE PLASTIC GLOVE, EVEN WHEN YOUR TEETH WAS CHATTERING.
TAKING ME TO THE VET OVER AND OVER, EVERY TIME I GOT SICK.
TAKING ME MIDDAY, SO JESSE WOULDN'T WONDER WHERE I WAS.
YOU TOOK CARE OF ME.
JESSE LOVED YOU.
IT WAS ENOUGH FOR ME.
BUT VETS ARE AT A PREMIUM.
HAVE YOU BEEN FEELING ALL RIGHT?
I HAVEN'T BEEN THINKING ABOUT IT.
SAY.
COULD WE BUY THAT FOR JESSE?
MY COLLAR'LL FETCH SOMETHING--IS IT IN YOUR BAG?
TCH.
THAT GIRL AND HORSES.

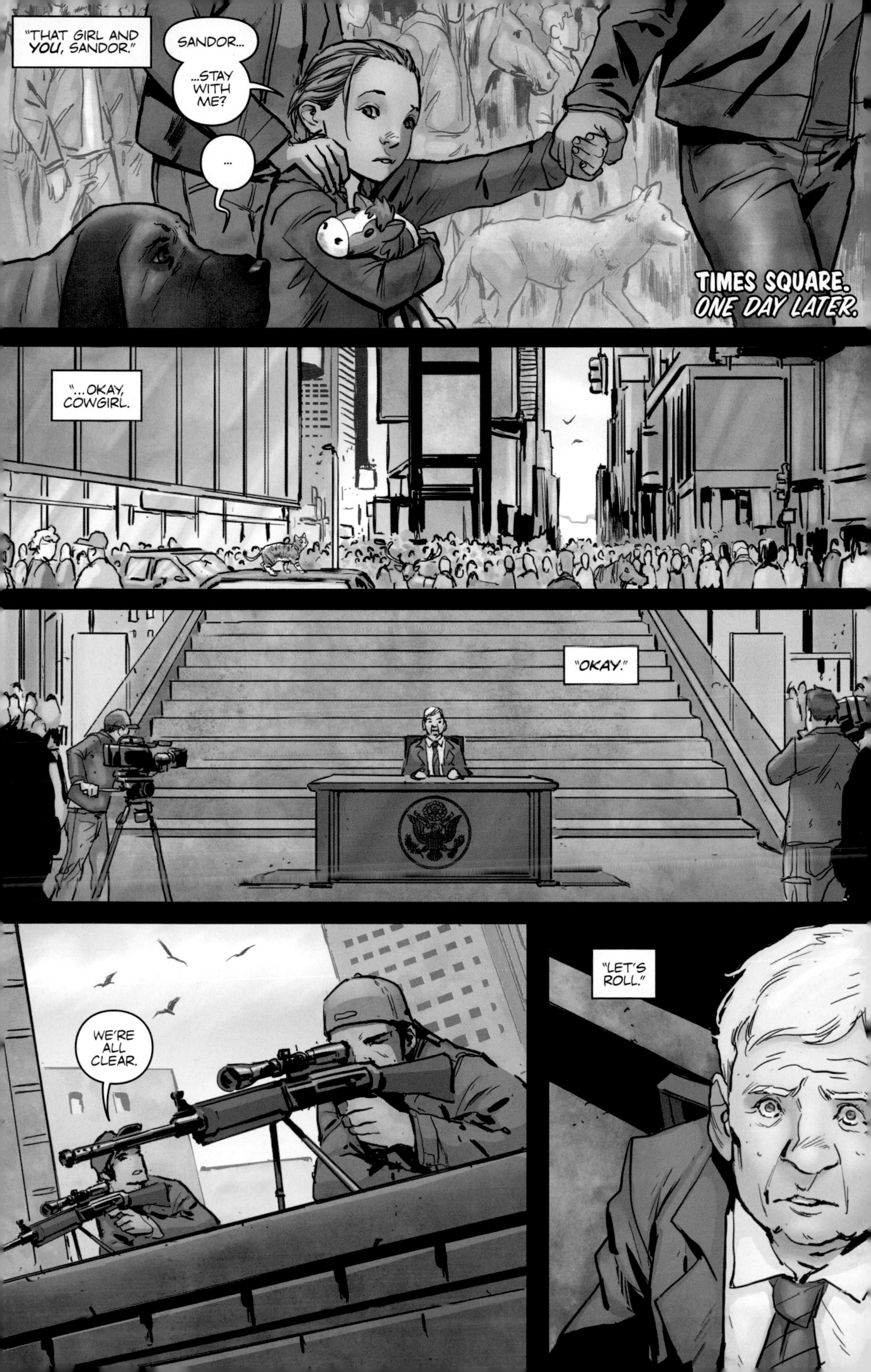
"THAT GIRL AND YOU, SANDOR."
SANDOR...
...STAY WITH ME?
...
TIMES SQUARE. ONE DAY LATER.
"...OKAY, COWGIRL.
"OKAY."
WE'RE ALL CLEAR.
"LET'S ROLL."

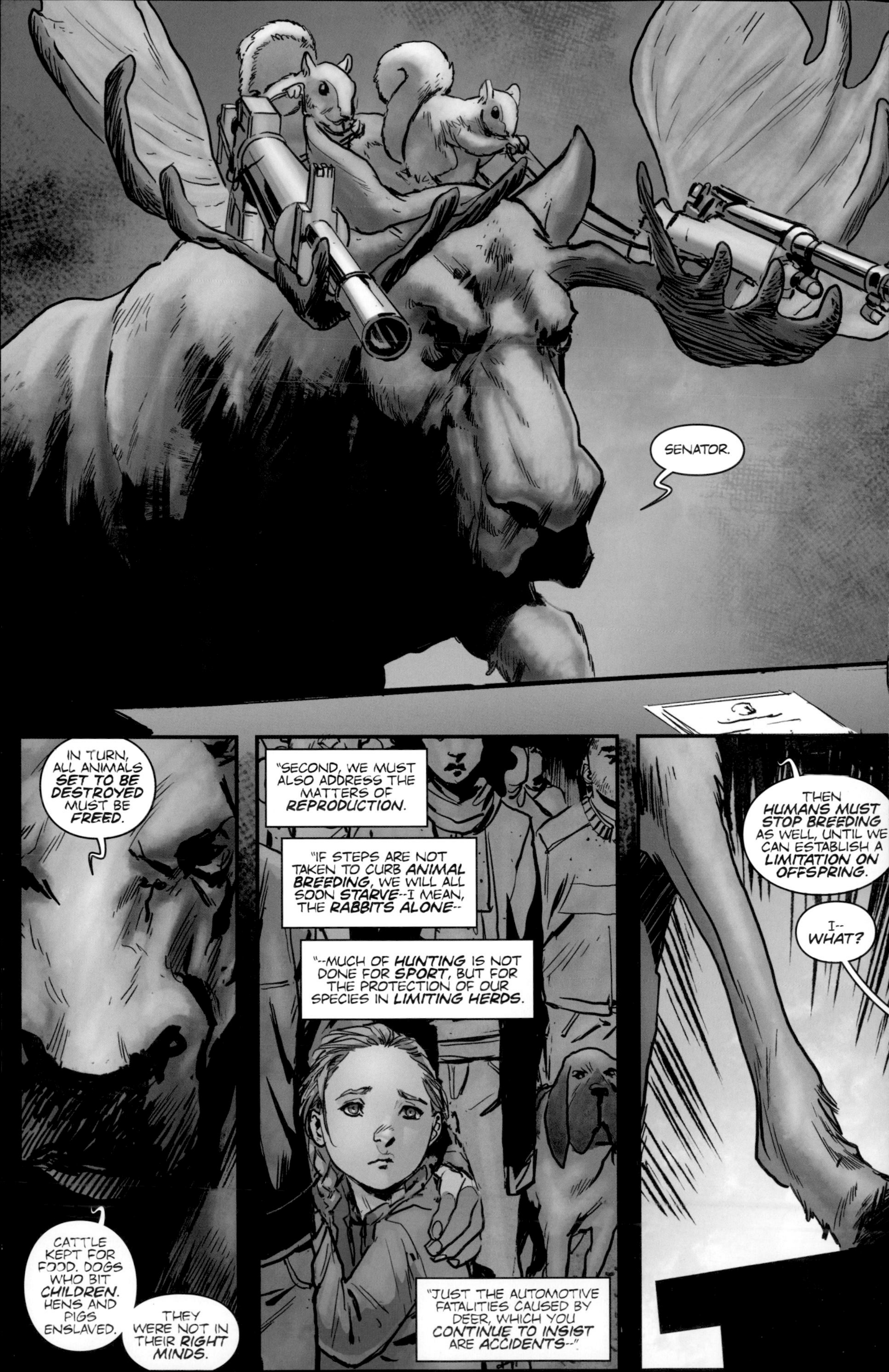
SENATOR.
IN TURN, ALL ANIMALS SET TO BE DESTROYED MUST BE FREED.
CATTLE KEPT FOR FOOD. DOGS WHO BIT CHILDREN. HENS AND PIGS ENSLAVED.
THEY WERE NOT IN THEIR RIGHT MINDS.
"SECOND, WE MUST ALSO ADDRESS THE MATTERS OF REPRODUCTION.
"IF STEPS ARE NOT TAKEN TO CURB ANIMAL BREEDING, WE WILL ALL SOON STARVE--I MEAN, THE RABBITS ALONE--
"--MUCH OF HUNTING IS NOT DONE FOR SPORT, BUT FOR THE PROTECTION OF OUR SPECIES IN LIMITING HERDS.
"JUST THE AUTOMOTIVE FATALITIES CAUSED BY DEER, WHICH YOU CONTINUE TO INSIST ARE ACCIDENTS--"
THEN HUMANS MUST STOP BREEDING AS WELL, UNTIL WE CAN ESTABLISH A LIMITATION ON OFFSPRING.
I-- WHAT?

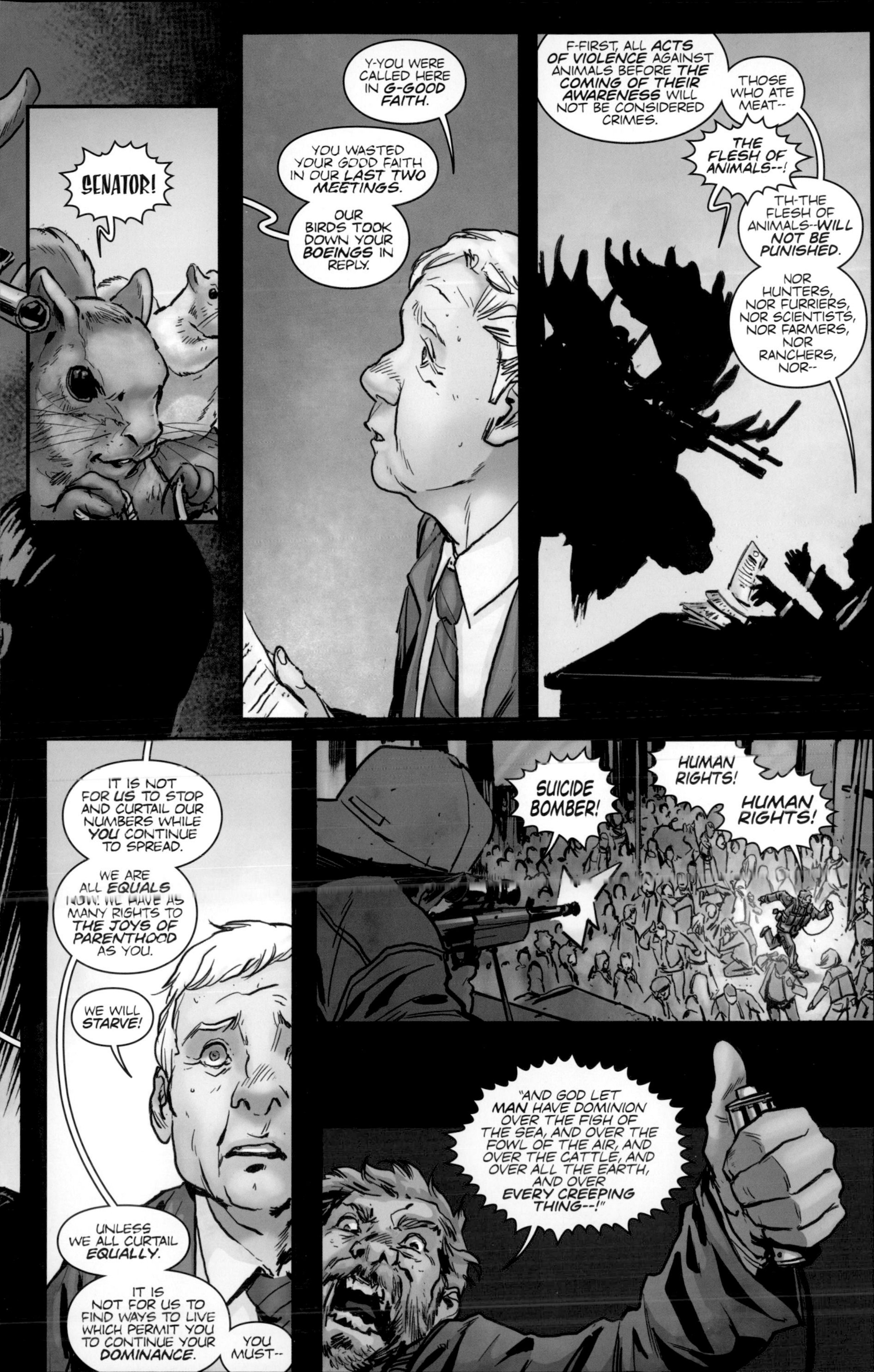
SENATOR!
Y-YOU WERE CALLED HERE IN G-GOOD FAITH.
YOU WASTED YOUR GOOD FAITH IN OUR LAST TWO MEETINGS.
OUR BIRDS TOOK DOWN YOUR BOEINGS IN REPLY.
F-FIRST, ALL ACTS OF VIOLENCE AGAINST ANIMALS BEFORE THE COMING OF THEIR AWARENESS WILL NOT BE CONSIDERED CRIMES.
THOSE WHO ATE MEAT--
THE FLESH OF ANIMALS--!
TH-THE FLESH OF ANIMALS--WILL NOT BE PUNISHED.
NOR HUNTERS, NOR FURRIERS, NOR SCIENTISTS, NOR FARMERS, NOR RANCHERS, NOR--
IT IS NOT FOR US TO STOP AND CURTAIL OUR NUMBERS WHILE YOU CONTINUE TO SPREAD.
WE ARE ALL EQUALS NOW! WE HAVE AS MANY RIGHTS TO THE JOYS OF PARENTHOOD AS YOU.
WE WILL STARVE!
UNLESS WE ALL CURTAIL EQUALLY.
IT IS NOT FOR US TO FIND WAYS TO LIVE WHICH PERMIT YOU TO CONTINUE YOUR DOMINANCE.
YOU MUST--
SUICIDE BOMBER!
HUMAN RIGHTS!
HUMAN RIGHTS!
"AND GOD LET MAN HAVE DOMINION OVER THE FISH OF THE SEA, AND OVER THE FOWL OF THE AIR, AND OVER THE CATTLE, AND OVER ALL THE EARTH, AND OVER EVERY CREEPING THING--!"

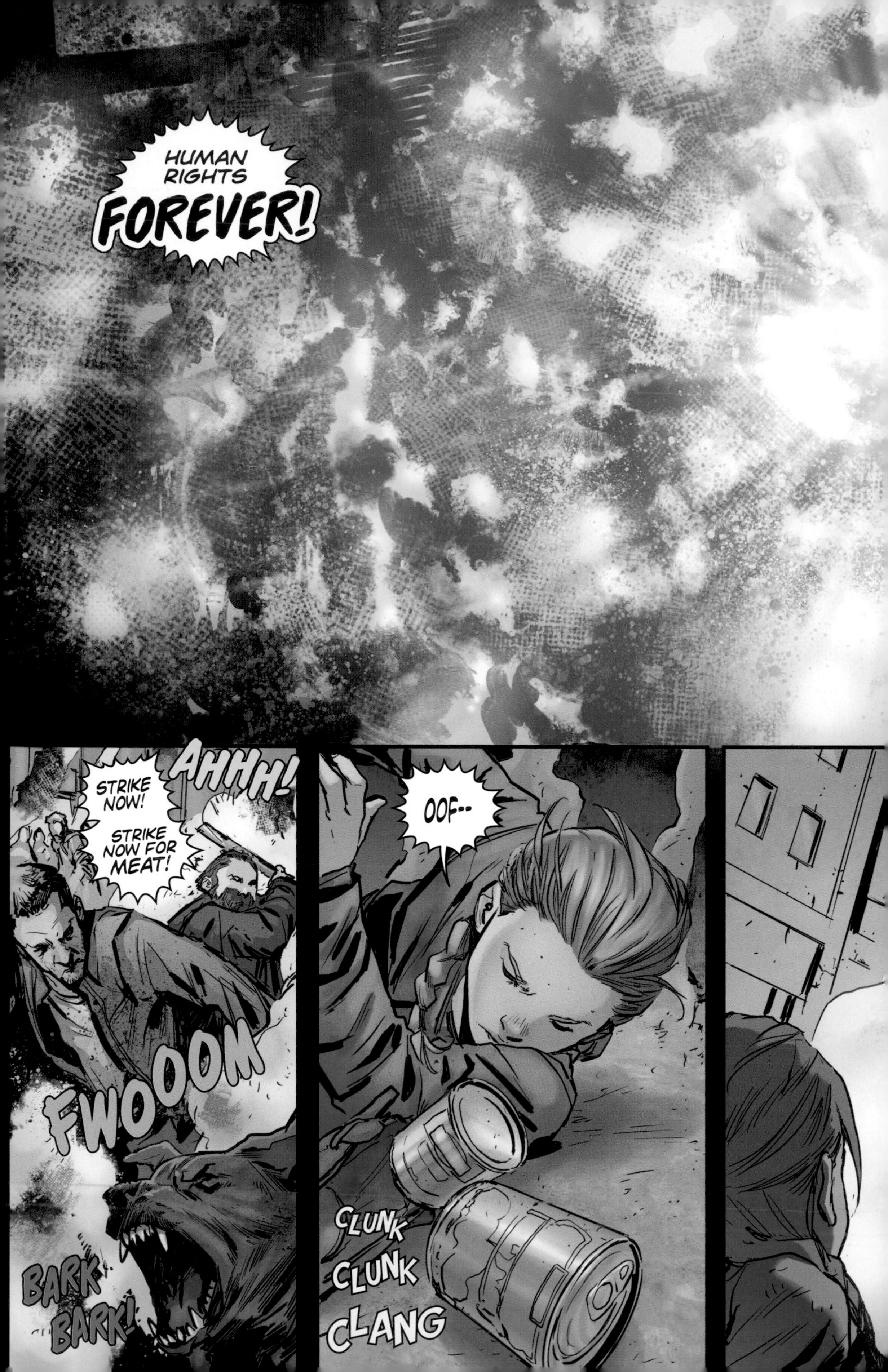
HUMAN RIGHTS FOREVER!
AHHH!
STRIKE NOW!
STRIKE NOW FOR MEAT!
FWOOOM
BARK BARK!
OOF--
CLUNK
CLUNK
CLANG

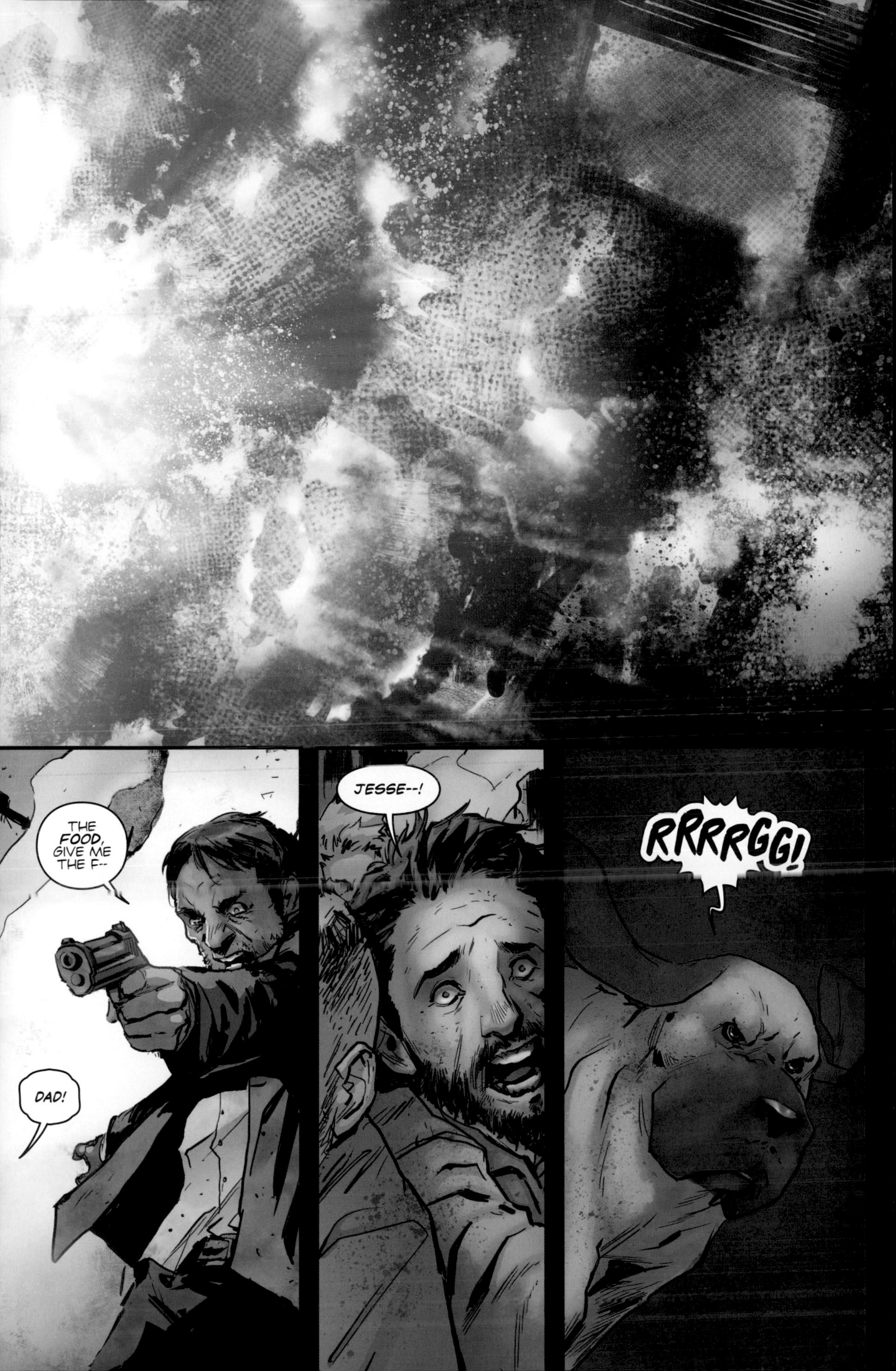
THE FOOD, GIVE ME THE F--
DAD!
JESSE--!
RRRRGG!

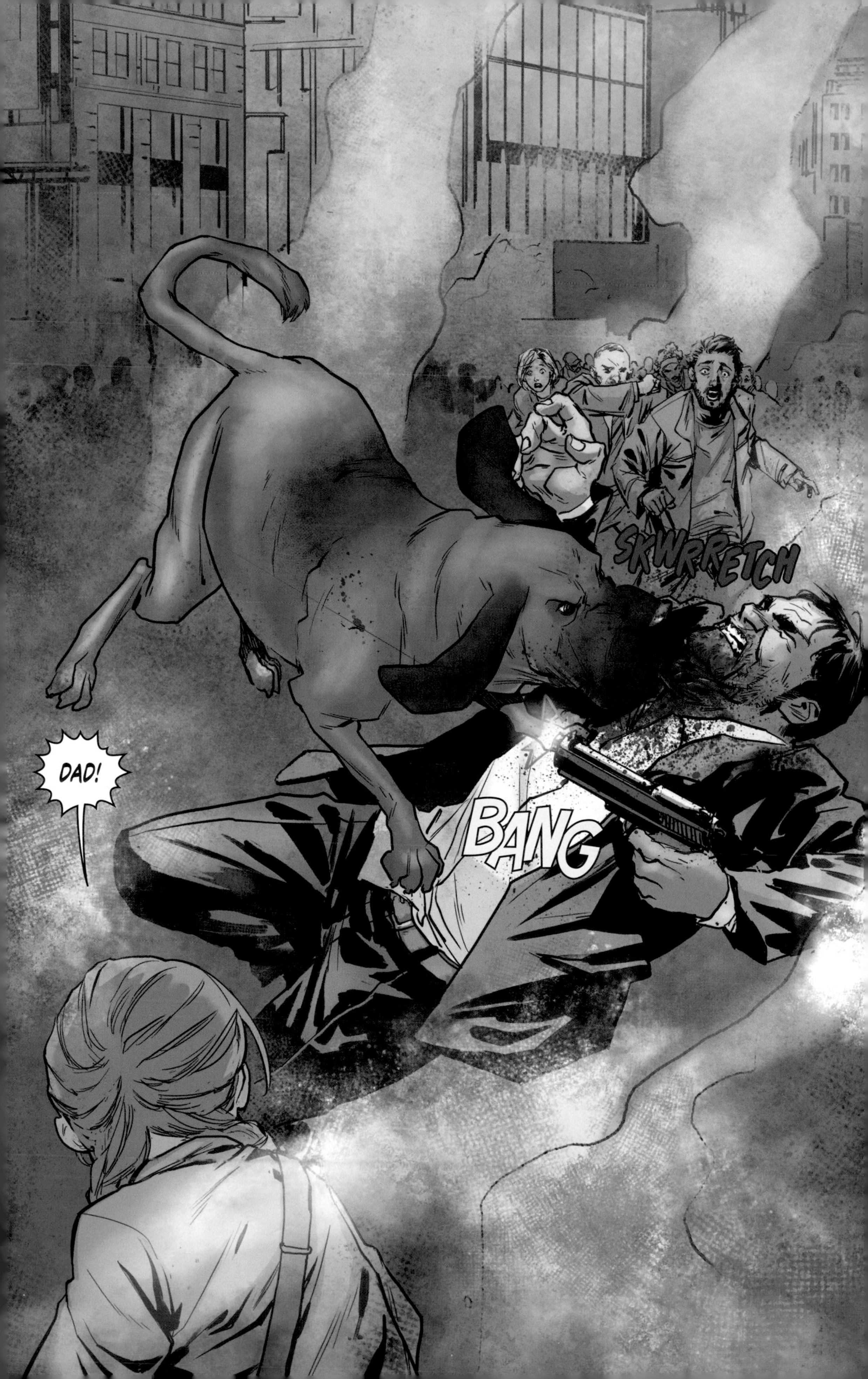
SKWRRETCH
DAD!
BANG

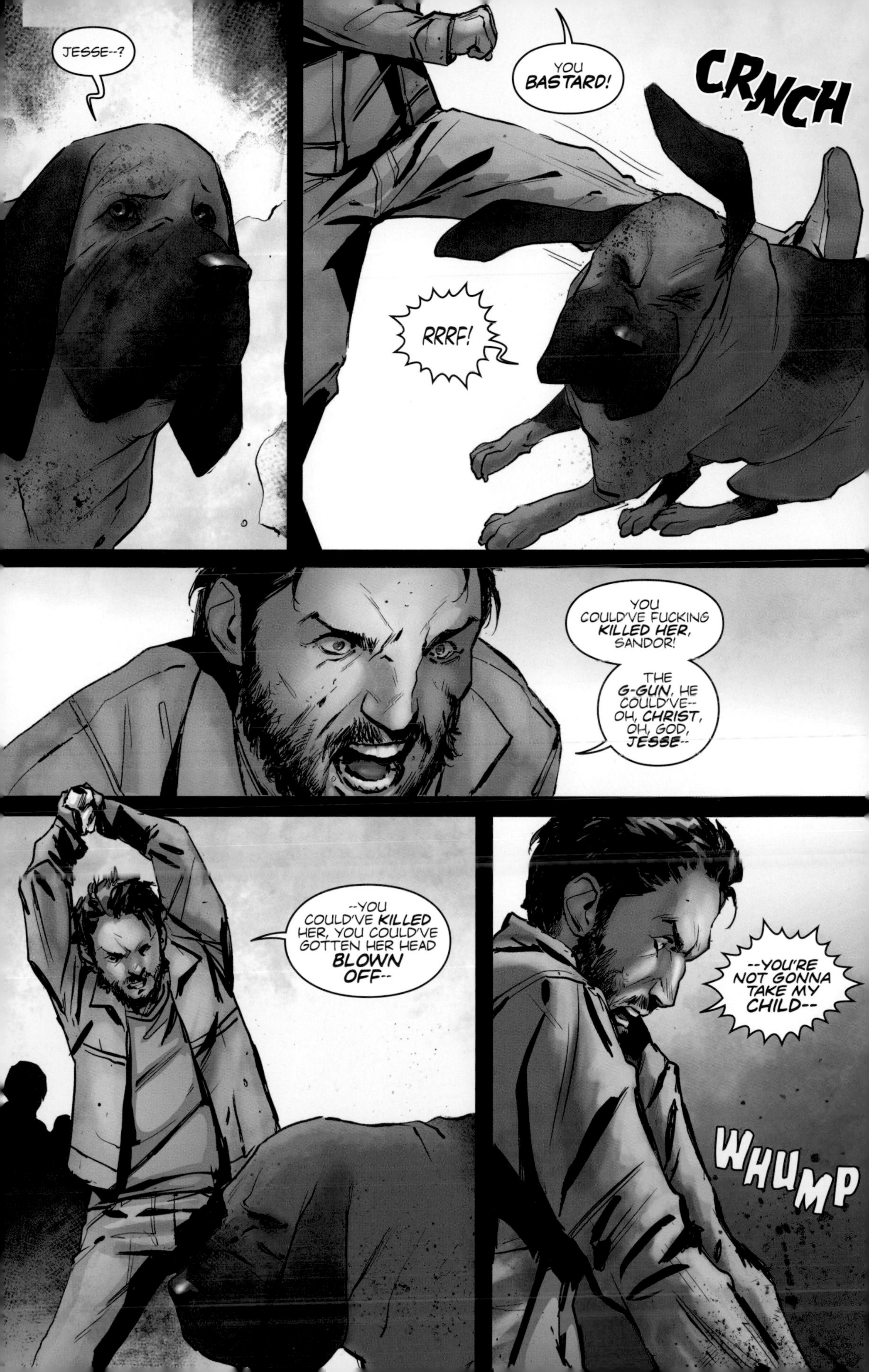
JESSE--?
YOU BASTARD!
CRNCH
RRRF!
YOU COULD'VE FUCKING KILLED HER, SANDOR!
THE G-GUN, HE COULD'VE-- OH, CHRIST, OH, GOD, JESSE--
--YOU COULD'VE KILLED HER, YOU COULD'VE GOTTEN HER HEAD BLOWN OFF--
--YOU'RE NOT GONNA TAKE MY CHILD--
WHUMP

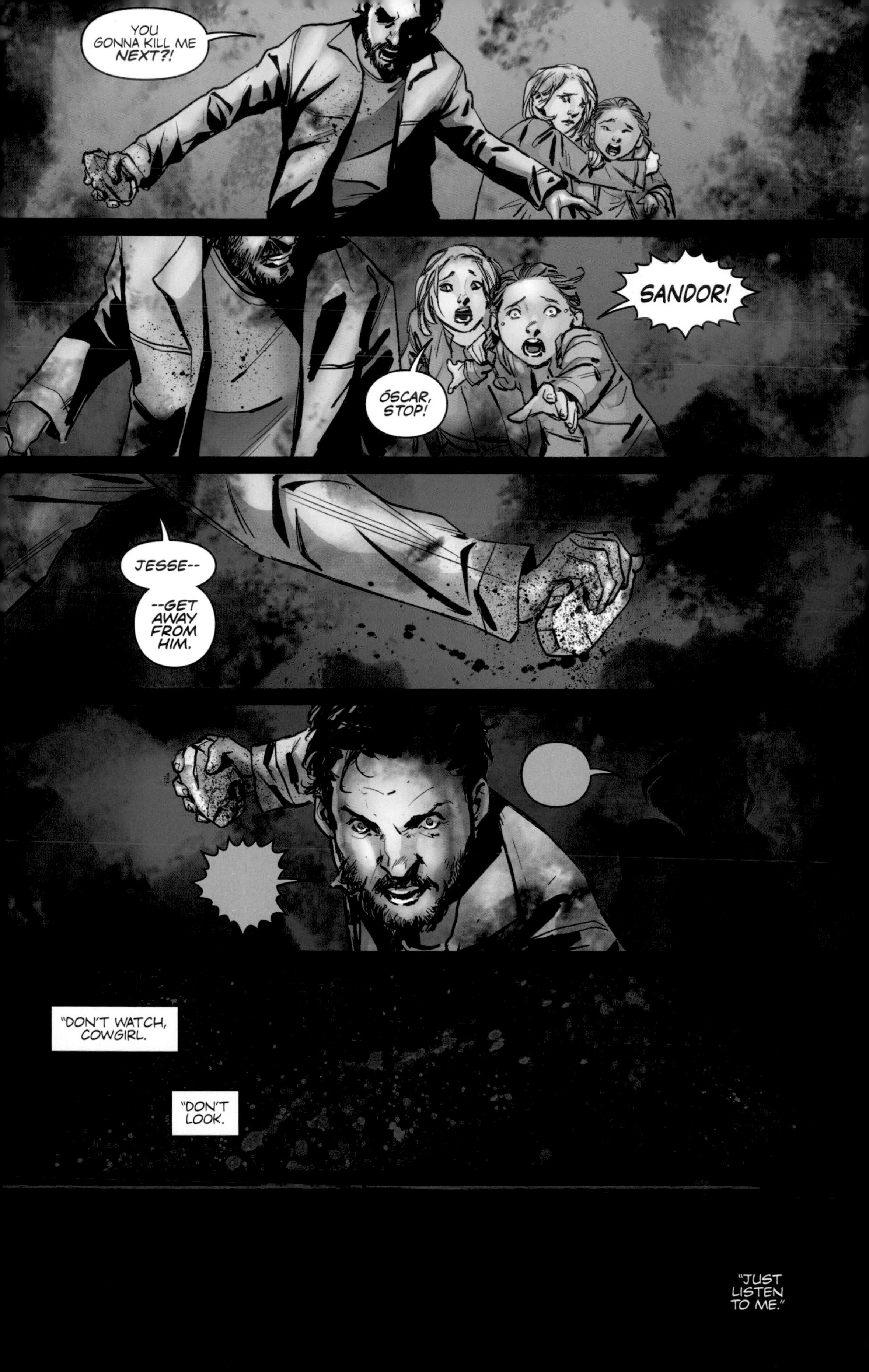

YOU GONNA KILL ME NEXT?!
SANDOR!
ÓSCAR, STOP!
JESSE--
--GET AWAY FROM HIM.
"DON'T WATCH, COWGIRL.
"DON'T LOOK.
"JUST LISTEN TO ME."

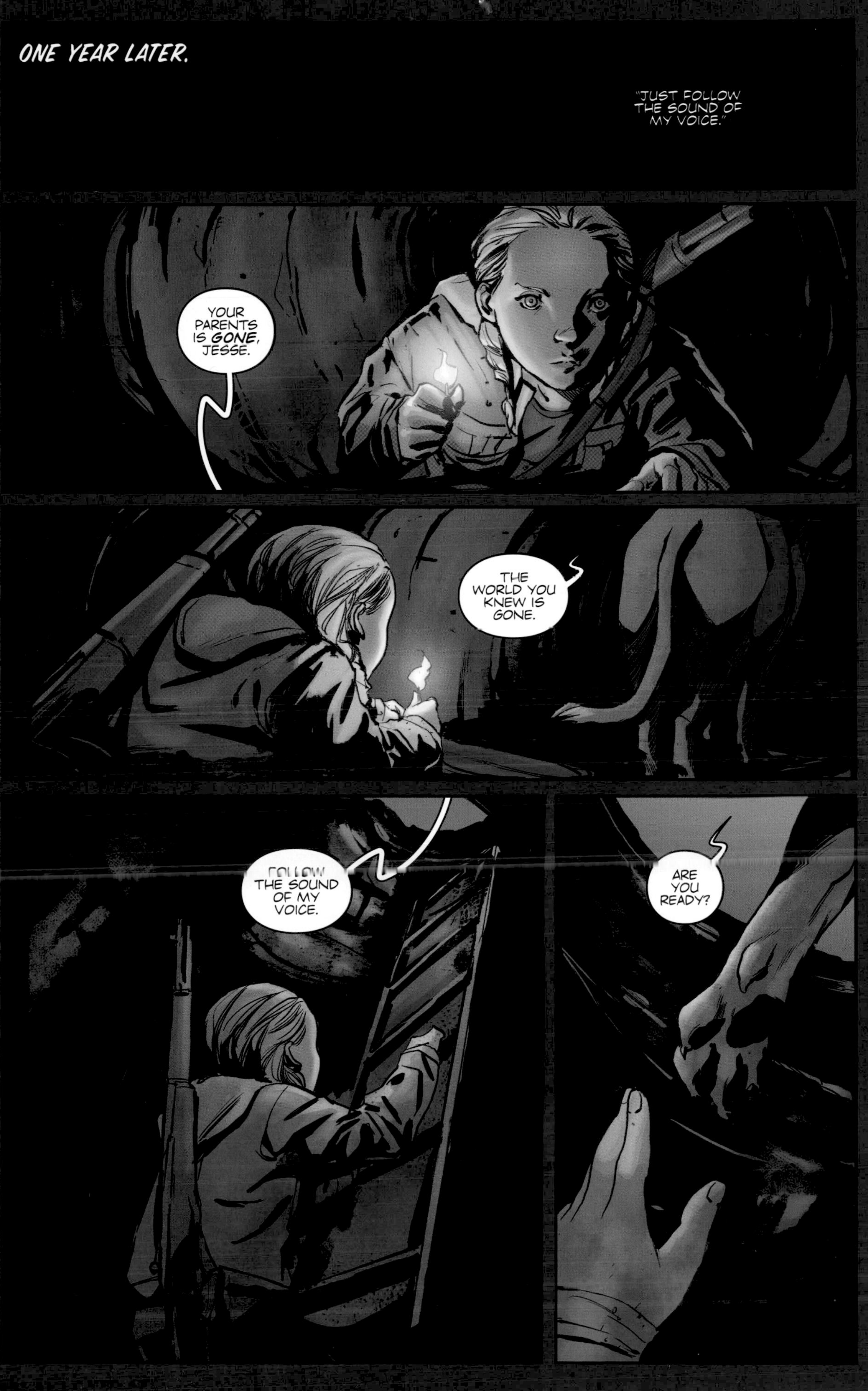
ONE YEAR LATER.
"JUST FOLLOW THE SOUND OF MY VOICE."
YOUR PARENTS IS GONE, JESSE.
THE WORLD YOU KNEW IS GONE.
FOLLOW THE SOUND OF MY VOICE.
ARE YOU READY?

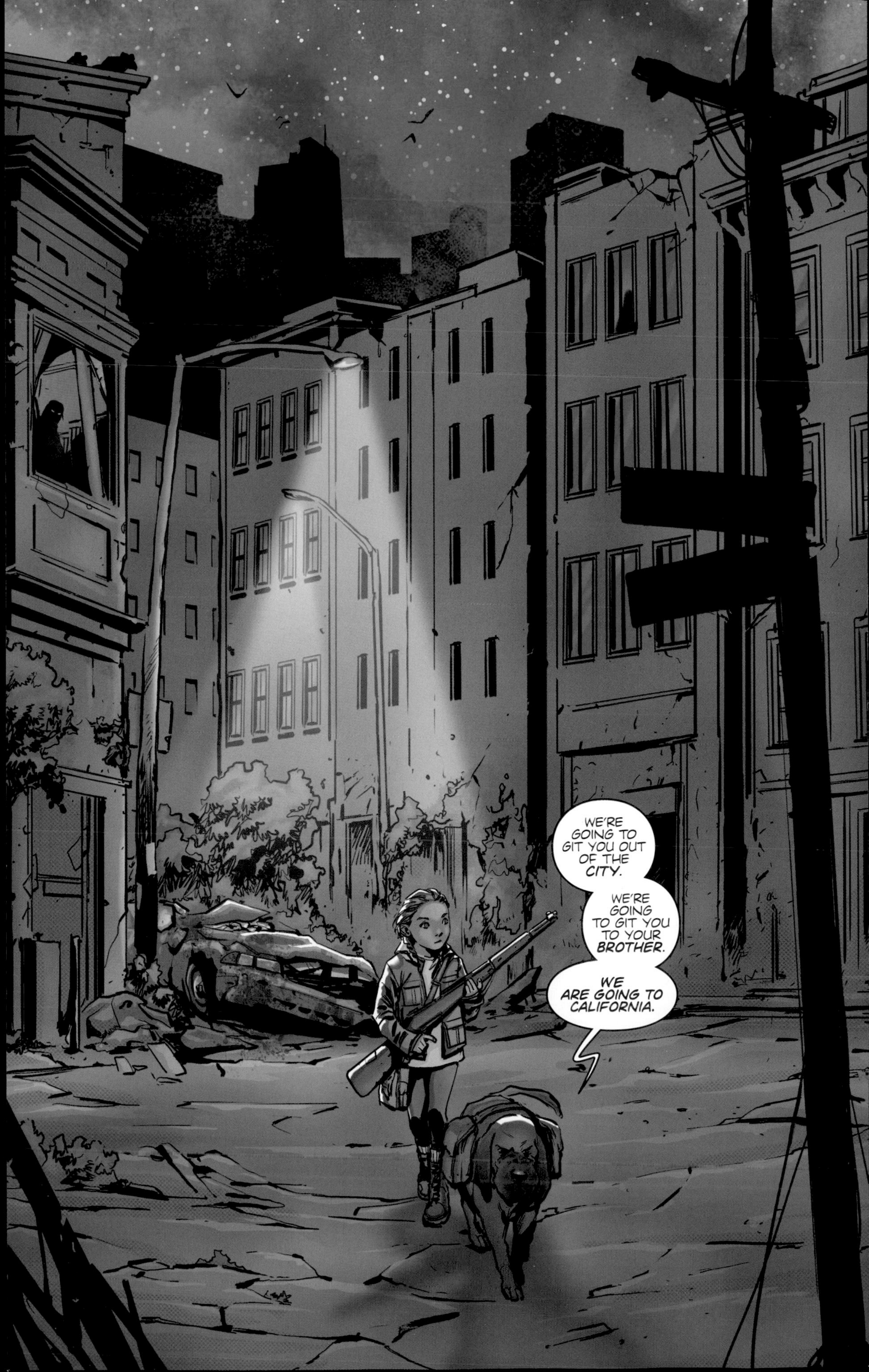
WE'RE GOING TO GIT YOU OUT OF THE CITY.
WE'RE GOING TO GIT YOU TO YOUR BROTHER.
WE ARE GOING TO CALIFORNIA.

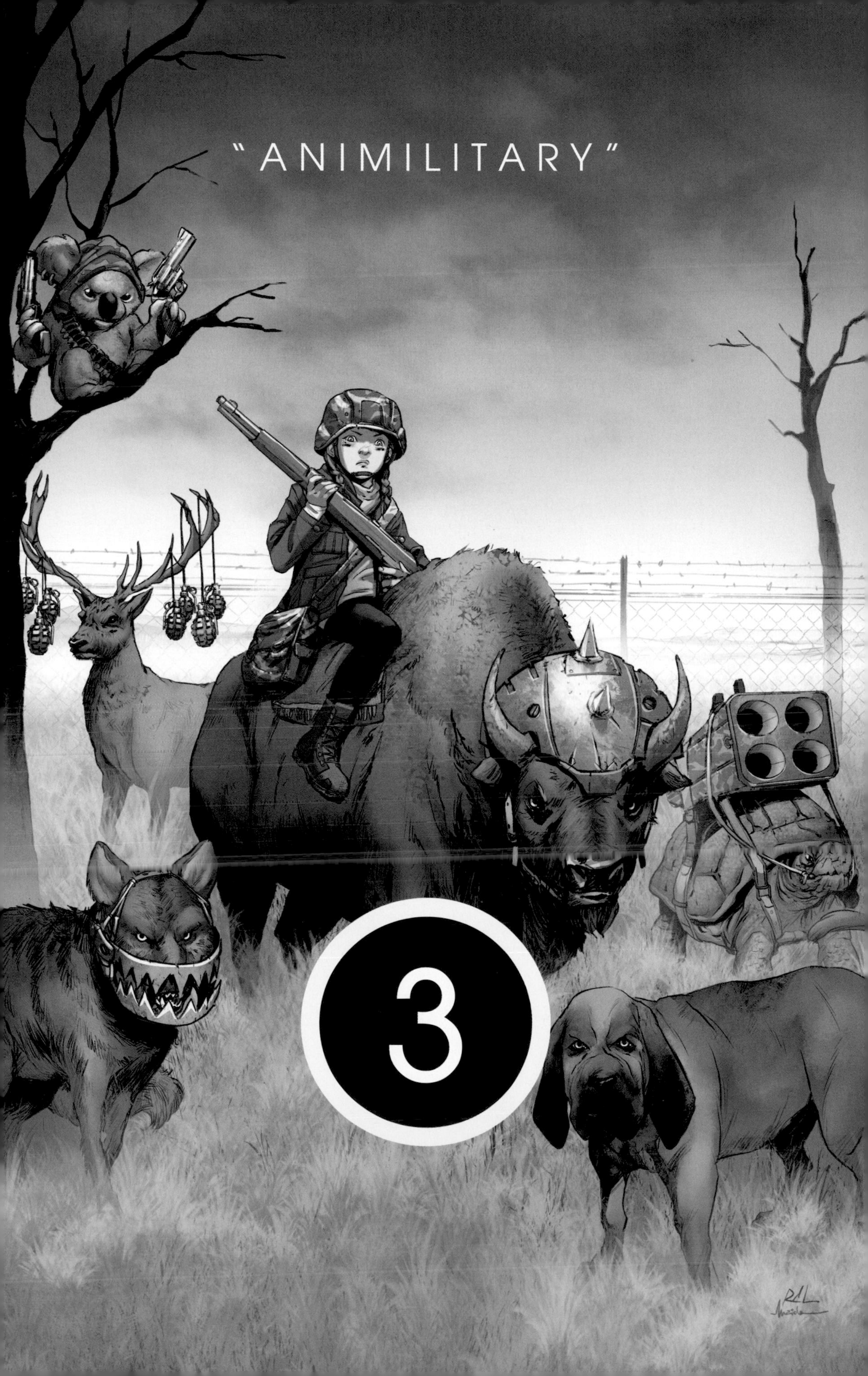
"ANIMILITARY"
3

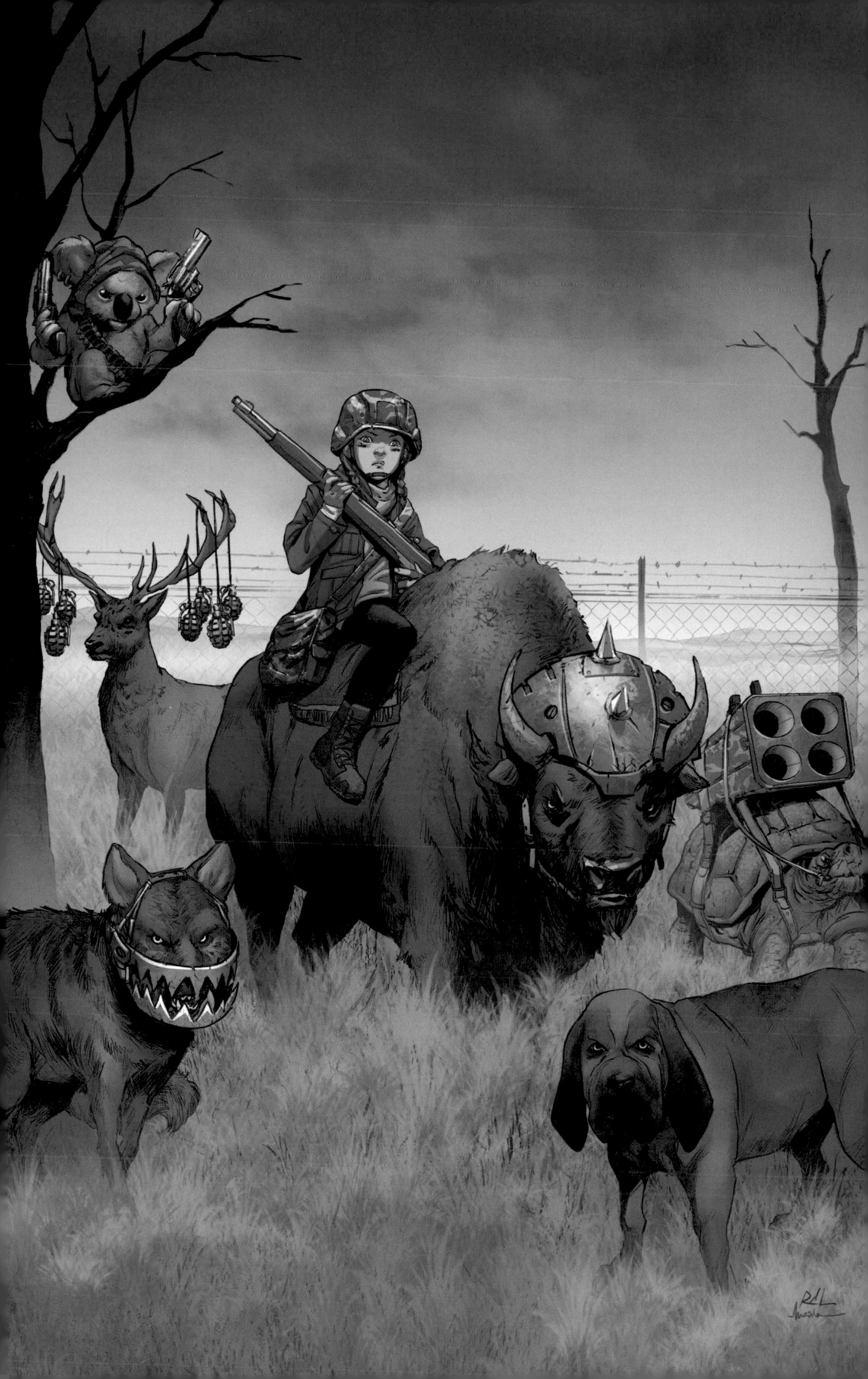

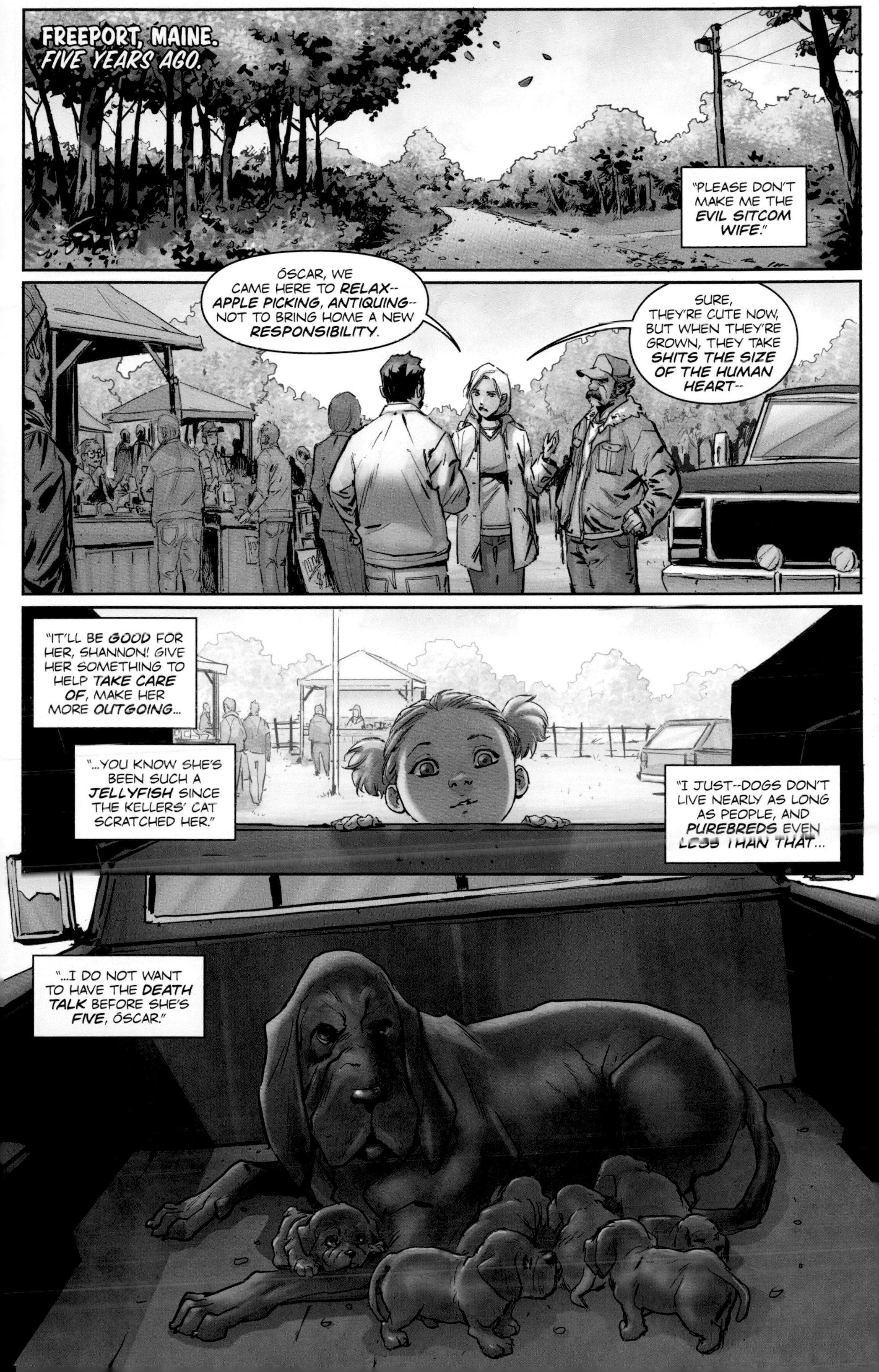
FREEPORT, MAINE.
FIVE YEARS AGO.
"PLEASE DON'T MAKE ME THE EVIL SITCOM WIFE."
ÓSCAR, WE CAME HERE TO RELAX-- APPLE PICKING, ANTIQUING-- NOT TO BRING HOME A NEW RESPONSIBILITY.
SURE, THEY'RE CUTE NOW, BUT WHEN THEY'RE GROWN, THEY TAKE SHITS THE SIZE OF THE HUMAN HEART--
"IT'LL BE GOOD FOR HER, SHANNON! GIVE HER SOMETHING TO HELP TAKE CARE OF, MAKE HER MORE OUTGOING...
"...YOU KNOW SHE'S BEEN SUCH A JELLYFISH SINCE THE KELLERS' CAT SCRATCHED HER."
"I JUST--DOGS DON'T LIVE NEARLY AS LONG AS PEOPLE, AND PUREBREDS EVEN LESS THAN THAT...
"...I DO NOT WANT TO HAVE THE DEATH TALK BEFORE SHE'S FIVE, ÓSCAR."

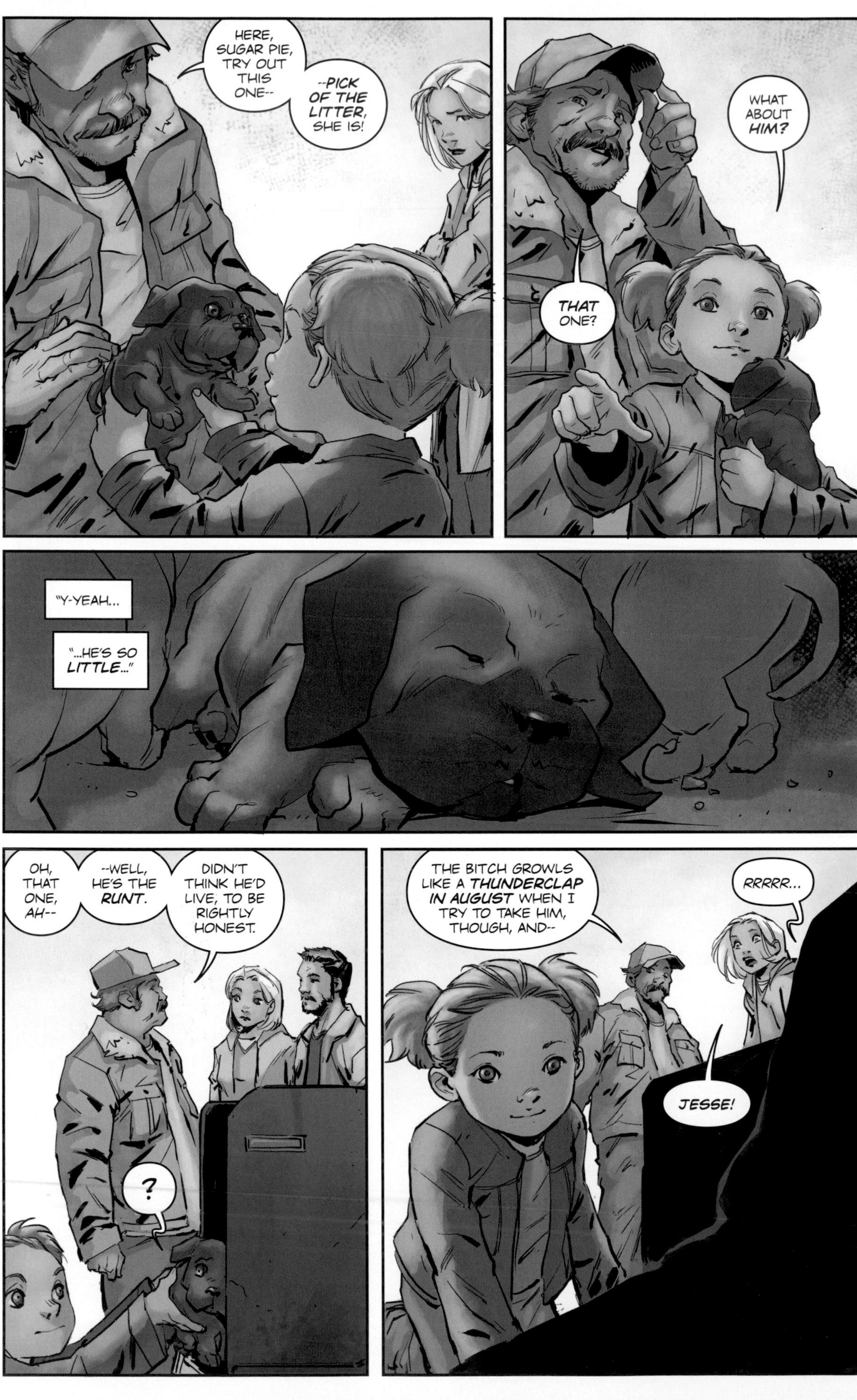
HERE, SUGAR PIE, TRY OUT THIS ONE--
--PICK OF THE LITTER, SHE IS!
WHAT ABOUT HIM?
THAT ONE?
"Y-YEAH...
"...HE'S SO LITTLE..."
OH, THAT ONE, AH--
--WELL, HE'S THE RUNT.
DIDN'T THINK HE'D LIVE, TO BE RIGHTLY HONEST.
?
THE BITCH GROWLS LIKE A THUNDERCLAP IN AUGUST WHEN I TRY TO TAKE HIM, THOUGH, AND--
RRRRR...
JESSE!

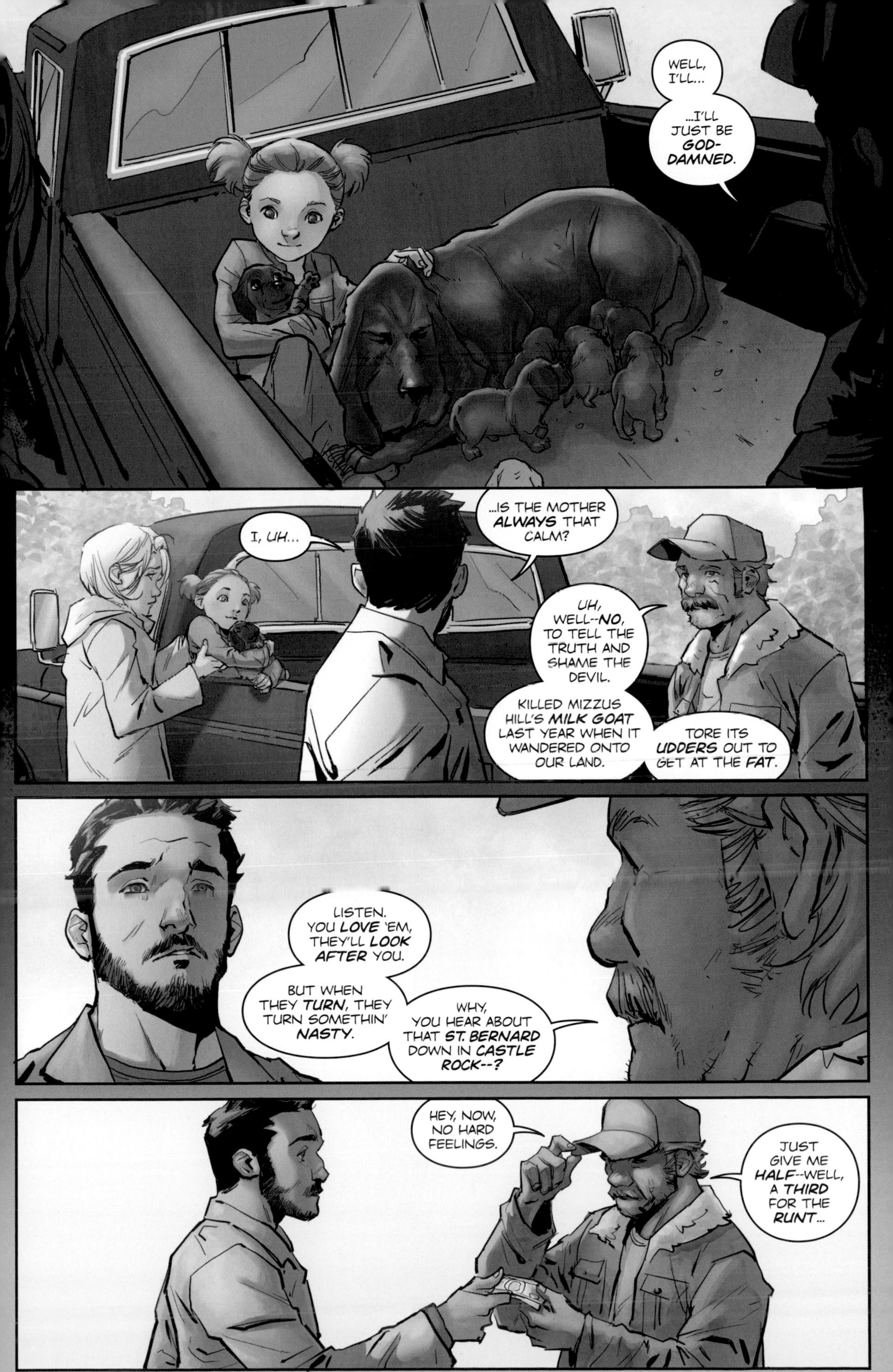
WELL, I'LL...
...I'LL JUST BE GOD-DAMNED.
I, UH...
...IS THE MOTHER ALWAYS THAT CALM?
UH, WELL--NO, TO TELL THE TRUTH AND SHAME THE DEVIL.
KILLED MIZZUS HILL'S MILK GOAT LAST YEAR WHEN IT WANDERED ONTO OUR LAND.
TORE ITS UDDERS OUT TO GET AT THE FAT.
LISTEN. YOU LOVE 'EM, THEY'LL LOOK AFTER YOU.
BUT WHEN THEY TURN, THEY TURN SOMETHIN' NASTY.
WHY, YOU HEAR ABOUT THAT ST. BERNARD DOWN IN CASTLE ROCK--?
HEY, NOW, NO HARD FEELINGS.
JUST GIVE ME HALF--WELL, A THIRD FOR THE RUNT...

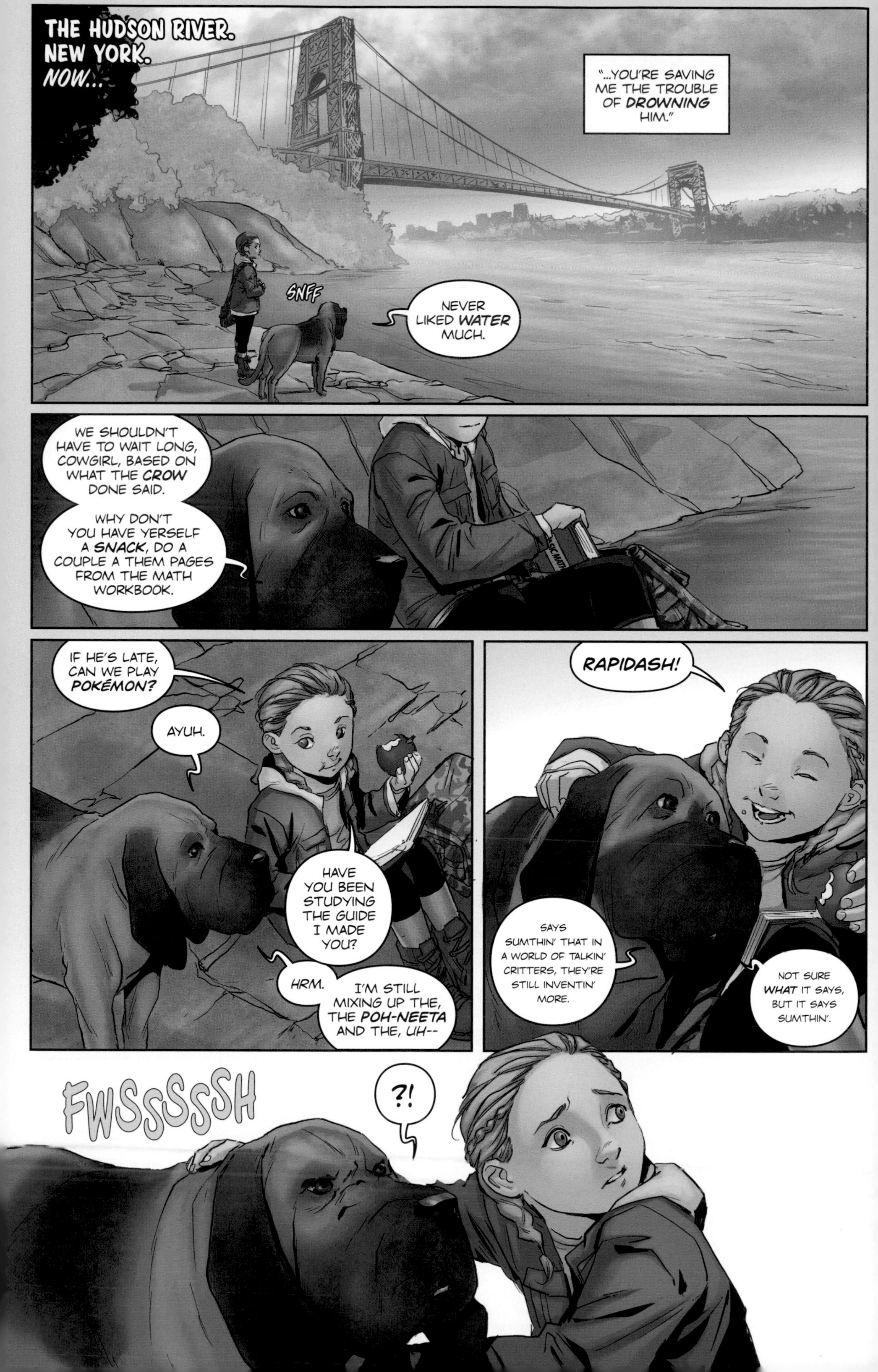
THE HUDSON RIVER. NEW YORK. NOW...
"...YOU'RE SAVING ME THE TROUBLE OF DROWNING HIM."
SNFF
NEVER LIKED WATER MUCH.
WE SHOULDN'T HAVE TO WAIT LONG, COWGIRL, BASED ON WHAT THE CROW DONE SAID.
WHY DON'T YOU HAVE YERSELF A SNACK, DO A COUPLE A THEM PAGES FROM THE MATH WORKBOOK.
IF HE'S LATE, CAN WE PLAY POKÉMON?
AYUH.
HAVE YOU BEEN STUDYING THE GUIDE I MADE YOU?
HRM.
I'M STILL MIXING UP THE, THE POH-NEETA AND THE, UH--
RAPIDASH!
SAYS SUMTHIN' THAT IN A WORLD OF TALKIN' CRITTERS, THEY'RE STILL INVENTIN' MORE.
NOT SURE WHAT IT SAYS, BUT IT SAYS SUMTHIN'.
FWSSSSSSH
?!

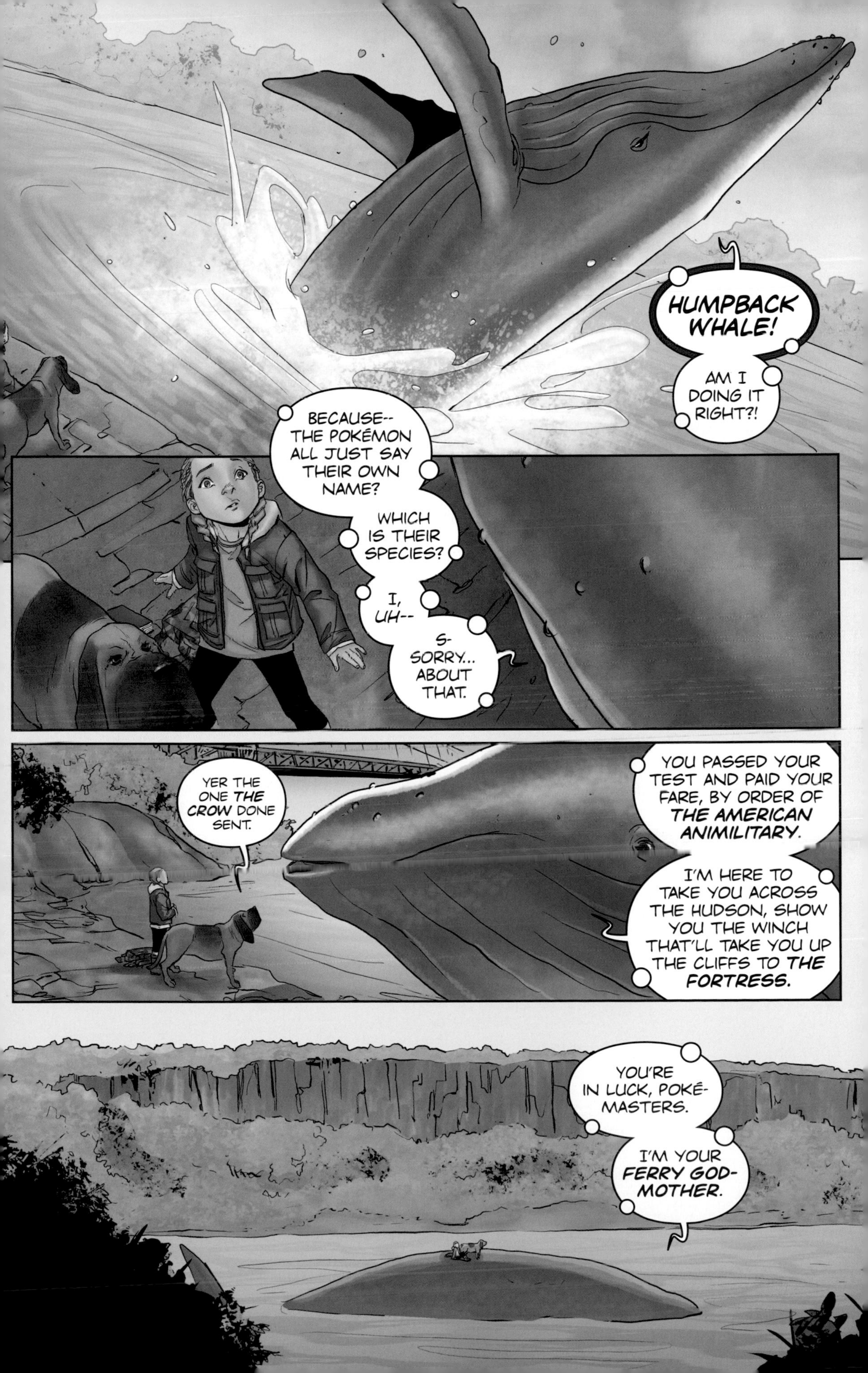
HUMPBACK WHALE!
AM I DOING IT RIGHT?!
BECAUSE-- THE POKÉMON ALL JUST SAY THEIR OWN NAME?
WHICH IS THEIR SPECIES?
I, UH--
S- SORRY... ABOUT THAT.
YER THE ONE THE CROW DONE SENT.
YOU PASSED YOUR TEST AND PAID YOUR FARE, BY ORDER OF THE AMERICAN ANIMILITARY.
I'M HERE TO TAKE YOU ACROSS THE HUDSON, SHOW YOU THE WINCH THAT'LL TAKE YOU UP THE CLIFFS TO THE FORTRESS.
YOU'RE IN LUCK, POKÉ-MASTERS.
I'M YOUR FERRY GOD-MOTHER.

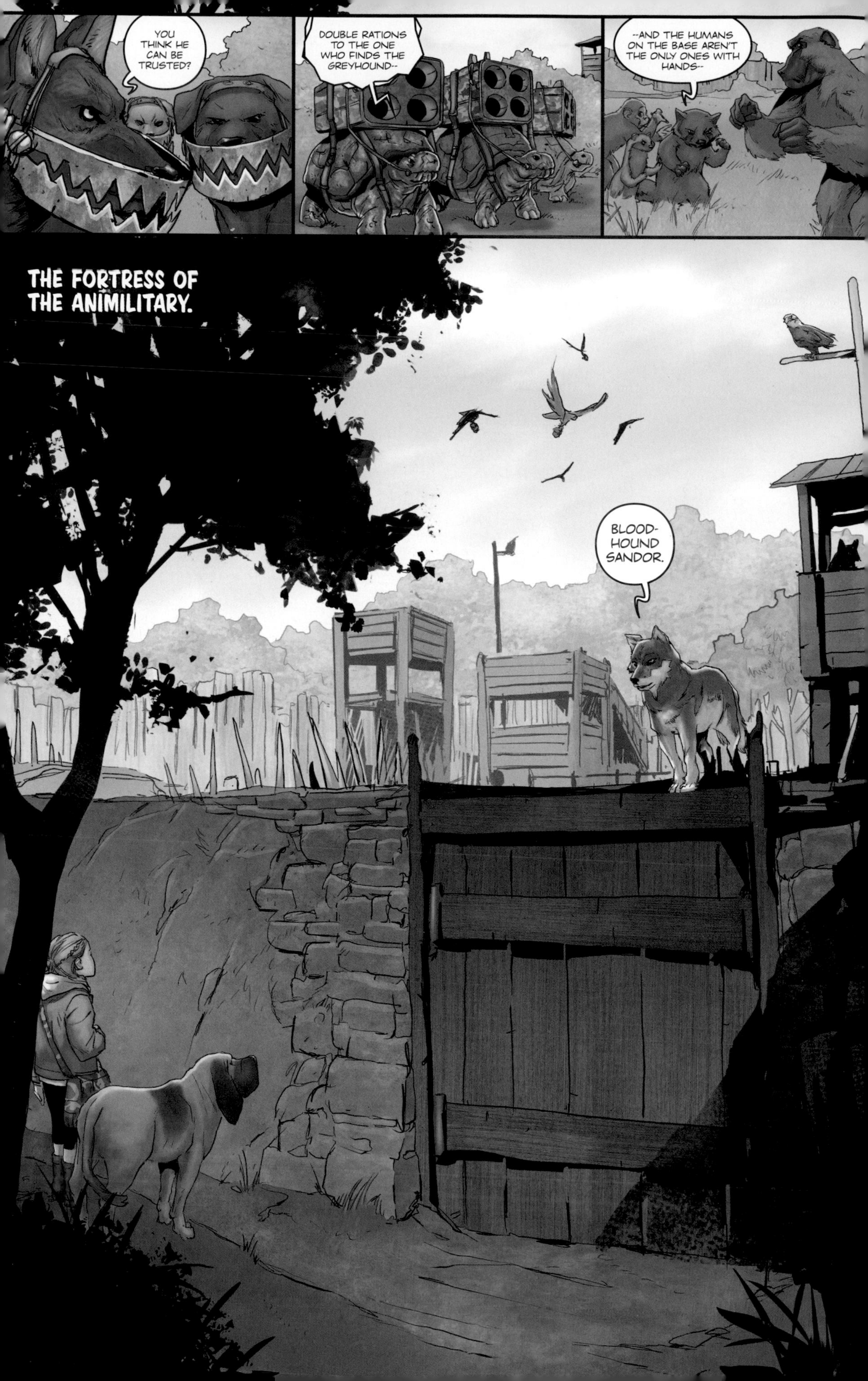
YOU THINK HE CAN BE TRUSTED?
DOUBLE RATIONS TO THE ONE WHO FINDS THE GREYHOUND--
--AND THE HUMANS ON THE BASE AREN'T THE ONLY ONES WITH HANDS--
THE FORTRESS OF THE ANIMILITARY.
BLOOD-HOUND SANDOR.

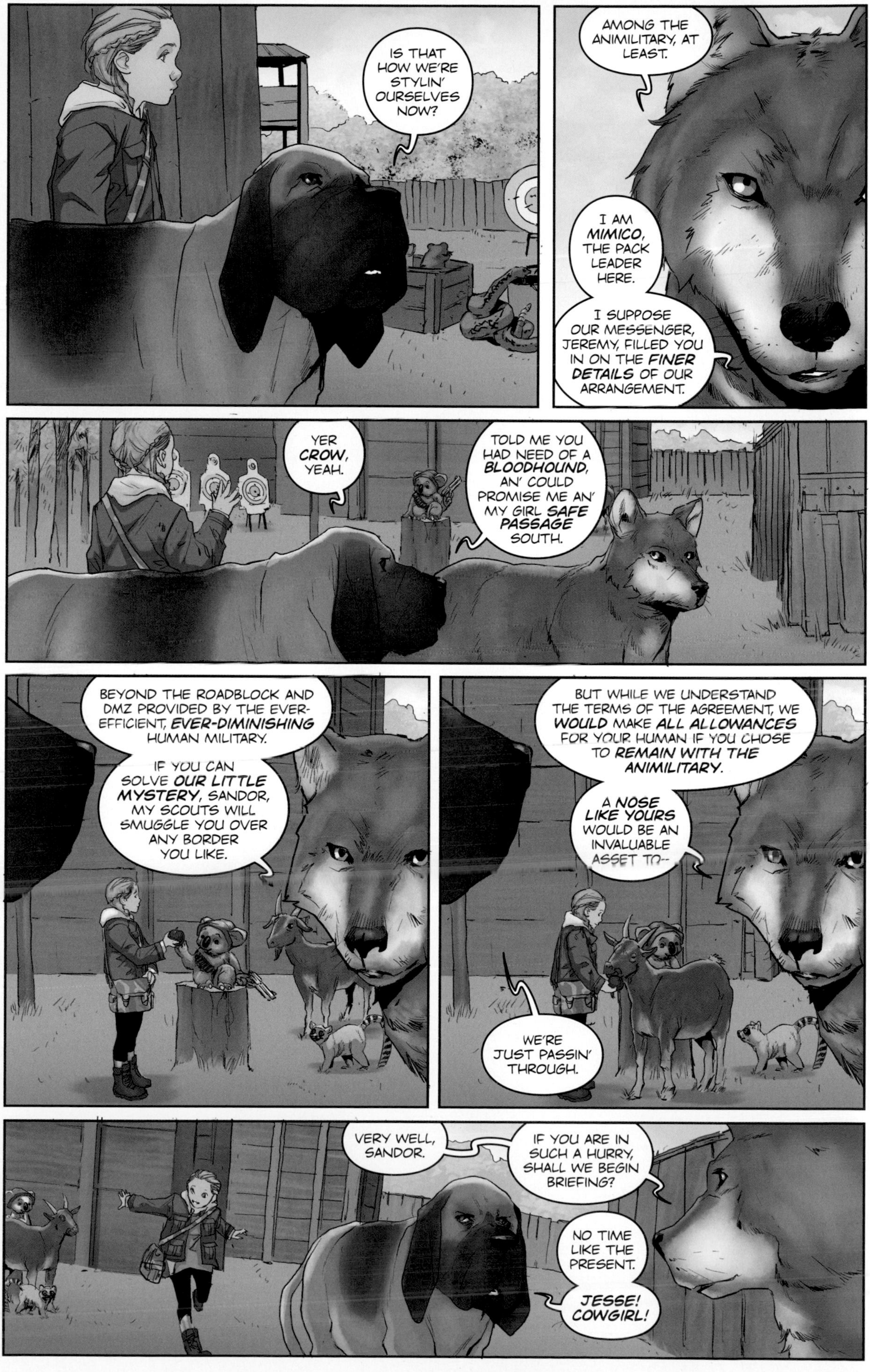
IS THAT HOW WE'RE STYLIN' OURSELVES NOW?
AMONG THE ANIMILITARY, AT LEAST.
I AM MIMICO, THE PACK LEADER HERE.
I SUPPOSE OUR MESSENGER, JEREMY, FILLED YOU IN ON THE FINER DETAILS OF OUR ARRANGEMENT.
YER CROW, YEAH.
TOLD ME YOU HAD NEED OF A BLOODHOUND, AN' COULD PROMISE ME AN' MY GIRL SAFE PASSAGE SOUTH.
BEYOND THE ROADBLOCK AND DMZ PROVIDED BY THE EVER-EFFICIENT, EVER-DIMINISHING HUMAN MILITARY.
IF YOU CAN SOLVE OUR LITTLE MYSTERY, SANDOR, MY SCOUTS WILL SMUGGLE YOU OVER ANY BORDER YOU LIKE.
BUT WHILE WE UNDERSTAND THE TERMS OF THE AGREEMENT, WE WOULD MAKE ALL ALLOWANCES FOR YOUR HUMAN IF YOU CHOSE TO REMAIN WITH THE ANIMILITARY.
A NOSE LIKE YOURS WOULD BE AN INVALUABLE ASSET TO--
WE'RE JUST PASSIN' THROUGH.
VERY WELL, SANDOR.
IF YOU ARE IN SUCH A HURRY, SHALL WE BEGIN BRIEFING?
NO TIME LIKE THE PRESENT.
JESSE! COWGIRL!

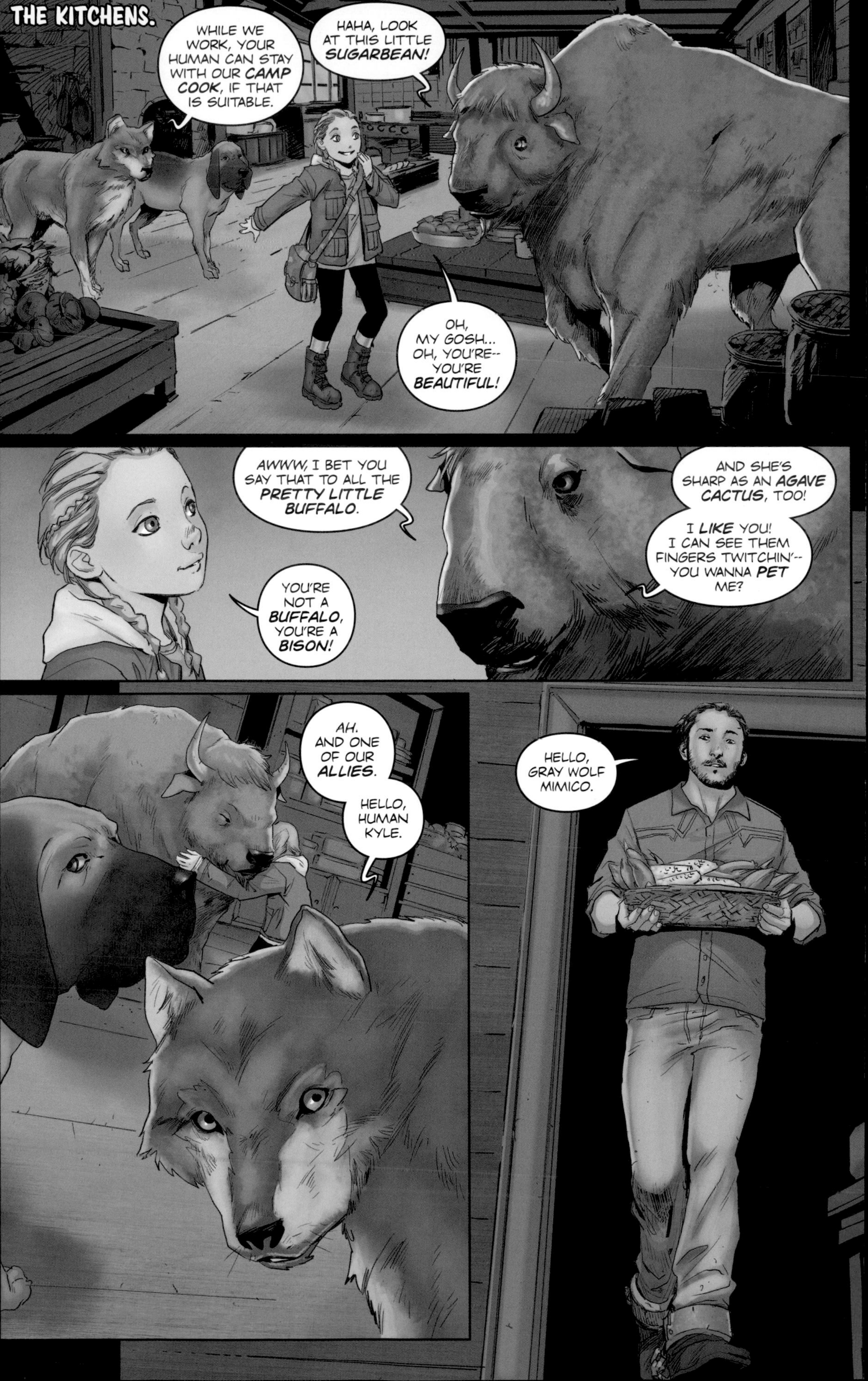
THE KITCHENS.
WHILE WE WORK, YOUR HUMAN CAN STAY WITH OUR CAMP COOK, IF THAT IS SUITABLE.
HAHA, LOOK AT THIS LITTLE SUGARBEAN!
OH, MY GOSH... OH, YOU'RE-- YOU'RE BEAUTIFUL!
AWWW, I BET YOU SAY THAT TO ALL THE PRETTY LITTLE BUFFALO.
YOU'RE NOT A BUFFALO, YOU'RE A BISON!
AND SHE'S SHARP AS AN AGAVE CACTUS, TOO!
I LIKE YOU! I CAN SEE THEM FINGERS TWITCHIN'-- YOU WANNA PET ME?
AH. AND ONE OF OUR ALLIES.
HELLO, HUMAN KYLE.
HELLO, GRAY WOLF MIMICO.

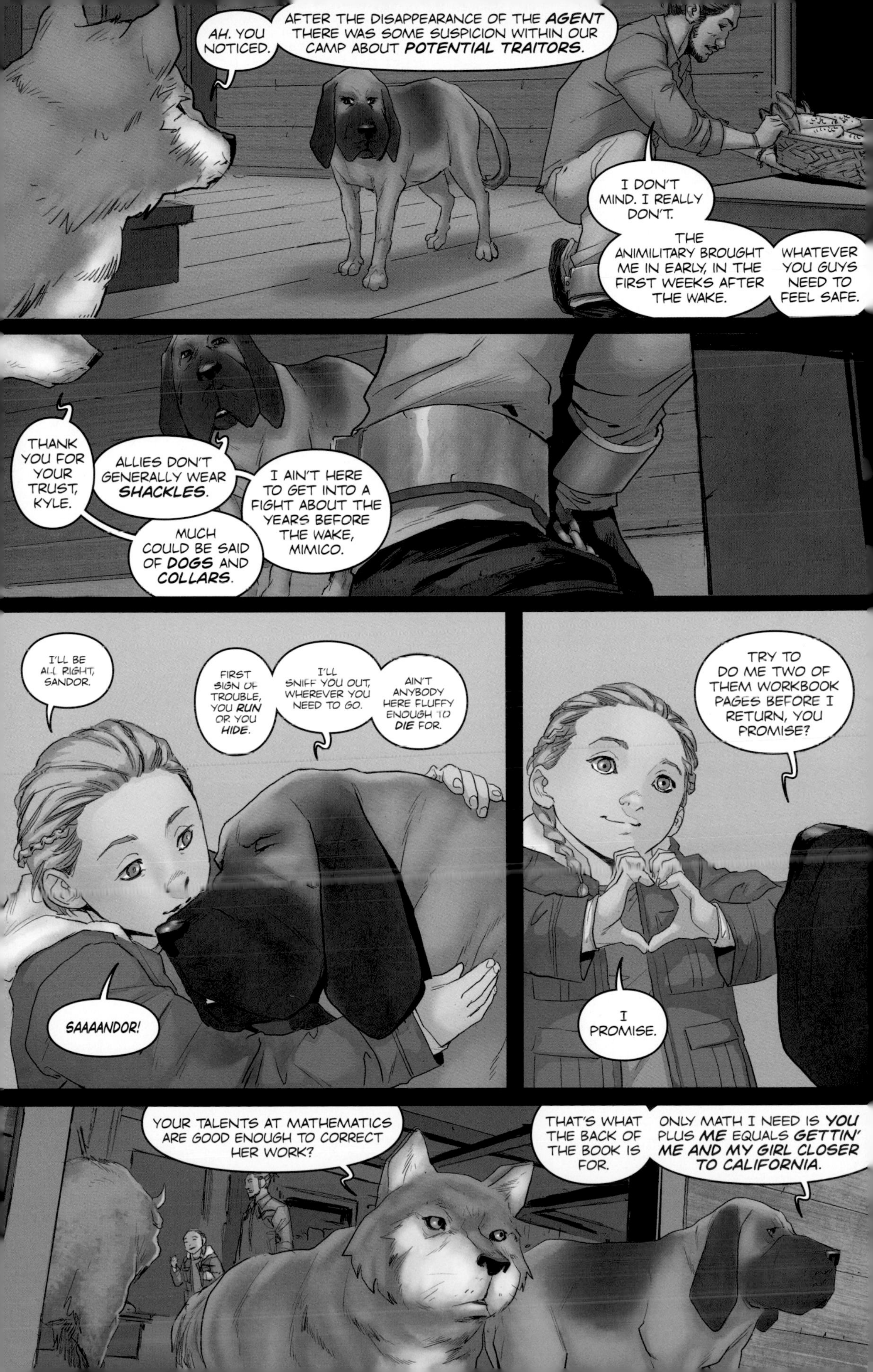
AH. YOU NOTICED.
AFTER THE DISAPPEARANCE OF THE AGENT THERE WAS SOME SUSPICION WITHIN OUR CAMP ABOUT POTENTIAL TRAITORS.
I DON'T MIND. I REALLY DON'T.
THE ANIMILITARY BROUGHT ME IN EARLY, IN THE FIRST WEEKS AFTER THE WAKE.
WHATEVER YOU GUYS NEED TO FEEL SAFE.
THANK YOU FOR YOUR TRUST, KYLE.
ALLIES DON'T GENERALLY WEAR SHACKLES.
MUCH COULD BE SAID OF DOGS AND COLLARS.
I AIN'T HERE TO GET INTO A FIGHT ABOUT THE YEARS BEFORE THE WAKE, MIMICO.
I'LL BE ALL RIGHT, SANDOR.
FIRST SIGN OF TROUBLE, YOU RUN OR YOU HIDE.
I'LL SNIFF YOU OUT, WHEREVER YOU NEED TO GO.
AIN'T ANYBODY HERE FLUFFY ENOUGH TO DIE FOR.
SAAAANDOR!
TRY TO DO ME TWO OF THEM WORKBOOK PAGES BEFORE I RETURN, YOU PROMISE?
I PROMISE.
YOUR TALENTS AT MATHEMATICS ARE GOOD ENOUGH TO CORRECT HER WORK?
THAT'S WHAT THE BACK OF THE BOOK IS FOR.
ONLY MATH I NEED IS YOU PLUS ME EQUALS GETTIN' ME AND MY GIRL CLOSER TO CALIFORNIA.

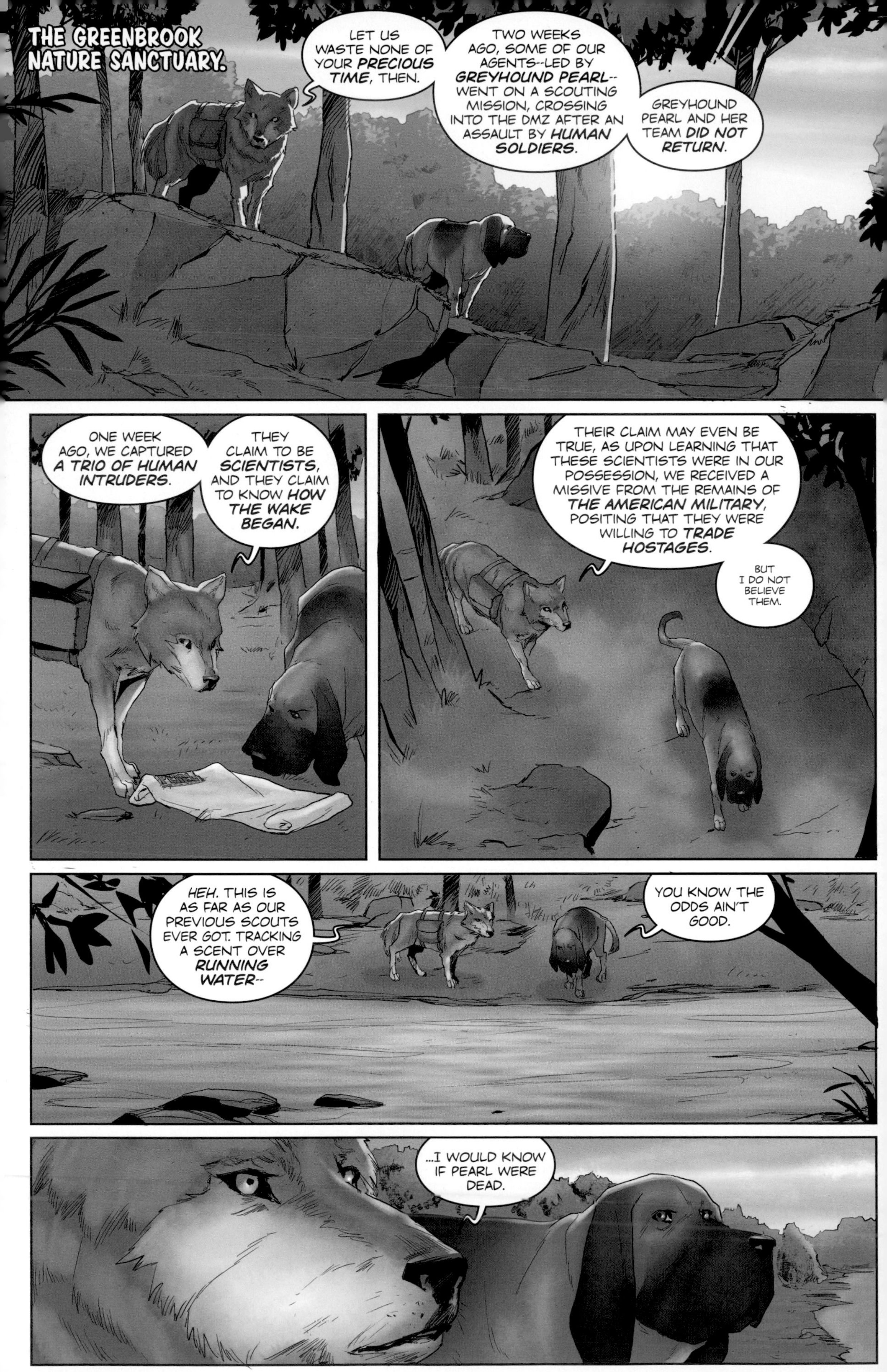
THE GREENBROOK NATURE SANCTUARY.
LET US WASTE NONE OF YOUR PRECIOUS TIME, THEN.
TWO WEEKS AGO, SOME OF OUR AGENTS--LED BY GREYHOUND PEARL--WENT ON A SCOUTING MISSION, CROSSING INTO THE DMZ AFTER AN ASSAULT BY HUMAN SOLDIERS.
GREYHOUND PEARL AND HER TEAM DID NOT RETURN.
ONE WEEK AGO, WE CAPTURED A TRIO OF HUMAN INTRUDERS.
THEY CLAIM TO BE SCIENTISTS, AND THEY CLAIM TO KNOW HOW THE WAKE BEGAN.
THEIR CLAIM MAY EVEN BE TRUE, AS UPON LEARNING THAT THESE SCIENTISTS WERE IN OUR POSSESSION, WE RECEIVED A MISSIVE FROM THE REMAINS OF THE AMERICAN MILITARY, POSITING THAT THEY WERE WILLING TO TRADE HOSTAGES.
BUT I DO NOT BELIEVE THEM.
HEH. THIS IS AS FAR AS OUR PREVIOUS SCOUTS EVER GOT. TRACKING A SCENT OVER RUNNING WATER--
YOU KNOW THE ODDS AIN'T GOOD.
...I WOULD KNOW IF PEARL WERE DEAD.

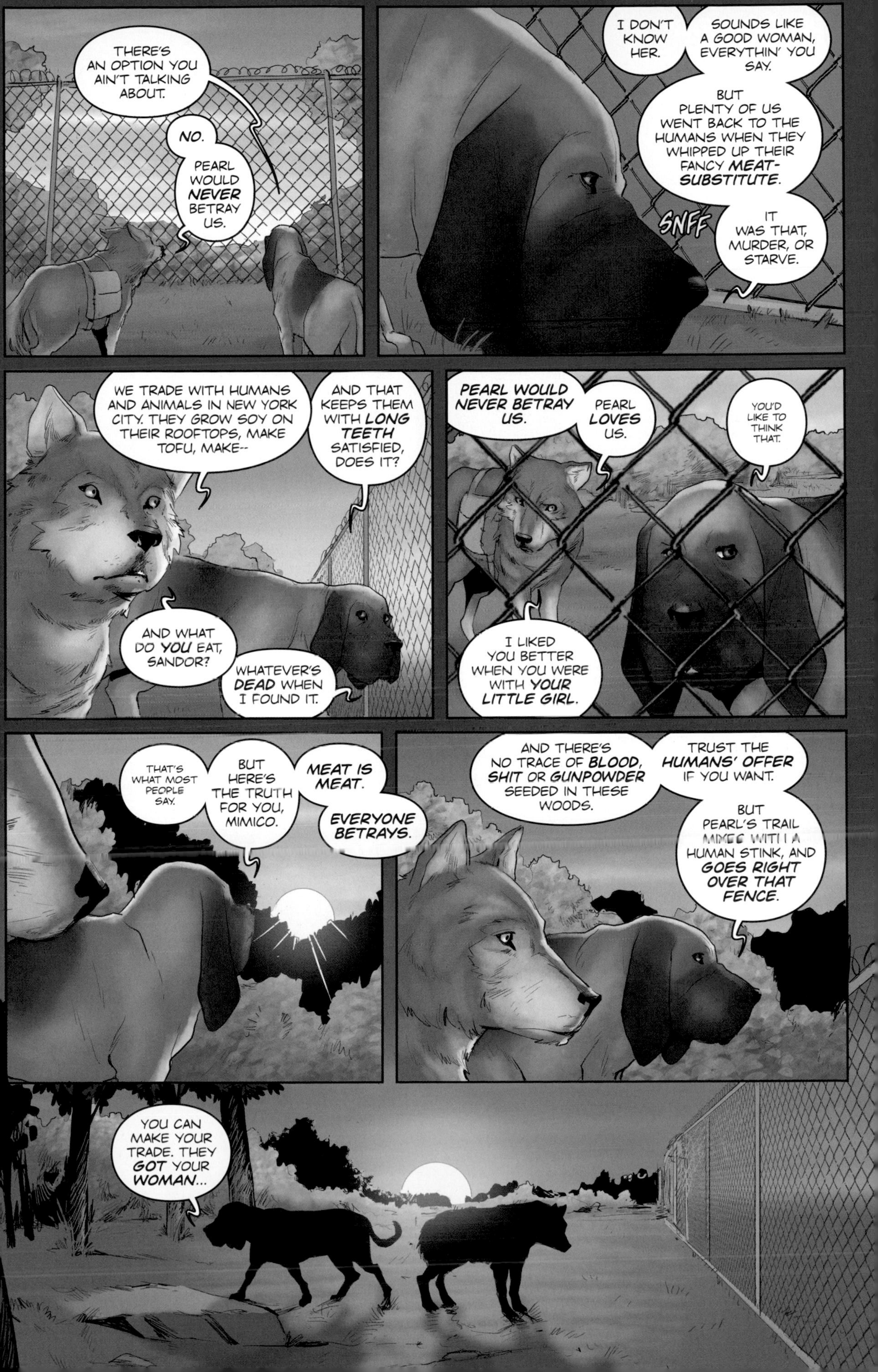
THERE'S AN OPTION YOU AIN'T TALKING ABOUT.
NO.
PEARL WOULD NEVER BETRAY US.
I DON'T KNOW HER.
SOUNDS LIKE A GOOD WOMAN, EVERYTHIN' YOU SAY.
BUT PLENTY OF US WENT BACK TO THE HUMANS WHEN THEY WHIPPED UP THEIR FANCY MEAT-SUBSTITUTE.
SNFF
IT WAS THAT, MURDER, OR STARVE.
WE TRADE WITH HUMANS AND ANIMALS IN NEW YORK CITY. THEY GROW SOY ON THEIR ROOFTOPS, MAKE TOFU, MAKE--
AND THAT KEEPS THEM WITH LONG TEETH SATISFIED, DOES IT?
AND WHAT DO YOU EAT, SANDOR?
WHATEVER'S DEAD WHEN I FOUND IT.
PEARL WOULD NEVER BETRAY US.
PEARL LOVES US.
YOU'D LIKE TO THINK THAT.
I LIKED YOU BETTER WHEN YOU WERE WITH YOUR LITTLE GIRL.
THAT'S WHAT MOST PEOPLE SAY.
BUT HERE'S THE TRUTH FOR YOU, MIMICO.
MEAT IS MEAT.
EVERYONE BETRAYS.
AND THERE'S NO TRACE OF BLOOD, SHIT OR GUNPOWDER SEEDED IN THESE WOODS.
TRUST THE HUMANS' OFFER IF YOU WANT.
BUT PEARL'S TRAIL MIXES WITH A HUMAN STINK, AND GOES RIGHT OVER THAT FENCE.
YOU CAN MAKE YOUR TRADE. THEY GOT YOUR WOMAN...

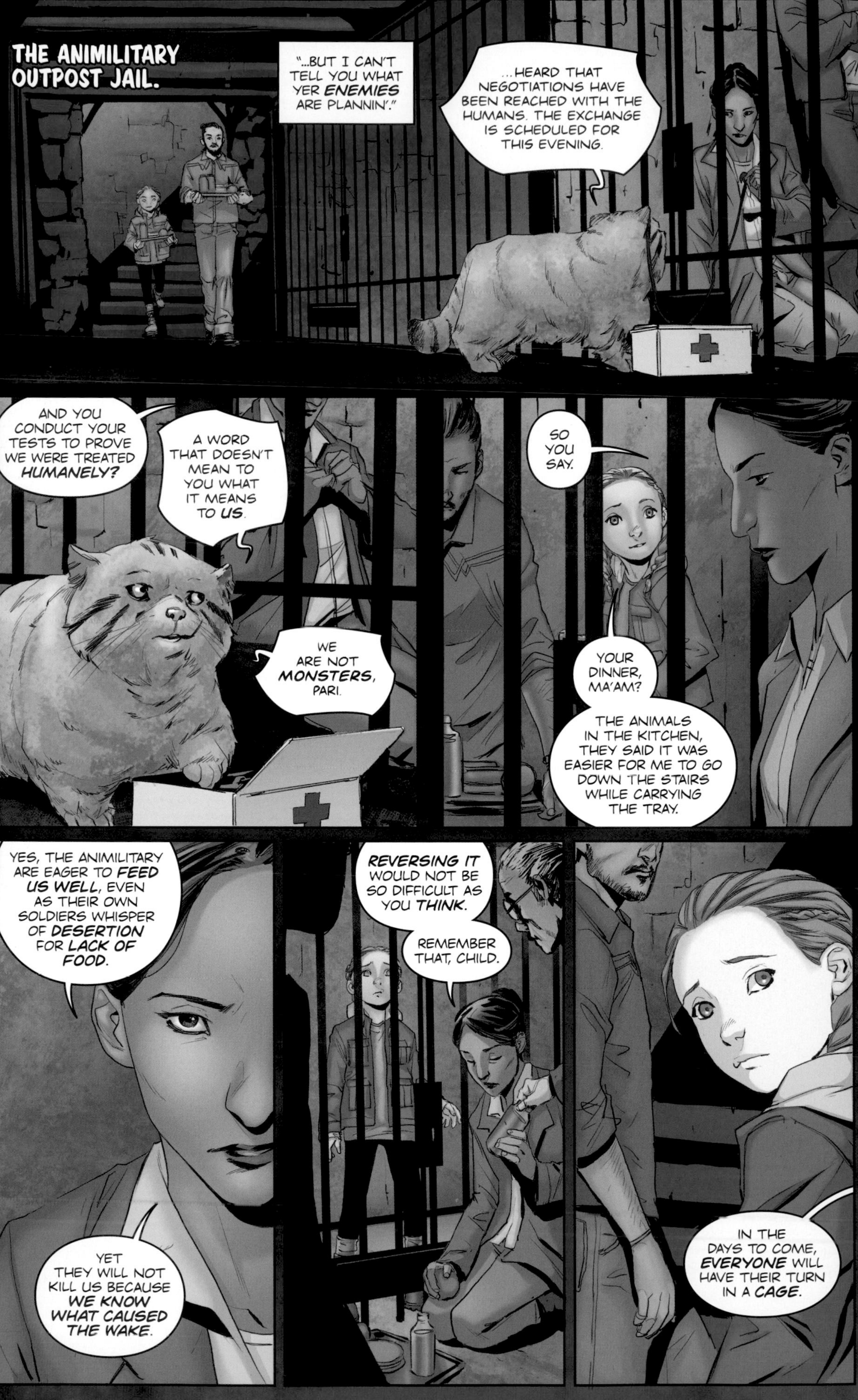
THE ANIMILITARY OUTPOST JAIL.
"...BUT I CAN'T TELL YOU WHAT YER ENEMIES ARE PLANNIN'."
...HEARD THAT NEGOTIATIONS HAVE BEEN REACHED WITH THE HUMANS. THE EXCHANGE IS SCHEDULED FOR THIS EVENING.
AND YOU CONDUCT YOUR TESTS TO PROVE WE WERE TREATED HUMANELY?
A WORD THAT DOESN'T MEAN TO YOU WHAT IT MEANS TO US.
WE ARE NOT MONSTERS, PARI.
SO YOU SAY.
YOUR DINNER, MA'AM?
THE ANIMALS IN THE KITCHEN, THEY SAID IT WAS EASIER FOR ME TO GO DOWN THE STAIRS WHILE CARRYING THE TRAY.
YES, THE ANIMILITARY ARE EAGER TO FEED US WELL, EVEN AS THEIR OWN SOLDIERS WHISPER OF DESERTION FOR LACK OF FOOD.
YET THEY WILL NOT KILL US BECAUSE WE KNOW WHAT CAUSED THE WAKE.
REVERSING IT WOULD NOT BE SO DIFFICULT AS YOU THINK.
REMEMBER THAT, CHILD.
IN THE DAYS TO COME, EVERYONE WILL HAVE THEIR TURN IN A CAGE.

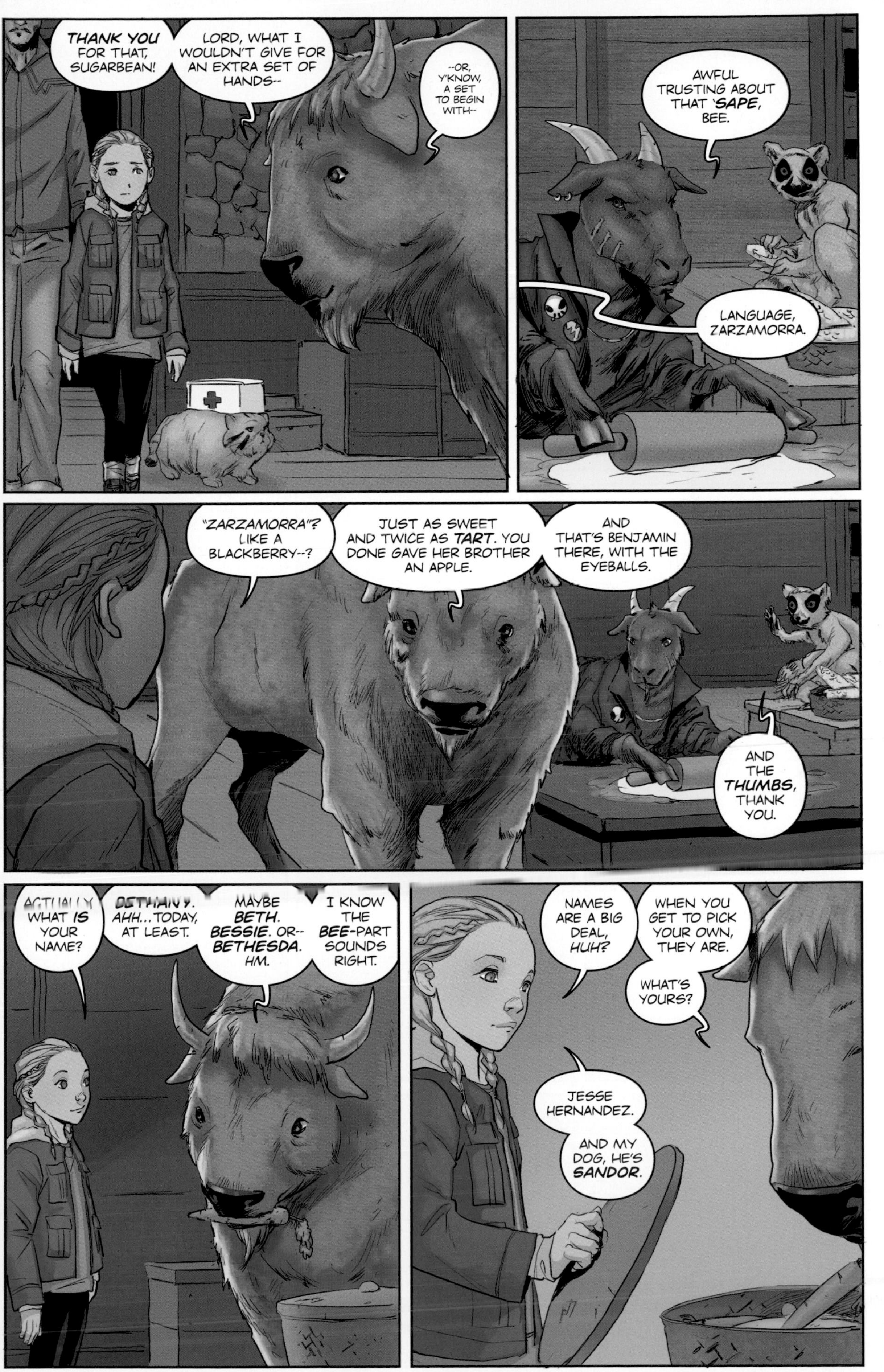
THANK YOU FOR THAT, SUGARBEAN!
LORD, WHAT I WOULDN'T GIVE FOR AN EXTRA SET OF HANDS--
--OR, Y'KNOW, A SET TO BEGIN WITH--
AWFUL TRUSTING ABOUT THAT 'SAPE, BEE.
LANGUAGE, ZARZAMORRA.
"ZARZAMORRA"? LIKE A BLACKBERRY--?
JUST AS SWEET AND TWICE AS TART. YOU DONE GAVE HER BROTHER AN APPLE.
AND THAT'S BENJAMIN THERE, WITH THE EYEBALLS.
AND THE THUMBS, THANK YOU.
ACTUALLY WHAT IS YOUR NAME?
BETHANY. AHH...TODAY, AT LEAST.
MAYBE BETH. BESSIE. OR-- BETHESDA. HM.
I KNOW THE BEE-PART SOUNDS RIGHT.
NAMES ARE A BIG DEAL, HUH?
WHEN YOU GET TO PICK YOUR OWN, THEY ARE.
WHAT'S YOURS?
JESSE HERNANDEZ.
AND MY DOG, HE'S SANDOR.

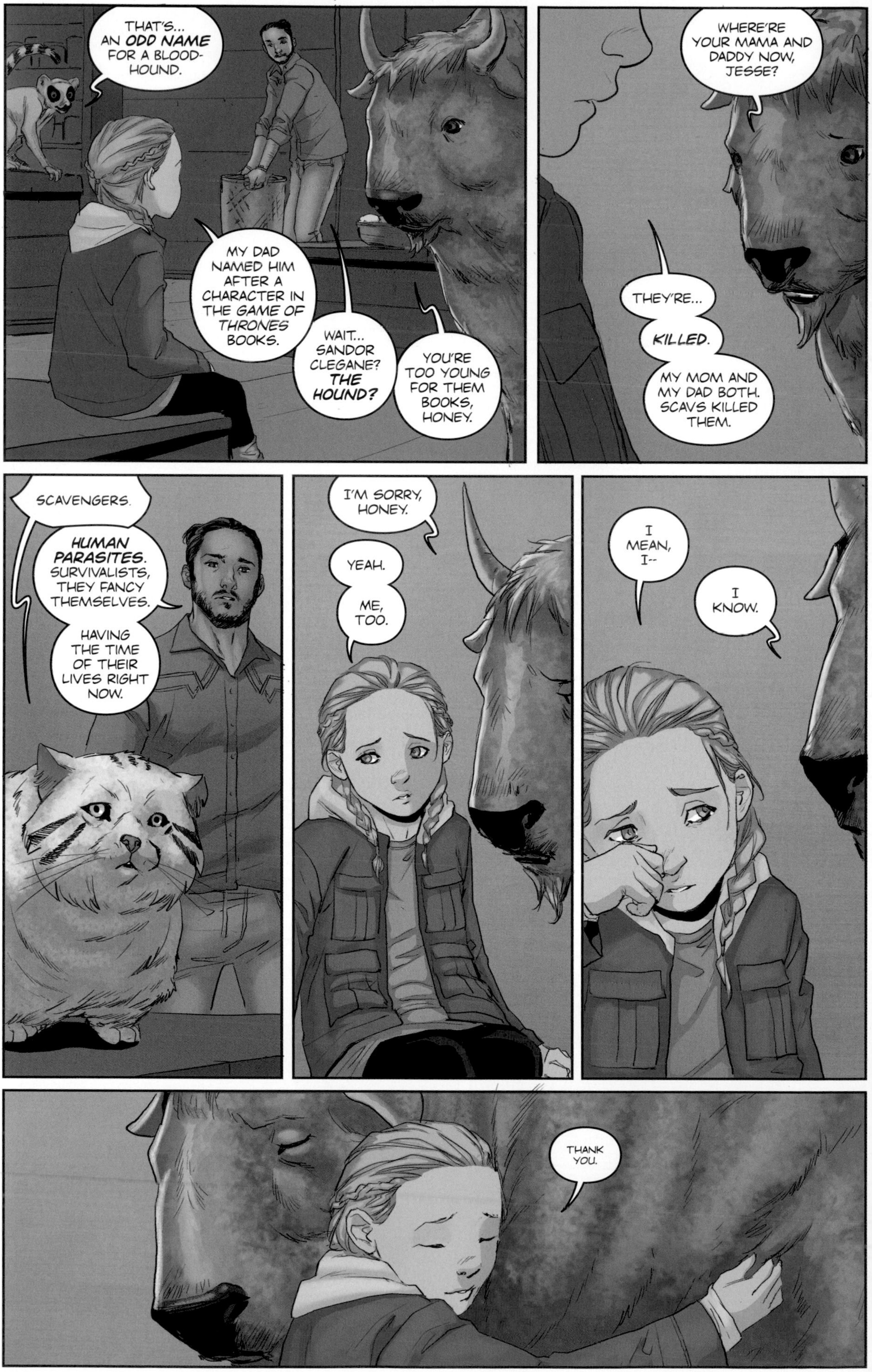
THAT'S... AN ODD NAME FOR A BLOOD-HOUND.
MY DAD NAMED HIM AFTER A CHARACTER IN THE GAME OF THRONES BOOKS.
WAIT... SANDOR CLEGANE? THE HOUND?
YOU'RE TOO YOUNG FOR THEM BOOKS, HONEY.
WHERE'RE YOUR MAMA AND DADDY NOW, JESSE?
THEY'RE...
KILLED.
MY MOM AND MY DAD BOTH. SCAVS KILLED THEM.
SCAVENGERS.
HUMAN PARASITES. SURVIVALISTS, THEY FANCY THEMSELVES.
HAVING THE TIME OF THEIR LIVES RIGHT NOW.
I'M SORRY, HONEY.
YEAH.
ME, TOO.
I MEAN, I--
I KNOW.
THANK YOU.

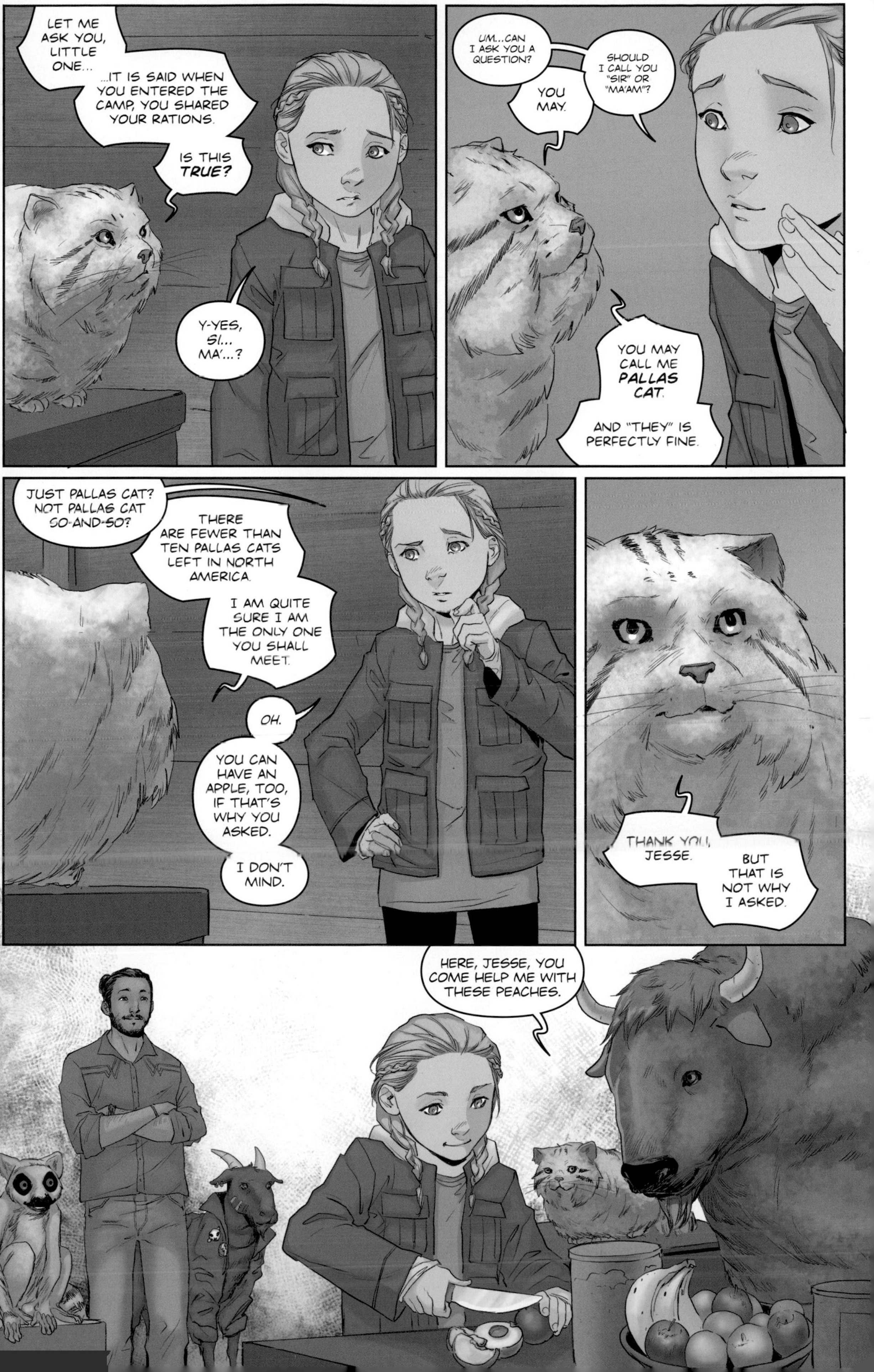
LET ME ASK YOU, LITTLE ONE...
...IT IS SAID WHEN YOU ENTERED THE CAMP, YOU SHARED YOUR RATIONS.
IS THIS TRUE?
Y-YES, SI... MA'...?
UM...CAN I ASK YOU A QUESTION?
YOU MAY.
SHOULD I CALL YOU "SIR" OR "MA'AM"?
YOU MAY CALL ME PALLAS CAT.
AND "THEY" IS PERFECTLY FINE.
JUST PALLAS CAT? NOT PALLAS CAT SO-AND-SO?
THERE ARE FEWER THAN TEN PALLAS CATS LEFT IN NORTH AMERICA.
I AM QUITE SURE I AM THE ONLY ONE YOU SHALL MEET.
OH.
YOU CAN HAVE AN APPLE, TOO, IF THAT'S WHY YOU ASKED.
I DON'T MIND.
THANK YOU, JESSE.
BUT THAT IS NOT WHY I ASKED.
HERE, JESSE, YOU COME HELP ME WITH THESE PEACHES.

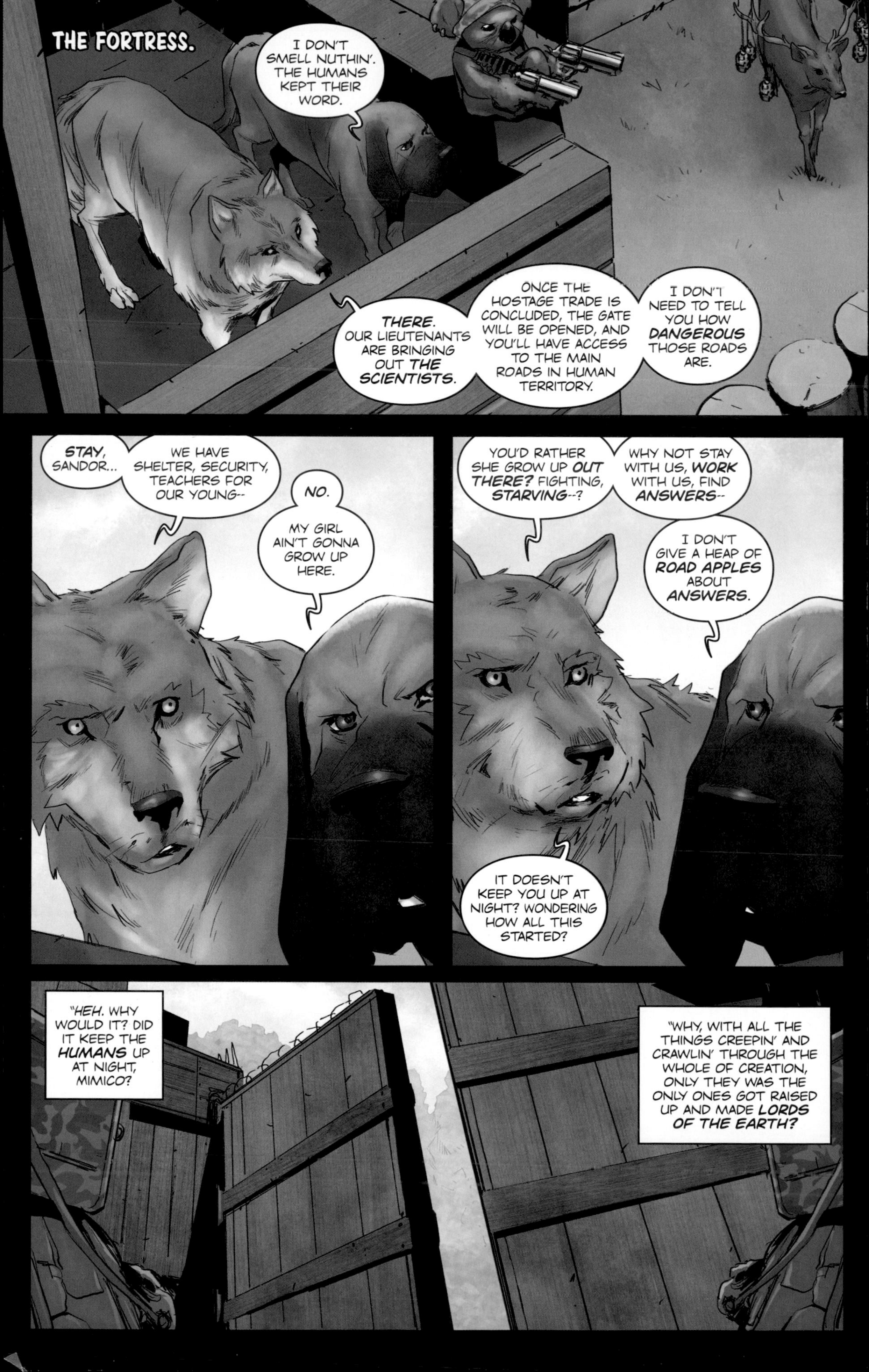
THE FORTRESS.
I DON'T SMELL NUTHIN'. THE HUMANS KEPT THEIR WORD.
THERE. OUR LIEUTENANTS ARE BRINGING OUT THE SCIENTISTS.
ONCE THE HOSTAGE TRADE IS CONCLUDED, THE GATE WILL BE OPENED, AND YOU'LL HAVE ACCESS TO THE MAIN ROADS IN HUMAN TERRITORY.
I DON'T NEED TO TELL YOU HOW DANGEROUS THOSE ROADS ARE.
STAY, SANDOR...
WE HAVE SHELTER, SECURITY, TEACHERS FOR OUR YOUNG--
NO.
MY GIRL AIN'T GONNA GROW UP HERE.
YOU'D RATHER SHE GROW UP OUT THERE? FIGHTING, STARVING--?
WHY NOT STAY WITH US, WORK WITH US, FIND ANSWERS--
I DON'T GIVE A HEAP OF ROAD APPLES ABOUT ANSWERS.
IT DOESN'T KEEP YOU UP AT NIGHT? WONDERING HOW ALL THIS STARTED?
"HEH. WHY WOULD IT? DID IT KEEP THE HUMANS UP AT NIGHT, MIMICO?
"WHY, WITH ALL THE THINGS CREEPIN' AND CRAWLIN' THROUGH THE WHOLE OF CREATION, ONLY THEY WAS THE ONLY ONES GOT RAISED UP AND MADE LORDS OF THE EARTH?

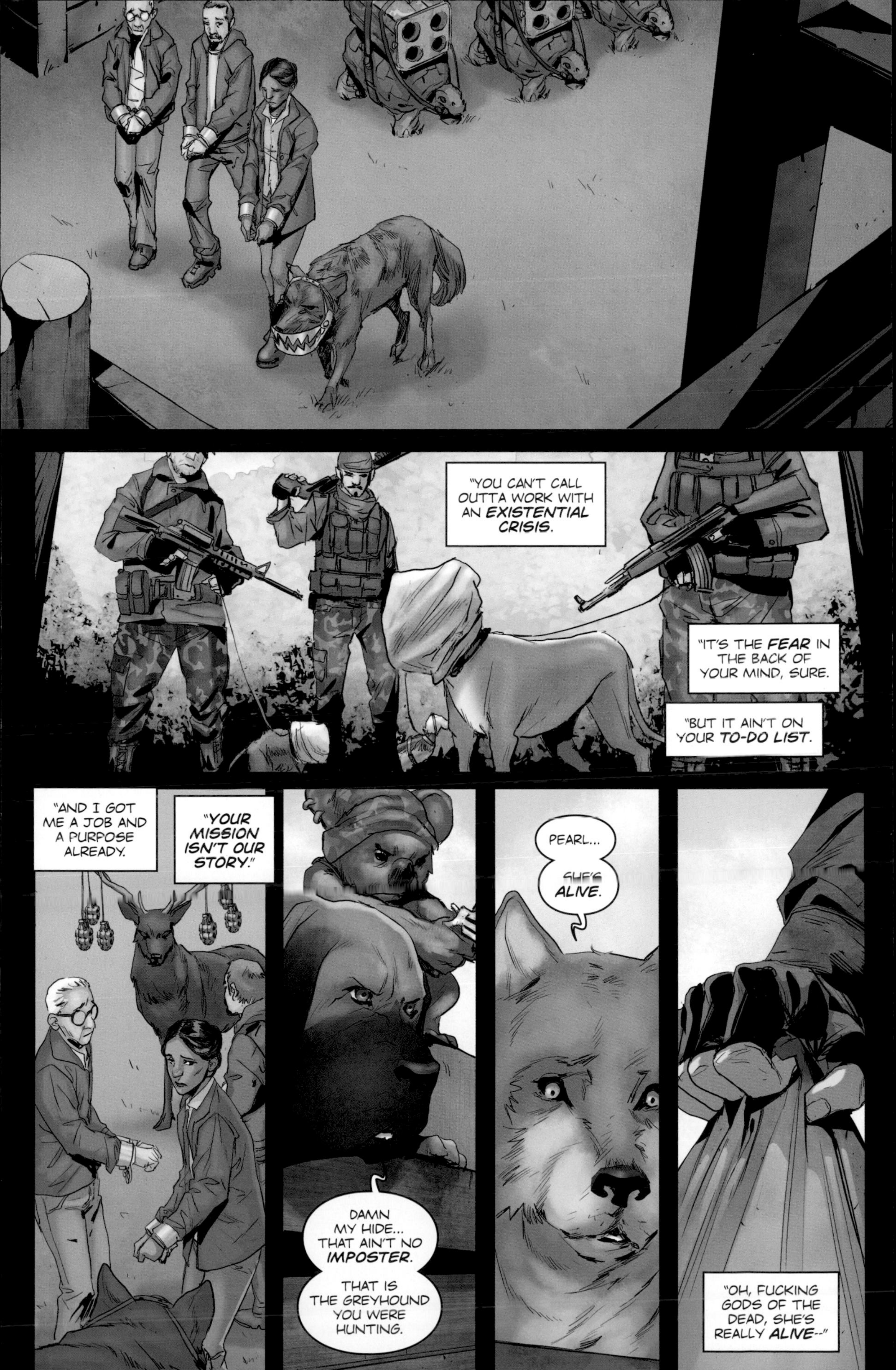

"YOU CAN'T CALL OUTTA WORK WITH AN EXISTENTIAL CRISIS.
"IT'S THE FEAR IN THE BACK OF YOUR MIND, SURE.
"BUT IT AIN'T ON YOUR TO-DO LIST.
"AND I GOT ME A JOB AND A PURPOSE ALREADY.
"YOUR MISSION ISN'T OUR STORY."
DAMN MY HIDE... THAT AIN'T NO IMPOSTER.
THAT IS THE GREYHOUND YOU WERE HUNTING.
PEARL...
SHE'S ALIVE.
"OH, FUCKING GODS OF THE DEAD, SHE'S REALLY ALIVE--"

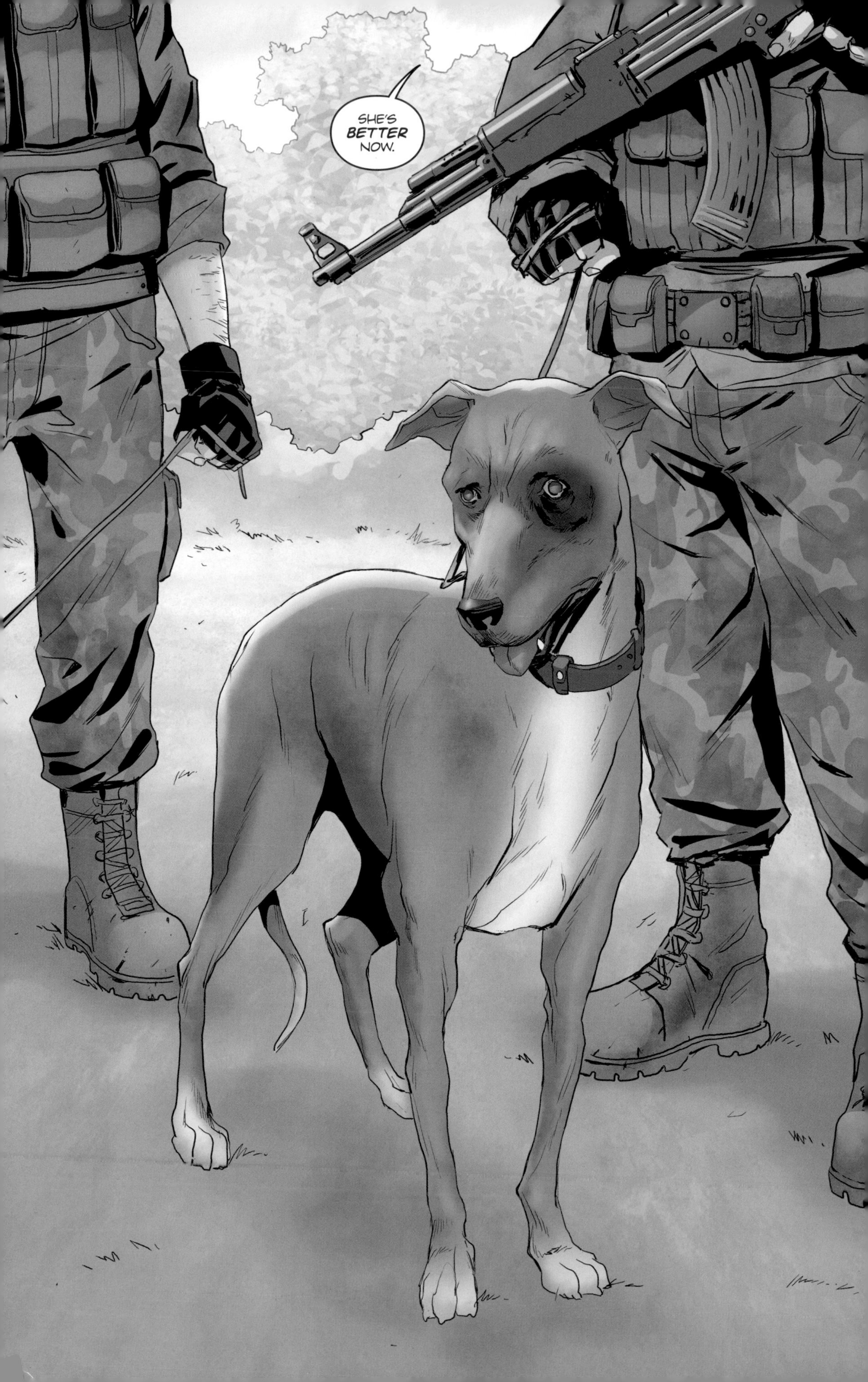
SHE'S **BETTER** NOW.

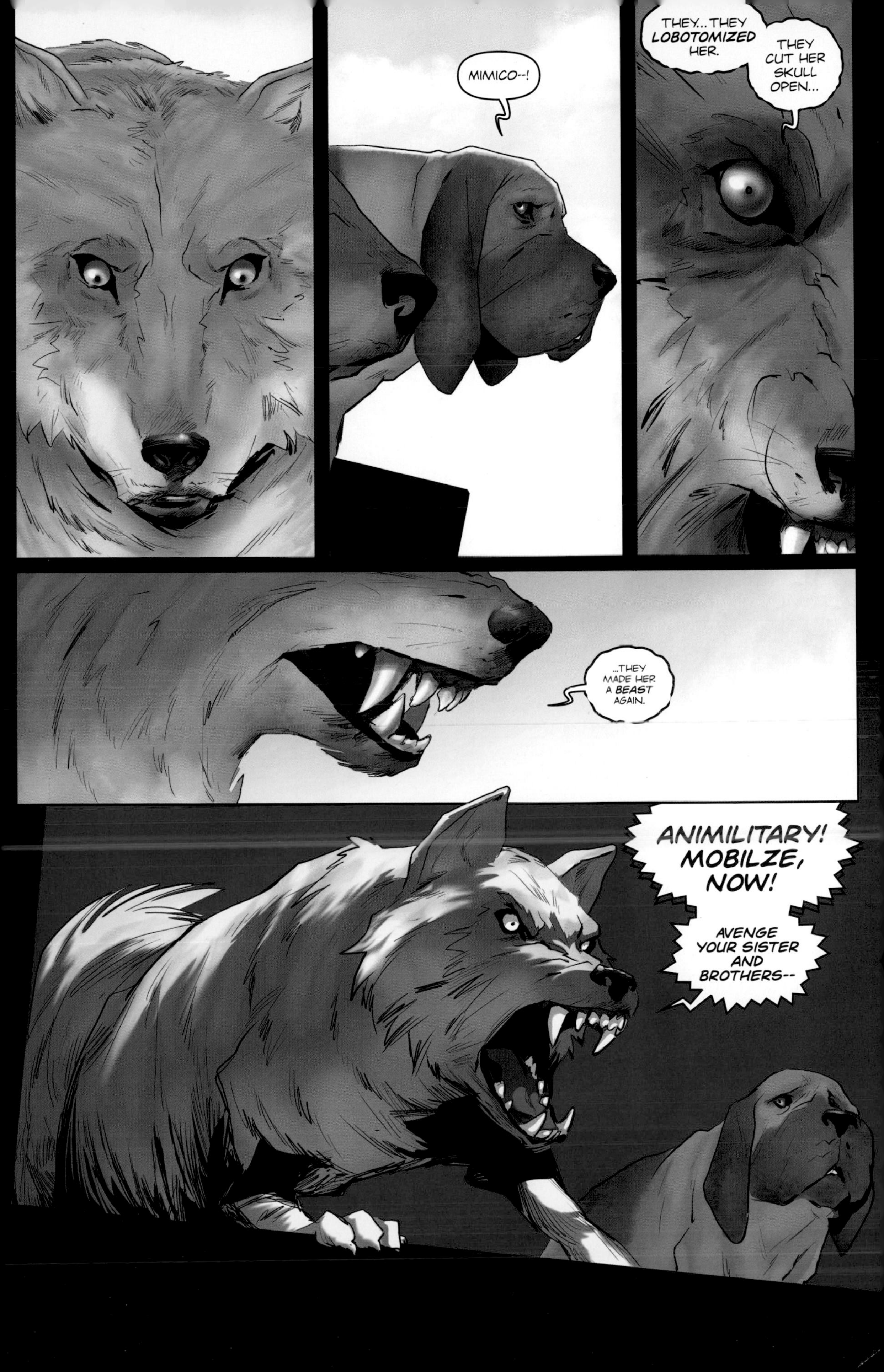
MIMICO--!
THEY... THEY LOBOTOMIZED HER.
THEY CUT HER SKULL OPEN...
...THEY MADE HER A BEAST AGAIN.
ANIMILITARY! MOBILZE, NOW!
AVENGE YOUR SISTER AND BROTHERS--

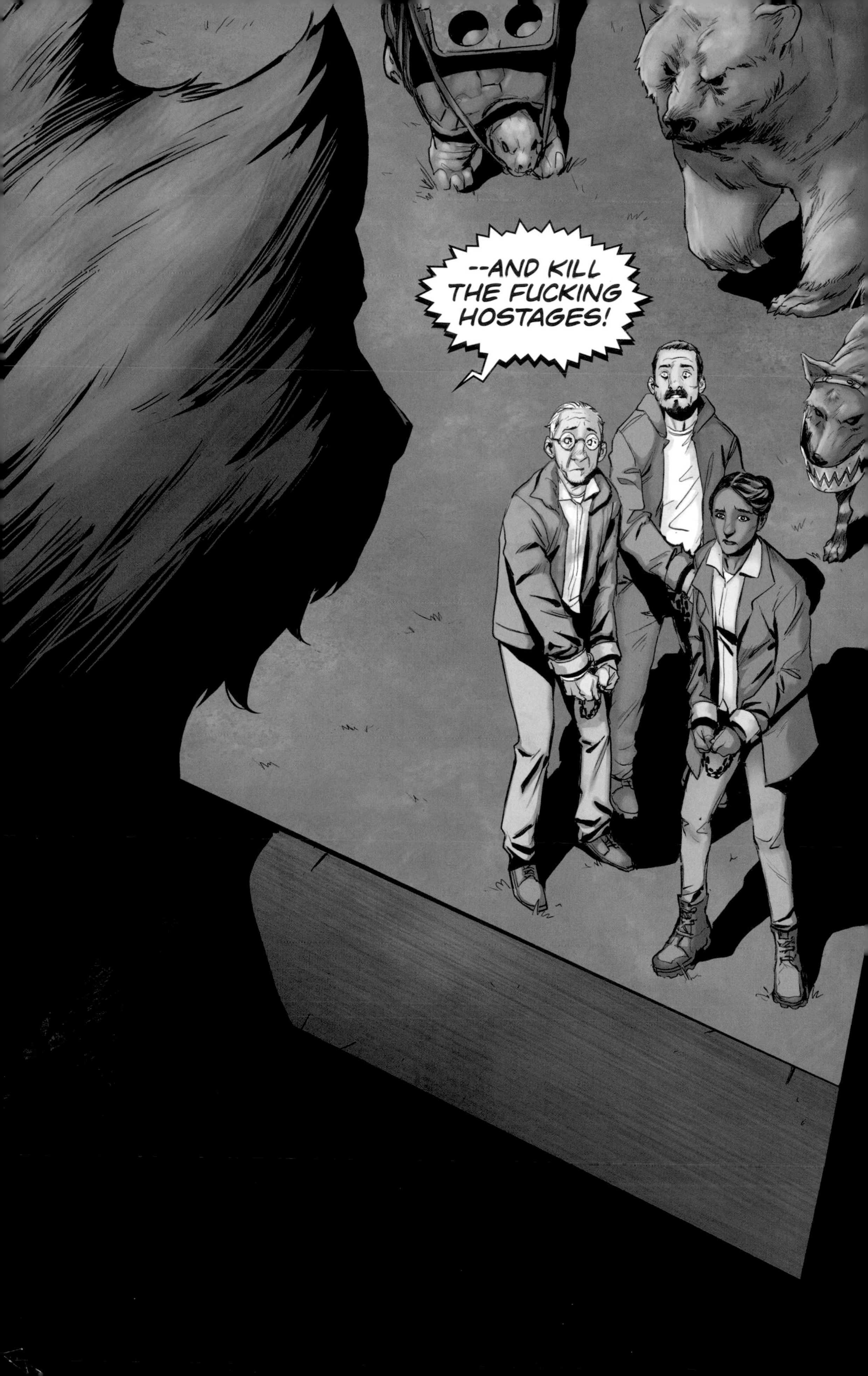
--AND KILL THE FUCKING HOSTAGES!

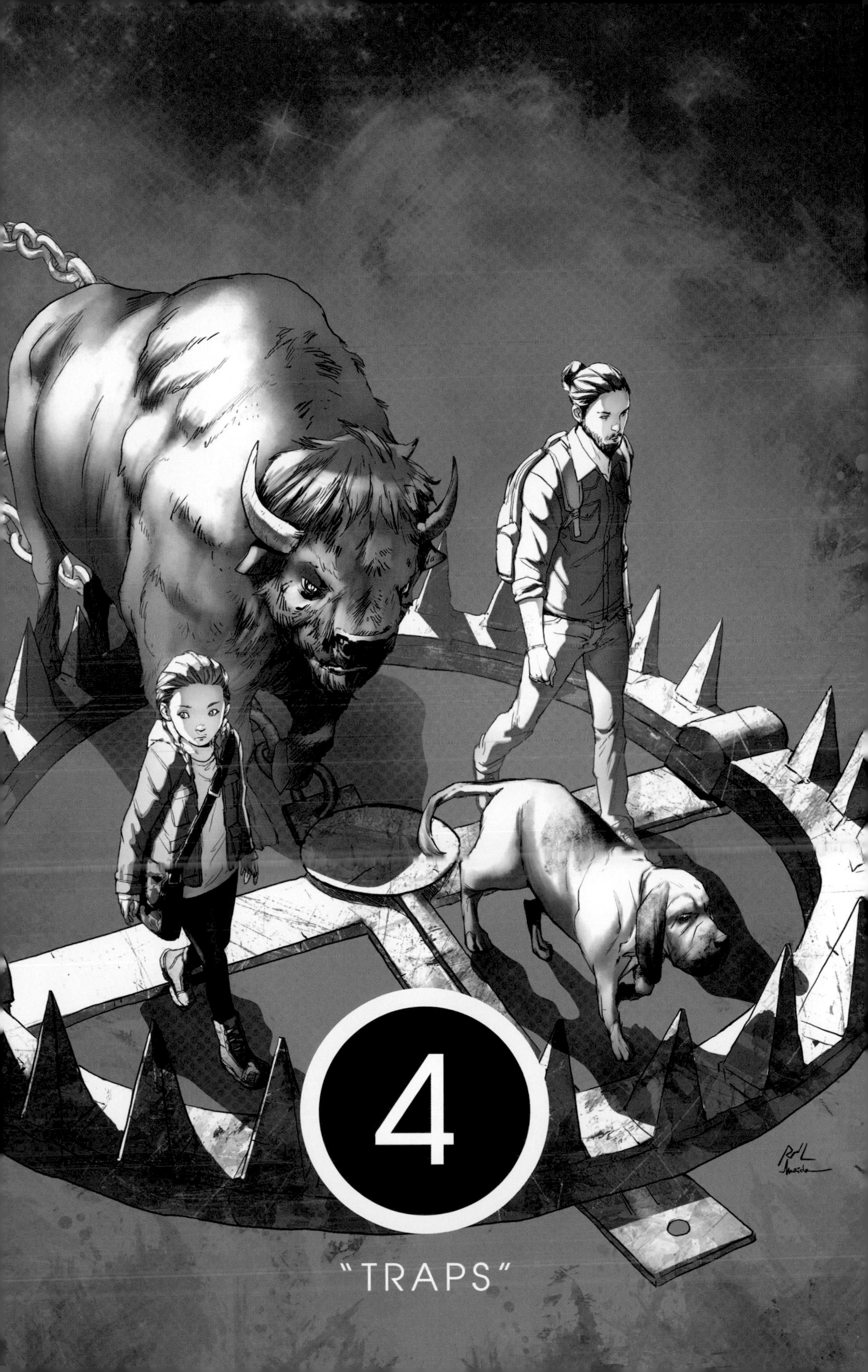
4
"TRAPS"

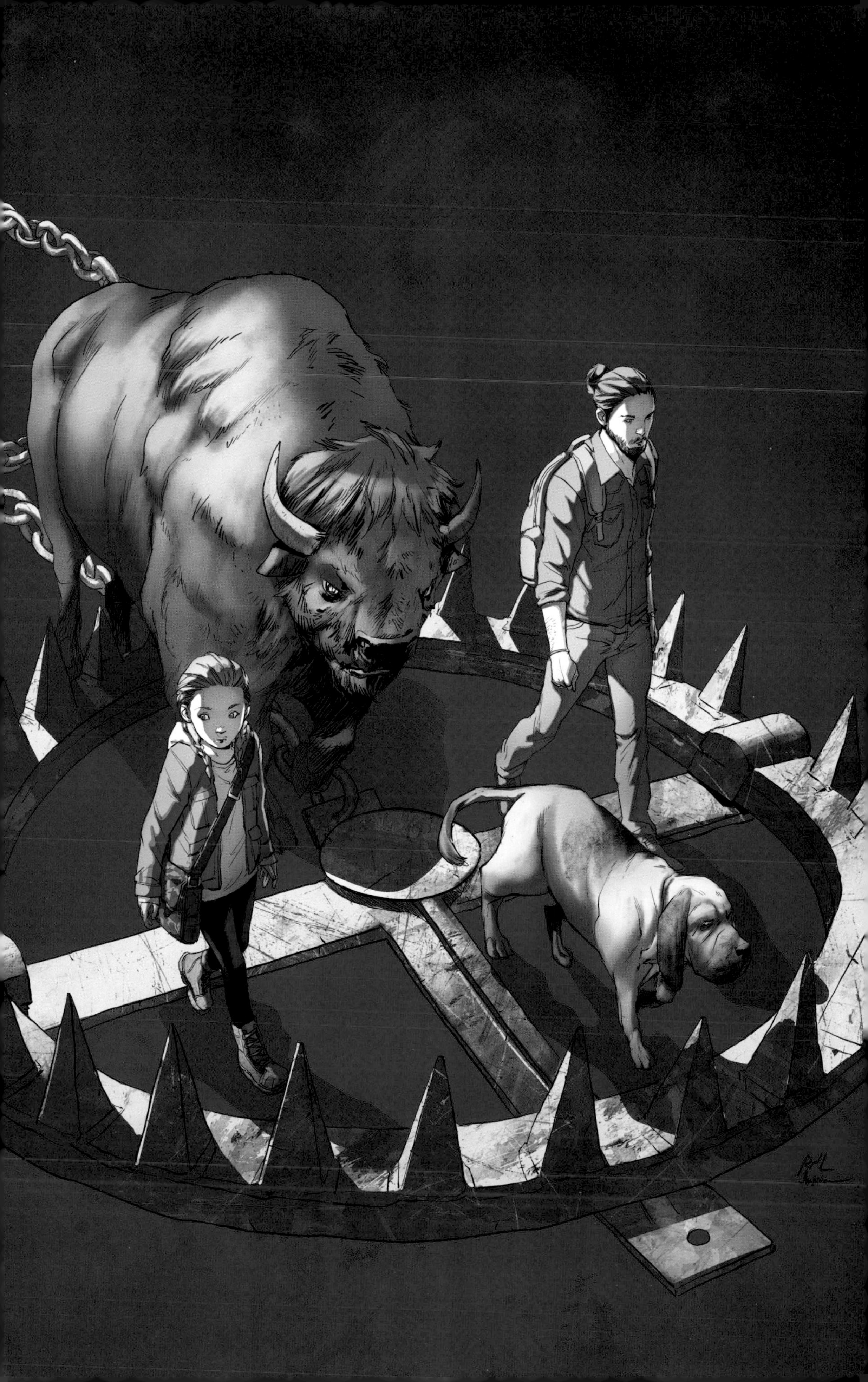

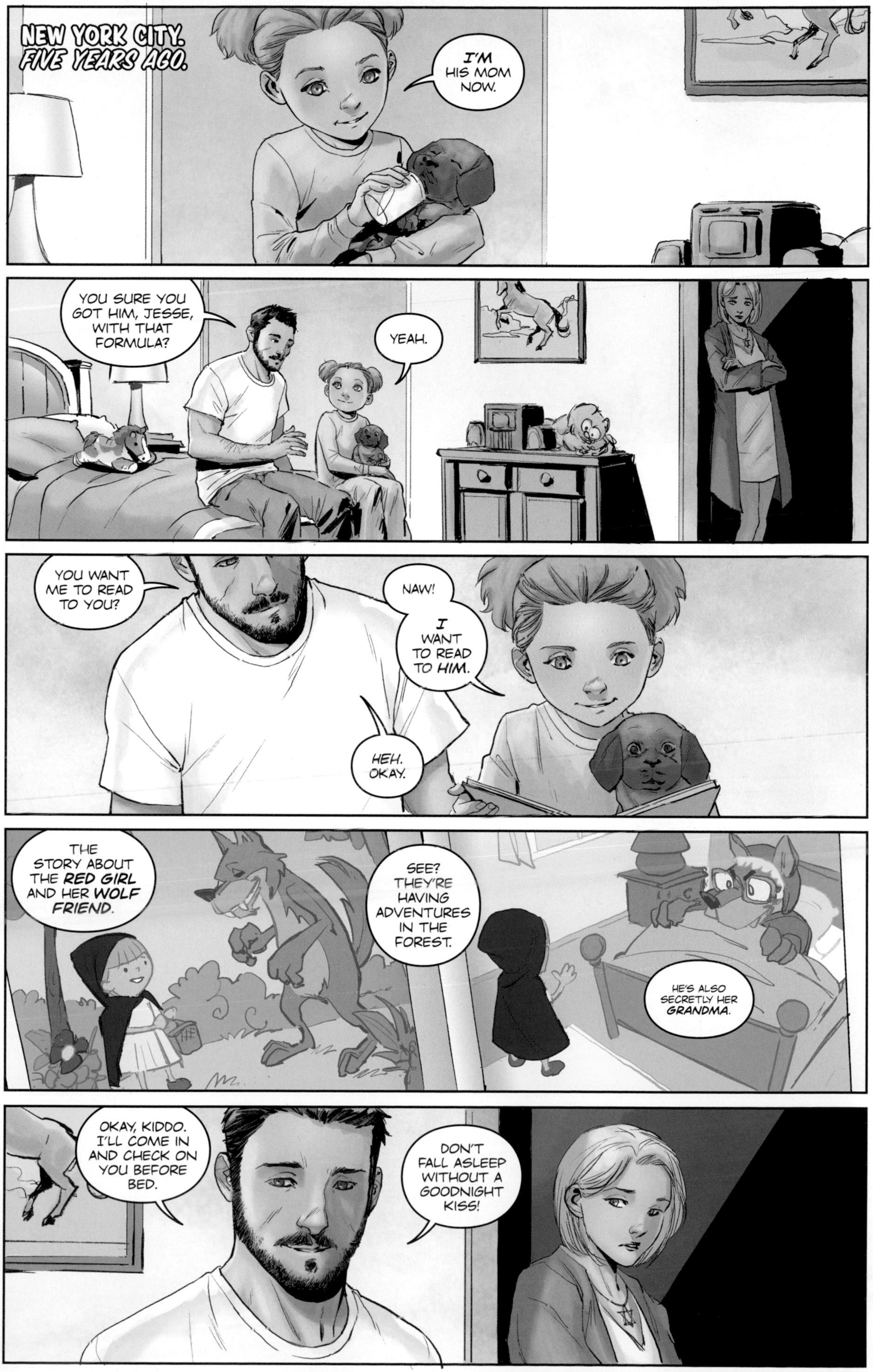

NEW YORK CITY. FIVE YEARS AGO.
I'M HIS MOM NOW.
YOU SURE YOU GOT HIM, JESSE, WITH THAT FORMULA?
YEAH.
YOU WANT ME TO READ TO YOU?
NAW!
I WANT TO READ TO HIM.
HEH. OKAY.
THE STORY ABOUT THE RED GIRL AND HER WOLF FRIEND.
SEE? THEY'RE HAVING ADVENTURES IN THE FOREST.
HE'S ALSO SECRETLY HER GRANDMA.
OKAY, KIDDO. I'LL COME IN AND CHECK ON YOU BEFORE BED.
DON'T FALL ASLEEP WITHOUT A GOODNIGHT KISS!

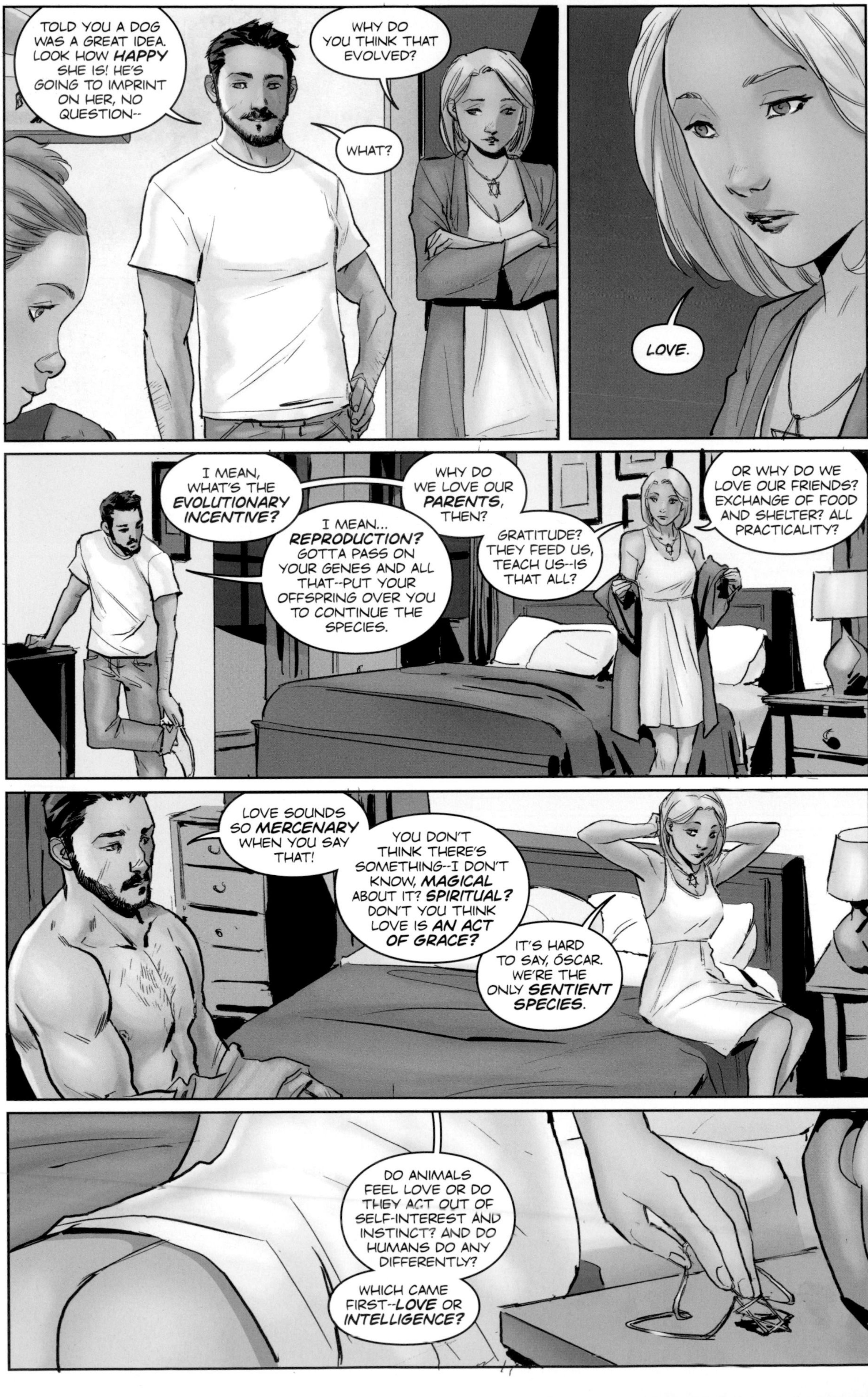
TOLD YOU A DOG WAS A GREAT IDEA. LOOK HOW HAPPY SHE IS! HE'S GOING TO IMPRINT ON HER, NO QUESTION--
WHY DO YOU THINK THAT EVOLVED?
WHAT?
LOVE.
I MEAN, WHAT'S THE EVOLUTIONARY INCENTIVE?
I MEAN... REPRODUCTION? GOTTA PASS ON YOUR GENES AND ALL THAT--PUT YOUR OFFSPRING OVER YOU TO CONTINUE THE SPECIES.
WHY DO WE LOVE OUR PARENTS, THEN?
GRATITUDE? THEY FEED US, TEACH US--IS THAT ALL?
OR WHY DO WE LOVE OUR FRIENDS? EXCHANGE OF FOOD AND SHELTER? ALL PRACTICALITY?
LOVE SOUNDS SO MERCENARY WHEN YOU SAY THAT!
YOU DON'T THINK THERE'S SOMETHING--I DON'T KNOW, MAGICAL ABOUT IT? SPIRITUAL? DON'T YOU THINK LOVE IS AN ACT OF GRACE?
IT'S HARD TO SAY, ÓSCAR. WE'RE THE ONLY SENTIENT SPECIES.
DO ANIMALS FEEL LOVE OR DO THEY ACT OUT OF SELF-INTEREST AND INSTINCT? AND DO HUMANS DO ANY DIFFERENTLY?
WHICH CAME FIRST--LOVE OR INTELLIGENCE?

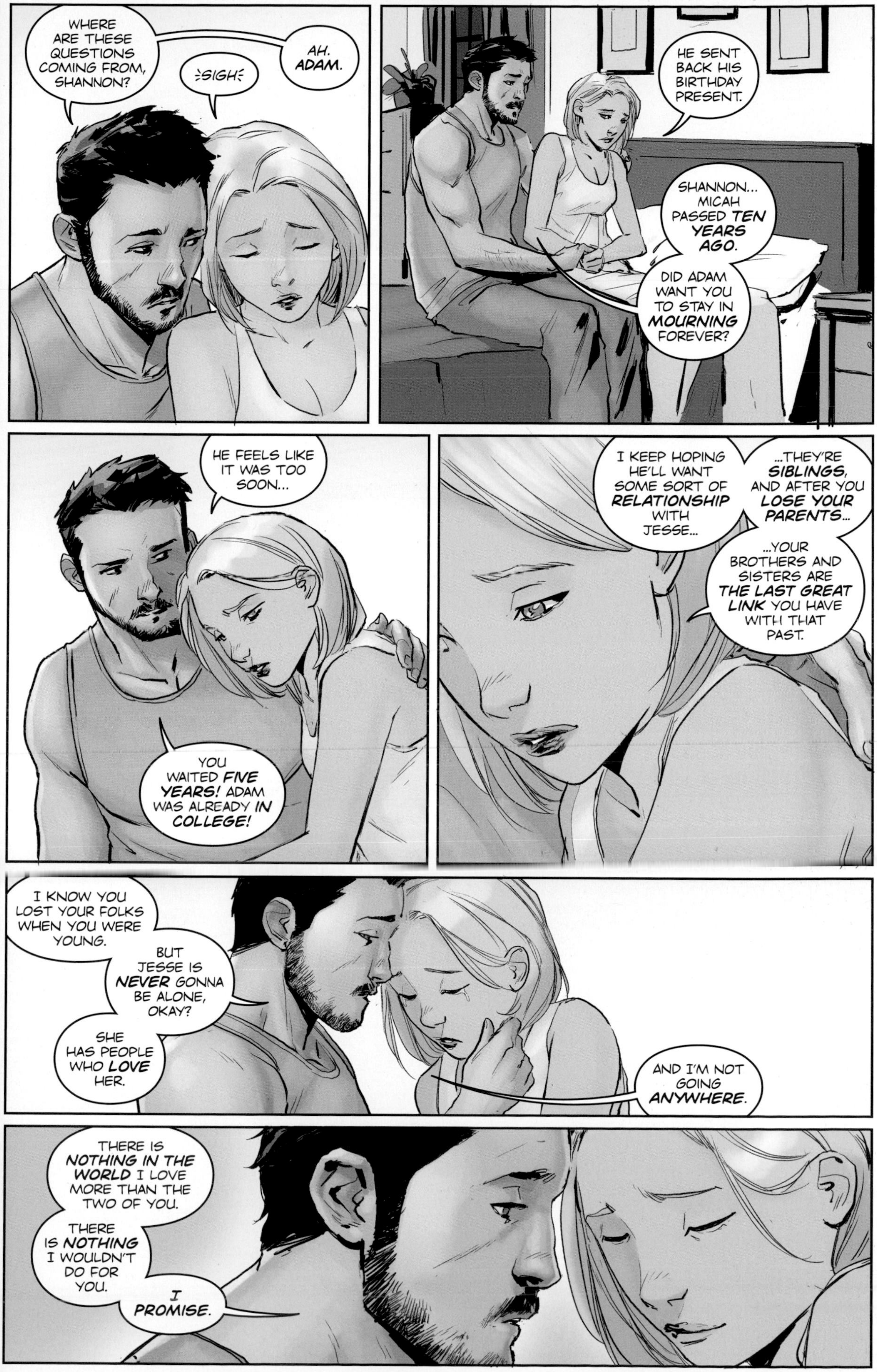
WHERE ARE THESE QUESTIONS COMING FROM, SHANNON?
SIGH
AH. ADAM.
HE SENT BACK HIS BIRTHDAY PRESENT.
SHANNON... MICAH PASSED TEN YEARS AGO.
DID ADAM WANT YOU TO STAY IN MOURNING FOREVER?
HE FEELS LIKE IT WAS TOO SOON...
YOU WAITED FIVE YEARS! ADAM WAS ALREADY IN COLLEGE!
I KEEP HOPING HE'LL WANT SOME SORT OF RELATIONSHIP WITH JESSE...
...THEY'RE SIBLINGS, AND AFTER YOU LOSE YOUR PARENTS...
...YOUR BROTHERS AND SISTERS ARE THE LAST GREAT LINK YOU HAVE WITH THAT PAST.
I KNOW YOU LOST YOUR FOLKS WHEN YOU WERE YOUNG.
BUT JESSE IS NEVER GONNA BE ALONE, OKAY?
SHE HAS PEOPLE WHO LOVE HER.
AND I'M NOT GOING ANYWHERE.
THERE IS NOTHING IN THE WORLD I LOVE MORE THAN THE TWO OF YOU.
THERE IS NOTHING I WOULDN'T DO FOR YOU.
I PROMISE.

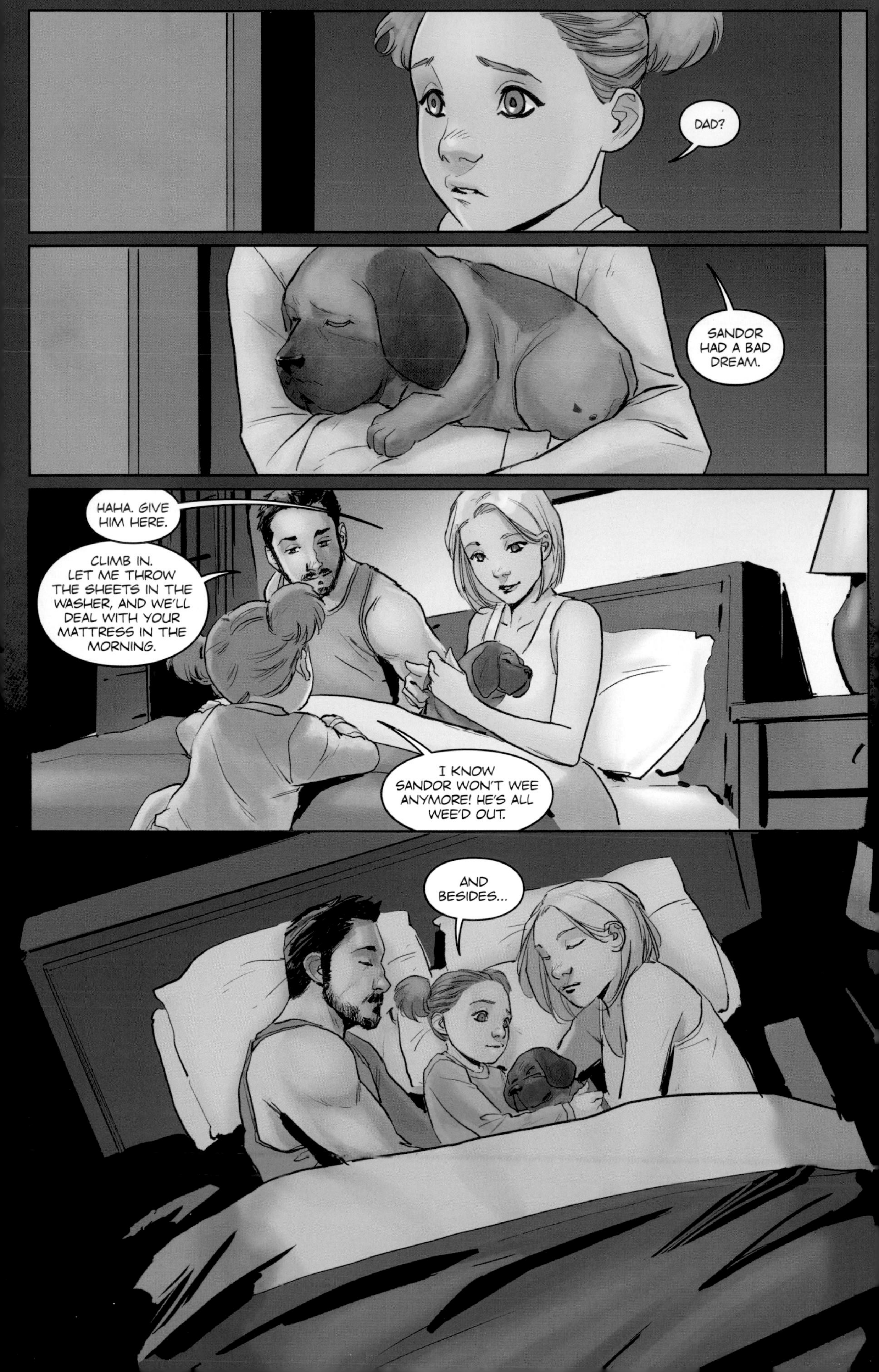
DAD?
SANDOR HAD A BAD DREAM.
HAHA. GIVE HIM HERE.
CLIMB IN. LET ME THROW THE SHEETS IN THE WASHER, AND WE'LL DEAL WITH YOUR MATTRESS IN THE MORNING.
I KNOW SANDOR WON'T WEE ANYMORE! HE'S ALL WEE'D OUT.
AND BESIDES...

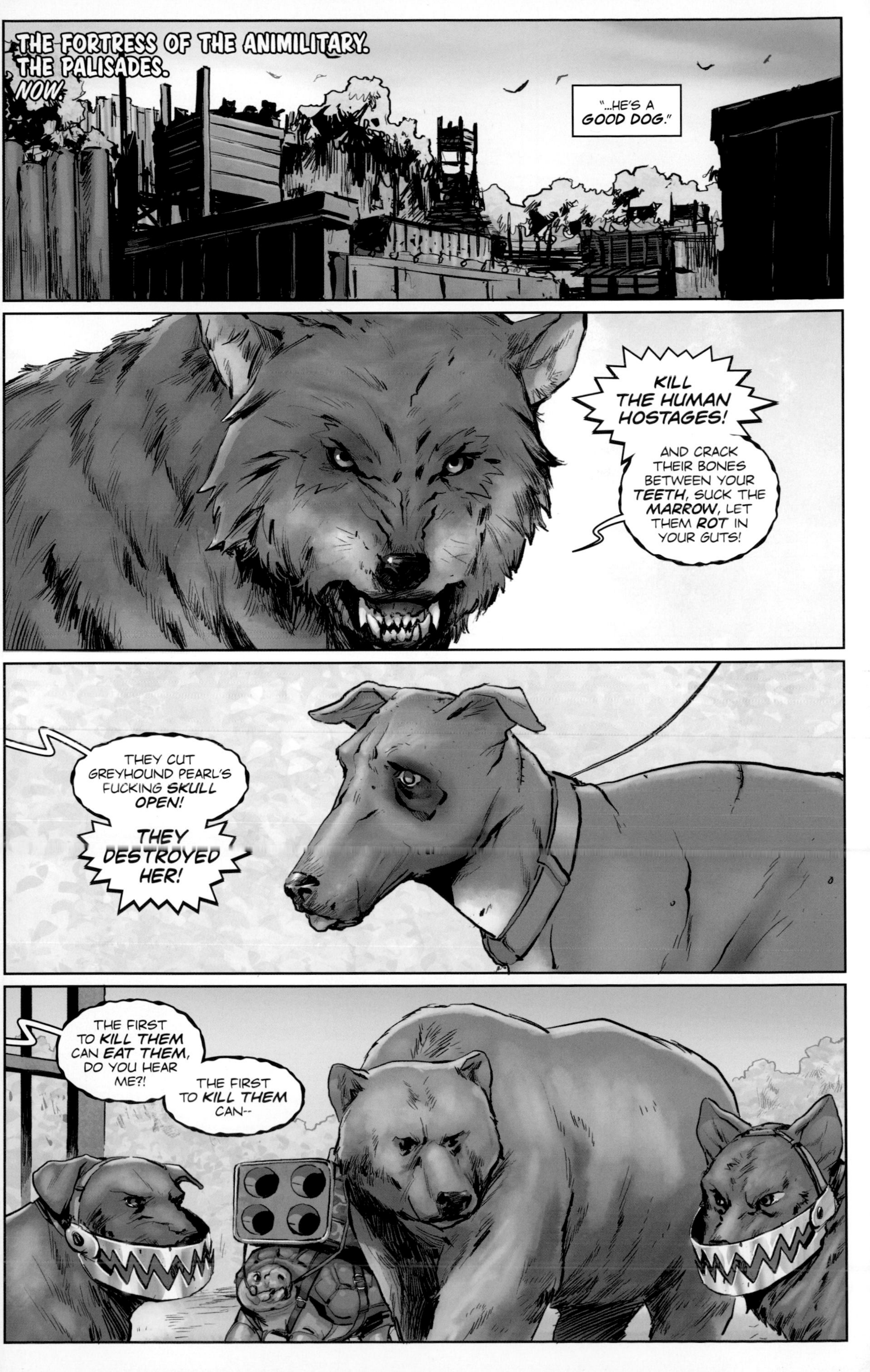
THE FORTRESS OF THE ANIMILITARY.
THE PALISADES.
NOW.
"...HE'S A GOOD DOG."
KILL THE HUMAN HOSTAGES!
AND CRACK THEIR BONES BETWEEN YOUR TEETH, SUCK THE MARROW, LET THEM ROT IN YOUR GUTS!
THEY CUT GREYHOUND PEARL'S FUCKING SKULL OPEN!
THEY DESTROYED HER!
THE FIRST TO KILL THEM CAN EAT THEM, DO YOU HEAR ME?!
THE FIRST TO KILL THEM CAN--

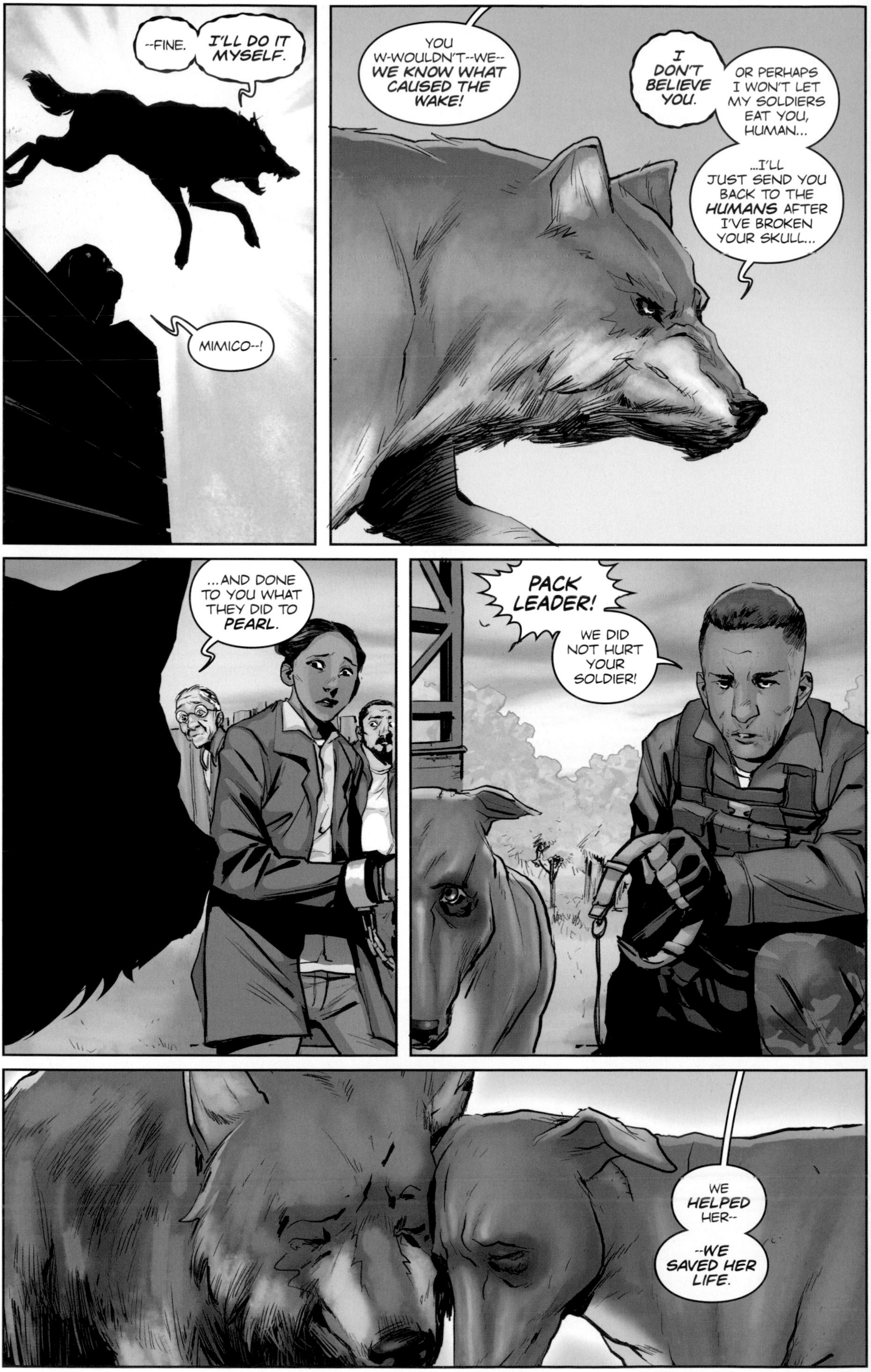
--FINE.
I'LL DO IT MYSELF.
MIMICO--!
YOU W-WOULDN'T--WE-- WE KNOW WHAT CAUSED THE WAKE!
I DON'T BELIEVE YOU.
OR PERHAPS I WON'T LET MY SOLDIERS EAT YOU, HUMAN...
...I'LL JUST SEND YOU BACK TO THE HUMANS AFTER I'VE BROKEN YOUR SKULL...
...AND DONE TO YOU WHAT THEY DID TO PEARL.
PACK LEADER!
WE DID NOT HURT YOUR SOLDIER!
WE HELPED HER--
--WE SAVED HER LIFE.

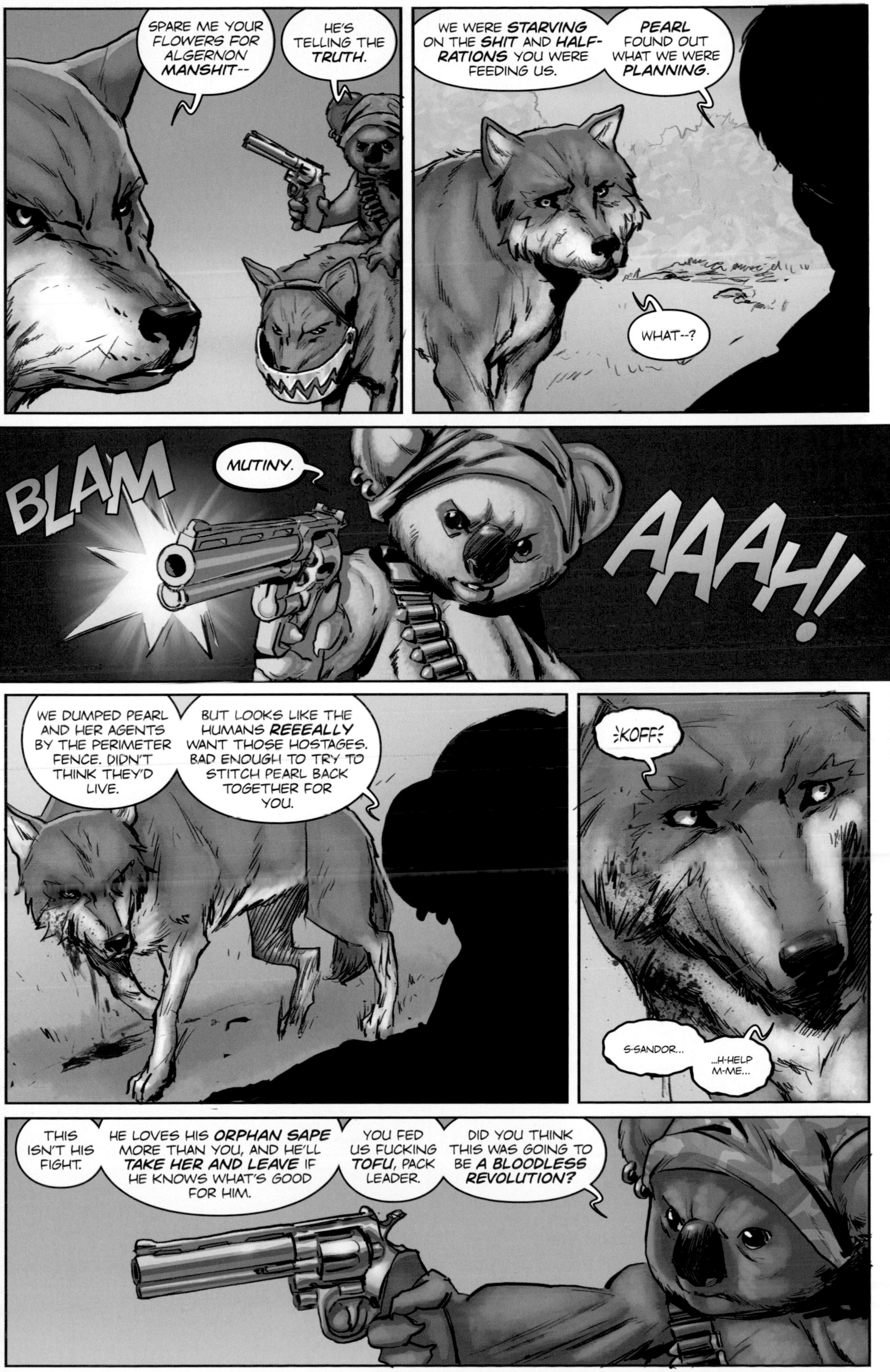
SPARE ME YOUR FLOWERS FOR ALGERNON MANSHIT--
HE'S TELLING THE TRUTH.
WE WERE STARVING ON THE SHIT AND HALF-RATIONS YOU WERE FEEDING US.
PEARL FOUND OUT WHAT WE WERE PLANNING.
WHAT--?
BLAM
MUTINY.
AAAH!
WE DUMPED PEARL AND HER AGENTS BY THE PERIMETER FENCE. DIDN'T THINK THEY'D LIVE.
BUT LOOKS LIKE THE HUMANS REEEALLY WANT THOSE HOSTAGES. BAD ENOUGH TO TRY TO STITCH PEARL BACK TOGETHER FOR YOU.
KOFF
S-SANDOR...
...H-HELP M-ME...
THIS ISN'T HIS FIGHT.
HE LOVES HIS ORPHAN SAPE MORE THAN YOU, AND HE'LL TAKE HER AND LEAVE IF HE KNOWS WHAT'S GOOD FOR HIM.
YOU FED US FUCKING TOFU, PACK LEADER.
DID YOU THINK THIS WAS GOING TO BE A BLOODLESS REVOLUTION?

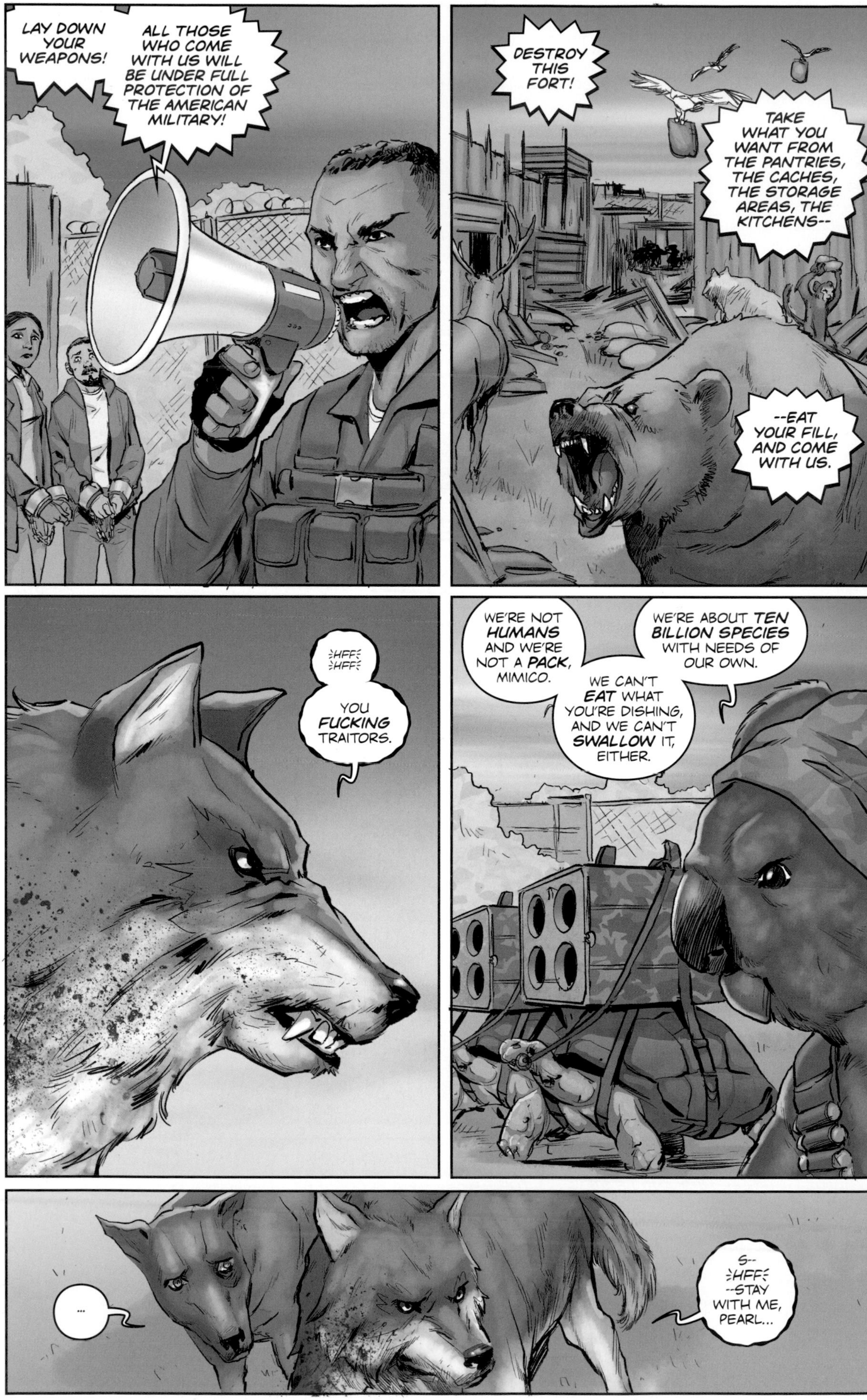
LAY DOWN YOUR WEAPONS!
ALL THOSE WHO COME WITH US WILL BE UNDER FULL PROTECTION OF THE AMERICAN MILITARY!
DESTROY THIS FORT!
TAKE WHAT YOU WANT FROM THE PANTRIES, THE CACHES, THE STORAGE AREAS, THE KITCHENS--
--EAT YOUR FILL, AND COME WITH US.
HFF HFF
YOU FUCKING TRAITORS.
WE'RE NOT HUMANS AND WE'RE NOT A PACK, MIMICO.
WE'RE ABOUT TEN BILLION SPECIES WITH NEEDS OF OUR OWN.
WE CAN'T EAT WHAT YOU'RE DISHING, AND WE CAN'T SWALLOW IT, EITHER.
...
S-- HFF --STAY WITH ME, PEARL...

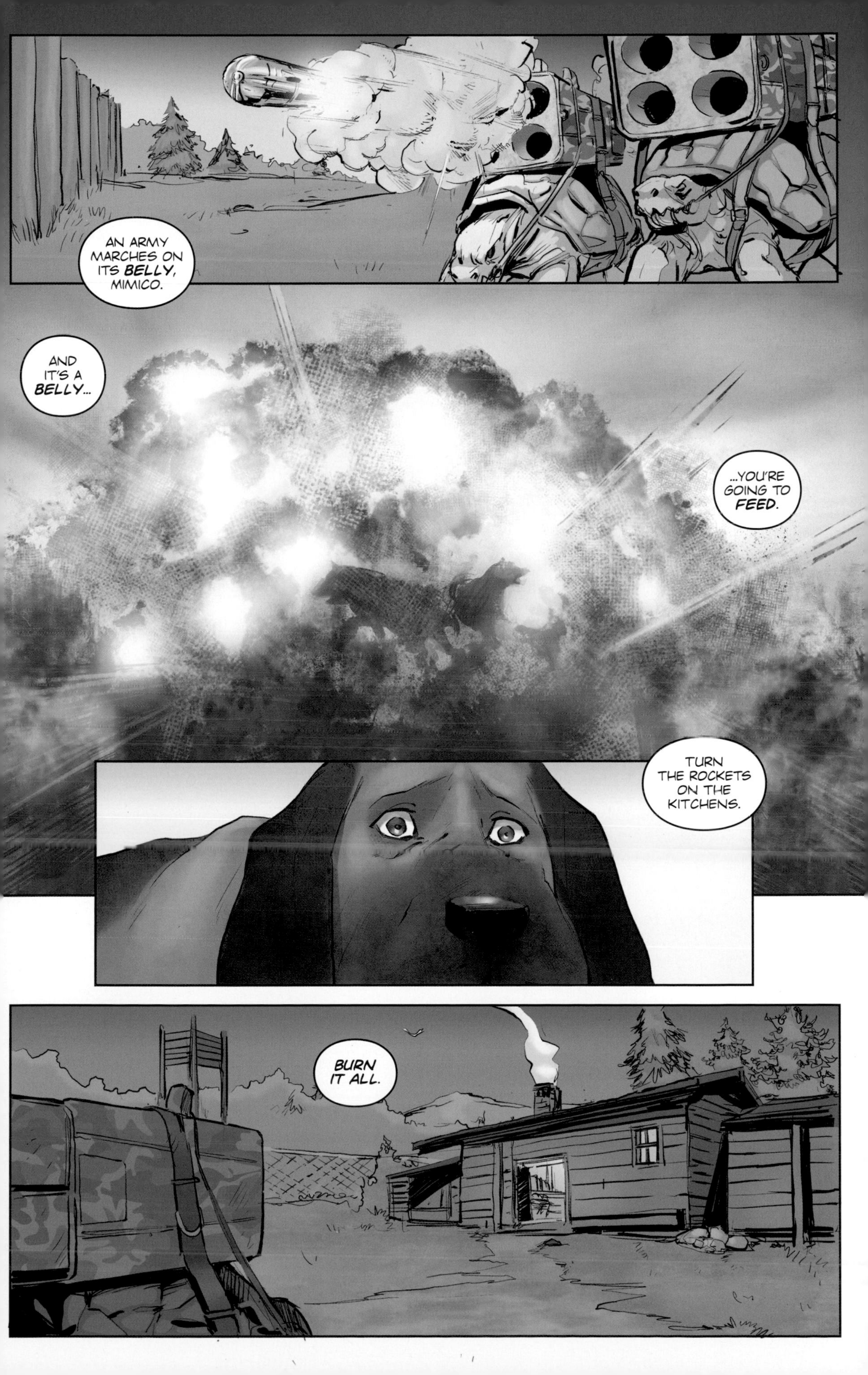
AN ARMY MARCHES ON ITS BELLY, MIMICO.
AND IT'S A BELLY...
...YOU'RE GOING TO FEED.
TURN THE ROCKETS ON THE KITCHENS.
BURN IT ALL.

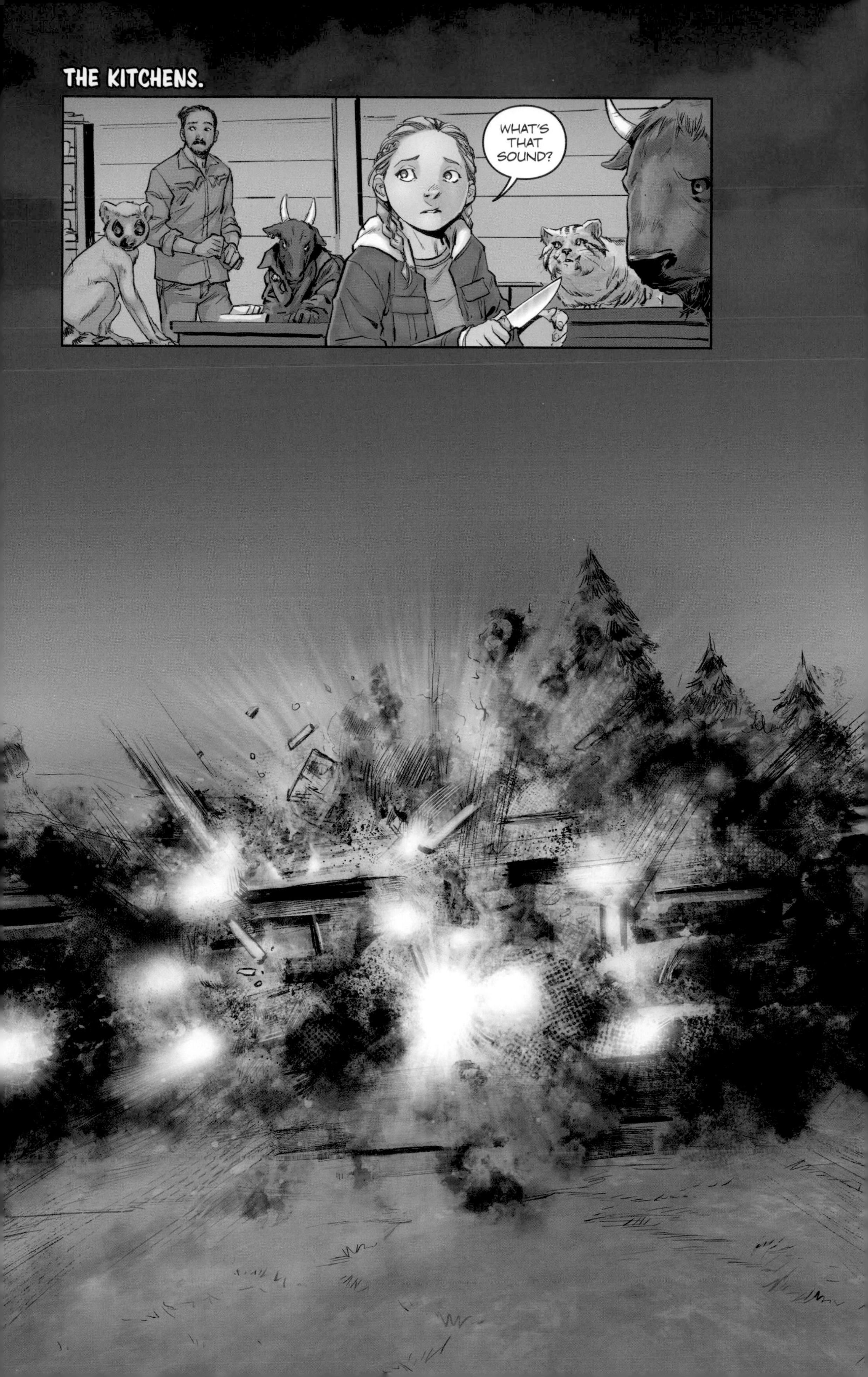
THE KITCHENS.
WHAT'S THAT SOUND?

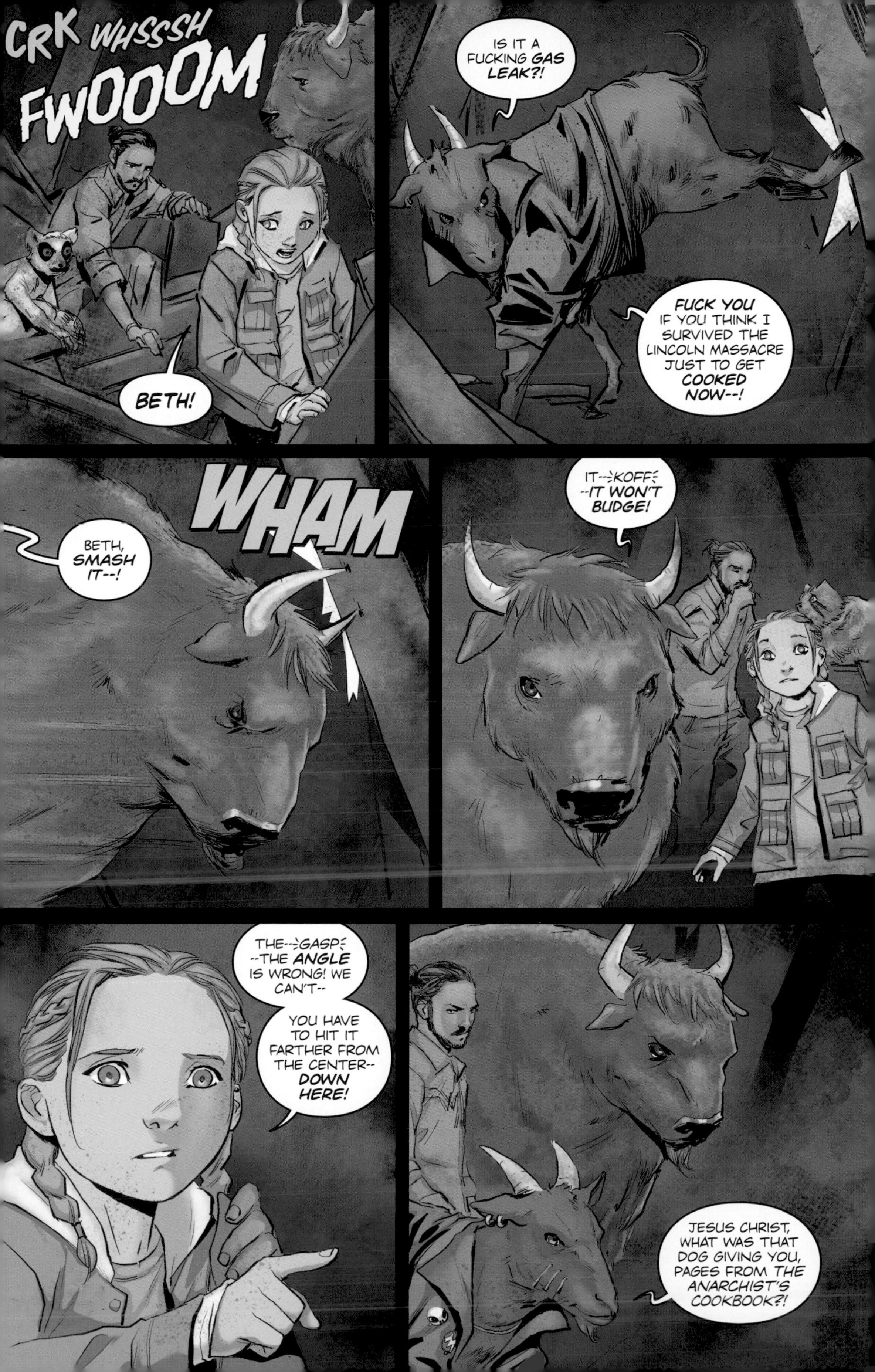
CRK WHSSSH
FWOOOM
BETH!
IS IT A FUCKING GAS LEAK?!
FUCK YOU IF YOU THINK I SURVIVED THE LINCOLN MASSACRE JUST TO GET COOKED NOW--!
WHAM
BETH, SMASH IT--!
IT--KOFF --IT WON'T BUDGE!
THE--GASP --THE ANGLE IS WRONG! WE CAN'T--
YOU HAVE TO HIT IT FARTHER FROM THE CENTER-- DOWN HERE!
JESUS CHRIST, WHAT WAS THAT DOG GIVING YOU, PAGES FROM THE ANARCHIST'S COOKBOOK?!

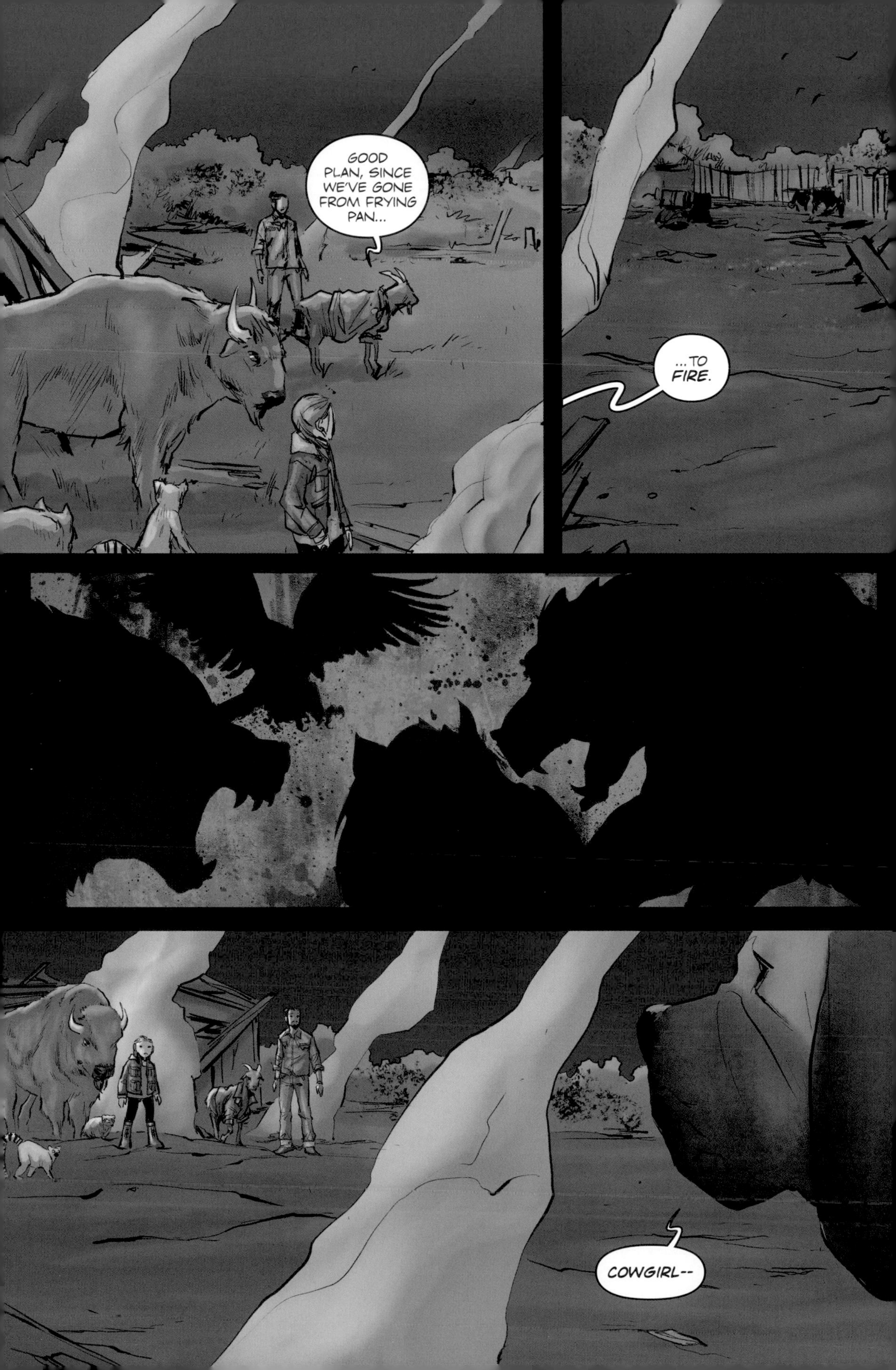
GOOD PLAN, SINCE WE'VE GONE FROM FRYING PAN...
...TO FIRE.
COWGIRL--

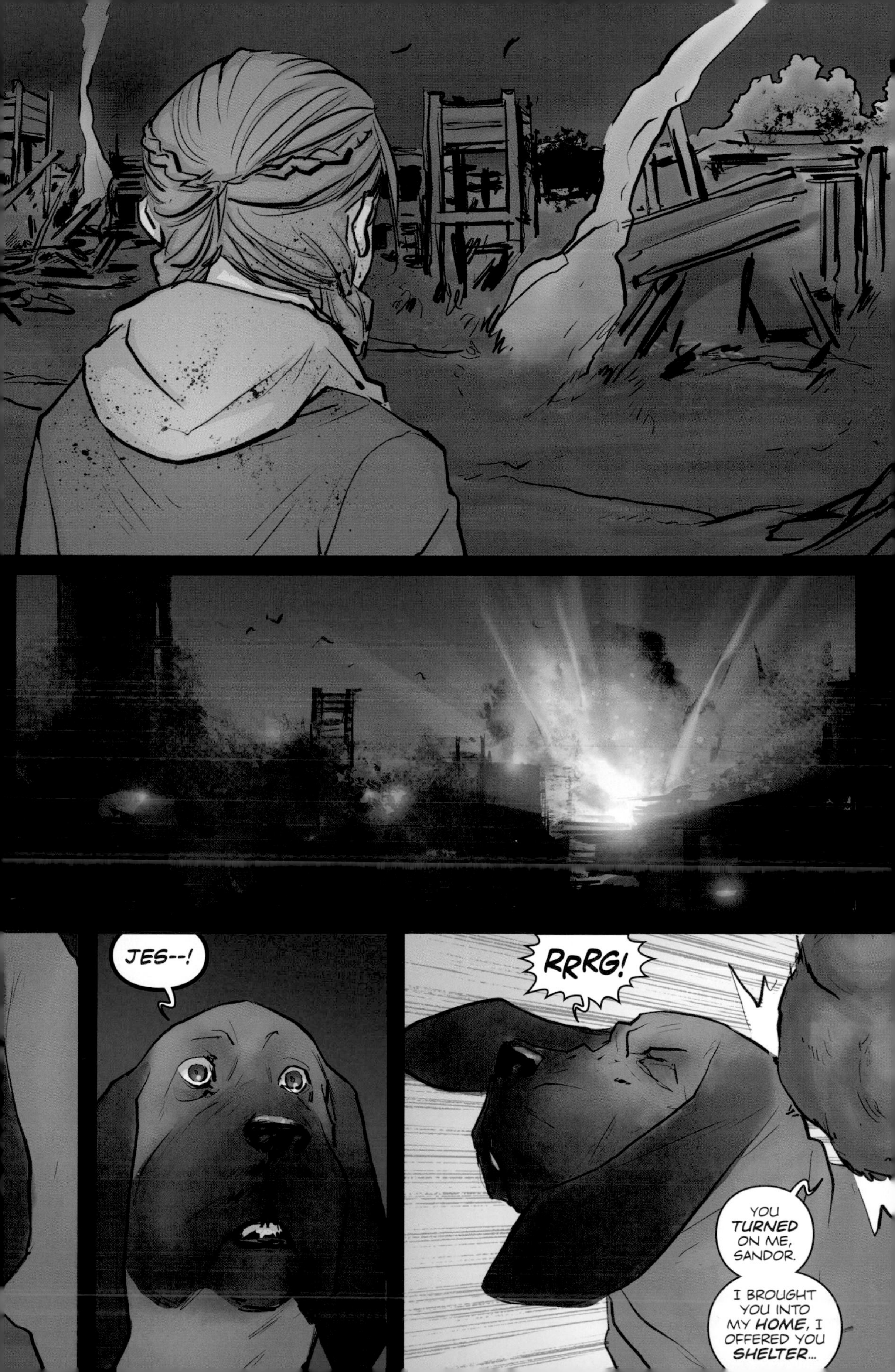
JES--!
RRRG!
YOU TURNED ON ME, SANDOR.
I BROUGHT YOU INTO MY HOME, I OFFERED YOU SHELTER...

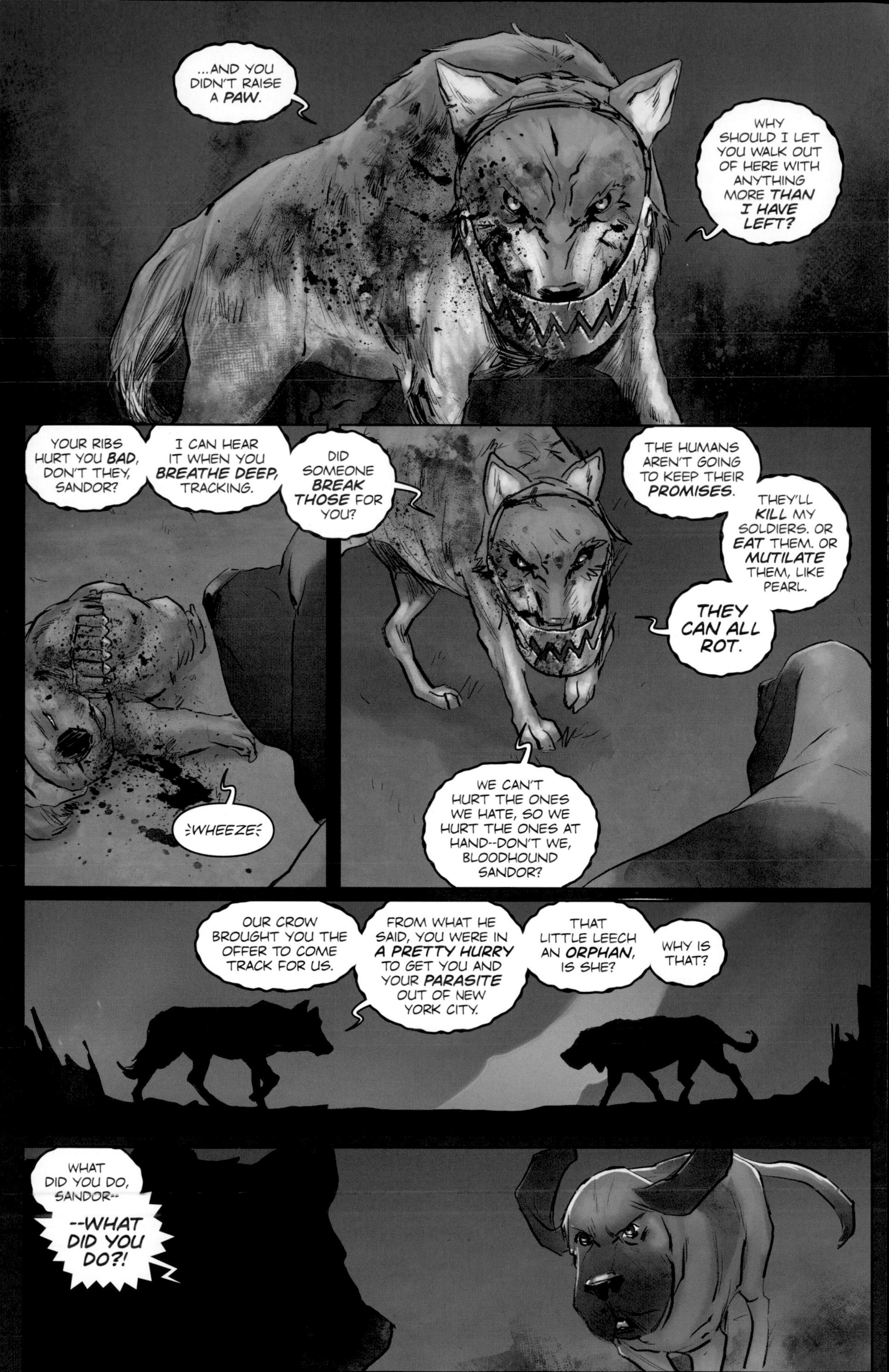
...AND YOU DIDN'T RAISE A **PAW**.
WHY SHOULD I LET YOU WALK OUT OF HERE WITH ANYTHING MORE **THAN I HAVE LEFT?**
YOUR RIBS HURT YOU **BAD**, DON'T THEY, SANDOR?
I CAN HEAR IT WHEN YOU **BREATHE DEEP**, TRACKING.
DID SOMEONE **BREAK THOSE** FOR YOU?
WHEEZE
THE HUMANS AREN'T GOING TO KEEP THEIR **PROMISES**.
THEY'LL **KILL** MY SOLDIERS. OR **EAT** THEM. OR **MUTILATE** THEM, LIKE PEARL.
THEY CAN ALL ROT.
WE CAN'T HURT THE ONES WE HATE, SO WE HURT THE ONES AT HAND--DON'T WE, BLOODHOUND SANDOR?
OUR CROW BROUGHT YOU THE OFFER TO COME TRACK FOR US.
FROM WHAT HE SAID, YOU WERE IN **A PRETTY HURRY** TO GET YOU AND YOUR **PARASITE** OUT OF NEW YORK CITY.
THAT LITTLE LEECH AN **ORPHAN**, IS SHE?
WHY IS THAT?
WHAT DID YOU DO, SANDOR--
--WHAT DID YOU DO?!

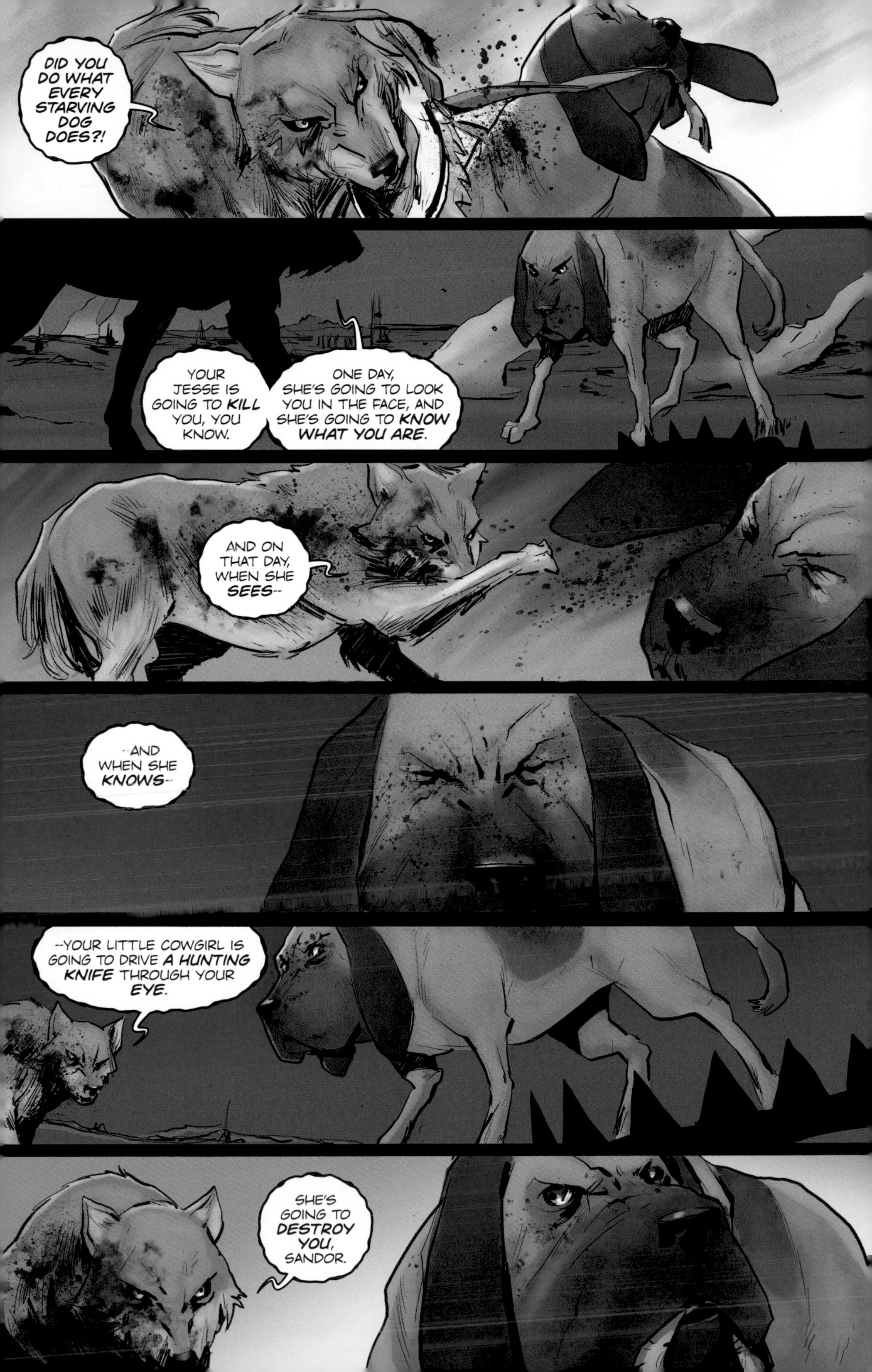
DID YOU DO WHAT EVERY STARVING DOG DOES?!
YOUR JESSE IS GOING TO KILL YOU, YOU KNOW.
ONE DAY, SHE'S GOING TO LOOK YOU IN THE FACE, AND SHE'S GOING TO KNOW WHAT YOU ARE.
AND ON THAT DAY, WHEN SHE SEES--
--AND WHEN SHE KNOWS--
--YOUR LITTLE COWGIRL IS GOING TO DRIVE A HUNTING KNIFE THROUGH YOUR EYE.
SHE'S GOING TO DESTROY YOU, SANDOR.

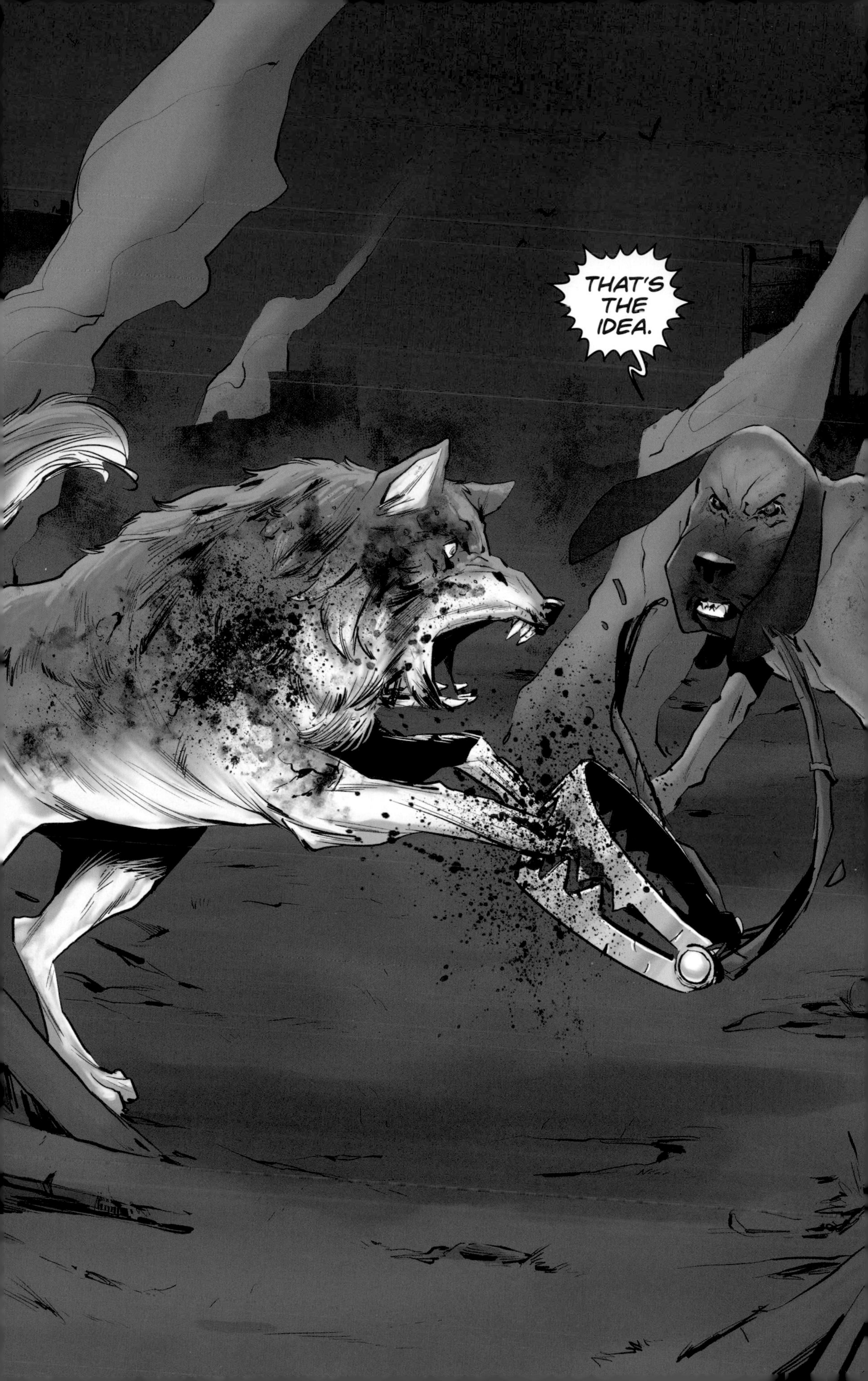
THAT'S THE IDEA.

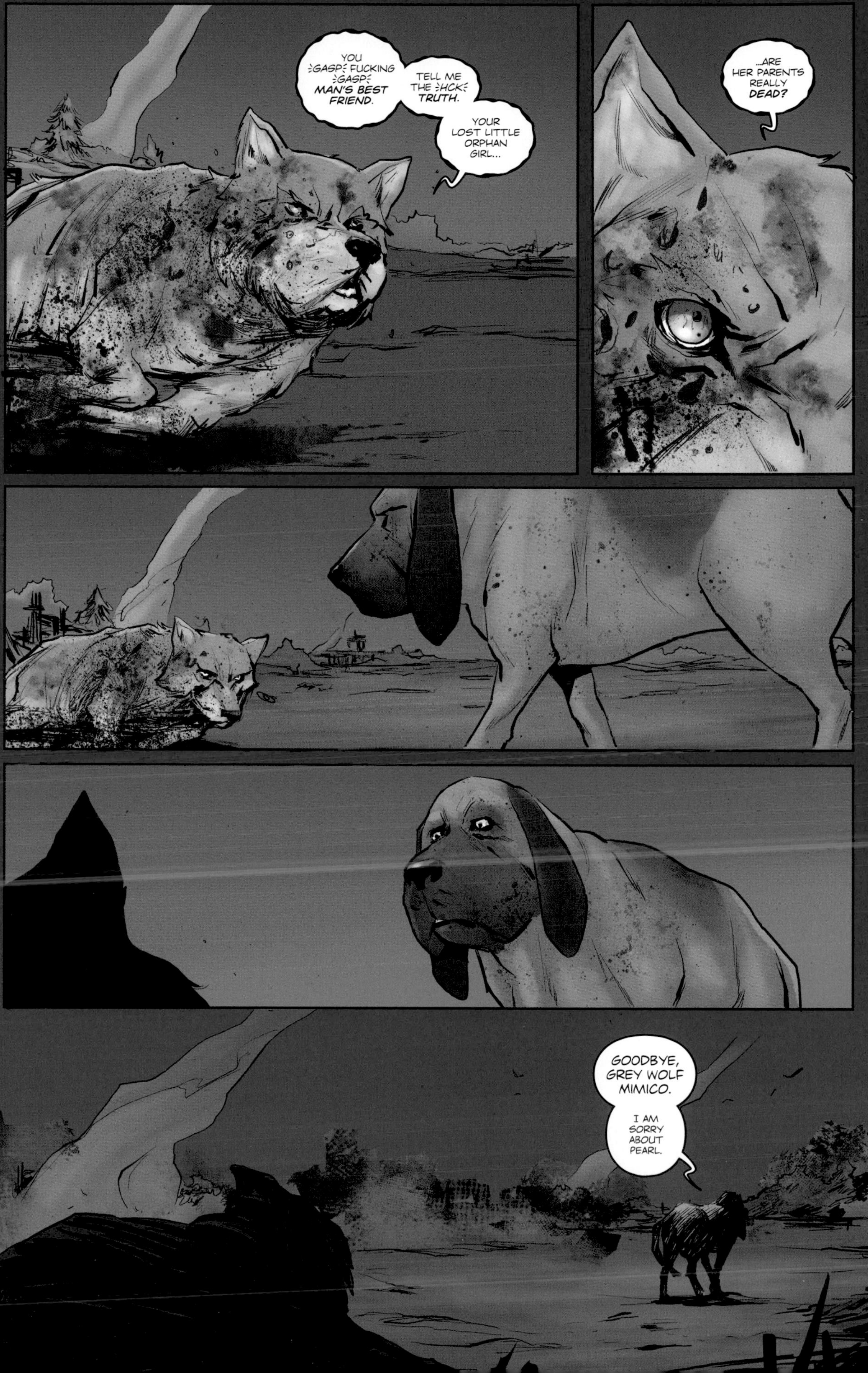
YOU ≶GASP≶ FUCKING ≶GASP≶ MAN'S BEST FRIEND.
TELL ME THE ≶HCK≶ TRUTH.
YOUR LOST LITTLE ORPHAN GIRL...
...ARE HER PARENTS REALLY DEAD?
GOODBYE, GREY WOLF MIMICO.
I AM SORRY ABOUT PEARL.

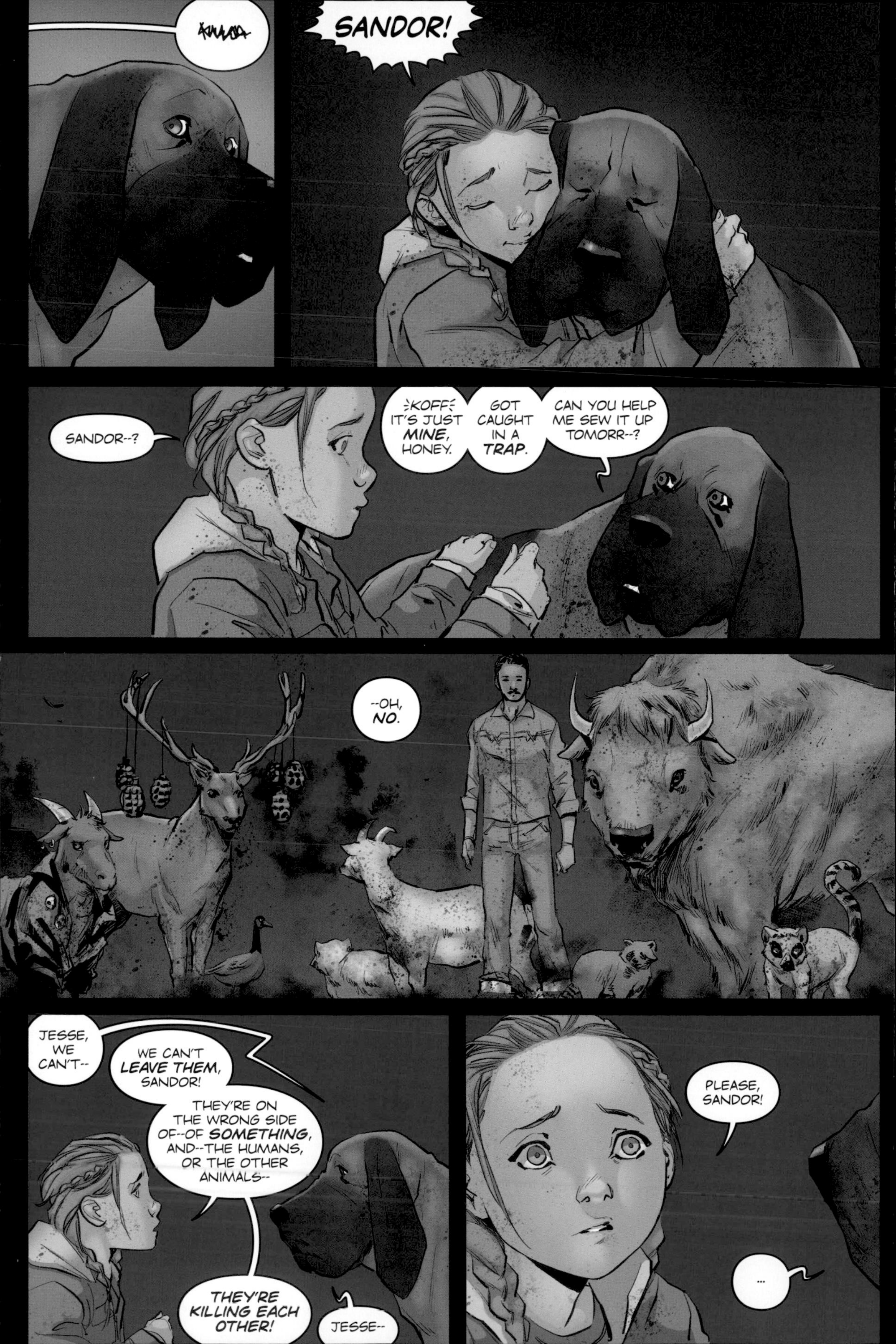
SANDOR!
SANDOR--?
KOFF IT'S JUST MINE, HONEY.
GOT CAUGHT IN A TRAP.
CAN YOU HELP ME SEW IT UP TOMORR--?
--OH, NO.
JESSE, WE CAN'T--
WE CAN'T LEAVE THEM, SANDOR!
THEY'RE ON THE WRONG SIDE OF--OF SOMETHING, AND--THE HUMANS, OR THE OTHER ANIMALS--
THEY'RE KILLING EACH OTHER!
JESSE--
PLEASE, SANDOR!
...

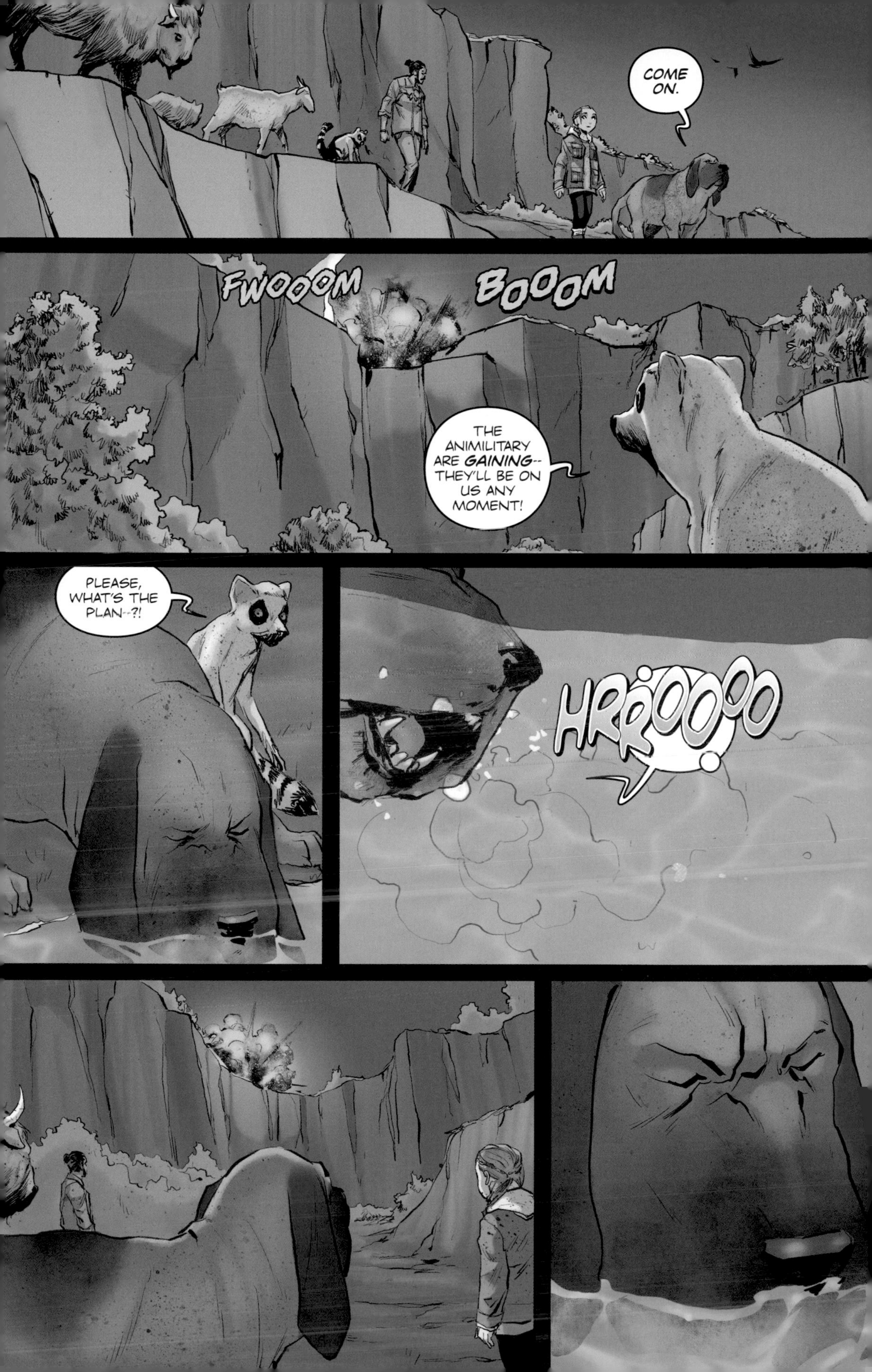
COME ON.
FWOOOM
BOOOM
THE ANIMILITARY ARE GAINING-- THEY'LL BE ON US ANY MOMENT!
PLEASE, WHAT'S THE PLAN--?!
HRROOOO

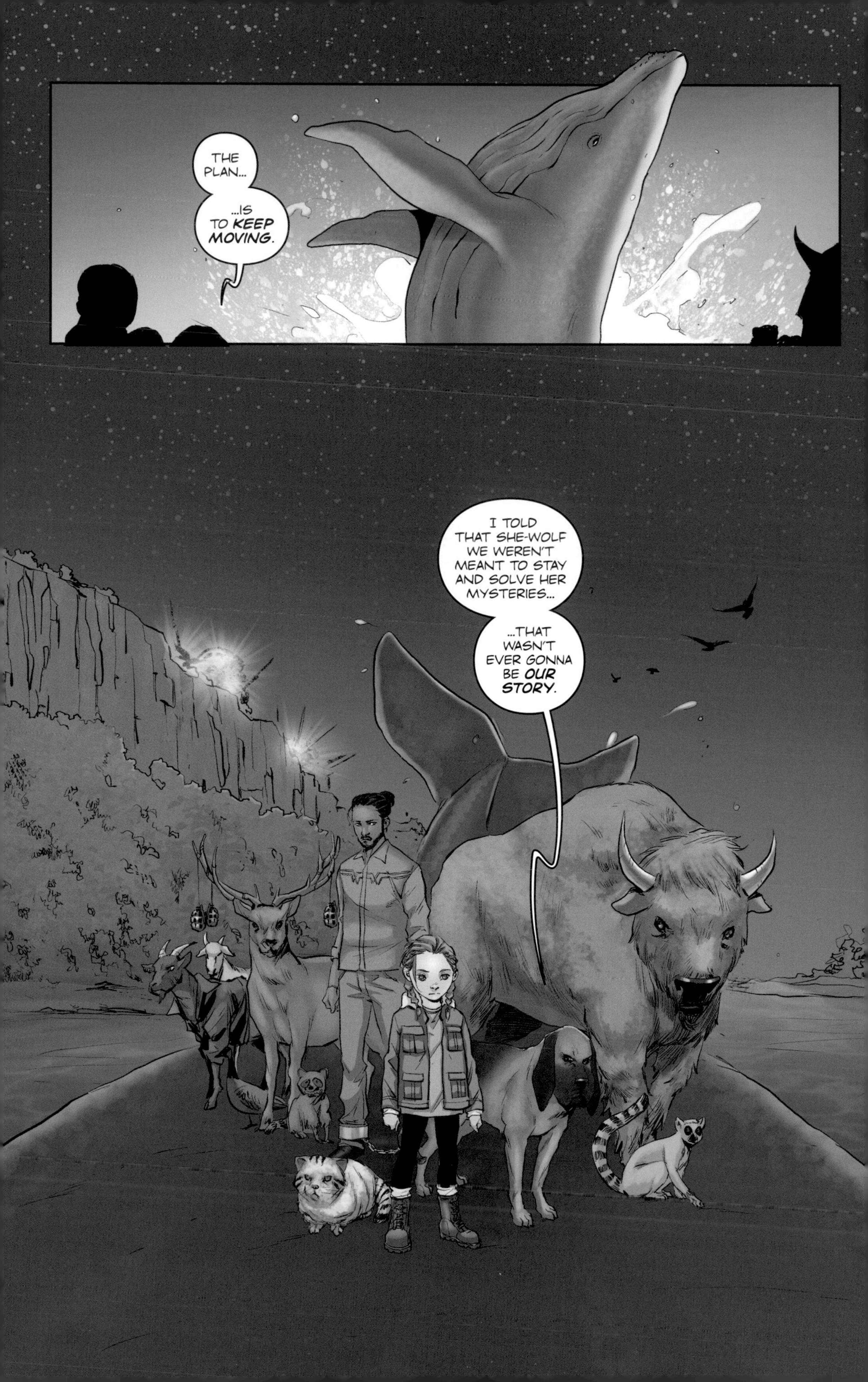
THE PLAN...
...IS TO KEEP MOVING.
I TOLD THAT SHE-WOLF WE WEREN'T MEANT TO STAY AND SOLVE HER MYSTERIES...
...THAT WASN'T EVER GONNA BE OUR STORY.

"HERE THERE BE DRAGONS"

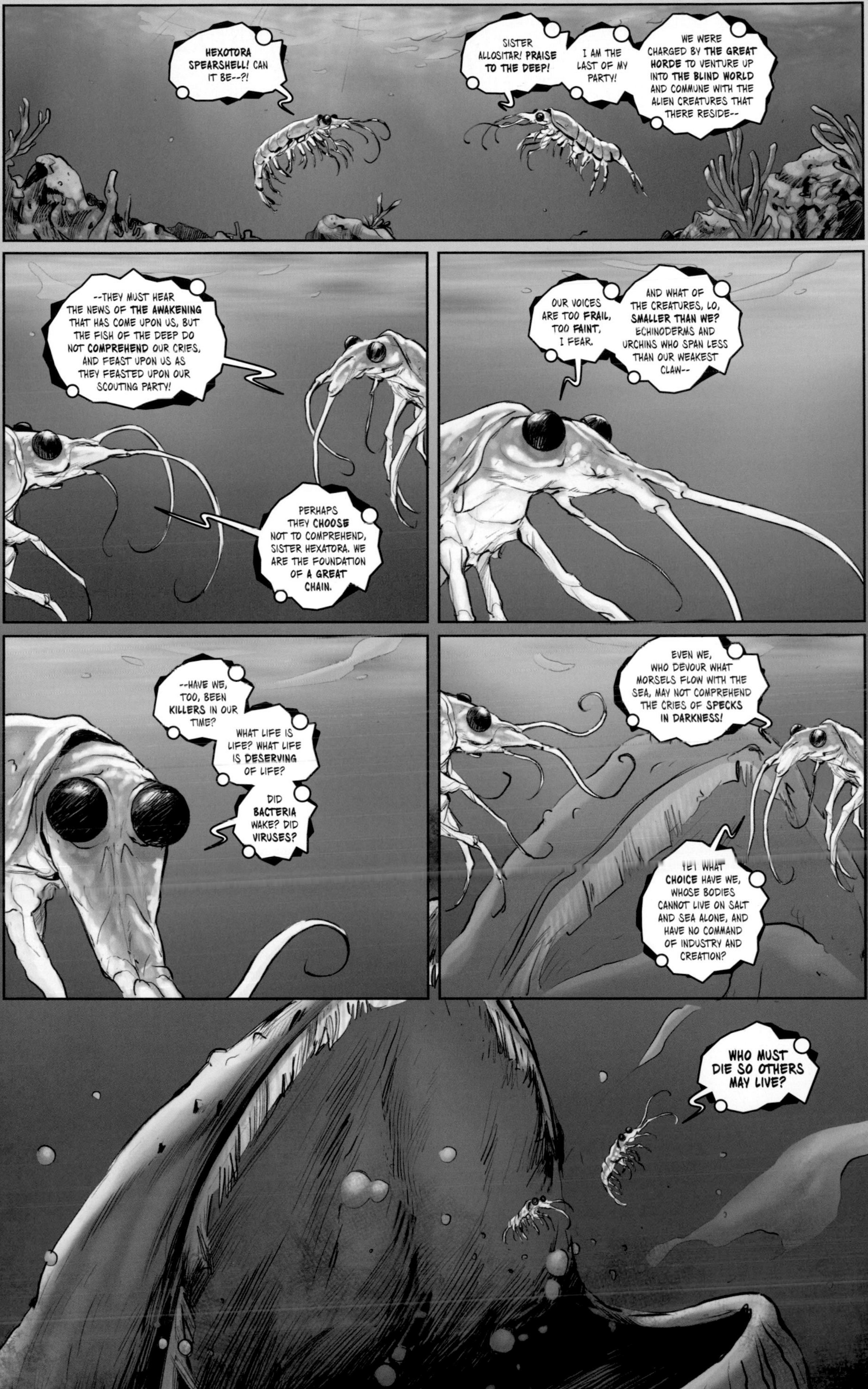
HEXOTORA SPEARSHELL! CAN IT BE--?!
SISTER ALLOSITAR! PRAISE TO THE DEEP!
I AM THE LAST OF MY PARTY!
WE WERE CHARGED BY THE GREAT HORDE TO VENTURE UP INTO THE BLIND WORLD AND COMMUNE WITH THE ALIEN CREATURES THAT THERE RESIDE--
--THEY MUST HEAR THE NEWS OF THE AWAKENING THAT HAS COME UPON US, BUT THE FISH OF THE DEEP DO NOT COMPREHEND OUR CRIES, AND FEAST UPON US AS THEY FEASTED UPON OUR SCOUTING PARTY!
PERHAPS THEY CHOOSE NOT TO COMPREHEND, SISTER HEXATORA. WE ARE THE FOUNDATION OF A GREAT CHAIN.
OUR VOICES ARE TOO FRAIL, TOO FAINT, I FEAR.
AND WHAT OF THE CREATURES, LO, SMALLER THAN WE? ECHINODERMS AND URCHINS WHO SPAN LESS THAN OUR WEAKEST CLAW--
--HAVE WE, TOO, BEEN KILLERS IN OUR TIME?
WHAT LIFE IS LIFE? WHAT LIFE IS DESERVING OF LIFE?
DID BACTERIA WAKE? DID VIRUSES?
EVEN WE, WHO DEVOUR WHAT MORSELS FLOW WITH THE SEA, MAY NOT COMPREHEND THE CRIES OF SPECKS IN DARKNESS!
YET WHAT CHOICE HAVE WE, WHOSE BODIES CANNOT LIVE ON SALT AND SEA ALONE, AND HAVE NO COMMAND OF INDUSTRY AND CREATION?
WHO MUST DIE SO OTHERS MAY LIVE?

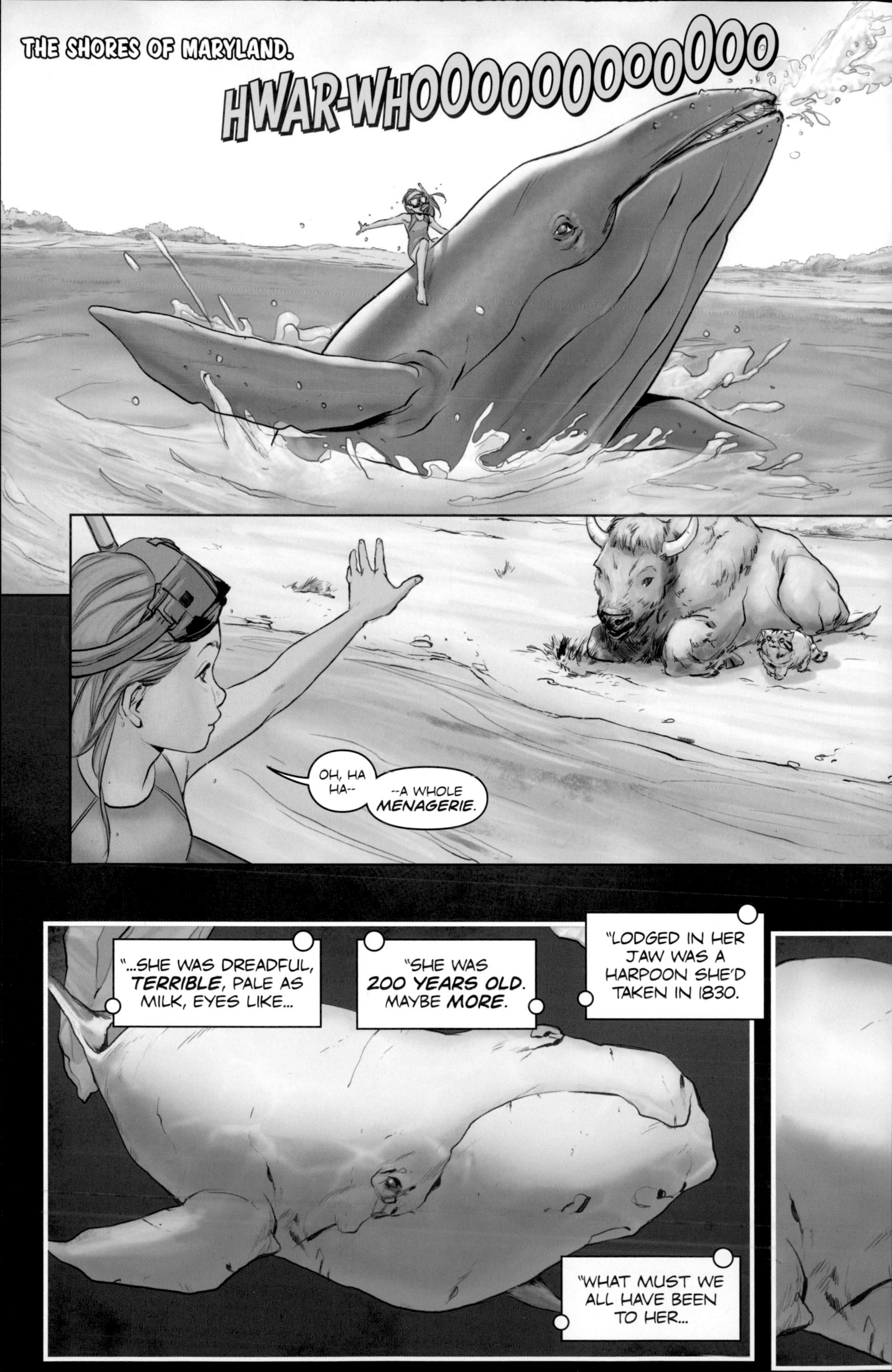
THE SHORES OF MARYLAND.
HWAR-WHOOOOOOOOOOOOO
OH, HA HA--
--A WHOLE MENAGERIE.
"...SHE WAS DREADFUL, TERRIBLE, PALE AS MILK, EYES LIKE...
"SHE WAS 200 YEARS OLD. MAYBE MORE.
"LODGED IN HER JAW WAS A HARPOON SHE'D TAKEN IN 1830.
"WHAT MUST WE ALL HAVE BEEN TO HER...

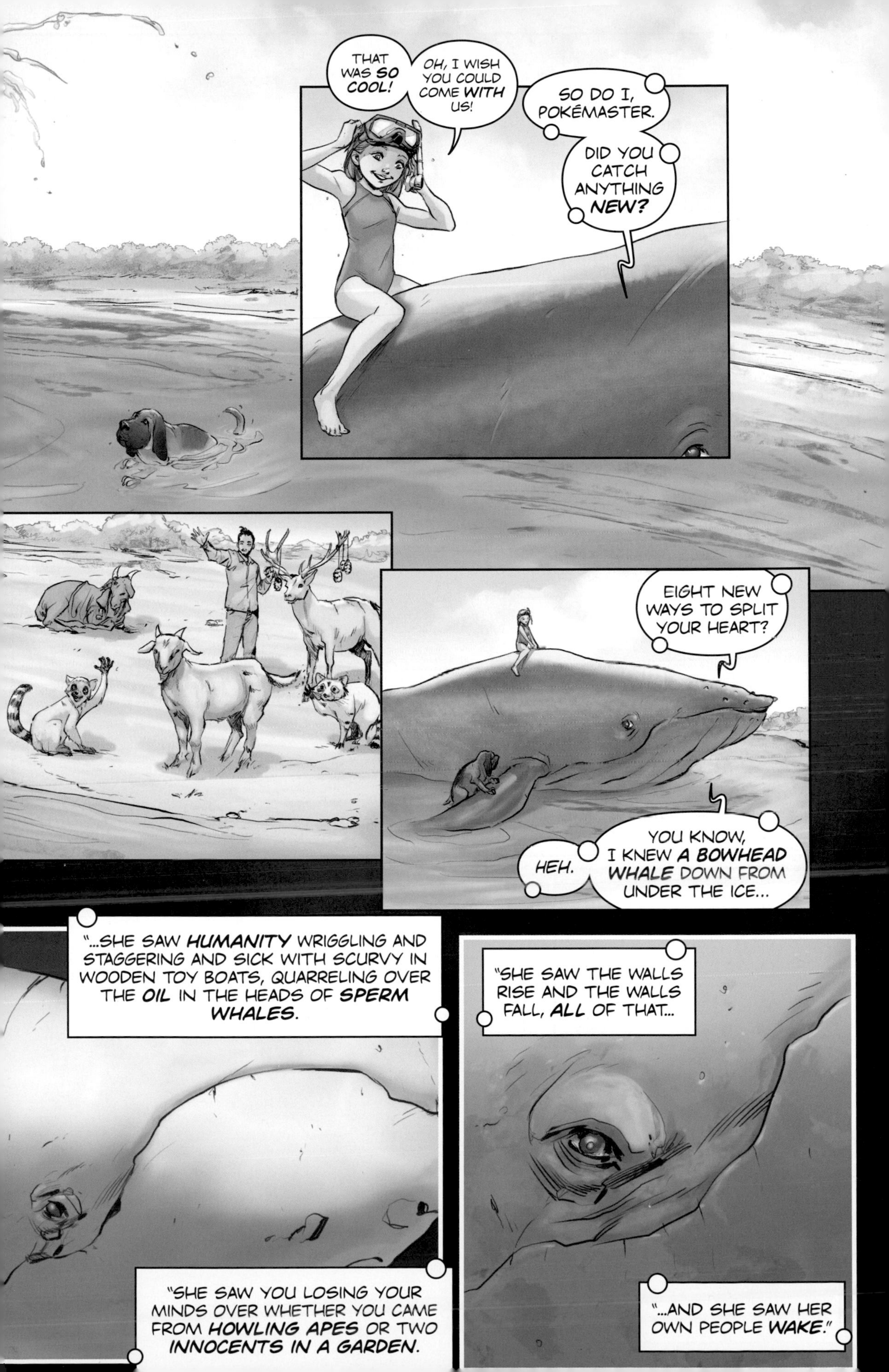
THAT WAS SO COOL!
OH, I WISH YOU COULD COME WITH US!
SO DO I, POKÉMASTER.
DID YOU CATCH ANYTHING NEW?
EIGHT NEW WAYS TO SPLIT YOUR HEART?
HEH.
YOU KNOW, I KNEW A BOWHEAD WHALE DOWN FROM UNDER THE ICE...
"...SHE SAW HUMANITY WRIGGLING AND STAGGERING AND SICK WITH SCURVY IN WOODEN TOY BOATS, QUARRELING OVER THE OIL IN THE HEADS OF SPERM WHALES.
"SHE SAW YOU LOSING YOUR MINDS OVER WHETHER YOU CAME FROM HOWLING APES OR TWO INNOCENTS IN A GARDEN.
"SHE SAW THE WALLS RISE AND THE WALLS FALL, ALL OF THAT...
"...AND SHE SAW HER OWN PEOPLE WAKE."

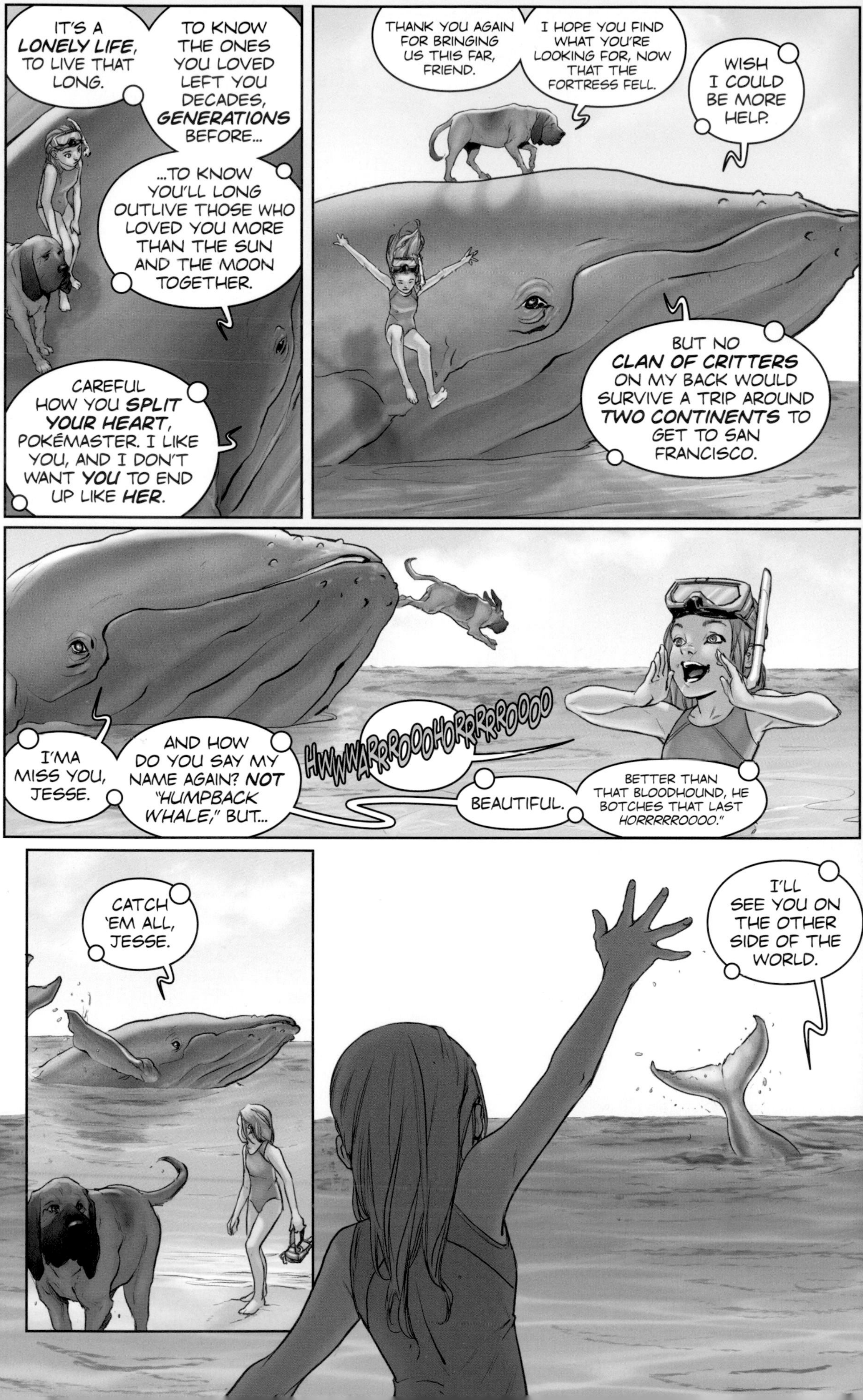
IT'S A LONELY LIFE, TO LIVE THAT LONG.
TO KNOW THE ONES YOU LOVED LEFT YOU DECADES, GENERATIONS BEFORE...
...TO KNOW YOU'LL LONG OUTLIVE THOSE WHO LOVED YOU MORE THAN THE SUN AND THE MOON TOGETHER.
CAREFUL HOW YOU SPLIT YOUR HEART, POKÉMASTER. I LIKE YOU, AND I DON'T WANT YOU TO END UP LIKE HER.
THANK YOU AGAIN FOR BRINGING US THIS FAR, FRIEND.
I HOPE YOU FIND WHAT YOU'RE LOOKING FOR, NOW THAT THE FORTRESS FELL.
WISH I COULD BE MORE HELP.
BUT NO CLAN OF CRITTERS ON MY BACK WOULD SURVIVE A TRIP AROUND TWO CONTINENTS TO GET TO SAN FRANCISCO.
I'MA MISS YOU, JESSE.
AND HOW DO YOU SAY MY NAME AGAIN? NOT "HUMPBACK WHALE," BUT...
HWWWARRROOOHORRRRROOOO
BEAUTIFUL.
BETTER THAN THAT BLOODHOUND, HE BOTCHES THAT LAST HORRRRROOOO."
CATCH 'EM ALL, JESSE.
I'LL SEE YOU ON THE OTHER SIDE OF THE WORLD.

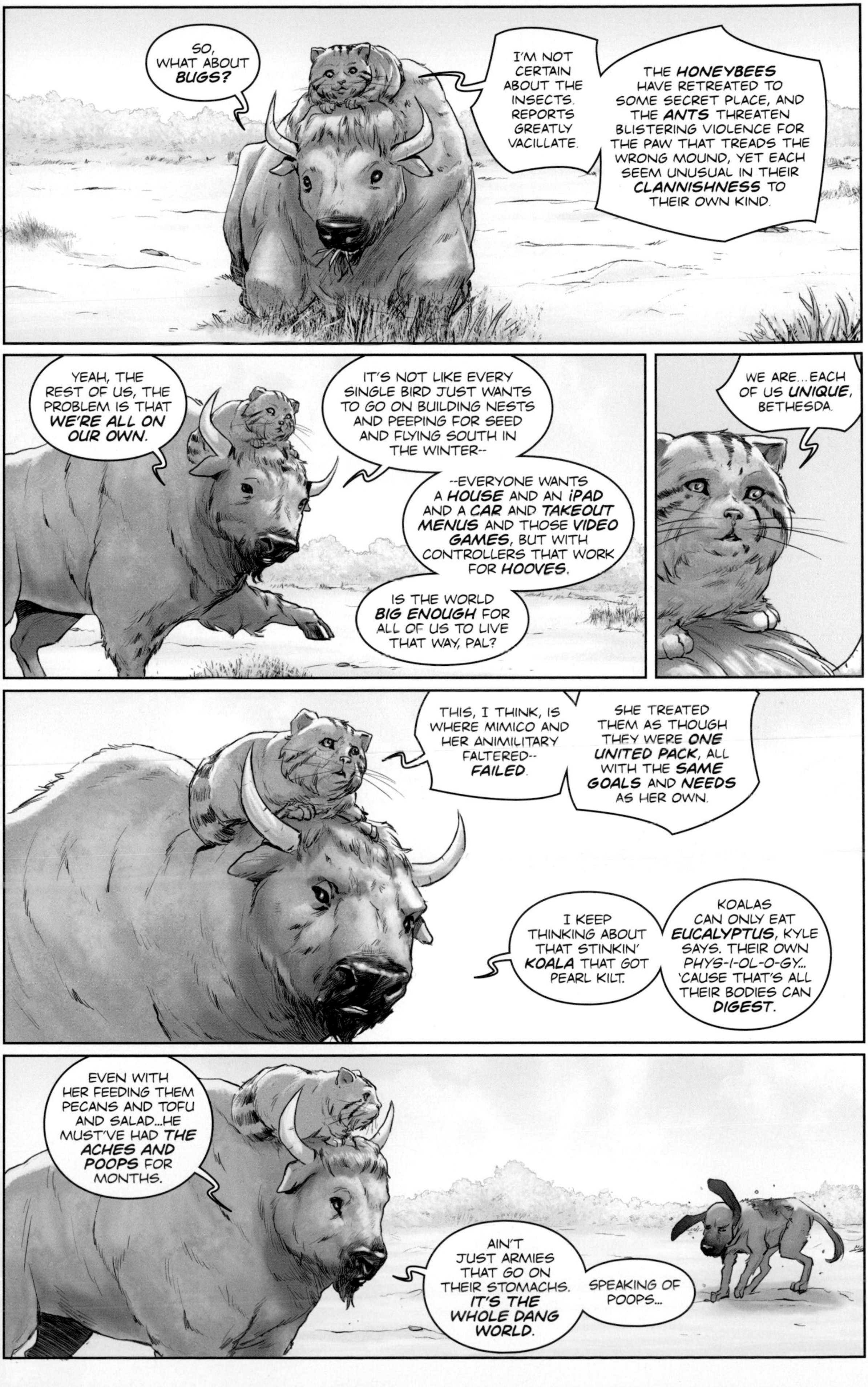

SO, WHAT ABOUT BUGS?
I'M NOT CERTAIN ABOUT THE INSECTS. REPORTS GREATLY VACILLATE.
THE HONEYBEES HAVE RETREATED TO SOME SECRET PLACE, AND THE ANTS THREATEN BLISTERING VIOLENCE FOR THE PAW THAT TREADS THE WRONG MOUND, YET EACH SEEM UNUSUAL IN THEIR CLANNISHNESS TO THEIR OWN KIND.
YEAH, THE REST OF US, THE PROBLEM IS THAT WE'RE ALL ON OUR OWN.
IT'S NOT LIKE EVERY SINGLE BIRD JUST WANTS TO GO ON BUILDING NESTS AND PEEPING FOR SEED AND FLYING SOUTH IN THE WINTER--
--EVERYONE WANTS A HOUSE AND AN iPAD AND A CAR AND TAKEOUT MENUS AND THOSE VIDEO GAMES, BUT WITH CONTROLLERS THAT WORK FOR HOOVES.
IS THE WORLD BIG ENOUGH FOR ALL OF US TO LIVE THAT WAY, PAL?
WE ARE...EACH OF US UNIQUE, BETHESDA.
THIS, I THINK, IS WHERE MIMICO AND HER ANIMILITARY FALTERED--FAILED.
SHE TREATED THEM AS THOUGH THEY WERE ONE UNITED PACK, ALL WITH THE SAME GOALS AND NEEDS AS HER OWN.
I KEEP THINKING ABOUT THAT STINKIN' KOALA THAT GOT PEARL KILT.
KOALAS CAN ONLY EAT EUCALYPTUS, KYLE SAYS. THEIR OWN PHYS-I-OL-O-GY... 'CAUSE THAT'S ALL THEIR BODIES CAN DIGEST.
EVEN WITH HER FEEDING THEM PECANS AND TOFU AND SALAD...HE MUST'VE HAD THE ACHES AND POOPS FOR MONTHS.
AIN'T JUST ARMIES THAT GO ON THEIR STOMACHS. IT'S THE WHOLE DANG WORLD.
SPEAKING OF POOPS...

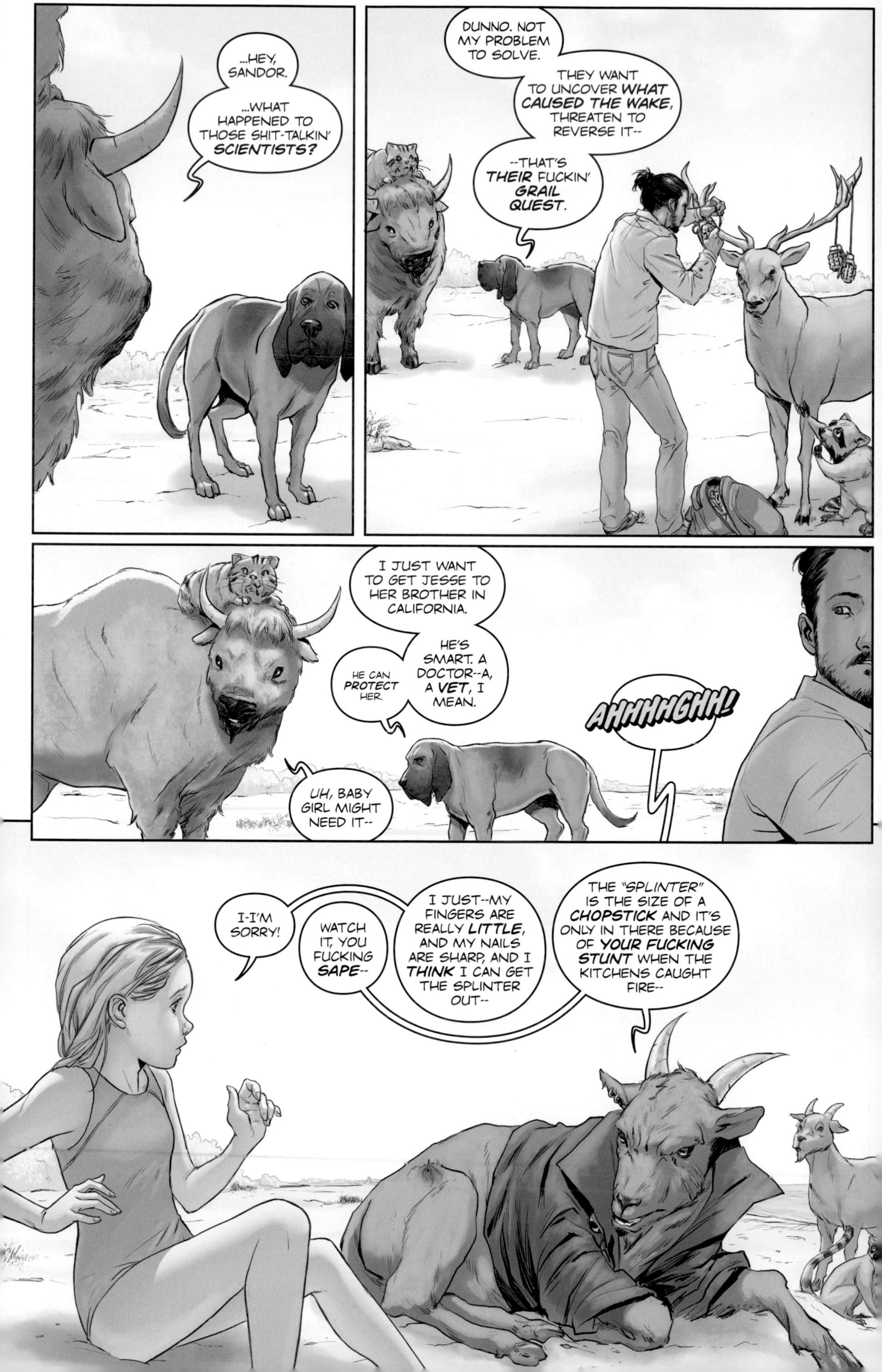
...HEY, SANDOR.
...WHAT HAPPENED TO THOSE SHIT-TALKIN' SCIENTISTS?
DUNNO. NOT MY PROBLEM TO SOLVE.
THEY WANT TO UNCOVER WHAT CAUSED THE WAKE, THREATEN TO REVERSE IT--
--THAT'S THEIR FUCKIN' GRAIL QUEST.
I JUST WANT TO GET JESSE TO HER BROTHER IN CALIFORNIA.
HE'S SMART. A DOCTOR--A, A VET, I MEAN.
HE CAN PROTECT HER.
UH, BABY GIRL MIGHT NEED IT--
AHHHHGHH!
I-I'M SORRY!
WATCH IT, YOU FUCKING SAPE--
I JUST--MY FINGERS ARE REALLY LITTLE, AND MY NAILS ARE SHARP, AND I THINK I CAN GET THE SPLINTER OUT--
THE "SPLINTER" IS THE SIZE OF A CHOPSTICK AND IT'S ONLY IN THERE BECAUSE OF YOUR FUCKING STUNT WHEN THE KITCHENS CAUGHT FIRE--

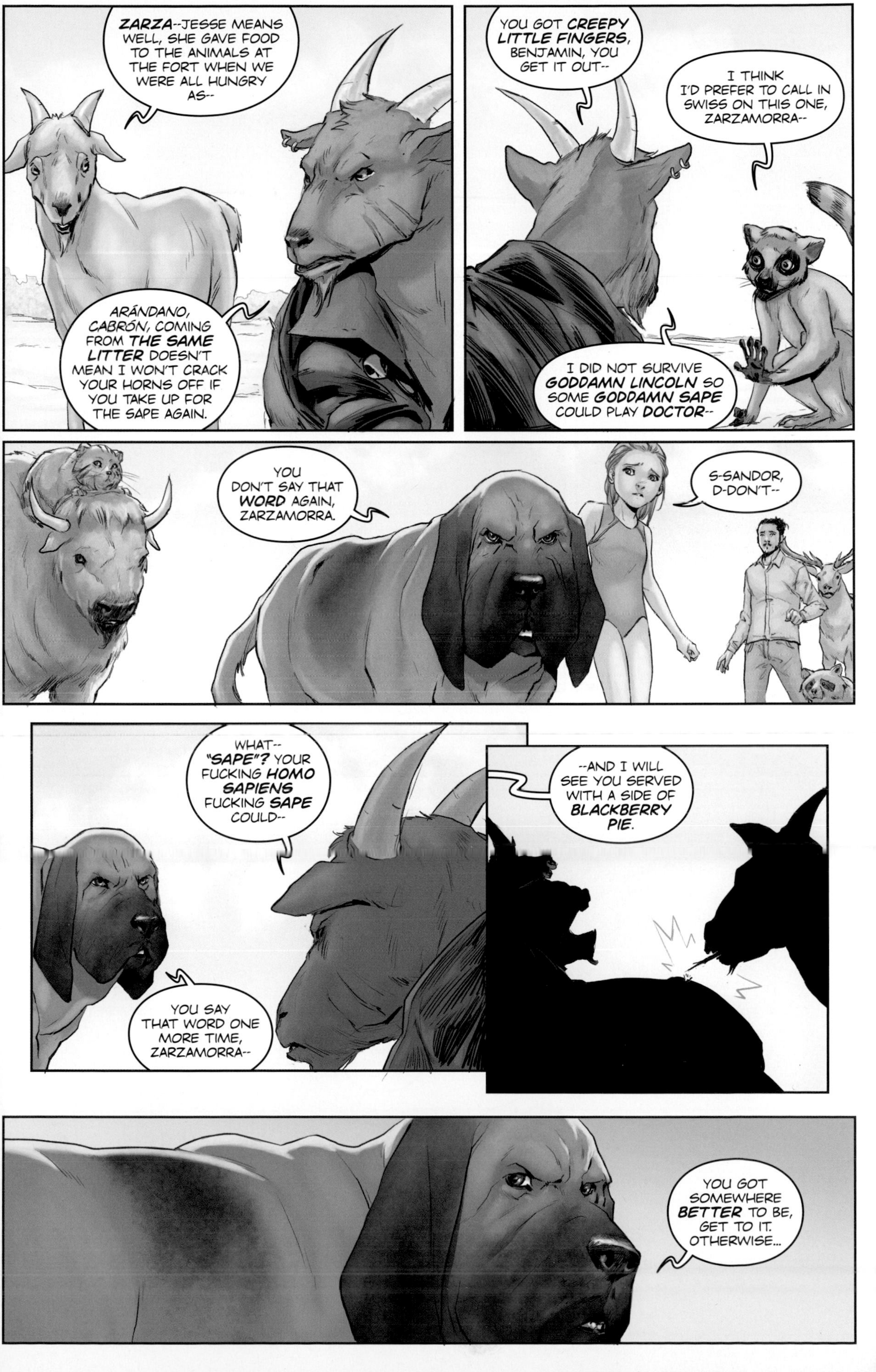
ZARZA--JESSE MEANS WELL, SHE GAVE FOOD TO THE ANIMALS AT THE FORT WHEN WE WERE ALL HUNGRY AS--
ARÁNDANO, CABRÓN, COMING FROM THE SAME LITTER DOESN'T MEAN I WON'T CRACK YOUR HORNS OFF IF YOU TAKE UP FOR THE SAPE AGAIN.
YOU GOT CREEPY LITTLE FINGERS, BENJAMIN, YOU GET IT OUT--
I THINK I'D PREFER TO CALL IN SWISS ON THIS ONE, ZARZAMORRA--
I DID NOT SURVIVE GODDAMN LINCOLN SO SOME GODDAMN SAPE COULD PLAY DOCTOR--
YOU DON'T SAY THAT WORD AGAIN, ZARZAMORRA.
S-SANDOR, D-DON'T--
WHAT-- "SAPE"? YOUR FUCKING HOMO SAPIENS FUCKING SAPE COULD--
YOU SAY THAT WORD ONE MORE TIME, ZARZAMORRA--
--AND I WILL SEE YOU SERVED WITH A SIDE OF BLACKBERRY PIE.
YOU GOT SOMEWHERE BETTER TO BE, GET TO IT. OTHERWISE...

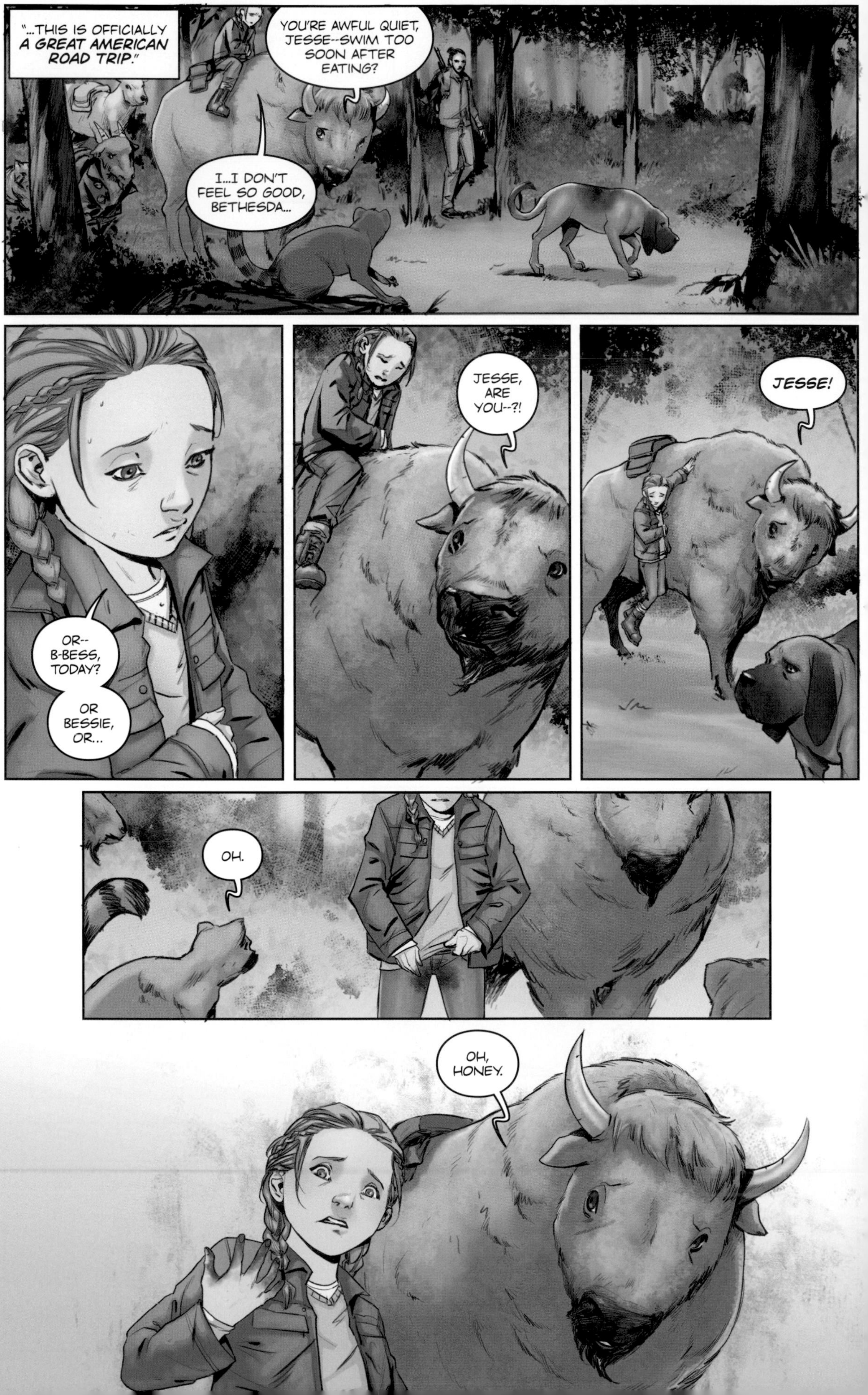
"...THIS IS OFFICIALLY A GREAT AMERICAN ROAD TRIP."
YOU'RE AWFUL QUIET, JESSE--SWIM TOO SOON AFTER EATING?
I...I DON'T FEEL SO GOOD, BETHESDA...
OR-- B-BESS, TODAY?
OR BESSIE, OR...
JESSE, ARE YOU--?!
JESSE!
OH.
OH, HONEY.

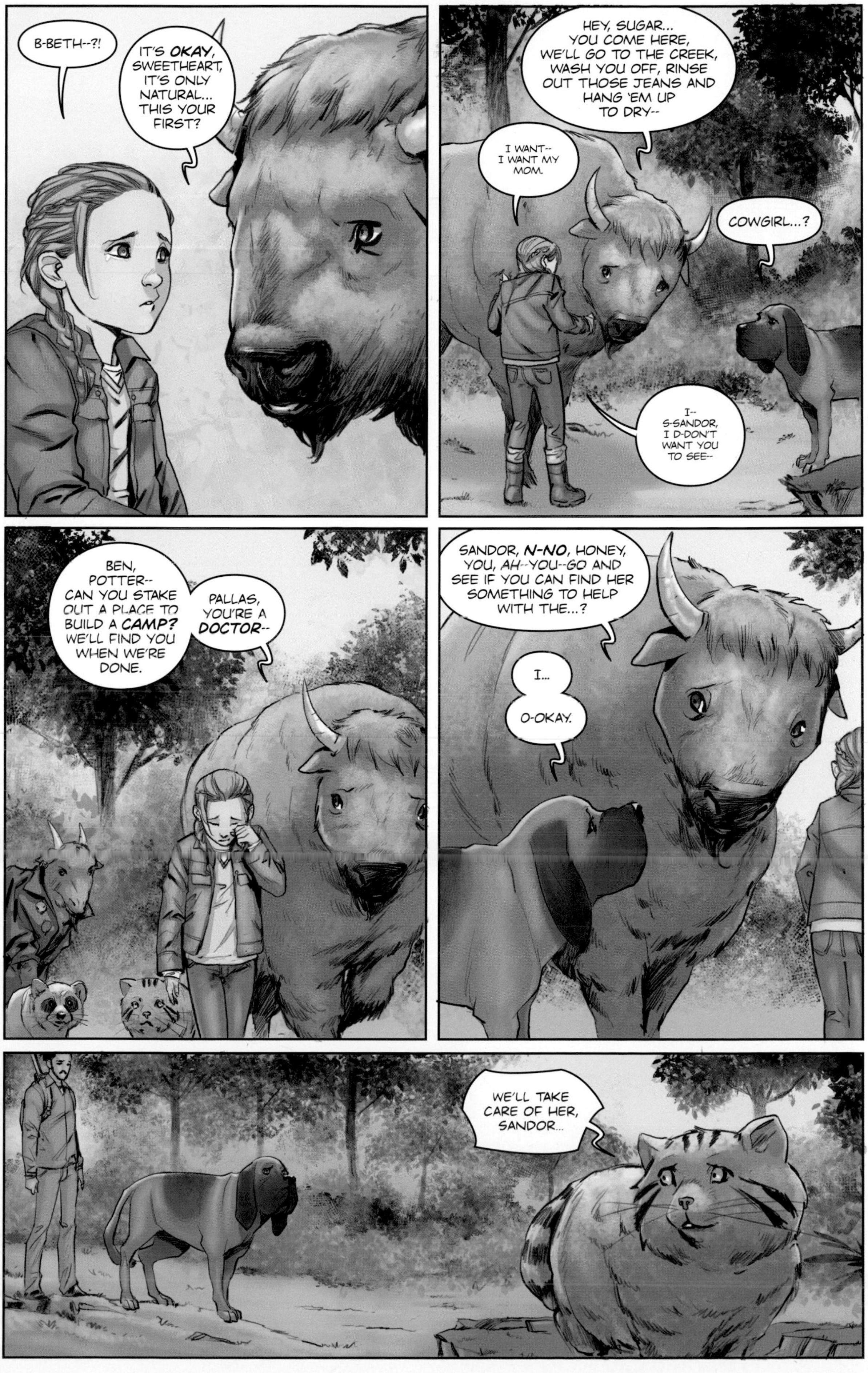
B-BETH--?!
IT'S OKAY, SWEETHEART, IT'S ONLY NATURAL... THIS YOUR FIRST?
HEY, SUGAR... YOU COME HERE, WE'LL GO TO THE CREEK, WASH YOU OFF, RINSE OUT THOSE JEANS AND HANG 'EM UP TO DRY--
I WANT-- I WANT MY MOM.
COWGIRL...?
I-- S-SANDOR, I D-DON'T WANT YOU TO SEE--
BEN, POTTER-- CAN YOU STAKE OUT A PLACE TO BUILD A CAMP? WE'LL FIND YOU WHEN WE'RE DONE.
PALLAS, YOU'RE A DOCTOR--
SANDOR, N-NO, HONEY, YOU, AH--YOU--GO AND SEE IF YOU CAN FIND HER SOMETHING TO HELP WITH THE...?
I...
O-OKAY.
WE'LL TAKE CARE OF HER, SANDOR...

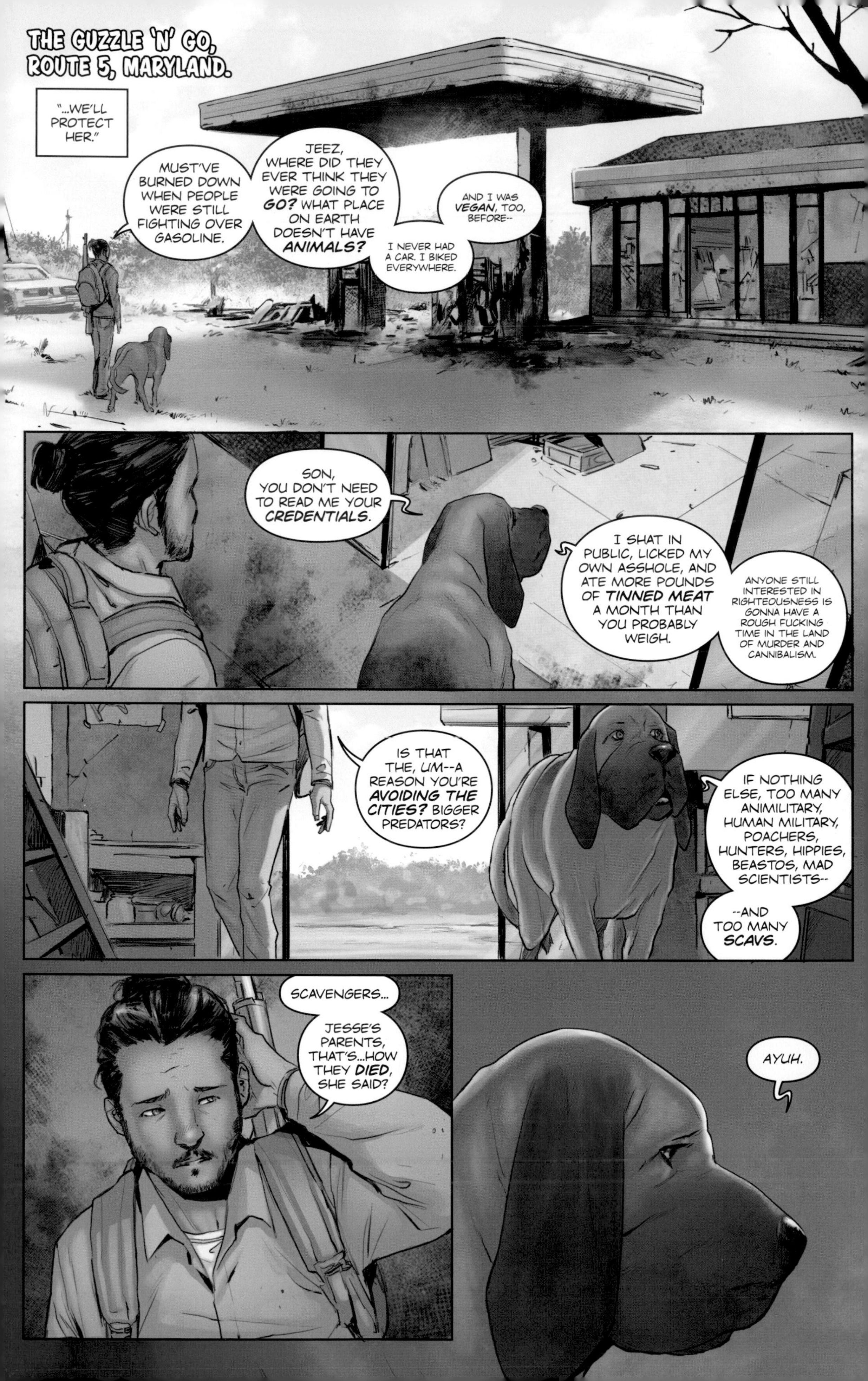
THE GUZZLE 'N' GO, ROUTE 5, MARYLAND.
"...WE'LL PROTECT HER."
MUST'VE BURNED DOWN WHEN PEOPLE WERE STILL FIGHTING OVER GASOLINE.
JEEZ, WHERE DID THEY EVER THINK THEY WERE GOING TO GO? WHAT PLACE ON EARTH DOESN'T HAVE ANIMALS?
I NEVER HAD A CAR. I BIKED EVERYWHERE.
AND I WAS VEGAN, TOO, BEFORE--
SON, YOU DON'T NEED TO READ ME YOUR CREDENTIALS.
I SHAT IN PUBLIC, LICKED MY OWN ASSHOLE, AND ATE MORE POUNDS OF TINNED MEAT A MONTH THAN YOU PROBABLY WEIGH.
ANYONE STILL INTERESTED IN RIGHTEOUSNESS IS GONNA HAVE A ROUGH FUCKING TIME IN THE LAND OF MURDER AND CANNIBALISM.
IS THAT THE, UM--A REASON YOU'RE AVOIDING THE CITIES? BIGGER PREDATORS?
IF NOTHING ELSE, TOO MANY ANIMILITARY, HUMAN MILITARY, POACHERS, HUNTERS, HIPPIES, BEASTOS, MAD SCIENTISTS--
--AND TOO MANY SCAVS.
SCAVENGERS...
JESSE'S PARENTS, THAT'S...HOW THEY DIED, SHE SAID?
AYUH.

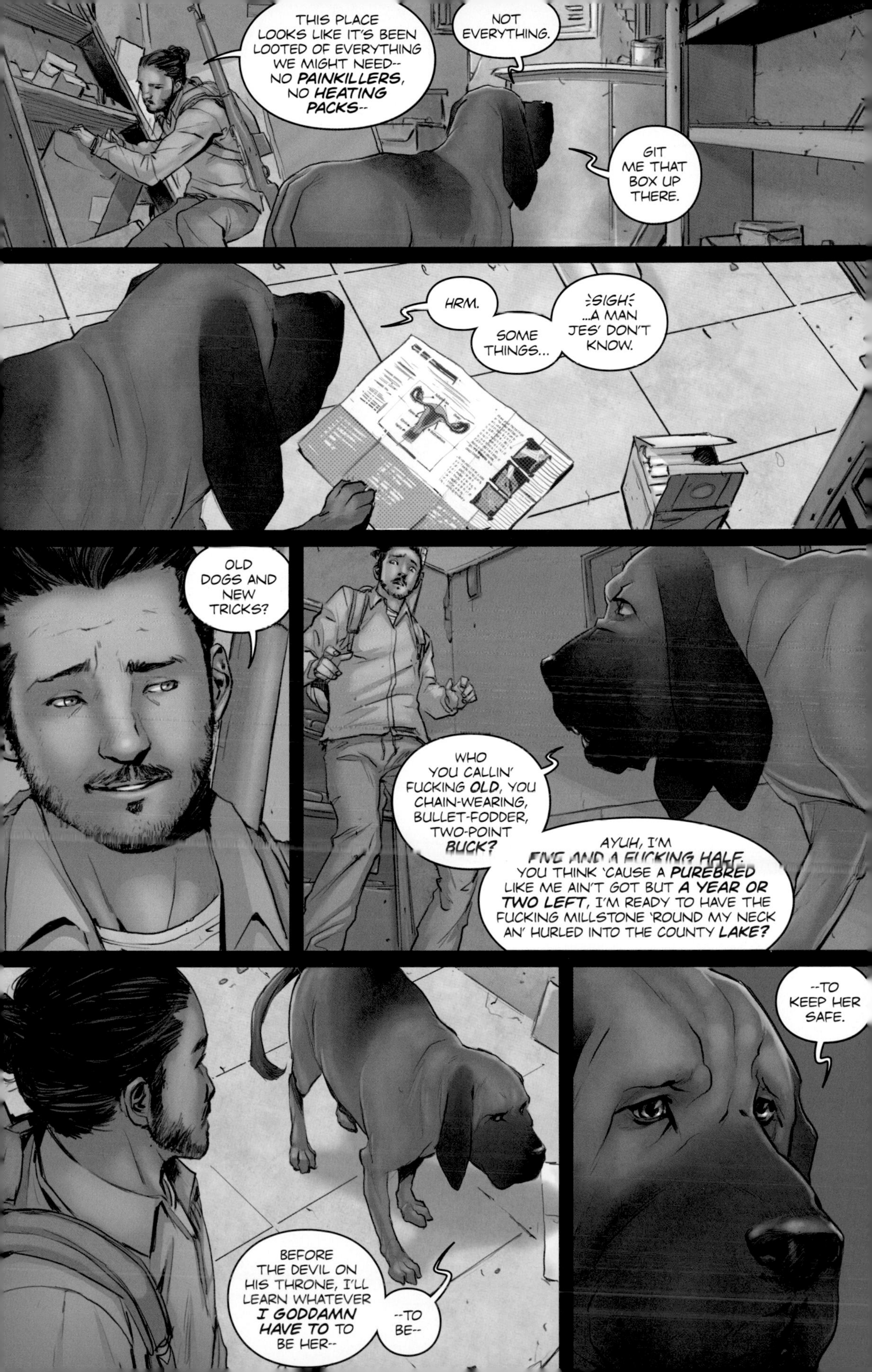
THIS PLACE LOOKS LIKE IT'S BEEN LOOTED OF EVERYTHING WE MIGHT NEED-- NO PAINKILLERS, NO HEATING PACKS--
NOT EVERYTHING.
GIT ME THAT BOX UP THERE.
HRM.
SOME THINGS...
SIGH ...A MAN JES' DON'T KNOW.
OLD DOGS AND NEW TRICKS?
WHO YOU CALLIN' FUCKING OLD, YOU CHAIN-WEARING, BULLET-FODDER, TWO-POINT BUCK?
AYUH, I'M FIVE AND A FUCKING HALF. YOU THINK 'CAUSE A PUREBRED LIKE ME AIN'T GOT BUT A YEAR OR TWO LEFT, I'M READY TO HAVE THE FUCKING MILLSTONE 'ROUND MY NECK AN' HURLED INTO THE COUNTY LAKE?
BEFORE THE DEVIL ON HIS THRONE, I'LL LEARN WHATEVER I GODDAMN HAVE TO TO BE HER--
--TO BE--
--TO KEEP HER SAFE.

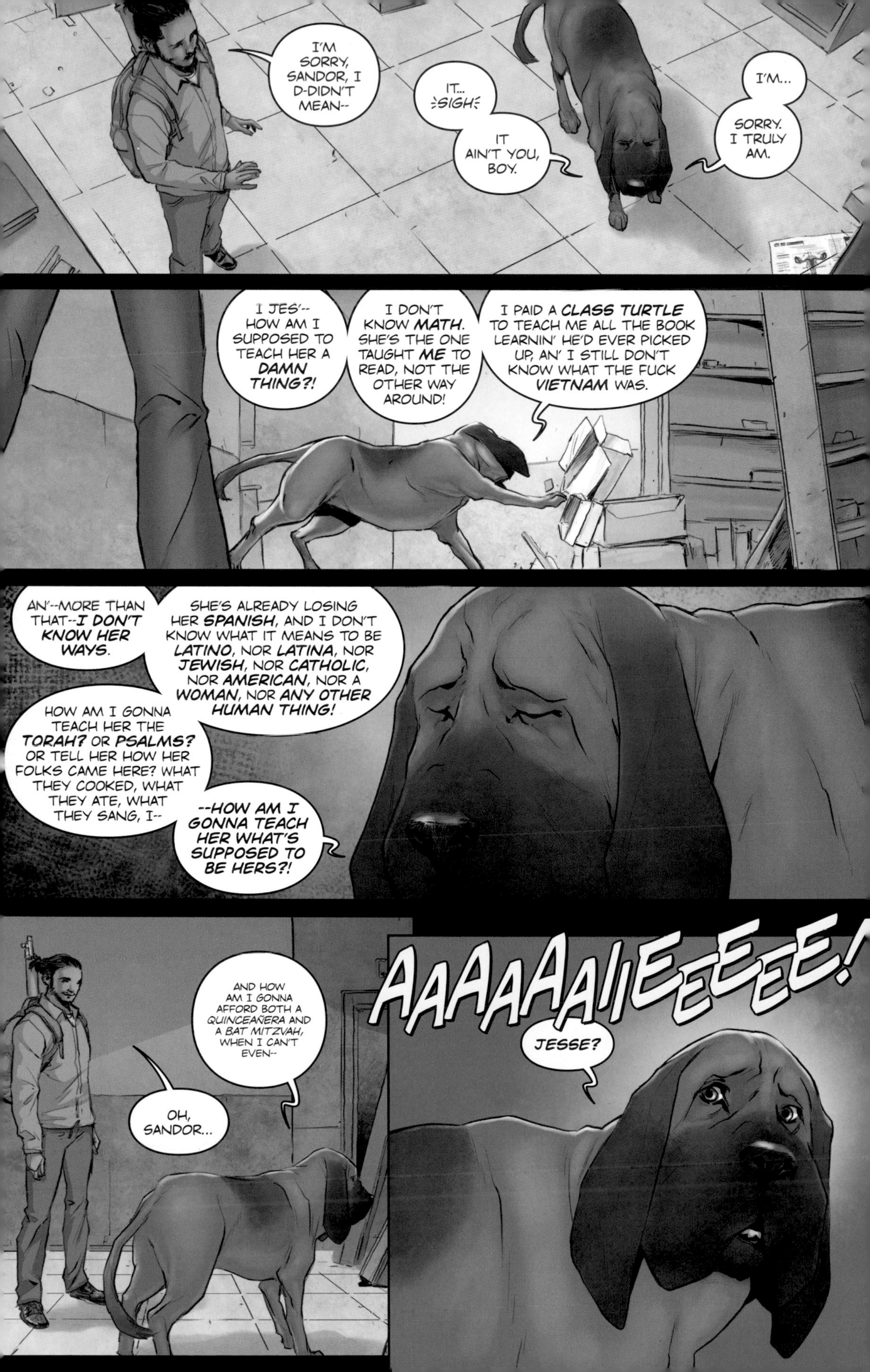
I'M SORRY, SANDOR, I D-DIDN'T MEAN--
IT... SIGH
IT AIN'T YOU, BOY.
I'M...
SORRY. I TRULY AM.
I JES'-- HOW AM I SUPPOSED TO TEACH HER A DAMN THING?!
I DON'T KNOW MATH. SHE'S THE ONE TAUGHT ME TO READ, NOT THE OTHER WAY AROUND!
I PAID A CLASS TURTLE TO TEACH ME ALL THE BOOK LEARNIN' HE'D EVER PICKED UP, AN' I STILL DON'T KNOW WHAT THE FUCK VIETNAM WAS.
AN'--MORE THAN THAT--I DON'T KNOW HER WAYS.
SHE'S ALREADY LOSING HER SPANISH, AND I DON'T KNOW WHAT IT MEANS TO BE LATINO, NOR LATINA, NOR JEWISH, NOR CATHOLIC, NOR AMERICAN, NOR A WOMAN, NOR ANY OTHER HUMAN THING!
HOW AM I GONNA TEACH HER THE TORAH? OR PSALMS? OR TELL HER HOW HER FOLKS CAME HERE? WHAT THEY COOKED, WHAT THEY ATE, WHAT THEY SANG, I--
--HOW AM I GONNA TEACH HER WHAT'S SUPPOSED TO BE HERS?!
AND HOW AM I GONNA AFFORD BOTH A QUINCEAÑERA AND A BAT MITZVAH, WHEN I CAN'T EVEN--
OH, SANDOR...
AAAAAAIIEEEEEE!
JESSE?

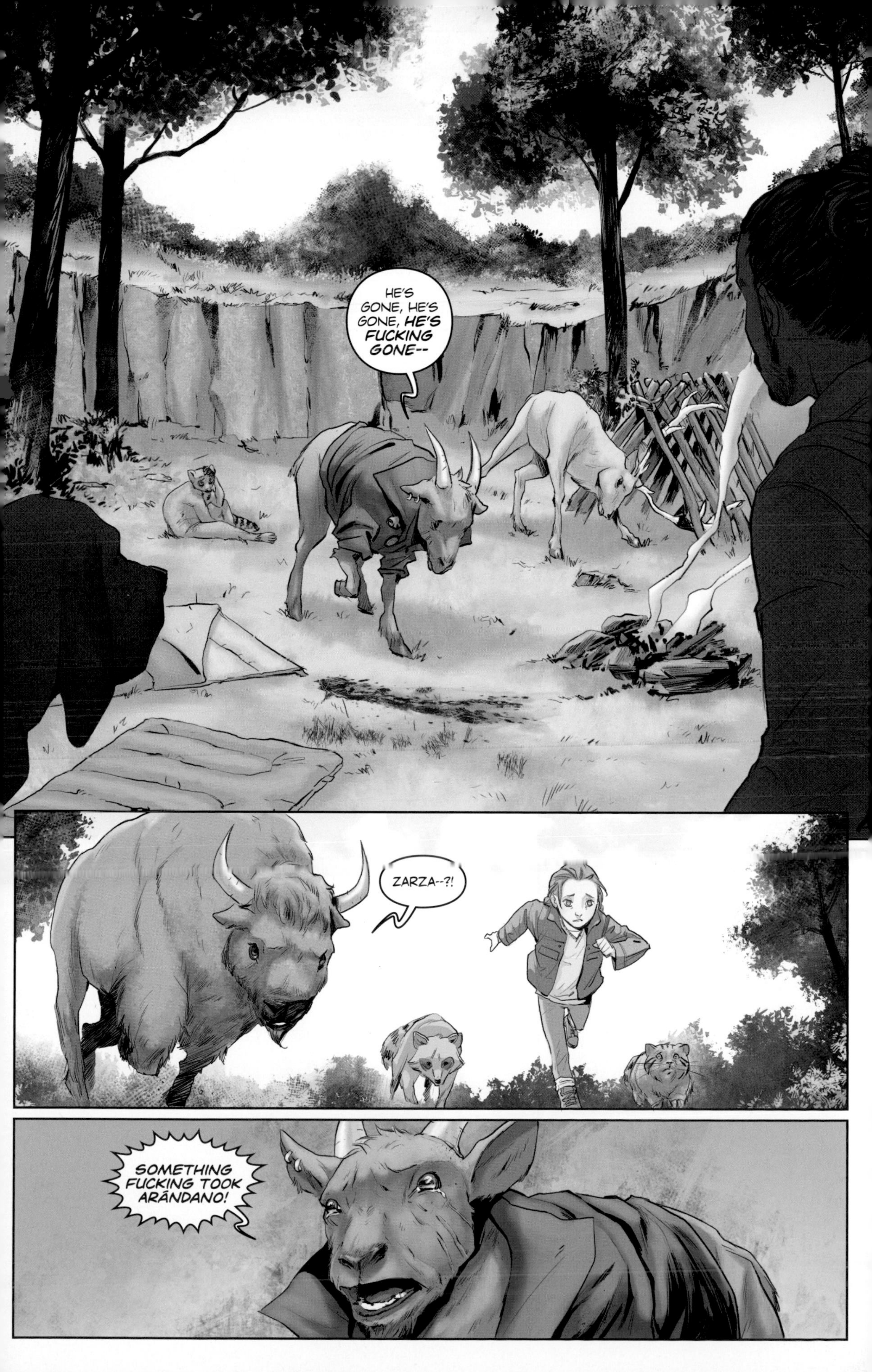
HE'S GONE, HE'S GONE, HE'S FUCKING GONE--
ZARZA--?!
SOMETHING FUCKING TOOK ARÁNDANO!

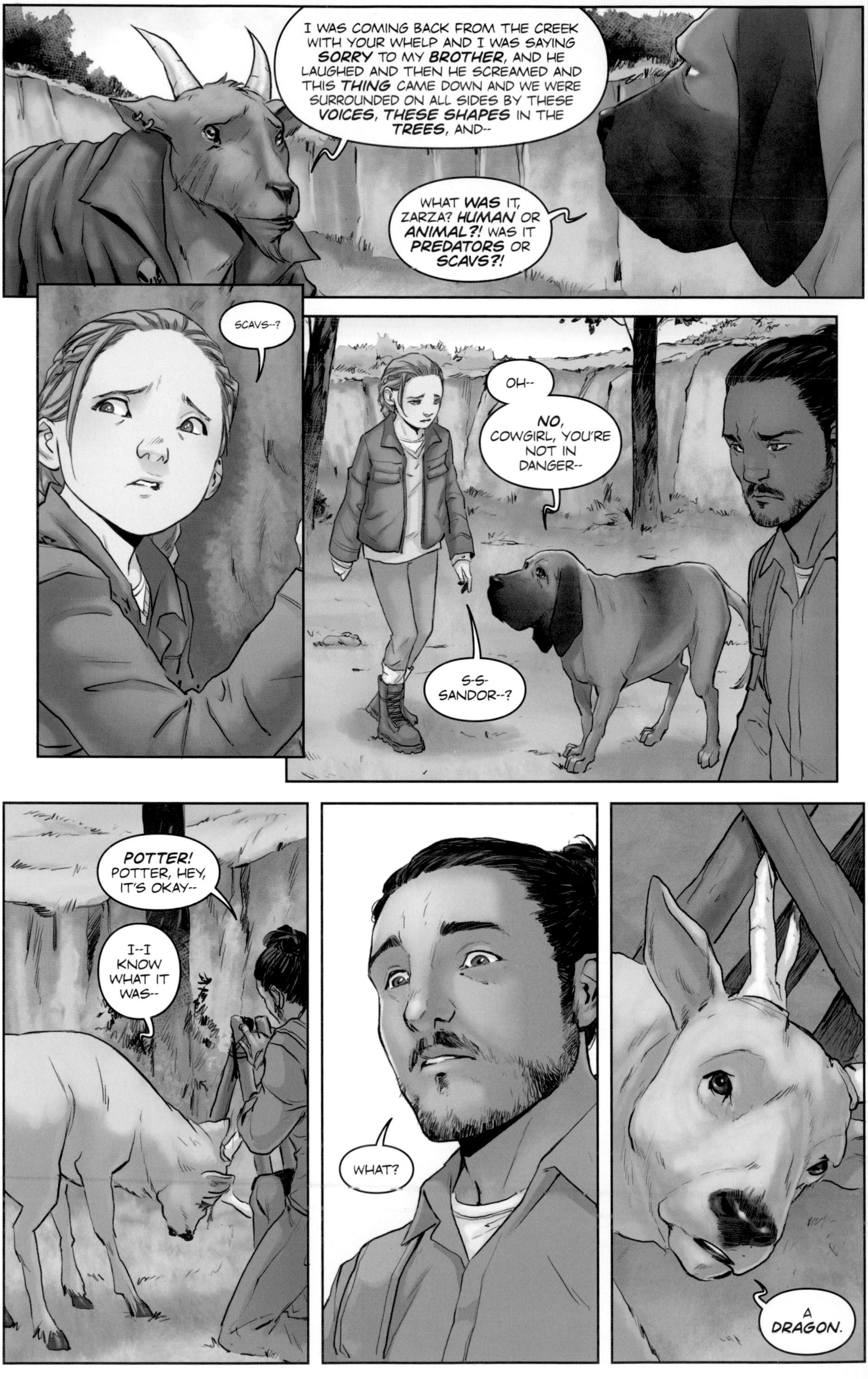
I WAS COMING BACK FROM THE CREEK WITH YOUR WHELP AND I WAS SAYING SORRY TO MY BROTHER, AND HE LAUGHED AND THEN HE SCREAMED AND THIS THING CAME DOWN AND WE WERE SURROUNDED ON ALL SIDES BY THESE VOICES, THESE SHAPES IN THE TREES, AND--
WHAT WAS IT, ZARZA? HUMAN OR ANIMAL?! WAS IT PREDATORS OR SCAVS?!
SCAVS--?
OH--
NO, COWGIRL, YOU'RE NOT IN DANGER--
S-S-SANDOR--?
POTTER! POTTER, HEY, IT'S OKAY--
I--I KNOW WHAT IT WAS--
WHAT?
A DRAGON.

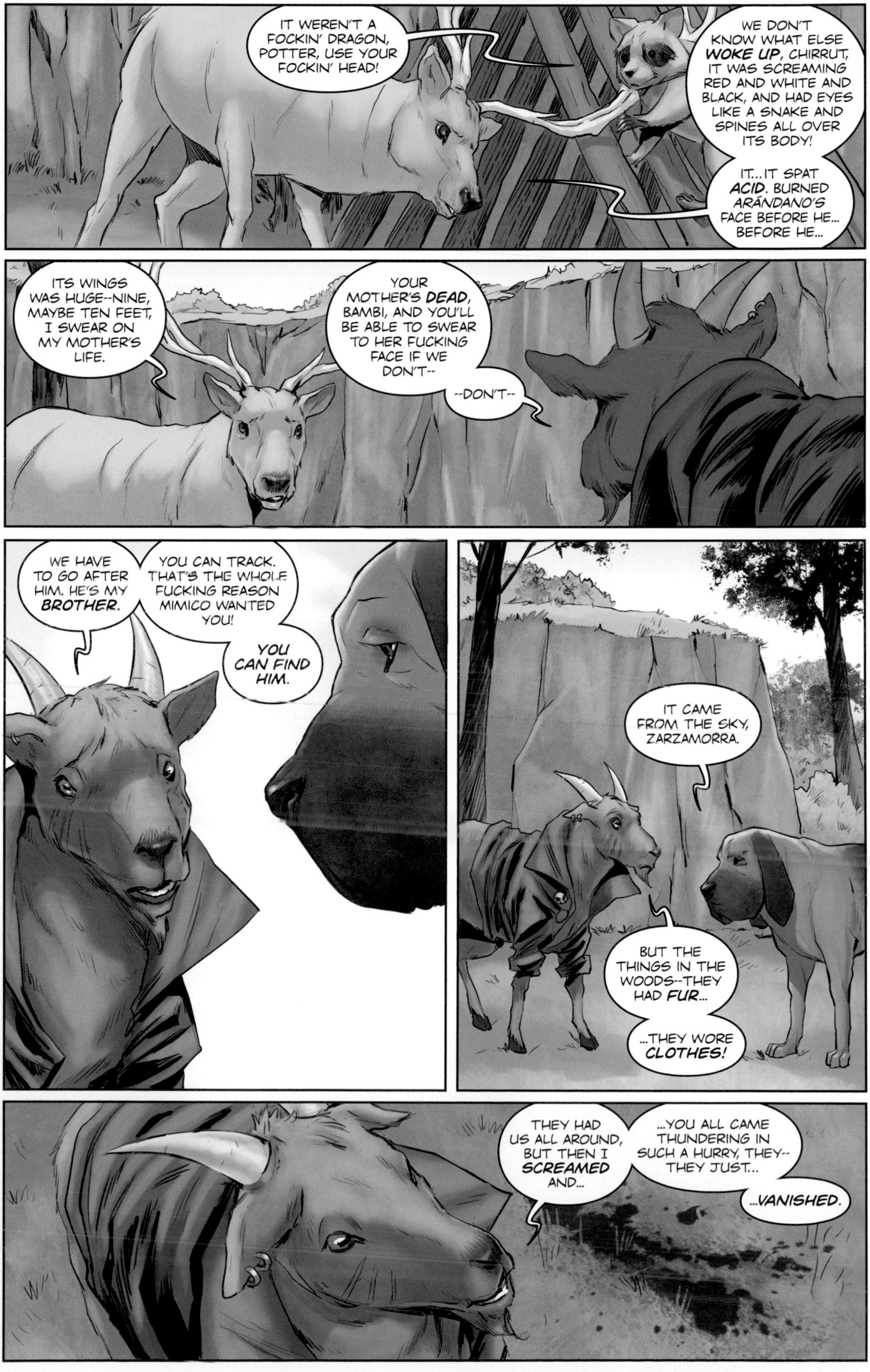
IT WEREN'T A FOCKIN' DRAGON, POTTER, USE YOUR FOCKIN' HEAD!
WE DON'T KNOW WHAT ELSE **WOKE UP**, CHIRRUT, IT WAS SCREAMING RED AND WHITE AND BLACK, AND HAD EYES LIKE A SNAKE AND SPINES ALL OVER ITS BODY!
IT... IT SPAT **ACID**. BURNED *ARÁNDANO'S* FACE BEFORE HE... BEFORE HE...
ITS WINGS WAS HUGE--NINE, MAYBE TEN FEET, I SWEAR ON MY MOTHER'S LIFE.
YOUR MOTHER'S **DEAD**, BAMBI, AND YOU'LL BE ABLE TO SWEAR TO HER FUCKING FACE IF WE DON'T--
--DON'T--
WE HAVE TO GO AFTER HIM. HE'S MY **BROTHER**.
YOU CAN TRACK. THAT'S THE WHOLE FUCKING REASON MIMICO WANTED YOU!
YOU CAN FIND HIM.
IT CAME FROM THE SKY, ZARZAMORRA.
BUT THE THINGS IN THE WOODS--THEY HAD **FUR**...
...THEY WORE **CLOTHES!**
THEY HAD US ALL AROUND, BUT THEN I **SCREAMED** AND...
...YOU ALL CAME THUNDERING IN SUCH A HURRY, THEY--THEY JUST...
...VANISHED.

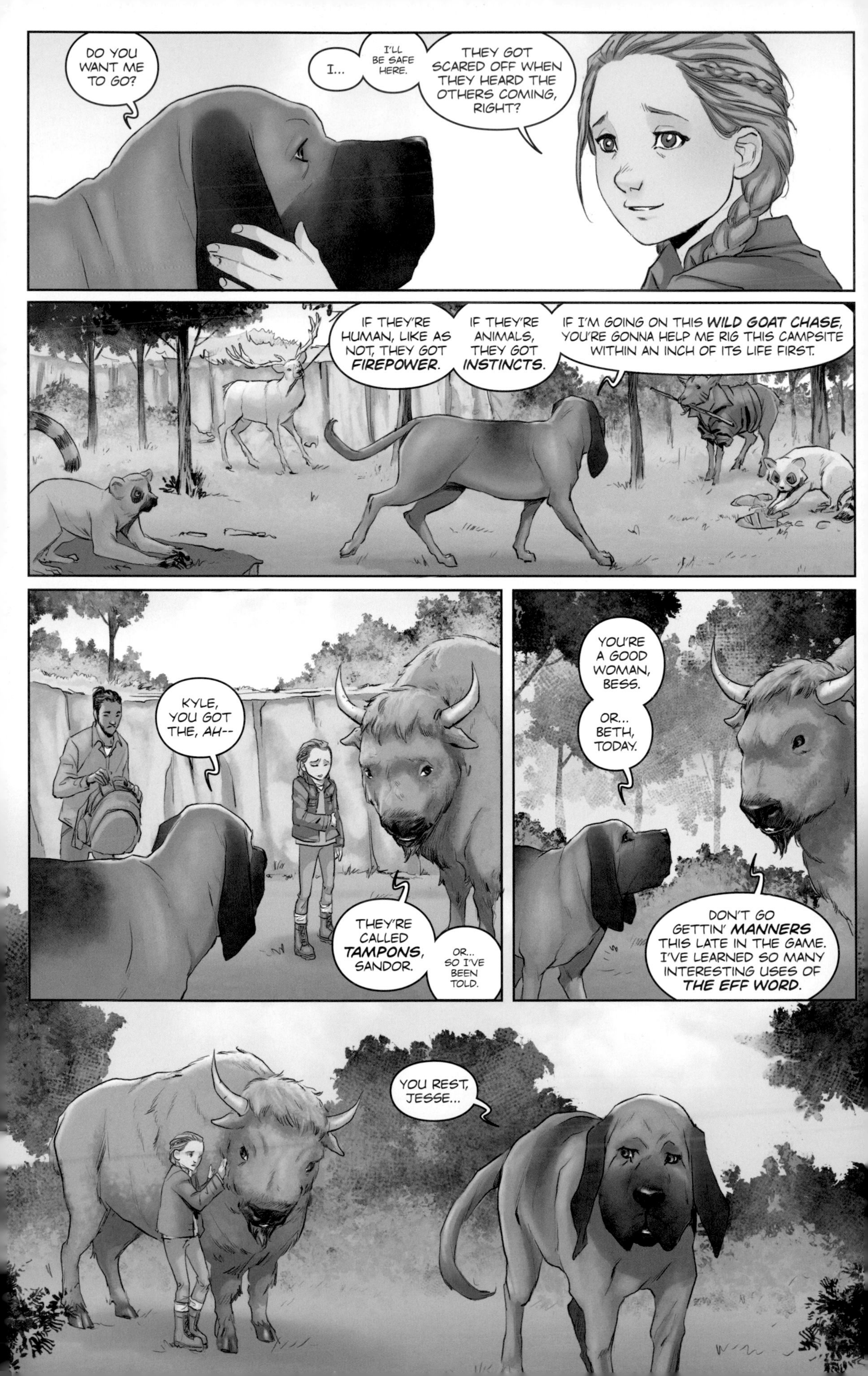
DO YOU WANT ME TO GO?
I...
I'LL BE SAFE HERE.
THEY GOT SCARED OFF WHEN THEY HEARD THE OTHERS COMING, RIGHT?
IF THEY'RE HUMAN, LIKE AS NOT, THEY GOT FIREPOWER.
IF THEY'RE ANIMALS, THEY GOT INSTINCTS.
IF I'M GOING ON THIS WILD GOAT CHASE, YOU'RE GONNA HELP ME RIG THIS CAMPSITE WITHIN AN INCH OF ITS LIFE FIRST.
KYLE, YOU GOT THE, AH--
THEY'RE CALLED TAMPONS, SANDOR.
OR... SO I'VE BEEN TOLD.
YOU'RE A GOOD WOMAN, BESS.
OR... BETH, TODAY.
DON'T GO GETTIN' MANNERS THIS LATE IN THE GAME. I'VE LEARNED SO MANY INTERESTING USES OF THE EFF WORD.
YOU REST, JESSE...

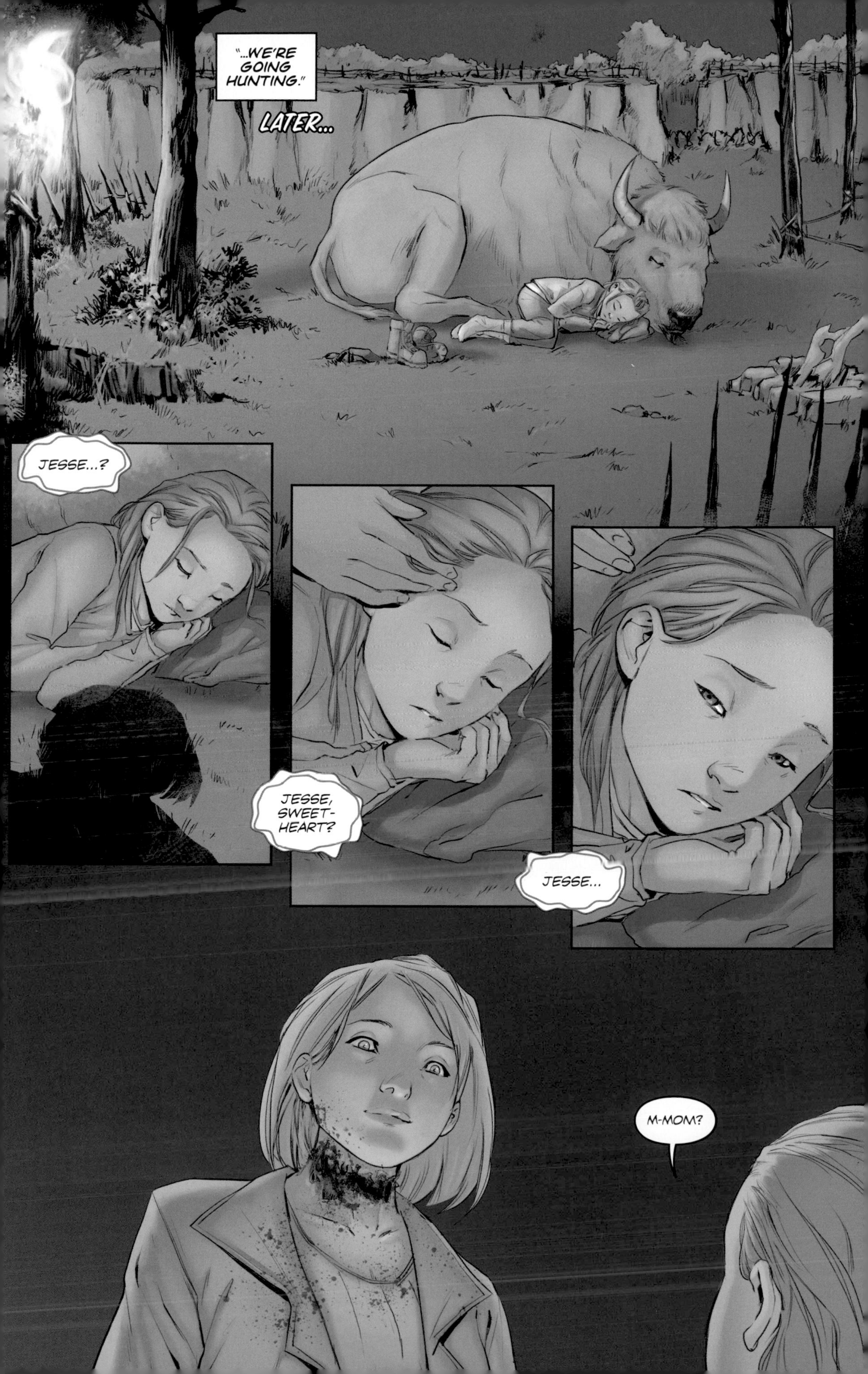

"...WE'RE GOING HUNTING."
LATER...
JESSE...?
JESSE, SWEET-HEART?
JESSE...
M-MOM?

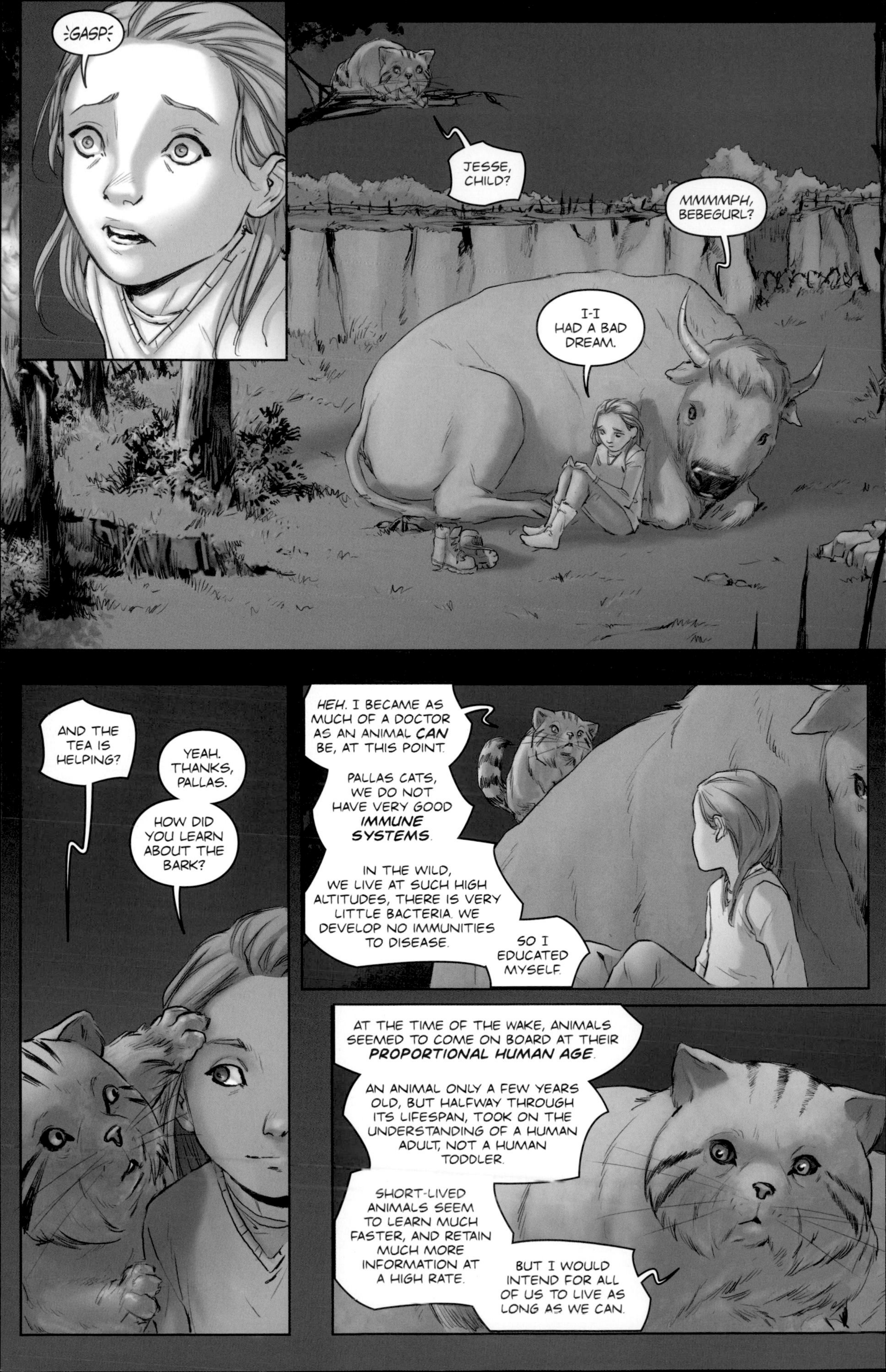

:GASP:
JESSE, CHILD?
MMMMPH, BEBEGURL?
I-I HAD A BAD DREAM.
AND THE TEA IS HELPING?
YEAH. THANKS, PALLAS.
HOW DID YOU LEARN ABOUT THE BARK?
HEH. I BECAME AS MUCH OF A DOCTOR AS AN ANIMAL CAN BE, AT THIS POINT.
PALLAS CATS, WE DO NOT HAVE VERY GOOD IMMUNE SYSTEMS.
IN THE WILD, WE LIVE AT SUCH HIGH ALTITUDES, THERE IS VERY LITTLE BACTERIA. WE DEVELOP NO IMMUNITIES TO DISEASE.
SO I EDUCATED MYSELF.
AT THE TIME OF THE WAKE, ANIMALS SEEMED TO COME ON BOARD AT THEIR PROPORTIONAL HUMAN AGE.
AN ANIMAL ONLY A FEW YEARS OLD, BUT HALFWAY THROUGH ITS LIFESPAN, TOOK ON THE UNDERSTANDING OF A HUMAN ADULT, NOT A HUMAN TODDLER.
SHORT-LIVED ANIMALS SEEM TO LEARN MUCH FASTER, AND RETAIN MUCH MORE INFORMATION AT A HIGH RATE.
BUT I WOULD INTEND FOR ALL OF US TO LIVE AS LONG AS WE CAN.

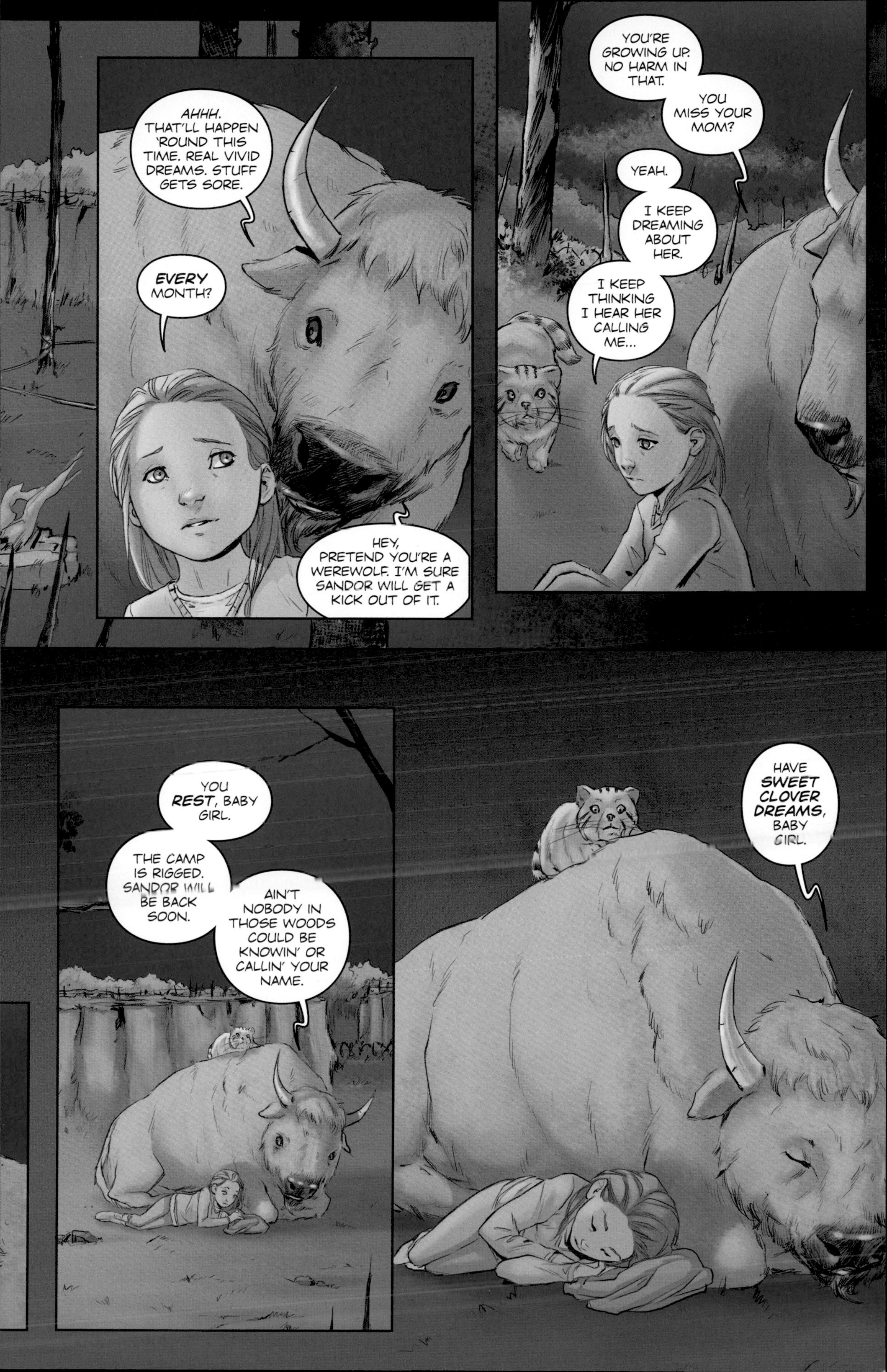
AHHH. THAT'LL HAPPEN 'ROUND THIS TIME. REAL VIVID DREAMS. STUFF GETS SORE.
EVERY MONTH?
HEY, PRETEND YOU'RE A WEREWOLF. I'M SURE SANDOR WILL GET A KICK OUT OF IT.
YOU'RE GROWING UP. NO HARM IN THAT.
YOU MISS YOUR MOM?
YEAH.
I KEEP DREAMING ABOUT HER.
I KEEP THINKING I HEAR HER CALLING ME...
YOU REST, BABY GIRL.
THE CAMP IS RIGGED. SANDOR WILL BE BACK SOON.
AIN'T NOBODY IN THOSE WOODS COULD BE KNOWIN' OR CALLIN' YOUR NAME.
HAVE SWEET CLOVER DREAMS, BABY GIRL.

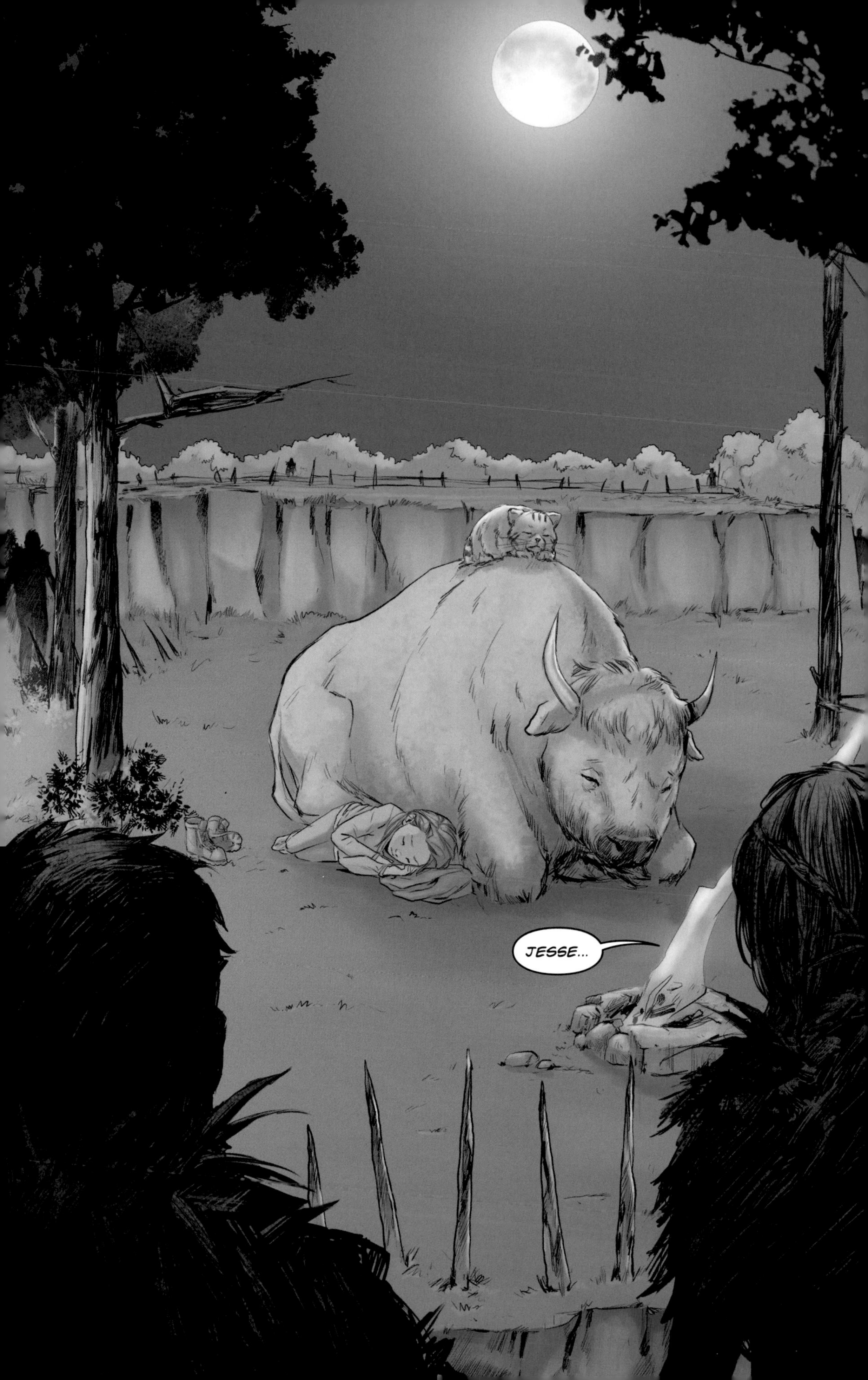
JESSE...

6

"WAKE UP"

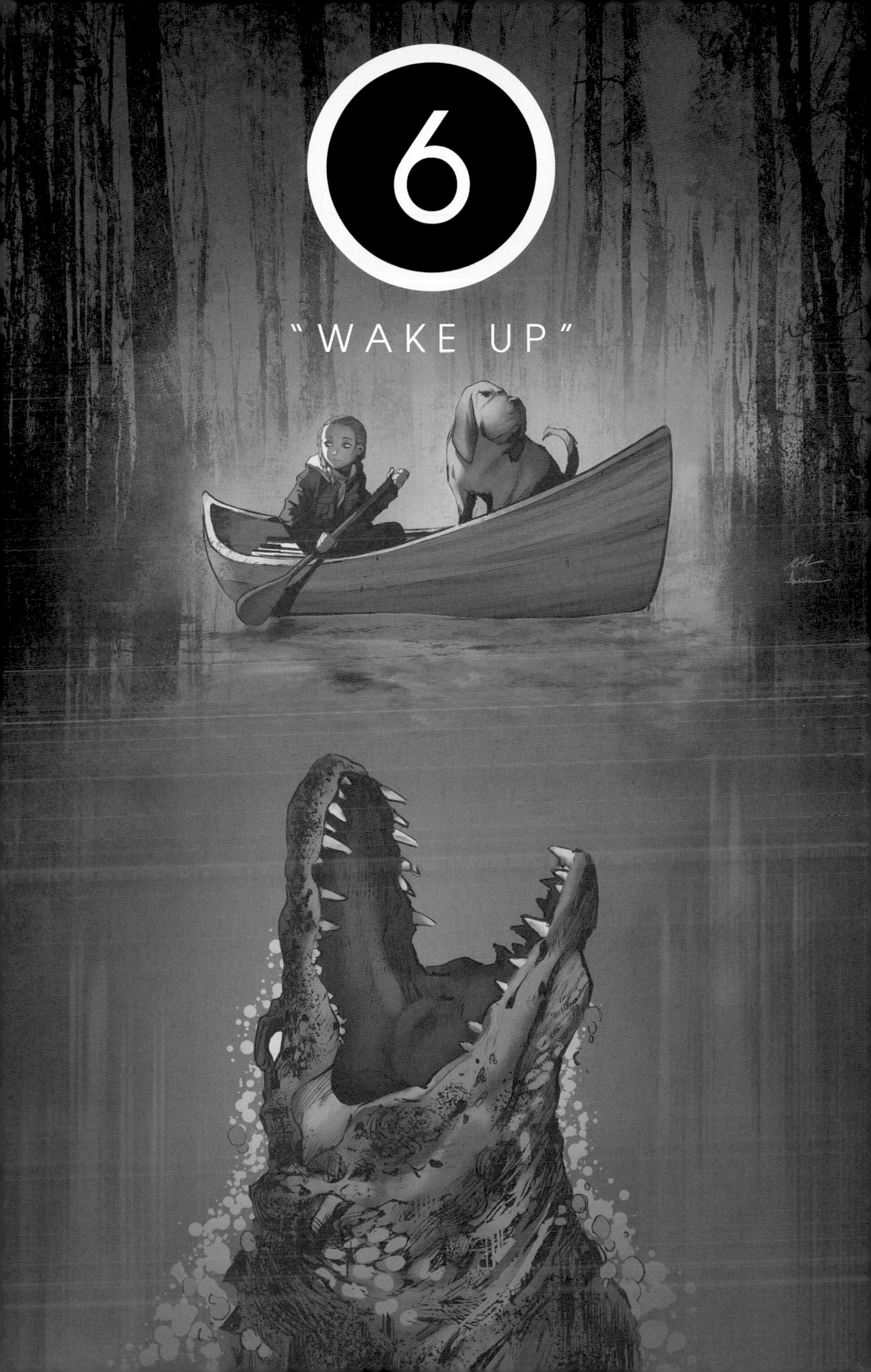

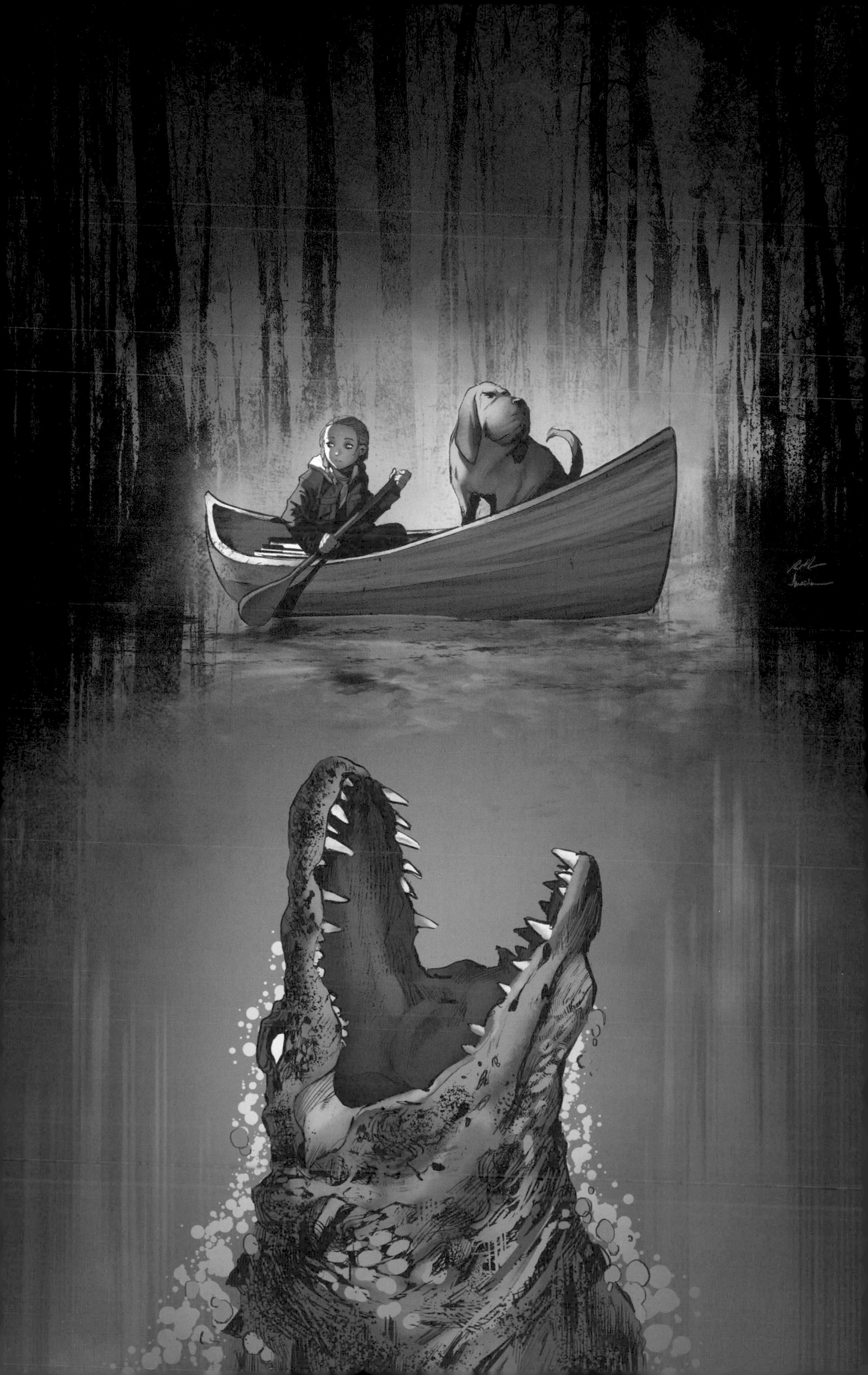

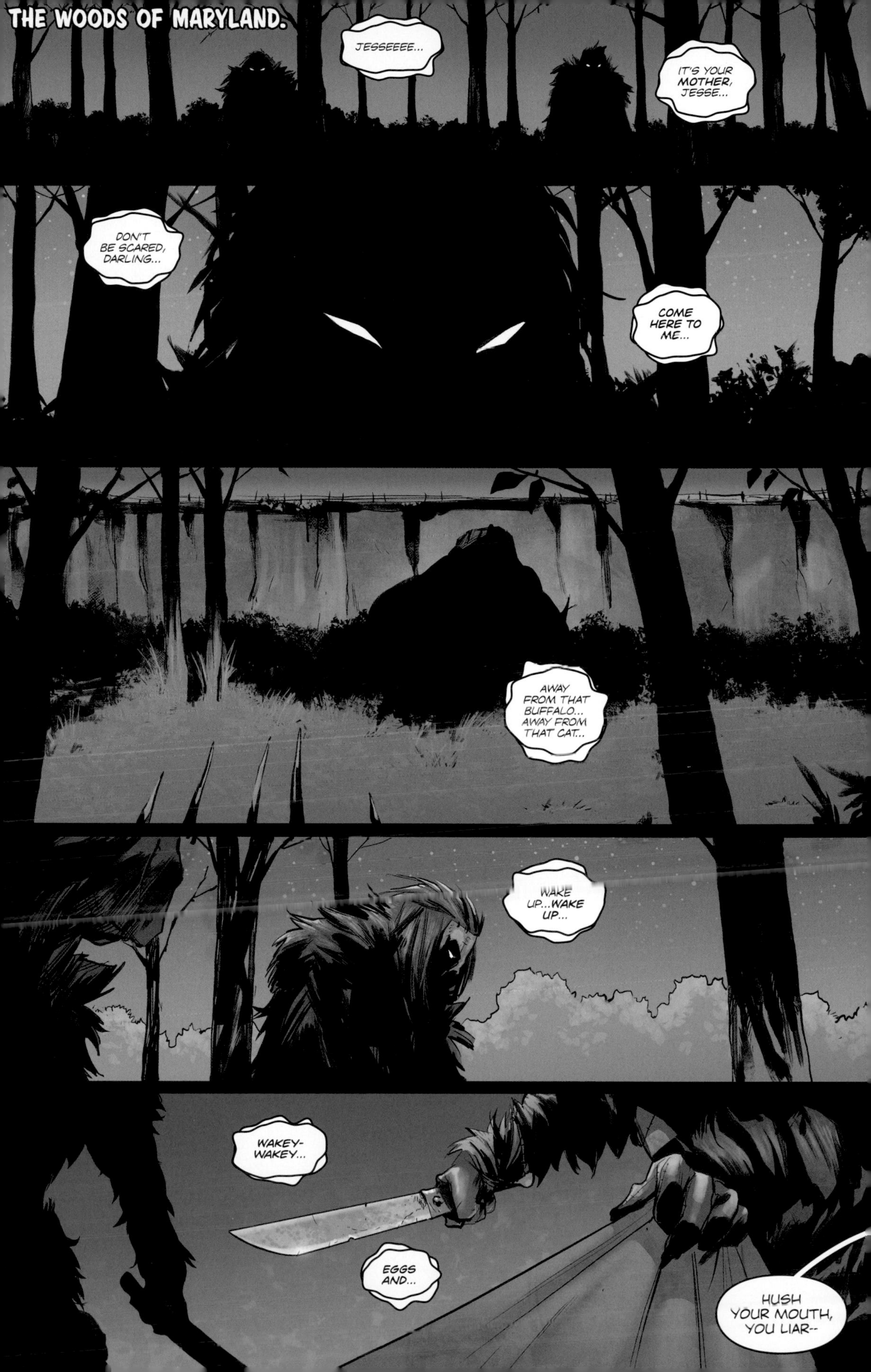
THE WOODS OF MARYLAND.
JESSEEEE...
IT'S YOUR MOTHER, JESSE...
DON'T BE SCARED, DARLING...
COME HERE TO ME...
AWAY FROM THAT BUFFALO... AWAY FROM THAT CAT...
WAKE UP...WAKE UP...
WAKEY-WAKEY...
EGGS AND...
HUSH YOUR MOUTH, YOU LIAR--

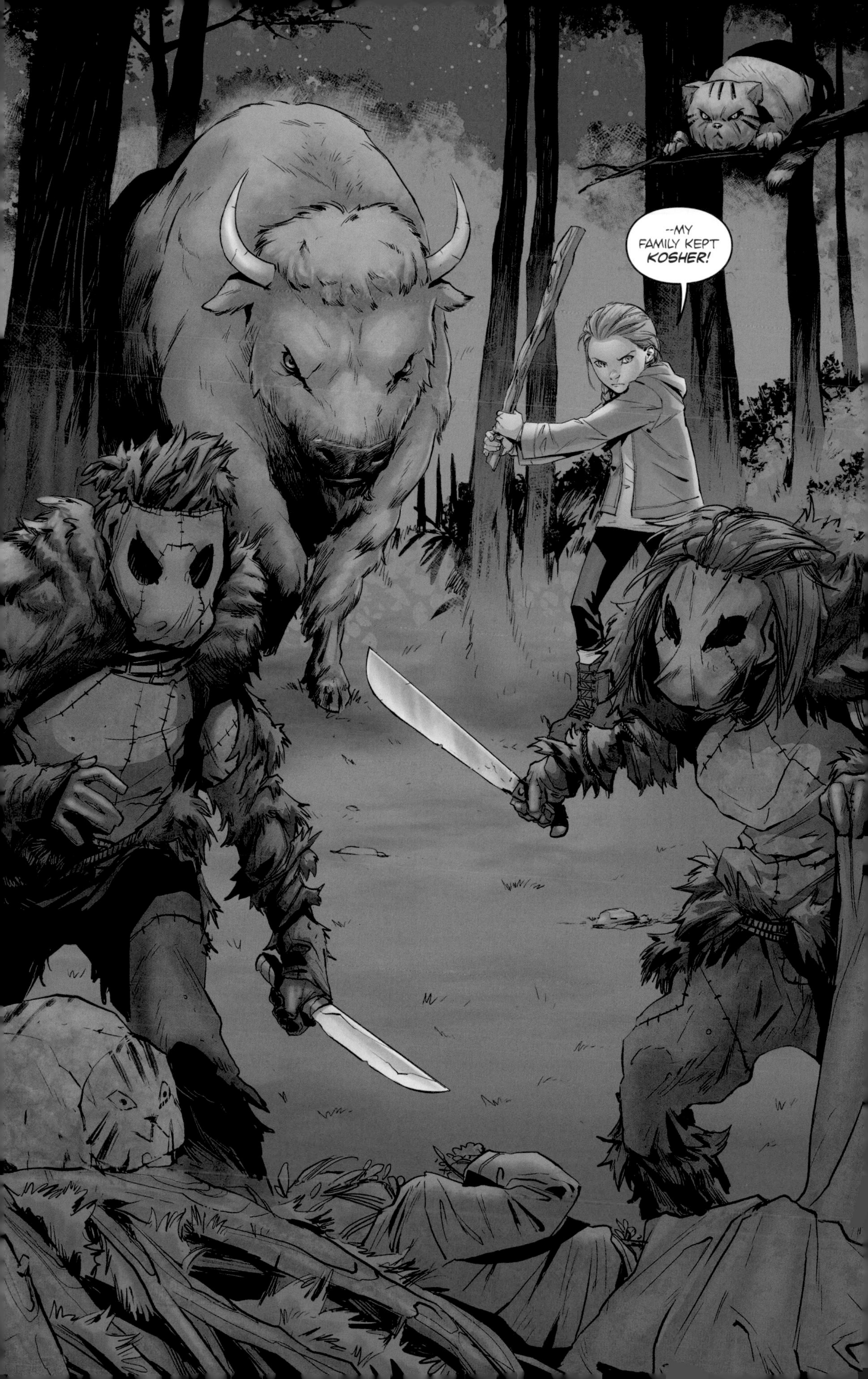
--MY FAMILY KEPT KOSHER!

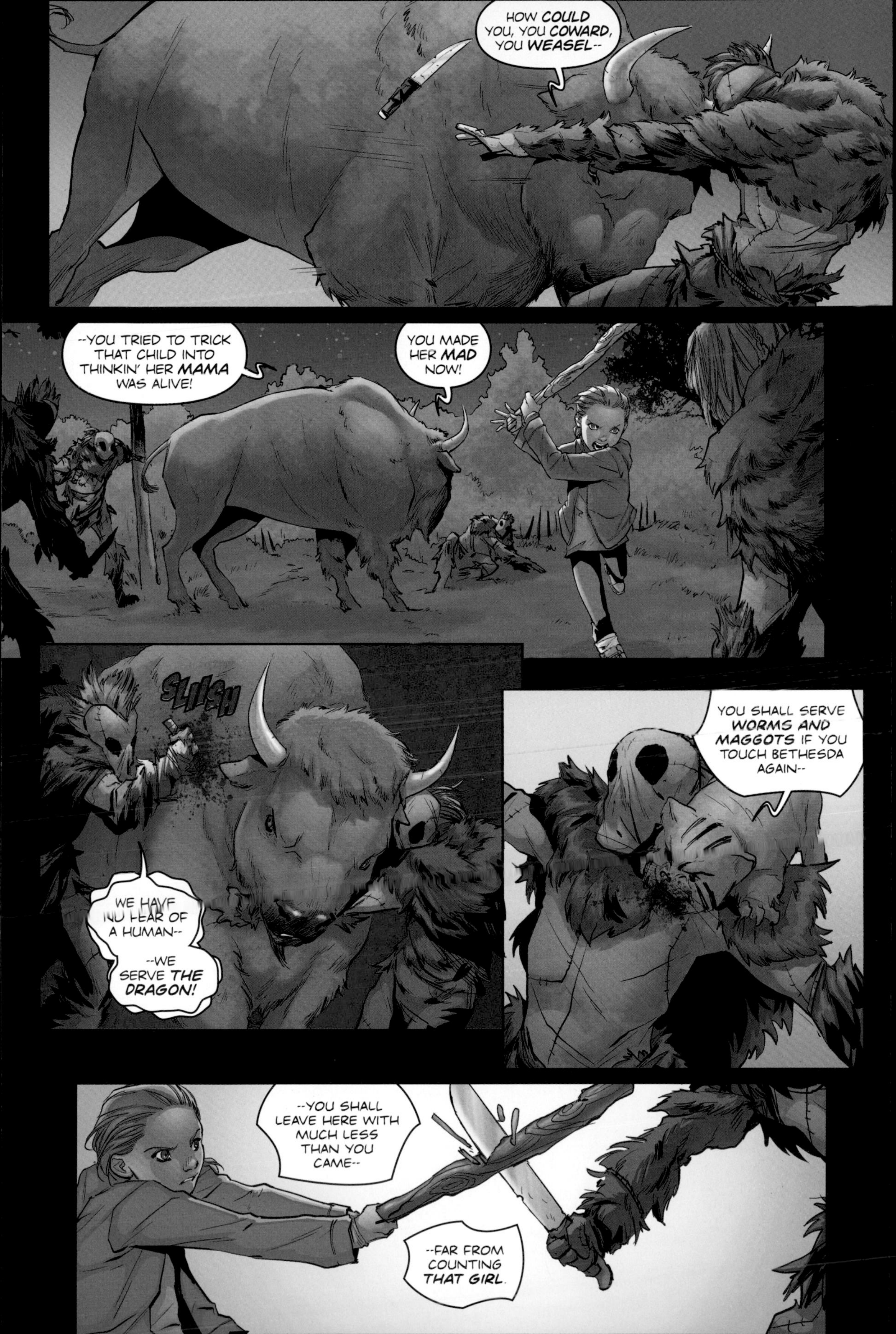
HOW COULD YOU, YOU COWARD, YOU WEASEL--
--YOU TRIED TO TRICK THAT CHILD INTO THINKIN' HER MAMA WAS ALIVE!
YOU MADE HER MAD NOW!
SLISH
WE HAVE NO FEAR OF A HUMAN--
--WE SERVE THE DRAGON!
YOU SHALL SERVE WORMS AND MAGGOTS IF YOU TOUCH BETHESDA AGAIN--
--YOU SHALL LEAVE HERE WITH MUCH LESS THAN YOU CAME--
--FAR FROM COUNTING THAT GIRL.

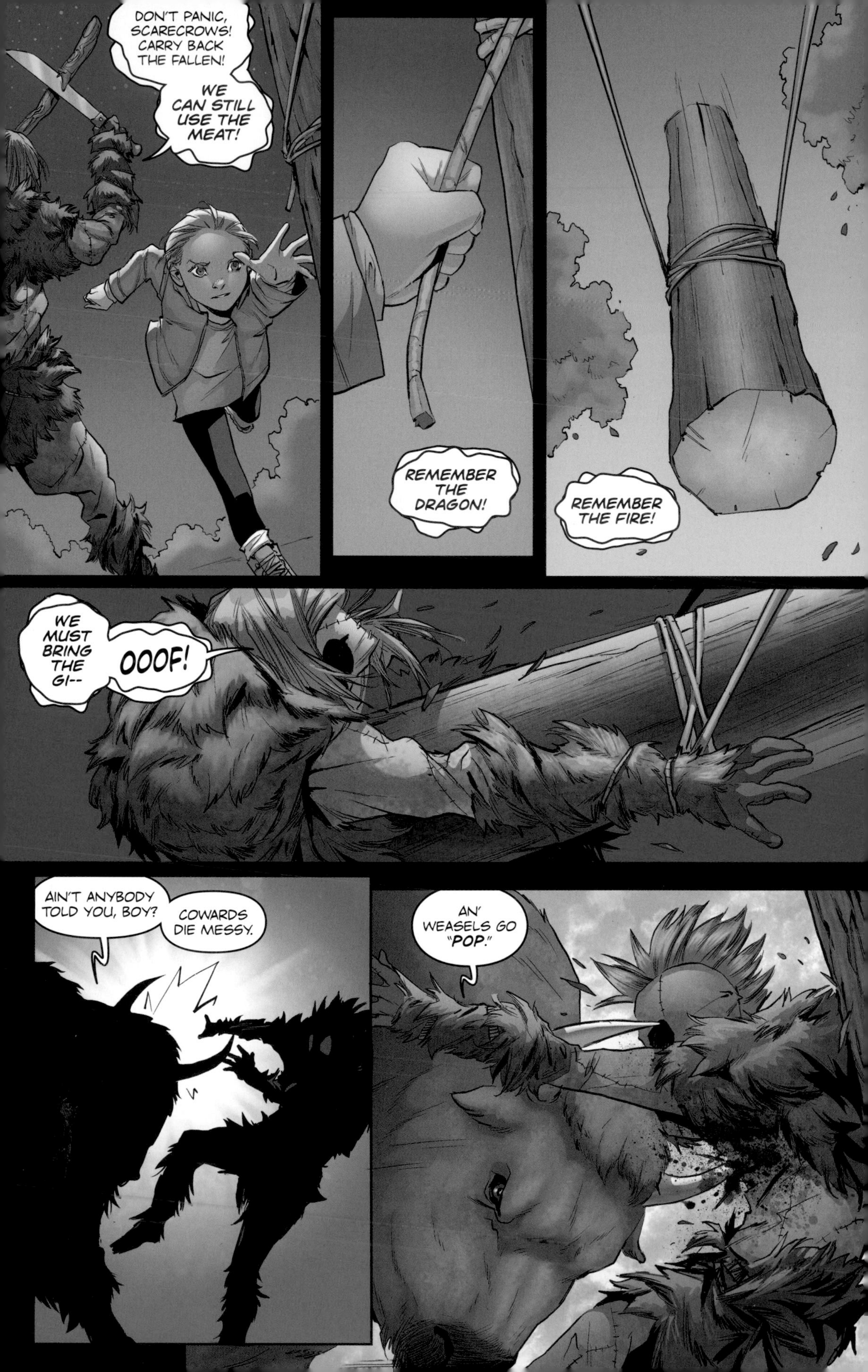
DON'T PANIC, SCARECROWS! CARRY BACK THE FALLEN!
WE CAN STILL USE THE MEAT!
REMEMBER THE DRAGON!
REMEMBER THE FIRE!
WE MUST BRING THE GI--
OOOF!
AIN'T ANYBODY TOLD YOU, BOY?
COWARDS DIE MESSY.
AN' WEASELS GO "POP."

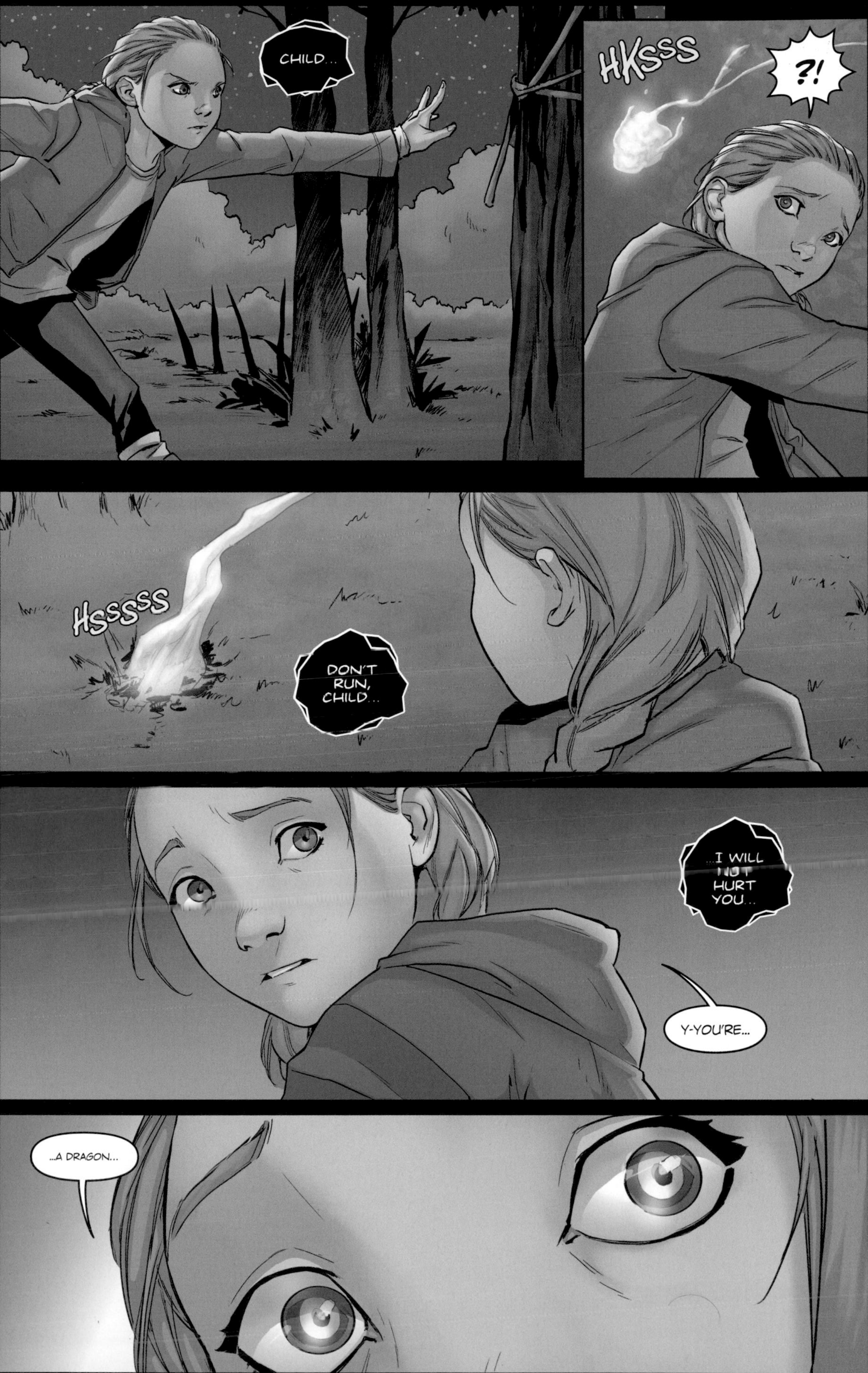

CHILD...
HKSSS
?!
HSSSSS
DON'T RUN, CHILD...
...I WILL NOT HURT YOU...
Y-YOU'RE...
...A DRAGON...

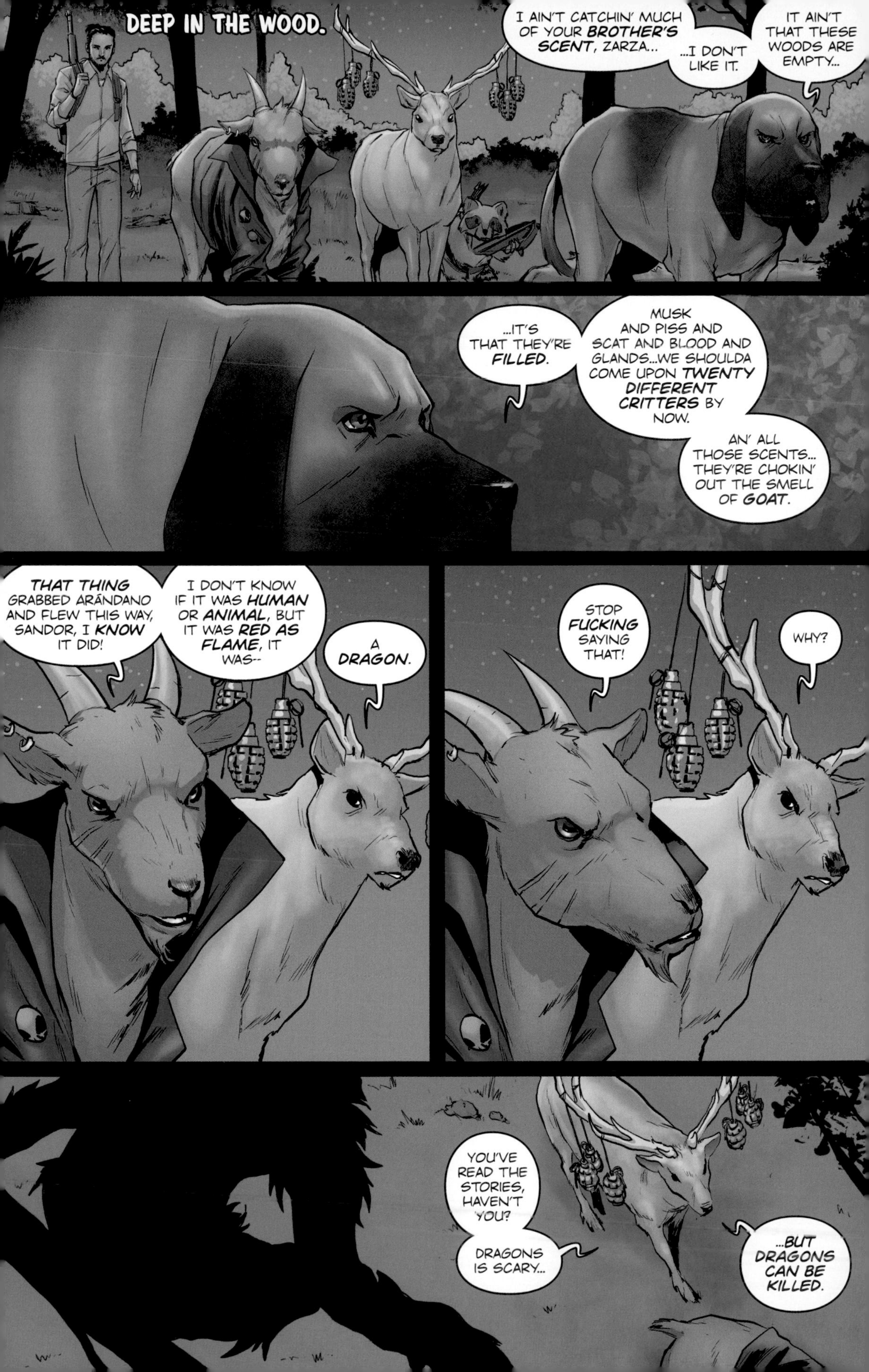
DEEP IN THE WOOD.
I AIN'T CATCHIN' MUCH OF YOUR BROTHER'S SCENT, ZARZA...
...I DON'T LIKE IT.
IT AIN'T THAT THESE WOODS ARE EMPTY...
...IT'S THAT THEY'RE FILLED.
MUSK AND PISS AND SCAT AND BLOOD AND GLANDS...WE SHOULDA COME UPON TWENTY DIFFERENT CRITTERS BY NOW.
AN' ALL THOSE SCENTS... THEY'RE CHOKIN' OUT THE SMELL OF GOAT.
THAT THING GRABBED ARÁNDANO AND FLEW THIS WAY, SANDOR, I KNOW IT DID!
I DON'T KNOW IF IT WAS HUMAN OR ANIMAL, BUT IT WAS RED AS FLAME, IT WAS--
A DRAGON.
STOP FUCKING SAYING THAT!
WHY?
YOU'VE READ THE STORIES, HAVEN'T YOU?
DRAGONS IS SCARY...
...BUT DRAGONS CAN BE KILLED.

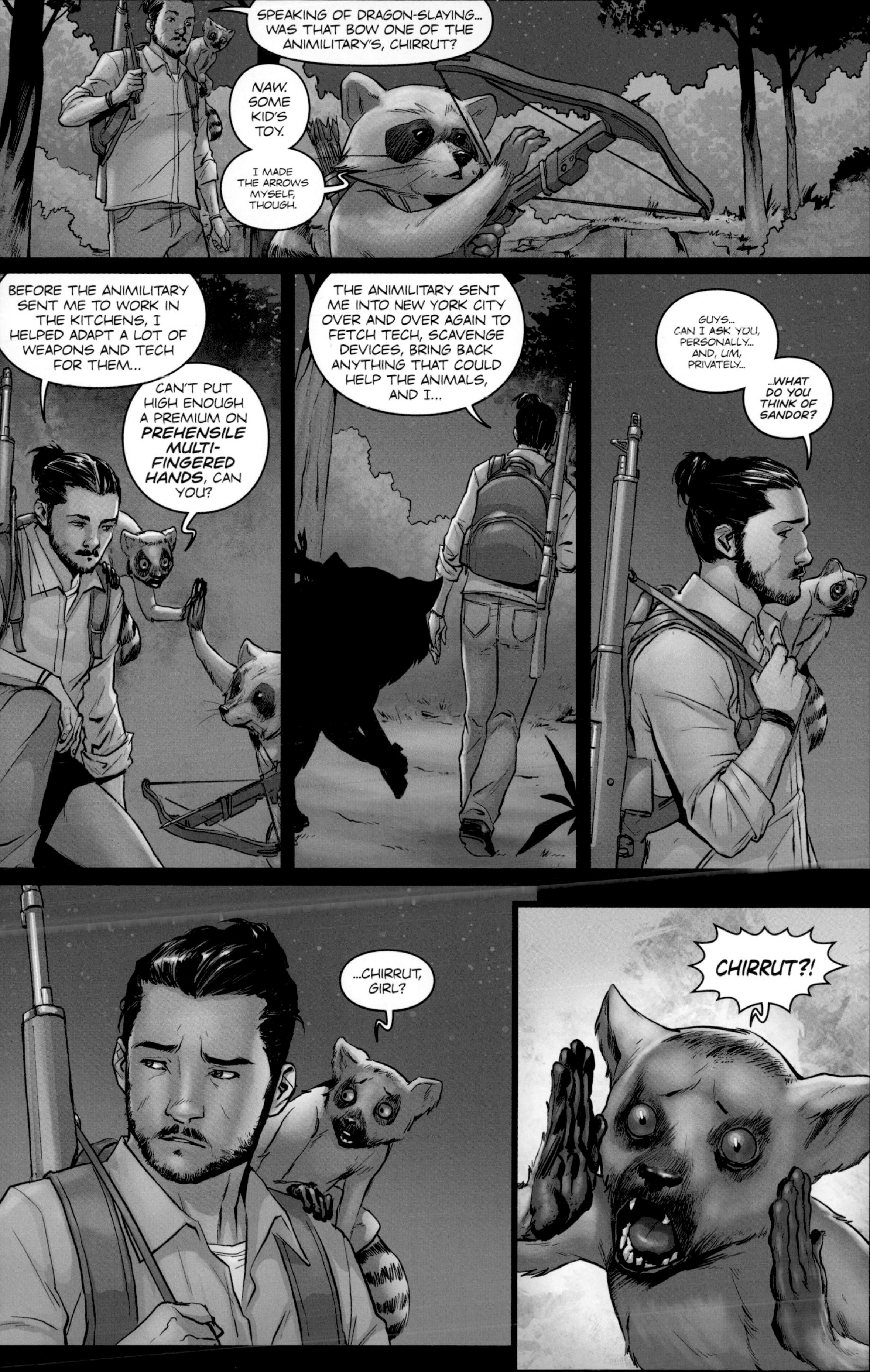
SPEAKING OF DRAGON-SLAYING... WAS THAT BOW ONE OF THE ANIMILITARY'S, CHIRRUT?
NAW. SOME KID'S TOY.
I MADE THE ARROWS MYSELF, THOUGH.
BEFORE THE ANIMILITARY SENT ME TO WORK IN THE KITCHENS, I HELPED ADAPT A LOT OF WEAPONS AND TECH FOR THEM...
CAN'T PUT HIGH ENOUGH A PREMIUM ON ***PREHENSILE MULTI-FINGERED HANDS***, CAN YOU?
THE ANIMILITARY SENT ME INTO NEW YORK CITY OVER AND OVER AGAIN TO FETCH TECH, SCAVENGE DEVICES, BRING BACK ANYTHING THAT COULD HELP THE ANIMALS, AND I...
GUYS... CAN I ASK YOU, PERSONALLY... AND, UM, PRIVATELY...
...WHAT DO YOU THINK OF SANDOR?
...CHIRRUT, GIRL?
CHIRRUT?!

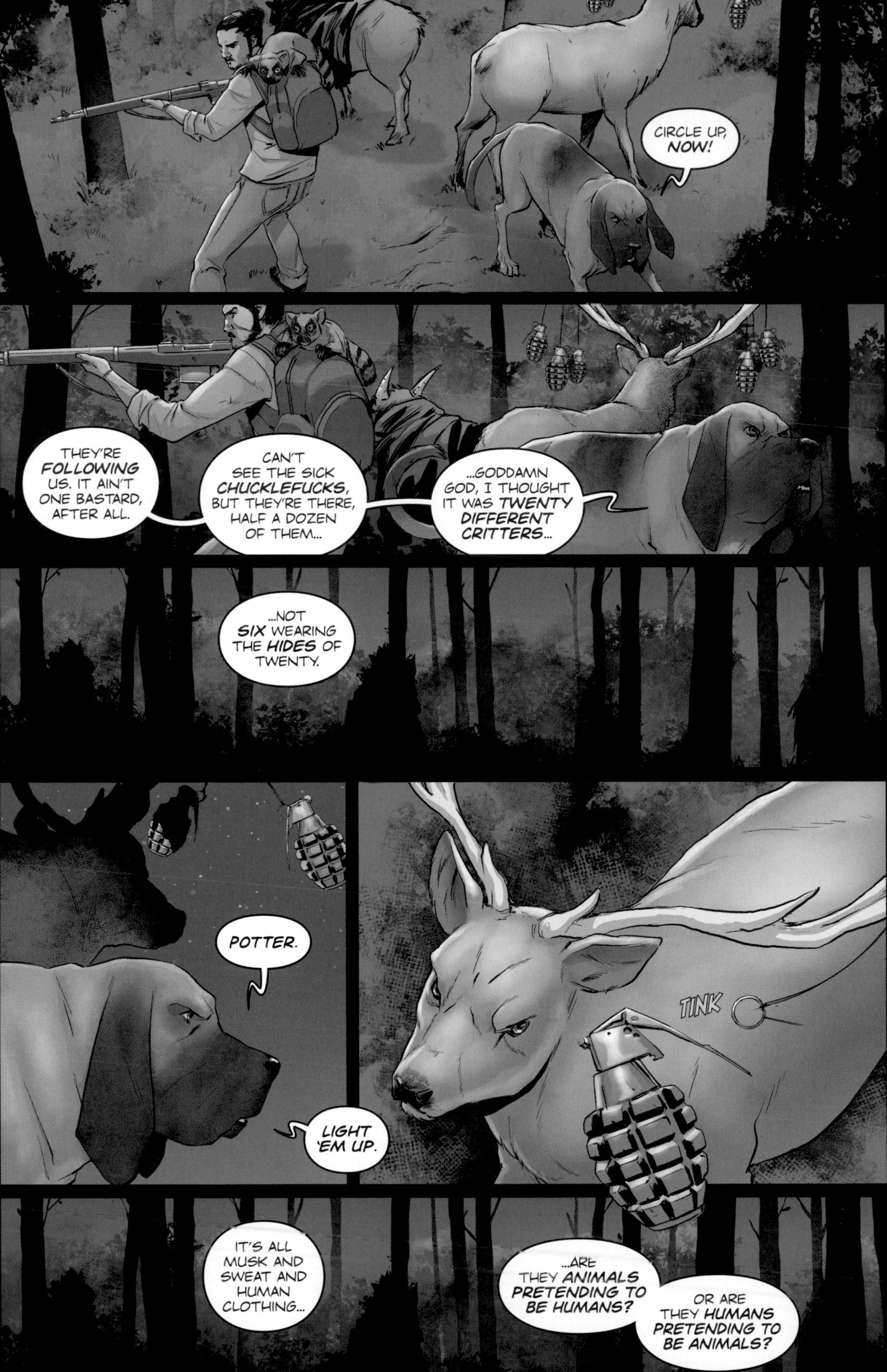
CIRCLE UP, NOW!
THEY'RE FOLLOWING US. IT AIN'T ONE BASTARD, AFTER ALL.
CAN'T SEE THE SICK CHUCKLEFUCKS, BUT THEY'RE THERE, HALF A DOZEN OF THEM...
...GODDAMN GOD, I THOUGHT IT WAS TWENTY DIFFERENT CRITTERS...
...NOT SIX WEARING THE HIDES OF TWENTY.
POTTER.
LIGHT 'EM UP.
TINK
IT'S ALL MUSK AND SWEAT AND HUMAN CLOTHING...
...ARE THEY ANIMALS PRETENDING TO BE HUMANS?
OR ARE THEY HUMANS PRETENDING TO BE ANIMALS?

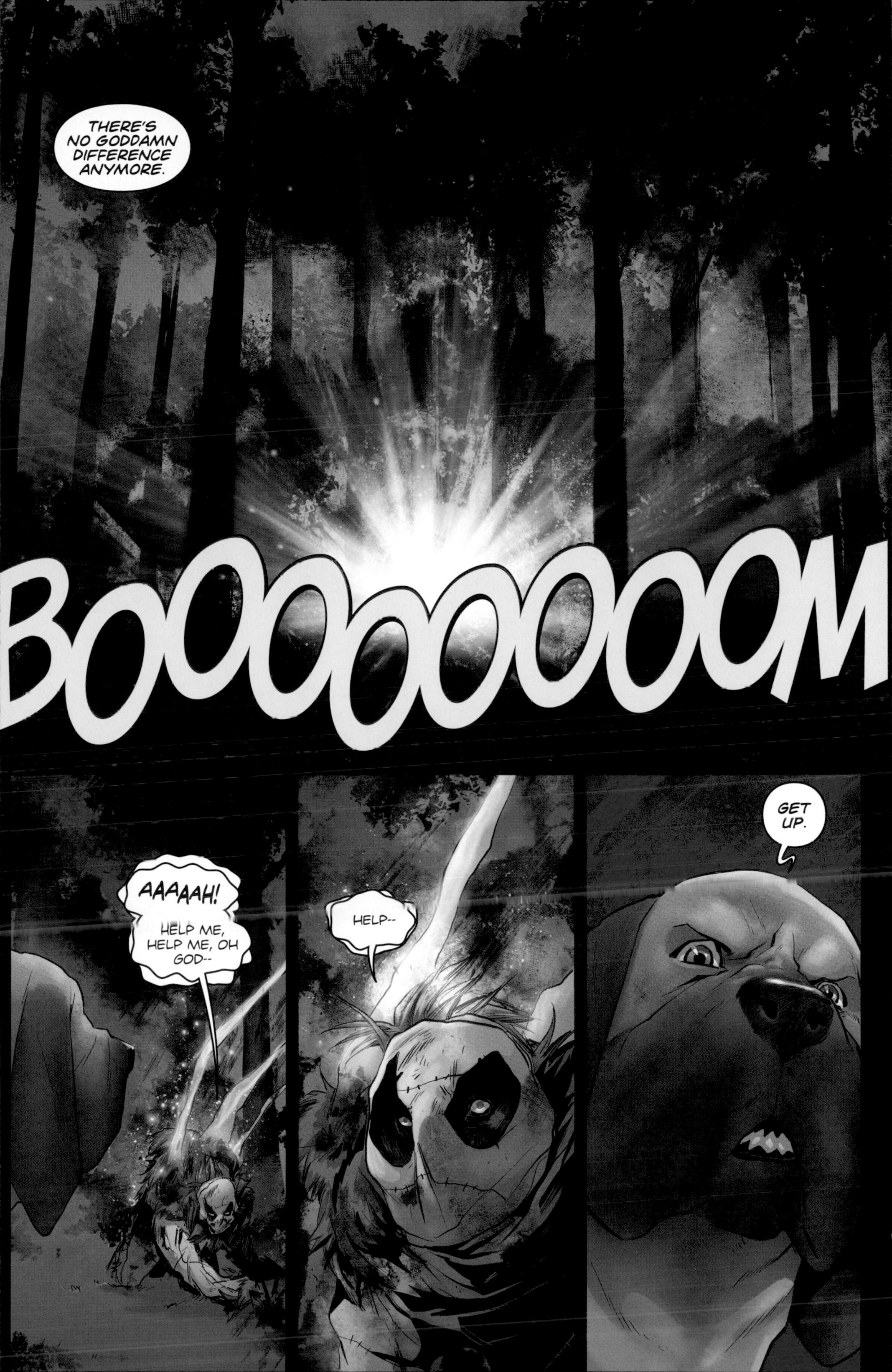
THERE'S NO GODDAMN DIFFERENCE ANYMORE.
BOOOOOOOOM
AAAAAH!
HELP ME, HELP ME, OH GOD--
HELP--
GET UP.

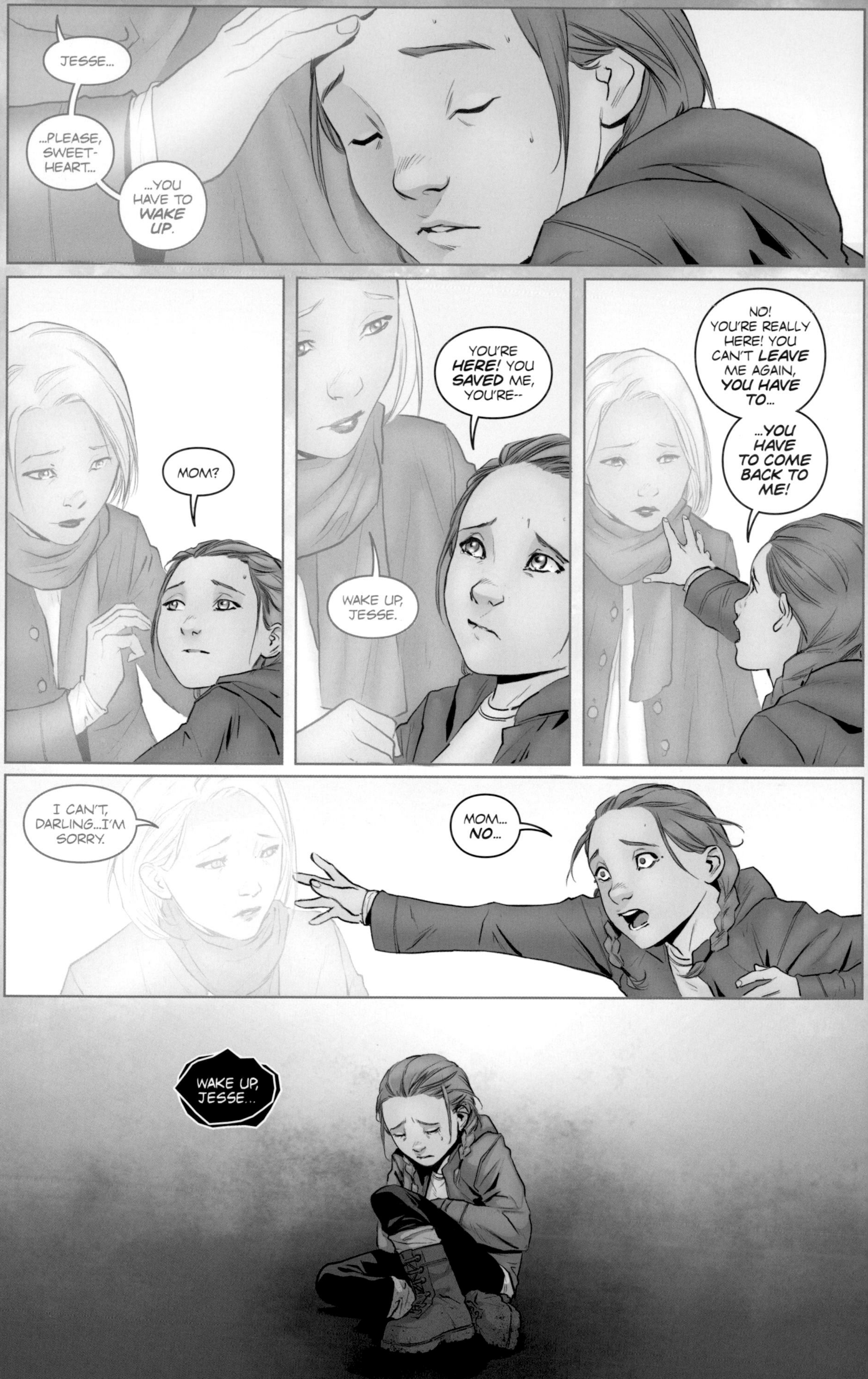
JESSE...
...PLEASE, SWEET-HEART...
...YOU HAVE TO WAKE UP.
MOM?
YOU'RE HERE! YOU SAVED ME, YOU'RE--
WAKE UP, JESSE.
NO! YOU'RE REALLY HERE! YOU CAN'T LEAVE ME AGAIN, YOU HAVE TO...
...YOU HAVE TO COME BACK TO ME!
I CAN'T, DARLING...I'M SORRY.
MOM... NO...
WAKE UP, JESSE...

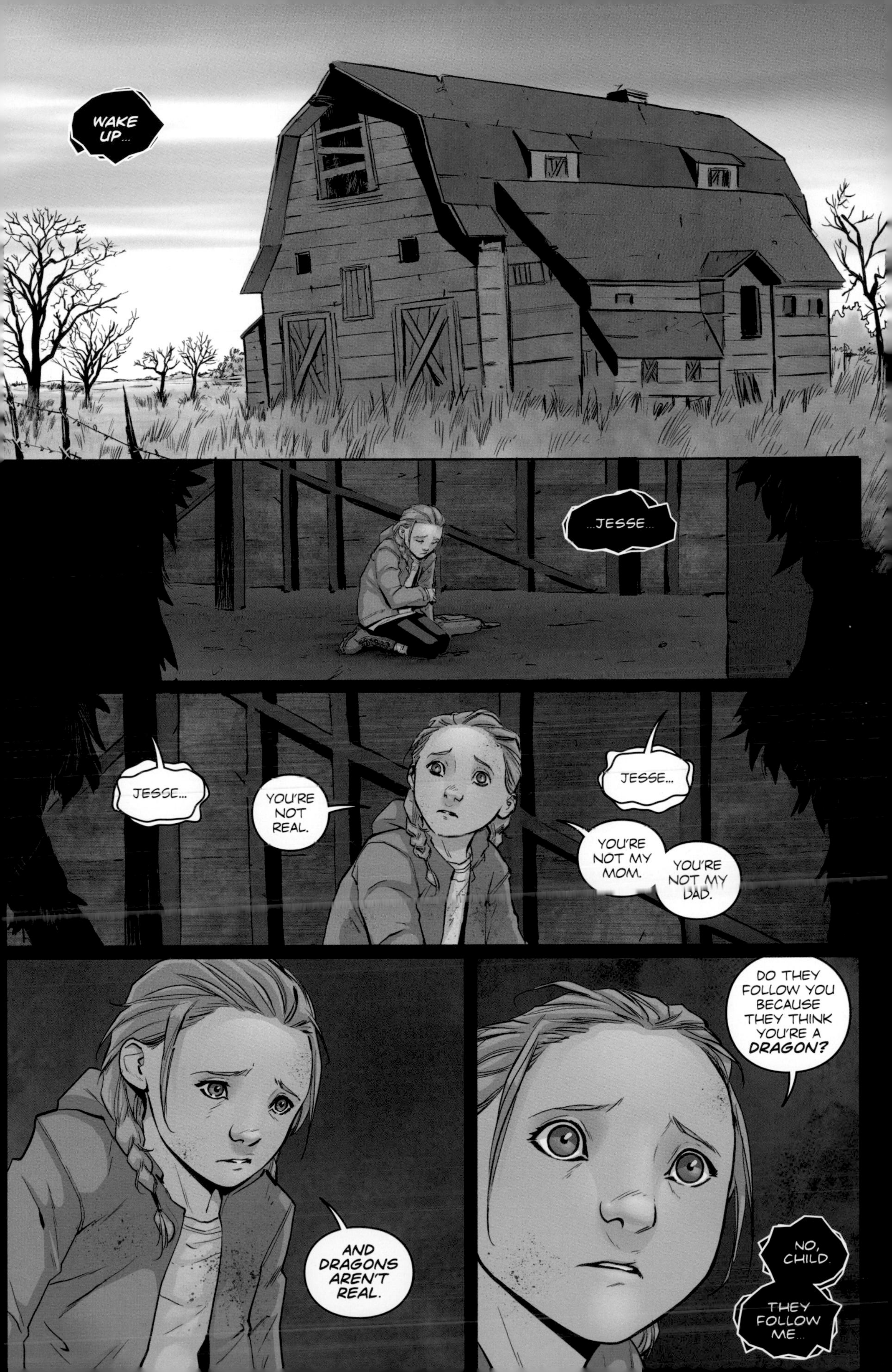
WAKE UP...
...JESSE...
JESSE...
YOU'RE NOT REAL.
JESSE...
YOU'RE NOT MY MOM.
YOU'RE NOT MY DAD.
AND DRAGONS AREN'T REAL.
DO THEY FOLLOW YOU BECAUSE THEY THINK YOU'RE A DRAGON?
NO, CHILD.
THEY FOLLOW ME...

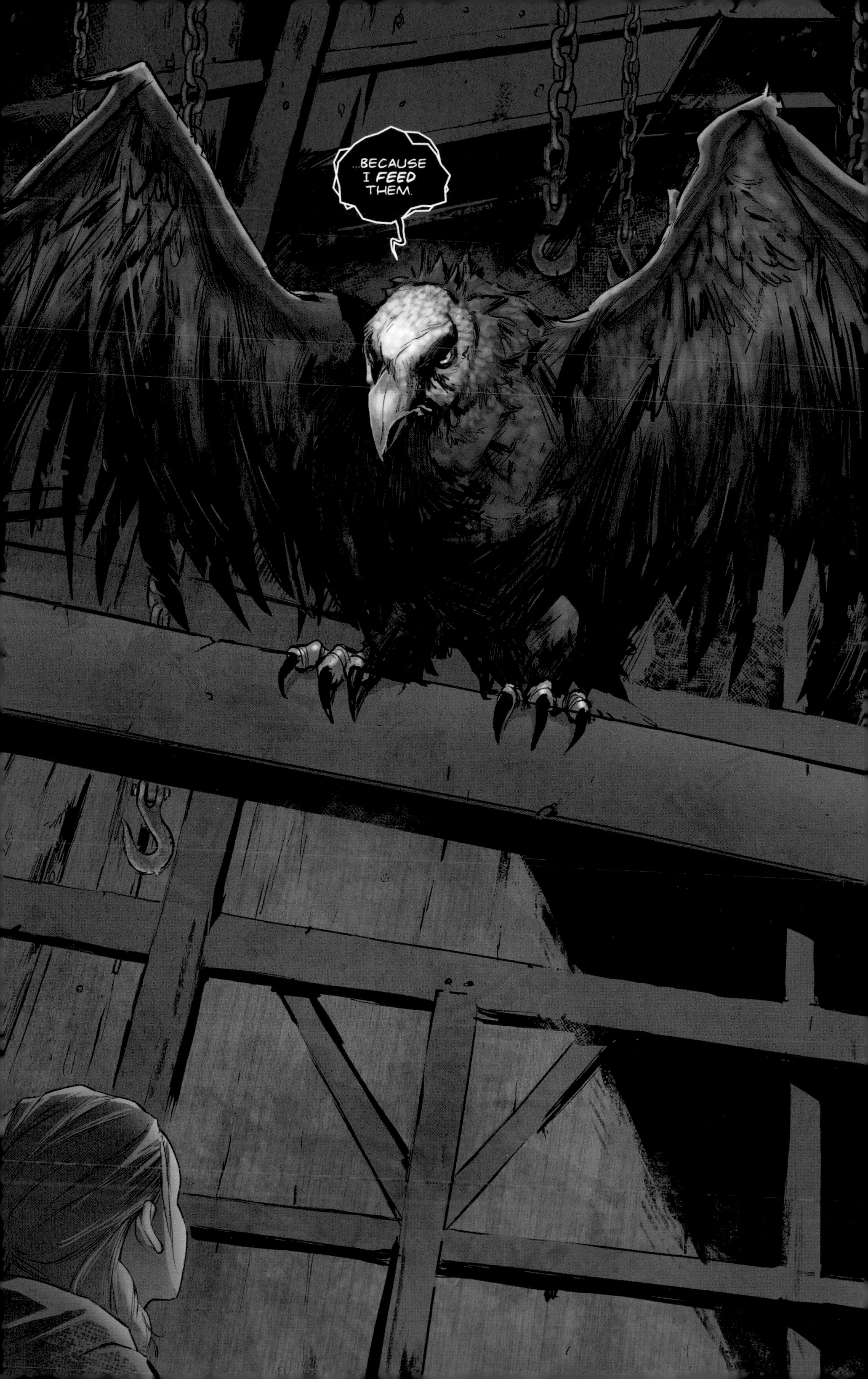
...BECAUSE I FEED THEM.

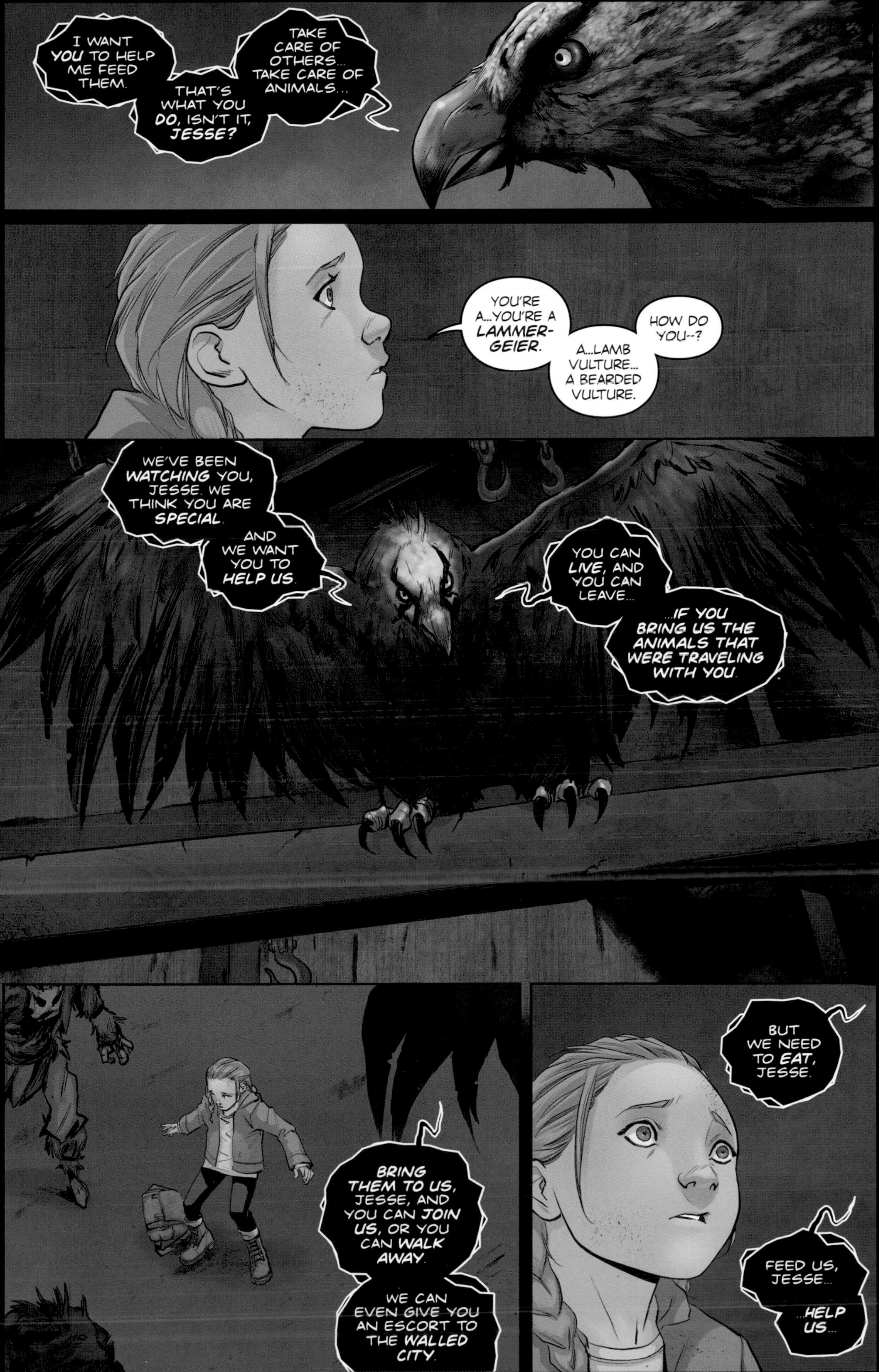
I WANT YOU TO HELP ME FEED THEM.
THAT'S WHAT YOU DO, ISN'T IT, JESSE?
TAKE CARE OF OTHERS... TAKE CARE OF ANIMALS...
YOU'RE A...YOU'RE A LAMMERGEIER.
A...LAMB VULTURE... A BEARDED VULTURE.
HOW DO YOU--?
WE'VE BEEN WATCHING YOU, JESSE. WE THINK YOU ARE SPECIAL.
AND WE WANT YOU TO HELP US.
YOU CAN LIVE, AND YOU CAN LEAVE...
...IF YOU BRING US THE ANIMALS THAT WERE TRAVELING WITH YOU.
BRING THEM TO US, JESSE, AND YOU CAN JOIN US, OR YOU CAN WALK AWAY.
WE CAN EVEN GIVE YOU AN ESCORT TO THE WALLED CITY.
BUT WE NEED TO EAT, JESSE.
FEED US, JESSE...
...HELP US...

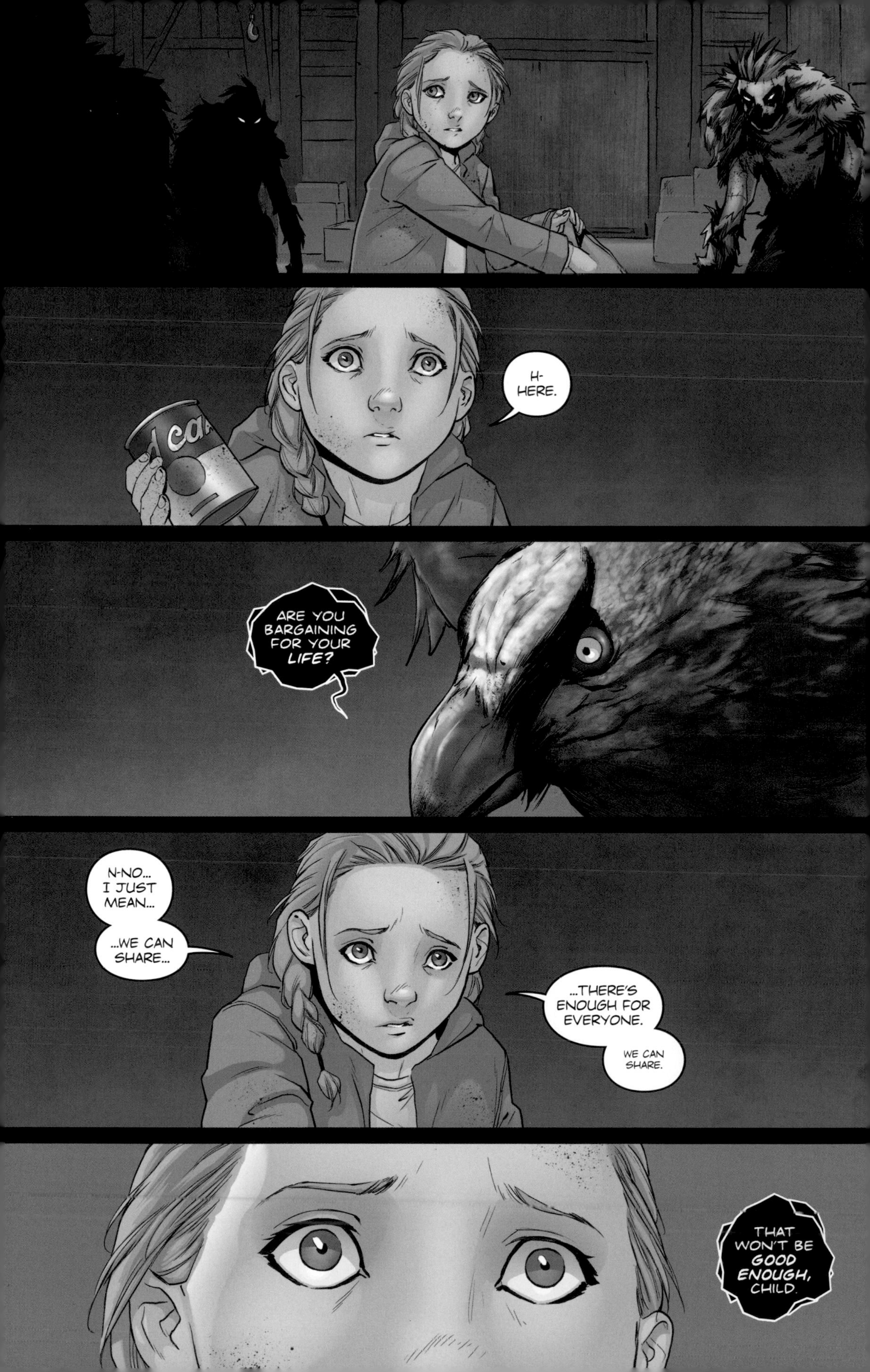
H-
HERE.
ARE YOU BARGAINING FOR YOUR *LIFE?*
N-NO... I JUST MEAN...
...WE CAN SHARE...
...THERE'S ENOUGH FOR EVERYONE.
WE CAN SHARE.
THAT WON'T BE *GOOD ENOUGH,* CHILD.

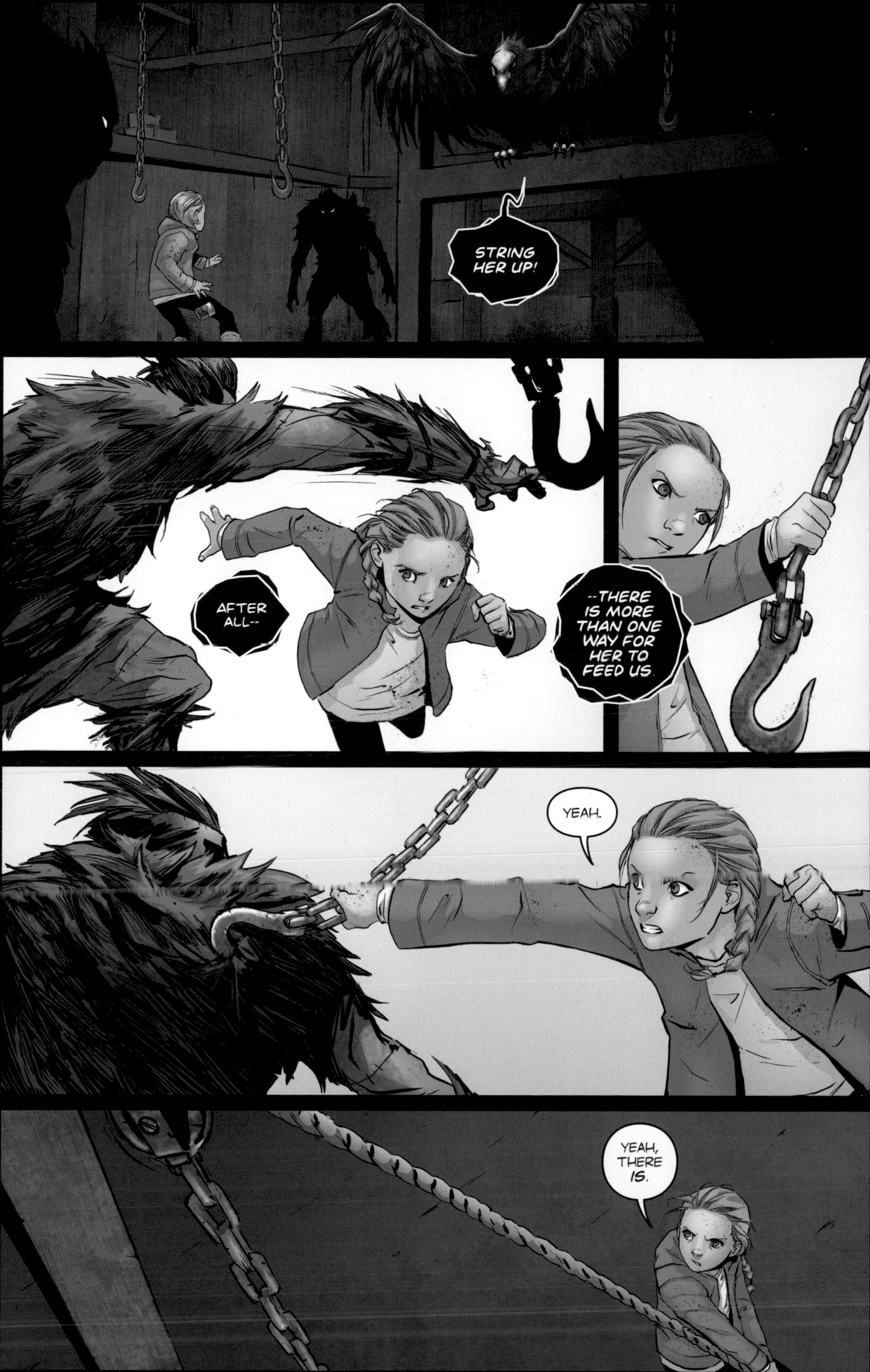
STRING HER UP!
AFTER ALL--
--THERE IS MORE THAN ONE WAY FOR HER TO FEED US.
YEAH.
YEAH, THERE IS.

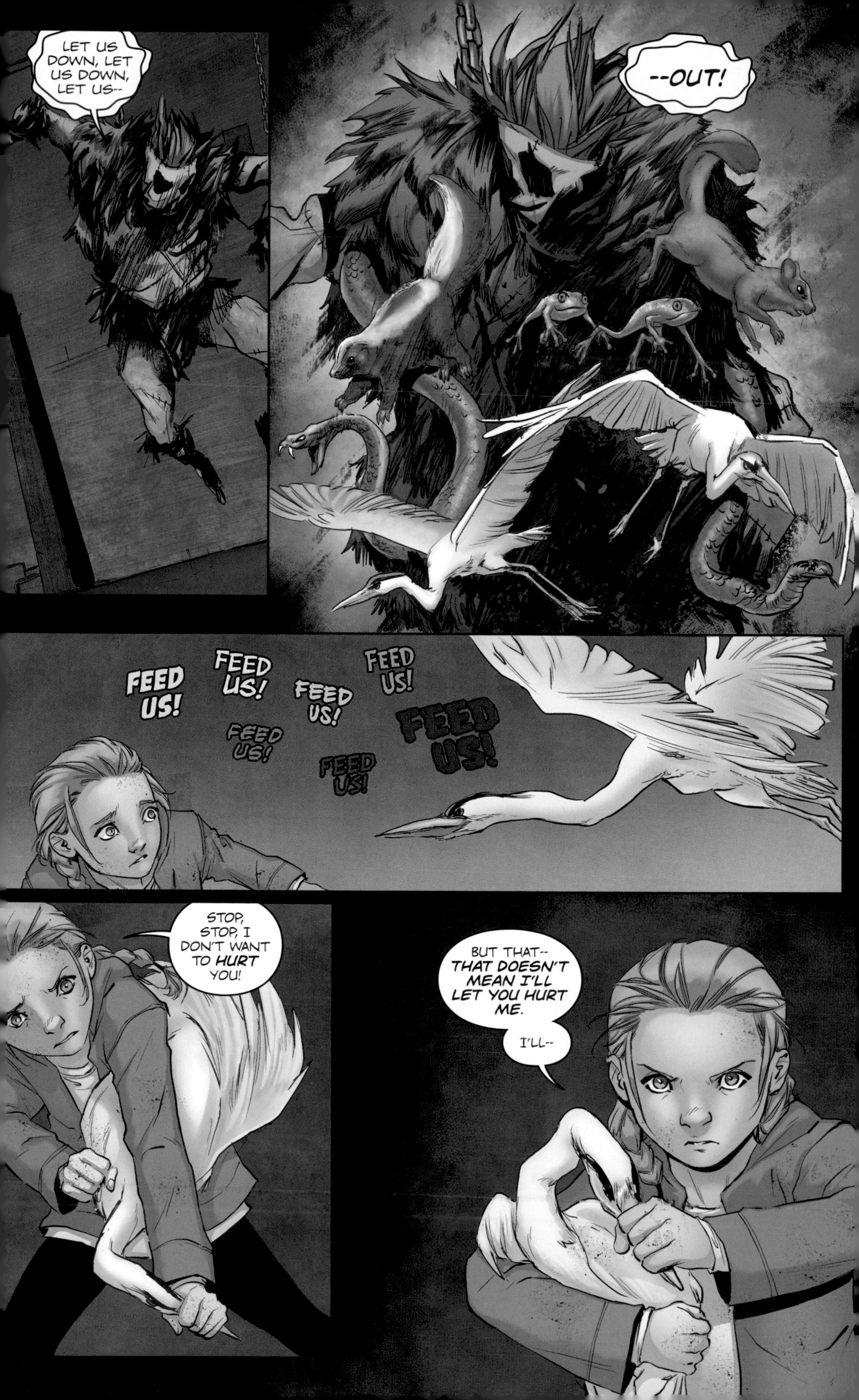
LET US DOWN, LET US DOWN, LET US--
--OUT!
FEED US!
FEED US!
FEED US!
FEED US!
FEED US!
FEED US!
FEED US!
STOP, STOP, I DON'T WANT TO **HURT** YOU!
BUT THAT-- **THAT DOESN'T MEAN I'LL LET YOU HURT ME.**
I'LL--

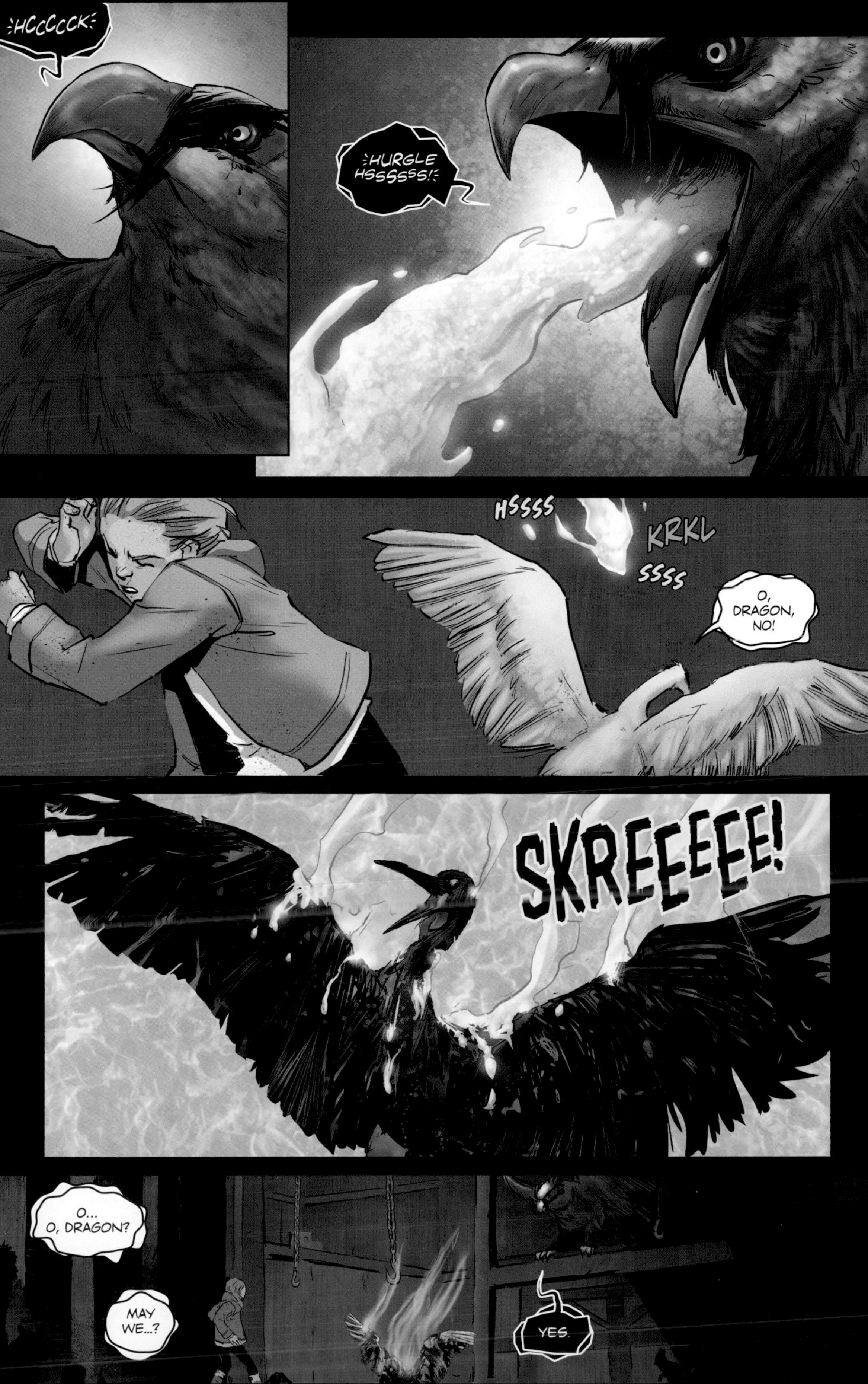
HCCCCCK
HURGLE HSSSSSS!
HSSSS
KRKL
SSSS
O, DRAGON, NO!
SKREEEEE!
O... O, DRAGON?
MAY WE...?
YES.

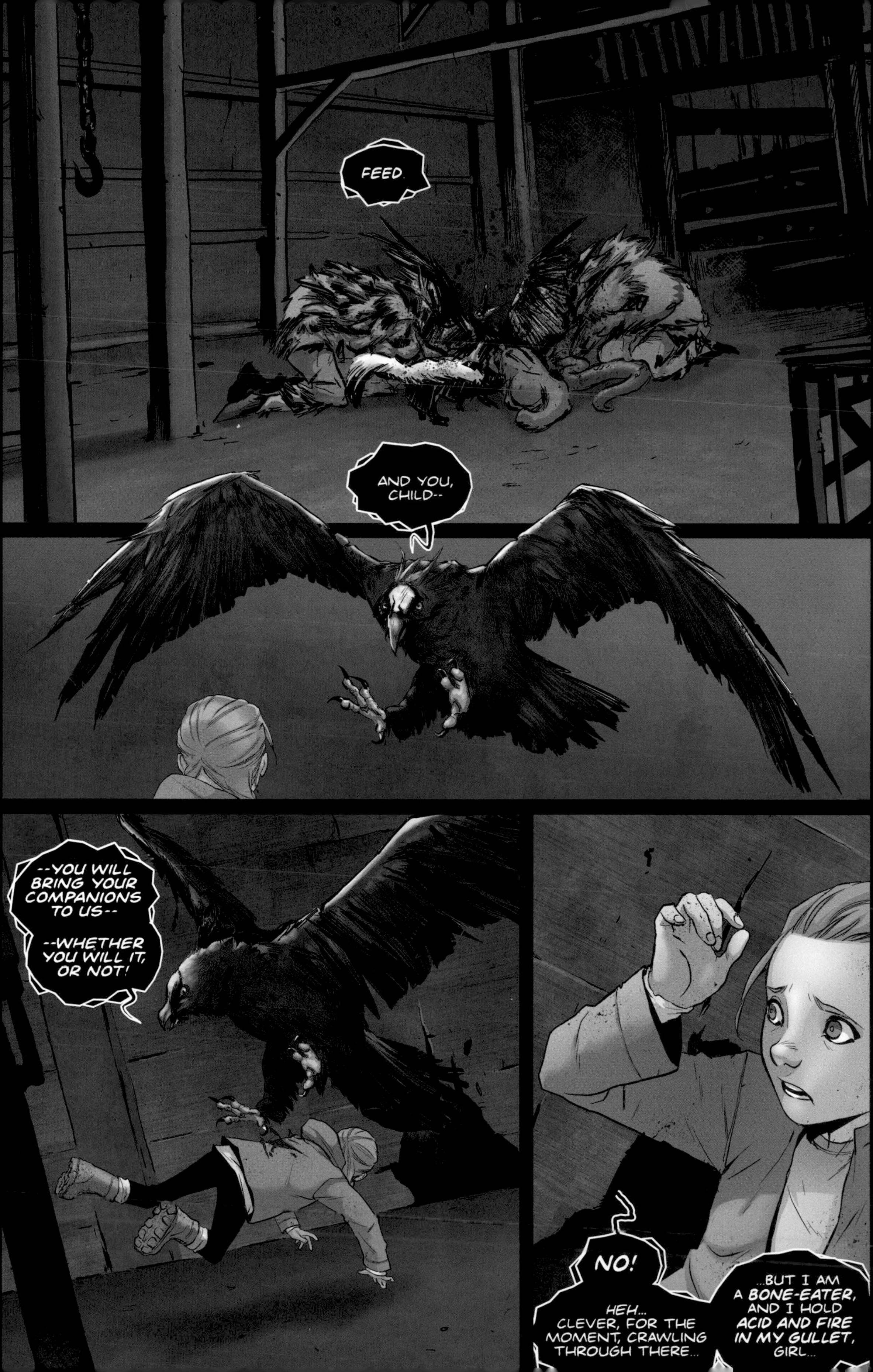
FEED.
AND YOU, CHILD--
--YOU WILL BRING YOUR COMPANIONS TO US--
--WHETHER YOU WILL IT, OR NOT!
NO!
HEH... CLEVER, FOR THE MOMENT, CRAWLING THROUGH THERE...
...BUT I AM A BONE-EATER, AND I HOLD ACID AND FIRE IN MY GULLET, GIRL...

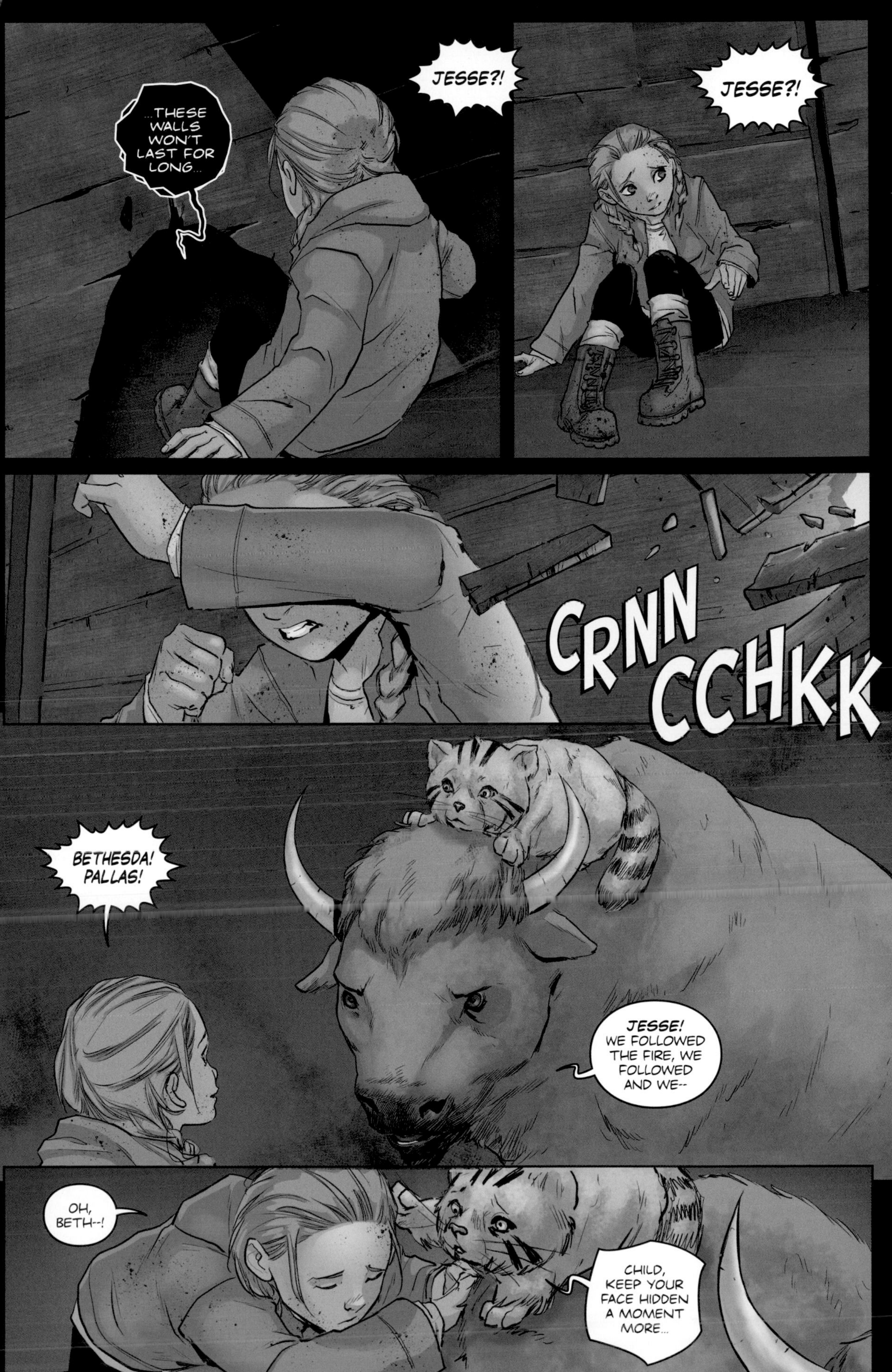
...THESE WALLS WON'T LAST FOR LONG...
JESSE?!
JESSE?!
CRNN
CCHKK
BETHESDA! PALLAS!
JESSE! WE FOLLOWED THE FIRE, WE FOLLOWED AND WE--
OH, BETH--!
CHILD, KEEP YOUR FACE HIDDEN A MOMENT MORE...

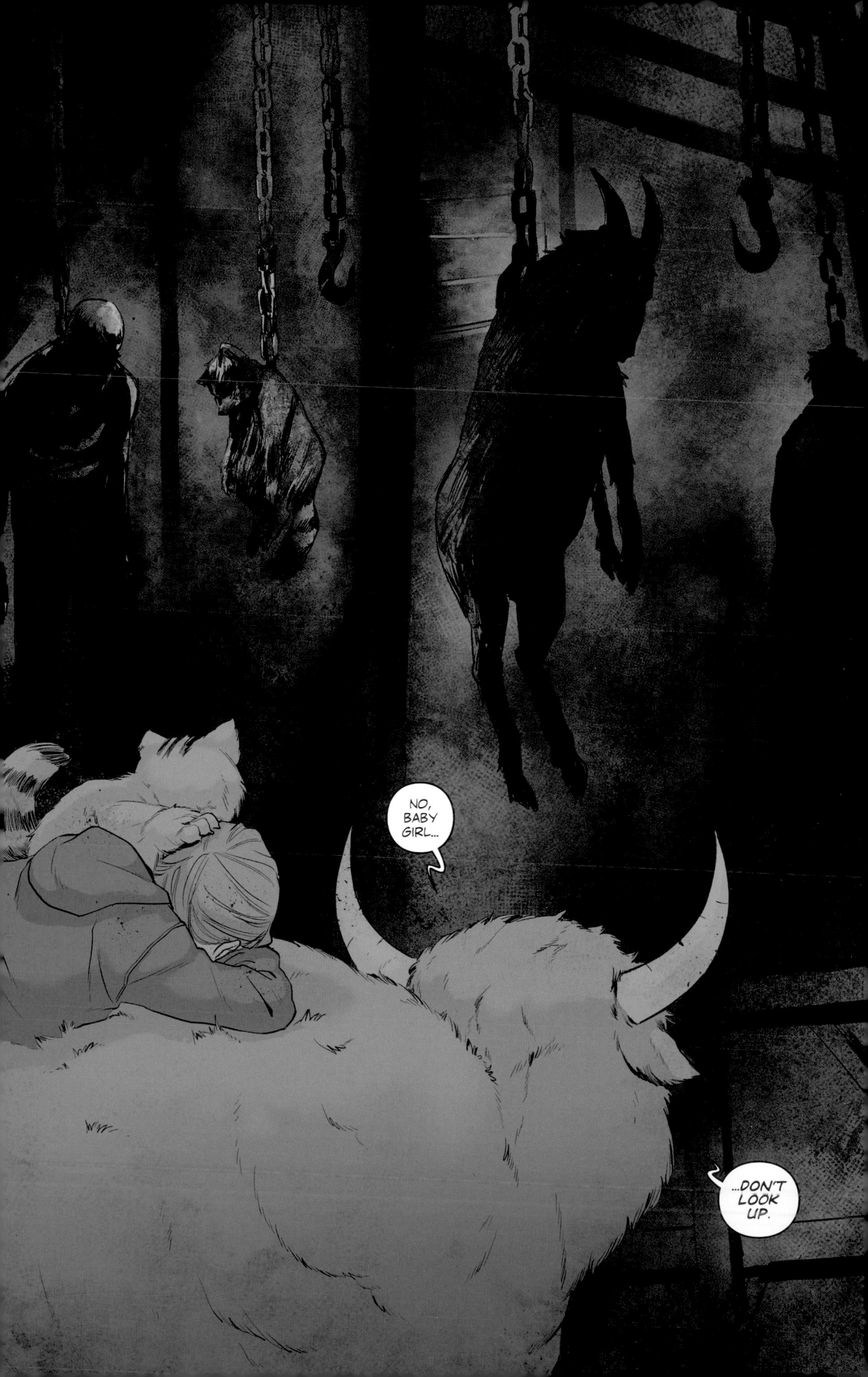

NO, BABY GIRL...
...DON'T LOOK UP.

"FEEDING TIME"

7

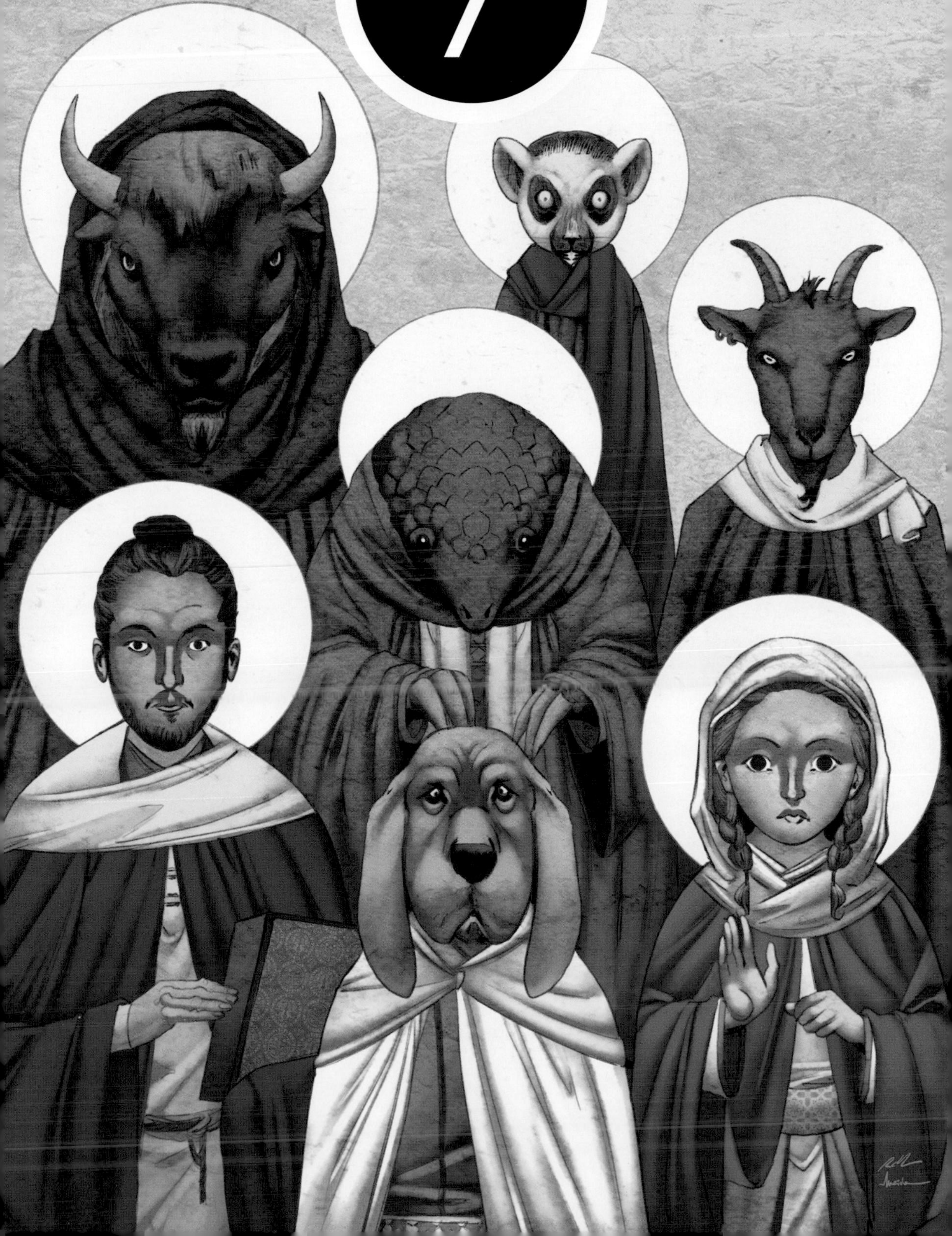

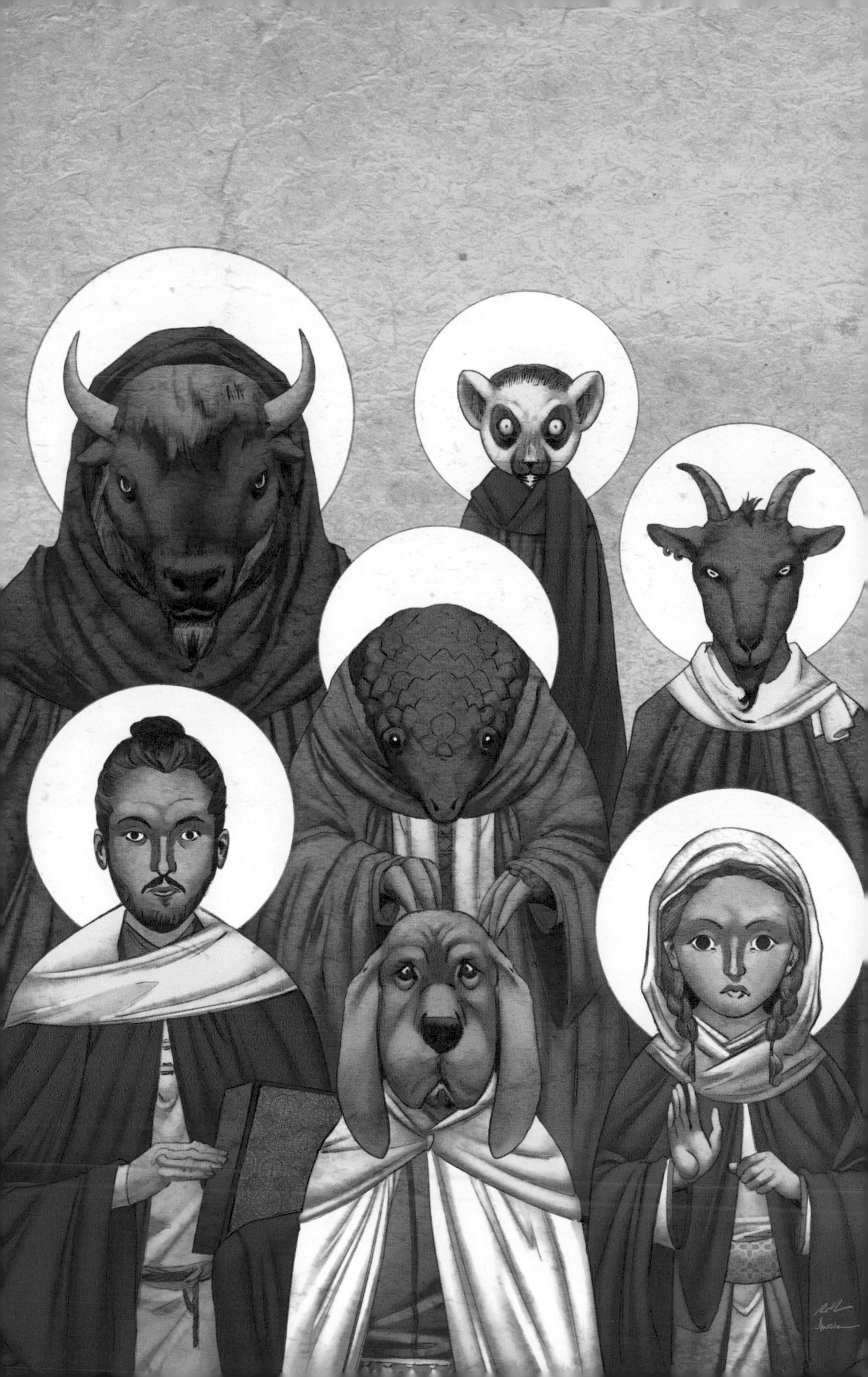

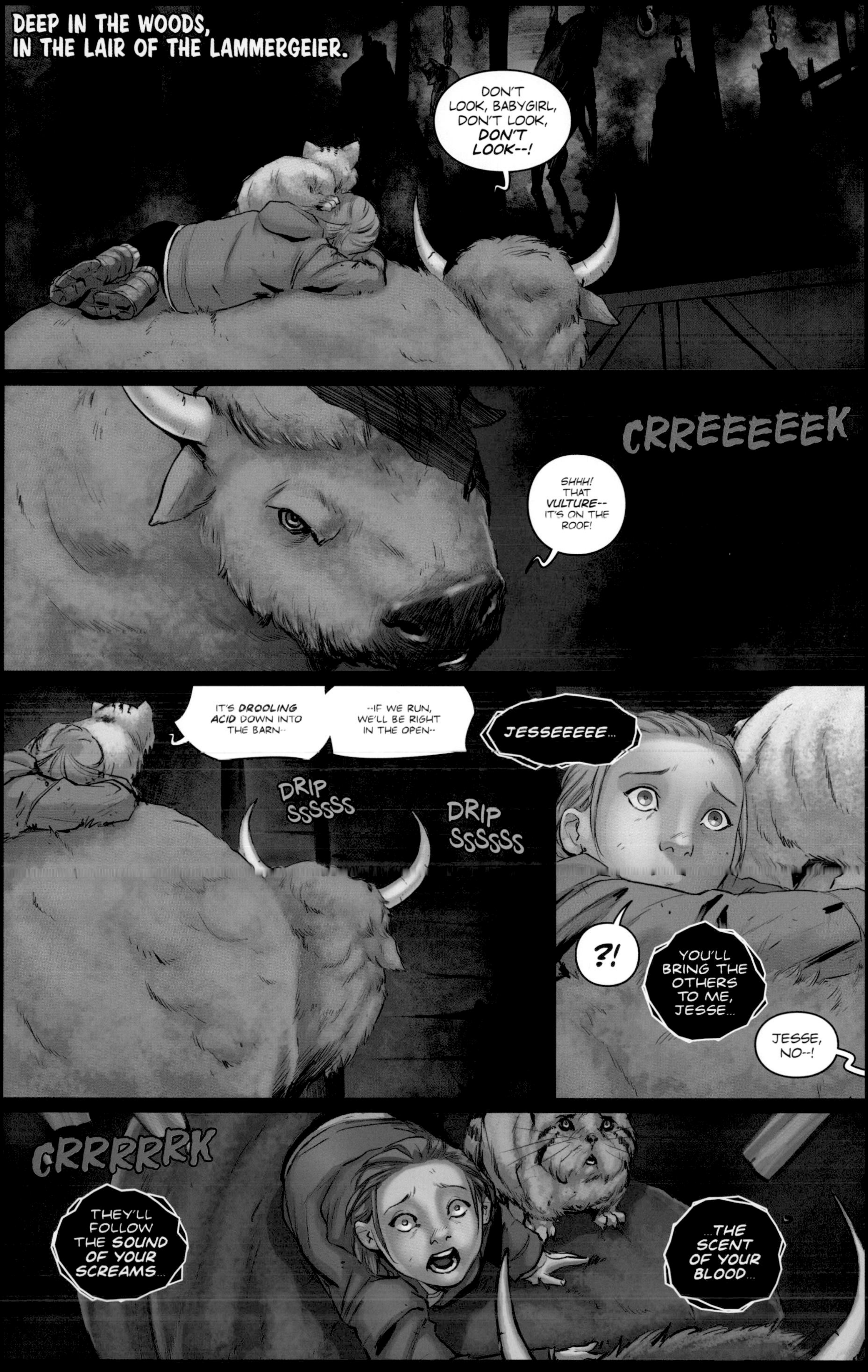
DEEP IN THE WOODS, IN THE LAIR OF THE LAMMERGEIER.
DON'T LOOK, BABYGIRL, DON'T LOOK, DON'T LOOK--!
CRREEEEEEK
SHHH! THAT VULTURE-- IT'S ON THE ROOF!
IT'S DROOLING ACID DOWN INTO THE BARN--
--IF WE RUN, WE'LL BE RIGHT IN THE OPEN--
DRIP SSSSSS
DRIP SSSSSS
JESSEEEEE...
?!
YOU'LL BRING THE OTHERS TO ME, JESSE...
JESSE, NO--!
CRRRRRK
THEY'LL FOLLOW THE SOUND OF YOUR SCREAMS...
...THE SCENT OF YOUR BLOOD...

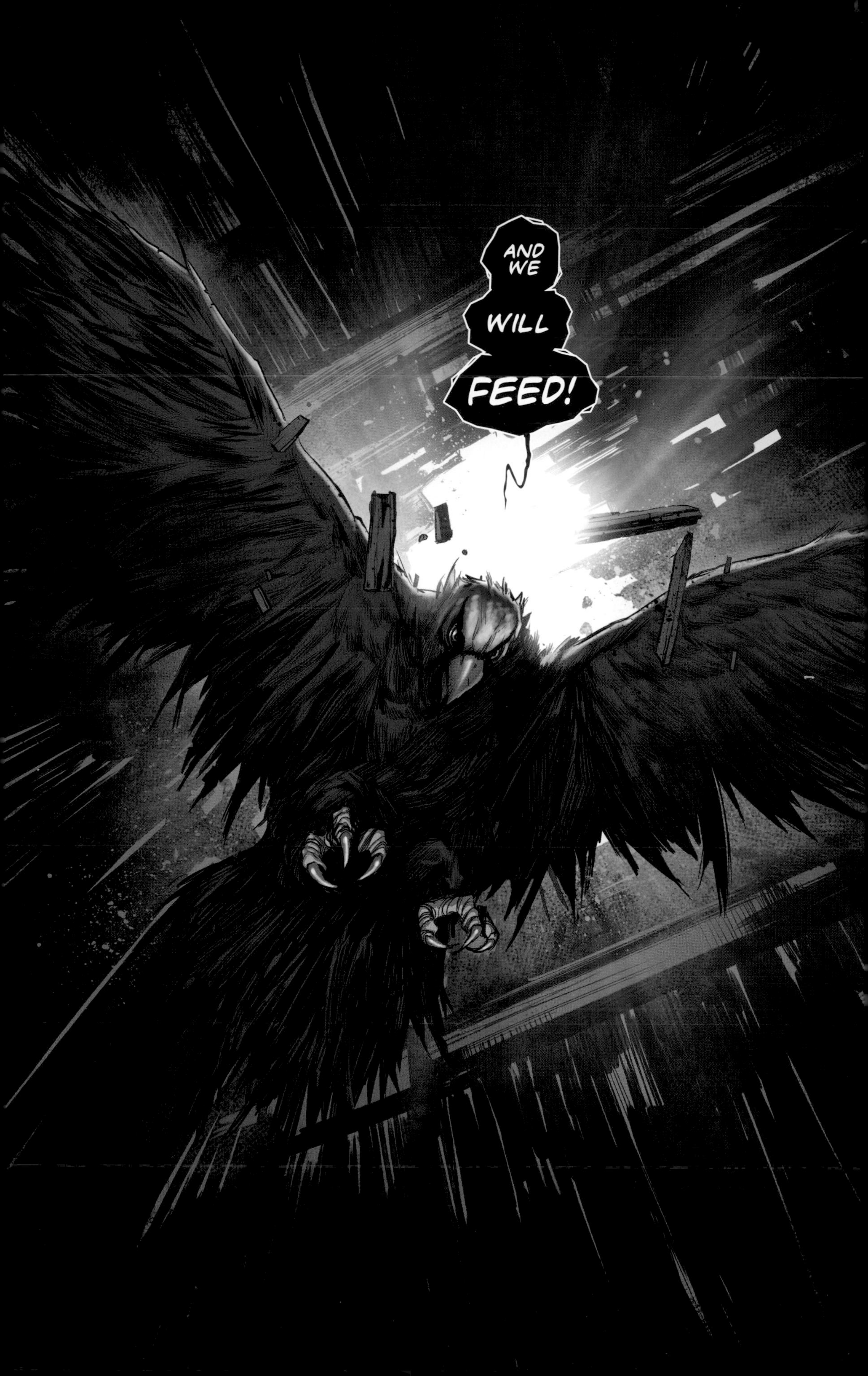
AND WE
WILL
FEED!

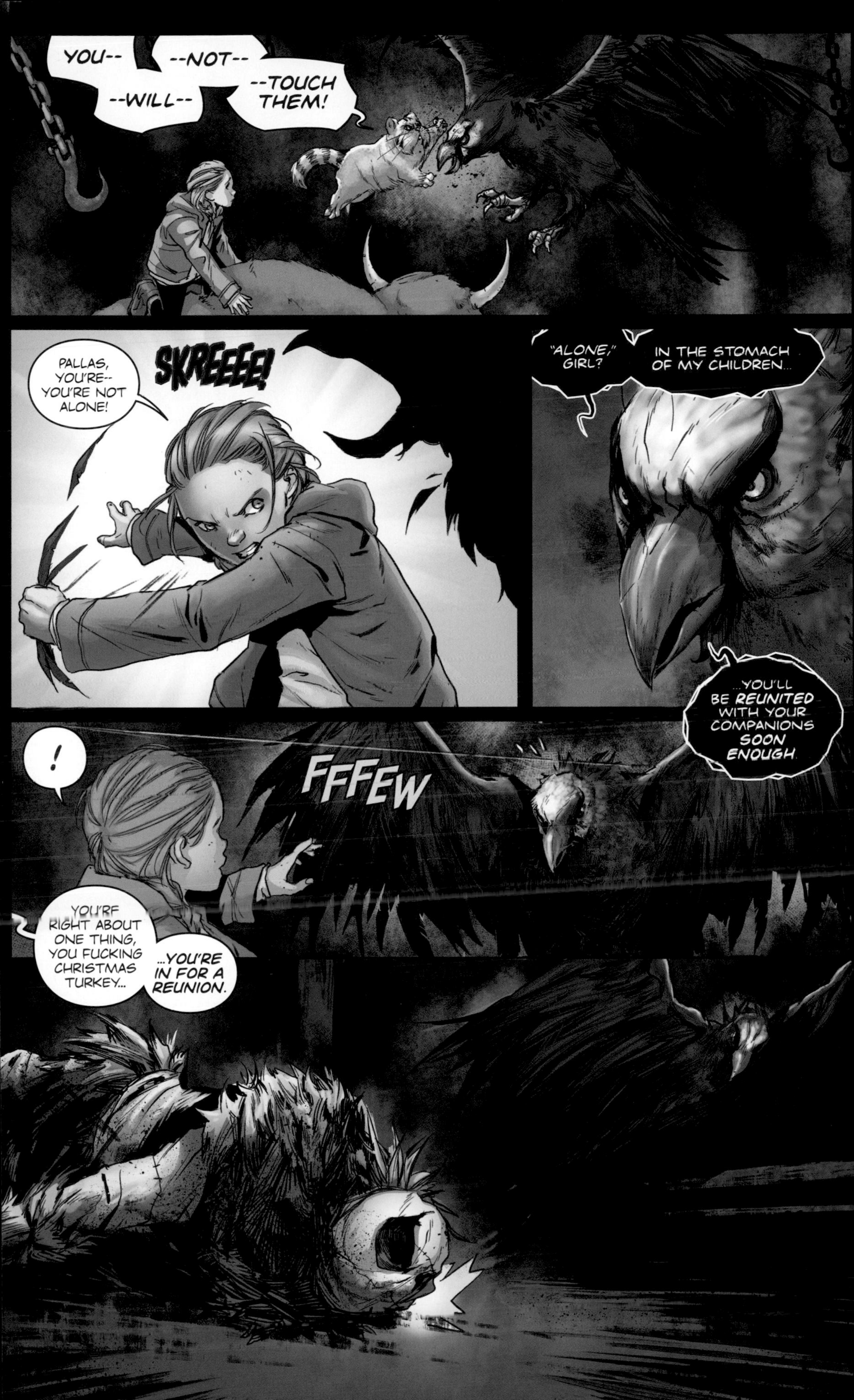
YOU--
--WILL--
--NOT--
--TOUCH THEM!
PALLAS, YOU'RE-- YOU'RE NOT ALONE!
SKREEEEE!
"ALONE," GIRL?
IN THE STOMACH OF MY CHILDREN...
...YOU'LL BE REUNITED WITH YOUR COMPANIONS SOON ENOUGH.
!
FFFEW
YOU'RF RIGHT ABOUT ONE THING, YOU FUCKING CHRISTMAS TURKEY...
...YOU'RE IN FOR A REUNION.

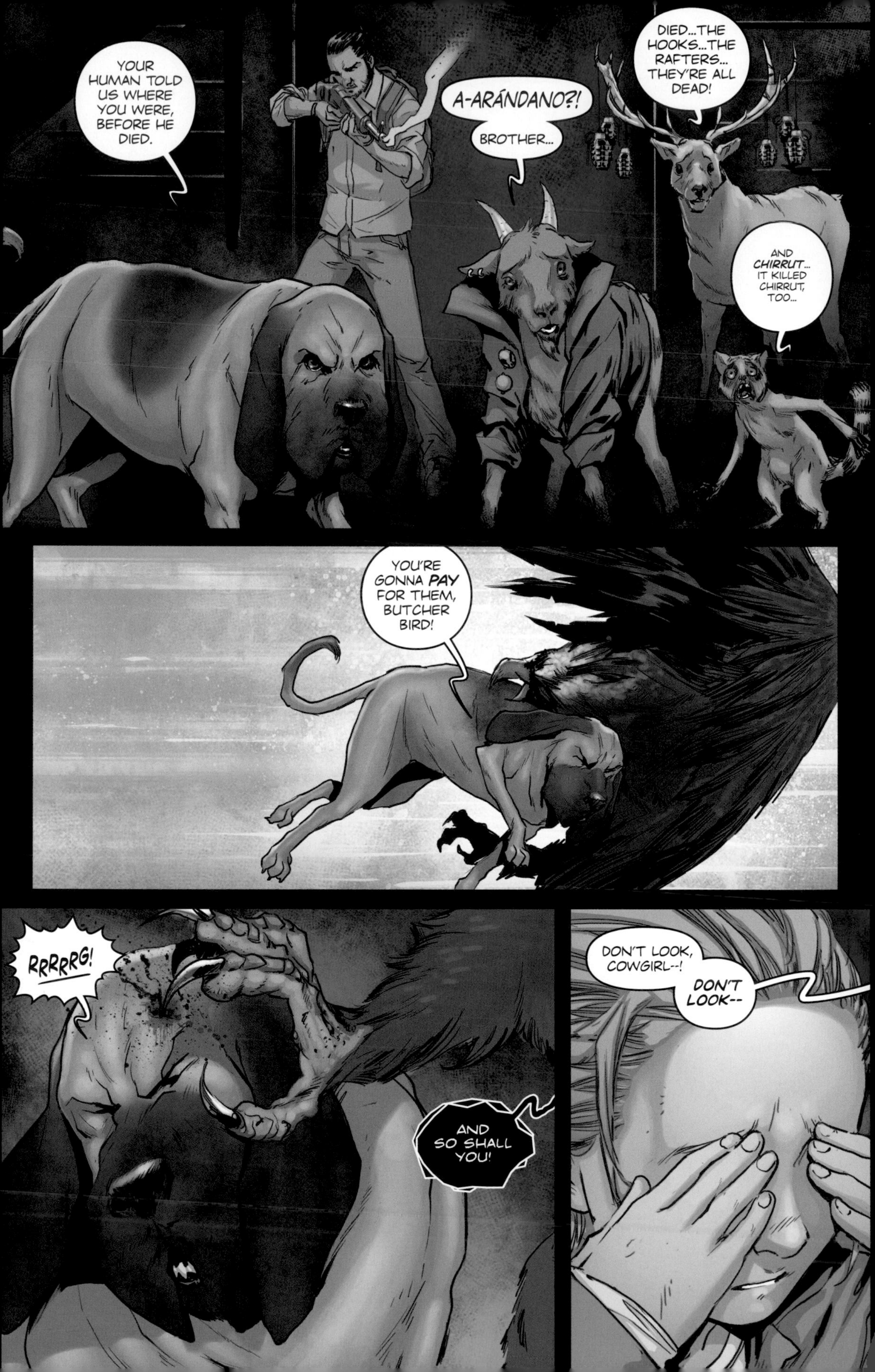
YOUR HUMAN TOLD US WHERE YOU WERE, BEFORE HE DIED.
A-ARÁNDANO?!
BROTHER...
DIED...THE HOOKS...THE RAFTERS... THEY'RE ALL DEAD!
AND CHIRRUT... IT KILLED CHIRRUT, TOO...
YOU'RE GONNA PAY FOR THEM, BUTCHER BIRD!
RRRRRG!
AND SO SHALL YOU!
DON'T LOOK, COWGIRL--!
DON'T LOOK--

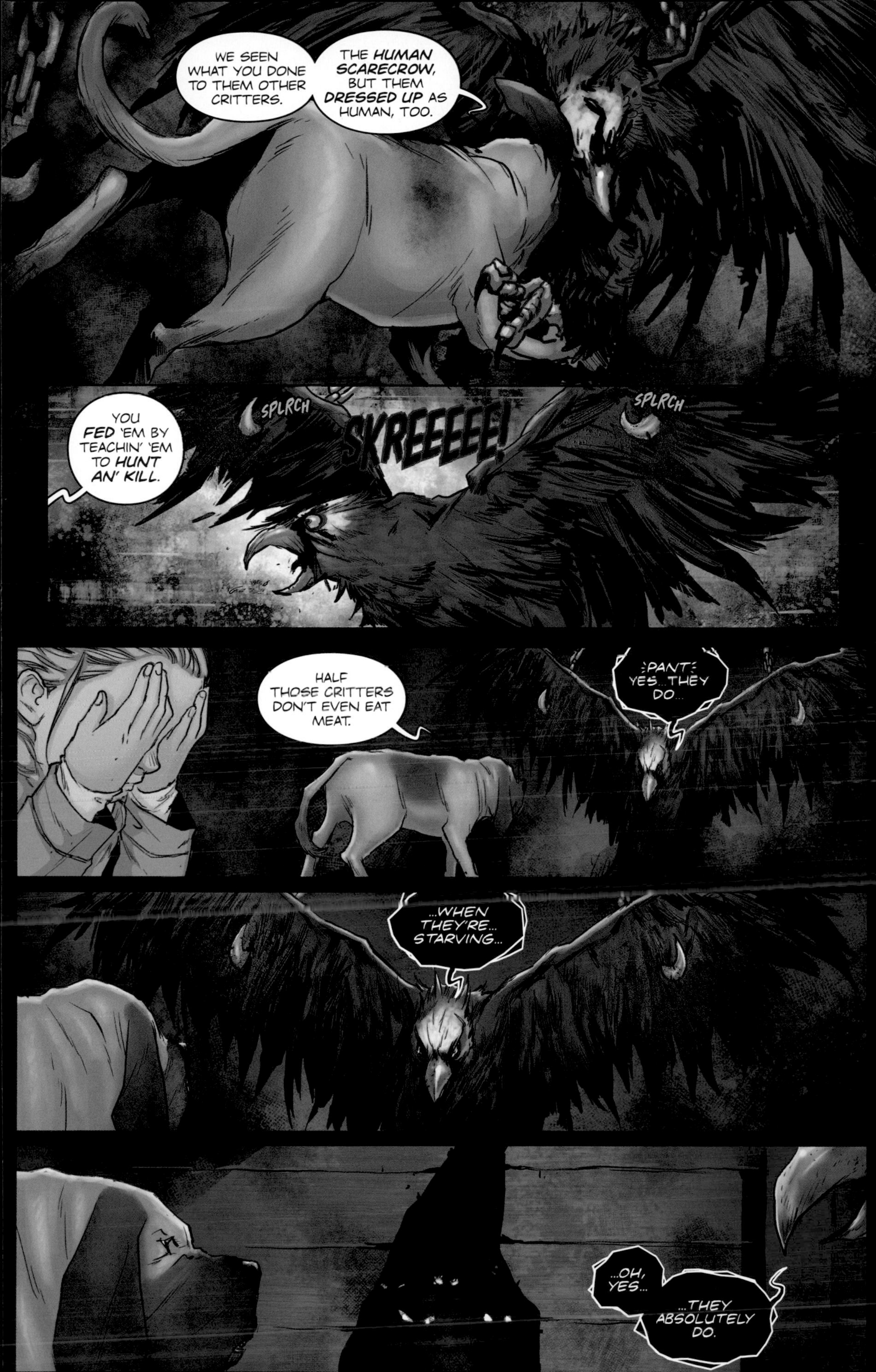
WE SEEN WHAT YOU DONE TO THEM OTHER CRITTERS.
THE HUMAN SCARECROW, BUT THEM DRESSED UP AS HUMAN, TOO.
YOU FED 'EM BY TEACHIN' 'EM TO HUNT AN' KILL.
SPLRCH
SKREEEEEE!
SPLRCH
HALF THOSE CRITTERS DON'T EVEN EAT MEAT.
:PANT: YES...THEY DO...
...WHEN THEY'RE... STARVING...
...OH, YES...
...THEY ABSOLUTELY DO.

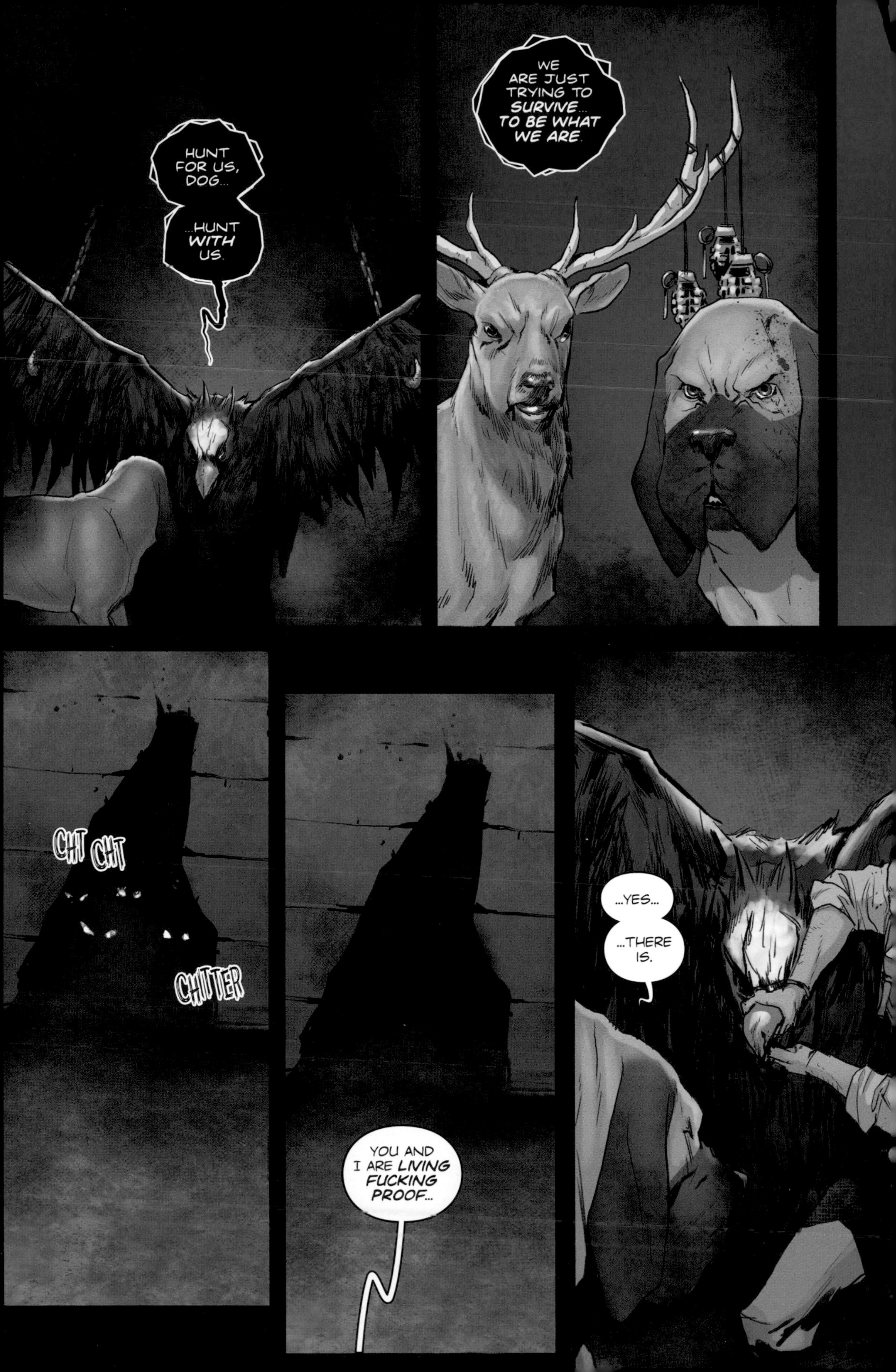
HUNT FOR US, DOG...
...HUNT WITH US.
WE ARE JUST TRYING TO SURVIVE... TO BE WHAT WE ARE.
CHT CHT
CHITTER
YOU AND I ARE LIVING FUCKING PROOF...
...YES...
...THERE IS.

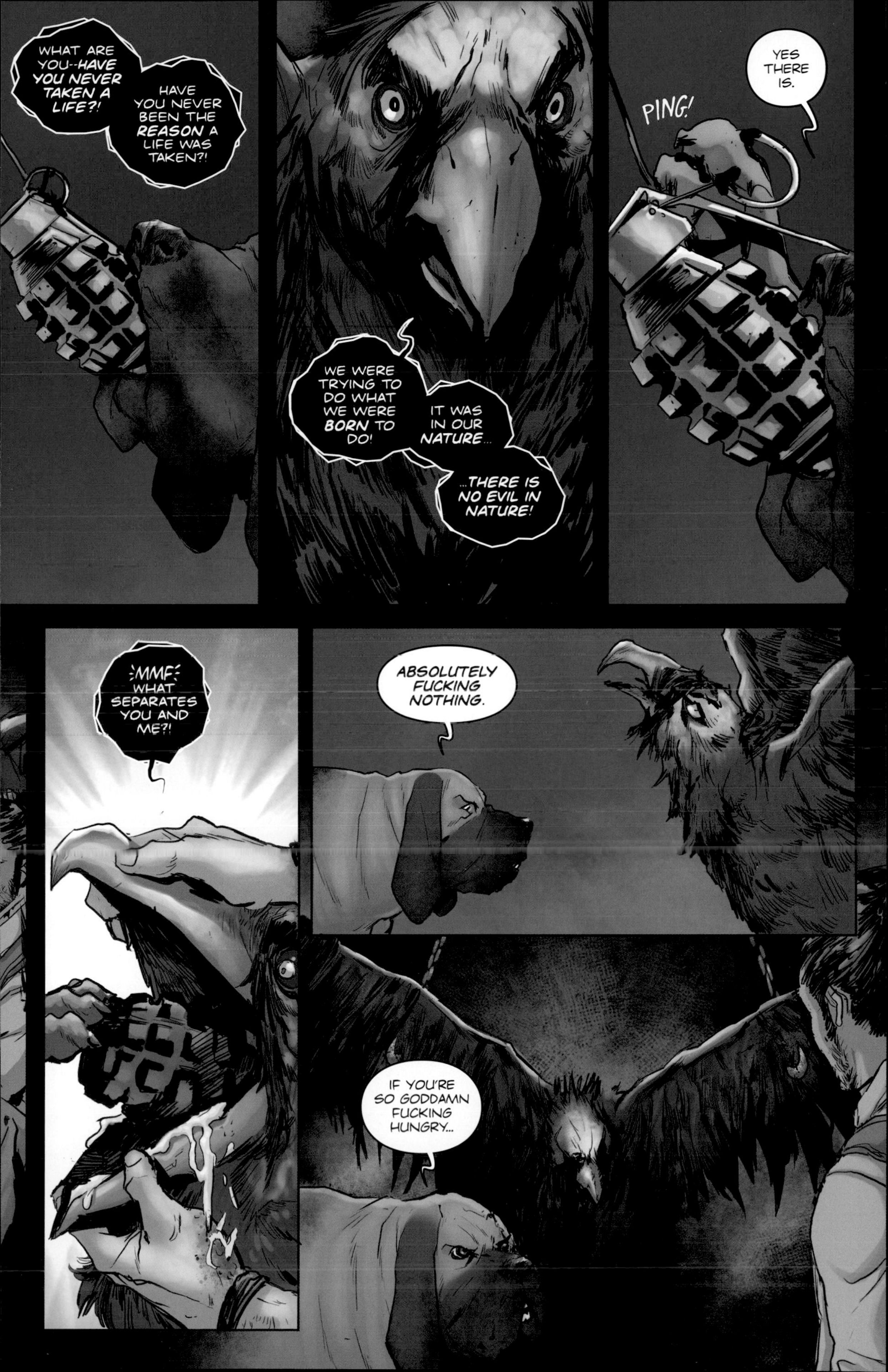
WHAT ARE YOU--HAVE YOU NEVER TAKEN A LIFE?!
HAVE YOU NEVER BEEN THE REASON A LIFE WAS TAKEN?!
WE WERE TRYING TO DO WHAT WE WERE BORN TO DO!
IT WAS IN OUR NATURE...
...THERE IS NO EVIL IN NATURE!
PING!
YES THERE IS.
MMF
WHAT SEPARATES YOU AND ME?!
ABSOLUTELY FUCKING NOTHING.
IF YOU'RE SO GODDAMN FUCKING HUNGRY...

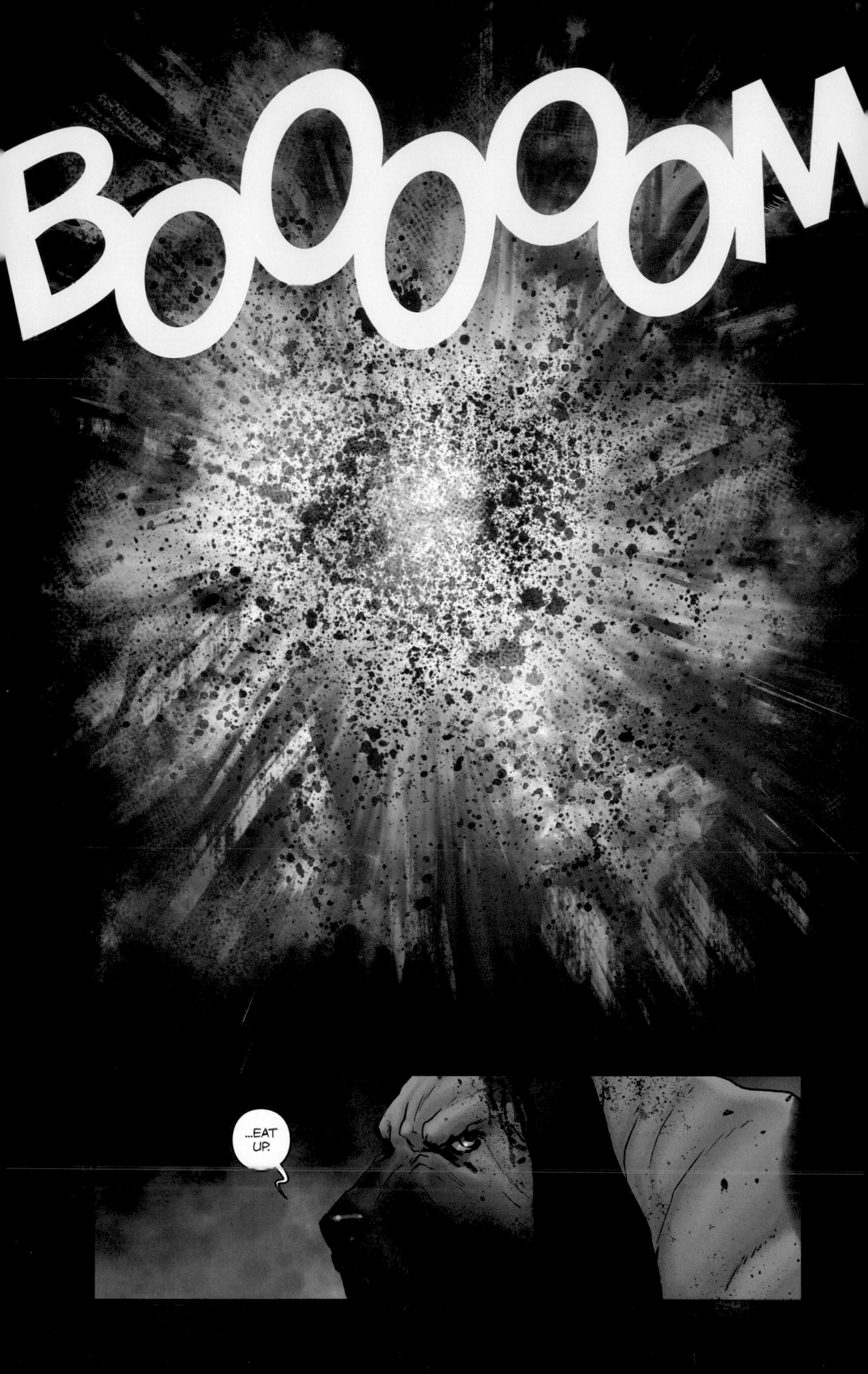
BOOOOOM
...EAT UP.

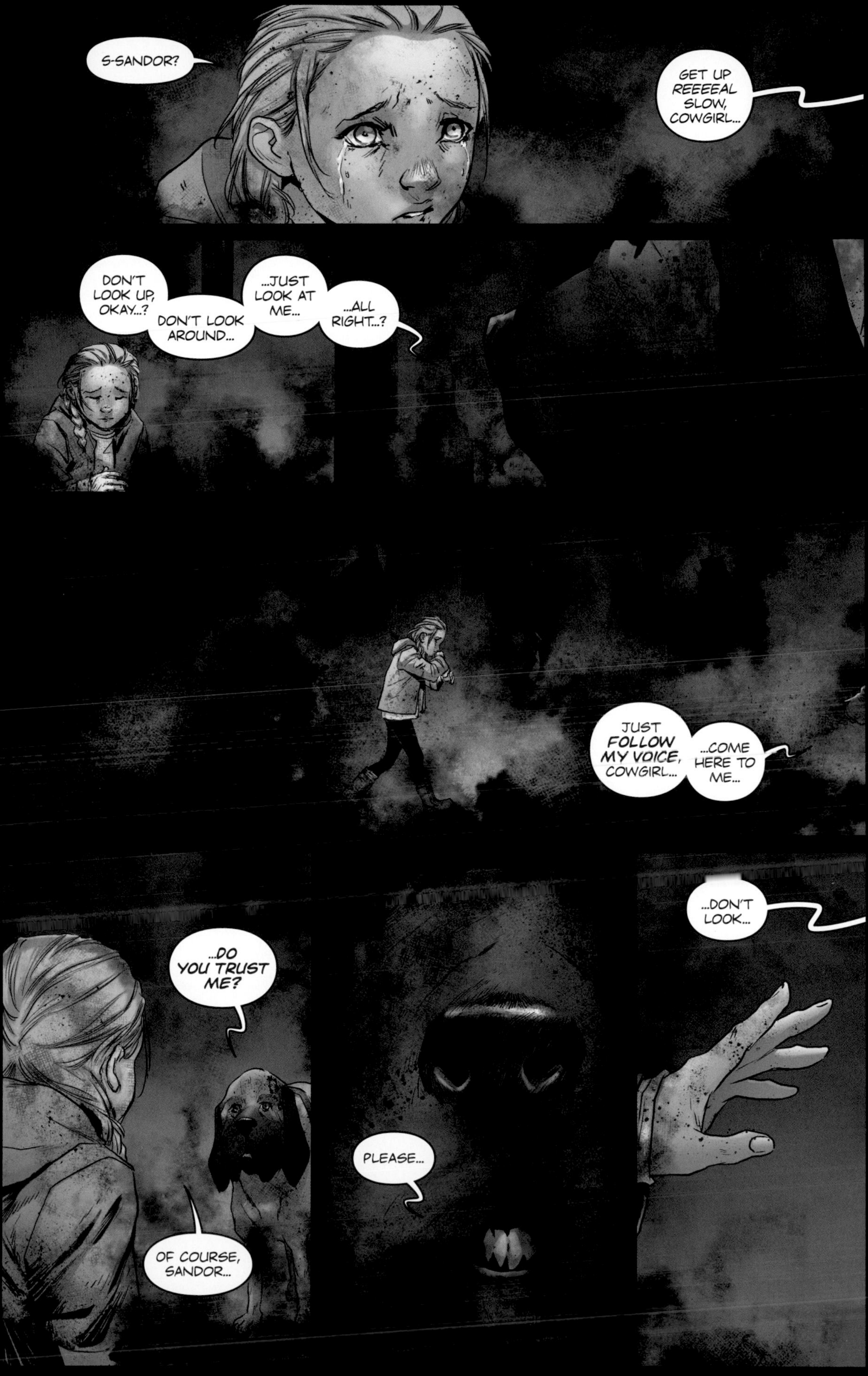
S-SANDOR?
GET UP REEEEAL SLOW, COWGIRL...
DON'T LOOK UP, OKAY...?
DON'T LOOK AROUND...
...JUST LOOK AT ME...
...ALL RIGHT...?
JUST FOLLOW MY VOICE, COWGIRL...
...COME HERE TO ME...
...DO YOU TRUST ME?
OF COURSE, SANDOR...
PLEASE...
...DON'T LOOK...

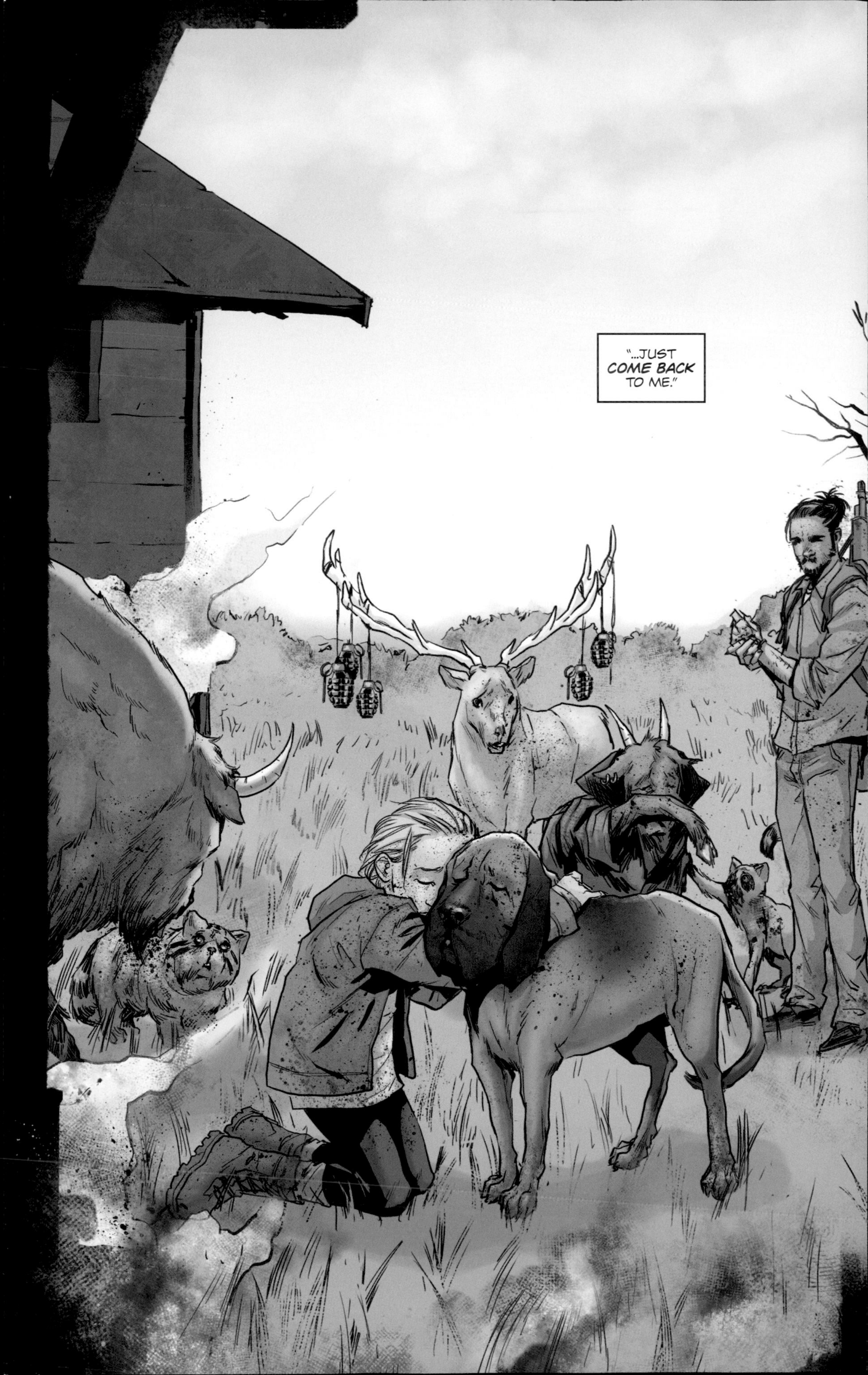
"...JUST COME BACK TO ME."

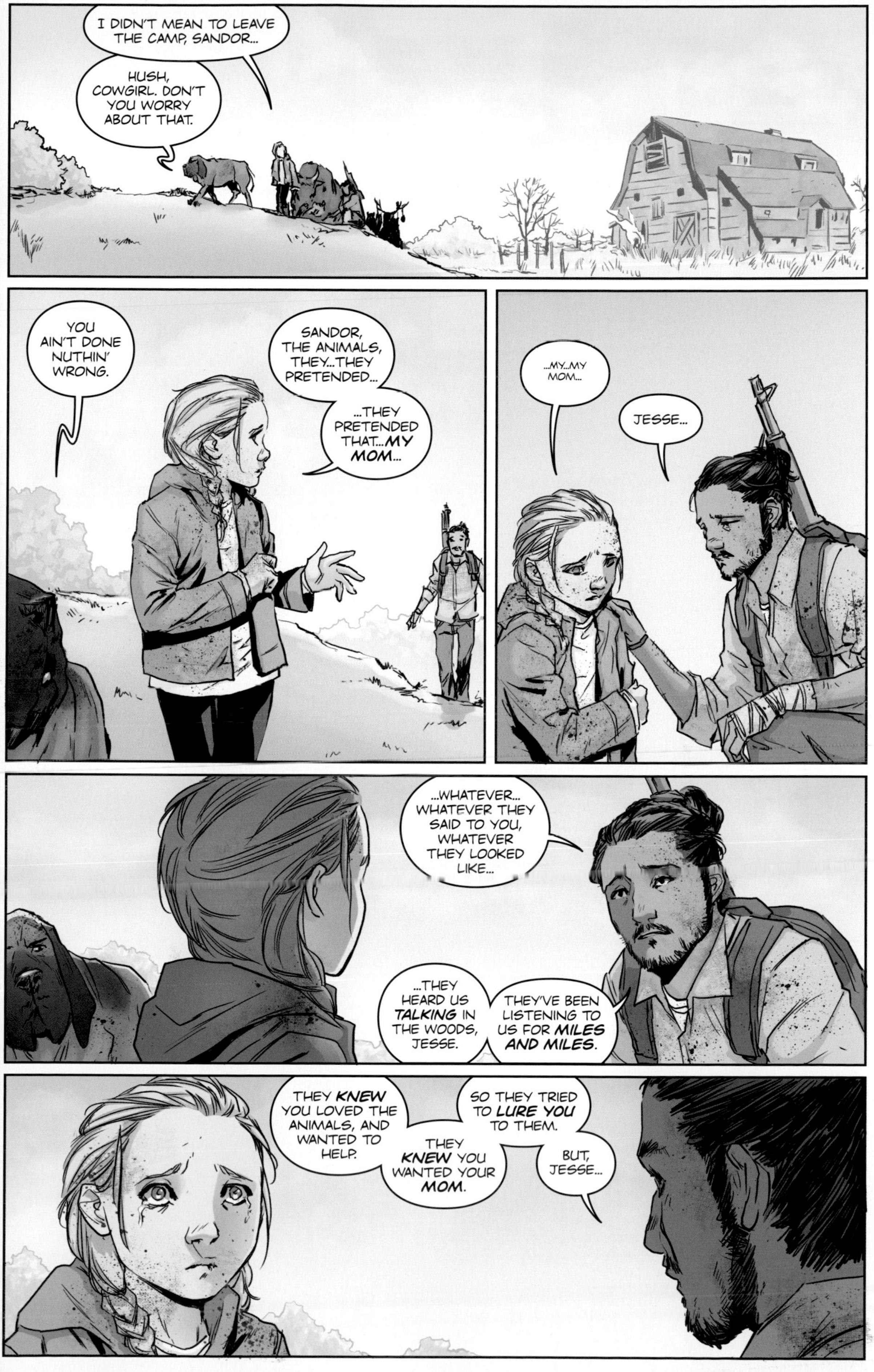
I DIDN'T MEAN TO LEAVE THE CAMP, SANDOR...
HUSH, COWGIRL. DON'T YOU WORRY ABOUT THAT.
YOU AIN'T DONE NUTHIN' WRONG.
SANDOR, THE ANIMALS, THEY...THEY PRETENDED...
...THEY PRETENDED THAT...**MY MOM**...
...MY...MY MOM...
JESSE...
...WHATEVER... WHATEVER THEY SAID TO YOU, WHATEVER THEY LOOKED LIKE...
...THEY HEARD US **TALKING** IN THE WOODS, JESSE.
THEY'VE BEEN LISTENING TO US FOR **MILES AND MILES**.
THEY **KNEW** YOU LOVED THE ANIMALS, AND WANTED TO HELP.
THEY **KNEW** YOU WANTED YOUR **MOM**.
SO THEY TRIED TO **LURE YOU** TO THEM.
BUT, JESSE...

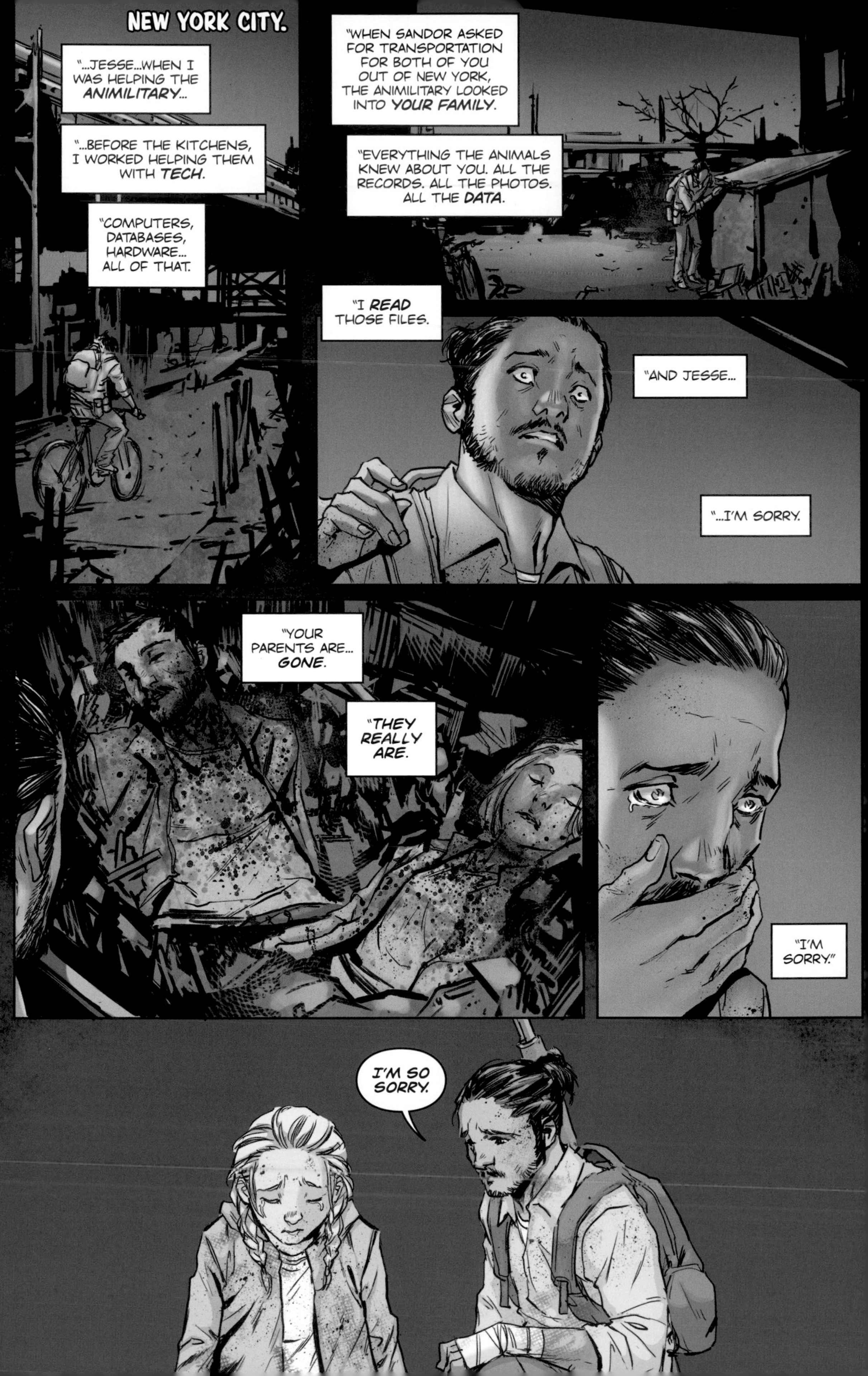
NEW YORK CITY.
"...JESSE...WHEN I WAS HELPING THE ANIMILITARY...
"...BEFORE THE KITCHENS, I WORKED HELPING THEM WITH TECH.
"COMPUTERS, DATABASES, HARDWARE... ALL OF THAT.
"WHEN SANDOR ASKED FOR TRANSPORTATION FOR BOTH OF YOU OUT OF NEW YORK, THE ANIMILITARY LOOKED INTO YOUR FAMILY.
"EVERYTHING THE ANIMALS KNEW ABOUT YOU. ALL THE RECORDS. ALL THE PHOTOS. ALL THE DATA.
"I READ THOSE FILES.
"AND JESSE...
"...I'M SORRY.
"YOUR PARENTS ARE... GONE.
"THEY REALLY ARE.
"I'M SORRY."
I'M SO SORRY.

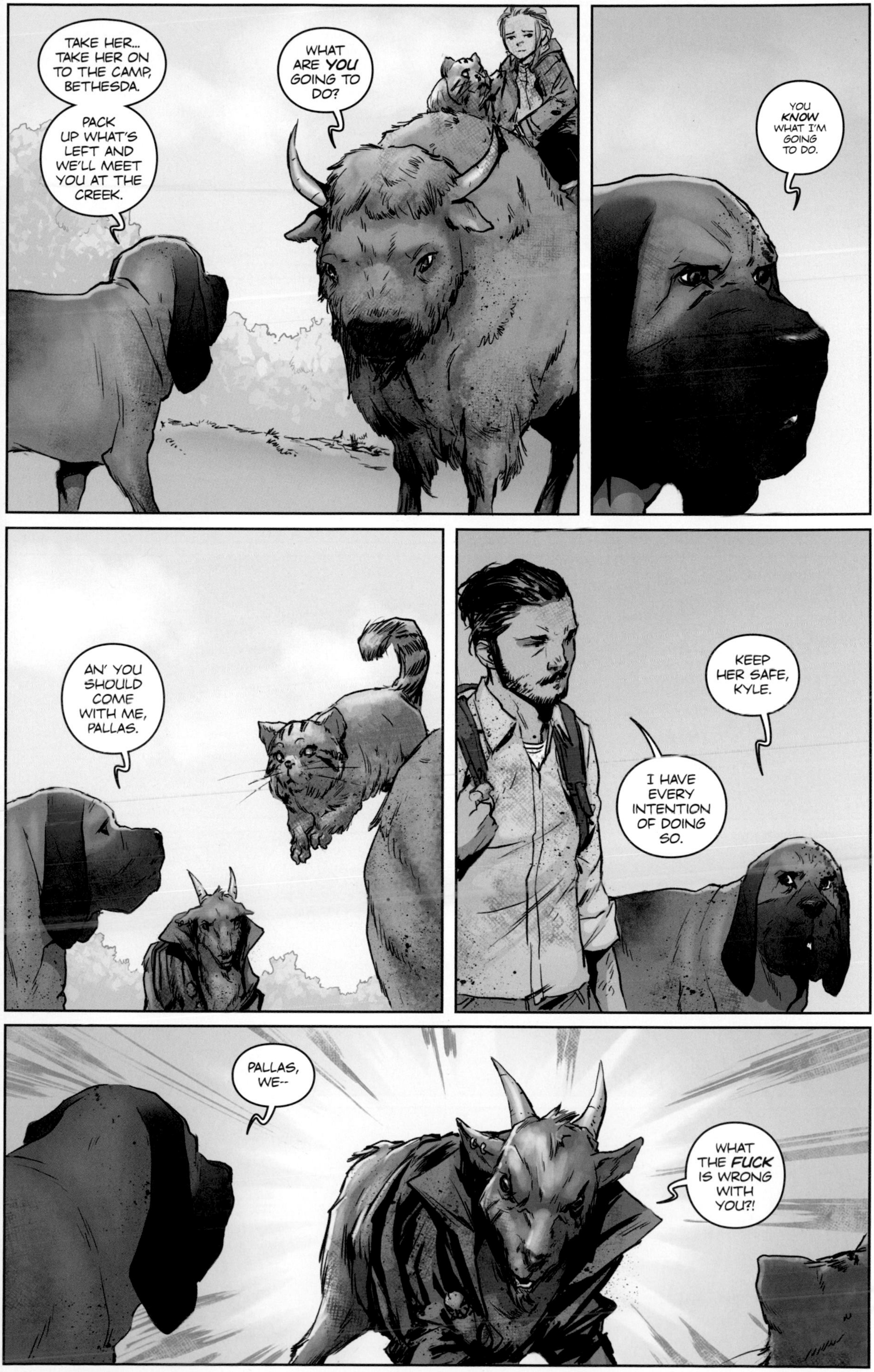
TAKE HER... TAKE HER ON TO THE CAMP, BETHESDA.
PACK UP WHAT'S LEFT AND WE'LL MEET YOU AT THE CREEK.
WHAT ARE YOU GOING TO DO?
YOU KNOW WHAT I'M GOING TO DO.
AN' YOU SHOULD COME WITH ME, PALLAS.
KEEP HER SAFE, KYLE.
I HAVE EVERY INTENTION OF DOING SO.
PALLAS, WE--
WHAT THE FUCK IS WRONG WITH YOU?!

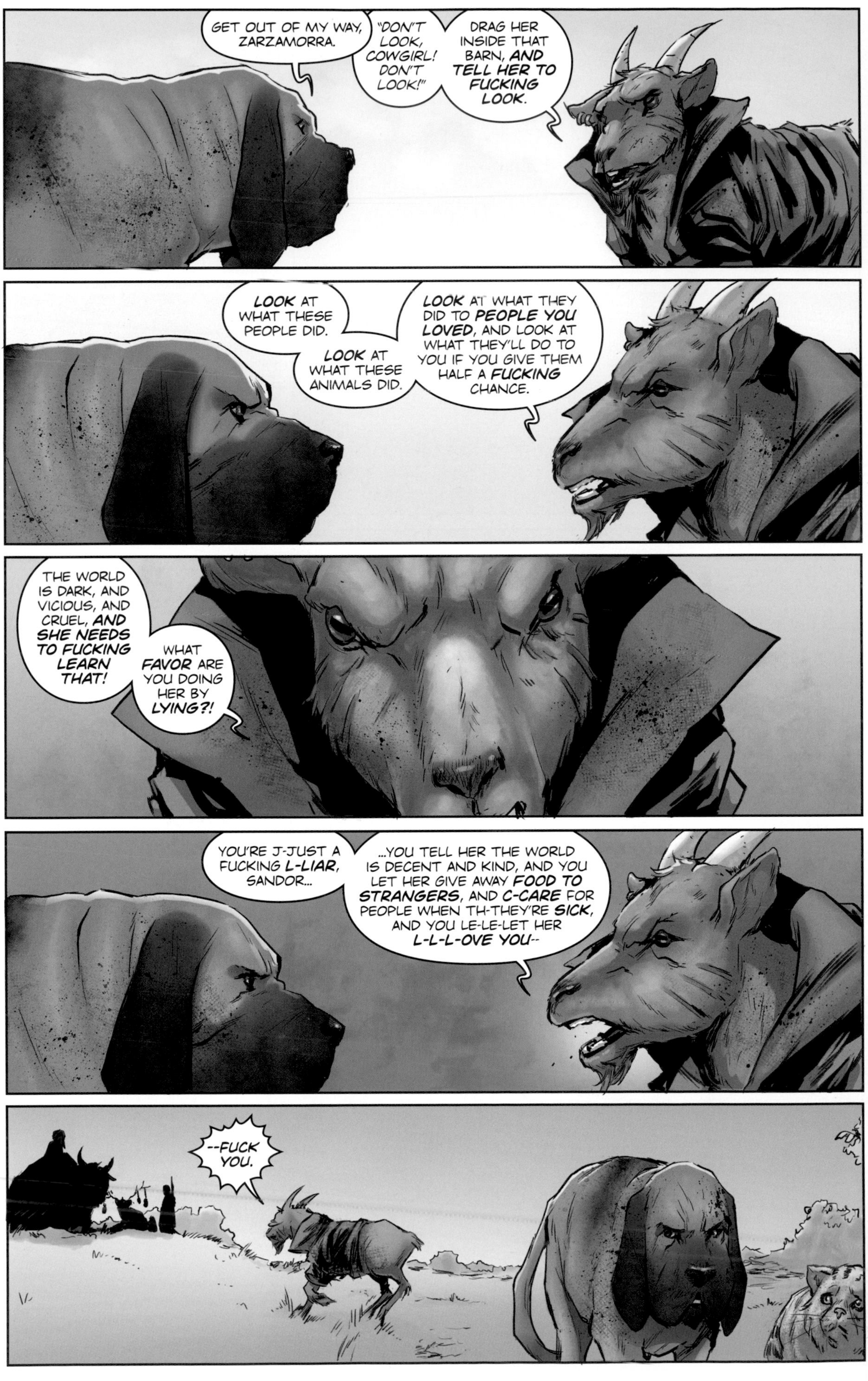
GET OUT OF MY WAY, ZARZAMORRA.
"DON'T LOOK, COWGIRL! DON'T LOOK!"
DRAG HER INSIDE THAT BARN, AND TELL HER TO FUCKING LOOK.
LOOK AT WHAT THESE PEOPLE DID.
LOOK AT WHAT THESE ANIMALS DID.
LOOK AT WHAT THEY DID TO PEOPLE YOU LOVED, AND LOOK AT WHAT THEY'LL DO TO YOU IF YOU GIVE THEM HALF A FUCKING CHANCE.
THE WORLD IS DARK, AND VICIOUS, AND CRUEL, AND SHE NEEDS TO FUCKING LEARN THAT!
WHAT FAVOR ARE YOU DOING HER BY LYING?!
YOU'RE J-JUST A FUCKING L-LIAR, SANDOR...
...YOU TELL HER THE WORLD IS DECENT AND KIND, AND YOU LET HER GIVE AWAY FOOD TO STRANGERS, AND C-CARE FOR PEOPLE WHEN TH-THEY'RE SICK, AND YOU LE-LE-LET HER L-L-L-OVE YOU--
--FUCK YOU.

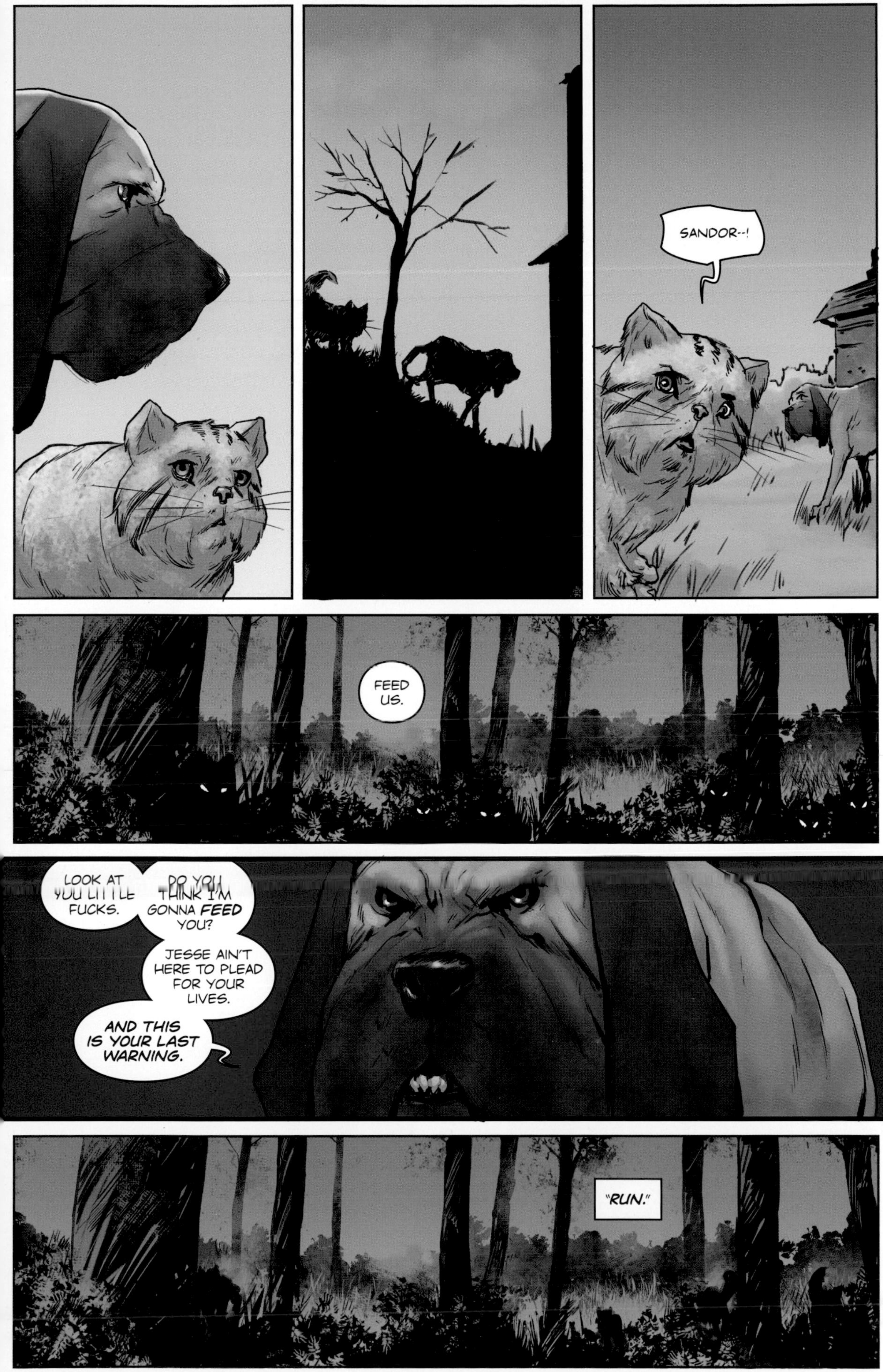
SANDOR--!
FEED US.
LOOK AT YOU LITTLE FUCKS.
DO YOU THINK I'M GONNA FEED YOU?
JESSE AIN'T HERE TO PLEAD FOR YOUR LIVES.
AND THIS IS YOUR LAST WARNING.
"RUN."

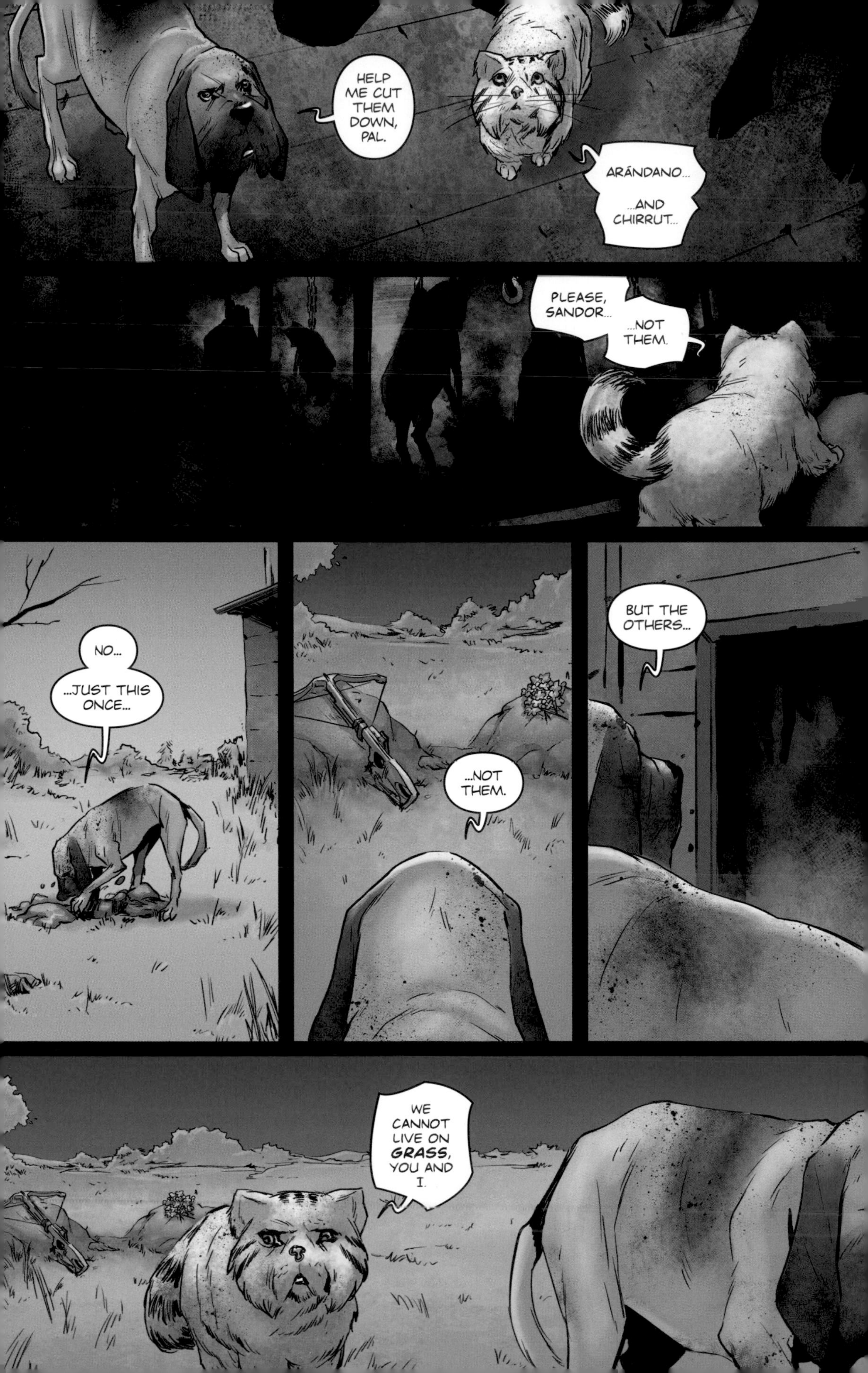
HELP ME CUT THEM DOWN, PAL.
ARÁNDANO...
...AND CHIRRUT...
PLEASE, SANDOR...
...NOT THEM.
NO...
...JUST THIS ONCE...
...NOT THEM.
BUT THE OTHERS...
WE CANNOT LIVE ON GRASS, YOU AND I.

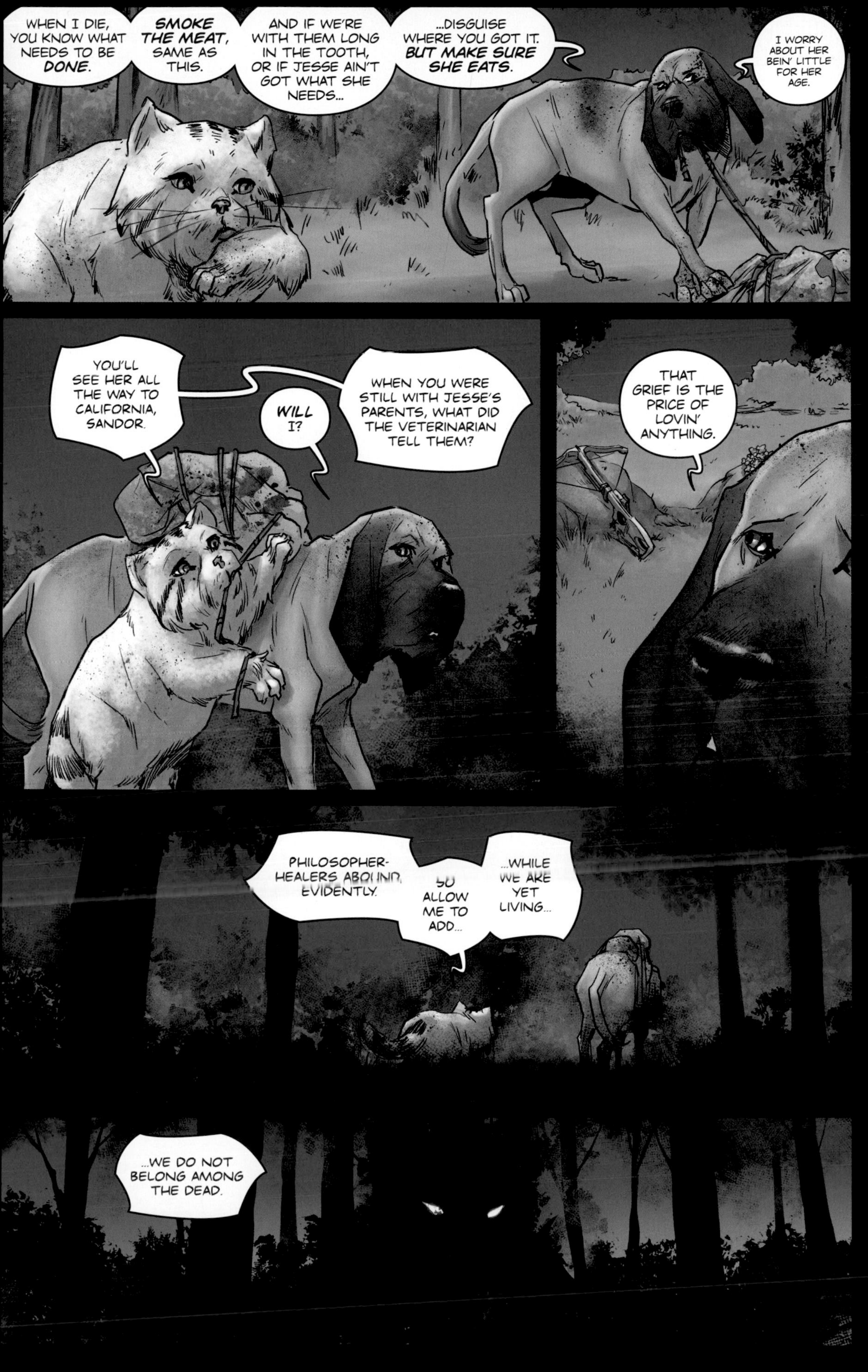
WHEN I DIE, YOU KNOW WHAT NEEDS TO BE **DONE**.
SMOKE THE MEAT, SAME AS THIS.
AND IF WE'RE WITH THEM LONG IN THE TOOTH, OR IF JESSE AIN'T GOT WHAT SHE NEEDS...
...DISGUISE WHERE YOU GOT IT. ***BUT MAKE SURE SHE EATS***.
I WORRY ABOUT HER BEIN' LITTLE FOR HER AGE.
YOU'LL SEE HER ALL THE WAY TO CALIFORNIA, SANDOR.
WILL I?
WHEN YOU WERE STILL WITH JESSE'S PARENTS, WHAT DID THE VETERINARIAN TELL THEM?
THAT GRIEF IS THE PRICE OF LOVIN' ANYTHING.
PHILOSOPHER-HEALERS ABOUND, EVIDENTLY.
SO ALLOW ME TO ADD...
...WHILE WE ARE YET LIVING...
...WE DO NOT BELONG AMONG THE DEAD.

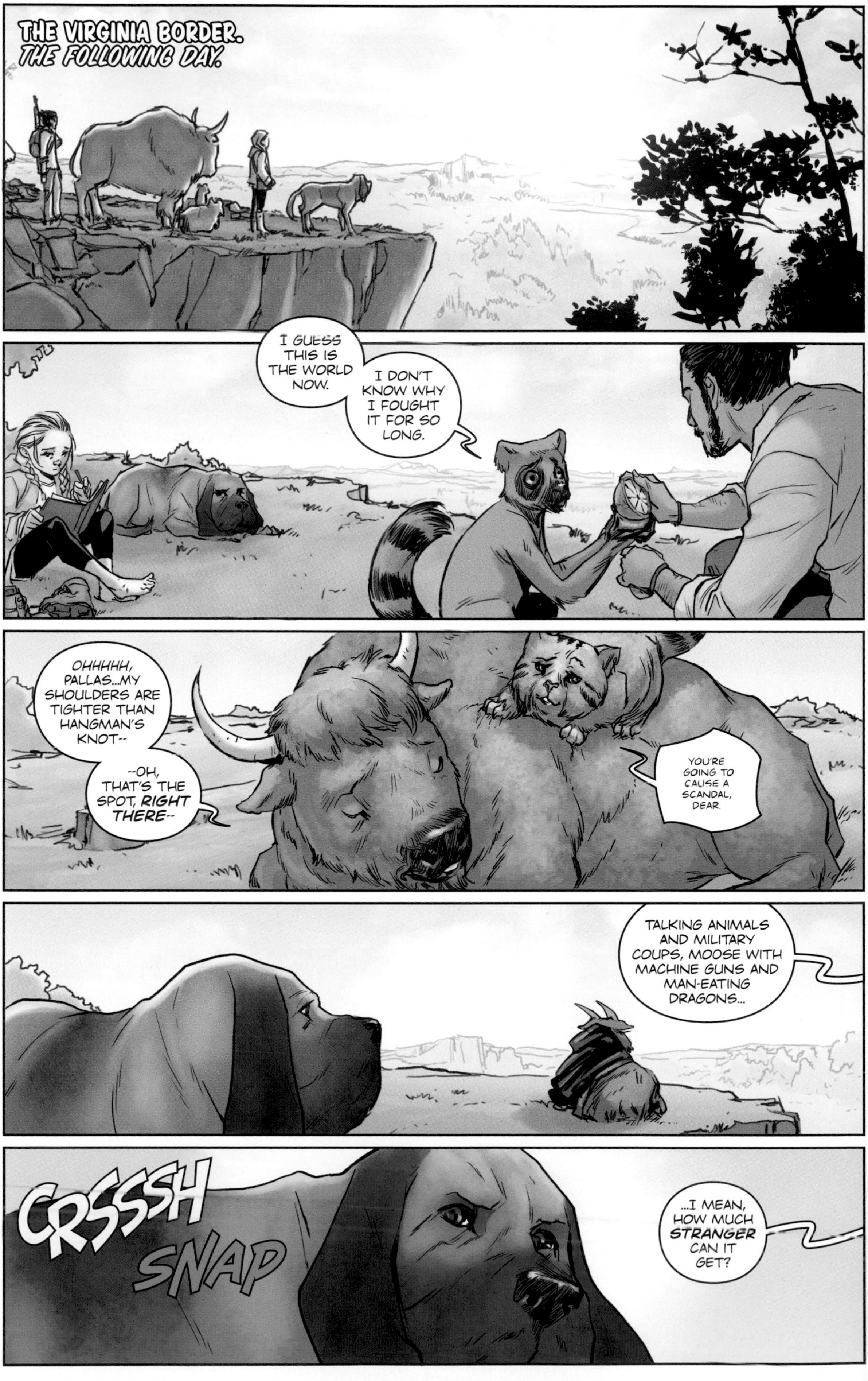
THE VIRGINIA BORDER.
THE FOLLOWING DAY.
I GUESS THIS IS THE WORLD NOW.
I DON'T KNOW WHY I FOUGHT IT FOR SO LONG.
OHHHHH, PALLAS...MY SHOULDERS ARE TIGHTER THAN HANGMAN'S KNOT--
--OH, THAT'S THE SPOT, RIGHT THERE--
YOU'RE GOING TO CAUSE A SCANDAL, DEAR.
TALKING ANIMALS AND MILITARY COUPS, MOOSE WITH MACHINE GUNS AND MAN-EATING DRAGONS...
CRSSSH
SNAP
...I MEAN, HOW MUCH STRANGER CAN IT GET?

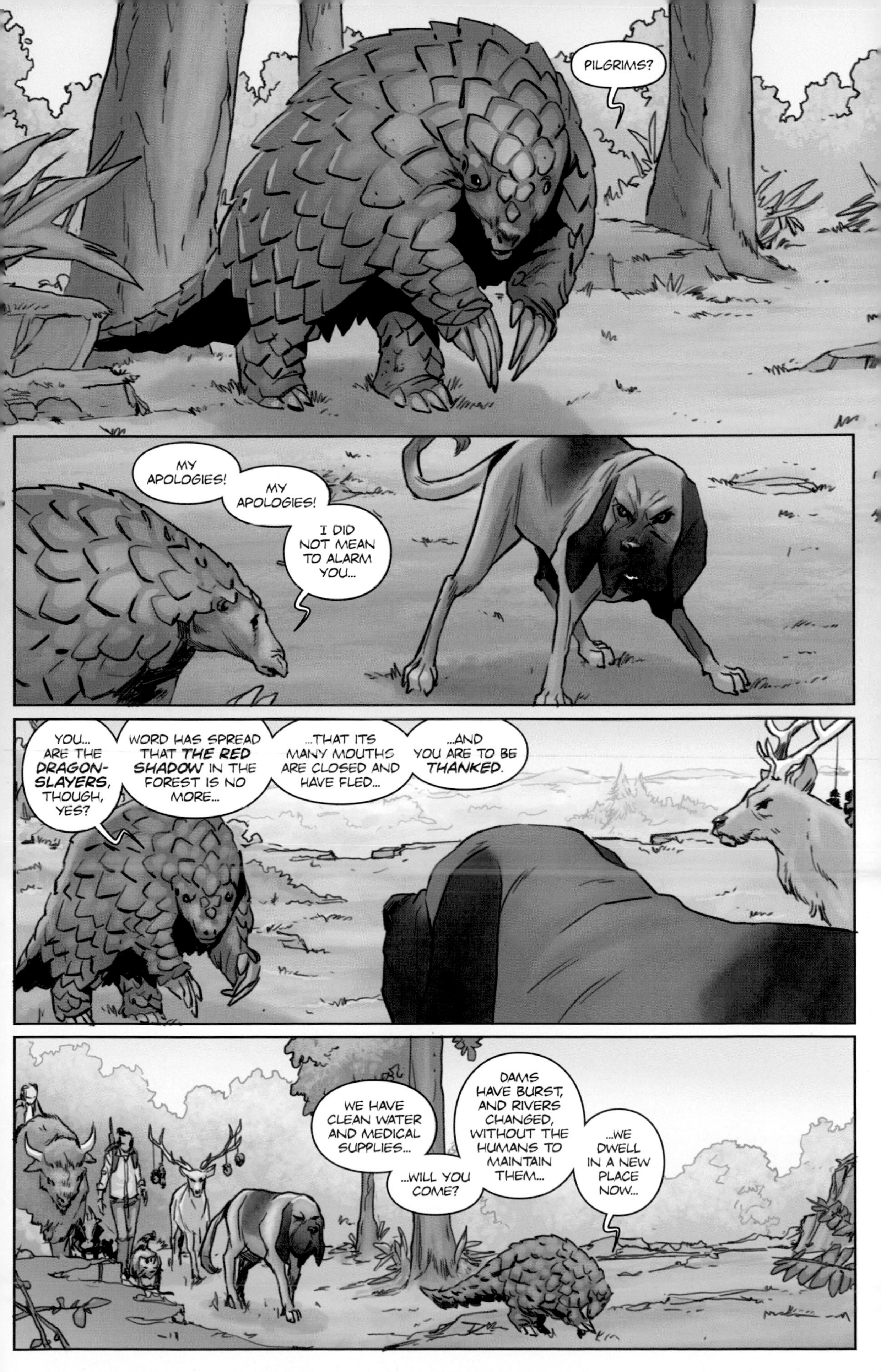
PILGRIMS?
MY APOLOGIES!
MY APOLOGIES!
I DID NOT MEAN TO ALARM YOU...
YOU... ARE THE DRAGON-SLAYERS, THOUGH, YES?
WORD HAS SPREAD THAT THE RED SHADOW IN THE FOREST IS NO MORE...
...THAT ITS MANY MOUTHS ARE CLOSED AND HAVE FLED...
...AND YOU ARE TO BE THANKED.
WE HAVE CLEAN WATER AND MEDICAL SUPPLIES...
...WILL YOU COME?
DAMS HAVE BURST, AND RIVERS CHANGED, WITHOUT THE HUMANS TO MAINTAIN THEM...
...WE DWELL IN A NEW PLACE NOW...

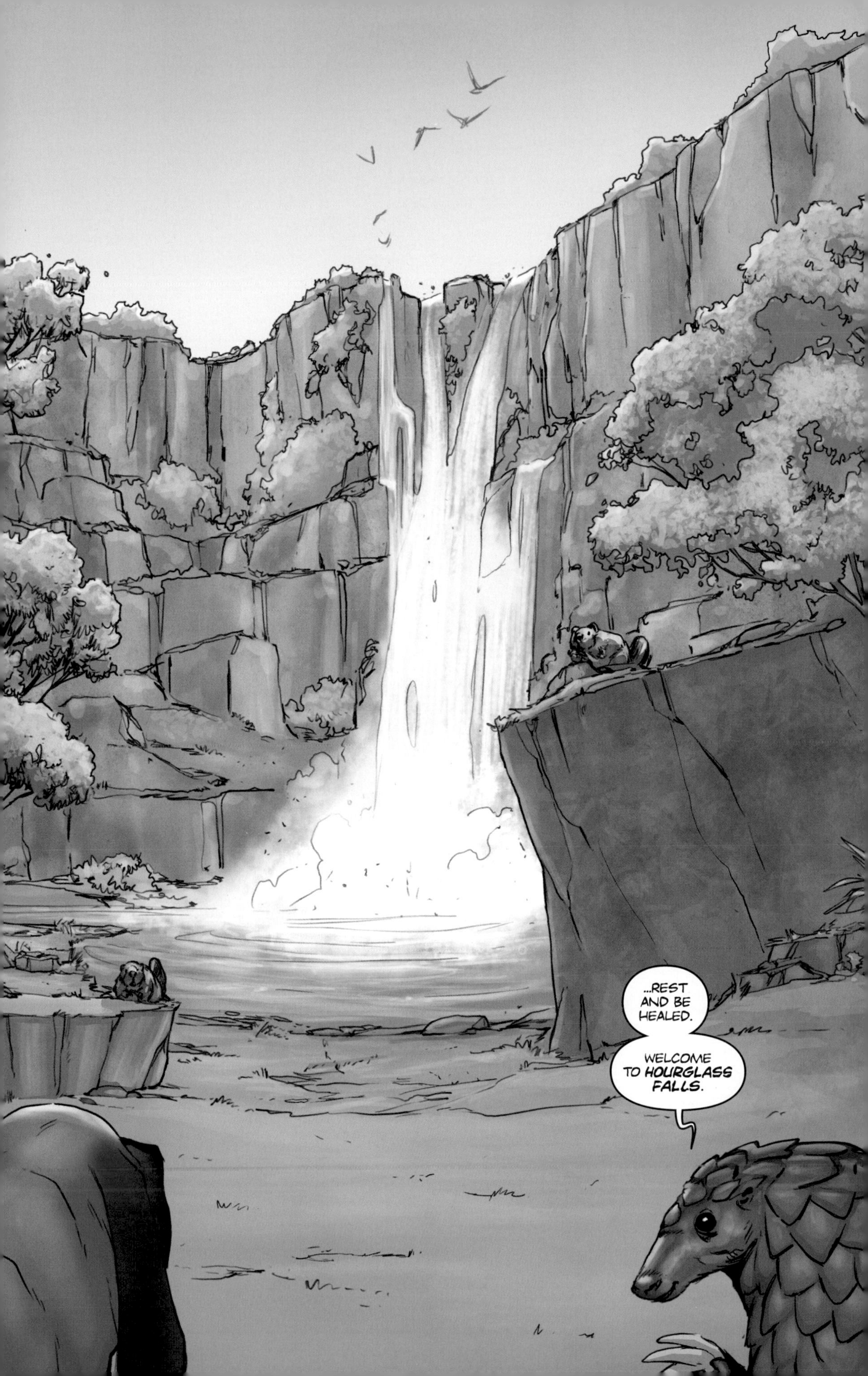
...REST AND BE HEALED.
WELCOME TO HOURGLASS FALLS.

"KINGDOM OF GOD"

8

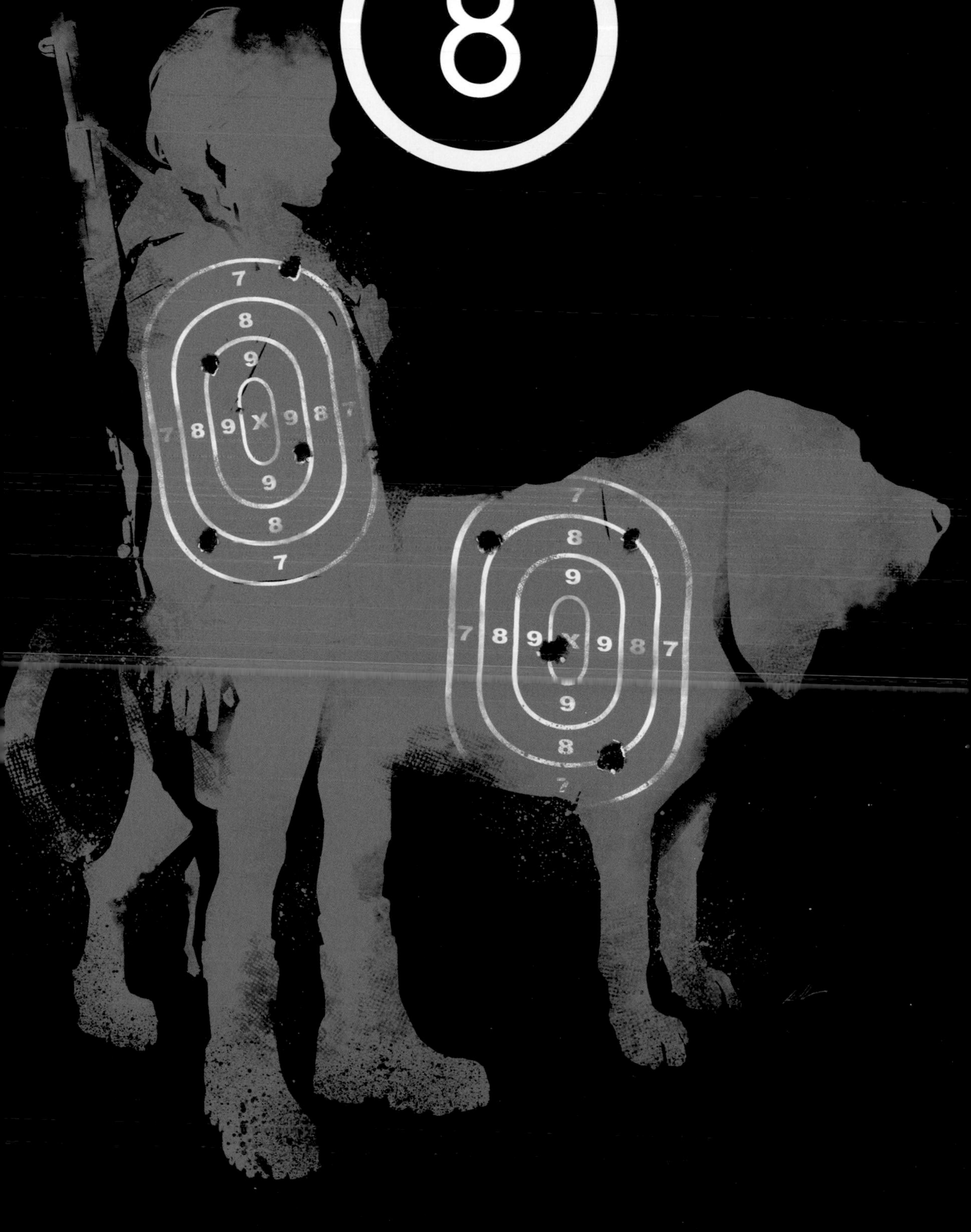
7
8
9
7 8 9 X 9 8 7
9
8
7
7
8
9
7 8 9 X 9 8 7
9
8
7

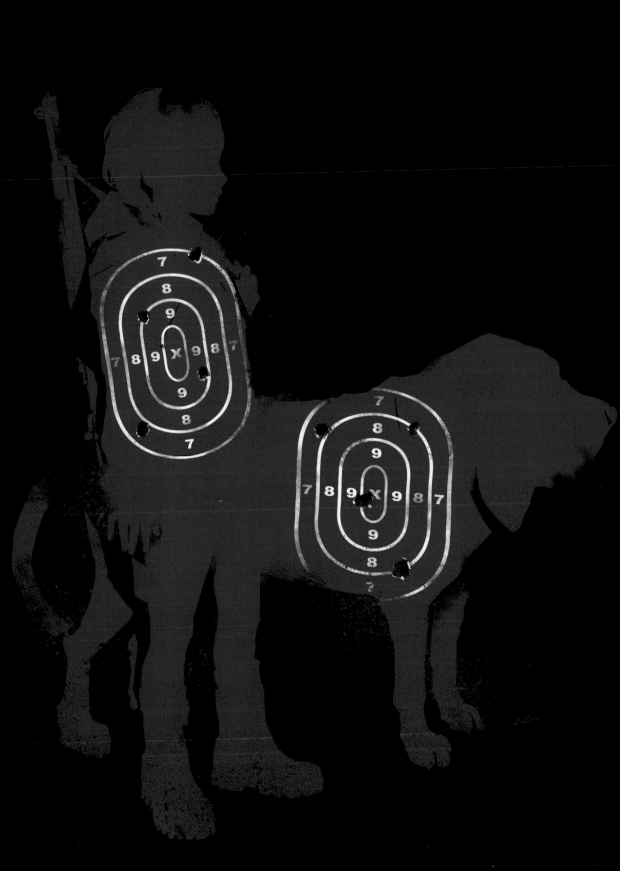

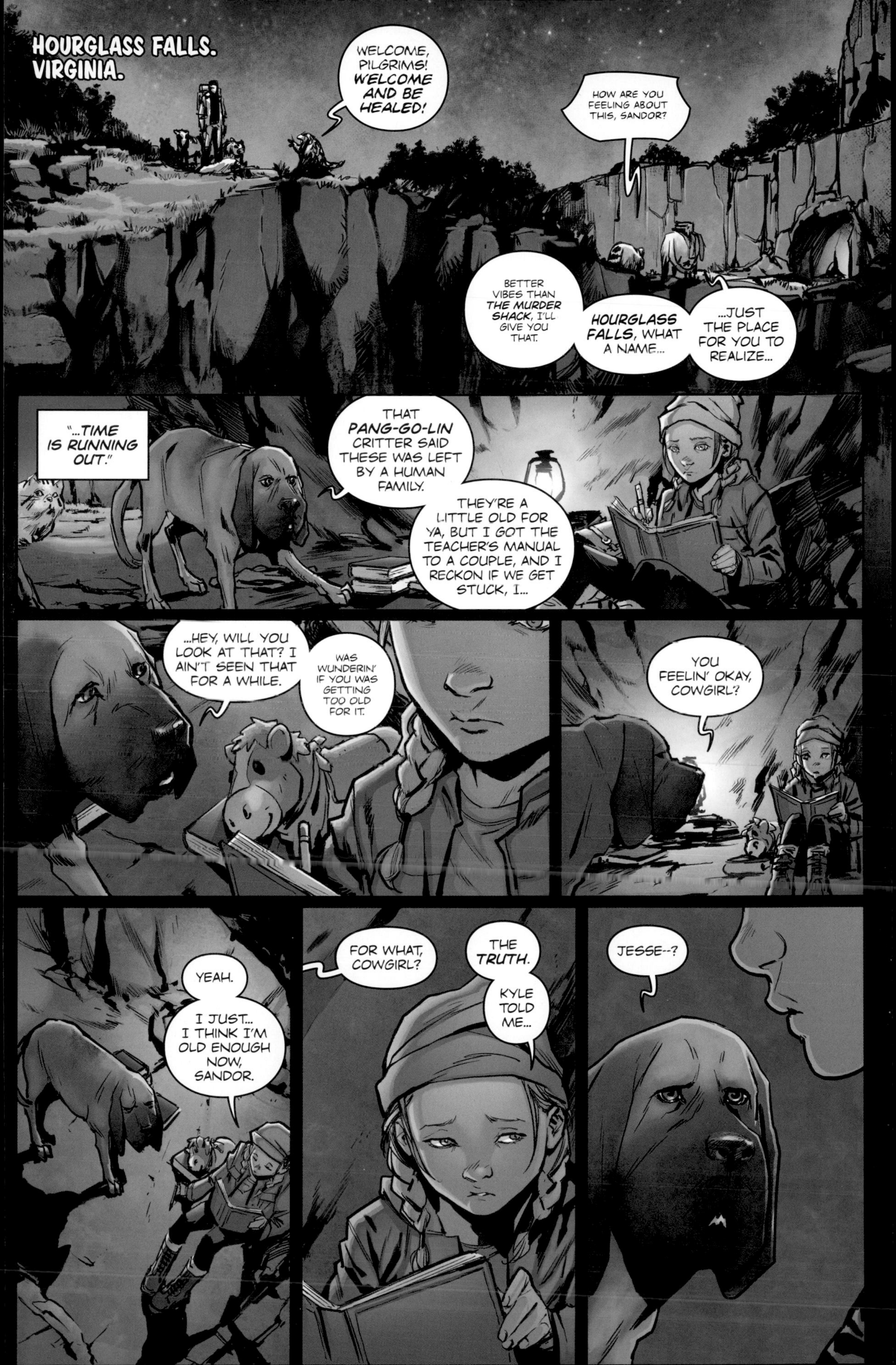
HOURGLASS FALLS. VIRGINIA.
WELCOME, PILGRIMS! WELCOME AND BE HEALED!
HOW ARE YOU FEELING ABOUT THIS, SANDOR?
BETTER VIBES THAN THE MURDER SHACK, I'LL GIVE YOU THAT.
HOURGLASS FALLS, WHAT A NAME...
...JUST THE PLACE FOR YOU TO REALIZE...
"...TIME IS RUNNING OUT."
THAT PANG-GO-LIN CRITTER SAID THESE WAS LEFT BY A HUMAN FAMILY.
THEY'RE A LITTLE OLD FOR YA, BUT I GOT THE TEACHER'S MANUAL TO A COUPLE, AND I RECKON IF WE GET STUCK, I...
...HEY, WILL YOU LOOK AT THAT? I AIN'T SEEN THAT FOR A WHILE.
WAS WUNDERIN' IF YOU WAS GETTING TOO OLD FOR IT.
YOU FEELIN' OKAY, COWGIRL?
YEAH.
I JUST... I THINK I'M OLD ENOUGH NOW, SANDOR.
FOR WHAT, COWGIRL?
THE TRUTH.
KYLE TOLD ME...
JESSE--?

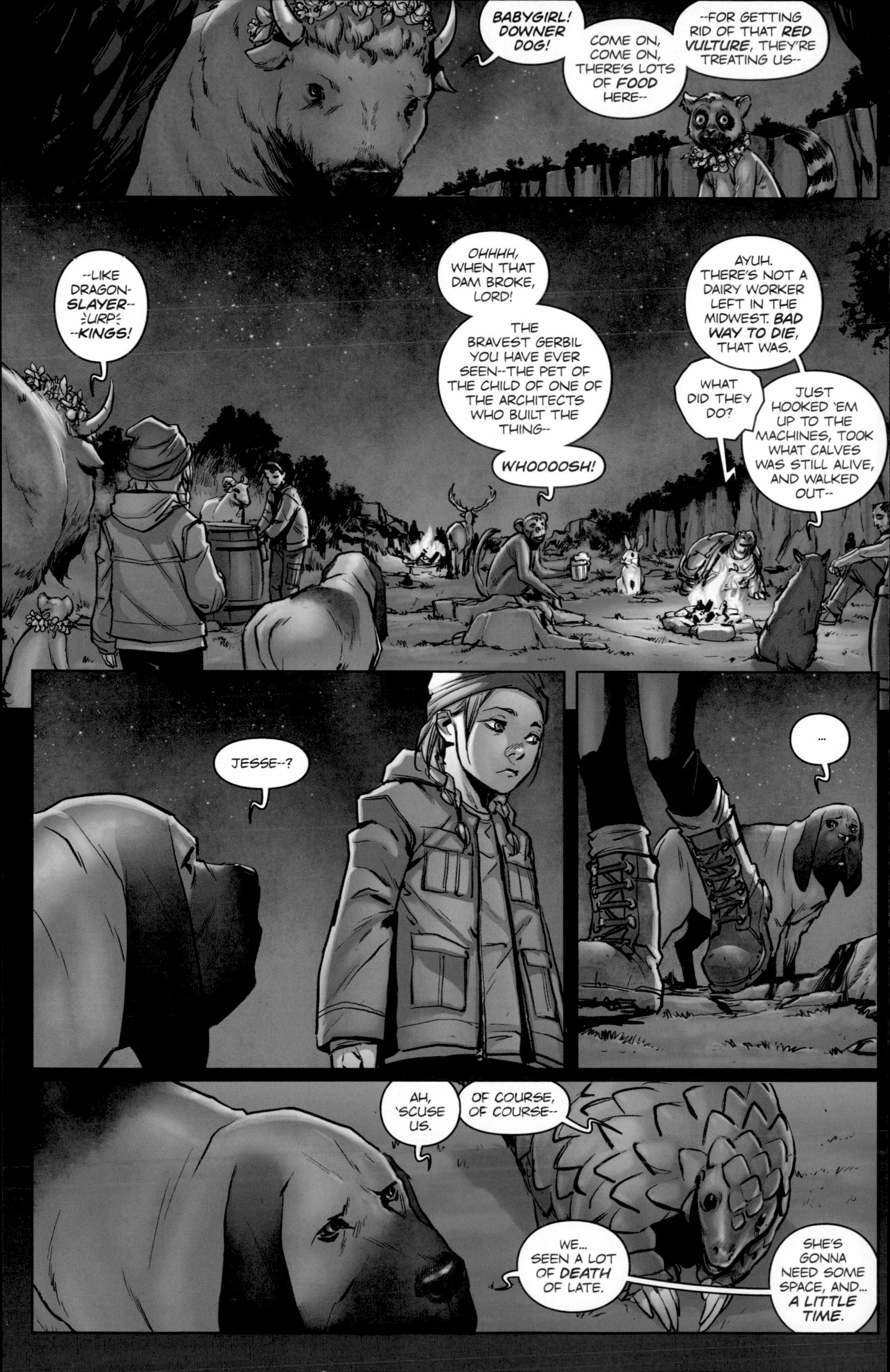
BABYGIRL! DOWNER DOG!
COME ON, COME ON, THERE'S LOTS OF FOOD HERE--
--FOR GETTING RID OF THAT RED VULTURE, THEY'RE TREATING US--
--LIKE DRAGON-SLAYER-- URP --KINGS!
OHHHH, WHEN THAT DAM BROKE, LORD!
THE BRAVEST GERBIL YOU HAVE EVER SEEN--THE PET OF THE CHILD OF ONE OF THE ARCHITECTS WHO BUILT THE THING--
WHOOOOSH!
AYUH. THERE'S NOT A DAIRY WORKER LEFT IN THE MIDWEST. BAD WAY TO DIE, THAT WAS.
WHAT DID THEY DO?
JUST HOOKED 'EM UP TO THE MACHINES, TOOK WHAT CALVES WAS STILL ALIVE, AND WALKED OUT--
JESSE--?
...
AH, 'SCUSE US.
OF COURSE, OF COURSE--
WE... SEEN A LOT OF DEATH OF LATE.
SHE'S GONNA NEED SOME SPACE, AND... A LITTLE TIME.

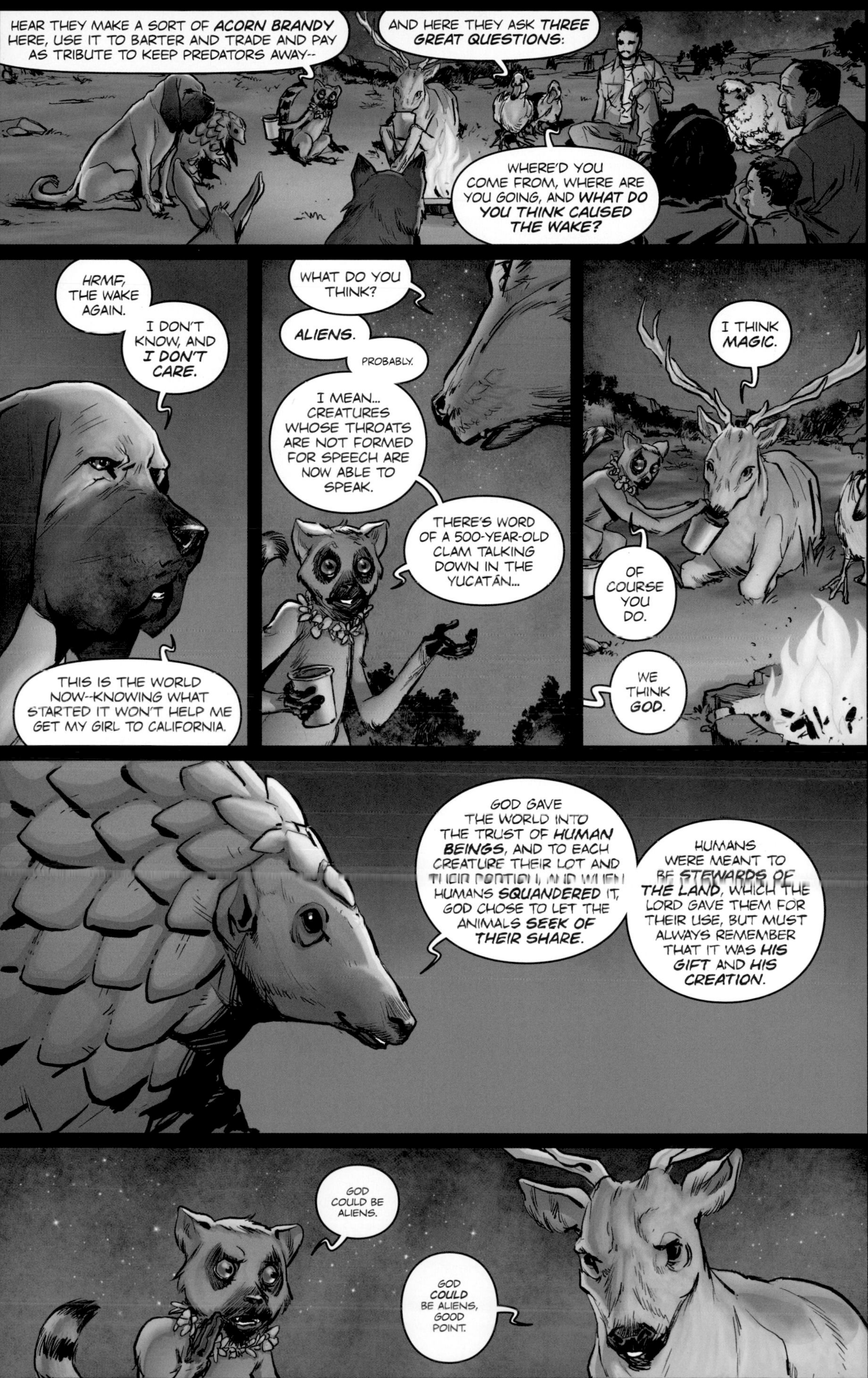
HEAR THEY MAKE A SORT OF ACORN BRANDY HERE, USE IT TO BARTER AND TRADE AND PAY AS TRIBUTE TO KEEP PREDATORS AWAY--
AND HERE THEY ASK THREE GREAT QUESTIONS:
WHERE'D YOU COME FROM, WHERE ARE YOU GOING, AND WHAT DO YOU THINK CAUSED THE WAKE?
HRMF, THE WAKE AGAIN.
I DON'T KNOW, AND I DON'T CARE.
THIS IS THE WORLD NOW--KNOWING WHAT STARTED IT WON'T HELP ME GET MY GIRL TO CALIFORNIA.
WHAT DO YOU THINK?
ALIENS.
PROBABLY.
I MEAN... CREATURES WHOSE THROATS ARE NOT FORMED FOR SPEECH ARE NOW ABLE TO SPEAK.
THERE'S WORD OF A 500-YEAR-OLD CLAM TALKING DOWN IN THE YUCATÁN...
I THINK MAGIC.
OF COURSE YOU DO.
WE THINK GOD.
GOD GAVE THE WORLD INTO THE TRUST OF HUMAN BEINGS, AND TO EACH CREATURE THEIR LOT AND THEIR PORTION, AND WHEN HUMANS SQUANDERED IT, GOD CHOSE TO LET THE ANIMALS SEEK OF THEIR SHARE.
HUMANS WERE MEANT TO BE STEWARDS OF THE LAND, WHICH THE LORD GAVE THEM FOR THEIR USE, BUT MUST ALWAYS REMEMBER THAT IT WAS HIS GIFT AND HIS CREATION.
GOD COULD BE ALIENS.
GOD COULD BE ALIENS, GOOD POINT.

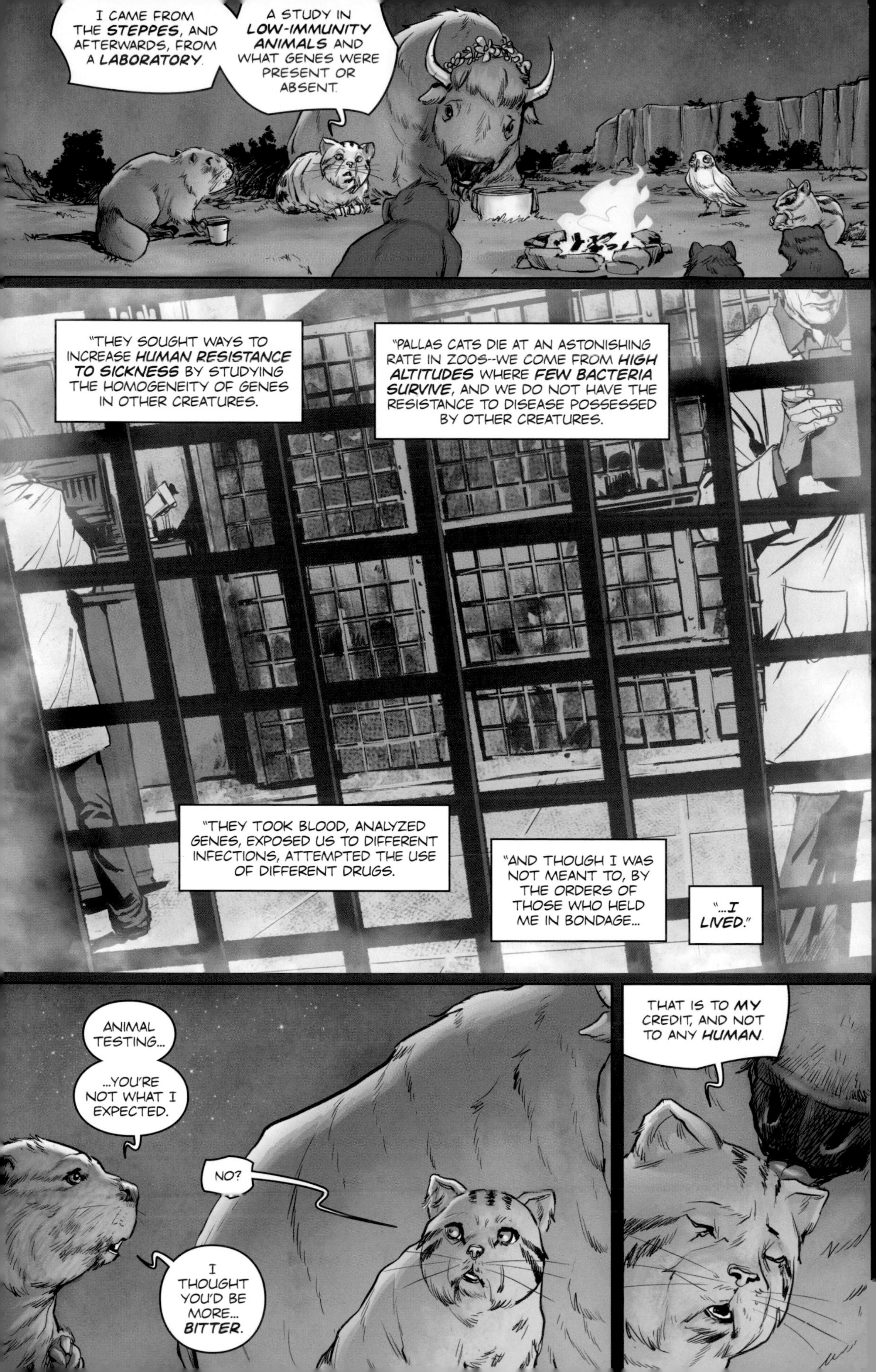
I CAME FROM THE STEPPES, AND AFTERWARDS, FROM A LABORATORY.
A STUDY IN LOW-IMMUNITY ANIMALS AND WHAT GENES WERE PRESENT OR ABSENT.
"THEY SOUGHT WAYS TO INCREASE HUMAN RESISTANCE TO SICKNESS BY STUDYING THE HOMOGENEITY OF GENES IN OTHER CREATURES.
"PALLAS CATS DIE AT AN ASTONISHING RATE IN ZOOS--WE COME FROM HIGH ALTITUDES WHERE FEW BACTERIA SURVIVE, AND WE DO NOT HAVE THE RESISTANCE TO DISEASE POSSESSED BY OTHER CREATURES.
"THEY TOOK BLOOD, ANALYZED GENES, EXPOSED US TO DIFFERENT INFECTIONS, ATTEMPTED THE USE OF DIFFERENT DRUGS.
"AND THOUGH I WAS NOT MEANT TO, BY THE ORDERS OF THOSE WHO HELD ME IN BONDAGE...
"...I LIVED."
ANIMAL TESTING...
...YOU'RE NOT WHAT I EXPECTED.
NO?
I THOUGHT YOU'D BE MORE... BITTER.
THAT IS TO MY CREDIT, AND NOT TO ANY HUMAN.

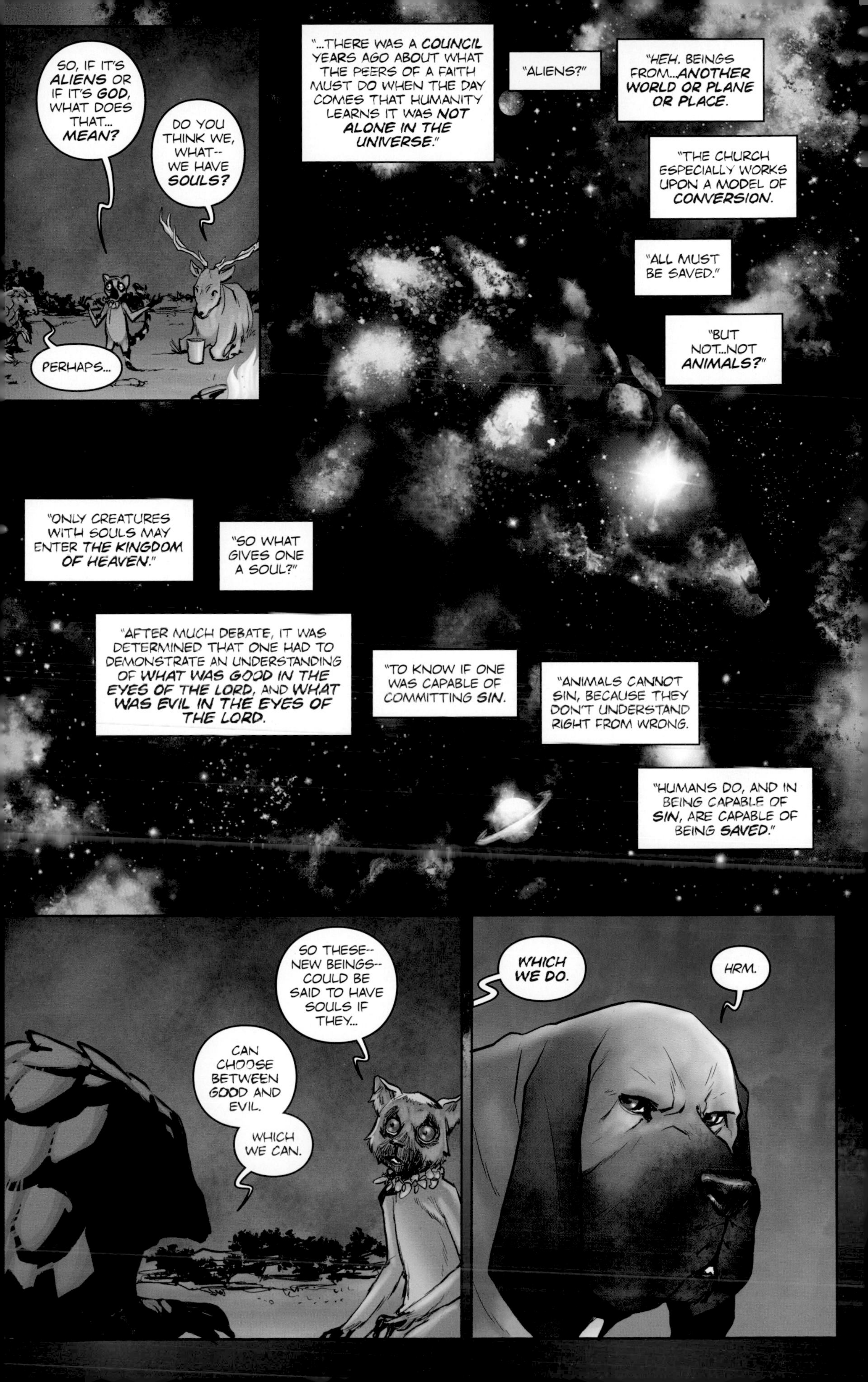

SO, IF IT'S ALIENS OR IF IT'S GOD, WHAT DOES THAT... MEAN?
DO YOU THINK WE, WHAT-- WE HAVE SOULS?
PERHAPS...
"...THERE WAS A COUNCIL YEARS AGO ABOUT WHAT THE PEERS OF A FAITH MUST DO WHEN THE DAY COMES THAT HUMANITY LEARNS IT WAS NOT ALONE IN THE UNIVERSE."
"ALIENS?"
"HEH. BEINGS FROM...ANOTHER WORLD OR PLANE OR PLACE.
"THE CHURCH ESPECIALLY WORKS UPON A MODEL OF CONVERSION.
"ALL MUST BE SAVED."
"BUT NOT...NOT ANIMALS?"
"ONLY CREATURES WITH SOULS MAY ENTER THE KINGDOM OF HEAVEN."
"SO WHAT GIVES ONE A SOUL?"
"AFTER MUCH DEBATE, IT WAS DETERMINED THAT ONE HAD TO DEMONSTRATE AN UNDERSTANDING OF WHAT WAS GOOD IN THE EYES OF THE LORD, AND WHAT WAS EVIL IN THE EYES OF THE LORD.
"TO KNOW IF ONE WAS CAPABLE OF COMMITTING SIN.
"ANIMALS CANNOT SIN, BECAUSE THEY DON'T UNDERSTAND RIGHT FROM WRONG.
"HUMANS DO, AND IN BEING CAPABLE OF SIN, ARE CAPABLE OF BEING SAVED."
SO THESE-- NEW BEINGS-- COULD BE SAID TO HAVE SOULS IF THEY...
CAN CHOOSE BETWEEN GOOD AND EVIL.
WHICH WE CAN.
WHICH WE DO.
HRM.

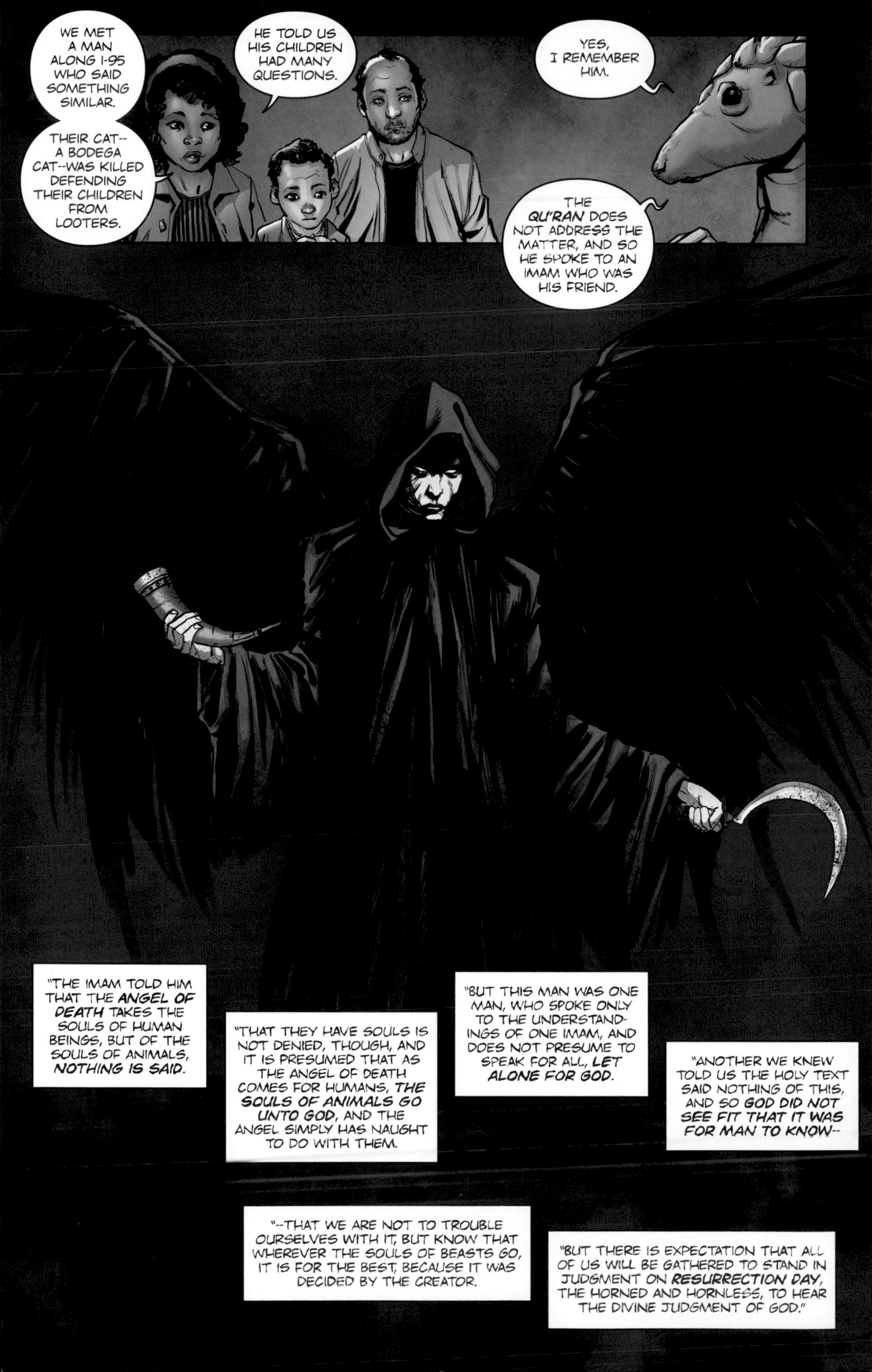

WE MET A MAN ALONG I-95 WHO SAID SOMETHING SIMILAR.
THEIR CAT-- A BODEGA CAT--WAS KILLED DEFENDING THEIR CHILDREN FROM LOOTERS.
HE TOLD US HIS CHILDREN HAD MANY QUESTIONS.
YES, I REMEMBER HIM.
THE QU'RAN DOES NOT ADDRESS THE MATTER, AND SO HE SPOKE TO AN IMAM WHO WAS HIS FRIEND.
"THE IMAM TOLD HIM THAT THE ANGEL OF DEATH TAKES THE SOULS OF HUMAN BEINGS, BUT OF THE SOULS OF ANIMALS, NOTHING IS SAID.
"THAT THEY HAVE SOULS IS NOT DENIED, THOUGH, AND IT IS PRESUMED THAT AS THE ANGEL OF DEATH COMES FOR HUMANS, THE SOULS OF ANIMALS GO UNTO GOD, AND THE ANGEL SIMPLY HAS NAUGHT TO DO WITH THEM.
"BUT THIS MAN WAS ONE MAN, WHO SPOKE ONLY TO THE UNDERSTANDINGS OF ONE IMAM, AND DOES NOT PRESUME TO SPEAK FOR ALL, LET ALONE FOR GOD.
"ANOTHER WE KNEW TOLD US THE HOLY TEXT SAID NOTHING OF THIS, AND SO GOD DID NOT SEE FIT THAT IT WAS FOR MAN TO KNOW--
"--THAT WE ARE NOT TO TROUBLE OURSELVES WITH IT, BUT KNOW THAT WHEREVER THE SOULS OF BEASTS GO, IT IS FOR THE BEST, BECAUSE IT WAS DECIDED BY THE CREATOR.
"BUT THERE IS EXPECTATION THAT ALL OF US WILL BE GATHERED TO STAND IN JUDGMENT ON RESURRECTION DAY, THE HORNED AND HORNLESS, TO HEAR THE DIVINE JUDGMENT OF GOD."

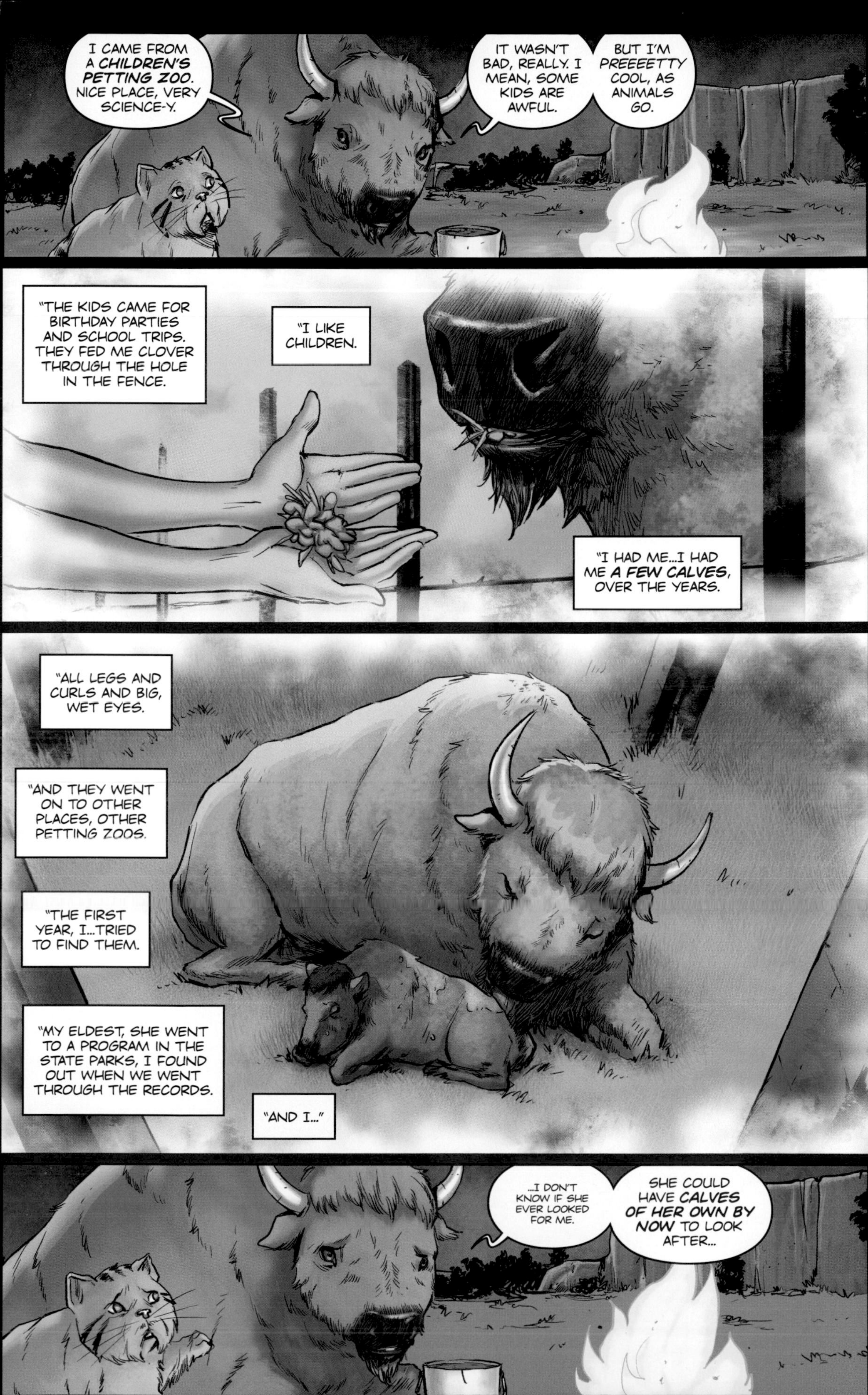
I CAME FROM A **CHILDREN'S PETTING ZOO.** NICE PLACE, VERY SCIENCE-Y.
IT WASN'T BAD, REALLY. I MEAN, SOME KIDS ARE AWFUL.
BUT I'M PREEEETTY COOL, AS ANIMALS GO.
"THE KIDS CAME FOR BIRTHDAY PARTIES AND SCHOOL TRIPS. THEY FED ME CLOVER THROUGH THE HOLE IN THE FENCE.
"I LIKE CHILDREN.
"I HAD ME...I HAD ME ***A FEW CALVES,*** OVER THE YEARS.
"ALL LEGS AND CURLS AND BIG, WET EYES.
"AND THEY WENT ON TO OTHER PLACES, OTHER PETTING ZOOS.
"THE FIRST YEAR, I...TRIED TO FIND THEM.
"MY ELDEST, SHE WENT TO A PROGRAM IN THE STATE PARKS, I FOUND OUT WHEN WE WENT THROUGH THE RECORDS.
"AND I..."
...I DON'T KNOW IF SHE EVER LOOKED FOR ME.
SHE COULD HAVE ***CALVES OF HER OWN BY NOW*** TO LOOK AFTER...

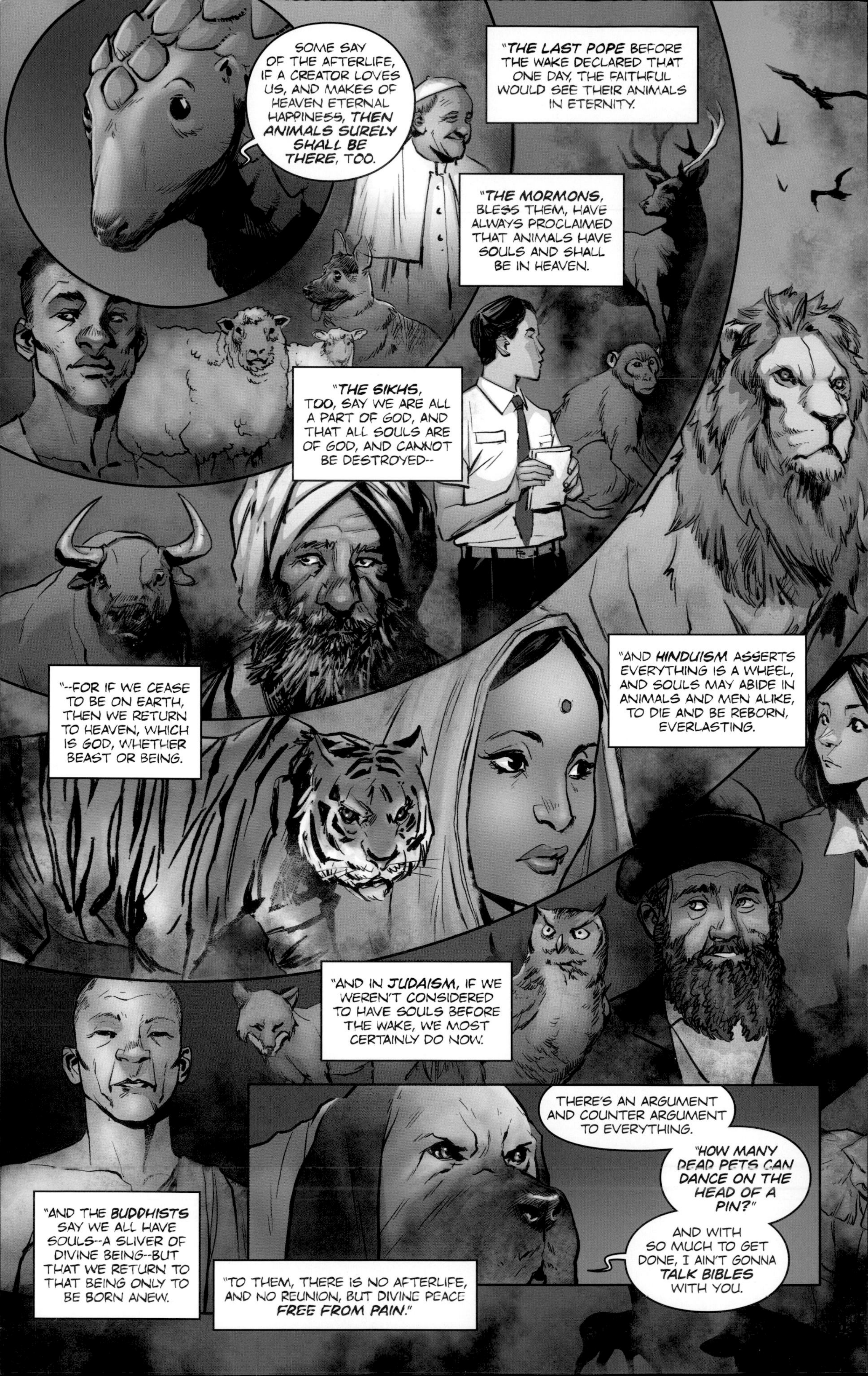

SOME SAY OF THE AFTERLIFE, IF A CREATOR LOVES US, AND MAKES OF HEAVEN ETERNAL HAPPINESS, THEN ANIMALS SURELY SHALL BE THERE, TOO.
"THE LAST POPE BEFORE THE WAKE DECLARED THAT ONE DAY, THE FAITHFUL WOULD SEE THEIR ANIMALS IN ETERNITY.
"THE MORMONS, BLESS THEM, HAVE ALWAYS PROCLAIMED THAT ANIMALS HAVE SOULS AND SHALL BE IN HEAVEN.
"THE SIKHS, TOO, SAY WE ARE ALL A PART OF GOD, AND THAT ALL SOULS ARE OF GOD, AND CANNOT BE DESTROYED--
"--FOR IF WE CEASE TO BE ON EARTH, THEN WE RETURN TO HEAVEN, WHICH IS GOD, WHETHER BEAST OR BEING.
"AND HINDUISM ASSERTS EVERYTHING IS A WHEEL, AND SOULS MAY ABIDE IN ANIMALS AND MEN ALIKE, TO DIE AND BE REBORN, EVERLASTING.
"AND IN JUDAISM, IF WE WEREN'T CONSIDERED TO HAVE SOULS BEFORE THE WAKE, WE MOST CERTAINLY DO NOW.
"AND THE BUDDHISTS SAY WE ALL HAVE SOULS--A SLIVER OF DIVINE BEING--BUT THAT WE RETURN TO THAT BEING ONLY TO BE BORN ANEW.
"TO THEM, THERE IS NO AFTERLIFE, AND NO REUNION, BUT DIVINE PEACE FREE FROM PAIN."
THERE'S AN ARGUMENT AND COUNTER ARGUMENT TO EVERYTHING.
"HOW MANY DEAD PETS CAN DANCE ON THE HEAD OF A PIN?"
AND WITH SO MUCH TO GET DONE, I AIN'T GONNA TALK BIBLES WITH YOU.

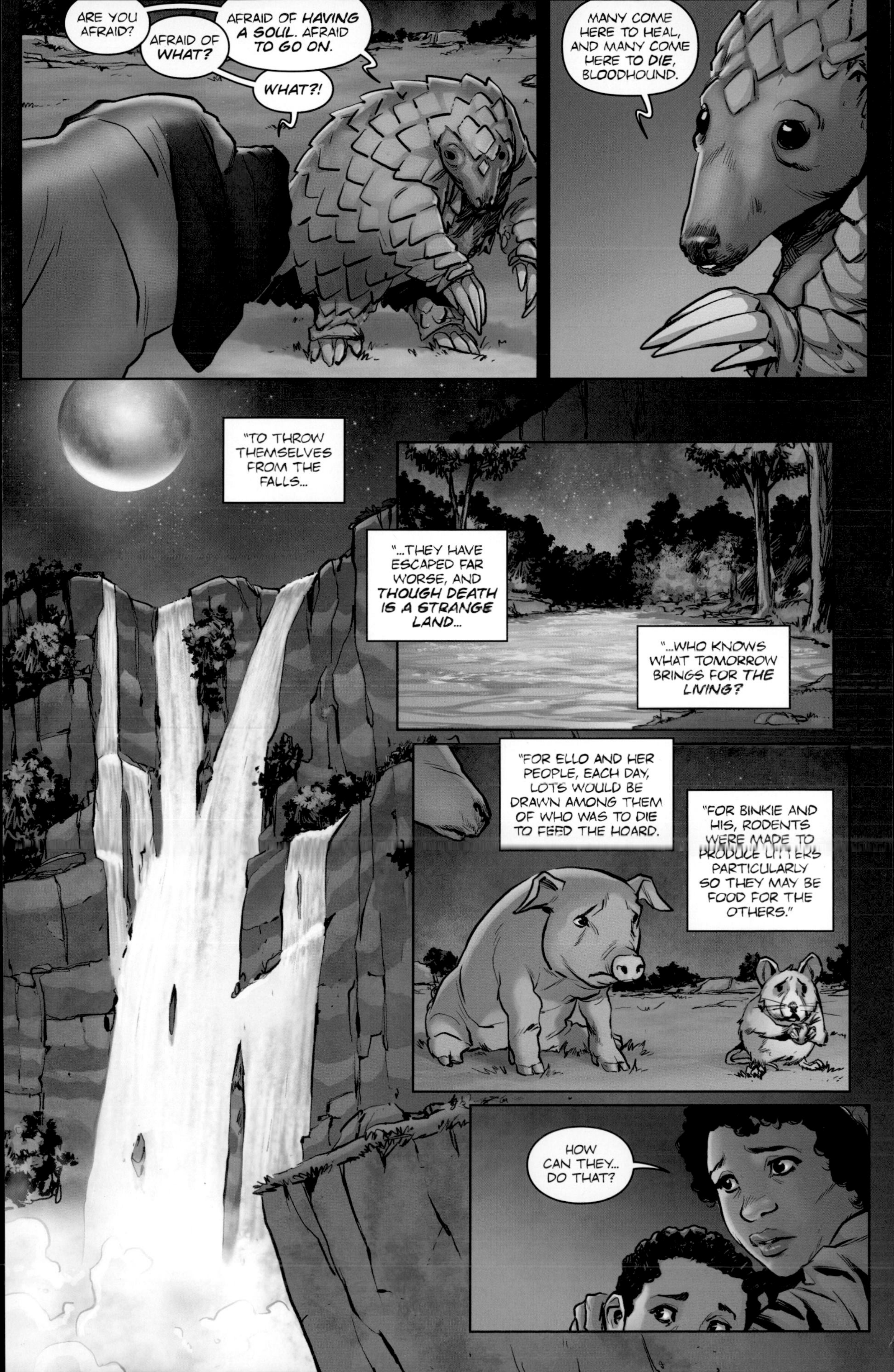
ARE YOU AFRAID?
AFRAID OF WHAT?
AFRAID OF *HAVING A SOUL*. AFRAID *TO GO ON*.
WHAT?!
MANY COME HERE TO HEAL, AND MANY COME HERE TO *DIE*, BLOODHOUND.
"TO THROW THEMSELVES FROM THE FALLS...
"...THEY HAVE ESCAPED FAR WORSE, AND *THOUGH DEATH IS A STRANGE LAND*...
"...WHO KNOWS WHAT TOMORROW BRINGS FOR *THE LIVING?*
"FOR ELLO AND HER PEOPLE, EACH DAY, LOTS WOULD BE DRAWN AMONG THEM OF WHO WAS TO DIE TO FEED THE HOARD.
"FOR BINKIE AND HIS, RODENTS WERE MADE TO PRODUCE LITTERS PARTICULARLY SO THEY MAY BE FOOD FOR THE OTHERS."
HOW CAN THEY... DO THAT?

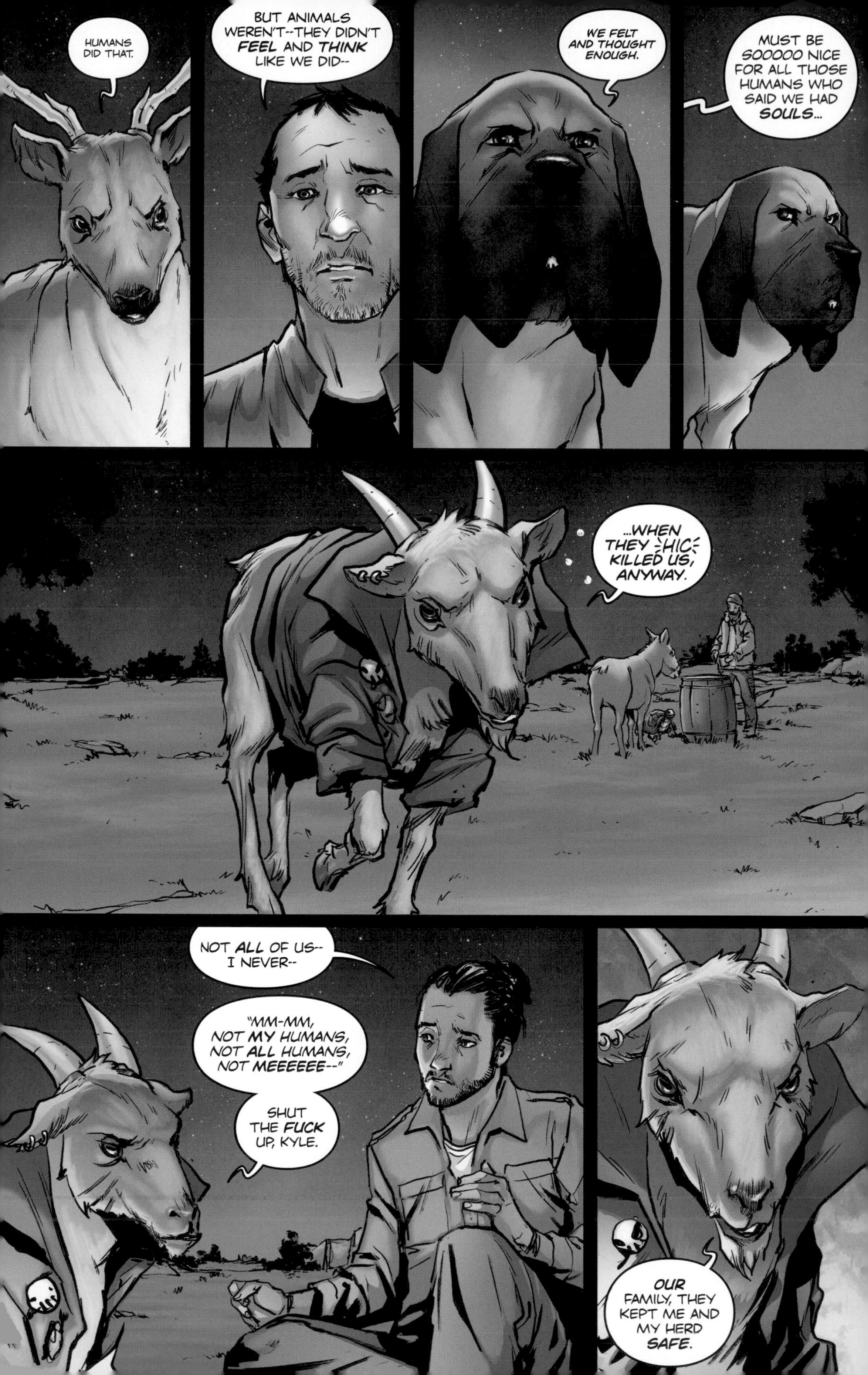
HUMANS DID THAT.
BUT ANIMALS WEREN'T--THEY DIDN'T FEEL AND THINK LIKE WE DID--
WE FELT AND THOUGHT ENOUGH.
MUST BE SOOOOOO NICE FOR ALL THOSE HUMANS WHO SAID WE HAD SOULS...
...WHEN THEY HIC KILLED US, ANYWAY.
NOT ALL OF US-- I NEVER--
"MM-MM, NOT MY HUMANS, NOT ALL HUMANS, NOT MEEEEEE--"
SHUT THE FUCK UP, KYLE.
OUR FAMILY, THEY KEPT ME AND MY HERD SAFE.

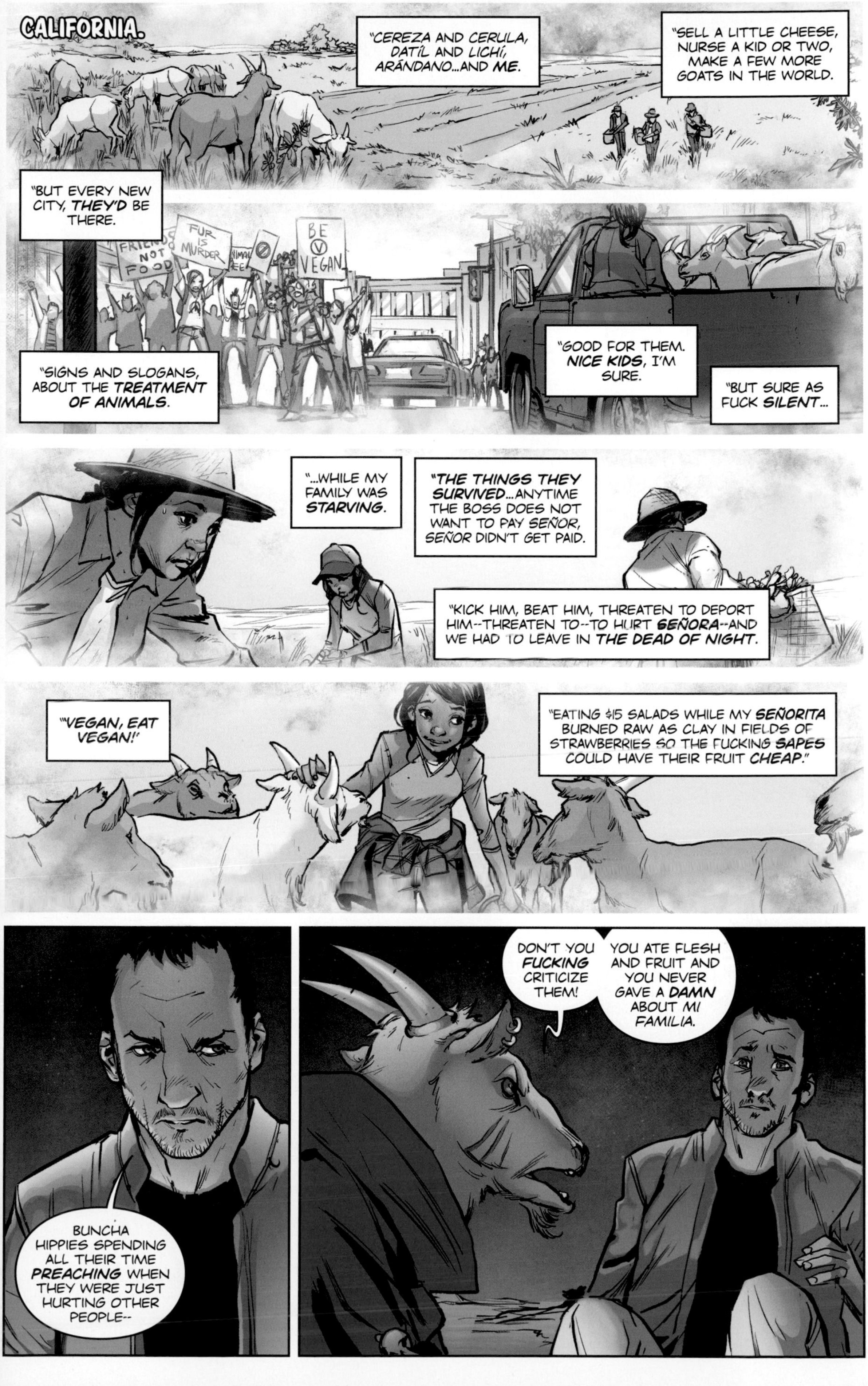
CALIFORNIA.
"CEREZA AND CERULA, DATÍL AND LICHÍ, ARÁNDANO...AND ME.
"SELL A LITTLE CHEESE, NURSE A KID OR TWO, MAKE A FEW MORE GOATS IN THE WORLD.
"BUT EVERY NEW CITY, THEY'D BE THERE.
FRIENDS NOT FOOD
FUR IS MURDER
BE V VEGAN
"SIGNS AND SLOGANS, ABOUT THE TREATMENT OF ANIMALS.
"GOOD FOR THEM. NICE KIDS, I'M SURE.
"BUT SURE AS FUCK SILENT...
"...WHILE MY FAMILY WAS STARVING.
"THE THINGS THEY SURVIVED...ANYTIME THE BOSS DOES NOT WANT TO PAY SEÑOR, SEÑOR DIDN'T GET PAID.
"KICK HIM, BEAT HIM, THREATEN TO DEPORT HIM--THREATEN TO--TO HURT SEÑORA--AND WE HAD TO LEAVE IN THE DEAD OF NIGHT.
"'VEGAN, EAT VEGAN!'
"EATING $15 SALADS WHILE MY SEÑORITA BURNED RAW AS CLAY IN FIELDS OF STRAWBERRIES SO THE FUCKING SAPES COULD HAVE THEIR FRUIT CHEAP."
BUNCHA HIPPIES SPENDING ALL THEIR TIME PREACHING WHEN THEY WERE JUST HURTING OTHER PEOPLE--
DON'T YOU FUCKING CRITICIZE THEM!
YOU ATE FLESH AND FRUIT AND YOU NEVER GAVE A DAMN ABOUT MI FAMILIA.

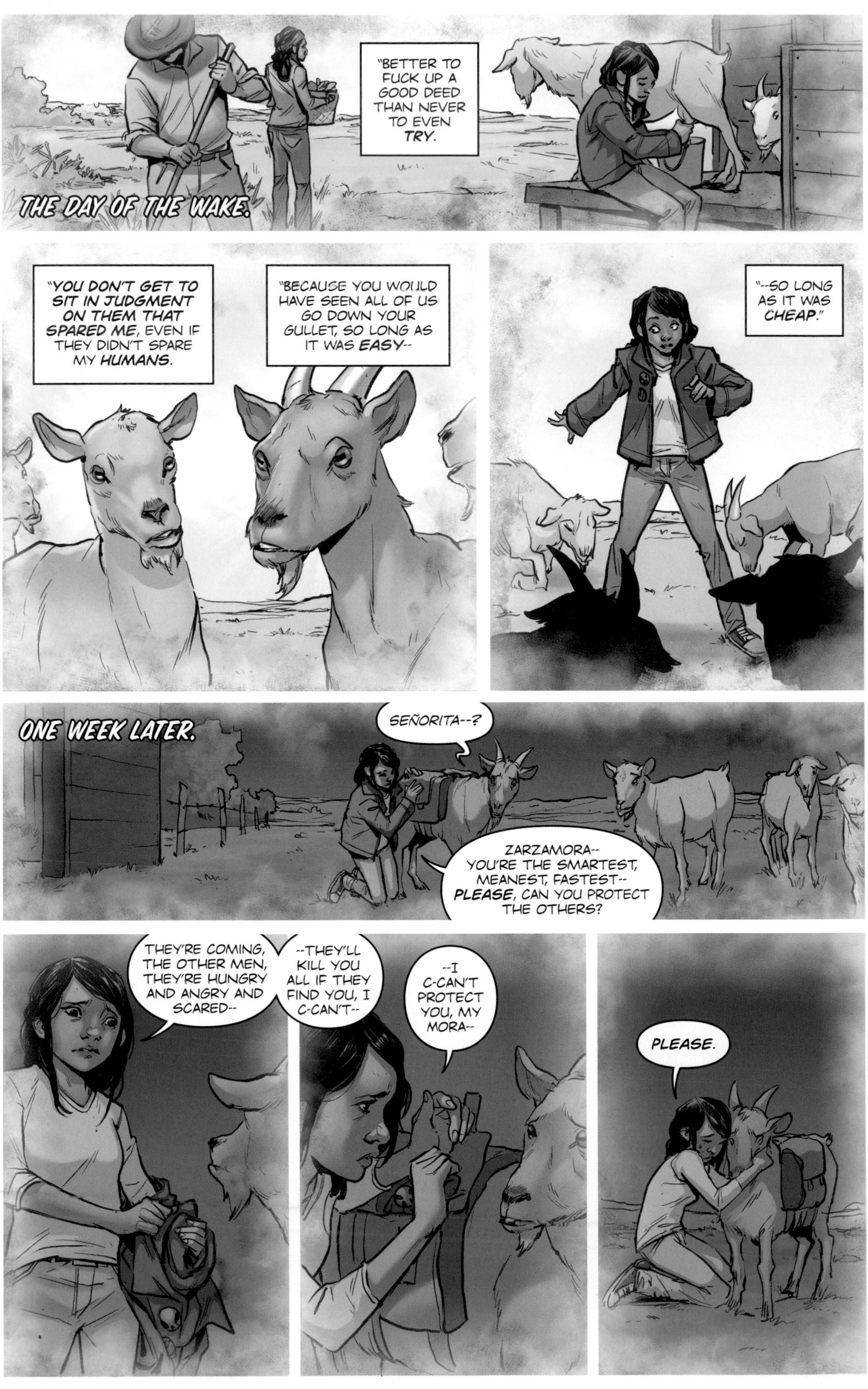
"BETTER TO FUCK UP A GOOD DEED THAN NEVER TO EVEN TRY.
THE DAY OF THE WAKE.
"YOU DON'T GET TO SIT IN JUDGMENT ON THEM THAT SPARED ME, EVEN IF THEY DIDN'T SPARE MY HUMANS.
"BECAUSE YOU WOULD HAVE SEEN ALL OF US GO DOWN YOUR GULLET, SO LONG AS IT WAS EASY--
"--SO LONG AS IT WAS CHEAP."
ONE WEEK LATER.
SEÑORITA--?
ZARZAMORA-- YOU'RE THE SMARTEST, MEANEST, FASTEST-- PLEASE, CAN YOU PROTECT THE OTHERS?
THEY'RE COMING, THE OTHER MEN, THEY'RE HUNGRY AND ANGRY AND SCARED--
--THEY'LL KILL YOU ALL IF THEY FIND YOU, I C-CAN'T--
--I C-CAN'T PROTECT YOU, MY MORA--
PLEASE.

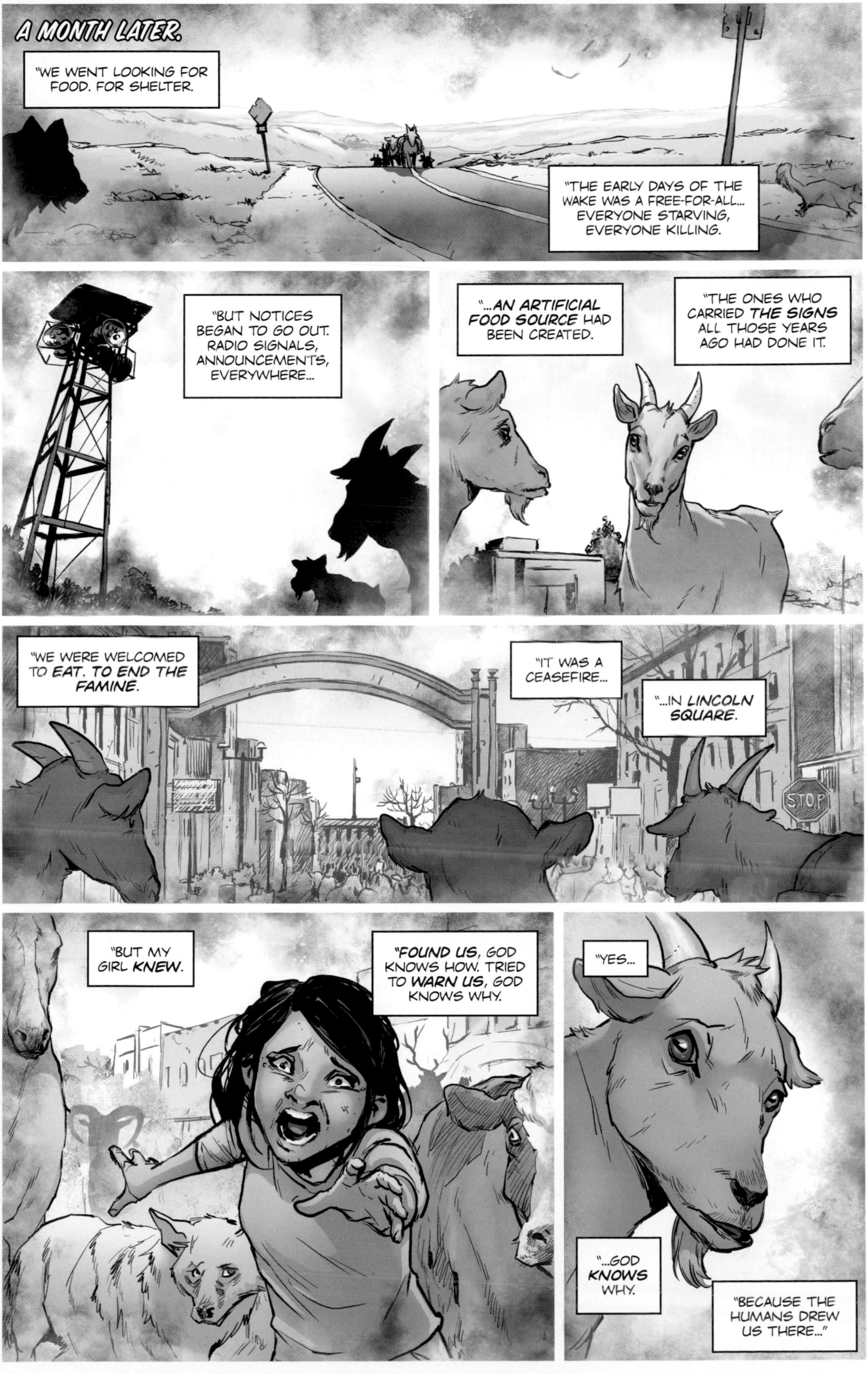
A MONTH LATER.
"WE WENT LOOKING FOR FOOD. FOR SHELTER.
"THE EARLY DAYS OF THE WAKE WAS A FREE-FOR-ALL... EVERYONE STARVING, EVERYONE KILLING.
"BUT NOTICES BEGAN TO GO OUT. RADIO SIGNALS, ANNOUNCEMENTS, EVERYWHERE...
"...AN ARTIFICIAL FOOD SOURCE HAD BEEN CREATED.
"THE ONES WHO CARRIED THE SIGNS ALL THOSE YEARS AGO HAD DONE IT.
"WE WERE WELCOMED TO EAT. TO END THE FAMINE.
"IT WAS A CEASEFIRE...
"...IN LINCOLN SQUARE.
STOP
"BUT MY GIRL KNEW.
"FOUND US, GOD KNOWS HOW. TRIED TO WARN US, GOD KNOWS WHY.
"YES...
"...GOD KNOWS WHY.
"BECAUSE THE HUMANS DREW US THERE..."

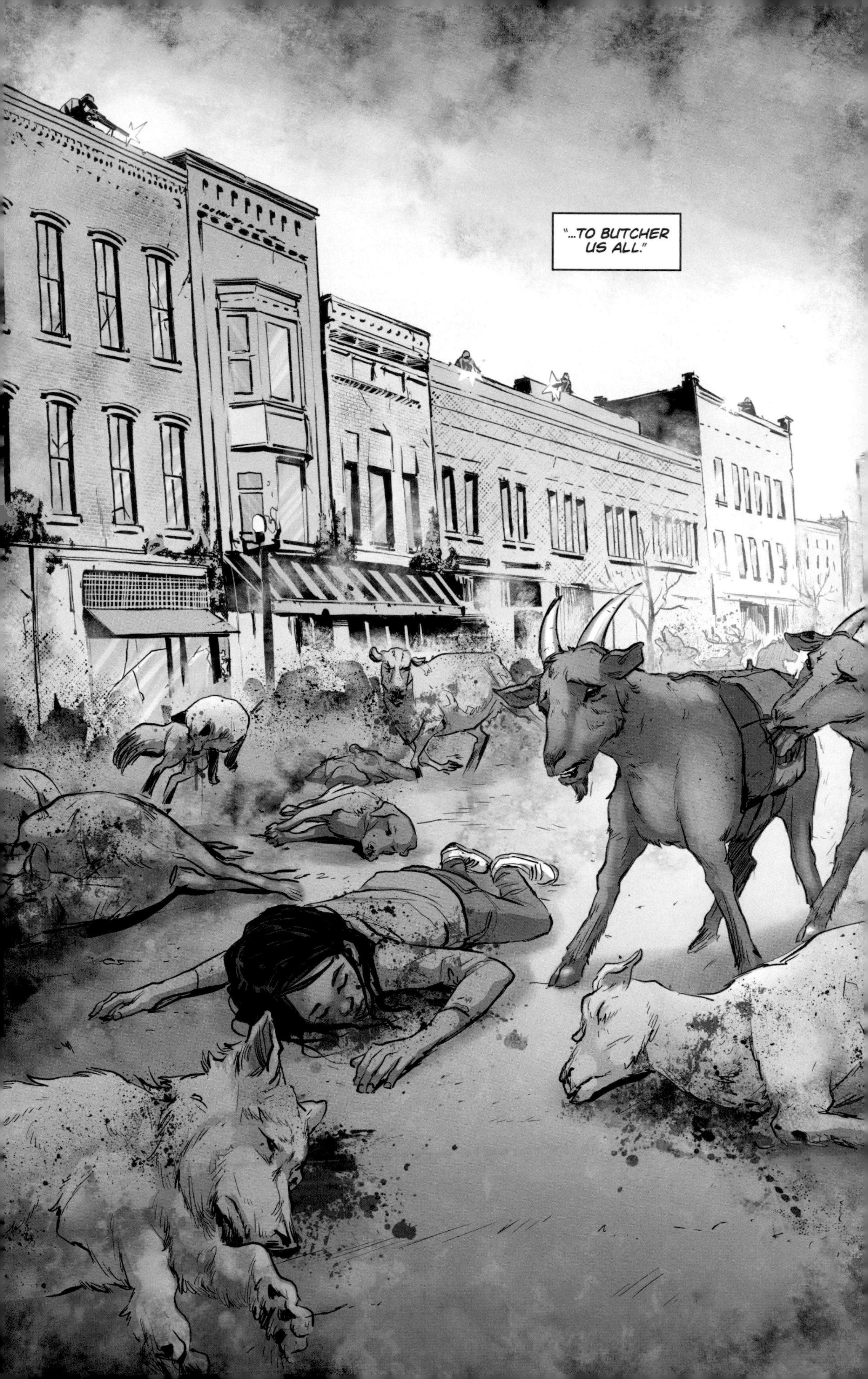
"...TO BUTCHER US ALL."

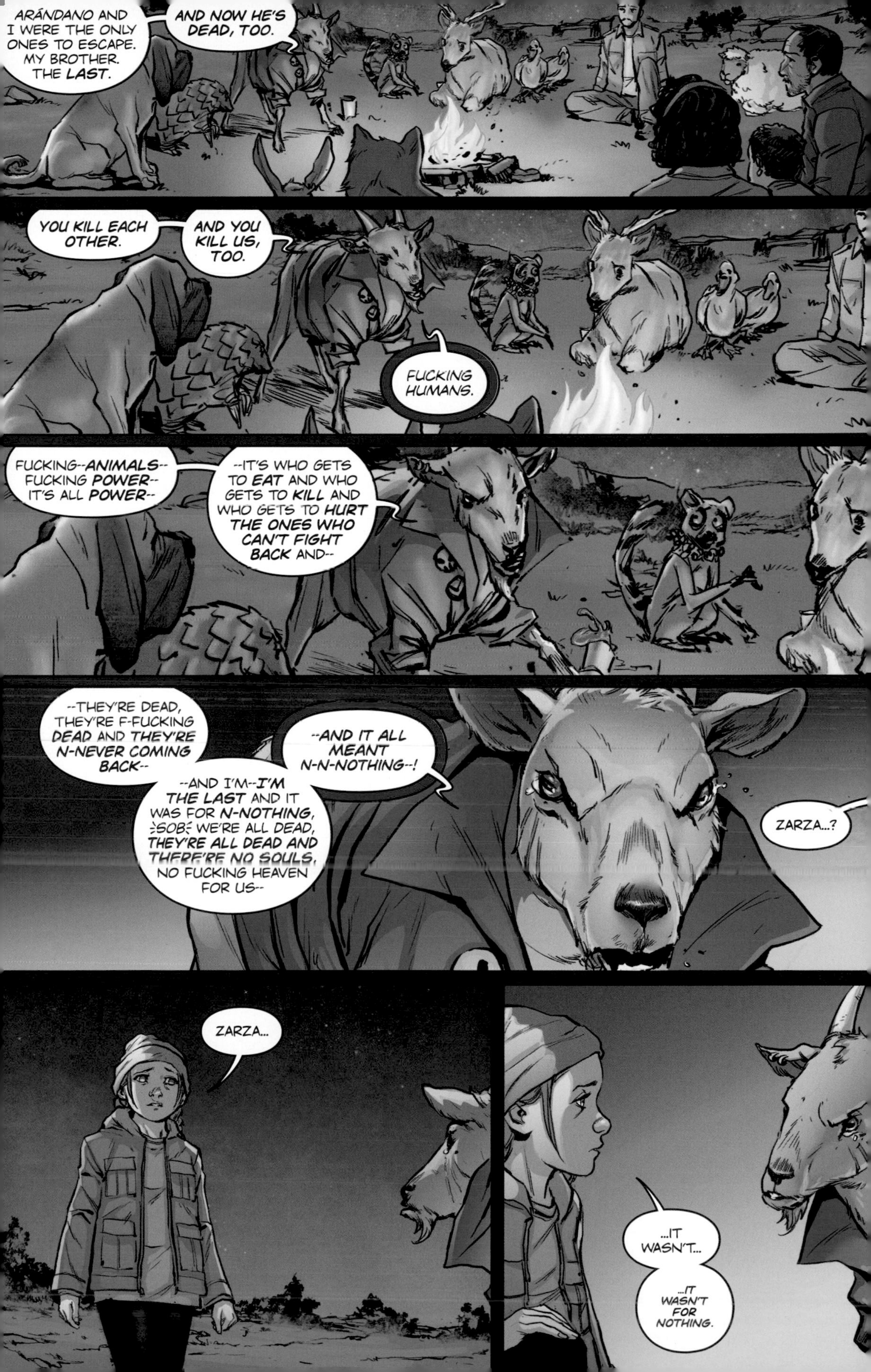
ARÁNDANO AND I WERE THE ONLY ONES TO ESCAPE. MY BROTHER. THE LAST.
AND NOW HE'S DEAD, TOO.
YOU KILL EACH OTHER.
AND YOU KILL US, TOO.
FUCKING HUMANS.
FUCKING--ANIMALS-- FUCKING POWER-- IT'S ALL POWER--
--IT'S WHO GETS TO EAT AND WHO GETS TO KILL AND WHO GETS TO HURT THE ONES WHO CAN'T FIGHT BACK AND--
--THEY'RE DEAD, THEY'RE F-FUCKING DEAD AND THEY'RE N-NEVER COMING BACK--
--AND IT ALL MEANT N-N-NOTHING--!
--AND I'M--I'M THE LAST AND IT WAS FOR N-NOTHING, SOB WE'RE ALL DEAD, THEY'RE ALL DEAD AND THERE'RE NO SOULS, NO FUCKING HEAVEN FOR US--
ZARZA...?
ZARZA...
...IT WASN'T...
...IT WASN'T FOR NOTHING.

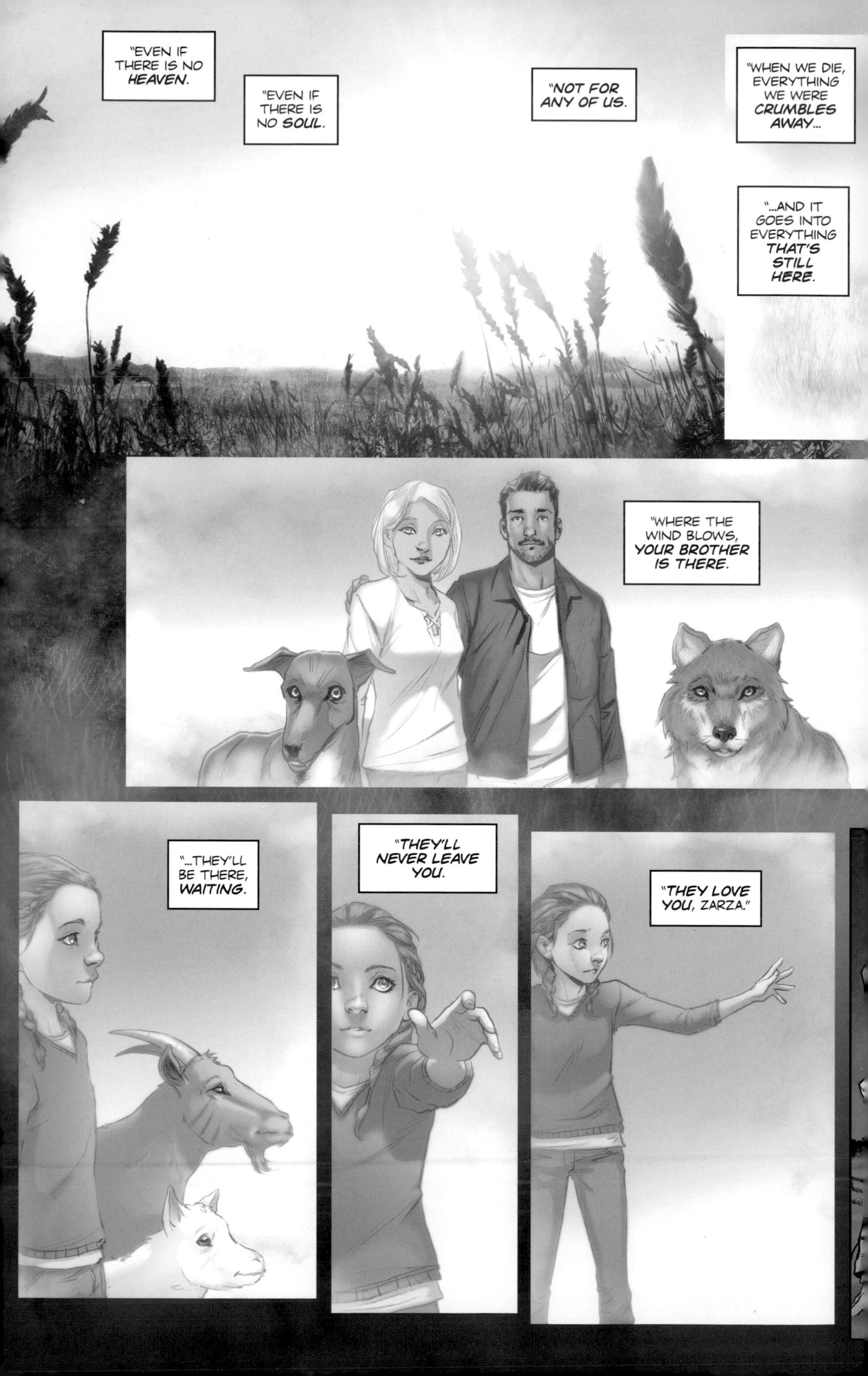
"EVEN IF THERE IS NO HEAVEN.
"EVEN IF THERE IS NO SOUL.
"NOT FOR ANY OF US.
"WHEN WE DIE, EVERYTHING WE WERE CRUMBLES AWAY...
"...AND IT GOES INTO EVERYTHING THAT'S STILL HERE.
"WHERE THE WIND BLOWS, YOUR BROTHER IS THERE.
"...THEY'LL BE THERE, WAITING.
"THEY'LL NEVER LEAVE YOU.
"THEY LOVE YOU, ZARZA."

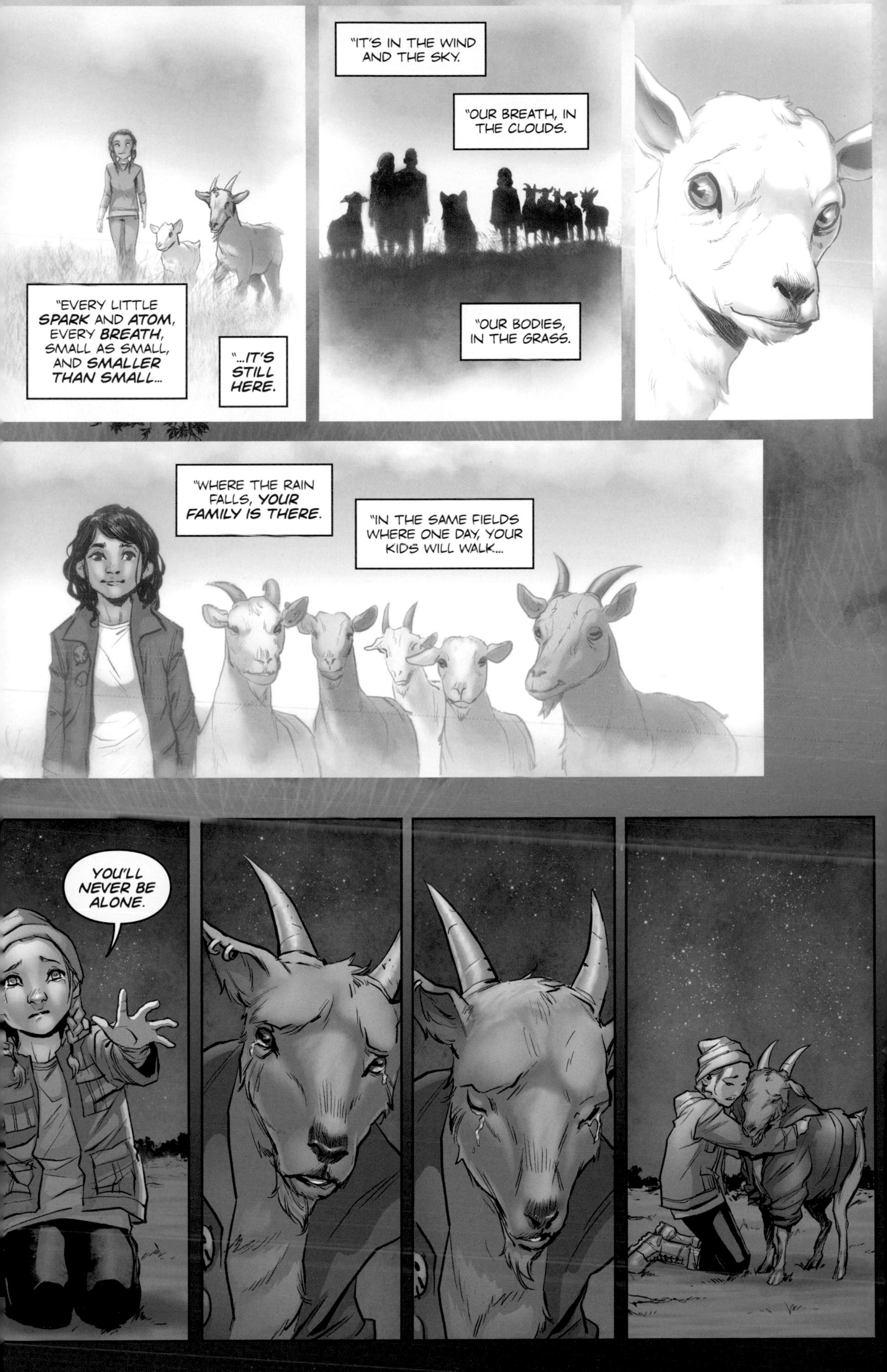
"EVERY LITTLE SPARK AND ATOM, EVERY BREATH, SMALL AS SMALL, AND SMALLER THAN SMALL...
"...IT'S STILL HERE.
"IT'S IN THE WIND AND THE SKY.
"OUR BREATH, IN THE CLOUDS.
"OUR BODIES, IN THE GRASS.
"WHERE THE RAIN FALLS, YOUR FAMILY IS THERE.
"IN THE SAME FIELDS WHERE ONE DAY, YOUR KIDS WILL WALK...
YOU'LL NEVER BE ALONE.

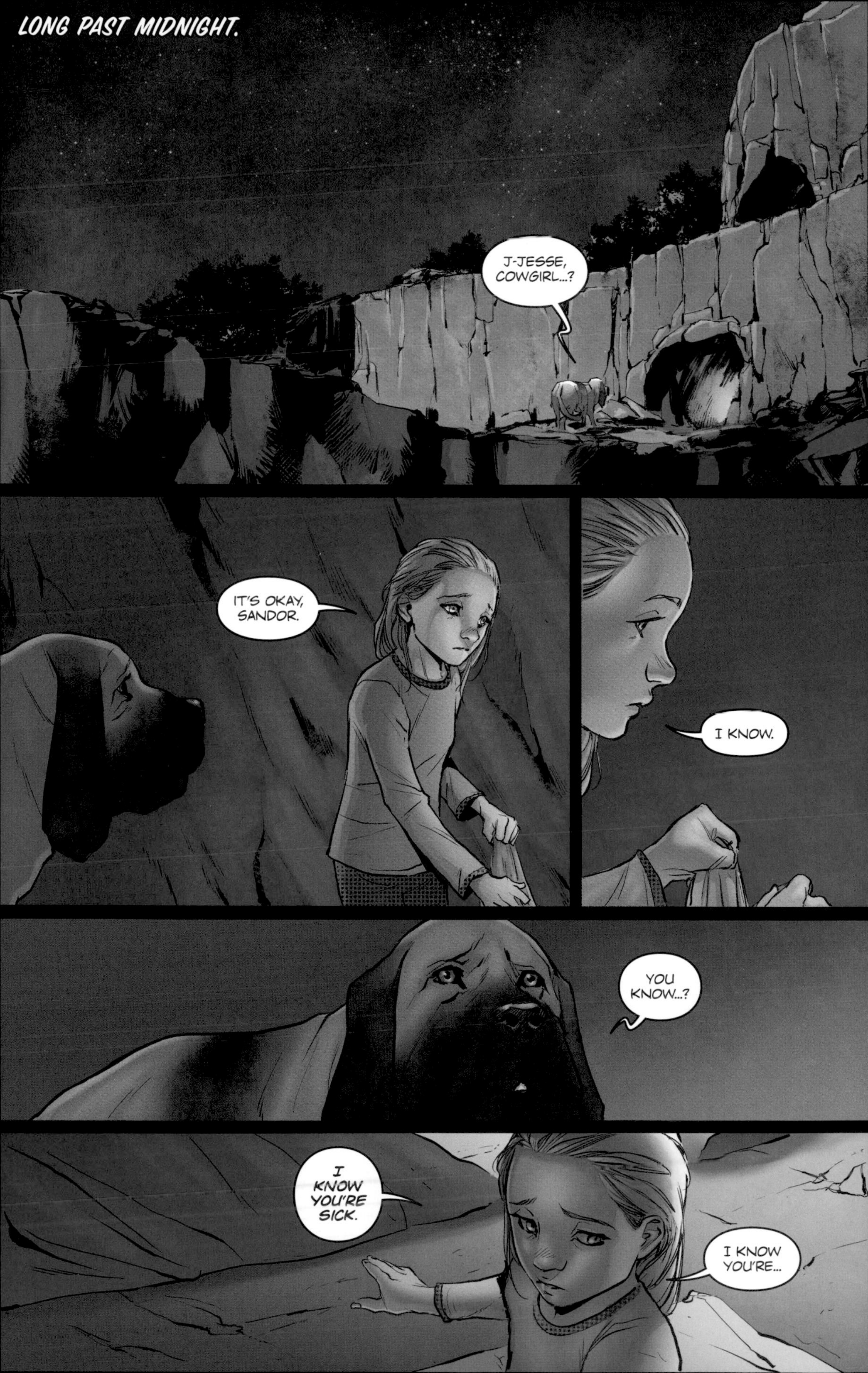
LONG PAST MIDNIGHT.
J-JESSE, COWGIRL...?
IT'S OKAY, SANDOR.
I KNOW.
YOU KNOW...?
I KNOW YOU'RE SICK.
I KNOW YOU'RE...

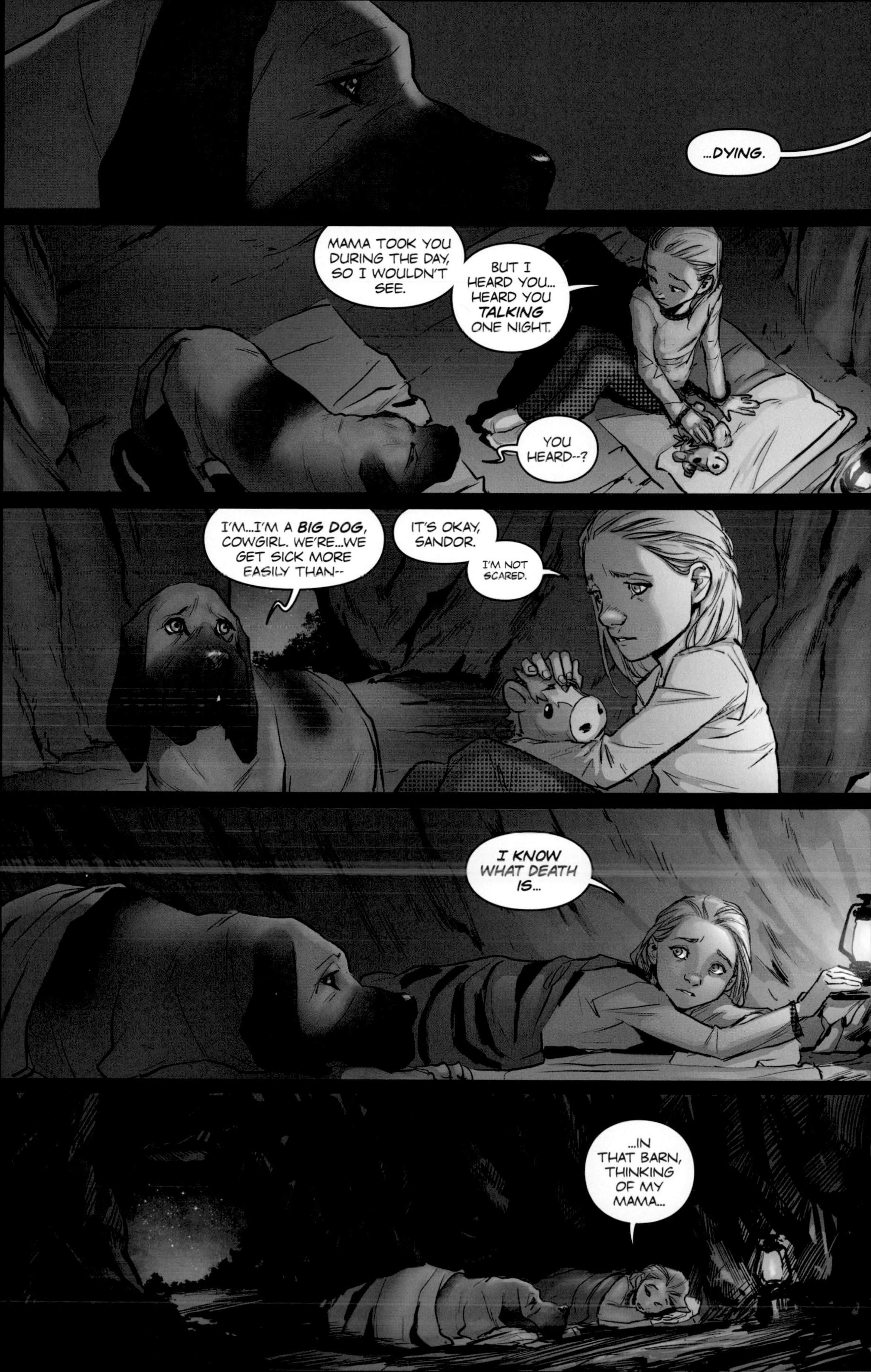
...DYING.
MAMA TOOK YOU DURING THE DAY, SO I WOULDN'T SEE.
BUT I HEARD YOU... HEARD YOU TALKING ONE NIGHT.
YOU HEARD--?
I'M...I'M A BIG DOG, COWGIRL. WE'RE...WE GET SICK MORE EASILY THAN--
IT'S OKAY, SANDOR.
I'M NOT SCARED.
I KNOW WHAT DEATH IS...
...IN THAT BARN, THINKING OF MY MAMA...

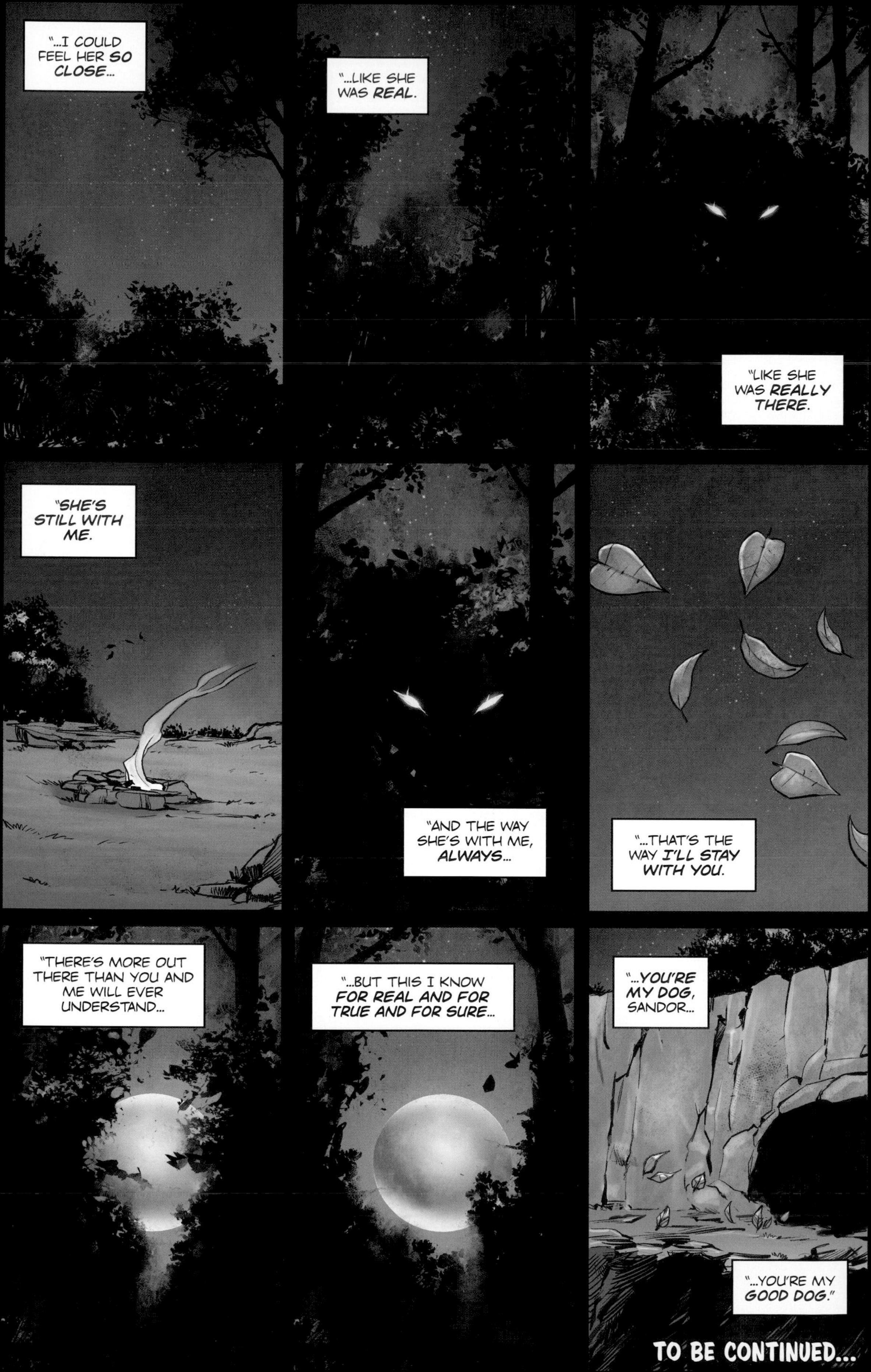
"...I COULD FEEL HER SO CLOSE...
"...LIKE SHE WAS REAL.
"LIKE SHE WAS REALLY THERE.
"SHE'S STILL WITH ME.
"AND THE WAY SHE'S WITH ME, ALWAYS...
"...THAT'S THE WAY I'LL STAY WITH YOU.
"THERE'S MORE OUT THERE THAN YOU AND ME WILL EVER UNDERSTAND...
"...BUT THIS I KNOW FOR REAL AND FOR TRUE AND FOR SURE...
"...YOU'RE MY DOG, SANDOR...
"...YOU'RE MY GOOD DOG."
TO BE CONTINUED...

"WORLD OF ANIMOSITY"

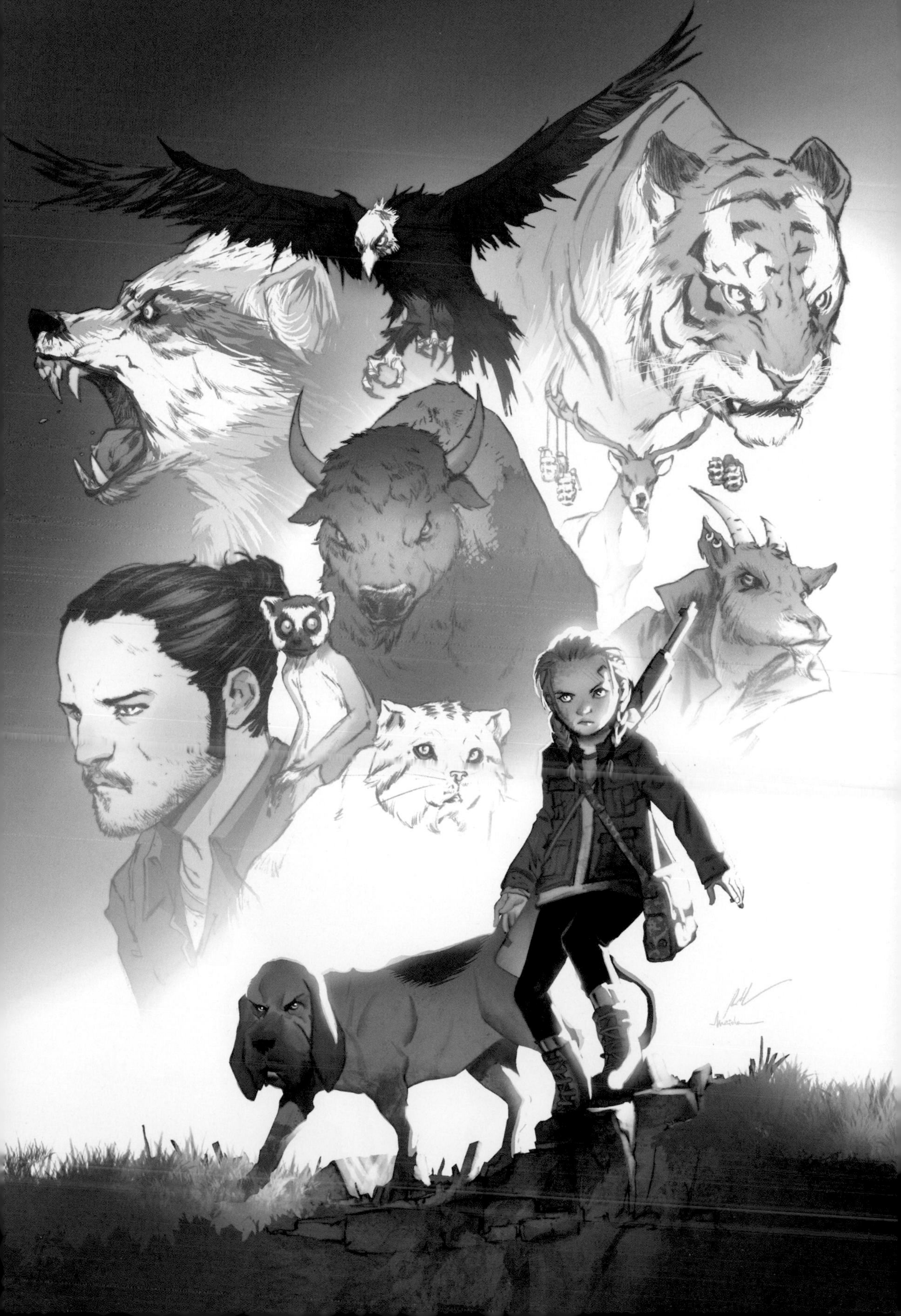

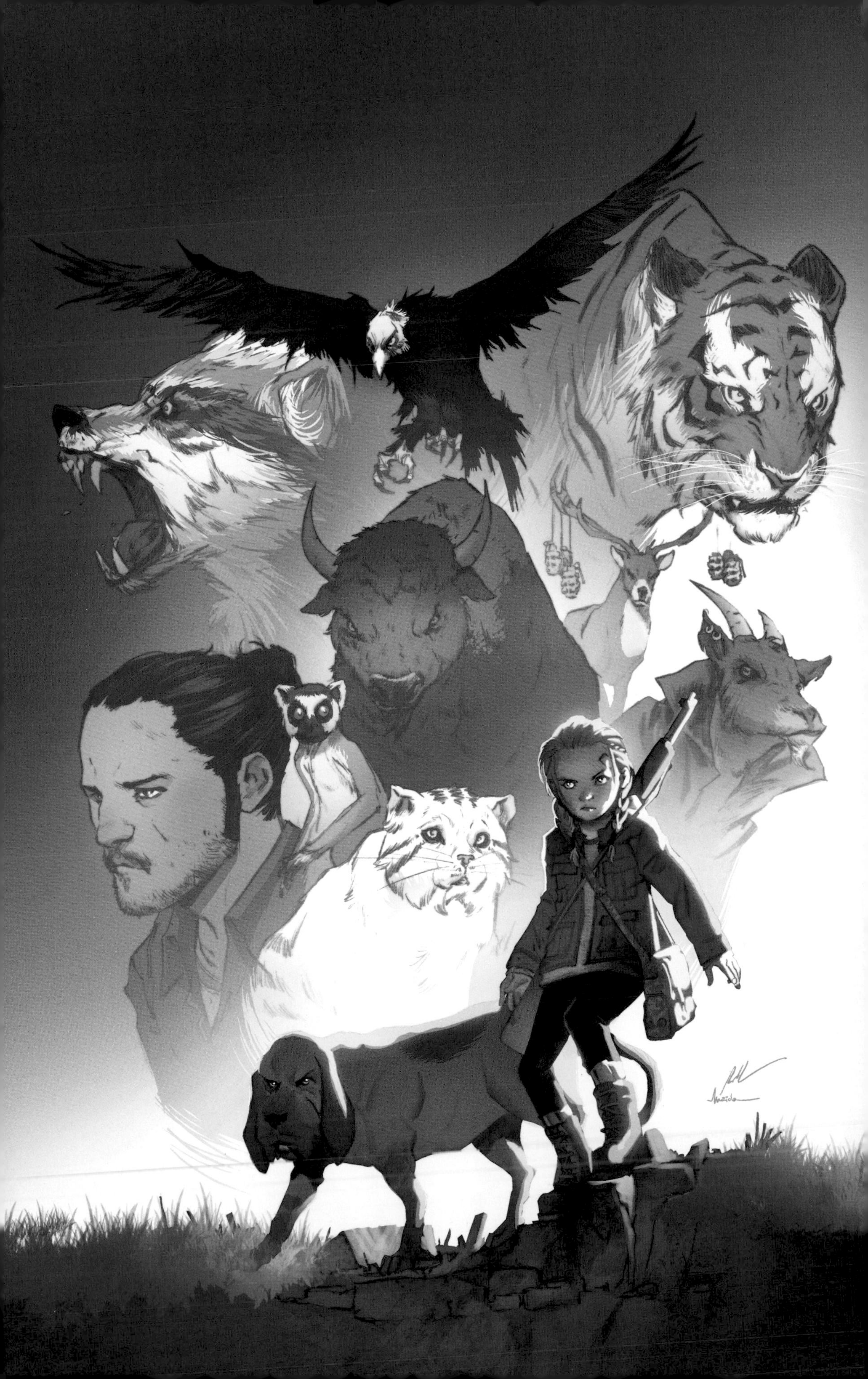

WORLD OF ANIMOSITY

THE PATH TO THE DOGHOUSE
Animosity issues #1 - #8

On the day of the Wake, the Animals did just that—they woke up.

They started thinking. They started talking. They started taking revenge.

An orca at SeaWorld rose from his tank, all gnashing jaws and saltwater spray, to the screams of terror from the audience, only to slam down his flippers and declare undying love for his trainer—and a dog in New York City woke up to realize who and what he was, where and how he existed, and that the girl in front of him—his girl, his protector, his child, his Jesse—was more important to him than the sun and the sky and all the life that ever had been or will be. He belonged to her, forever.

But something happened in that city. No one's saying what.

And one year later, Jesse's parents are gone, and Sandor, her dog, her lone guardian, is getting her out—getting her far, far, away, across the wild green yonder of America and all the way to the distant coast. There, in San Francisco, a city seized by the Animals, is Jesse's estranged half-brother, Adam.

Sandor did this because he has a secret.

Sandor is dying.

Purebred dogs of his ilk don't last long in the world, and he's had five good years—but now, he's got a ticking clock and a daughter he wants to see grow up happy and true.

Liaising with an agent of the Animilitary—an armed force of Animals seeking to create a separate and protected society—Sandor arranged for safe transport out of the princedom of New York City. In exchange, Sandor—a bloodhound with a keen sense of smell—had to find one of the Animilitary's missing scouts. The trail uncovered a violent coup within the Animilitary, which had been facing a food crisis in the struggle to provide for all the Animals—carnivores, herbivores and omnivores alike—on a bloodless diet that could not sustain them. The coup exploded with Sandor and Jesse inside the camp, and they managed to make it out—along with certain Animals that Jesse had befriended—before the entire fortress was overrun by rebels and the vestiges of the American military.

Riding the back of the humpback whale who had originally ferried them across the Hudson River, Sandor, Jesse and their new companions moved down the coast until the path was clear and safe enough to begin a cross-country road trip.

Jesse is growing up, and signs of it frighten Sandor more than they even frighten her. Sandor fears, so much, that he will be unable to protect Jesse from all pain, all terror, aware that he will not be there for her adulthood.

But in the forests of Maryland came a dreaded specter—a creature like a great red dragon, vomiting fire and carrying off some of their companions. Sandor and some of the survivors go on the hunt, while two dear friends remain to guard Jesse—but the Red Dragon comes for them next.

The Red Dragon is revealed as a *lammergeier*, a red-bearded vulture with an eight-foot wingspan a belly of acid that dissolves bone. It rules its cult of men-masquerading-as-beasts and beasts-masquerading-as-men, compelling them to hunt in its name, and dividing the spoils among the squalid horde. The men-beasts of the woods listened closely to Jesse and her companions, marking their rivalries, their fears and their insecurities. They attempted to divide the band, snatching the smallest and weakest, separating them in the disorientating darkness of the woods. The beast-men sought to lure Jesse from her guardians, pretending to be her parents, calling to her as she slept—but Jesse awoke, discovered their true nature, and fought back.

Jesse, Sandor, and their companions destroyed the Red Dragon and its horde, with Sandor pleading for Jesse not to look, to protect her from seeing the true cost of her safety. Reunited, and mourning for their dead, the companions moved on through the hills—followed by a shadow shaped like the ghost of Jesse's mother—or the shape of the man-beast that had impersonated her.

The companions sought rest at Hourglass Falls, an isolated waterfall in the hills of Virginia, where creatures—human and Animal alike—come for a moment of peace on their way to greater journeys. The companions told their tales and origins, and speculated on the future of their lives now—what they believe is left in life, and what they believe might be waiting for them in the great hereafter.

In this place, Jesse told Sandor that she knew of his secret. Sandor at last admitted the truth—his days are numbered, and he knows that he will eventually have to leave her. Jesse knows what death is now, and while she is unafraid, she will stay with him, and love him, because he is her dog—her good dog.

The specter of Jesse's mother's ghost—if that is what it was—dissolves into shadow and moonlight, and Jesse and Sandor fall sleep beneath the haze of stars.

JESSE HERNANDEZ

Species: Human *(Homo sapiens)*

Age: 11 years of expected 81 years

Location Born: New York City

Mother: Shannon Mandel

Father: Óscar Hernandez

Siblings: Adam North, maternal half-brother

Height: 4'6"

Weight: 72 lbs

Hair Color: Dark blonde

Eye Color: Amber

Vorous: Omnivore

Profile:

Jesse Hernandez just wants everybody to be happy, please—happy and safe, okay? And maybe nice to each other, even if they don't always deserve it. She doesn't know what happy means anymore, or safe, or nice—not since she lost her parents, not since she lost the world she knew—but she's trying to remember, or, if she never knew, she's trying to find out.

Jesse was always shy and small for her age, and despite the best efforts of her parents, an early trauma rendered her lonely and anxious. Jesse never knew what it was she was supposed to be. If you're sweet, people say you're naïve, or boring, or manipulative, or stupid. If you're quiet, people say you're bitter, or judgmental, or needy, or doing it for attention. If she spoke in Hebrew with her mama, people called her one name, and if she spoke Spanish with her daddy, people called her a whole other one—and if you didn't know the name, you could tell in their voice what they were trying to say.

Before the Wake, people that Jesse didn't love always needed something from her, always expected something from her, whether it was teachers saying she didn't try hard enough with other students, or friends' parents trying to decide if she was "the right kind" of playmate for their daughter—whether it was old ladies telling her not to get dirty or men shouting things out of car windows that she didn't understand.

People were too much—too frantic, too frenetic, too busy, too demanding, too angry—Jesse wanted to just run up the stairs and into the elevator and up into her parents' New York apartment and slam the door and bury her face in a book and breathe in the warm, soft, blood-bay fur of her hound dog, Sandor. Sandor never asked her for anything, other than that she stay with him. Sandor just let her be the thing she was, just be and grow and grow and be, and he loved her a thousand fold.

After the devastating loss of her parents in the first year after the Wake, Jesse did not know what would become of her, and spent many days wishing she could go to sleep, in the same way that the Animals woke up—then she would never have to feel pain like this again. Only at Sandor's insistence, her goal is to reach her half-brother in San Francisco. Though Adam is a stranger to her, he is her only living kin, but she doesn't much care where she goes anymore—so long as Sandor, her Bloodhound, is with her.

Due to Sandor's stern methods, Jesse has been extraordinarily sheltered in the brave new world of the Animals. This allows her to greet others with kindness and generosity, but also opens her up to intense hazards and deceives her about the nature of the dangers ahead. Jesse has long allowed Sandor to think that his lies keep her in the dark—but about some things, she is no longer pretending.

SANDOR

Species: Bloodhound *(Canis lupus familiaris)*

Age: 5 years of expected 7 years

Location Born: Freeport, Maine

Mother: Belladonna

Father: Unknown

Siblings: Six puppies

Height: 2'6"

Weight: 110 lbs

Hair Color: Red-brown

Eye Color: Hazel

Vorous: Omnivore

Profile:

Sandor's entire mission in life is to give up the one thing that gives his own life any meaning.

Sandor was born to a Maine farmer whose prized hunting dog had a tryst with an unknown hound dog father who jumped the fence. Though he was the runt of the litter, Jesse picked him out when they were both little children. She guarded him, carried him, raised him, and on the day of the Wake, their roles switched—he became the caretaker, the protector, and she was his little girl.

Sandor was devoted to Shannon, Jesse's mother, but often clashed with Jesse's father, Óscar, over how best to protect and provide for the family. Far from the reluctant anti-hero, Sandor ardently strives to protect Jesse, but he is an ill-made knight—his intentions are powerful, but he is brutal, clumsy, earnest and vicious in defense of his child. He has done many things he isn't proud of, and a few things he *is* proud of that still won't see the light of day.

Sandor lies through his many sharp teeth to keep Jesse from understanding the ugliness of the world. He is frightened that one day his lies won't be good enough, and Jesse will see the world—and him—for what he believes both truly are.

As a large, deep-chested purebred dog, Sandor's life expectancy is winding down, and he is racing time

itself to carry Jessie through rivers, forests, mountains and plains to the one person he believes will take her in, the one person he believes could love her next to as much as he does—her half-brother Adam. Sandor's reasons for believing this are his own.

The whole momentum of Sandor's life is now in the flat-out race to bear his child to that safe haven—to see that she is happy, healthy, beloved and secure—and then, to lose her forever. Sandor's only happy ending is the thing he most fears—but isn't that true for all parents?

...Isn't it?

...Isn't it?

(Please, God, someone tell me what I'm doing is right.)

THE FORMER UNITED

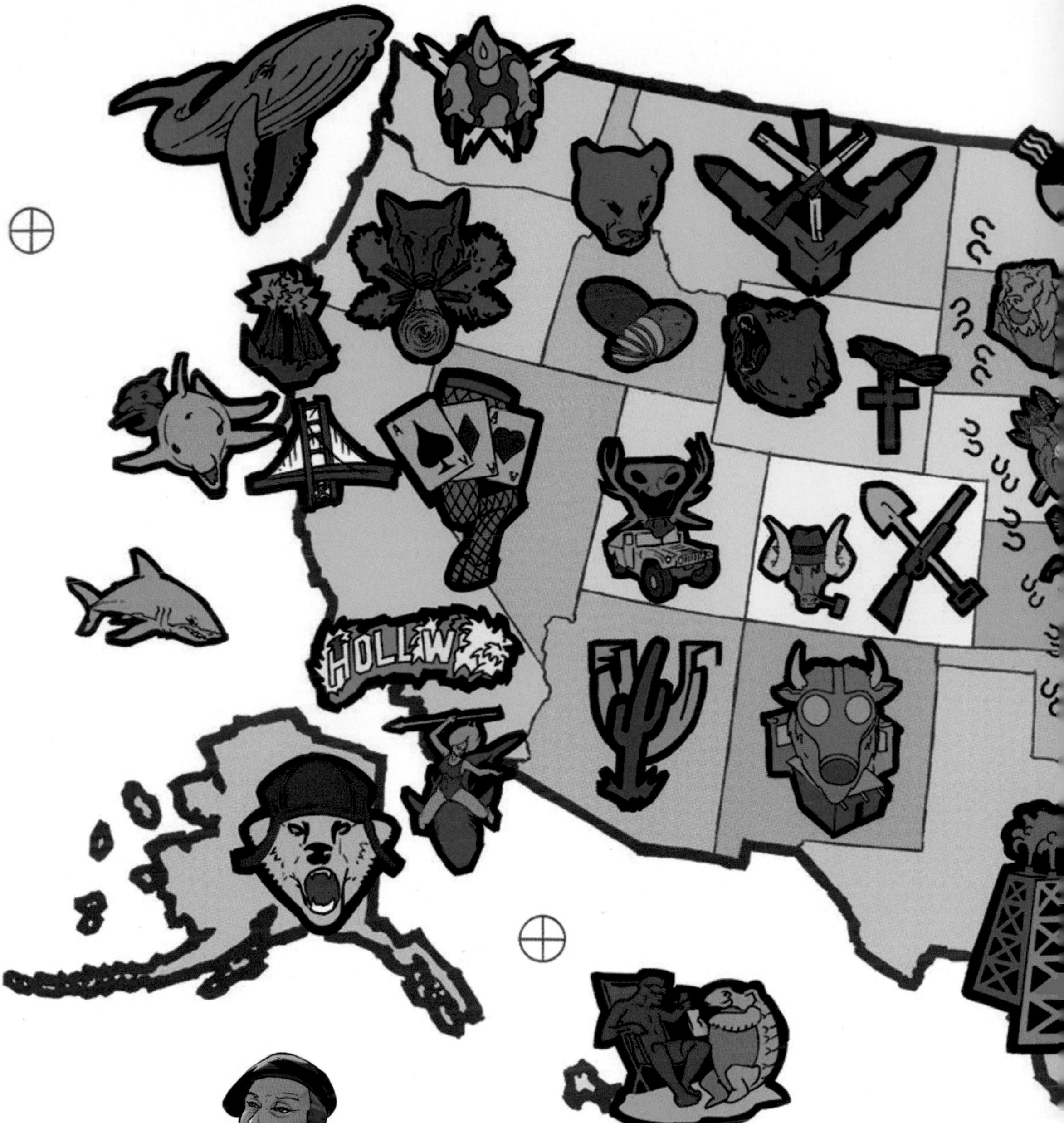

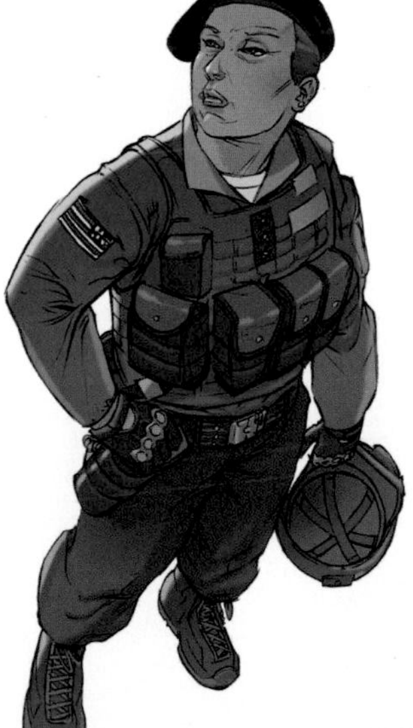

NYOTA GUTIÉRREZ

STATES OF AMERICA

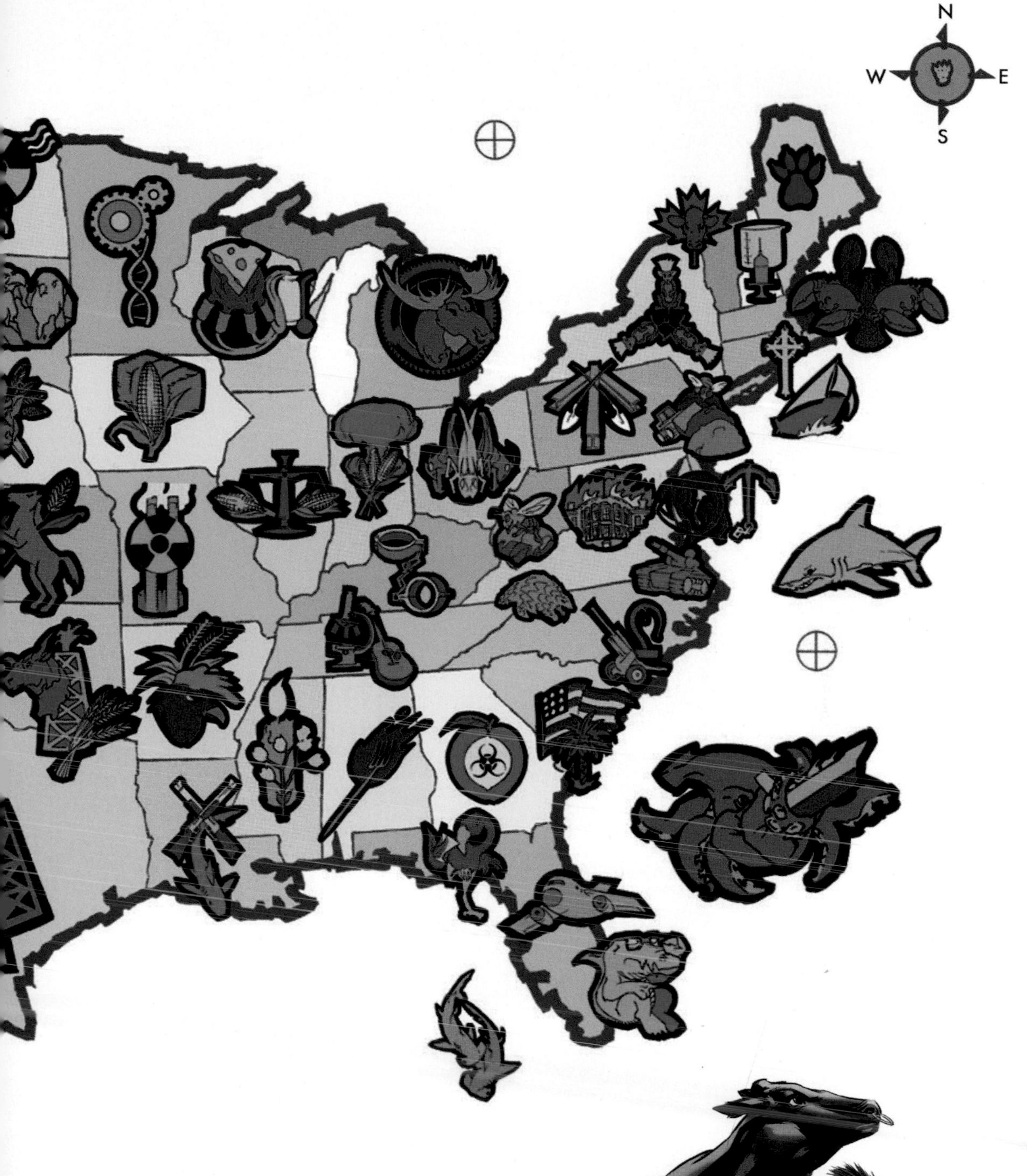
N
W
E
S

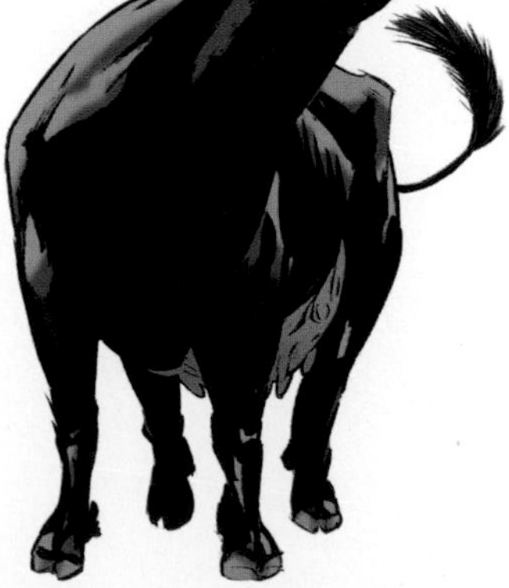

THE MAIDEN

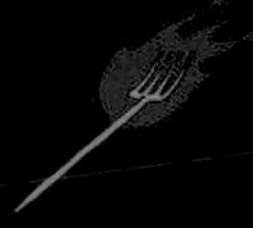

ALABAMA

In the initial crisis, the humans concerned themselves more with attacking each other in the chaos than defending one another against the Animal uprising. The conflict ended in a ferocious Animal victory after the Animals seized the Air Force and military bases and divided the vehicles, munitions and weaponry among themselves.

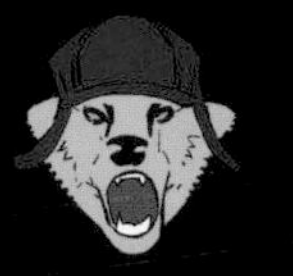

ALASKA

Conditions unknown. Communications were seized and severed during and shortly after the Wake.

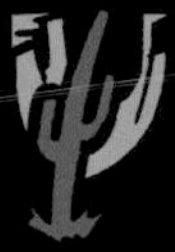

ARIZONA

In the dissolution of any formal government authority on the continent, several Native reservations opened and expanded their borders, seized local power and negotiated truces among the Animal populations. These territories now operate as safe havens. Forces that have attempted to quell them have not been seen again.

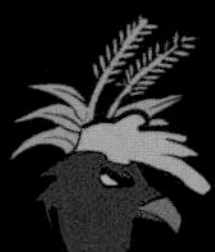

ARKANSAS

Rich in rice and livestock, Animals seized many farms, and after initial acts of revenge, they maintain individual truces with human farming families. Individual farms allied themselves with Animal mercenaries to defend against invaders. Raids from other factions and other states are ongoing.

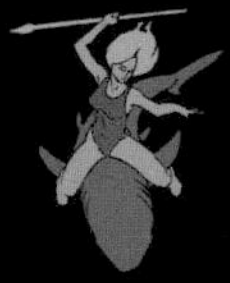

CALIFORNIA

To the north, the redwoods and sequoia forests have become notoriously haunted by spectral creatures of species unknown. In San Francisco, the Animals seized power with the smallest loss of life seen in a city of this size, and currently struggle to rebuild a functioning society where humans and Animals might live together. To the south, looting and debauchery are rampant as many humans and Animals welcome the end of the world and live out their numbered days in hedonism.

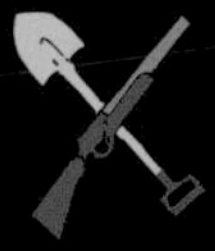

COLORADO

The only known location in the United States where an Animal force—led by Brutus, a bighorn sheep—has seized a nuclear silo. The society is isolated and well defended, and little additional information has been attained. Military fighters sent to bomb the area were taken down by individual birds who sacrificed themselves by diving into the engines of the planes or flying into the paths of oncoming missiles before the payload neared the city.

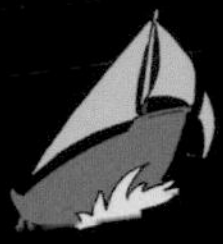

CONNECTICUT

On the day of the Wake, wealthy humans attempted to hole up in suburban homes, but Animals, anxious and eager for comfort, entered these luxurious neighborhoods house by house, seeking beds, pillows, air conditioning and bathtubs. The human population tried to flee by boat, presuming that the Wake had not extended to the ocean, and many were sunk on private sailboats and yachts by the less-than-sympathetic creatures of the sea, despite the attempts of many Animals to rescue them. The surviving humans are currently held for ransom against whoever will redeem them.

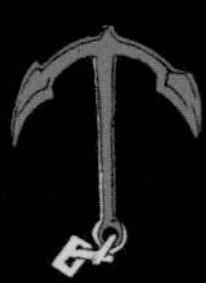

DELAWARE

Humans retreated to the massive shipping yards, which became bunkers against Animal invasion. The Animals soon lost interest in pursuing the humans, and some humans tentatively reemerged. Other human colonies still sit in the harbors, self-contained within the ships and their various cargos, utterly isolated against the outside world, and forming mad, miniscule new societies within these strange, floating cells.

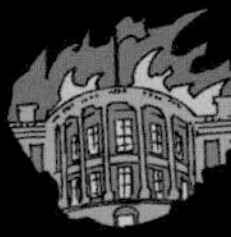

DISTRICT OF COLUMBIA

Bo, Socks, Barney and Buddy could be trusted. This pet couldn't be.

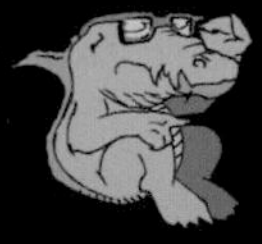

FLORIDA

Dinosaurs vs. Florida Man, live on Pay-Per-View. The happiest place on earth to enjoy the end of days.

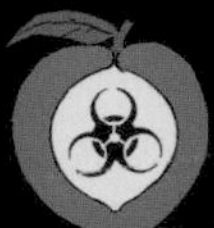

GEORGIA

The Center for Disease Control in Atlanta—which houses the United States' cache of ferociously deadly diseases—is besieged by Animals. Scientists within struggle to find a way to defend humankind with bioweaponry, while Animals seek to prevent the use of these viruses against them. Both human and Animal radicals seek to control fatal strains of plague that could be released upon the world.

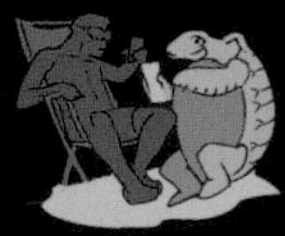

HAWAII

"We live in peace, mostly. Agreed just to kill and eat the fish and live as pescetarians."

"Don't the fish scream?"

"Of course they scream! You just…you just try not to hear it, after a while."

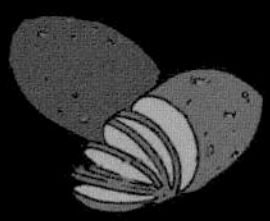

IDAHO

Idaho faired quite well among the fates of the United States. The high agricultural production from potatoes and the low human population permitted the humans and Animals to reach a tense, if tidy, trade agreement to mutually harvest the crop. While monotonous, and undoubtedly contributing to a kind of madness through boredom, Idaho was never plagued by starvation and is largely secure post-Wake.

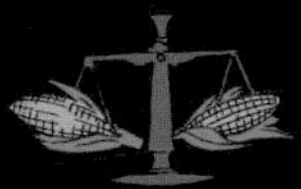

ILLINOIS

In Illinois, the bedraggled vestiges of human lawmakers desperately attempted to assess the legality of this bizarre new world. What rights do Animals have? What rights do humans? Where does property enter into all of this? What is now considered murder? Can you be tried retroactively for violence committed before the Wake? Who owns what? What happens now? Oh God, oh God–

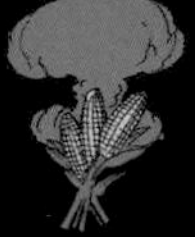

INDIANA

Human separatists poisoned huge fields of corn, killing hordes of Animals and securing their own store of food from the bodies of the dead. However, the poison—a rare fungus—mutated, and massive areas were bombed to prevent the spores from spreading.

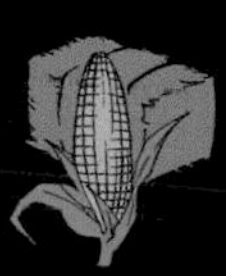

IOWA

Much of Iowa was divided and annexed for food production. Various powers rode in to conquer and kill those in power, but those laboring in the fields—whether enslaved or free—largely stayed the same. One of the only states not to suffer starvation, but one of the only ones to suffer spontaneous civil wars every few weeks.

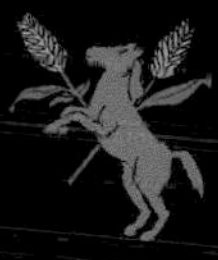

KANSAS

The heart of the kingdom of the Horse Lords, radicals advocate for a separate Animal nation of herbivores in the breadbasket of the former United States. They are led by the triumvirate of the mare Angharrad, the gelding Incitatus, and the stallion No Name, and offer citizenship only in exchange for labor and abiding by their strict, Draconian laws.

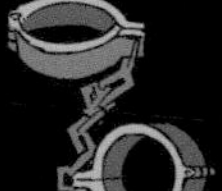

KENTUCKY

The humans in rural Kentucky currently hold their own, maintaining as close to a pre-Wake society as possible, paying or forcing the Animals to abide in their original roles. The mountains are currently targeted by Animal rebels who are planning a siege of the hills.

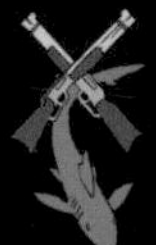

LOUISIANA

In Louisiana, the sprawling prison system orchestrated a mass release of inmates who were offered full pardons in exchange for fighting the Animal uprising. Many fought for the humans, and many defected to the side of the Animals in exchange for the security of their families. The conflict is brutal and ongoing.

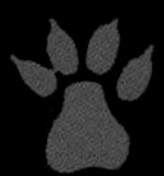

MAINE

Despite extraordinary resourcefulness by the humans, the state fell to the Animals, who were able to use the dense foliage, fog and forest to their advantage. The state has been sealed, and is rumored to be controlled by a creature who rises at night from the crossroads.

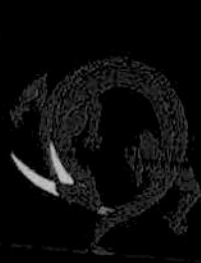

MARYLAND

The forest of Maryland is home to the legend of a bloody red dragon who sprays fire and acid from its throat and devours creatures whole. The dragon is said to be served by a slave-army of shambling man-beasts and beast-men who worship it in exchange for food and protection. To enter these forests is certain death, for these creatures keep the old ways of blood and bone and, above all, hunger.

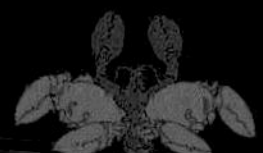

MASSACHUSETTS

The dense urban area created a bottleneck for humans seeking to flee, and the coasts became the major source of danger as crabs, lobsters and other crustaceans surged onto the beaches and up from the sewers, while sharks, dolphins and some whales entered the cities through rivers and reservoirs. Two-thirds of the cities have been conceded to the Animals, who have gone about remaking them to their own tastes, dressed in seaweed, the streets flooded and drains overflowing. Conflict is ongoing as humans fight back, including a secret rebel militia wielding Red Sox bats.

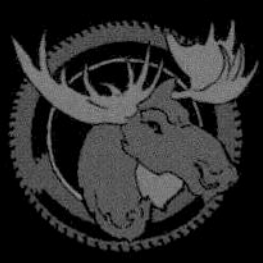

MICHIGAN

Megafauna and other animals from the Great Lakes invaded and seized the means of production of vehicles. While all cars currently in circulation are still functioning, at least until the final consumption of the remaining oil and gasoline, the Animals are currently engaged in the creation of new armored vehicles designed for their own purposes. Production has already begun.

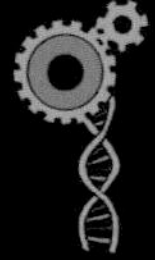

MINNESOTA

Humans valiantly defended the factories and industries, winning in some places, losing in others, and striking tense bargains for the Animals to use the machines for their own purposes in exchange for Animal-made goods (whether wool, honey, milk, eggs or the flesh of those who had been killed or died of natural causes). Elsewhere, a laboratory deeply invested in biomedical engineering tries desperately to discover the cause—and perhaps cure—of the Wake.

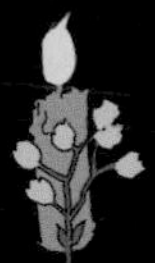

MISSISSIPPI

The site of a dark and mysterious act of grace where Animals came from their fields, slow and silent, and walked up to the trembling humans, some armed, who awaited them. Some Animals knelt. Some lay their heads in the laps of the people who had cared for them. Even those who had done evil to their Animals were offered a chance at forgiveness. Those who did not surrender to this act of grace were turned upon and attacked and viciously slain—not by the Animals, but by the forgiven humans, who fell soon after to weeping and a grief so deep, they often never recovered.

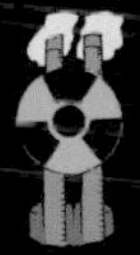

MISSOURI

The site of a nuclear silo and stockpile, humans and Animals raced to keep the deadly weaponry from one another's hands and paws. A savage, barbaric siege took place, but humans and Animals worked together to overthrow a third combined force comprised of those who desired to trigger the missiles and end this mad new world.

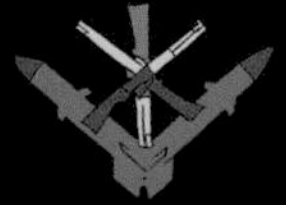

MONTANA

As a state with one of the lowest human population densities, one of the highest gun ownerships, and one of the highest shooting incident reports, Montana remains an intense survival zone. Denizens live with only individual truces in a sometimes peaceful, sometimes bloody free-for-all.

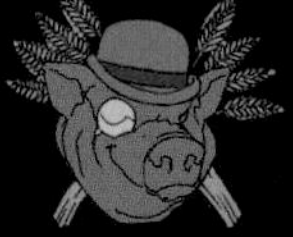

NEBRASKA

The large population of swine attempted a political coup with the goal of integrating Animals into the human systems and society already in place. The hogs—insisting that their intelligence before the Wake guaranteed them increased intelligence after the Wake—negotiated with humans to extend political rights to Animals, though their Orwellian motives were fairly predictable in the end. The state is marked for annexation by the Horse Lords, particularly by the warlike stallion Tencendor.

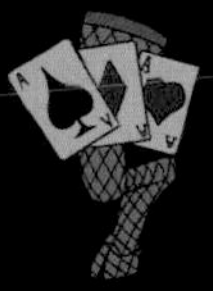

NEVADA

One of the strangest territories, Nevada is now host to those who wish to spend their final days in hedonism. Few acts of revenge took place during the Wake, with most creatures—both human and Animal—giving themselves up to debauchery amid the violence of the day. The human/Animal sex trade thrives in the overgrown and crumbling ruins of the former hotels and casinos, and is self-regulated by squads and gangs protecting the interests of their own. Elsewhere, cultists gather in the desert, certain that alien intervention caused the Wake and attempting passionately to make contact with supposed visitors from another world.

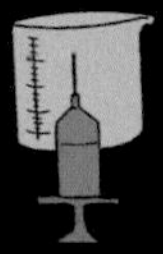

NEW HAMPSHIRE

The site of an underground laboratory and bunker engaged in intense and unethical experimentation on post-Wake Animals. Humans and Animals alike are hunting for it to free those within—and harvest whatever information they may have gathered.

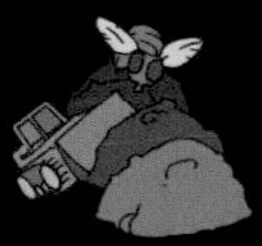

NEW JERSEY

Hordes of Animals began unearthing the landfills, sorting, cleaning, dividing, trading and selling the salvage. The task is far less repulsive to Animals, many of whom are used to scavenging or already dwell in the landfill. The collection of plastics, electronics and machinery is now precious, given the trade agreements, the production of energy and manufacturing which have now come to a screeching halt.

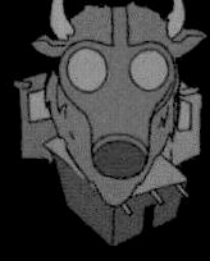

NEW MEXICO

Home of the Los Alamos Lab, studying everything from the origins of the Wake, to plagues deadly to both humans and Animals, to futuristic superweapons. The state is contested territory currently under expansion by Native tribes imprisoned for decades on dwindling reservations, aided by Animals keen to overthrow the remains of the American authorities still in the area.

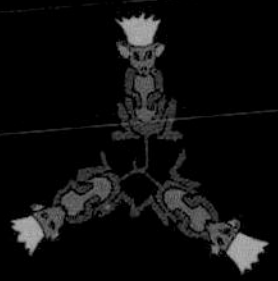

NEW YORK

The Three Princes of New York—together, known as the Rat King—rule the sewers of New York City. Manhattan is an isolated city, and entrance or exit is forbidden and punishable by death and devouring. The rat population has exploded post-Wake, and they use their human citizens to maintain the city. Life is neither so good nor so terrible, and each remaining human and Animal has their duties in this dystopia. Art, Literature, science and education thrive despite the tyranny of the rats. A strange, jagged new society is emerging.

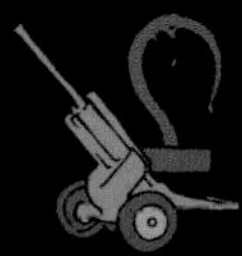

NORTH CAROLINA

The site of the largest slaughterhouse in America, North Carolina was home to horrific violence long before the Wake. The livestock within led a dreadful and terrible uprising, helmed by a black heifer who was born with a number instead of a name. "The Maiden," as she is now known, is a herald and prophetess to her people, who are engaged in a staggering and Biblical rebellion.

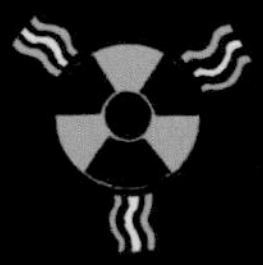

NORTH DAKOTA

The location of a nuclear silo, and a state surrounded in much mystery. Something terrible happened here within twenty-four hours of the Wake, and the nuclear facility poisoned much of the surrounding area. An explosion? A meltdown? The details and participants are unknown, and no one hazards to go anywhere near this territory any longer. Insects and birds exposed to even strong breezes die quickly, and human beings suffer rashes, bleeding and radiation poisoning the closer to the site they come.

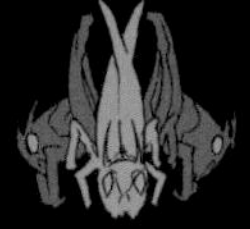

OHIO

A horde of insects, swarms dense enough to blacken the sky, swept through the agricultural territory of Ohio. Grasshoppers, crickets, beetles, cockroaches, butterflies, etc. met as if in a terrible summit, and stripped every shred of green from the fields and forests. The super-horde moved unpredictably through the country, a plague out of the End Times, devouring all food they come across.

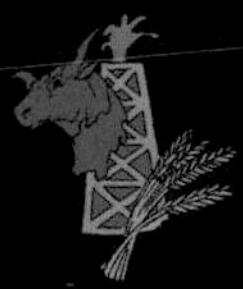

OKLAHOMA

The site of a failed Animal uprising. Humans maintain much control of the precious oil fields, working with Animal mercenaries, but their hold is tenuous, and their food supplies were poisoned by Animal conspirators. The Horse Lords plan to seize this territory as well, under the military command of the ruthless mare Matsukaze.

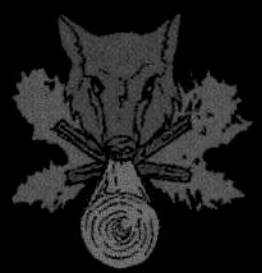

OREGON

Many Animals retreated to the forests to establish separatist communities, and live in the mist and pines there, haunted by ghostly specters. Small societies have sprung up in the trees, especially the Lupercal, the largest orphanage in the known world. Here, Animal communities work together to provide for the children—human and Animal alike—orphaned in the Wake. All are raised as Animals, and trade lumber and labor to the humans in exchange for goods.

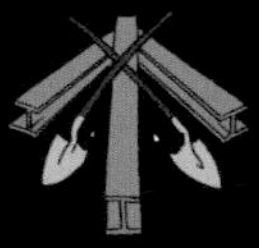

PENNSYLVANIA

Humans and Animals alike labor in the mines and mills for resources, which they trade to forces and factions in other states. The new society is squalid and often violent, with hunger-driven conflicts on both sides, but the clannish communities provide for their own first and their neighbors second, and ferociously defend those of their own territories above anyone from outside the state. The deer alone are saboteurs, viciously killing any human they come across.

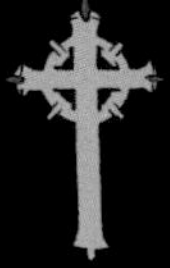

RHODE ISLAND

The Archdiocese of Rhode Island declared Animals to be rational beings with souls, capable of sin and salvation, who will enter heaven or hell depending on their actions on Earth. This pronouncement swelled the ranks of the Church with Animal soldiers willing to defend them, outraged human believers over the audacity of the declaration, and was also met with sublime indifference by many other Animals who ate their way through the pantries of several local churches.

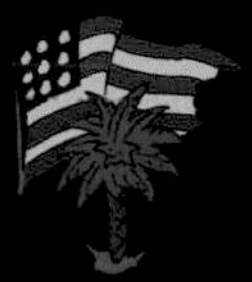

SOUTH CAROLINA

The new Capital of the United States, and retreat of the last of the American leaders. Many American heads of state fell during the Wake, from the rogue bald eagle who took down Air Force One to the Mad Million, several allied colonies of ants that burrowed, infiltrated, sabotaged and detonated a bunker housing many human world leaders. The functional remains of the United States government are protected by General Nyota Gutiérrez, the highest-ranking officer among those who escaped the firebombing of the White House.

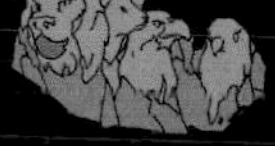

SOUTH DAKOTA

Some ultimately very rude graffiti that probably wasn't an incredibly good use of someone's time during the apocalypse.

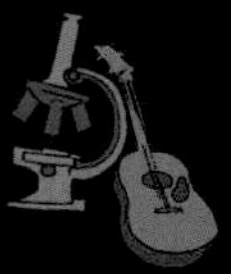

TENNESSEE

Home of the Oak Ridge National Laboratory, where human and Animal scientists are tentatively working together to study the Wake, under the assurance that this laboratory will in no way try to control, reverse, or attempt to cure it. Much of the Wake defies scientific explanation, especially the Animal's ability to speak without the existence of vocal cords designed for that purpose. Some Animals rumored to speak do not have brains, but these cases have not yet been proven. It is also the site of some sweet country music, if you're looking to drink yourself through the End Times.

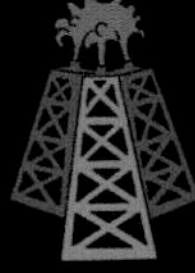

TEXAS

Texas has split into several oil kingdoms, where barons rule vast swathes of territory, complete with armed human knights and peasant livestock who work the land. The kings of Texas operate as if they are countries unto themselves; living and dying brutally in the vast grasslands and deserts, and trading or selling supplies to all visitors. Survivalists are having a blast. Those caught in the middle, human and Animal alike, less so.

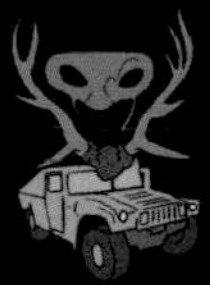

UTAH

The site of a lingering pocket of the US Military desperately trying to reunite with command. The Mormons, who got to feel pretty swell for being the first among the Christian faiths to declare that Animals have souls, were largely left undisturbed. However, a massive population of pets and domestic animals turned on owners that they had witnessed being abusive to those dependent on them. The remaining families were treated quite well by the post-Wake Animals, and adopted into Animal clans who provided for them with great loyalty. However, a splinter cell of Animals went into the mountains, believing themselves now to be the final and most favored children of God, and no one is entirely sure what they are doing out in the wilds.

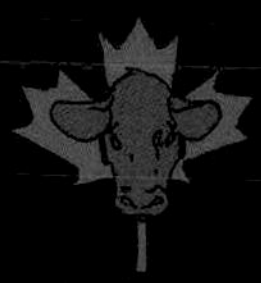

VERMONT

Site of the House of Red Clover, the first formal school for the Animals. Led by Sugar Maple, a former dairy cow, and taught by senior Animals pooling their accumulated knowledge, the school is aided by human allies. Class sizes number in the hundreds to thousands as the Animals are taught languages, writing, mathematics, technical skills, history, science and technology heretofore unknown to them.

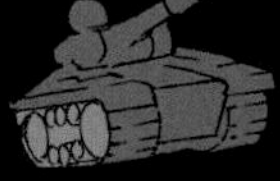

VIRGINIA

The site of Hourglass Falls, a safe haven where many humans and Animals have passed to rest, or to peacefully end their lives. Virginia was also the location of a massive military and naval force, particularly in Norfolk, where many American battleships were stationed. The Virginia branches of the military—including some Animal allies—were essential in ushering the remains of the United States government through a 500-mile battle zone to South Carolina, where they were able to regroup in a secret fortress.

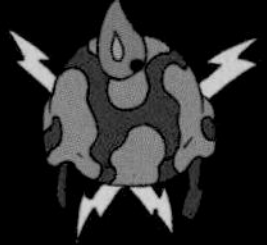

WASHINGTON

On the night of the Wake, in a pouring rainstorm, human engineers and workers united to protect the plants and dams from enraged Animals seeking to disrupt and destroy human supremacy. The humans were outnumbered, ten-to-one in biomass alone, when they were joined by massive flocks, herds, schools and swarms of Animals seeking to protect the source of the electricity, which they felt essential to the protection of Animal-kind and the function of a new and peaceful society. The immense battle—during which some plants fell in dazzling explosions of electricity through the flooded areas, leading to devastating electrocutions and blasts that lit up the sky—ended in a victory for the humans and their Animal rescuers, who attempted to maintain the power for both human and Animal benefit.

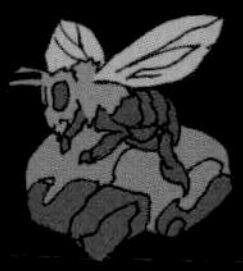

WEST VIRGINIA

The Animals work in the mines alongside humans to bring up the coal, which they trade for resources from other states. Treachery and cannibalism are not unheard of, but the clannishness of the communities prioritizes those of one's own family and township above even one's species. Communities act ruthlessly with one another, but are sternly protective of their own.

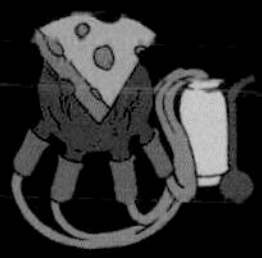

WISCONSIN

A hub of the dairy industry, and site of some of the cruelest and most vile discoveries both before and after the Wake. What happened here is not spoken of by either humans or Animals.

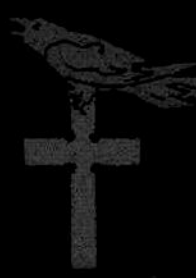

WYOMING

Allied flocks of birds, turning on other species, claimed huge parts of this territory for themselves, and they have managed to keep it. They have begun to construct a humanoid society all their own, complete with garments, songs, customs, and massive structures to which they contribute. Ground-dwelling Animals respond with human weaponry and poisoned corn, but the Nation of the Birds will undoubtedly become a terrible and efficient power in the near future. Also the site of a small cult that believes this to be the end of days, though they are not above doing occasional labor for the birds in exchange for food.

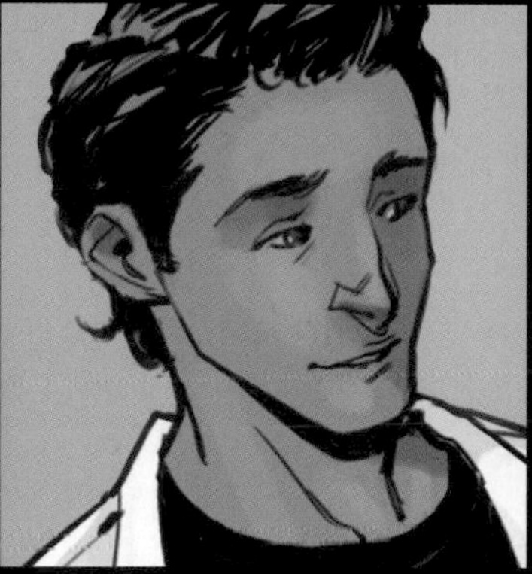

ADAM NORTH

Species: Human *(Homo sapiens)*

Age: 29 years of expected 78 years

Location Born: Boston, Massachusetts

Vorous: Omnivore

Weight: 180 lbs

Height: 6′1″

Profile:

Insecure, anxious, and always longing to do the right thing, Adam North is one of the precious few veterinarians remaining to San Francisco. Jesse's estranged half-brother, he is unaware of her journey to his door. He struggles to find—and dedicate himself to—the ultimate good in any situation. He fears doing harm.

Adam feels divided, unable to fit into any home, family or community. He has thought, at times, that his identity—bisexual, biracial and estranged from his mother, half-sister and stepfather—contributed to this feeling of alienation, but he worries that however or whenever he was born, he would still struggle to fit in.

He often preferred the company of animals because of the simplicity and honesty of their emotions, of their indifference to the fact that he was unlike them—they merely loved him, without ever expecting him to be like them.

He feels particular regret for the breakdown of his relationship with his mother, Shannon, after the death of his father, Micah, who lost his battle with cancer when Adam was ten. His half-sister, Jesse, is a total stranger to him.

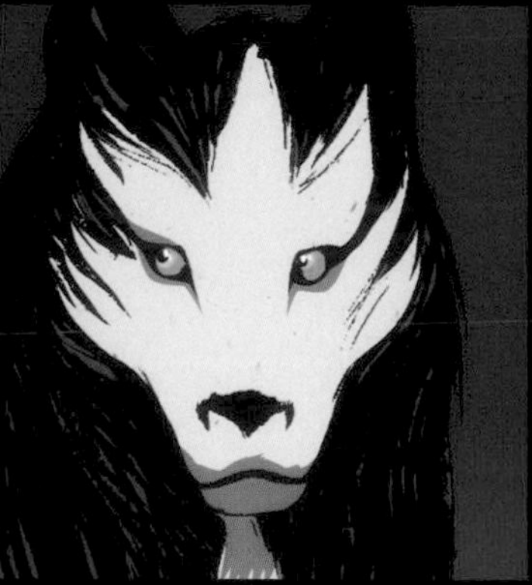

WINTERMUTE

Species: Wolf-Malamute hybrid *(Canis lupus x Canis lupus familiaris)*

Age: [redacted]

Location Born: [redacted]

Vorous: [redacted]

Weight: 110 lbs

Height: 2′5″

Profile:

[redacted] Wintermute was born under sterile conditions in a laboratory owned by Pham Industries. [redacted] She struggles to maintain peace and prosperity for Animal and human alike in the City by the Sea.

BETHESDA

Species: American Bison *(Bison bison)*

Age: 10 years of expected 25 years

Location Born: Bethesda, Maryland

Vorous: Herbivore

Weight: 1,100 lbs

Height: 5'9"

Profile:

Beth can't help the evil that was done to her before and after the Wake, but she has resolved not to let it take root in her heart. Her resilience and kindness are often taken for granted. Beth cares for and looks after others, but only Pallas understands that Beth, too, needs care and looking after.

Beth—known in turn as Bethesda, Bessie, Bette, etc. as she struggles to affix her identity in an often shifting world—is particularly affectionate to children and other small, lost, troubled things. She fears she cares for these creatures because she cannot care for her own calves, born in charitable captivity and taken to various nature preserves Lord knows where.

While Beth feels she has been fortunate—she was born a bison, not a dairy cow or head of cattle—she struggles with the idea that she should be grateful for her position. She longs to be reunited with her lost children, but was thwarted in her search and the trail has since gone cold. Despite and because of her considerable size and strength, she is a prime target for hunters, scavengers and meat-eaters. She is safest with a group, and feels adrift without a family or herd around her.

Bethesda intends to help Jesse to San Francisco out of the hope that the Animals there—reputed to have built a massive, functioning society with advanced technology—will be able to help her find her lost calves. She is kind and loyal until provoked, and wants for her loved ones simply to be happy.

PALLAS

Species: Pallas's cat *(Otocolobus manul)*

Age: Unknown years of expected 11 years

Location Born: The Himalayan Plateau

Vorous: Carnivore

Weight: 8 lbs

Height: 2'1"

Profile:

Pallas was born in the steppes of the Himalayan Plateau, and lived a largely solitary life, occasionally outsmarting hunters amidst the wilds. Eventually, they were poached and brought to a laboratory as a test animal in an experiment to study the immune systems of various mammals when exposed to different diseases. Pallas's cats—also known as manuls—have notoriously poor immune systems, as they live at such intense heights where few viruses survive.

After the Wake, Pallas remained in the laboratory, studying the medical texts and interacting with the surviving scientists, doctors and veterinarians. Their keen intelligence and prodigious memory aided their education, though they are hindered by the limits of human technology designed for human hands. Pallas served as a doctor and medic to the Animilitary, the White Wings, and other forces during and after the Wake. Pallas's main focus is the alleviation of pain and the prevention of harm.

Pallas is genderqueer, and is indifferent to the distinctions that humans make regarding the roles assigned to and expected of various genders. They are calm, thoughtful, intelligent and reasonably sympathetic to others. They have begun to develop a deep attachment to Beth, and consequently only express any sudden or excessive emotion when Beth is threatened or unhappy.

KYLE KHAHN

Species: Human *(Homo sapiens)*

Age: 26 years of expected 78 years

Location Born: Unknown

Vorous: Vegan

Weight: 164 lbs

Height: 5'11"

Profile:

Kyle was a Computer Science student who was expelled from several universities before the coming of the Wake. He was employed in the kitchens and cafeterias of the majority of the schools as part of a work/study program, as well as in several Brooklyn restaurants. His family situation is unknown.

Kyle has always struggled to live his life ethnically— abstaining from meat, from products created in sweatshops, from attending events in venues built by slave labor, etc. Others resented his efforts as performative and accused him of evangelization.

Kyle turned himself over to the creatures who would later become the Animilitary within days of the Wake, and served them faithfully until the coup by the American

military and dissidents within the Animilitary's ranks. He felt it was the right thing to do.

When speaking to Jesse, Kyle alleges that he read her parents' case history in a file while working for the Animilitary, when in fact, Kyle discovered the bodies of Jesse's parents in New York City while he was there on a scavenging mission for Mimico, the Animilitary's leader.

Kyle struggles to maintain his sympathy for others when they do not return it.

KEEKIRIKEE

Species: Giant golden-crowned flying fox *(Acerodon jubatus)*

Age: 3 years of expected 15 years

Location Born: Maitum, Sarangani, Philippines

Vorous: Frugivore

Weight: 2.5 lbs

Wingspan: 5'5"

Profile:

Keekirikee came from the Philippines on a shipping freighter containing fresh mangoes and pineapples. As a stowaway entering to a new land, she escaped and hid out with flocks of bats along the California coast, preying on the orchards of inland farmers. Her native colony of bats numbered in the hundreds of thousands, and her new colony held around twenty thousand.

Moody and secretive, swaying between sudden intense cravings for affection or intensely despising those around her, Keekirikee is a creature of contradictions. She works as the primary guardian animal and chaperone of Adam North in San Francisco, and she seems at a loss as to whether she would prefer many friends and family or none at all.

Keekirikee resents that the Wake brought human awareness—and the burden of human sadness—into her life. She often considers that she was happier as a mere fruit bat, and though she knows the gift of her cognizance is just that—a gift—she struggles with feeling ungrateful. She envies humans for their ability to cope with sentience, and enjoys human hobbies, like swimming, and human jewelry and clothing. She is prone to outbursts of sudden teasing, flirting and jokes, but follows them just as suddenly with icy silence. She wishes she were happier, but doesn't know what would give her life meaning.

SHANNON MANDEL

Species: Human *(Homo sapiens)*

Age: 40 years at time of death

Location Born: Boston, Massachusetts

Vorous: Omnivore

Weight: 132 lbs

Height: 5'6"

Profile:

The only daughter of an old family, and a noted physicist in her own right, Shannon lived the majority of her life in great loneliness. She was an exemplary student, a debutante and pioneer in her field, but often felt hollow—was this all there was to life?

At twenty-five, she married the novelist Micah North, who she felt understood her fears, and for a few years, she, Micah and their son Adam were very happy. When Micah was diagnosed and ultimately lost his battle with cancer, Shannon was devastated and sank into a profound depression. Years later, she would be tempted from her gloom by a charming literature teacher, Óscar Hernadez, who she met at a reading of one of Micah's posthumous collections.

After her wedding to Óscar and their whirlwind honeymoon, Shannon suffered from post-partum depression and feared being unable to bond with her newborn daughter, Jesse. This grief magnified through the increasing rejections of Adam, who never forgave her for remarrying five years after the death of his father.

Shannon often wondered if much of her life was a mistake, and during her days working at home, she confided—sometimes over a glass of wine—in the family dog, Sandor, who could not understand. This dog, on the day of the Wake, would recollect her years of loneliness, unhappiness, and confession with sympathy.

ÓSCAR HERNANDEZ

Species: Human *(Homo sapiens)*

Age: 39 years at time of death

Location Born: Queens, New York City

Vorous: Omnivore

Weight: 159 lbs

Height: 5'10"

Profile:

A mechanic turned high school literature teacher turned award-winning college professor, Óscar was immensely proud to be a self-made man. Separated from his own family through the foster system at a young age, and raised by various distant relatives in turn, the tumult of his childhood and youth gave Óscar a profound sense of what he longed for in a family. All of his achievements have been in service to his wife, Shannon, and their daughter, Jesse.

Loving but jealous, Óscar employed the very furthest extents of his power to give Jesse every kindness and advantage he could, from the best books, to the best schools, to the most enriching experiences, to a newborn

Sandor Clegane, in one of his favorite fantasy epics, *A Game of Thrones*.

Óscar endured a great deal of tension with the ghosts of Shannon's past, fueled by insecurities of never being good enough as a provider for his wife and child. He compared himself first to Micah North, Shannon's late husband, and then to Adam, Shannon and Micah's son. During the Wake, when Sandor became another competitive figure in Óscar's life, threatening the stability and safety of the family—and Óscar's place in it—tensions escalated to the point of explosion.

THE REST OF

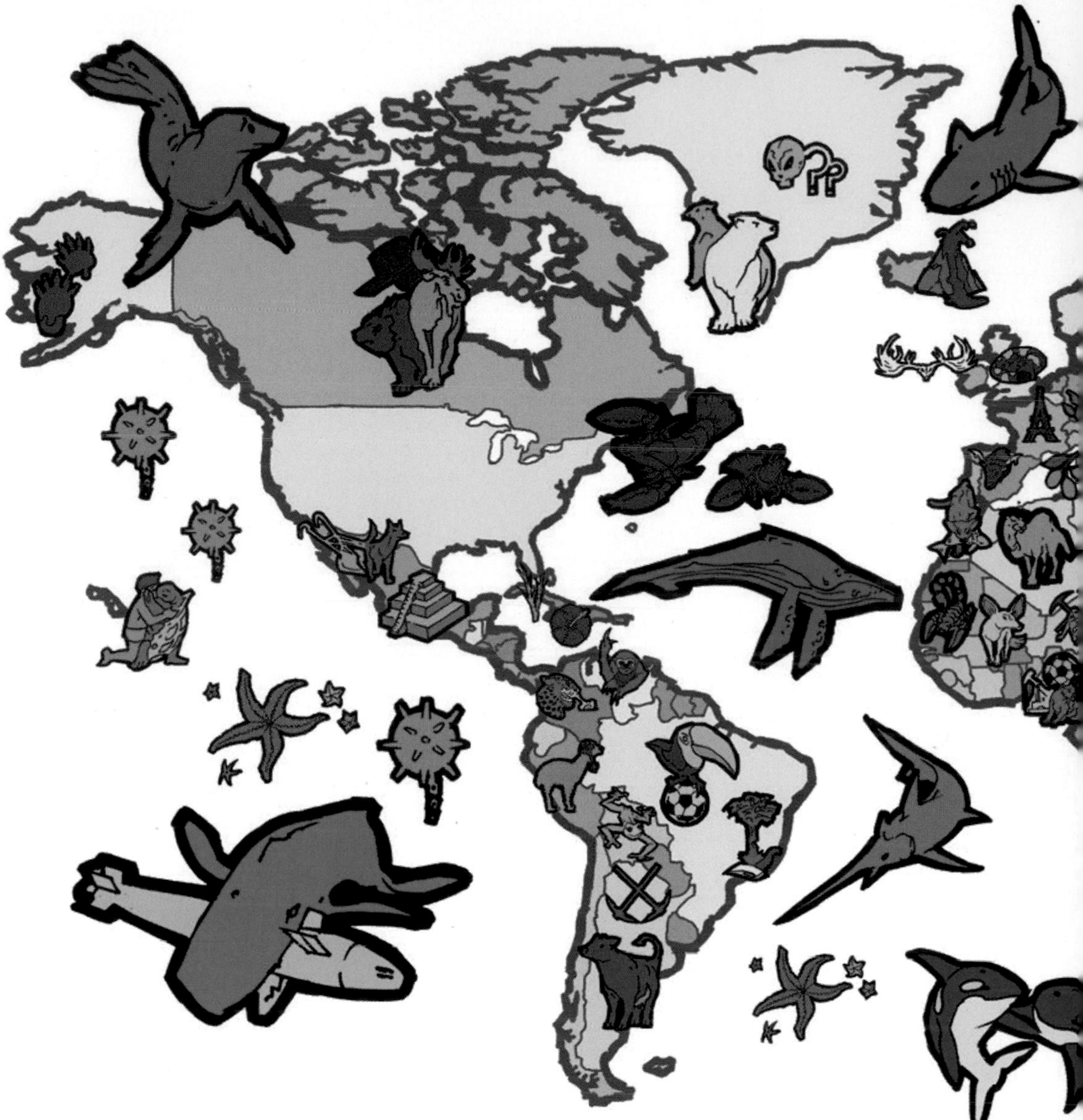

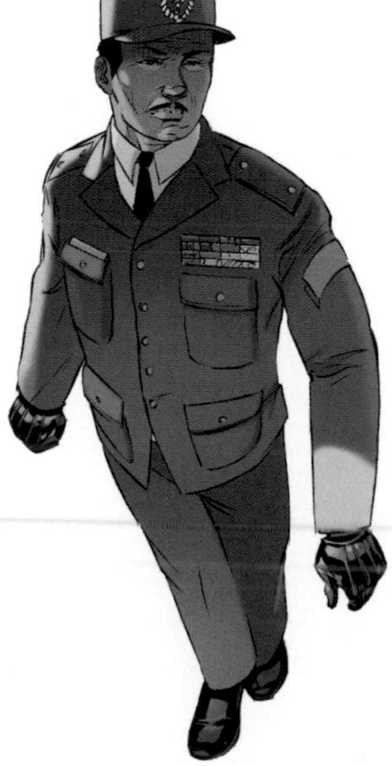

MAJOR DIEGO SINGH

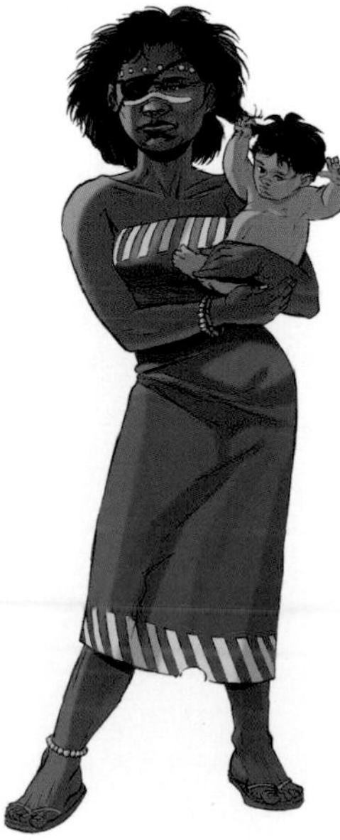

RUBY

THE WORLD

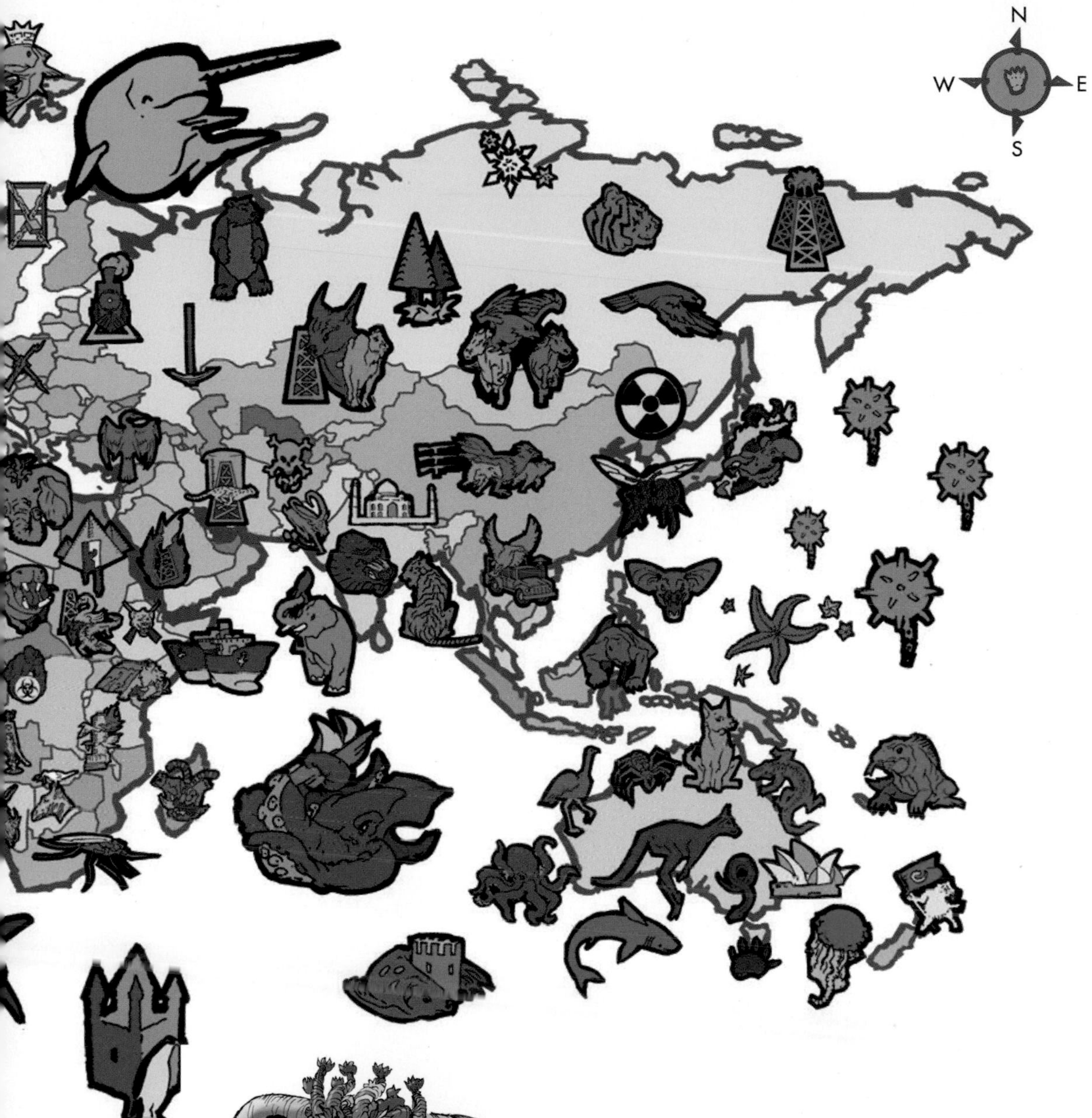
N
W
E
S

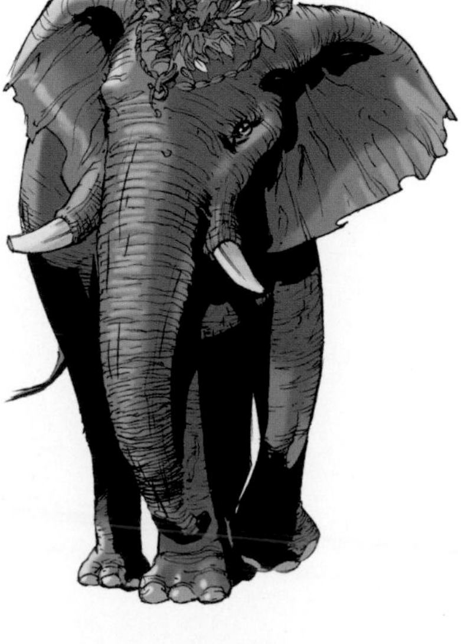

HASANA THE JUST

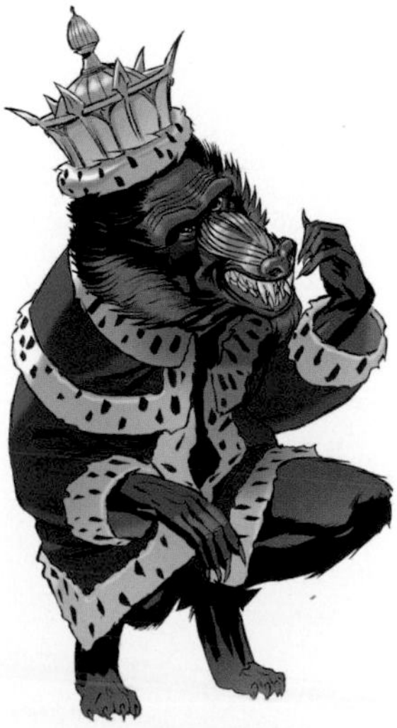

KING HAX

AFRICA

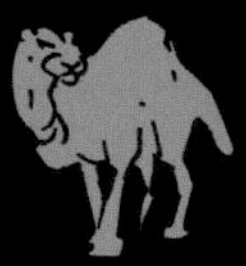
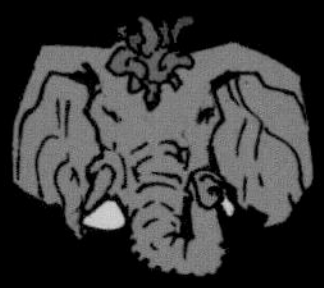
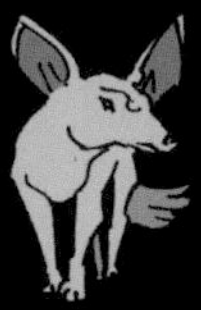

ALGERIA/LIBYA/MALI/MAURITANIA

This united territory is ruled by an elephant matriarch named Hasana who is advised and attended by a select council of humans and Animals alike. Hasana herself is revered as the symbolic grandmother of all the elephant herds in the upper two-thirds of the continent. She is the bitter, sworn enemy of the hyena matriarch Big Teeth, who killed her youngest grandcalf during a raid abetted by stolen motorcycles provided by Somali pirates. Animals of all species flocked to Hasana to protect her until she had amassed a mighty army, from the proudest lions to the smallest ants.

Hasana's campaign progressed through the nations of the north, quelling disputes and gathering new followers whom she fed, clothed and sheltered from predation. City by city, village by village, even humans swore her allegiance, and soon nearly the entire Animal population of the upper half of Africa pledged her their loyalty. She soon redistributed the land and resources for farming, setting Animals to solving crises of water, and settling hard disputes among families.

Unbeknownst to many of her loyal followers, but well known to her bitter enemies, is that Hasana has kept her power through the orchestration of a massive truce with the mosquitos of the continent. She offered her enemies and those cities unwilling to kneel as prey to the insects infected with malaria, while negotiating that those under her protection were to be spared the dreaded sickness. Her devotees call her "Queen Solomon," and her enemies call her "The Bloody Trumpet."

DEMOCRATIC REPUBLIC OF THE CONGO

Intense outbreaks of new zoonotic diseases carried by apes and monkeys reached critical peaks as Animals flooded from the jungles and into high-density human populations. Ebola, sleeping sickness and complications arising from mutations of HIV all poured forth with the exodus of the Animals.

EGYPT

The site of a notoriously bloody riot in Cairo as livestock stampeded out of meat markets, killing hundreds, and were gunned down by soldiers. Cairo arranged a mass extermination of all Animals thought to be "infected," though many families hid their beloved pets or smuggled them outside of city limits. Animals claiming to be gods or the avatars of long-dead pharaohs seized upon Ancient Egyptian mythology, and devotees flocked to their numbers, while the crocodiles took control of the Nile and threatened to poison sources of fresh water if Animal demands are not met.

ETHIOPIA

The hyena called Big Teeth, a military matriarch, is head of a counsel of humans and Animals, governing a "pack" of three hundred thousand souls as raiders in a mobile camp over several hundred miles. Her reliance on technology, from tanks to torpedoes, makes her a formidable threat, but one whose *modus operandi* is as a reaver and raider with no plan for the future beyond survival.

KENYA

A whole lot of lionesses murdered a whole lot of lions over the routine butchery of cubs to whom the sauntering male lions were not related. Less than 10% of the original number of adult male lions in the nation are left, while the lionesses formed nations of their own. One lioness, called the Scarred One, declared that humankind is safe from her people, so long as they leave huge swaths of territory and the national parks to the lions, and mind their own business in the cities. The herbivores were not invited to comment.

MADASCGAR

One of the most biodiverse nations on Earth, with 90% of its wildlife occurring nowhere else on the planet, Madagascar is self-sustaining and largely having a party as it watches what the rest of the world plans to do.

MOROCCO

Morocco has become a vast port city where people and Animals can trade and sell goods, or arrange secret travel on smugglers' ships, to any destination in the world.

NAMIBIA

Antelopes, springboks, dik-diks, wildebeest, klipspringers, kudus, oryxes, gemboks, water buffalo, etc. murdered the absolute ever-loving shit out of tourism hunters and poachers, dragged the bodies to the border, and dumped them in South Africa.

NIGERIA

The technological advances of Nigeria meant that it had more to lose in the Wake. Nigeria successfully maintained control of the nation, due in part to the extermination of rebel squads of Animals, but suffered some of the lowest loss of human life on the continent. Animals entered the major urban areas in droves, looking for food, care and explanations of their current state, and were housed on soccer fields and in sporting arenas until employment could be found for them.

SENEGAL/GUINEA/COTE D'IVOIRE/ SIERRA LEONE/GHANA/BURKINA FASO

An enormous barricade, over a thousand miles long, was erected to separate Senegal, Guinea, Cote d'Ivoire, Sierra Leone, Ghana and Burkina Faso from the rest of the continent, though there are gaps in this massive defense system that are exploited by smugglers. The barricade, initially erected to prevent disease and the onrush of Animals and refugees alike from overwhelming the coast in mass starvation, has largely protected it. Land Animals and humans have formed alliances against the fish, and work together to hold off famine—but hoarding, betrayal and concealment of disease are strenuously punished.

SOMALIA

Human pirates, aided now by sea birds and sea creatures, have become one of the most formidable forces on the seas. Certain Animals now helm their own ships in a huge pirate navy directed by a Captain Afrax and his bloodthirsty ostrich wife.

SOUTH AFRICA

Humans in any form of power were expelled en masse from the country, some fleeing by plane and others by yacht, as the Animals burned large portions of the country to the ground, and seized food caches to redistribute among those remaining. Humans willing to fight with the Animals were spared and rewarded. Humans who fought for the leaders who were ejected were driven into the shallow water as gifts of alliance to the sharks.

ANTARTICA

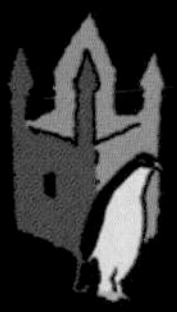
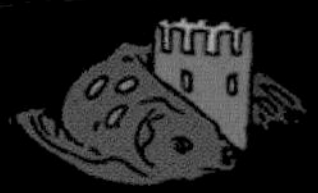

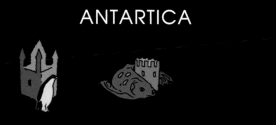

ANTARTICA

The last unclaimed kingdom, all but devoid of humanity. Only a few thousand humans were present at scientific research stations during the Wake. Some became hostages, others became allies to the Animals, others attempted to flee, others attempted to do their scientific duties and study the events, and others were slain by warring clans of Animals attempting to seize human facilities (and in at least one case) human slaves. The continent is divided into warring clans of penguins attempting to seize power and ease the brutal struggles of their lives, while leopard seals and killer whales make devious alliances in the seas.

ASIA

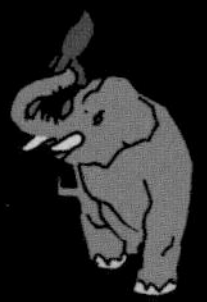 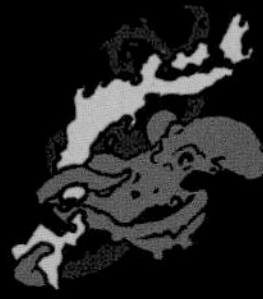 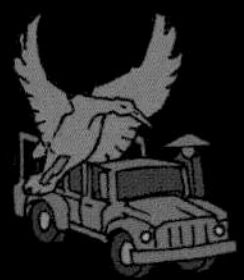

AFGHANISTAN

The site of a dreaded outbreak of the smallpox. The bacteria, which had been considered extinct, was uncovered in an isolated village and carried in infected carrion by a vulture. Humanity, which no longer vaccinates against the disease, was unprepared, and the plague burned through huge swaths of the country. The world was in such chaos that little medical aid could be sent to stop the spread. Animals, immune to the smallpox strain, acted as guardians, liaisons, doctors and runners to acquire the vaccine for the humans left uninfected, and sit as caretakers of the dying and protectors of the living. This is one of the only known cases where the human nation was paralyzed, and relied on the kindness of the Animals for survival.

CHINA

As the country with the largest population of humans in the world, so too did China have the largest population of livestock. The billions of cows, pigs, sheep, chickens and more rose up in a devastating civil war, sparking a massive famine and colossal conflict, leaving hundreds of millions dead.

FIJI

With air travel collapsing on the day of the Wake, and the seas far too dangerous with vengeful ocean life, anyone on Fiji during the Wake is still on Fiji after the Wake. Animals and humans, after some initial bewilderment, are making the best of their environments, redistributing the wealth and resources, and many taking up housing in the luxury resorts. A pretty swell time, to be honest, especially since if anyone tries to take more than his fair share, you can feed him to the lizards.

INDIA

Areas with the highest population density suffered intense violence as humans and Animals, in a panic, lashed out at one another—human against human, Animal against Animal, and everyone against each other in a desperate bid to protect their loved ones. Looting, burning and panic caused huge devastation in the most populated cities, and the military was unable to control any Animal populations without unforgivable costs to human life, and so did not fire upon any urban areas.

Power was seized by one Mandrill, the imported pet of a notorious gangster, who declared himself at first to be a king and then a god. The Mandrill, called Hax, seized control of huge caches of food and weaponry, and all lesser monkeys and apes swore fealty to him. He lives as a king in villas abandoned during the violence, and controls human populations through the threat of infection and disease and the seizing and raising of human infants to be his own soldiers.

In turn, an eight-year-old she-elephant calf called Tapani beseeched that the Animals and humans live peacefully, and led huge communities away from the cities to live in small farming villages where they might care for each other in accordance to their needs and abilities. The Animals and humans work the land as stably as possible, with Animals adopting human dress and custom, and attempt to stave off famine.

INDONESIA

Fighting gamecocks exploded out of the ring, turning on many who had gathered to watch the bloodsport and declaring that the humans would now have to fight and die in gladiatorial combat for the pleasure of the roosters and their wives and chicks. Those in urban areas suffered most, usually due to panic, while those in more remote areas were able to swiftly orchestrate alliances with the Animals to protect their territory from those fleeing the cities. Komodo dragons have established themselves as pagan gods who raise armies of lizards to raid human villages, while the Animals of the faithful do their best to defend their humans and understand their own identities and roles in this brave new world.

IRAN

In the chaos of the Wake, cities have isolated themselves, shutting their doors and attempting to survive in small, insulated units. In one such city, the University dominates the community, and one man, known as the Professor, tries to ethically explore and understand the nature of the Wake. His companion, in the small garden and courtyard of the library that is his domain, is a she-cheetah, with whom he discusses the philosophy of the world and the will of God. She will one day be the death of him, but he does not know that yet.

IRAQ

In the power vacuum left by years of brutality and instability, the chaos of the Wake has largely triggered a free-for-all, with Animals seizing whatever they can and attempting to have a massive orgy of food, mating, fun and chaos before what is surely the end of the world. The so-called "Prince of Baghdad" is a golden jackal who had orchestrated a vast network of Animals (armed with luxury cars and automatic weapons) to trade oil stores for whatever they might desire.

JAPAN

Besieged by sea Animals, Japan is targeted for its cache of experimental biotechnology, included advanced prosthetic and synthetic limbs intended to be attached to systems suffering from intense nerve damage. Animals loyal to the humans now fight back viciously to protect their loved ones, but the seas team with life and far outnumber those on land. Sea life carried in by mercenary birds or creeping up through canals and reservoirs hold scientists hostage, offering lesser creatures such as oysters, fish and urchins as food in exchange for the technology.

KAZAKHSTAN

Animals, great or small, were immediately rounded up for extermination by the humans. Those who would swear loyalty and occupy their pre-Wake roles were allowed to return to them, though speaking is punished with death. Those who refused were culled. Separatist groups hide in the hills.

MONGOLIA

Little has changed.

NORTH KOREA

A meltdown of a malformed nuclear reactor has rendered the country utterly silent, though some civilian survivors have been rumored to have slipped over the borders, aided by wild Animals.

PAKISTAN

Humans and Animals alike worked together to prevent the nuclear armaments of the country from falling into the hands of those who believed that the end of days had come. The massive civil war that ensued erased much of the leadership of the nation, while in the hills, wise creatures of every species gather to teach whoever would come and listen.

THE PHILIPPINES

The Philippines were the epicenter for a massive outbreak of nipah virus carried by infected bats, causing hemorrhaging, respiratory failure, encephalitis and meningitis. The country has been sealed. Status unknown.

SAUDI ARABIA

Human forces, beset by powerful Animal rebels, drove and lured many rampaging creatures onto the oil fields, where they set the fields themselves ablaze to shatter the Animal resistance.

SOUTH KOREA

A dreaded swarm of Asian giant hornets, the largest and most vicious hornets in the world, coalesced upon the most densely populated cities, causing devastation to humans and Animals alike. The stings resulted in anaphylactic shock, cardiac arrest and organ failure, in addition to collisions caused by drivers and conductors swarmed by the insects. The hornets harvested everything that could be devoured or carried off, but many seemed to kill only for the sake of killing. Intense gas bombing of the cities drove the giant hornets into the countryside, where alliances between human and Animal populations—particularly birds—turned upon them.

THAILAND/LAOS/CAMBODIA/VIETNAM

Humans and birds quickly established truces among themselves to defend against the grasping hands and paws of other Animals and other nations who might seize power during this crisis and vulnerability. Birds were granted rights above all other Animals, though individual alliances are made with domestic Animals such as oxen. Cats, for example, were employed by the state to keep down the population of vermin. Creatures assumed new duties, though some now had power, and others lived just as before, though now they were cognizant of the horror of their fate.

TURKEY

Animals in urban areas were exterminated or driven out, leading to a food crisis. Non-human Animals were declared illegal, and forbidden in the nation. The country crumbled, expending resources on trying to protect its people from Animals, firing bullets at birds in the sky, seeding the ground with poison against insects. The only anti-Animal isolationist nation, it will be short-lived as winter draws near.

AUSTRALIA

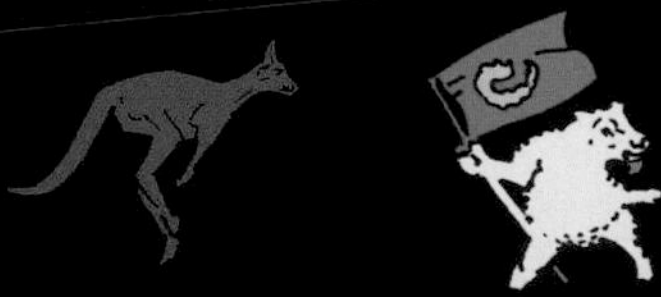

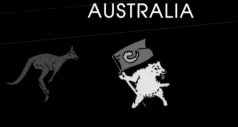

AUSTRALIA

The deadly Animals of Australia may truly have met their match in the ferocity of its people, but the humans were too few. The detention centers (where imprisoned refugees were held for attempting to enter the country without documentation) were opened in the hopes of granting citizenship in exchange for taking up arms against the Animals. The Animals, who bowed only to the ancient peoples of the continent, sought the counsel of one named Ruby, a human woman who rose to usher in an uneasy end to the bloodshed. She beseeched the Animals to tear down the prisons that held the refugees, and with an army of the mightiest and deadliest creatures in the world at her back, offered all of the humans this alternative: live in peace, together, or die as invaders in a stolen land.

NEW ZEALAND

Guess.

EUROPE

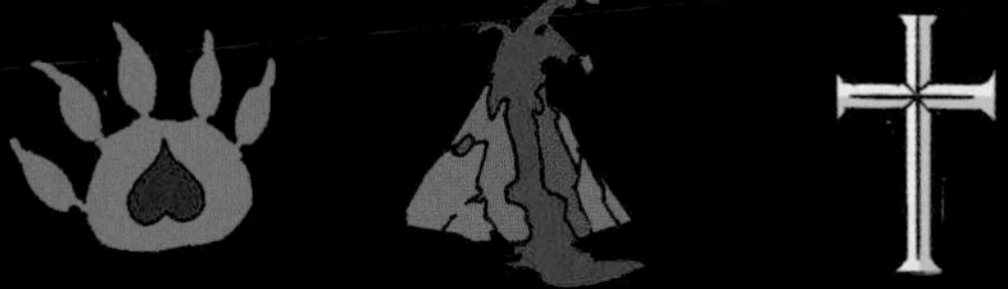

EASTERN EUROPE

A vast survival zone, where strength, skill and the needs of one's family and community—whatever species that may be—triumph over all other considerations.

FINLAND/NORWAY/SWEDEN

Believing the Wake to be caused by a plague or some other infectious origin, the Northern countries sealed their borders, and no human has gone in or out—though birds report the strangest tales of madness, occultism and heroism.

FRANCE/GERMANY/POLAND

The intense bonds between humans and their domesticated Animals became a complex issue during the Wake. The humans displayed clear love for the Animals they kept as pets, while showing indifference or pleasantly enjoying the benefits of the deaths of Animals of other species. Many humans were executed under Animal law, while other Animals yet intervened on behalf of their humans. Some Animals were executed with their humans as traitors, and still others declare their love for one another and live as married couples. Chaos reigns, and town to town, community to community, often seem like separate worlds.

ICELAND

Some believe the Wake was caused by ancient gods beneath the Earth, and have gone to find the gods and either thank or appease them.

ITALY

The Pope was sealed within the Vatican for his protection, but is besieged on all sides by humans anticipating the end of days, and Animals begging for souls and the right to enter Heaven.

RUSSIA

For Animals, speaking is punishable by death. Animal rebels coalesce in the hills and sewers, seeking a way to rebel and free their kin. Pre-Wake roles are rigidly enforced, and new livestock have their vocal cords removed at birth, though the full effect of this is not understood, as many Animals without vocal cords became capable of speech during the Wake. Whole human cities, when besieged by birds or insects, have elected to bomb themselves flat so long as the Animals go with them. Many human leaders have proven that they would rather go out as masters of the Earth than see themselves on equal footing with the Animals. The tigers to the East are seeking allies to rescue the remaining Animals under human control.

NORTH AMERICA

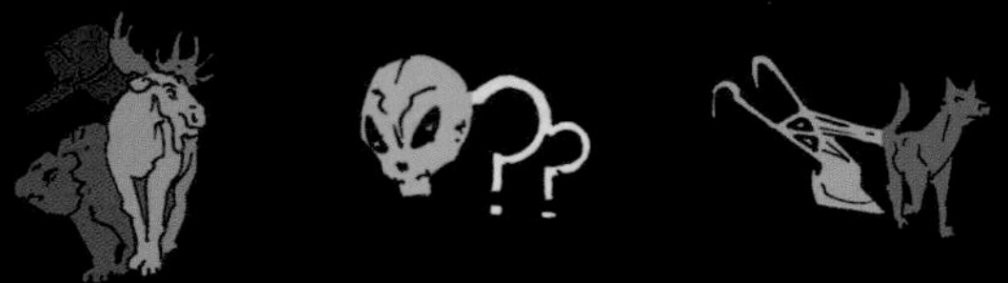

CANADA

The Canadians fought well and honorably, but the Animals were far, far too many, and the moose, especially, fought dirty. The Animals keep the humans largely as pets and very indulged house servants. The country has one of the highest qualities of living in the world post-Wake, and Toronto alone has enough condos to house vast populations of Animals.

GREENLAND

Home of the Greenland sharks, which live to be over 500 years old. The sharks are living libraries who gather students to whom they might tell the oral histories of the seas, lest the knowledge be lost forever. Also the site of where certain humans believe that extraterrestrials visited Earth in order to cause the Wake, though none of these theories have been verified.

MEXICO

In urban areas with the most intense population density, immediate violence—human against Animal, Animal against human, human against human, and all species of Animal against one another—was explosive. The close quarters and immense claustrophobia of these environments led to 90% mortality in the worst cases, though this does not mean that mortality rate was equal among all species. After a week of incredible violence, the survivors emerged to a vastly altered landscape, and began to scavenge among the ruins.

In rural areas, however, the violence was dramatically decreased, and after the initial panic and chaos, family and community units did their best to stave off famine through working together, especially given that the initial violence had reduced the number of mouths to feed, and greatly increased the available arable land.

UNITED STATES

Please see "The Former United States of America" section earlier in this issue.

SOUTH AMERICA

ARGENTINA

Animal uprisings among cattle ranches were immense and enormously bloody, and Animal separatist nations were formed over the previous grazing land. The Cattle Land now permits select humans to enter their territory to perform actions that the livestock are unable to perform themselves, and in exchange, they offer those who have died of old age as meat.

BOLIVIA

Humans will die if they enter the forest. That is the Animals' only law and request. If an Animal escapes to the forest, it will not be pursued. If an Animal escapes to the forest, humans may not pursue it. How the Animals rule among themselves is unknown.

BRAZIL

The humans of Brazil put up one of the most spectacular civilian displays of power, holding back Animal forces for months after the Wake. The cities became battlegrounds as Animals flooded from the forests into urban areas, with humans up in high-rises, sniping with weaponry abandoned by the retreating army. Treachery plagued the factions, from humans going over to the Animals, wild Animals going over to the humans, and pets operating as heroic and conniving double agents to both sides.

The abandoned Olympic stadium was the site of a climactic and terrible battle, with flocks of parrots and toucans reigning down flaming torches from the sky, to swarms of insects blackening the atmosphere, to explosions of snakes writhing up from abandoned swimming pools. Both sides, mighty and exhausted, staggered to tense, uneasy truces that threaten at any moment to open again into total civil war.

COLOMBIA

Animals have seized control of nearly all of the countries resources— natural, manufactured, legal and illegal, including the leopards, who have taken over the drug trade. Diego Singh, a major abruptly promoted through the ranks due to the immense violence during the initial week of the Wake, emerged as a force bent on restoring control to the country at any cost –so long as that control is a human control.

CUBA

Large Animals and most mammals were immediately removed from the human population and taken to distant locations, where they were restrained and set to labor in agricultural fields. Human fatalities were few, but the birds and insects remain free, and are currently plotting a massive overthrow of the humans on the island.

HAITI

Humans fleeing from other nations were welcomed to Haiti, so long as they abided by Animal law. Animals require humans to operate machinery designed for human needs, and threw themselves into agricultural endeavors at the expense of all else, determined that the island would not starve. Religious leaders, confounded as to the meaning of the Wake, initially believed it indicated the end of days, but revised to view the Animals as angelic messengers sent to aid the faithful and drive out human tyrants.

SPAIN

After some initial bloodthirsty revenge, the Animals went off for a drink. Spain, exhausted, legalized pretty much everything and called it a day.

Foxes on horseback meticulously located, tracked and captured those who voted on the return of foxhunting. With hordes of hounds beside them, they ran their prey to the ground, panting and bleeding. With their quarry surrounded, the foxes carefully brought forth one of their own number infected with rabies, bound in a straightjacket, frothing mad, and managed to use him with the utmost care. This infected fox was led to administer several bites to the captured party, who was then released into a forest guarded on all sides by the hounds, and left without treatment to die a very, very terrible death.

Humans with pets were largely defended by them, and survival came down to family units—those who foreswore eating meat, to those who would survive at any cost, to those who made plans about where they might go from here. Mother cats formed a network of communication through the cities and towns, striking deals with birds for information from abroad.

The entire world waits and watches and asks, "Where do we go from here?"

VENEZUELA

Venezuela endured the total dissolution of its previous government, with Animals and humans alike uniting to drive out the remains of the former regime. The rebelling populace seized all factories and farmland, and is now desperately at work on how to offset famine with so many more mouths to feed. Animals proved most efficient at combating the military, as ants contaminated fuel storage and rodents destroyed interior machinery, rendering many vehicles useless, though armed soldiers managed to kill hundreds of thousands of both humans and Animals. The people are currently engaged in a massive rebellion—perhaps the only one where humans and Animals are allied uniting against a common national enemy. Though famine looms, the country may be the first to reincorporate Animals into its laws when the nation is rebuilt.

A brave new world is coming.

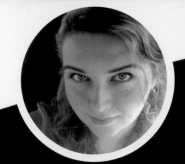

MARGUERITE BENNETT • JUAN DOE
ANIMOSITY
THE RISE
"...just jump in. You won't regret it." IGN.COM
"...this is the book to read." ComicsAlliance.com
MARSHALL DILLON
AFTERSHOCK

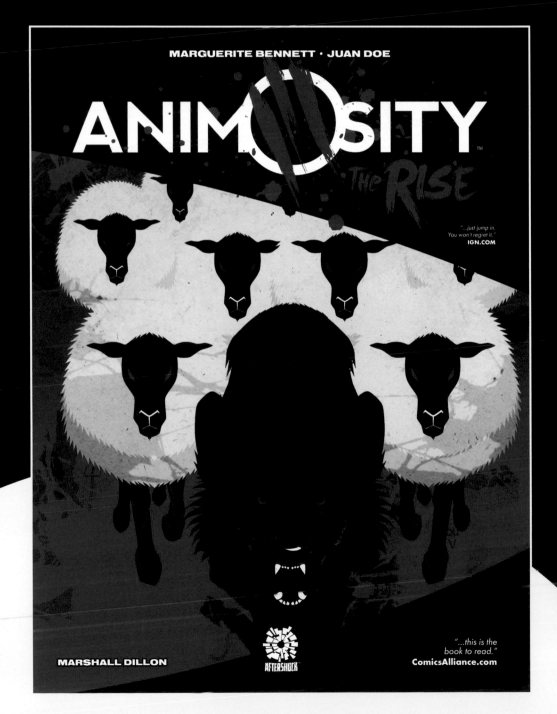

ANIMSITY

EXTRAS

AFTERSHOCK

PAGE TWO

2.1
SPLASH PAGE.

JOE is devoured alive by RATS as ADAM turns in shock and horror. Rats are burrowing into Joe's open throat, burrowing under his skin, ripping at his ears, etc. We're not looking for gore, but the suggestion of something unspeakable. (The truly horrible things are going on out of sight under his clothes). If there's space, the family in the background is equally horrified and the PUPPY is standing protectively in front of the family (thematic foreshadowing, but not necessary if it clutters the page).

1 RATS:	DIE, YOU BASTARD
2 RATS:	RAT BASTARD
3 RATS:	RAT BASTARD
4 RATS:	DIE BASTARD
5 RATS:	DIE DIE DIE

script by
MARGUERITE BENNETT

PAGE
02
PROCESS

pencils by
RAFAEL DE LATORRE

inks by
RAFAEL DE LATORRE

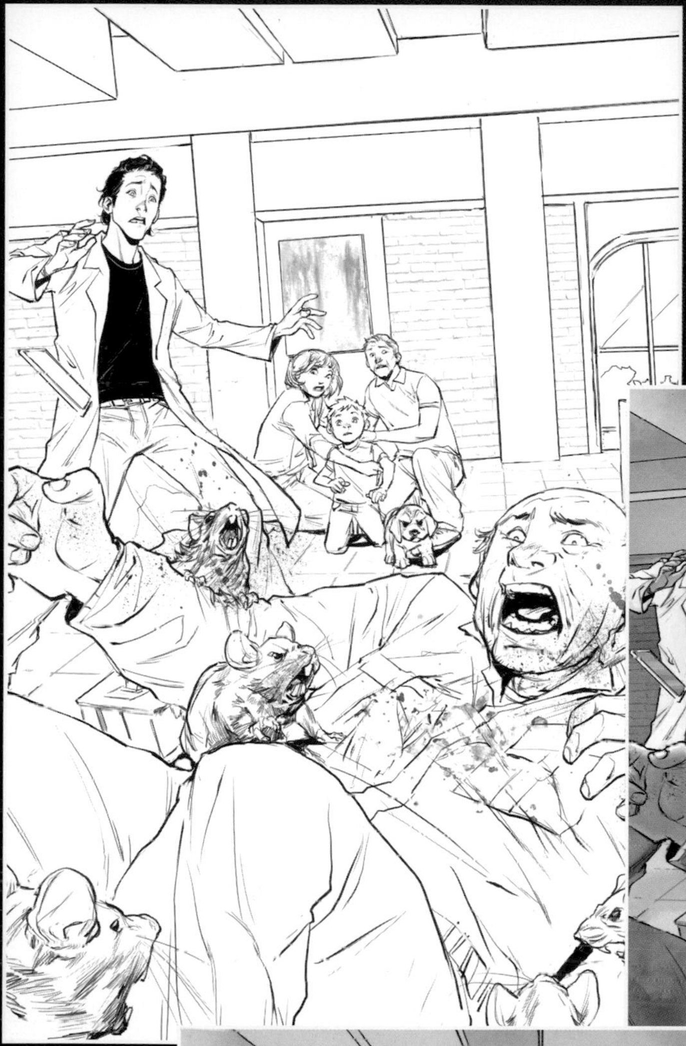

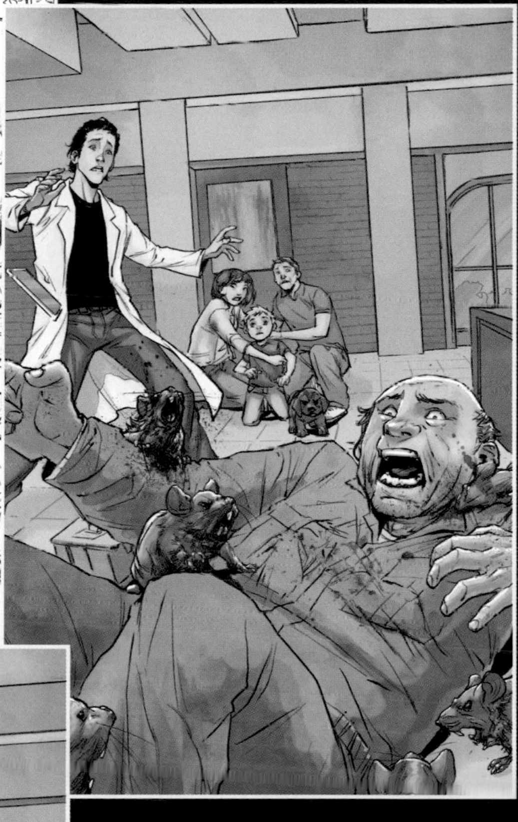

colors by
ROB SCHWAGER

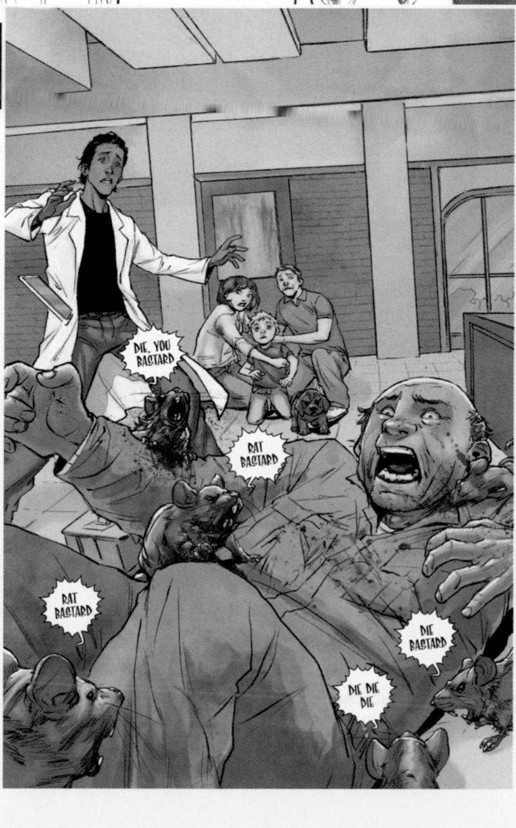
DIE, YOU BASTARD
RAT BASTARD
RAT BASTARD
DIE BASTARD
DIE DIE DIE

lettering by
MARSHALL DILLON

ANIMOSITY #2

PAGE SEVENTEEN

17.1
SANDOR turns, his muzzle and face all bloody. He is stricken, hopeful, looking for
JESSE.

1 SANDOR: Jesse--?

17.2
SANDOR is kicked savagely in the RIBS. (It's Jesse's father, though we can't quite see
him yet. Sandor's ribs are actually broken by the end of this sequence, and will pain
him for the rest of the series.)

2 SFX: CRNCH

3 SANDOR: RRRF!!

17.3
JESSE'S FATHER towers over SANDOR. JESSE'S FATHER'S rage from helplessness and terror—
his inability to protect his family, his consuming fear of his daughter being killed.

4 FATHER: You BASTARD.

17.4
JESSE'S FATHER kicks SANDOR in the ribs again. SANDOR snarls this time, trying to
dodge.

2 FATHER: You could've KILLED her.

3 SANDOR: RRRF!!

17.5
JESSE'S FATHER brings a rock down at SANDOR'S HEAD. He's beating him because he can't
beat the dead man, because he can't beat the entire world into a pulp for endangering
his child. We're going to revisit this scene (with Sandor as Father, and someone else
in Sandor's proverbial shoes) later in the series.

4 FATHER: You could've KILLED her, you could've gotten her head BLOWN OFF--

script by
MARGUERITE BENNETT

pencils by
RAFAEL DE LATORRE

inks by
RAFAEL DE LATORRE

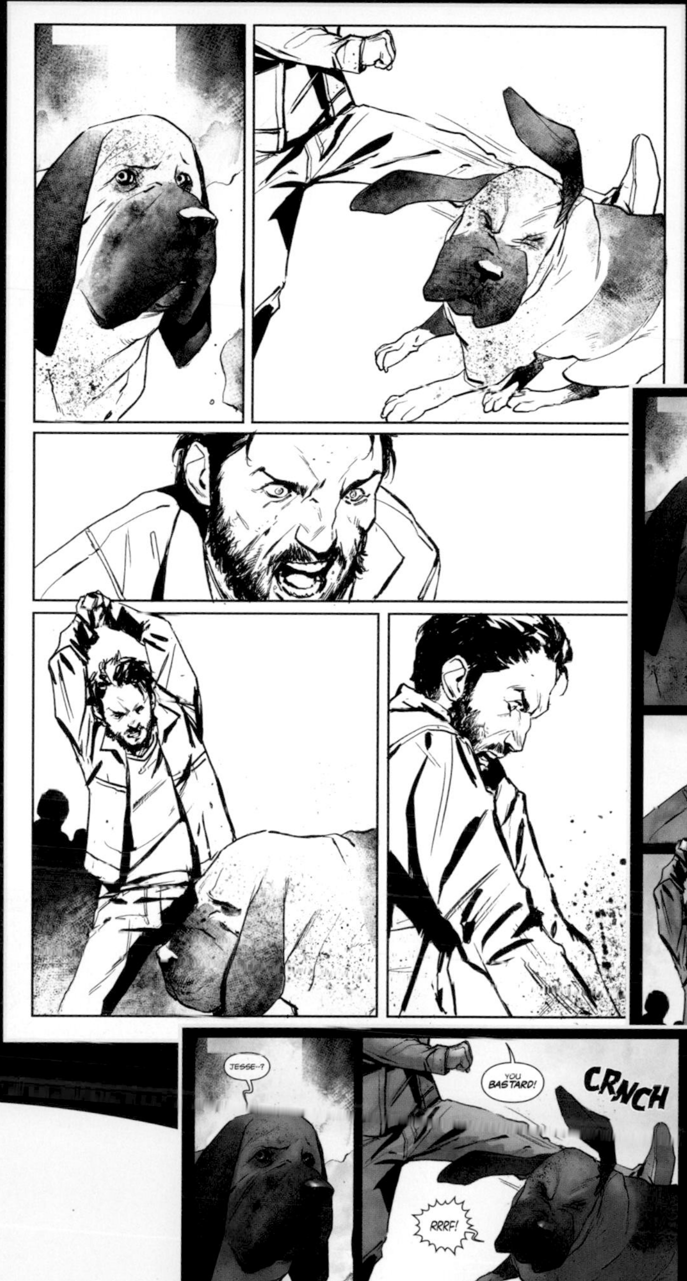

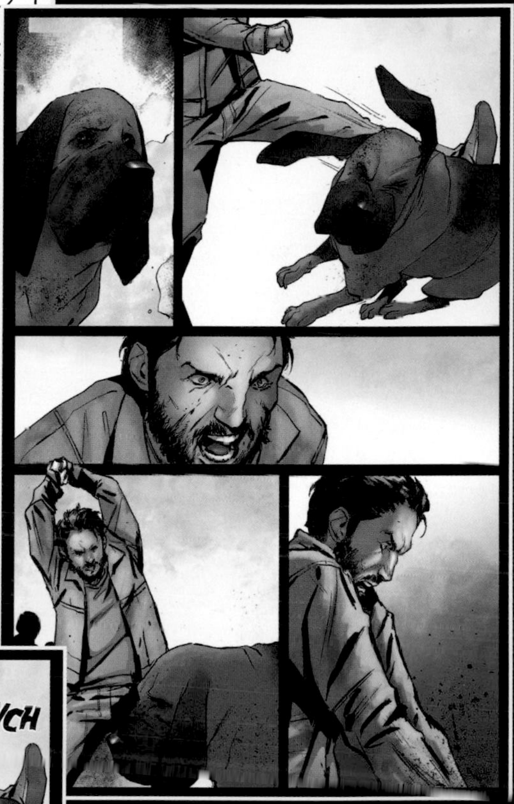

colors by
ROB SCHWAGER

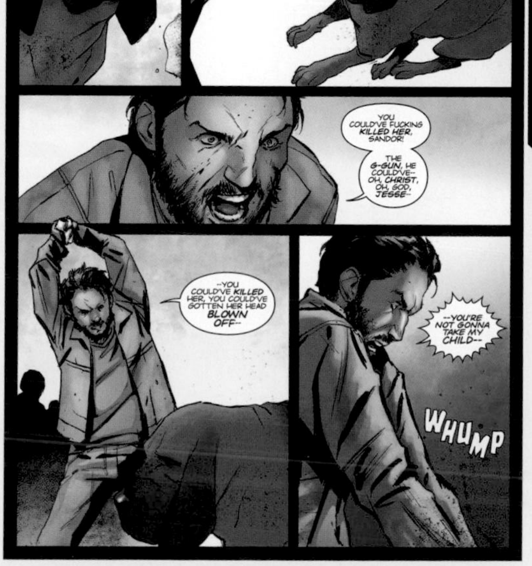
JESSE--?
YOU BASTARD!
CRNCH
RRRF!
YOU COULD'VE FUCKING KILLED HER, SANDOR!
THE G-GUN, HE COULD'VE-- OH, CHRIST, OH, GOD, JESSE--
--YOU COULD'VE KILLED HER, YOU COULD'VE GOTTEN HER HEAD BLOWN OFF--
--YOU'RE NOT GONNA TAKE MY CHILD--
WHUMP

lettering by
MARSHALL DILLON

ANIMOSITY #3

script by
MARGUERITE BENNETT

PAGE EIGHT

8.1

MIMICO ushers SANDOR and JESSE into the Fortress's kitchen, in which an enormous AMERICAN BISON is standing. The KITCHEN has been engineered so everything is at half the height it would be in a normal kitchen—the stove is very low and separate from the oven, which is also low. The knives, ladles, spoons, etc, all have very long handles (so the bison can grip them in her teeth). There are buttons instead of switches for everything. (Jesse is delighted.) Mimico's posture is always erect, like a politician displaying something they are proud of; SANDOR'S posture is lower, more suspicious, lower.

1 MIMICO: While we work, your human can stay with our **camp cook**, if that is suitable.

2 BETH: Oh, look at this little *sugarbean!*

3 JESSE: Oh my gosh!

8.2

BETH, amused, beams down at JESSE. JESSE looks delighted.

4 BETH: Yeah, I bet you say that to all the pretty buffalo.

5 JESSE: You're not a buffalo, you're a *bison!*

6 BETH: Oh, I **like** you. Do you want to pet me?

8.3

JESSE hugs BETH. SANDOR is ruefully amused. He's letting JESSE hug a strange ANIMAL without feeling the least bit jealous, either. MIMICO is turning to greet KYLE, who is off screen.

7 MIMICO: Ah. And one of our **allies**.

8 MIMICO: Hello, Human Kyle.

8.4

SANDOR turns as KYLE enters the kitchen. KYLE, as described, is the perfect Brooklyn hipster, the save-the-Earth vegan who wants to be an ally to the animals and be accepted by them so damn badly. KYLE is carrying a large basket of CORN. His ANKLES have been shackled together by a short length of chain.

9 KYLE: Hello, Gray Wolf Mimico.

PAGE
08
PROCESS

pencils by
RAFAEL DE LATORRE

inks by

RAFAEL DE LATORRE

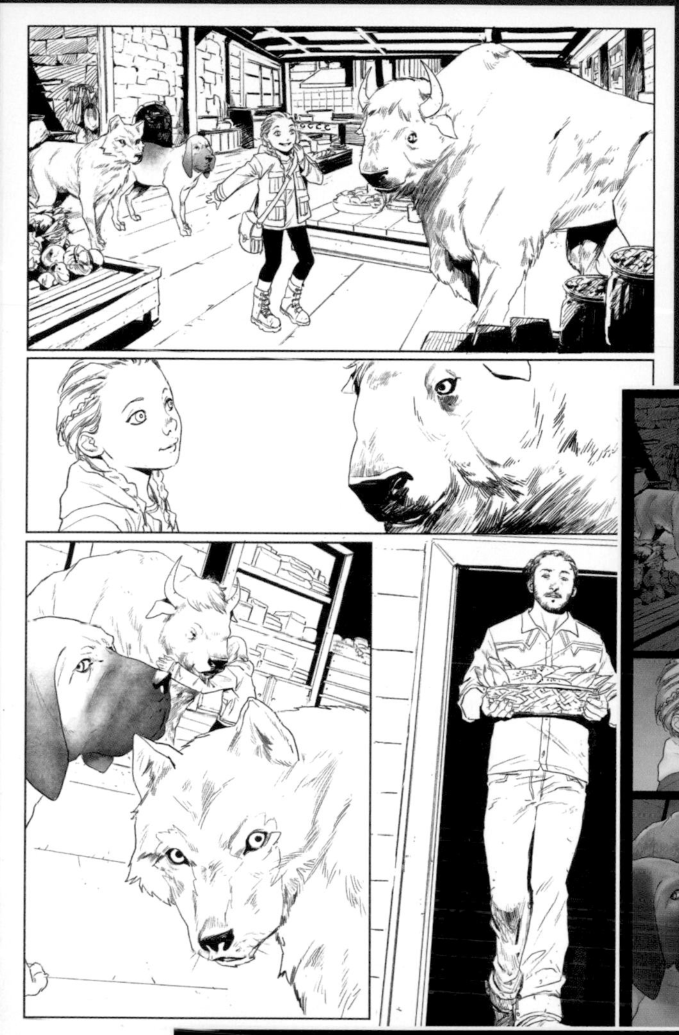

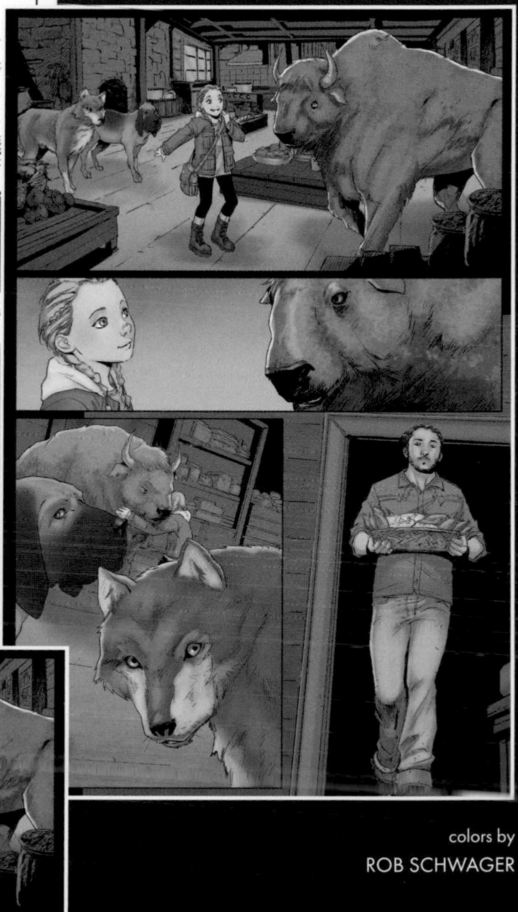

colors by

ROB SCHWAGER

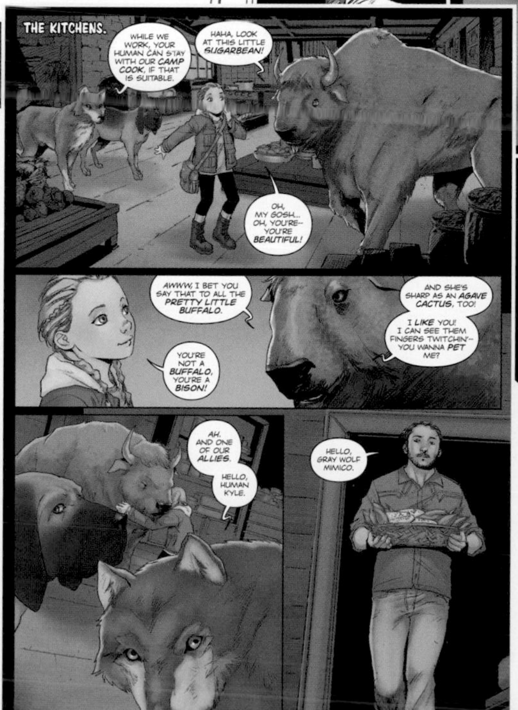
THE KITCHENS.
WHILE WE WORK, YOUR HUMAN CAN STAY WITH OUR CAMP COOK, IF THAT IS SUITABLE.
HAHA, LOOK AT THIS LITTLE SUGARBEAN!
OH, MY GOSH... OH, YOU'RE-- YOU'RE BEAUTIFUL!
AWWW, I BET YOU SAY THAT TO ALL THE PRETTY LITTLE BUFFALO.
YOU'RE NOT A BUFFALO, YOU'RE A BISON!
AND SHE'S SHARP AS AN AGAVE CACTUS, TOO!
I LIKE YOU! I CAN SEE THEM FINGERS TWITCHIN'-- YOU WANNA PET ME?
AH. AND ONE OF OUR ALLIES.
HELLO, HUMAN KYLE.
HELLO, GRAY WOLF MIMICO.

lettering by

MARSHALL DILLON

·ANIM SITY #4

PAGE NINE

9.1
The TORTOISES fire.

NO COPY

9.2
Largest panel. MIMICO and PEARL are consumed (though Mimico is not actually killed!) in a burst of FIRE from the explosion of the Tortoises' Rocket.

NO COPY

9.3
SANDOR stares in horror.

NO COPY

9.4
The TORTOISES aim for a low building with smoke rising from the CHIMNEY.

TORTOISE: Burn it all.

script by
MARGUERITE BENNETT

PAGE 9 PROCESS

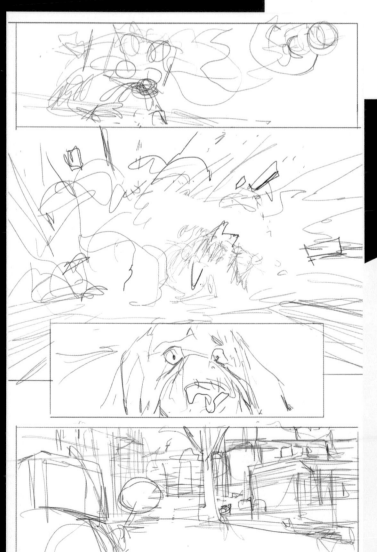

pencils by
RAFAEL DE LATORRE

inks by

RAFAEL DE LATORRE

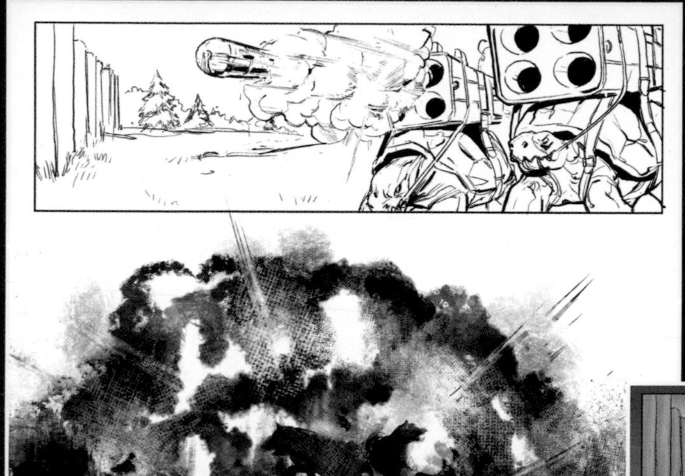

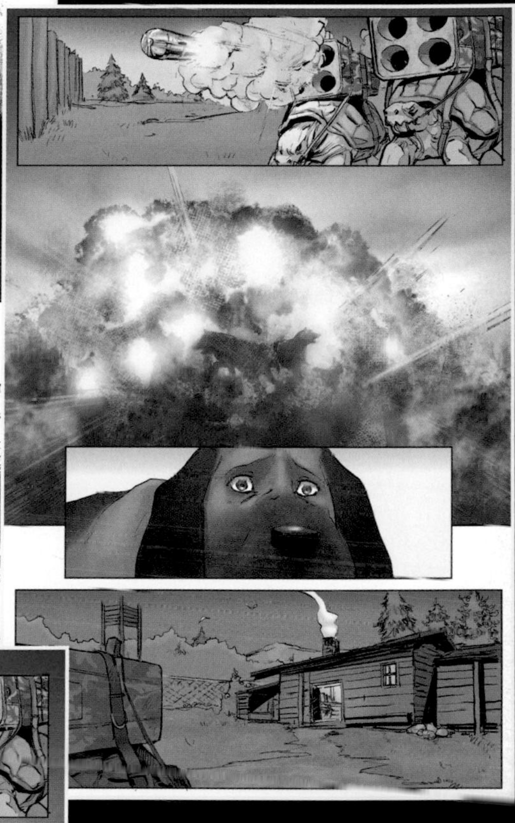

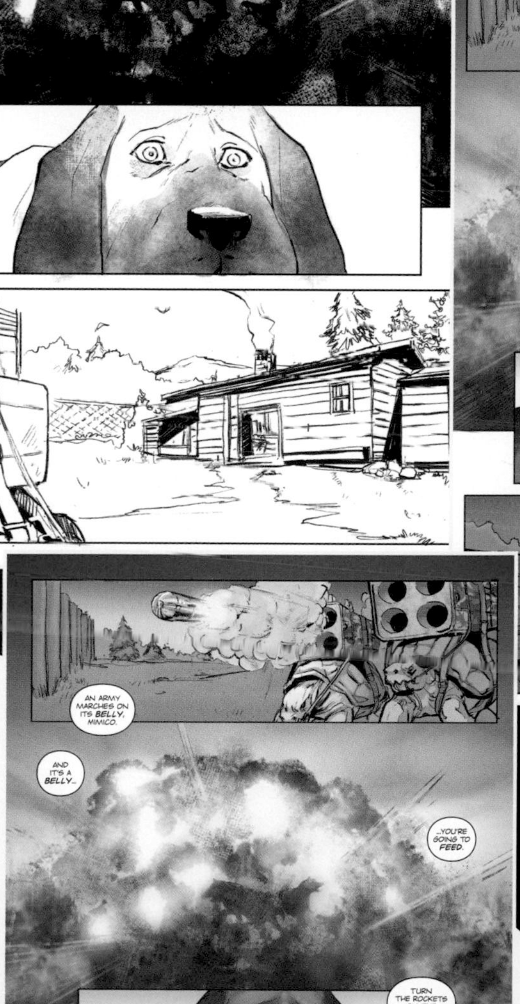

AN ARMY MARCHES ON ITS BELLY, MIMICO.
AND IT'S A BELLY...
...YOU'RE GOING TO FEED.
TURN THE ROCKETS ON THE KITCHENS.
BURN IT ALL.

colors by

ROB SCHWAGER

lettering by

MARSHALL DILLON

21 QUESTIONS

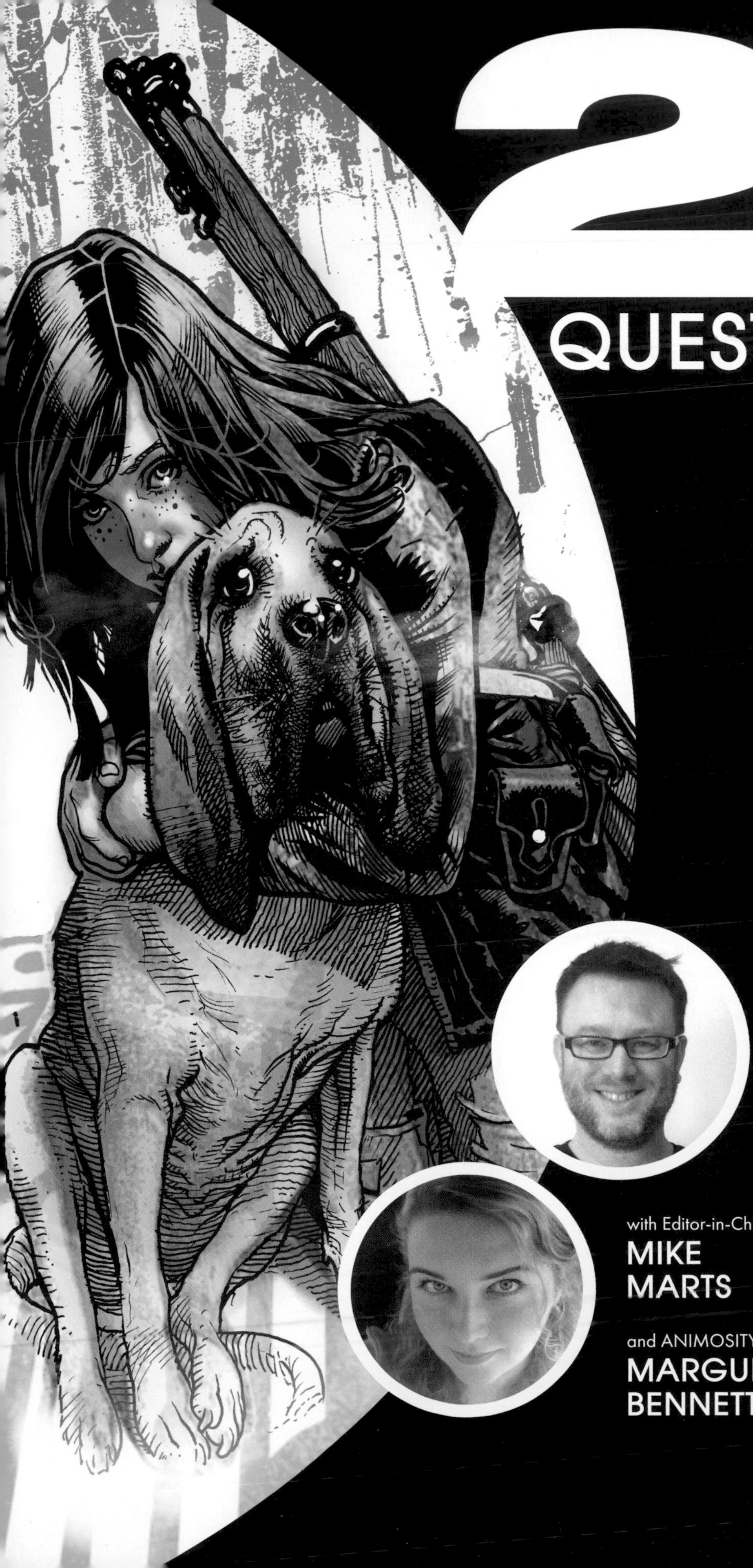

with Editor-in-Chief
MIKE MARTS

and ANIMOSITY writer
MARGUERITE BENNETT

1

MIKE MARTS: Spot the moment you knew you wanted to be a comic book writer...

MARGUERITE BENNETT: I knew I wanted to write words and dialogue that went over pictures all the way back to when I was a tiny child. In the head of a tiny child, though, that means children's books. As a proper comic book writer, I suppose I was seventeen, though I believed it was as much of a pipe dream as being an astronaut. Or, screw it, a unicorn. I was pretty thoroughly gatekept out of comics as a teenager and college student. I didn't genuinely think I could do this—let alone that I might be good at it, honestly—until Scott Snyder kept me after class and straight up told me I could.

2

Who's the mentor who knows they're your mentor, and who's the mentor that doesn't know?

The mentor who knows is Scott Snyder. The mentor who doesn't know is you. (Whoops. Fuck. I spoiled it.)

3

Movie that should have been a comic first but wasn't.

I'm actually going to go with the HARRY POTTER books because I am wildly selfish and always need more Harry Potter in my life. Would've been a wonderful way to introduce young readers to the medium, and movies could always come after.

4

Comic that should have become a movie but didn't.

NECROPOLIS, by Jake Wyatt, done in stop motion Harry Selick animation a la CORALINE. That would be something chilling and dazzling to see.

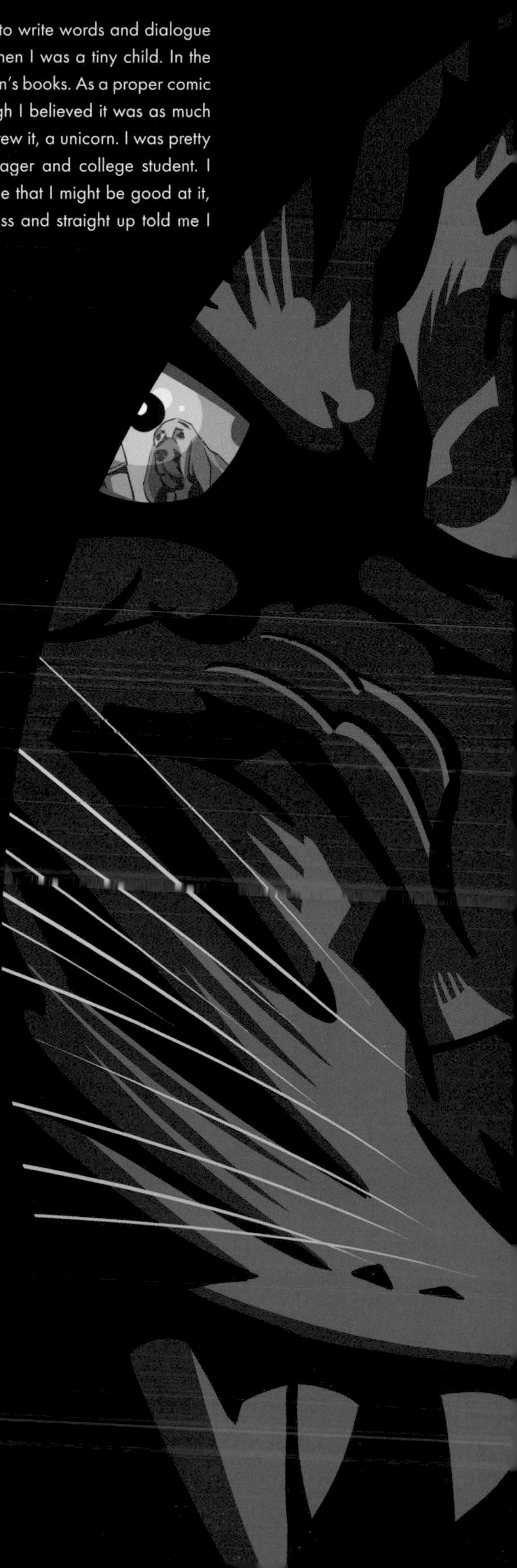

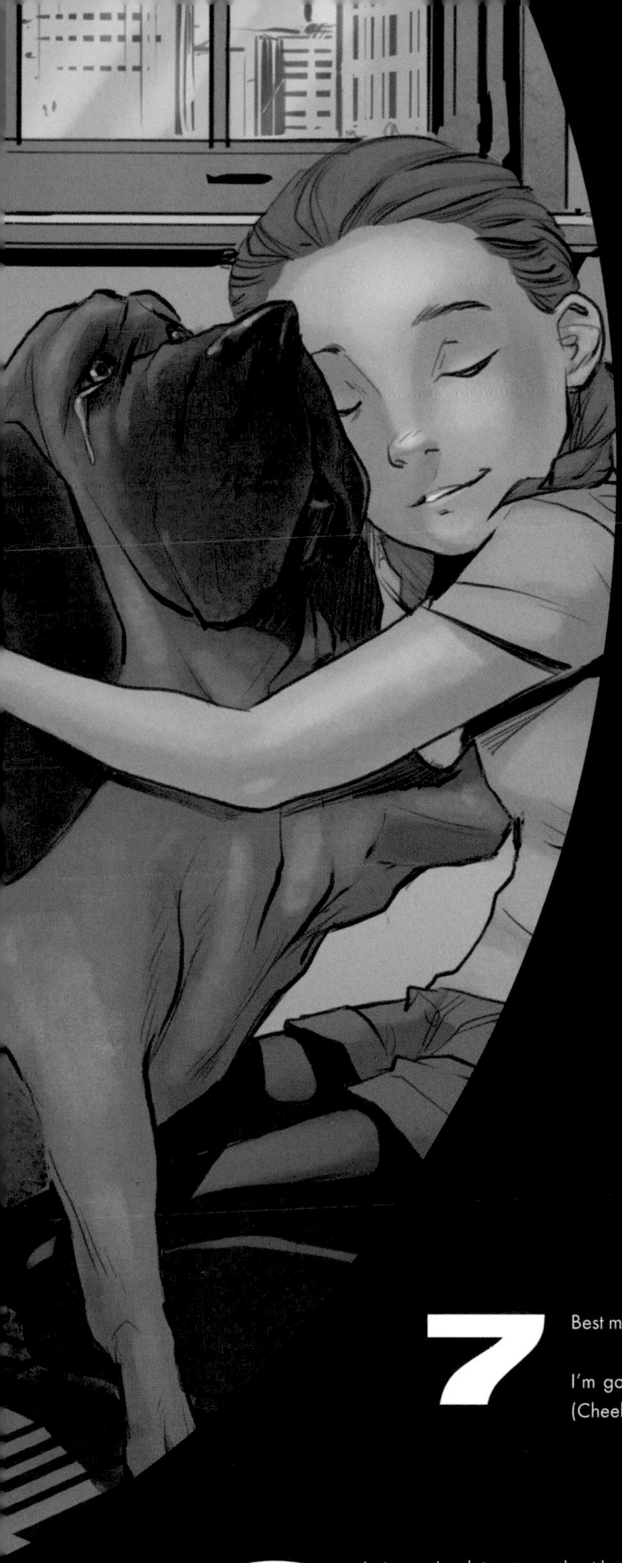

5

Do you listen to music while writing?

Oh, God, yes. I'm a junkie for movie and video game soundtracks. So many superheroine fight scenes are going to be written to *The Force Awakens* soundtracks, you don't even know. INSEXTS was largely written to Dario Marianelli and Rammstein, incidentally.

6

Best moment of your career that's happened so far...

The night Scott asked me to write BATMAN with him. He pulled me aside after one of the evening classes, my second year of grad school. It was January, with snow on the ground, and it was so, so cold and so, so dark. On the drive home, I had to pull over onto the side of the road and screw up my eyes and stare at the ceiling to keep myself from crying. I just thought over and over, "I'm saved, I'm saved. Thank you, whatever's out there, for the gift of my life." Everything started that night. I have never been so grateful.

7

Best moment of your career that hasn't happened yet...

I'm gonna get a kiss from Emi Lenox if I can manage it. (Cheeks kisses are also acceptable.)

8

Artist you're dying to work with.

Sean Gordon Murphy. We've been joking about an S&M gangster comic for a long time. One day I'm going to collect and we're both going to be wanted in twelve states.

If you could only co-write for the rest of your career, who would be your partner?

Kieron Gillen. He's kind, funny, generous, gentle and talented as all goddamn get-out. He has minded me when I was new and awkward, he has celebrated with me in my best triumphs, and he has been with me during my darkest tempers. He listens when you talk story. He always finds something to improve upon, and is always supportive when you're passionate about something in turn.

Favorite creation of yours.

INSEXTS, haha! Though if I can't say INSEXTS, I'm mighty proud of the work I've done on BOMBSHELLS. One of the vexing things about most team stories, but superhero stories in general, is the minimal number of women. If you have a team of six dudes and one woman, that one woman suddenly has to bear the burden of validating and representing the experiences of all women, which is impossible, and also dumb. Only thing dumber is how the woman is often then cut to avoid controversy, criticism and scrutiny. I write mostly women (something I genuinely never thought I'd do) and it allows me to get at different elements of different experiences, which creates, I hope, a richer and more complex art for readers.

Describe your workplace.

I live in a beautiful house with Noelle Stevenson, and we call our home Galhalla. It's a pert, charming, hundred-year-old, whitewashed house in Los Angeles, with high, pale ceilings covered in bookcases, a bright and airy living room, a shining and dark dining room table, an opulent liquor cabinet, a cozy kitchen, and a perfect backyard for parties. I cycle through all of these over the course of a week. I write certain projects sitting at the dining room table; I write certain projects in my bathrobe, lying in bed like a queen under a pile of furs, quilts and sheepskins. I can't work in the same place; my mind needs different sorts of stimulation for each scene and book.

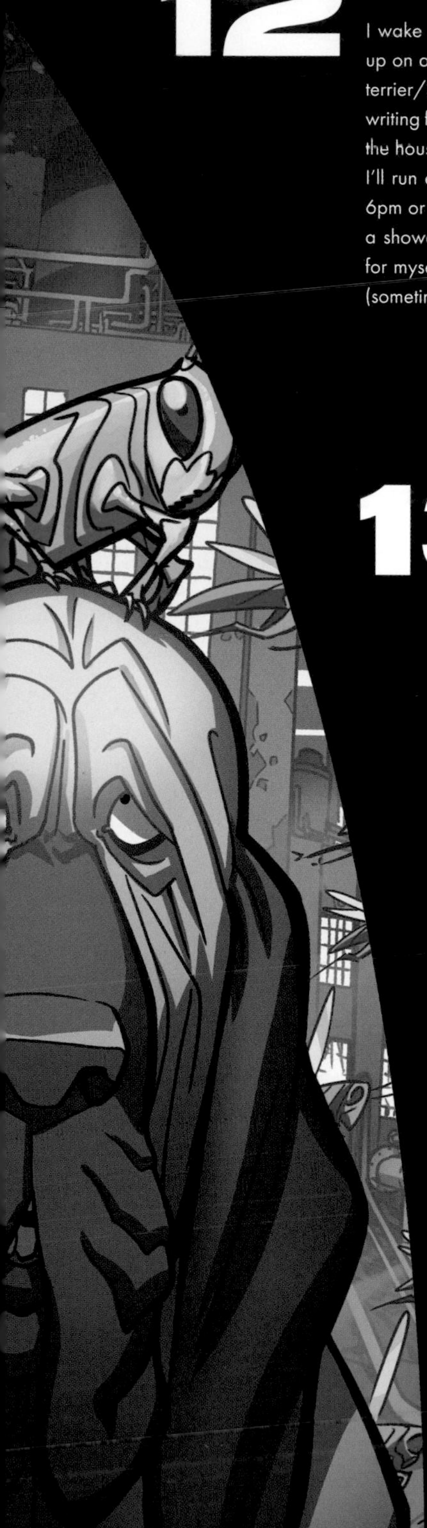

12

Describe your typical day of writing.

I wake up at 5am to look over art from artists in different time zones and catch up on any fires, social media or other crises. At 6am, I usually walk Winston, our terrier/Schnauzer mix, and at 6:45am, answer East Coast e-mails. At 8am, I begin writing for East Coast, which runs until about noon. Then I break for lunch and clean the house. Around 1:30pm, I begin writing for West Coast until about 4pm, when I'll run errands, do chores, or else nap and recharge for the evening's work. At 6pm or 7pm, I'll have dinner (or decompress) with Noelle. I'll clean up and have a shower. At 8:30pm, I finish up work for West Coast and begin prose writing for myself, until about 10:30pm. Curl up in bed at 11pm and read until midnight (sometimes comics, sometimes prose).

13

I've seen you get into the "writing zone". Describe that.

Ha! It's a sight. For a lot of things, I start with an emotion or image that resonates with me, and retro-engineer a story to convey it. I ask what the worst thing is that could happen to get us there, what the best thing might be. From there come characters who could carry the message and power of those images or emotions, and then it's essentially LARPing through the house, trying to live my day-to-day life as them until I feel like I have their voices, desires, fears, and flaws down. It's a very silly process.

14

World's about to end and you can pick one comic character, one fellow creator and one Hollywood type to pal around with as the "last people on Earth". Go.

I'm gonna say Sandor Clegane, aka The Hound, from GAME OF THRONES (technically a comic!). I want to spent my final days protected from zombies and able to annoy someone who could bend me into a pretzel but won't because he's broken and lonely, I guess? For creator, James Tynion. He's my (6 weeks younger) older brother and he's been with me since the very beginning. I see him every week, text him most every day, and talk to him about every story and major project I embark on. We're siblings, the Snyder children, making it off on our own. He's brilliant, loyal, ambitious, generous and caring. I'll always go to bat for him and I couldn't imagine life without him.

15

Last good book you read was...

DARK PLACES, Gillian Flynn (the author of GONE GIRL)'s second novel. I love mean, confident, capable female protagonists, especially if they are unlikeable, cunning, and have their shit together. I like women who don't have to learn lessons, and I love books where I have no idea what is going to happen, even up to the very last pages.

16

The title to the comic about you would be called...

Handmaiden. It would be a very sharp memoir, about how young women in the workforce, social circles and home life are used (particularly as that we are valued as supporting characters, help-meets and, frankly, handmaidens for the work, art and attentions of older men). It would be very fun, witty and scandalous, but it would be very mean.

17

Best comic that everyone might not be reading yet but should be...

The People Inside, by Ray Fawkes. That graphic novel absolutely cut my throat. Intense, formulist approach to love, loss, grief, joy, healing and the passage of time. Honestly, forget this garbage about my process! That book is the most important thing you could take away from this interview, haha. I'm not kidding. Go on Amazon and buy it before you forget. You close the back cover with the most fantastic sense of poignancy.

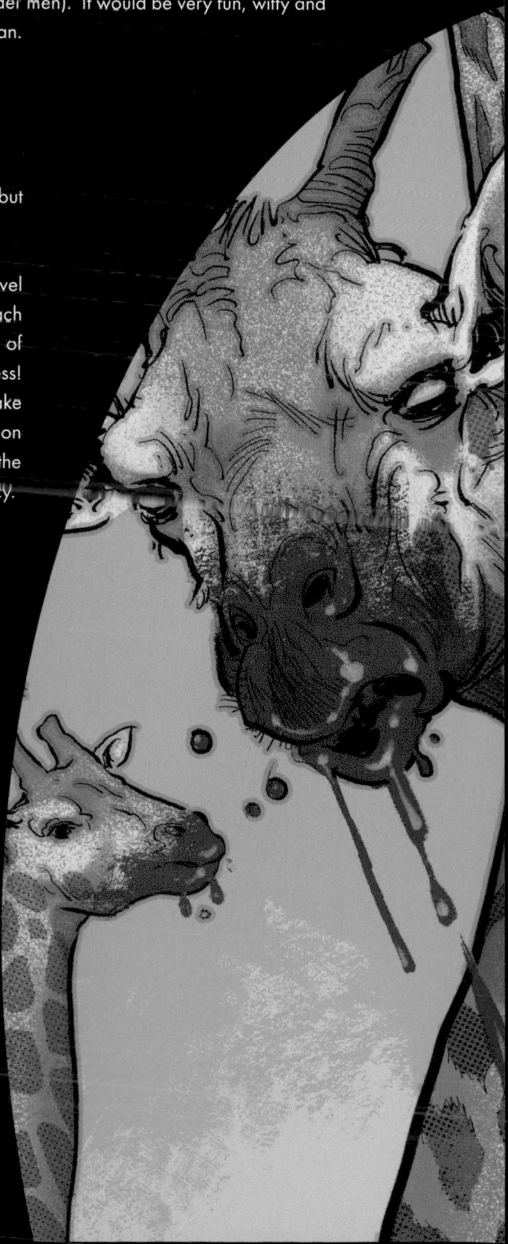

18

Why AfterShock?

The absolute creative freedom, the fantastic support and encouragement, the many reminders that our stories and energy and endeavors are appreciated, the ease and accessibility of every voice at the company, the chance to work with artists I adore who I know are valued and protected, and teams across the board that I trust. I know I will work with AfterShock for a long while and I am incredibly happy about that.

19 Favorite actor...

I'd say Donald Sutherland. He's very smart, very soothing, very dapper and I imagine he'd have some wonderful stories. I could listen to his voice for ages. I listen to his reading of *"The Old Man and the Sea"* with regularity. He means a lot to me as a muse and he plays such phenomenal villains.

20 Favorite movie...

My favorite movie is *The Fall* by Tarsem Singh. Gorgeous, brutal story of a 1920s stuntman who tells a little migrant girl a fairy tale epic to convince her to steal the drugs he needs to kill himself. Utterly beautiful and unlike anything I've ever seen.

21 Favorite late night snack...

Dried figs or bleu cheese stuffed olives. I walk around the house in my bathrobe, popping them in my mouth like candy, muttering about plot points to myself.

AFTERSHOCK™

YEAR ONE COVER PROCESS

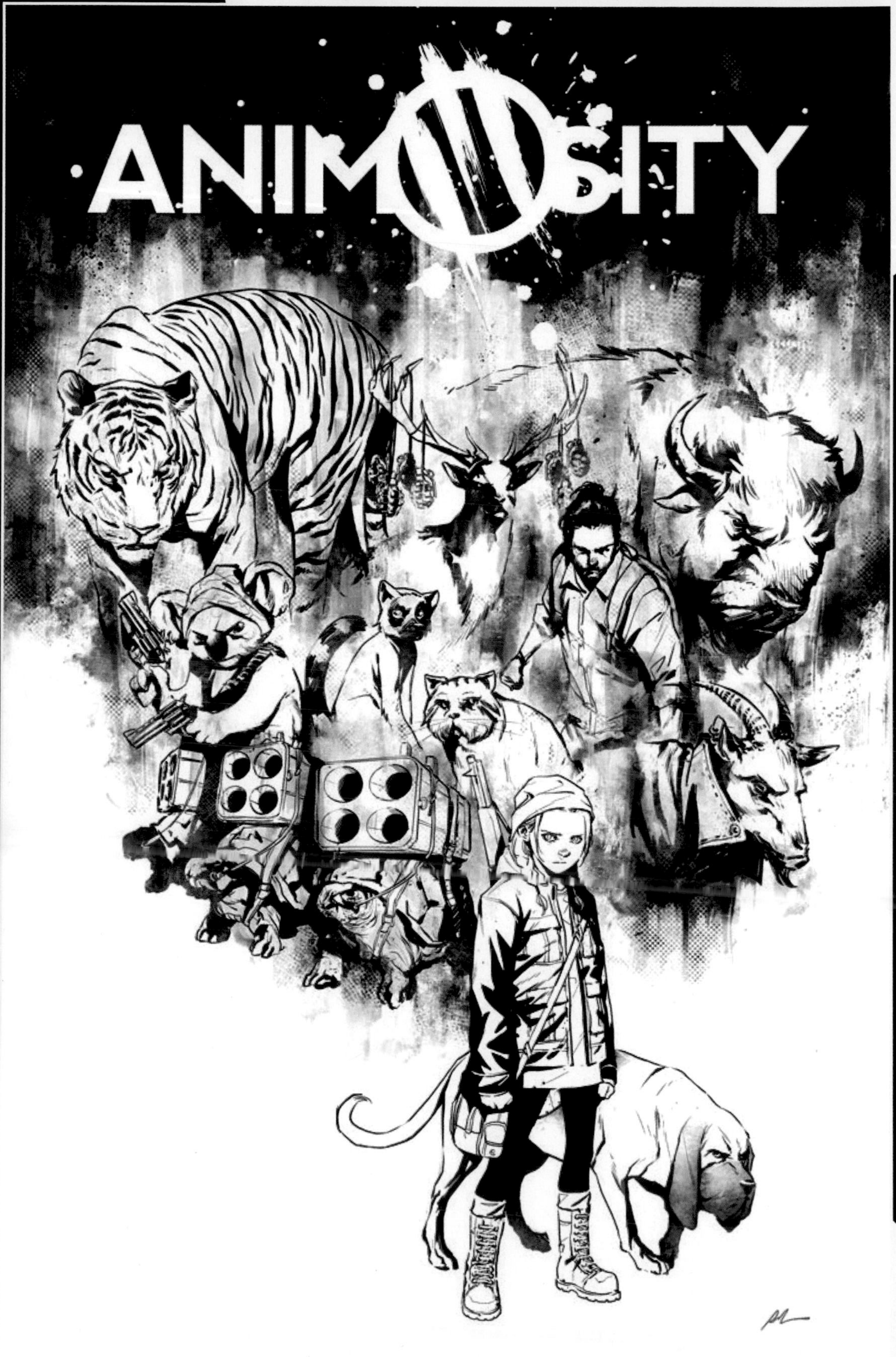
ANIMOSITY

ANIMOSITY YEAR ONE
final cover inks by
RAFAEL DE LATORRE

YEAR ONE COVER PROCESS

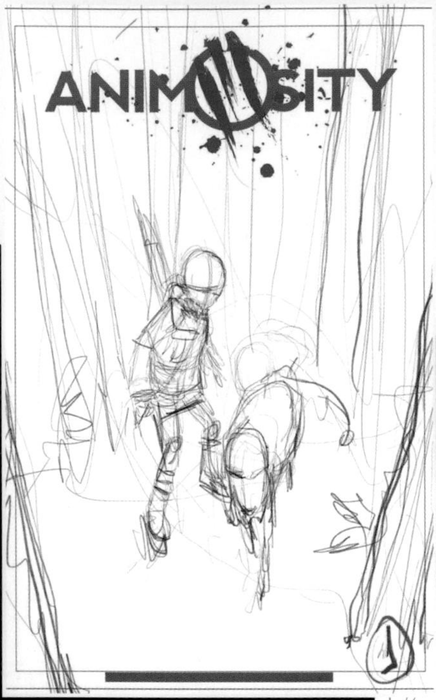
ANIMOSITY
1

cover sketch
version 1

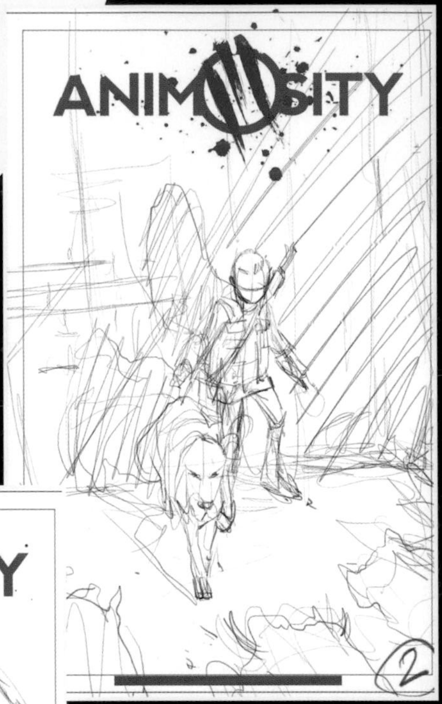
ANIMOSITY
2

cover sketch
version 2

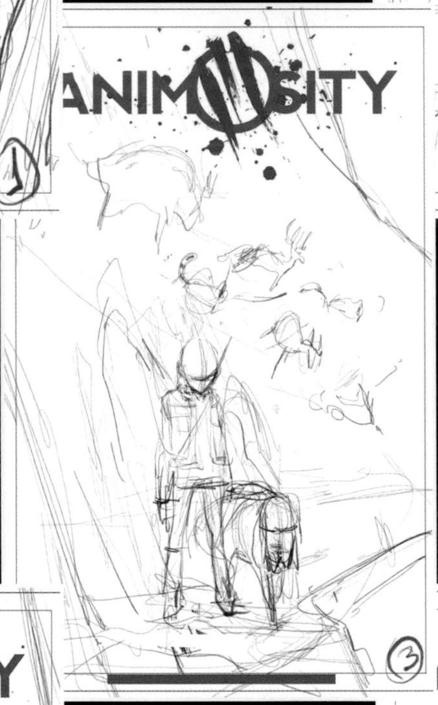
ANIMOSITY
3

cover sketch
version 3

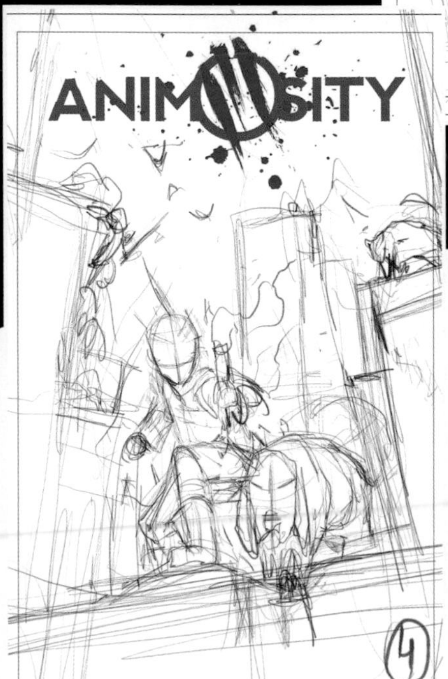
ANIMOSITY
4

cover sketch
version 4

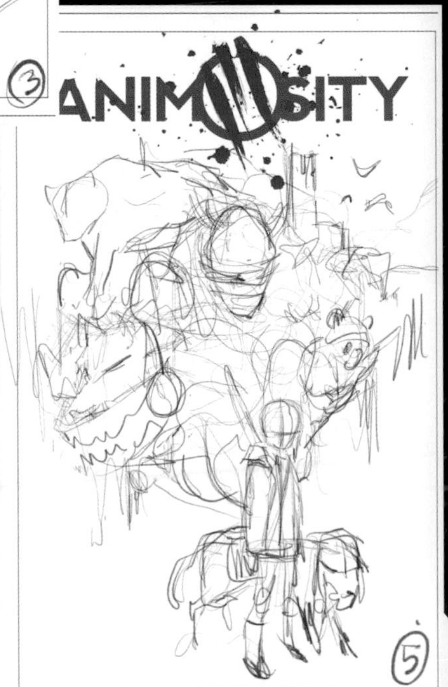
ANIMOSITY
5

cover sketch
version 5

ANIMOSITY LETTERING PROCESS

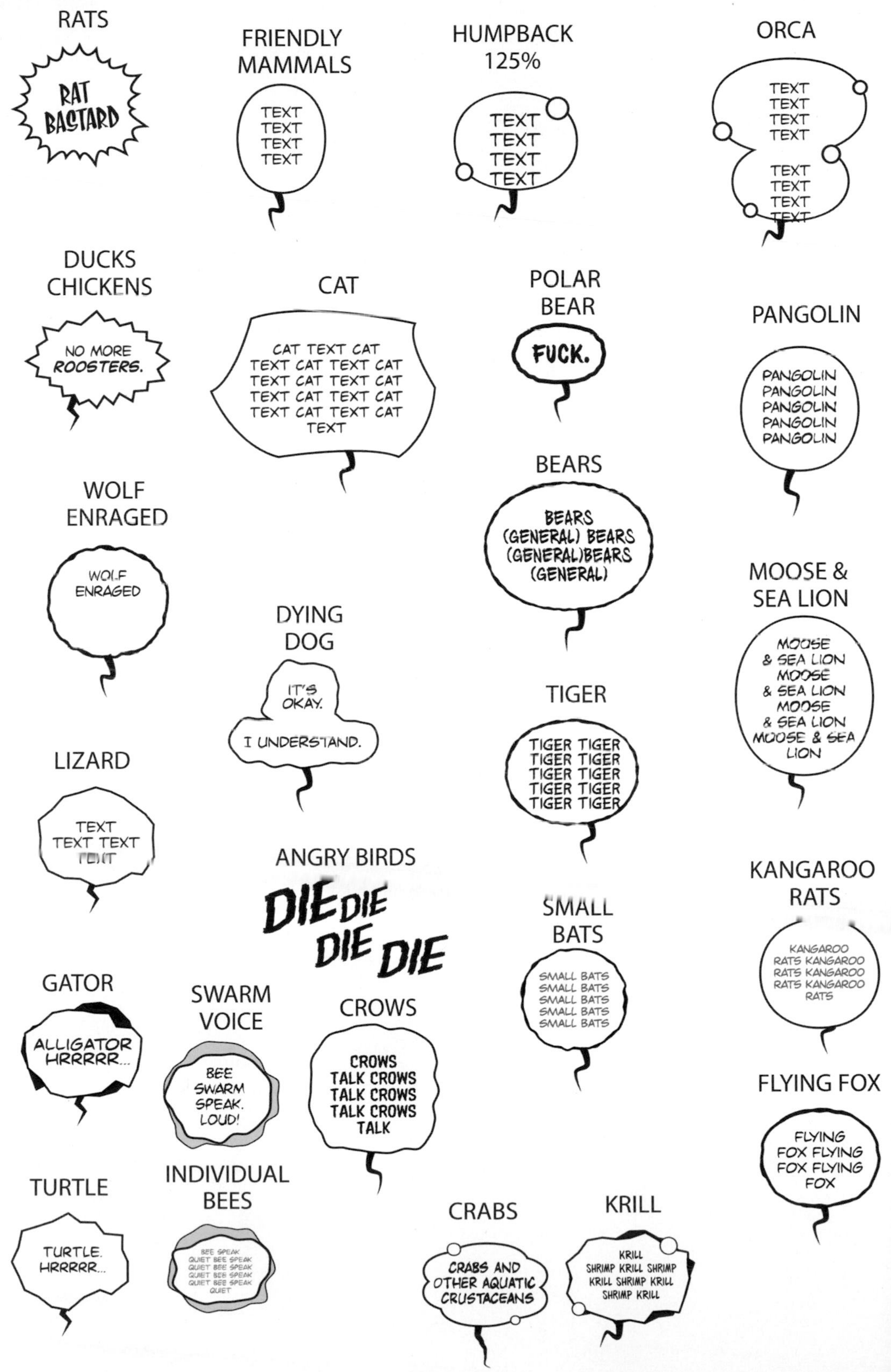

RATS
RAT BASTARD
FRIENDLY MAMMALS
TEXT TEXT TEXT TEXT
HUMPBACK 125%
TEXT TEXT TEXT TEXT
ORCA
TEXT TEXT TEXT TEXT
TEXT TEXT TEXT TEXT
DUCKS CHICKENS
NO MORE ROOSTERS.
CAT
CAT TEXT CAT TEXT CAT TEXT CAT TEXT CAT TEXT CAT TEXT CAT TEXT CAT TEXT CAT TEXT CAT TEXT
POLAR BEAR
FUCK.
PANGOLIN
PANGOLIN PANGOLIN PANGOLIN PANGOLIN PANGOLIN
BEARS
BEARS (GENERAL) BEARS (GENERAL)BEARS (GENERAL)
WOLF ENRAGED
WOLF ENRAGED
MOOSE & SEA LION
MOOSE & SEA LION MOOSE & SEA LION MOOSE & SEA LION MOOSE & SEA LION
DYING DOG
IT'S OKAY.
I UNDERSTAND.
TIGER
TIGER TIGER TIGER TIGER TIGER TIGER TIGER TIGER TIGER TIGER
LIZARD
TEXT TEXT TEXT TEXT
ANGRY BIRDS
DIE DIE DIE DIE
KANGAROO RATS
KANGAROO RATS KANGAROO RATS KANGAROO RATS KANGAROO RATS
SMALL BATS
SMALL BATS SMALL BATS SMALL BATS SMALL BATS SMALL BATS
GATOR
ALLIGATOR HRRRRR...
SWARM VOICE
BEE SWARM SPEAK. LOUD!
CROWS
CROWS TALK CROWS TALK CROWS TALK CROWS TALK
FLYING FOX
FLYING FOX FLYING FOX FLYING FOX
TURTLE
TURTLE. HRRRRR...
INDIVIDUAL BEES
BEE SPEAK QUIET BEE SPEAK QUIET BEE SPEAK QUIET BEE SPEAK QUIET BEE SPEAK QUIET
CRABS
CRABS AND OTHER AQUATIC CRUSTACEANS
KRILL
KRILL SHRIMP KRILL SHRIMP KRILL SHRIMP KRILL SHRIMP KRILL

Animosity Lettering Tests by
MARSHALL DILLON

ANIMOSITY COVER GALLERY

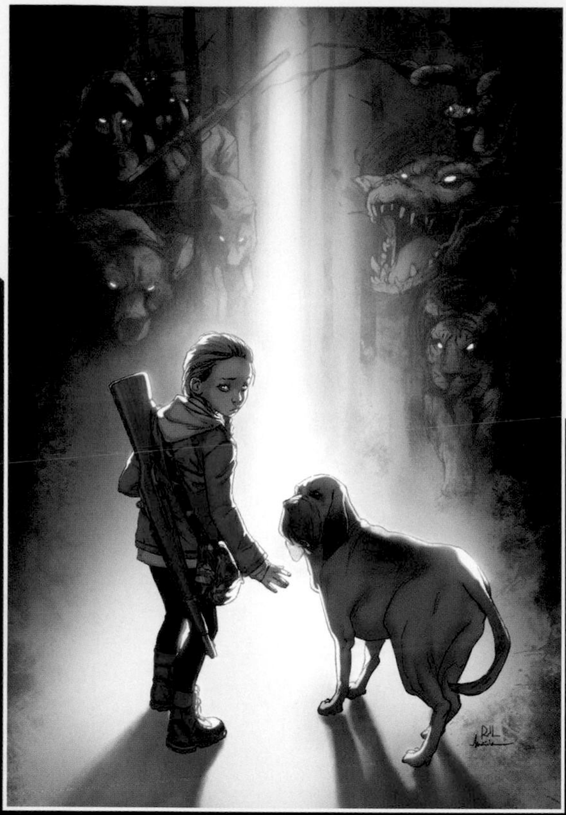

issue #1 cover
RAFAEL DE LATORRE & MARCELO MAIOLO

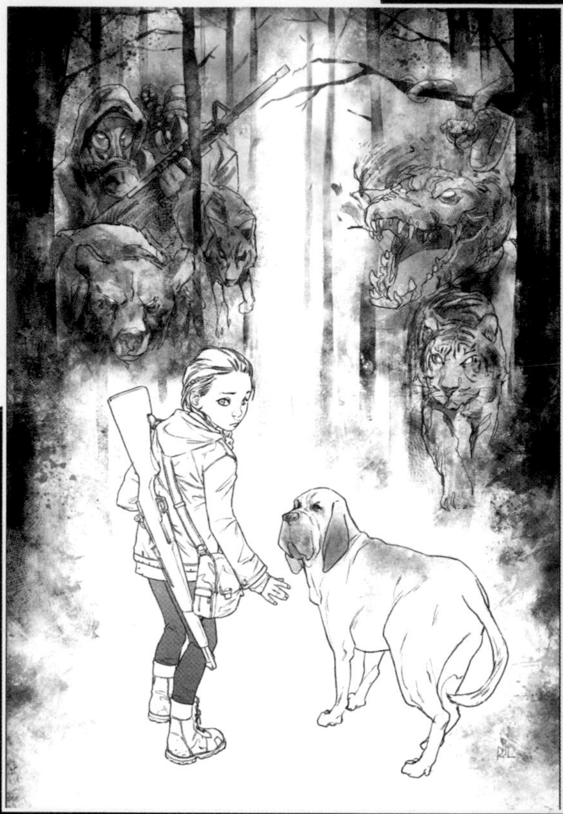

issue #1 Baltimore Retailer Summit b/w variant
RAFAEL DE LATORRE & MARCELO MAIOLO

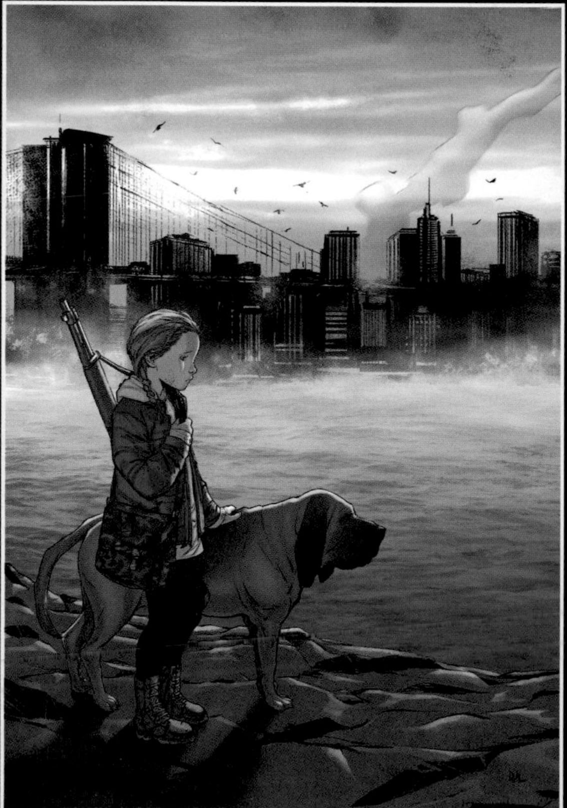

issue #1 Blindbox variant cover
RAFAEL DE LATORRE & MARCELO MAIOLO

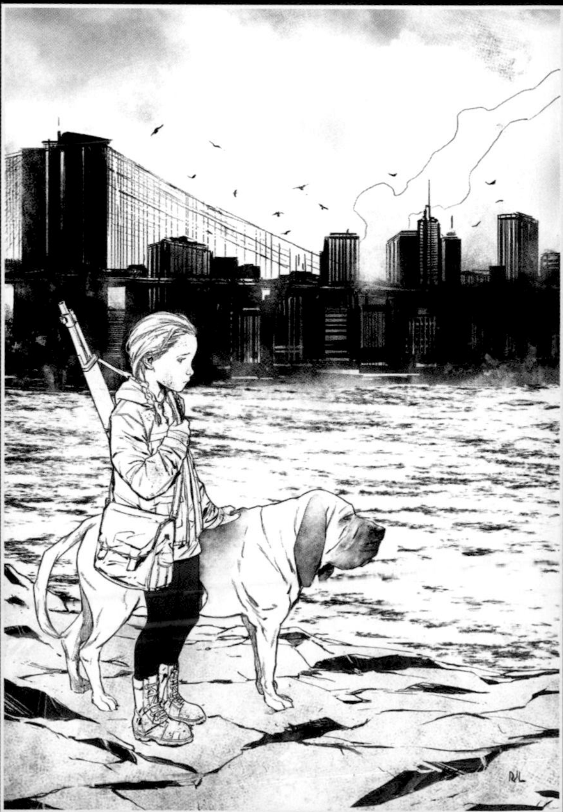

issue #1 Blindbox b/w variant cover
RAFAEL DE LATORRE & MARCELO MAIOLO

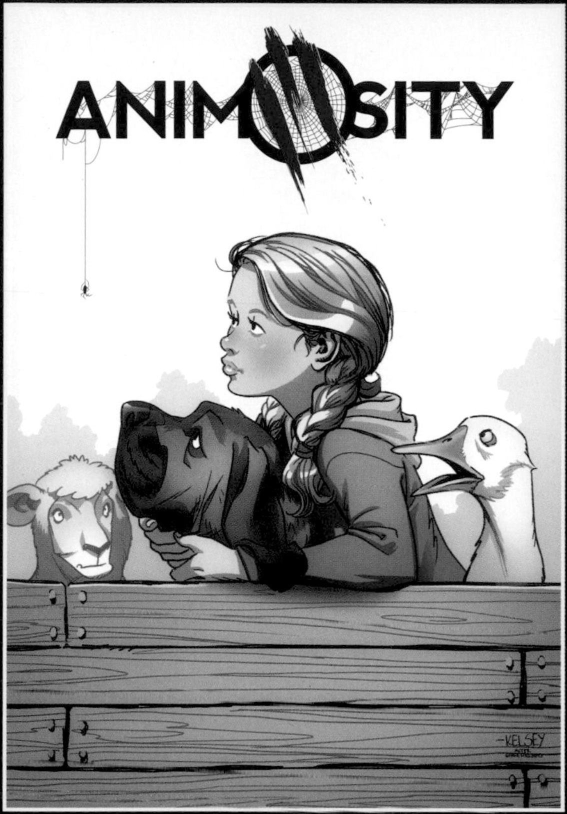
ANIMOSITY
issue #1 Blindbox variant cover A
KELSEY SHANNON

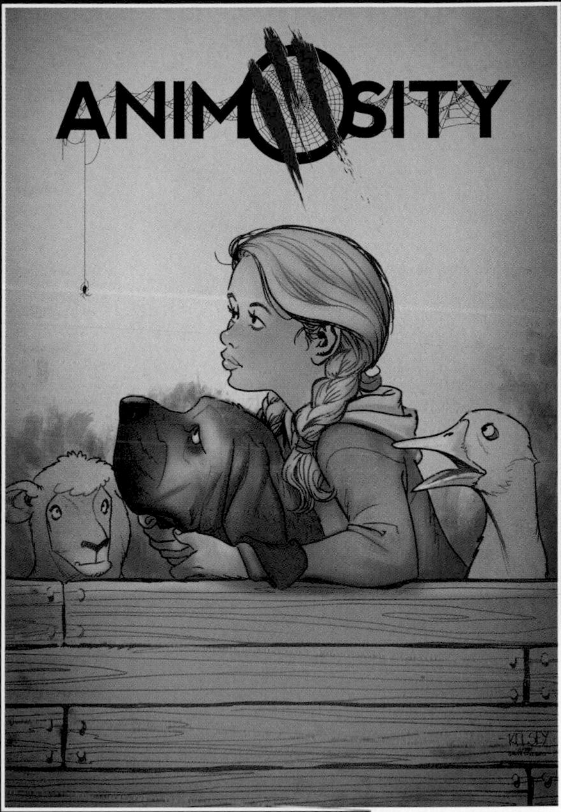
ANIMOSITY
issue #1 Blindbox variant cover B
KELSEY SHANNON

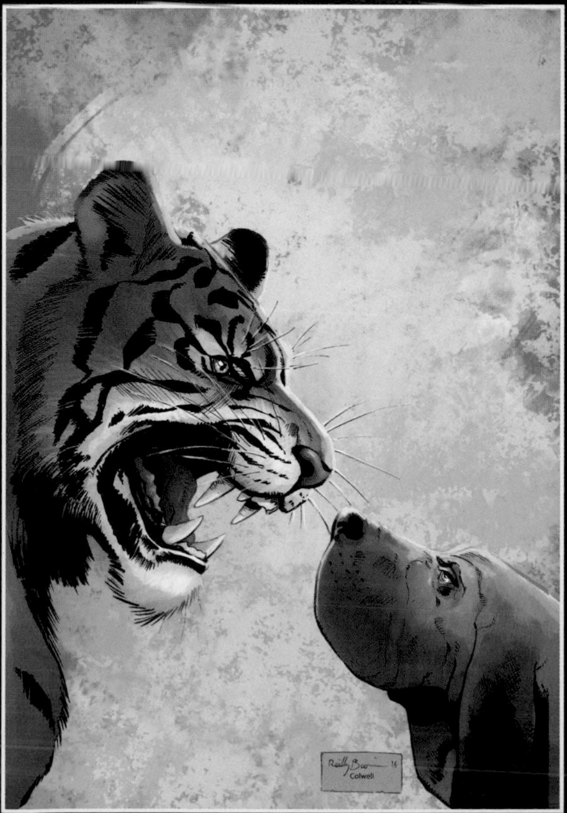
issue #1 Little Shop of Comics variant cover
REILLY BROWN & JEREMY COLWELL

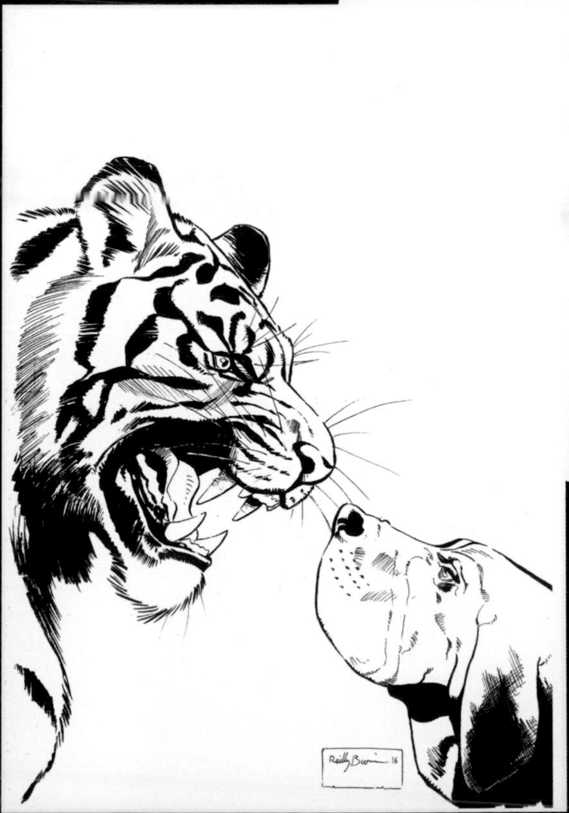
issue #1 Little Shop of Comics b/w variant cover
REILLY BROWN & JEREMY COLWELL

ANIMOSITY COVER GALLERY

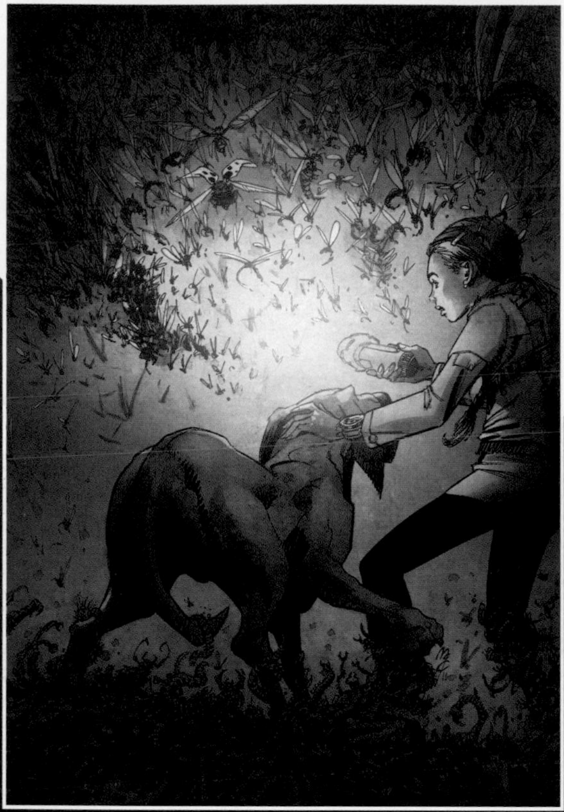

issue #1 The Comic Mint variant cover
JOHN McCREA

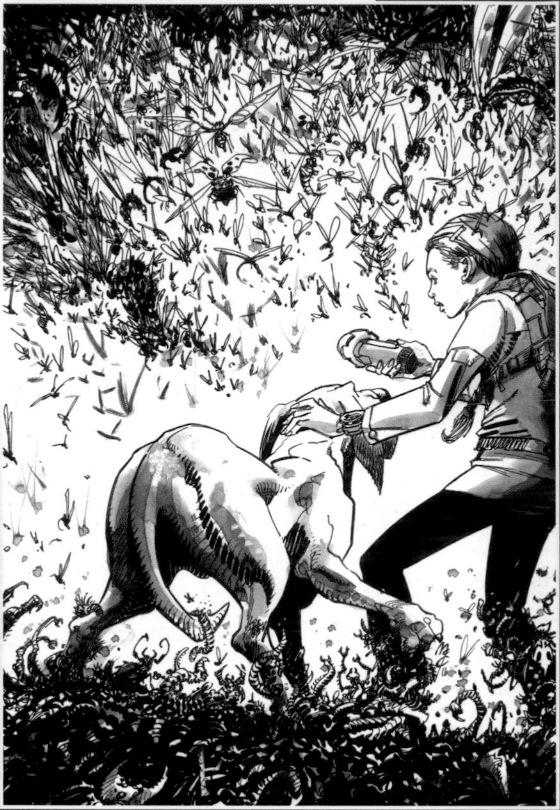

issue #1 The Comic Mint b/w variant cover
JOHN McCREA

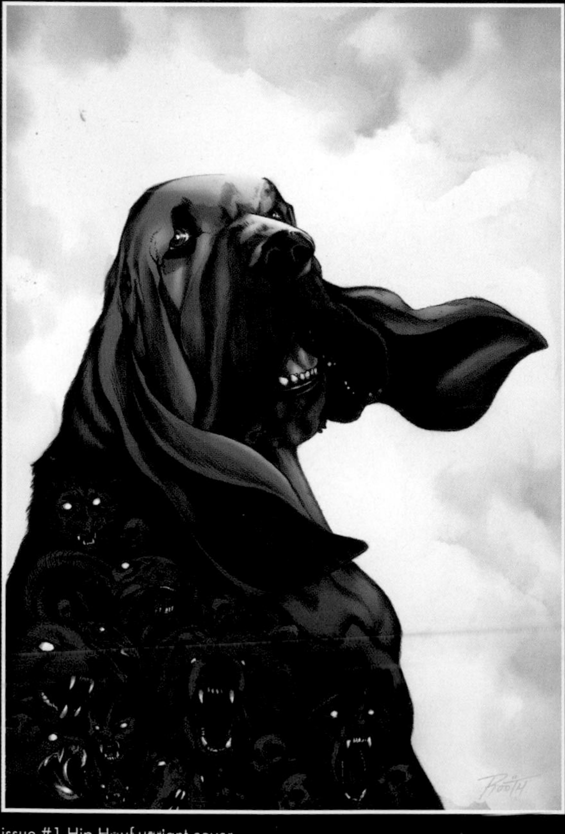

issue #1 Hip Hopf variant cover

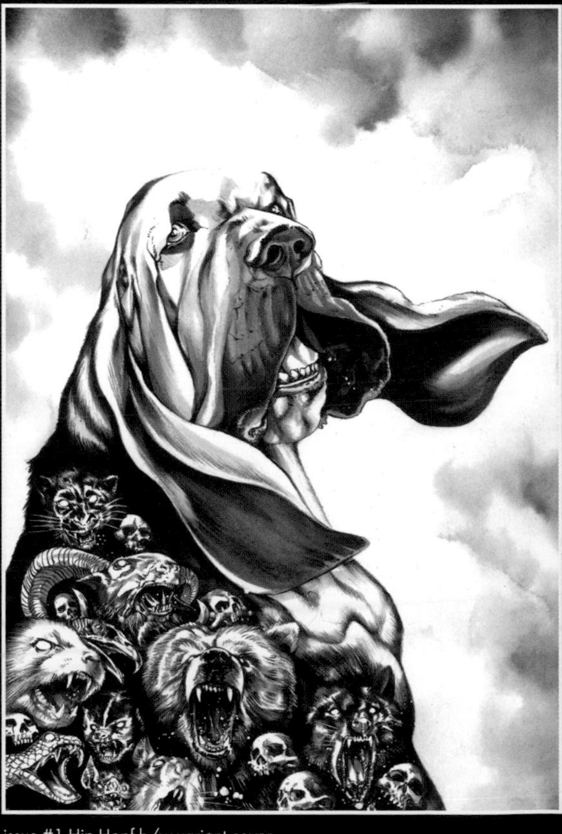

issue #1 Hip Hopf b/w variant cover

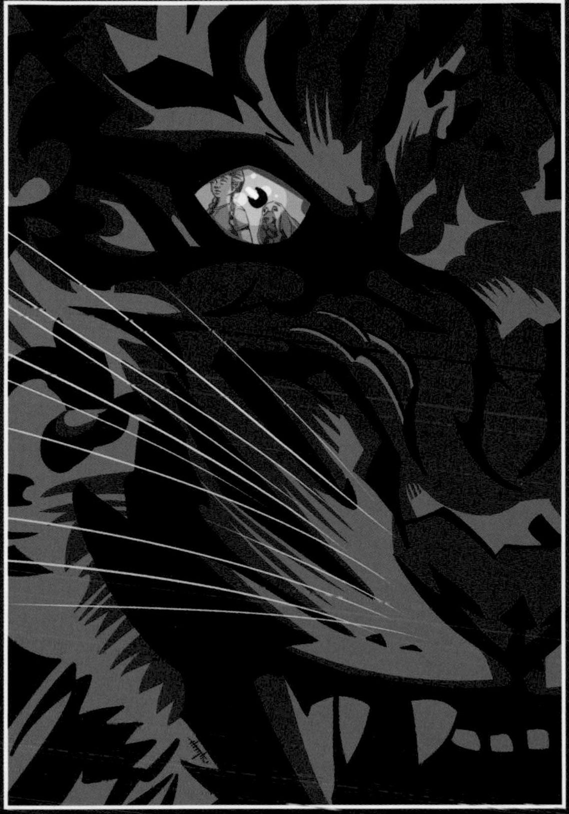

issue #1 Frankie's Comics fifth printing cover
HOYT SILVA

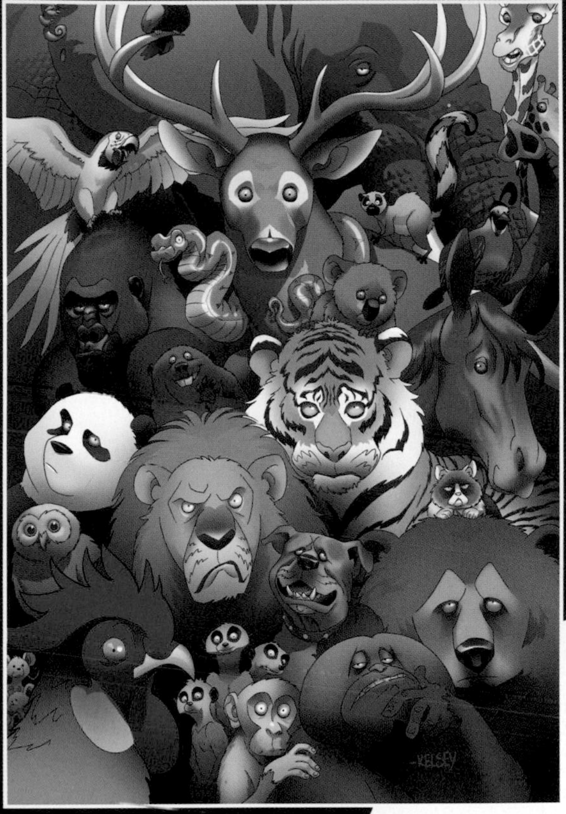
KELSEY

issue #1 variant cover
KELSEY SHANNON

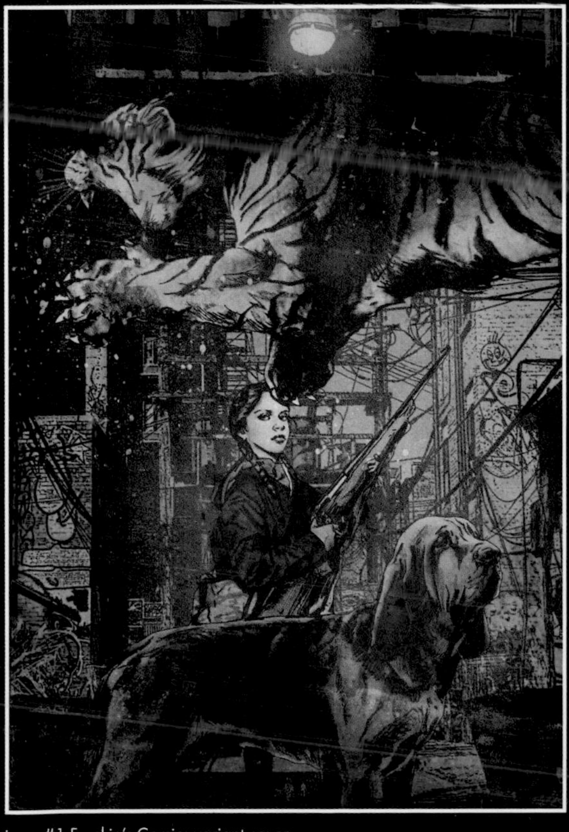

issue #1 Frankie's Comics variant cover

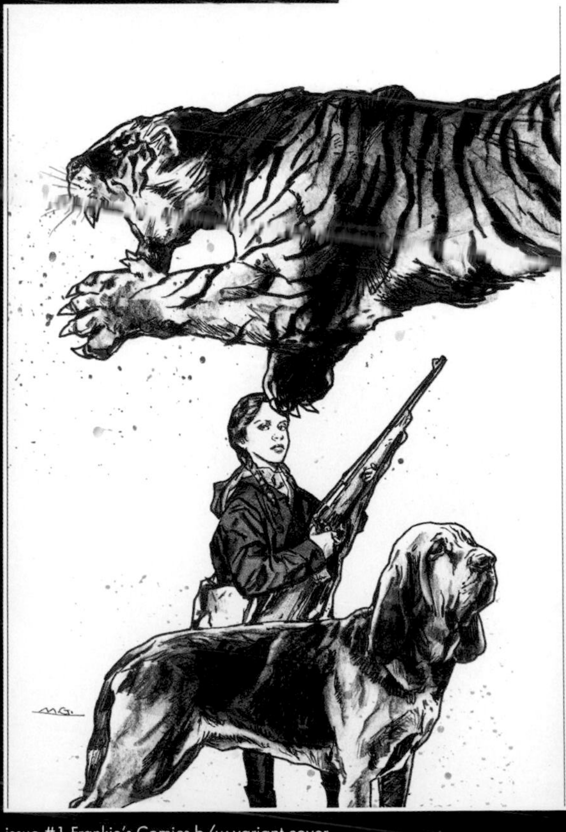

issue #1 Frankie's Comics b/w variant cover

ANIMOSITY COVER GALLERY

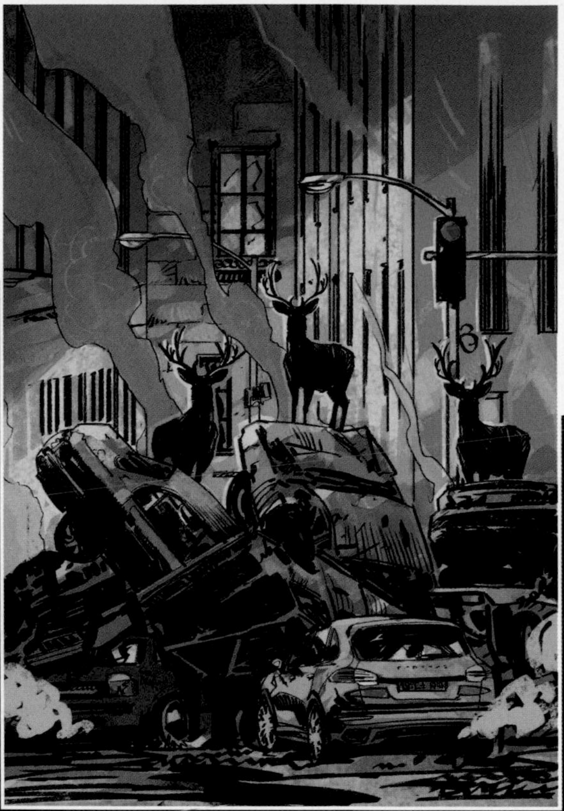

issue #1 Ssalefish variant cover
GARRY BROWN

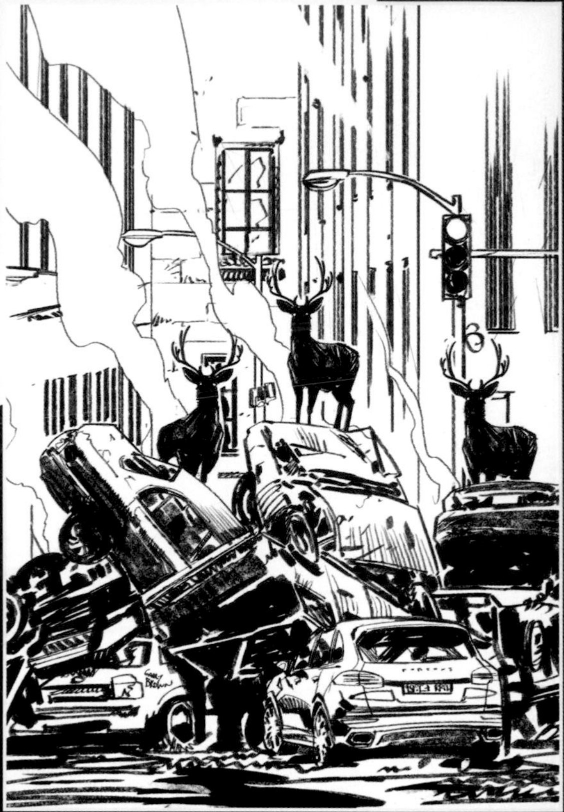

issue #1 Ssalefish b/w variant cover
GARRY BROWN

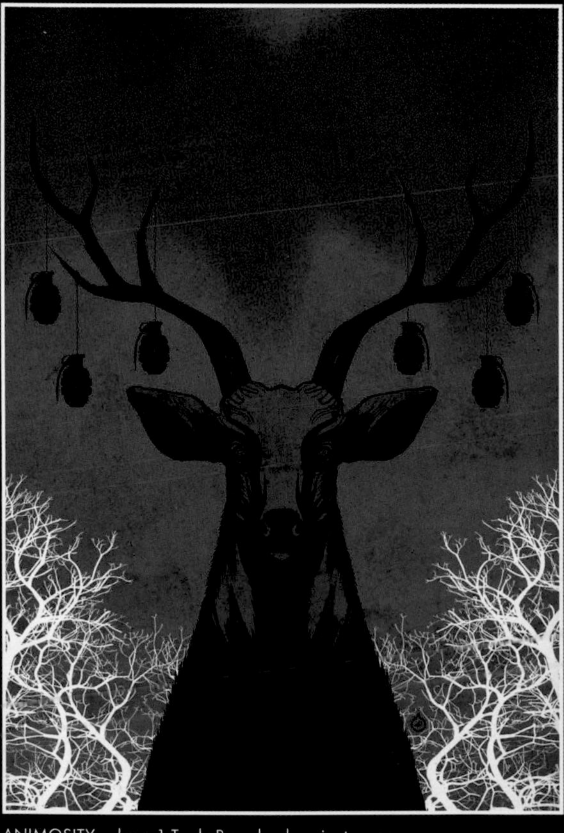

ANIMOSITY volume 1 Trade Paperback variant cover

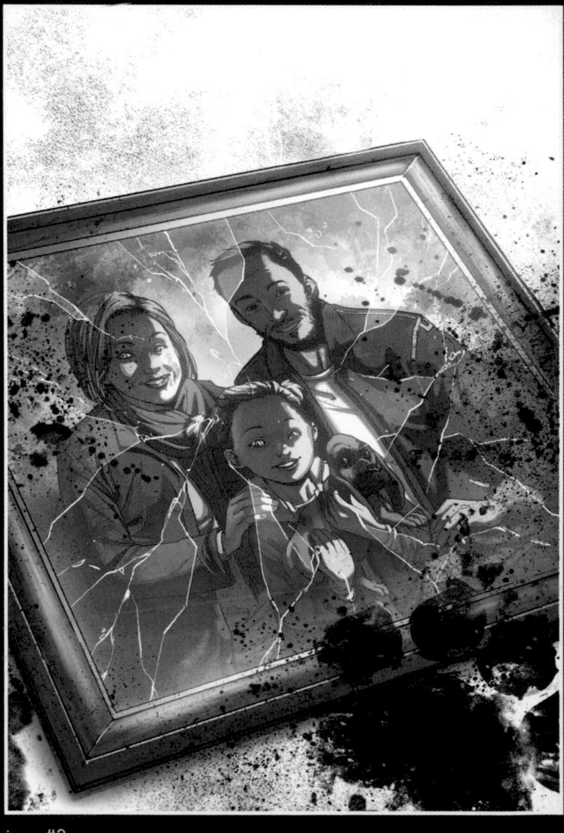

issue #2 cover

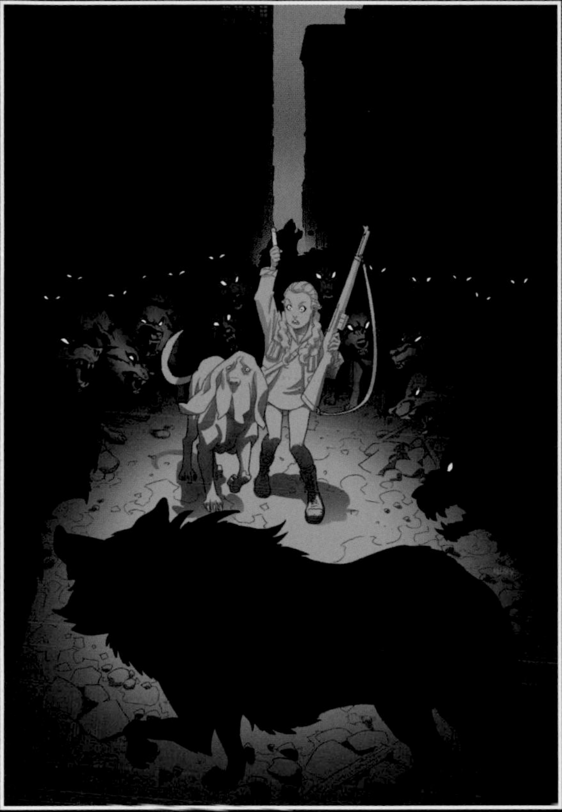

issue #2 The Comic Mint variant cover
KELSEY SHANNON

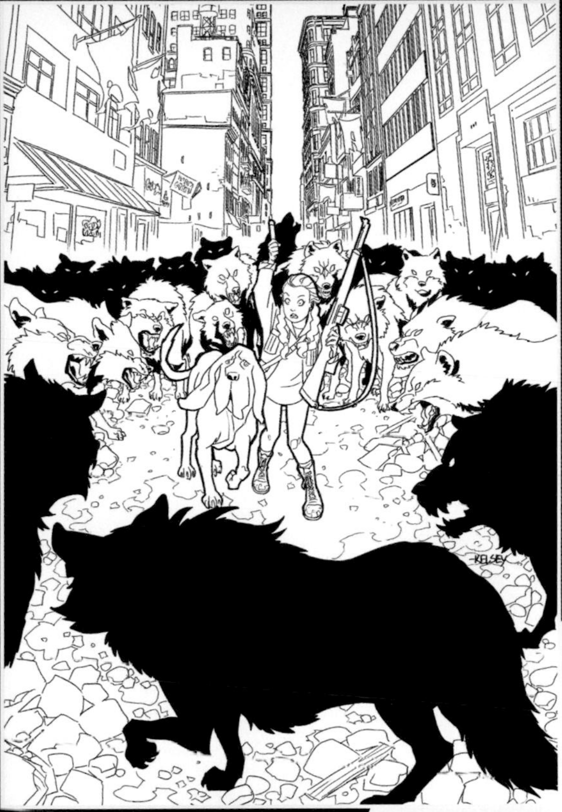
KELSEY

issue #2 The Comic Mint b/w variant cover
KELSEY SHANNON

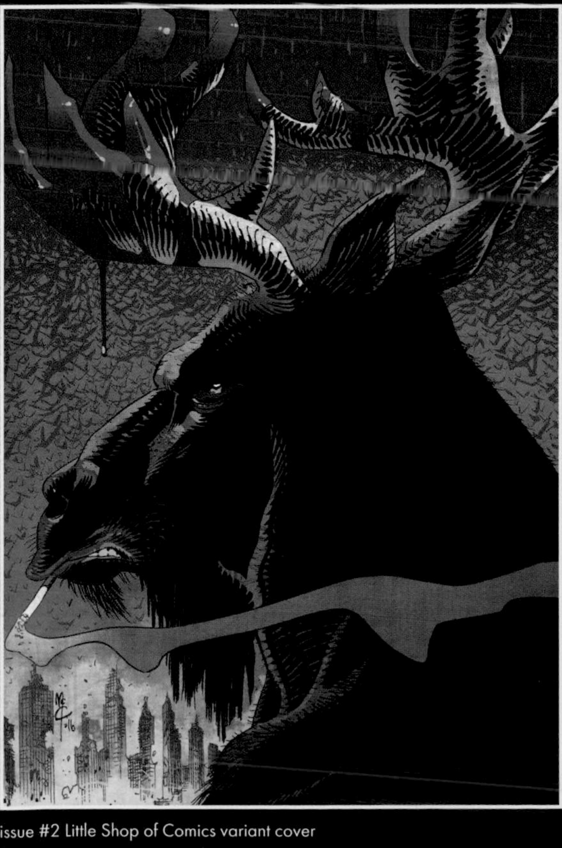

issue #2 Little Shop of Comics variant cover
JOHN McCREA

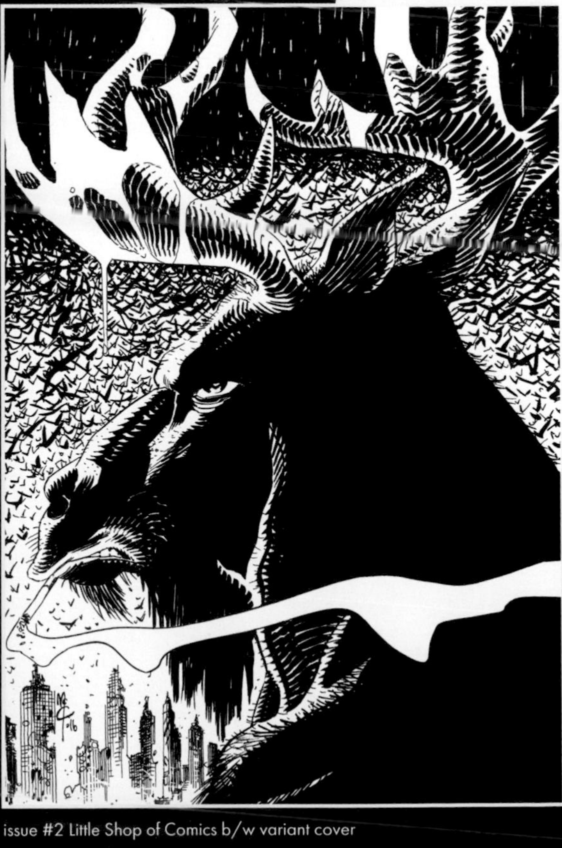

issue #2 Little Shop of Comics b/w variant cover
JOHN McCREA

ANIMOSITY COVER GALLERY

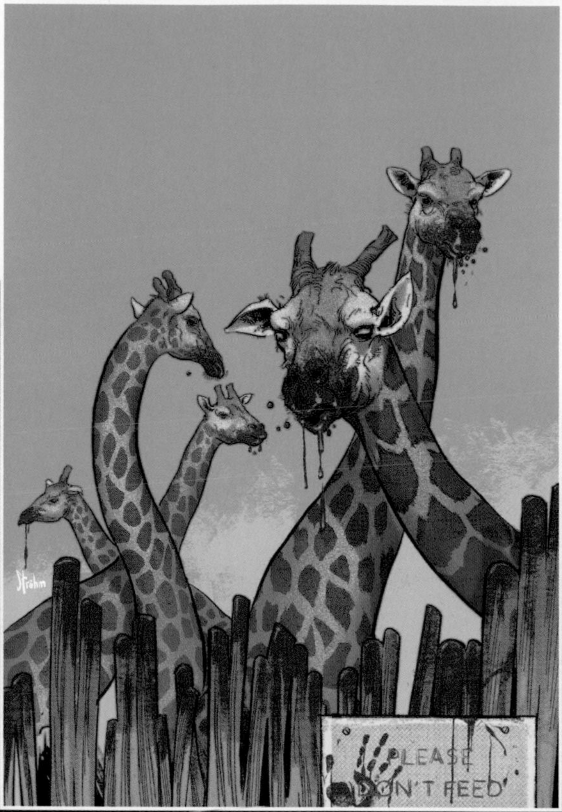
PLEASE
DON'T FEED

issue #2 Frankie's Comics variant cover
KYLE STRAHM & GREG SMALLWOOD

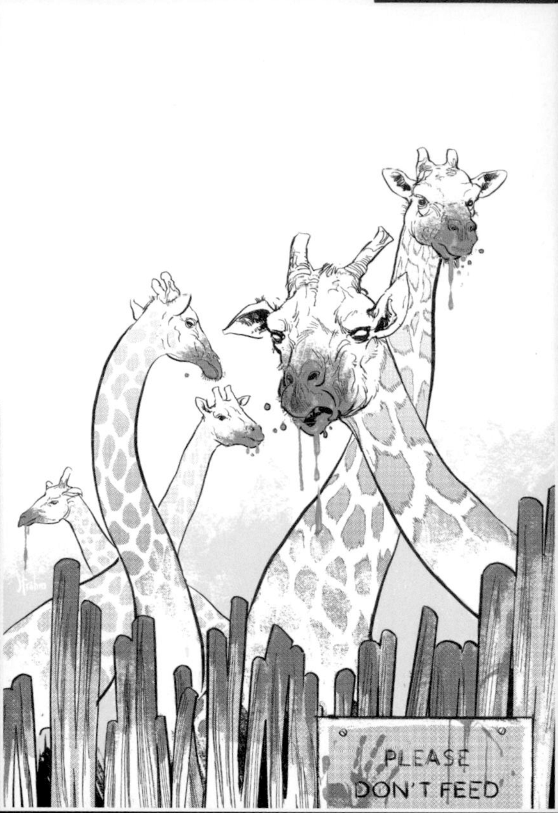
PLEASE
DON'T FEED

issue #2 Frankie's Comics b/w variant cover
KYLE STRAHM & GREG SMALLWOOD

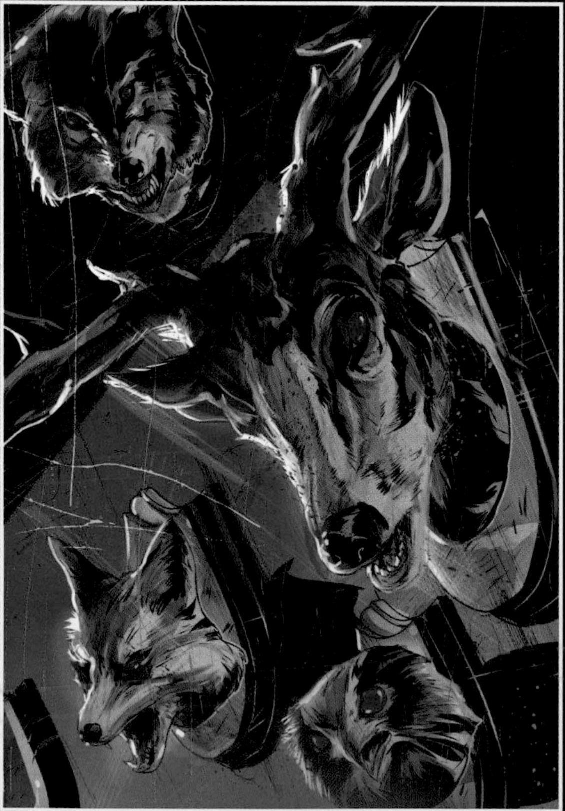

issue #2 NYCC Exclusive variant cover

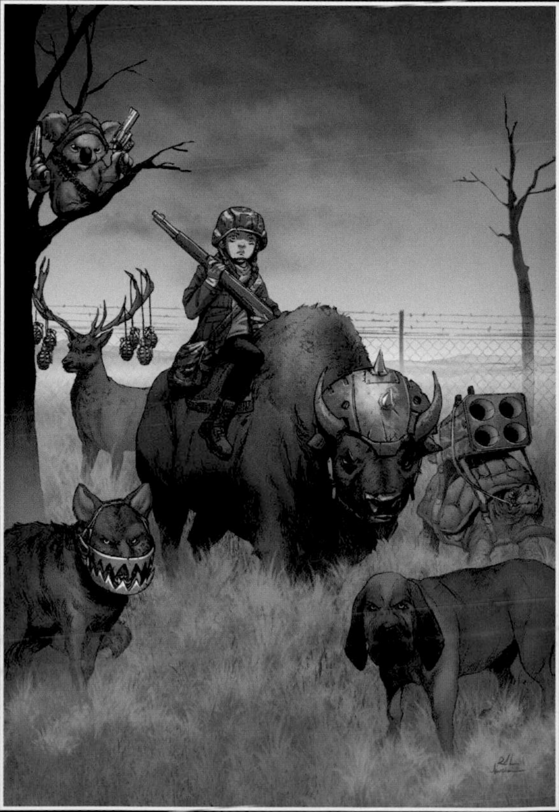

issue #3 cover

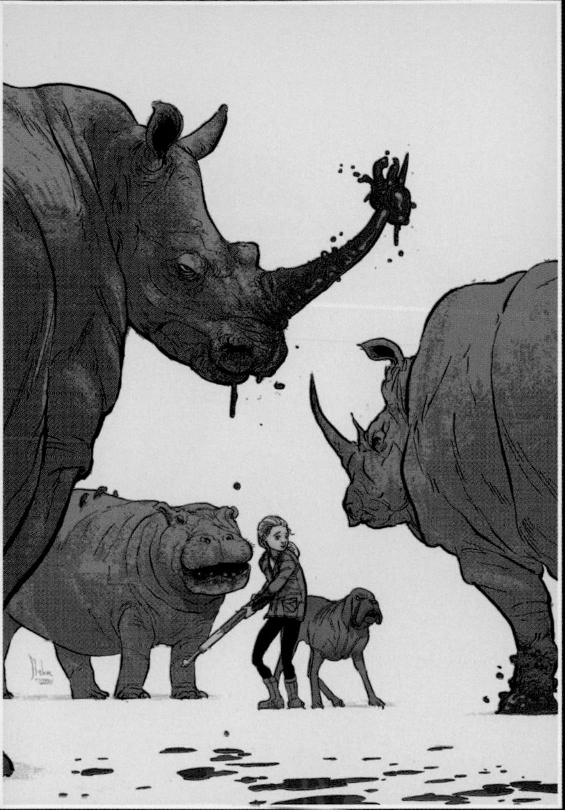

issue #3 Frankie's Comics variant cover
KYLE STRAHM & GREG SMALLWOOD

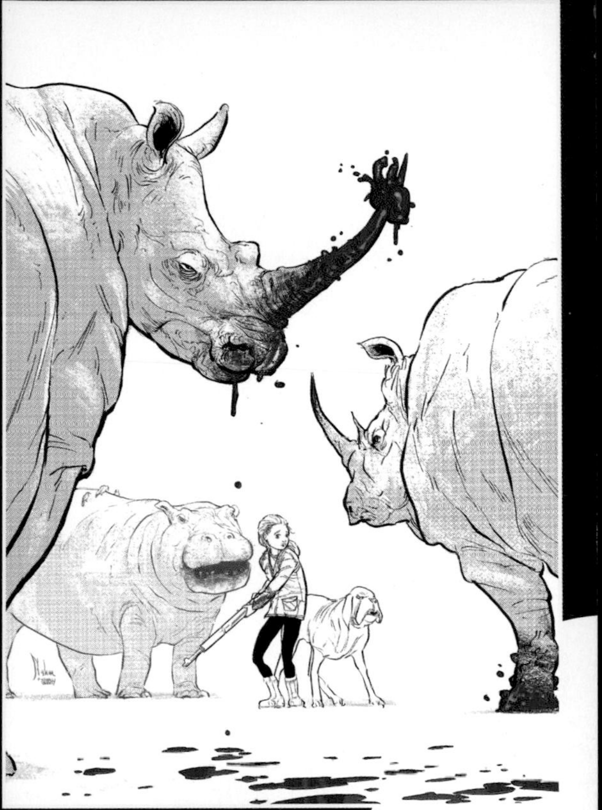

issue #3 Frankie's Comics b/w variant cover
KYLE STRAHM & GREG SMALLWOOD

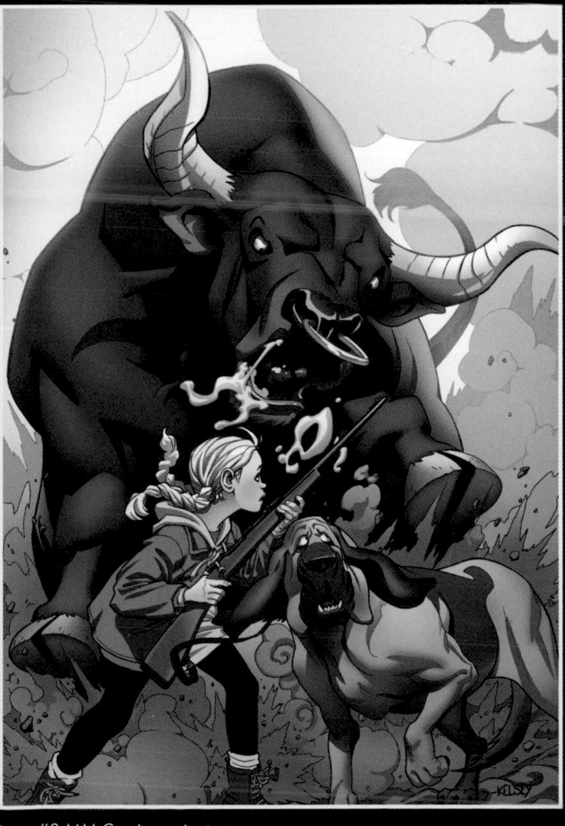
KELSEY

issue #3 MM Comics variant cover

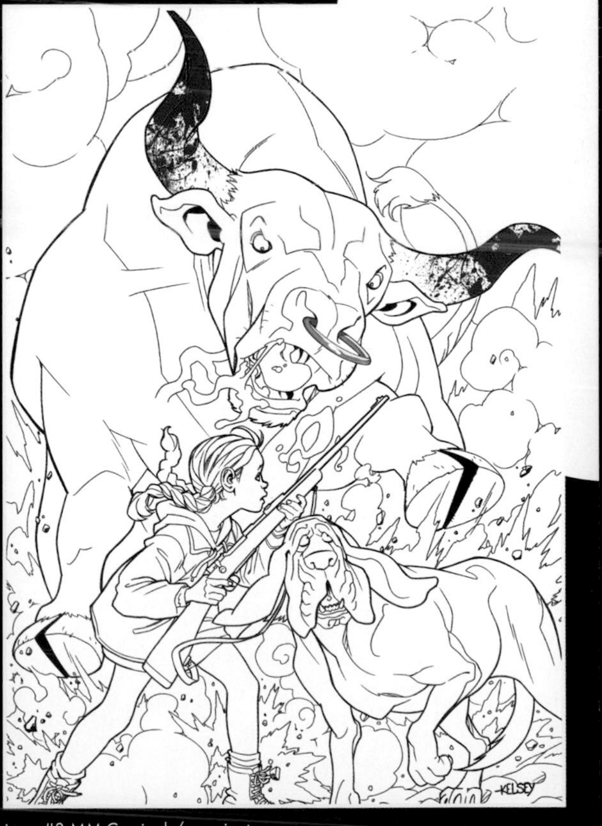
KELSEY

issue #3 MM Comics b/w variant cover

ANIMOSITY COVER GALLERY

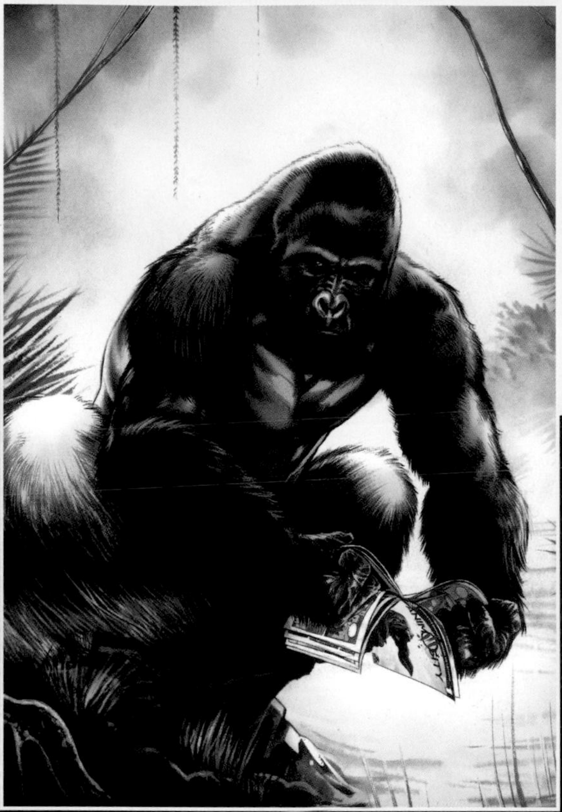

issue #3 Hip Hopf variant cover
MIKE ROOTH

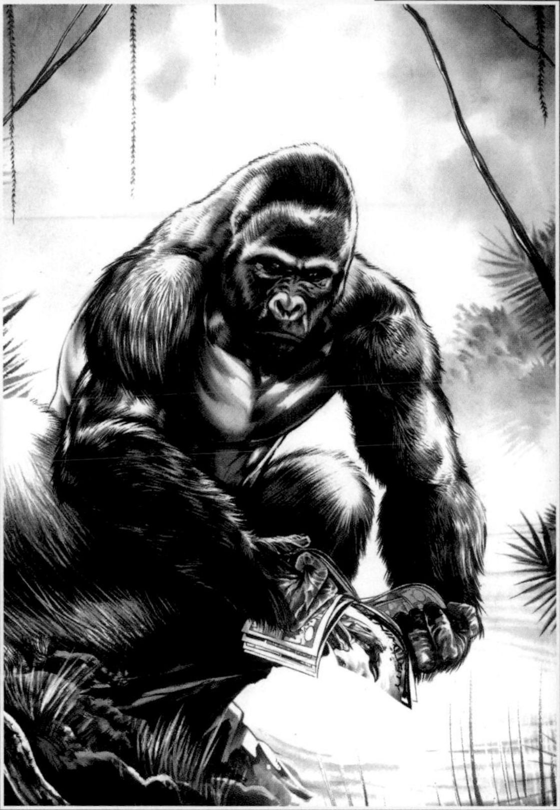

issue #3 Hip Hopf b/w variant cover
MIKE ROOTH

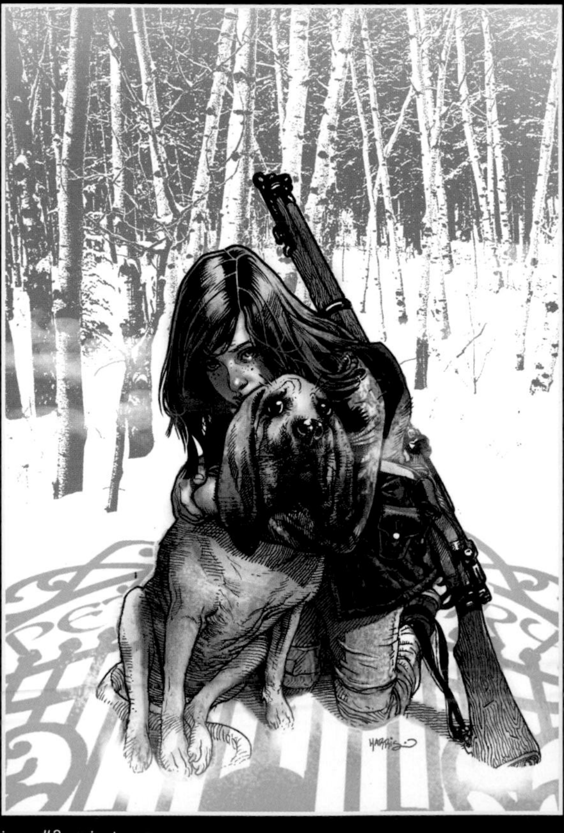

issue #3 variant cover

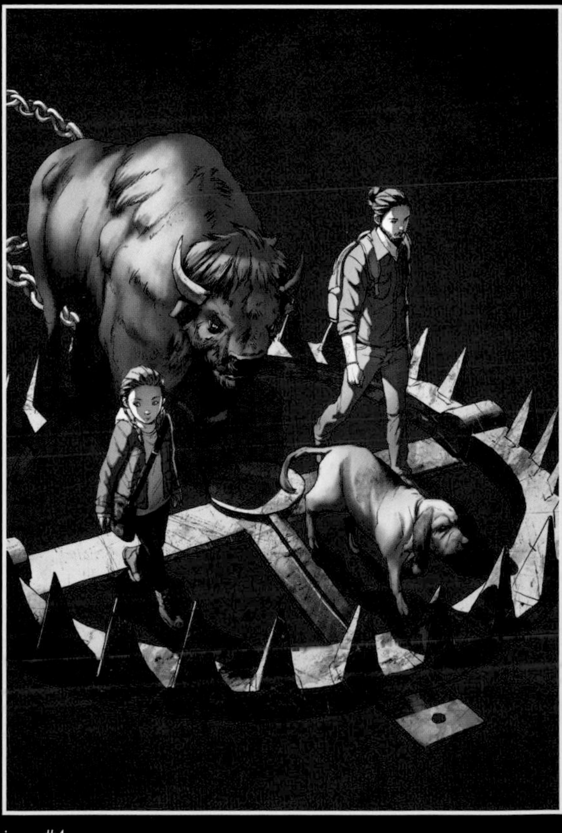

issue #4 cover

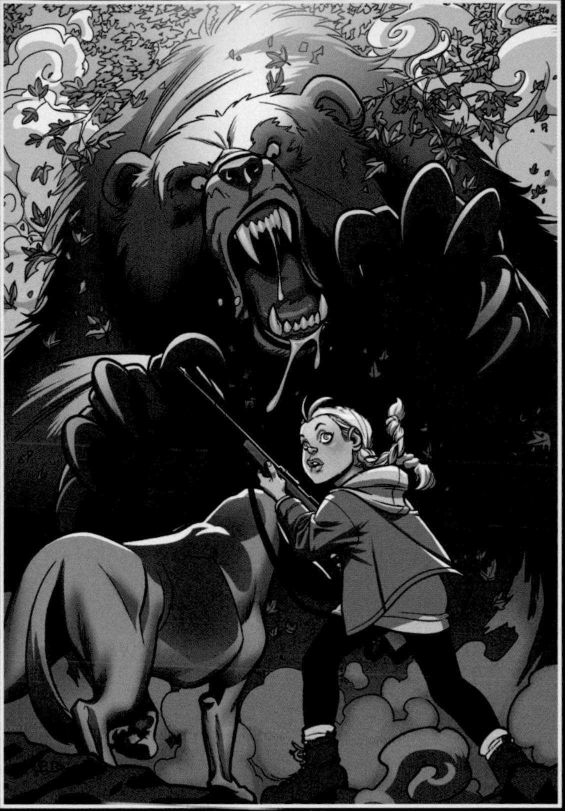

issue #4 MM Comics variant cover
KELSEY SHANNON

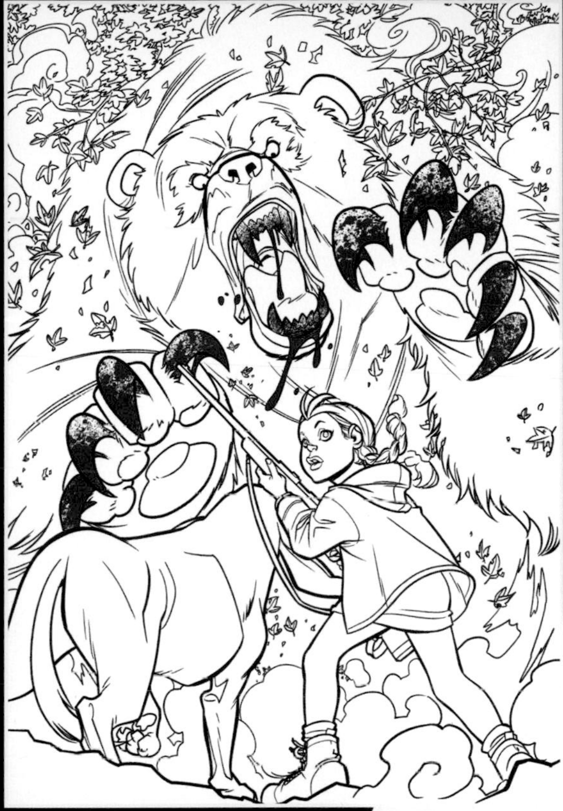

issue #4 MM Comics b/w variant cover
KELSEY SHANNON

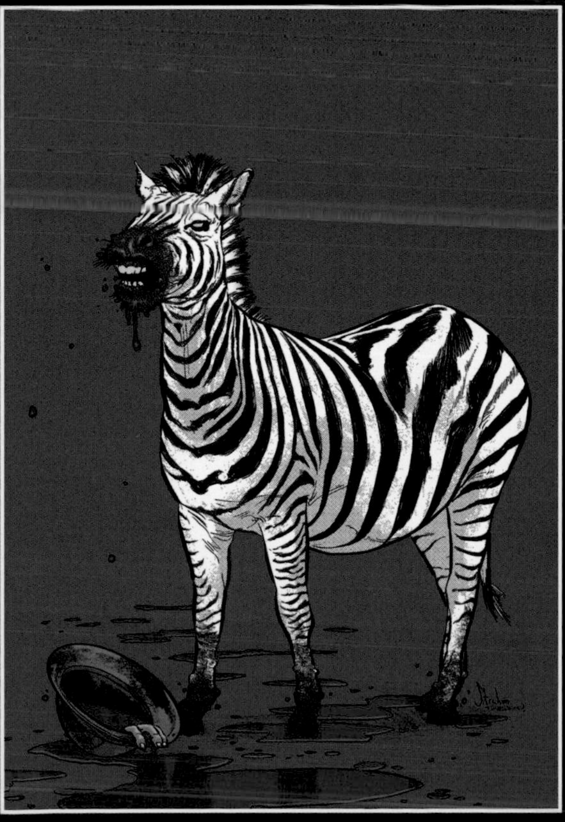

issue #4 Frankie's Comics variant cover

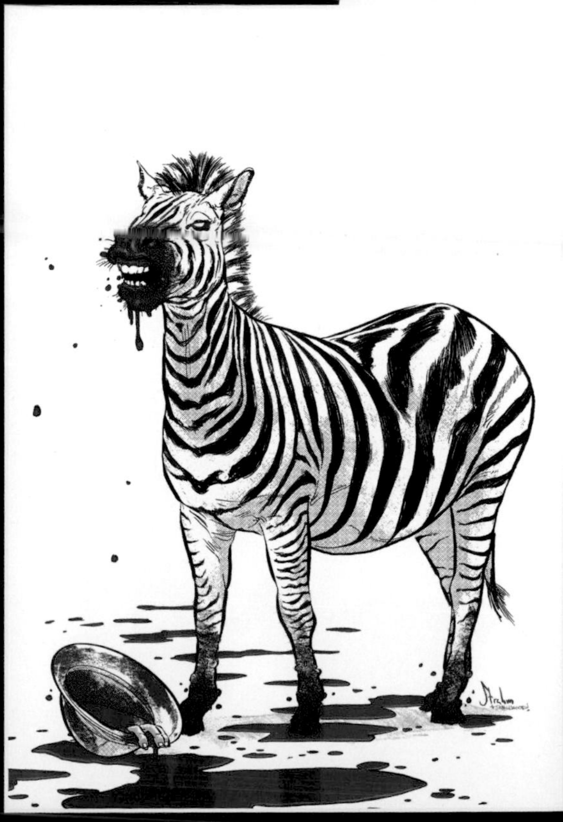

issue #4 Frankie's Comics b/w variant cover

ANIMOSITY COVER GALLERY

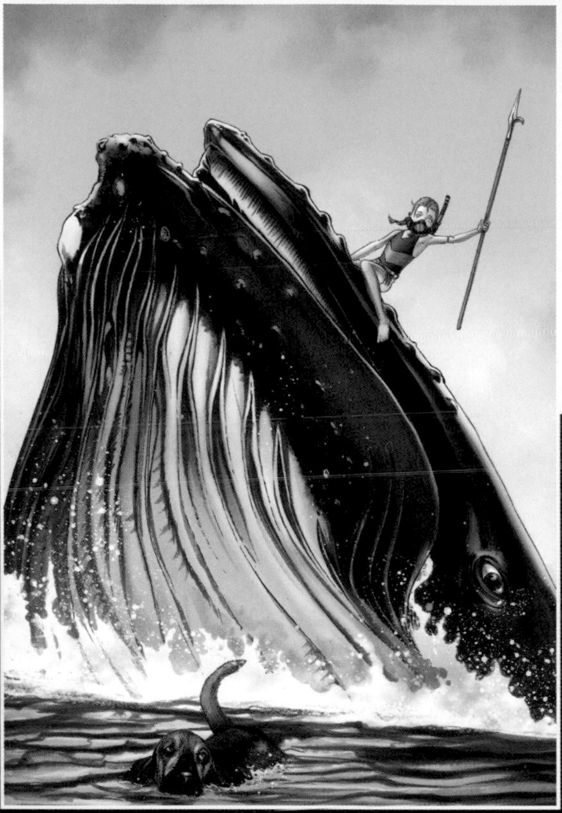

issue #4 Hip Hopf variant cover
MIKE ROOTH

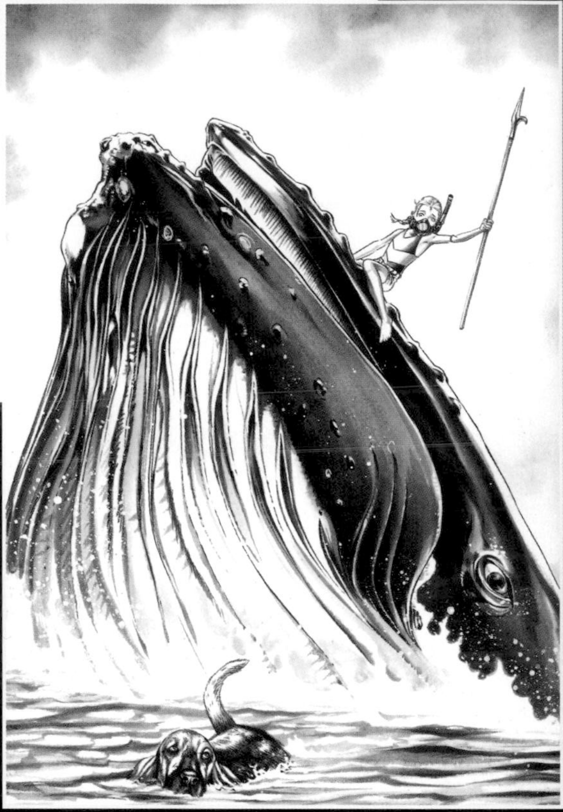

issue #4 Hip Hopf b/w variant cover
MIKE ROOTH

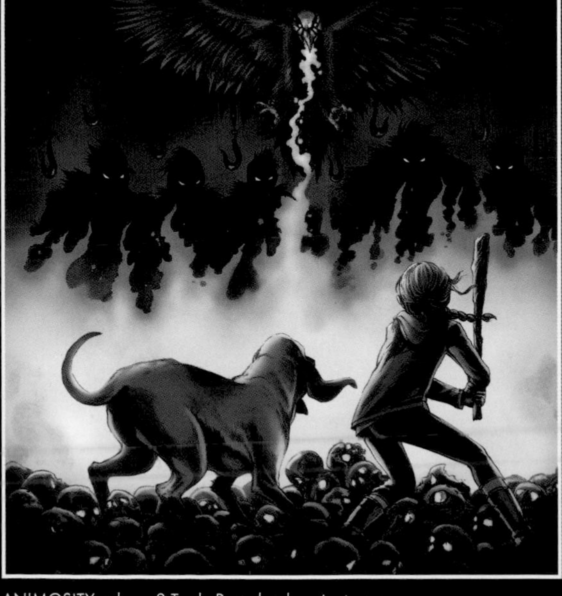

ANIMOSITY volume 2 Trade Paperback variant cover

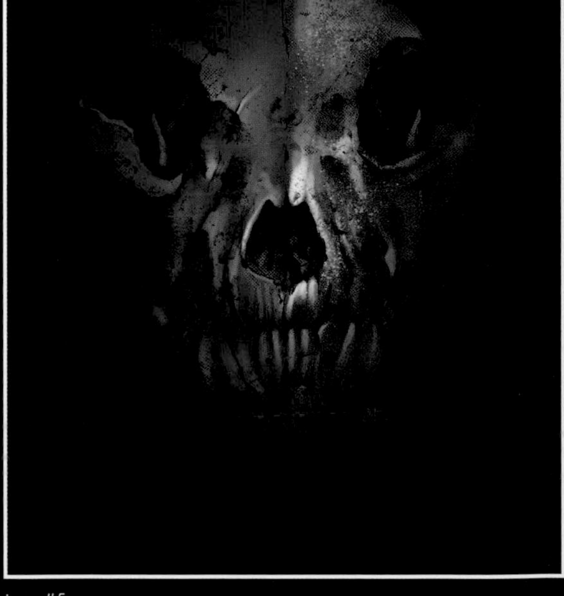

issue #5 cover

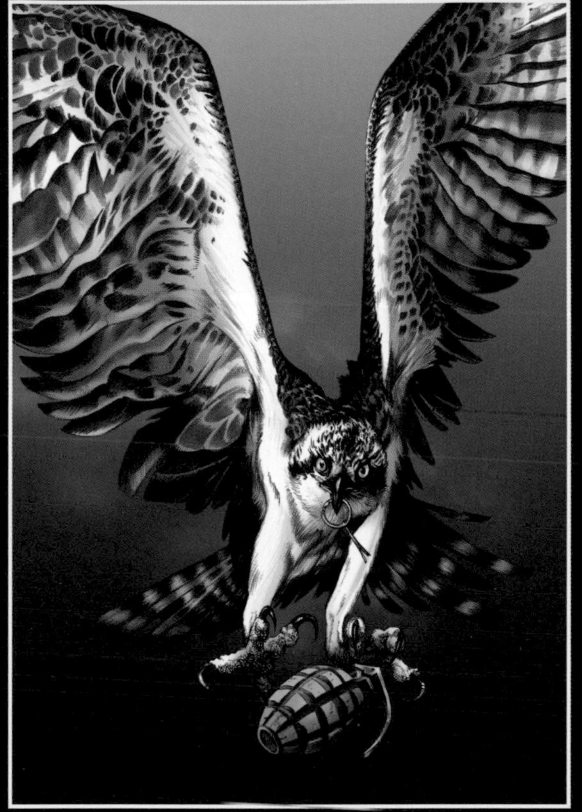

issue #5 Emerald City Comicon variant cover
MIKE ROOTH

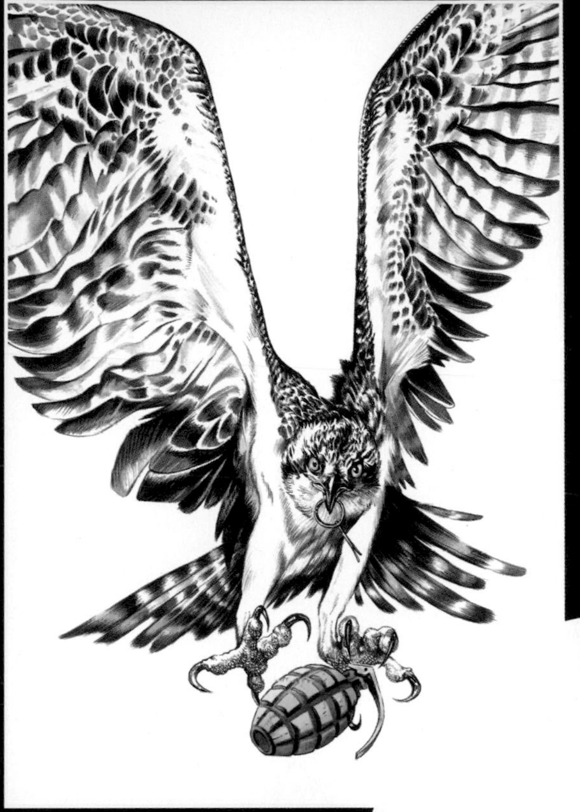

issue #5 CBCS b/w variant cover
MIKE ROOTH

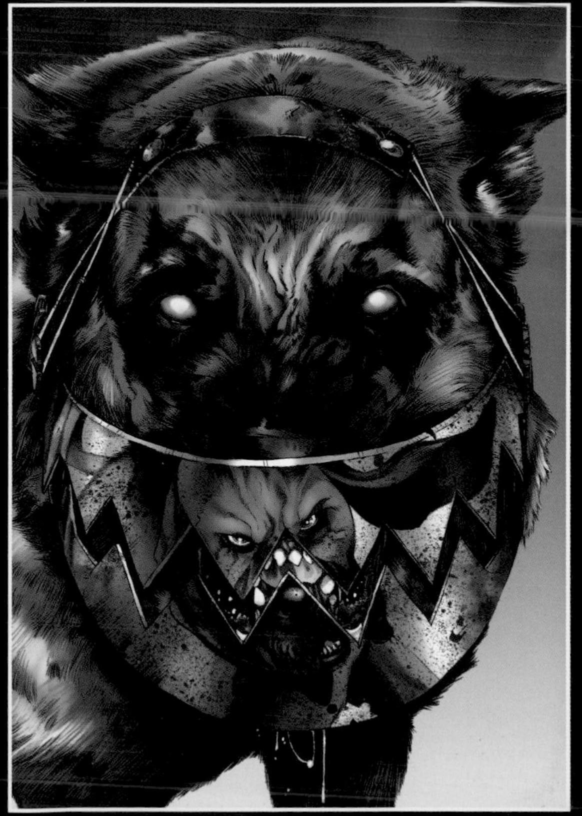

issue #5 Hip Hopf Comics variant cover

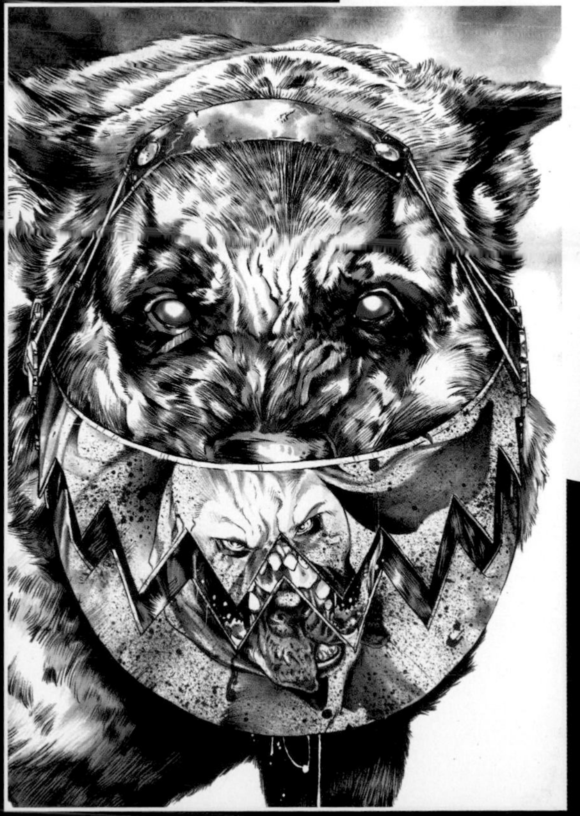

issue #5 Hip Hopf Comics b/w variant cover

ANIMOSITY COVER GALLERY

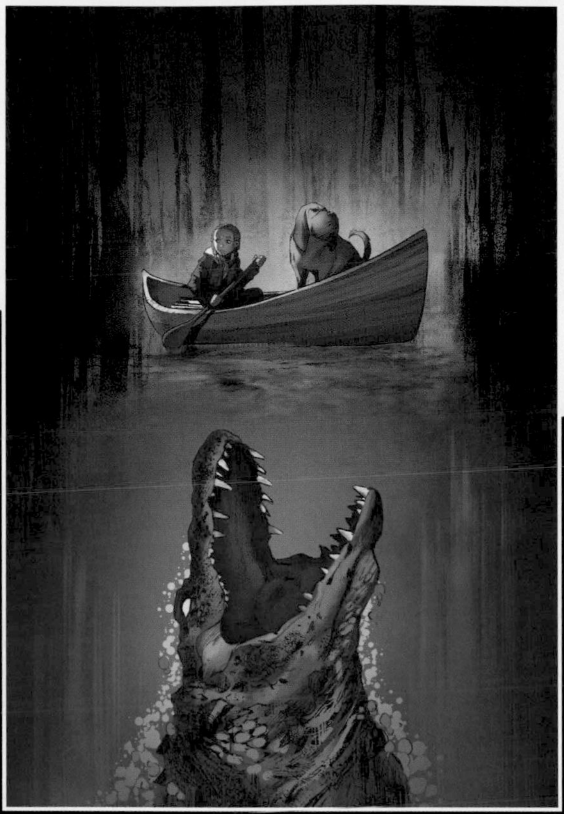

issue #6 cover
RAFAEL DE LATORRE & MARCELO MAIOLO

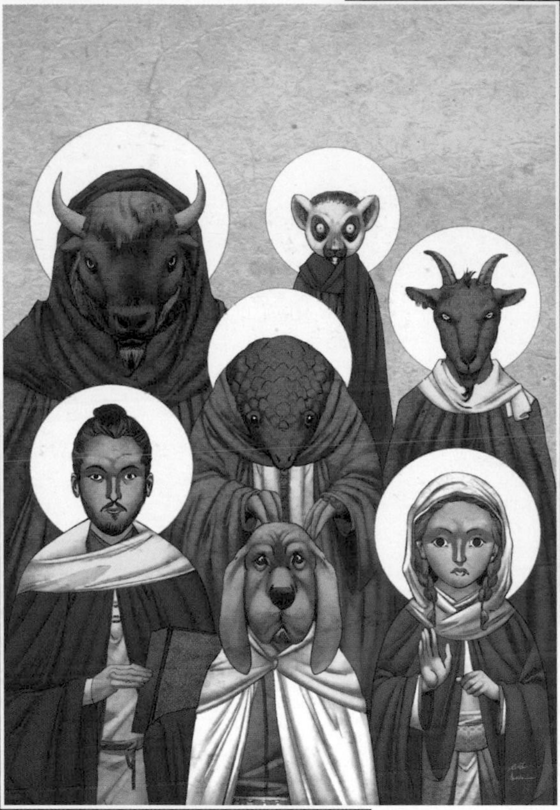

issue #7 cover
RAFAEL DE LATORRE & MARCELO MAIOLO

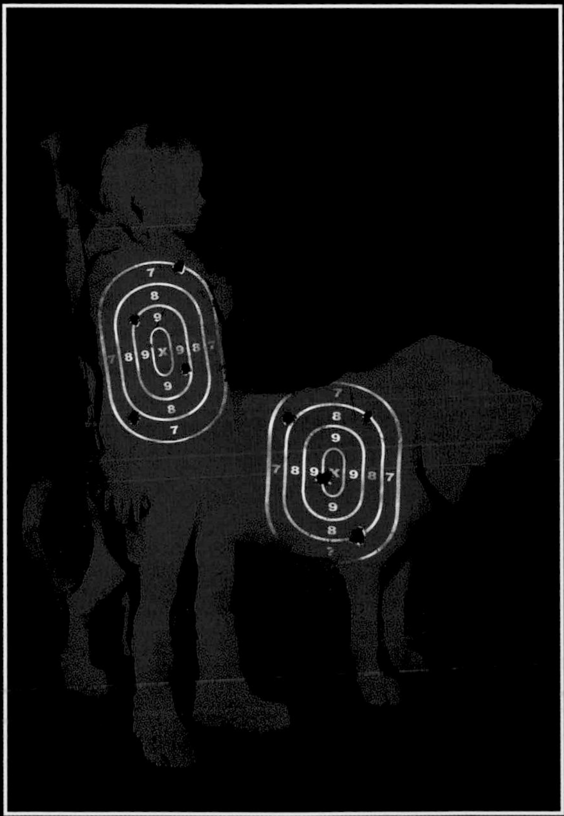

issue #8 cover
RAFAEL DE LATORRE & MARCELO MAIOLO

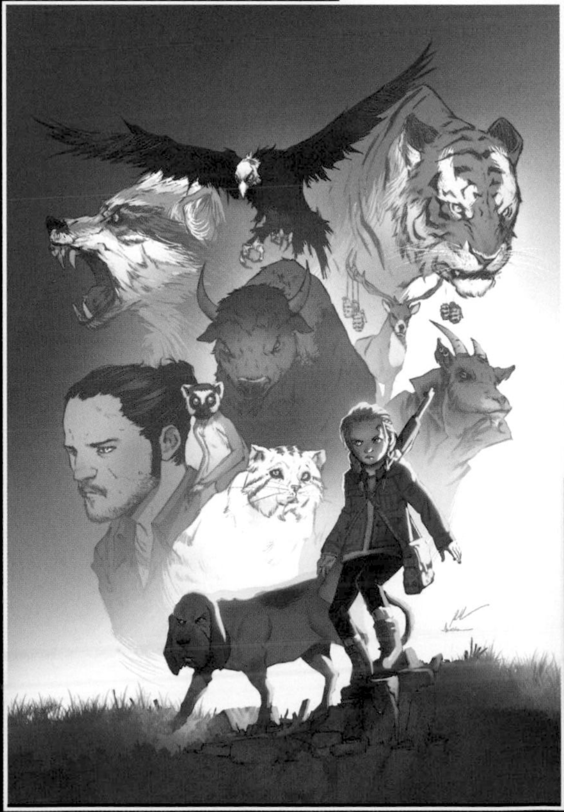

World of Animosity cover
RAFAEL DE LATORRE & MARCELO MAIOLO

ANIMOSITY CHARACTER SKETCHES

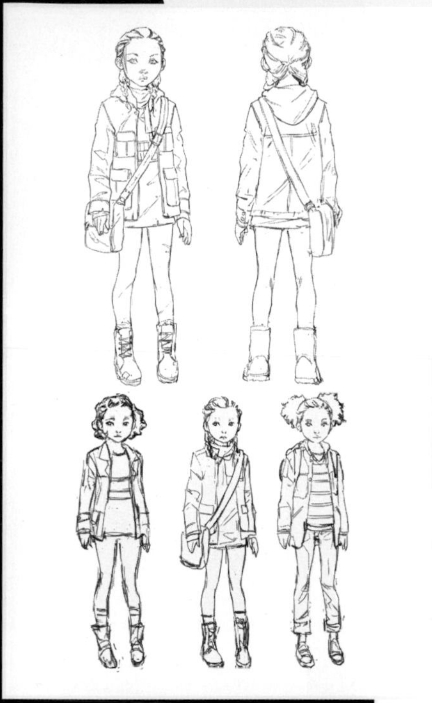

Jesse sketch

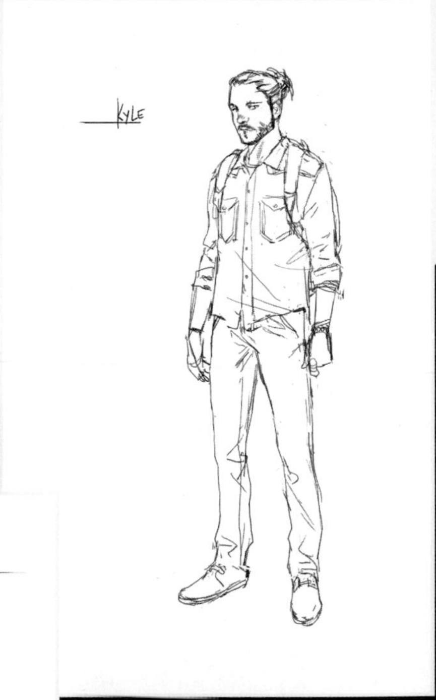
KYLE

Kyle sketch

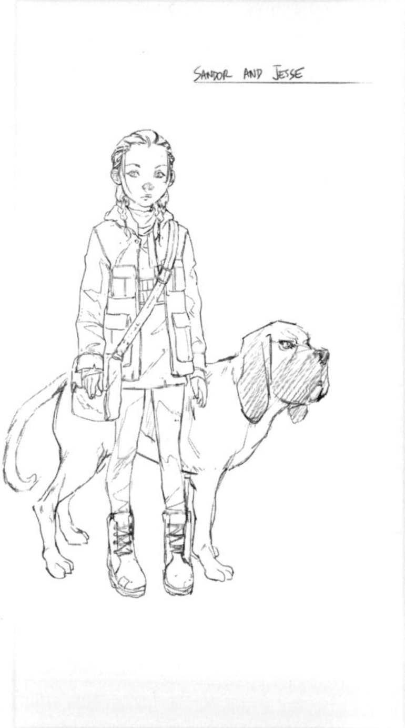
SANDOR AND JESSE

Jesse and Sandor sketch

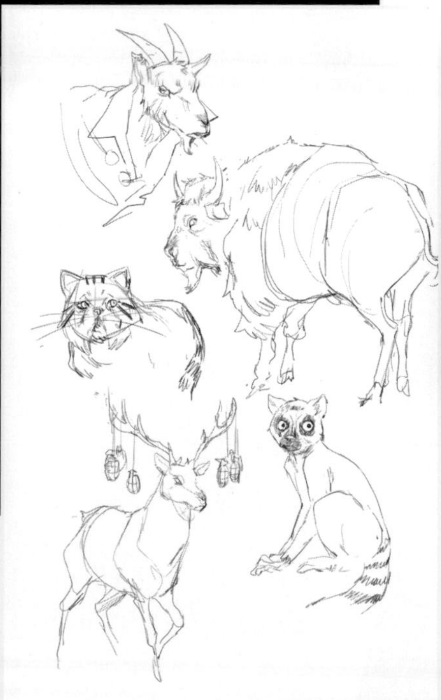

animals sketch

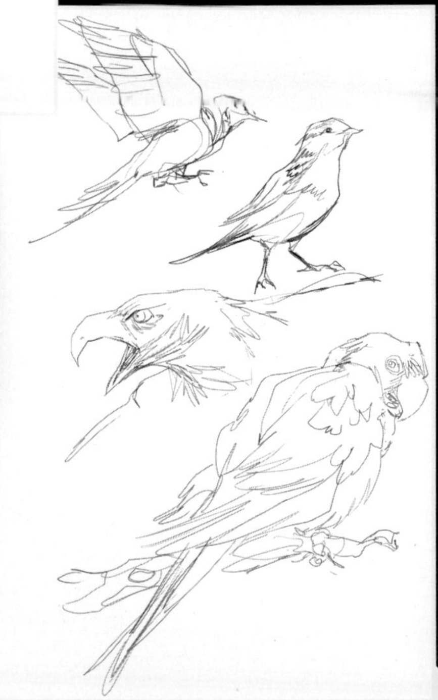

birds sketch

ANIMOSITY COVER PROCESS

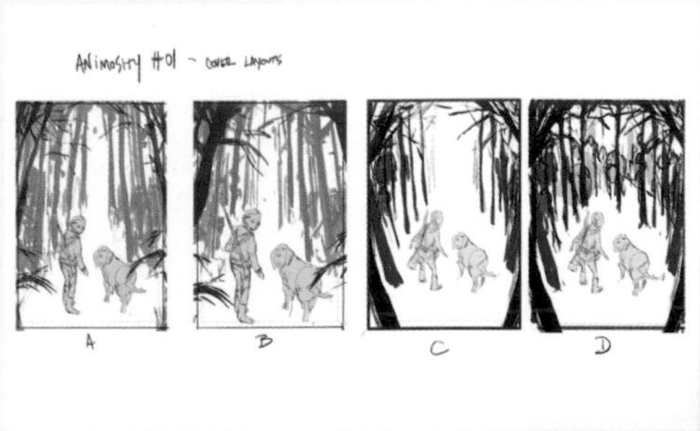
Animosity #01 – cover layouts
A
B
C
D

issue #1 cover layouts

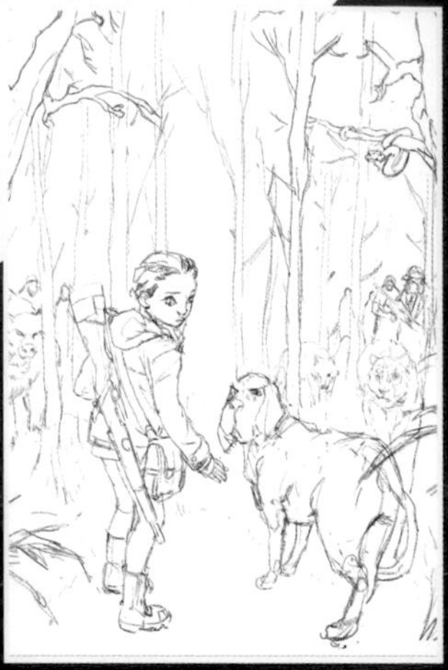

issue #1 cover pencils

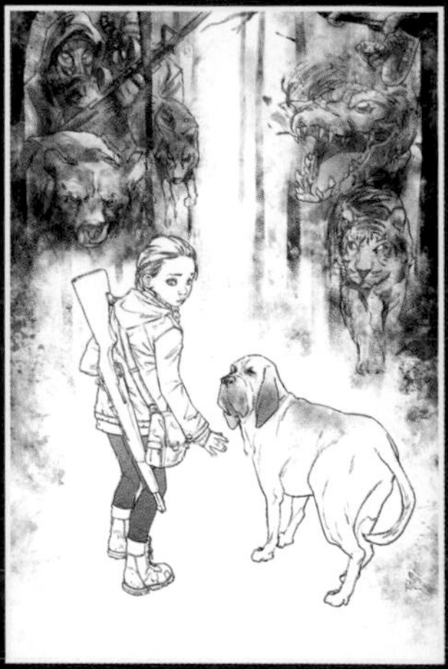

issue #1 cover inks

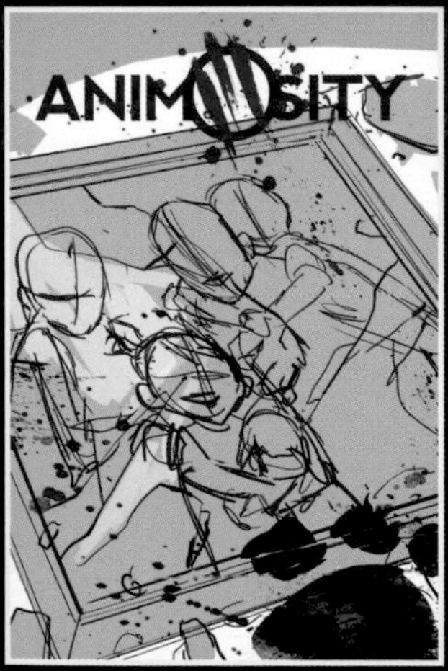
ANIMOSITY

issue #2 cover layout

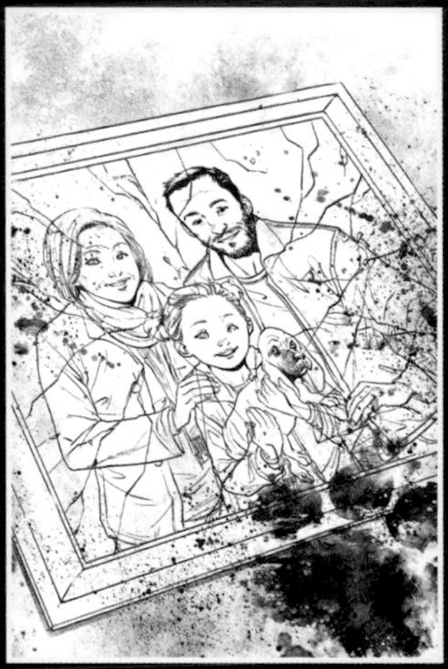

issue #2 cover inks

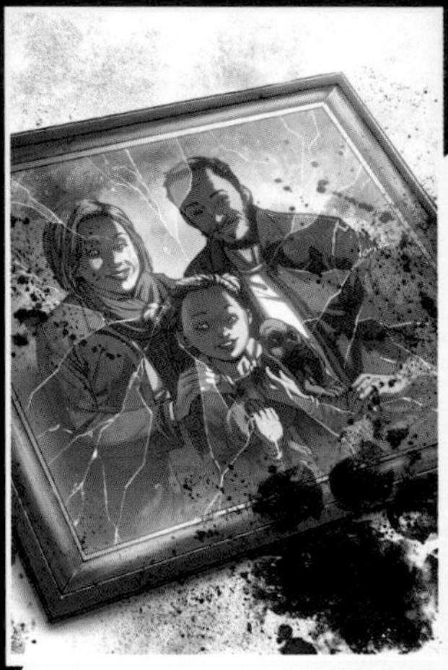

issue #2 cover color

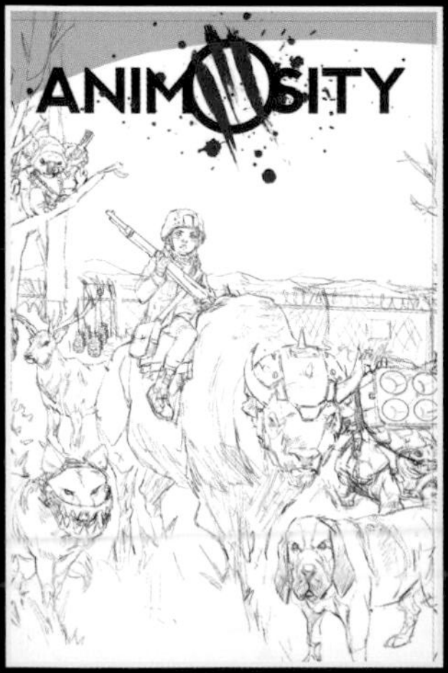
ANIMOSITY

issue #3 cover pencils

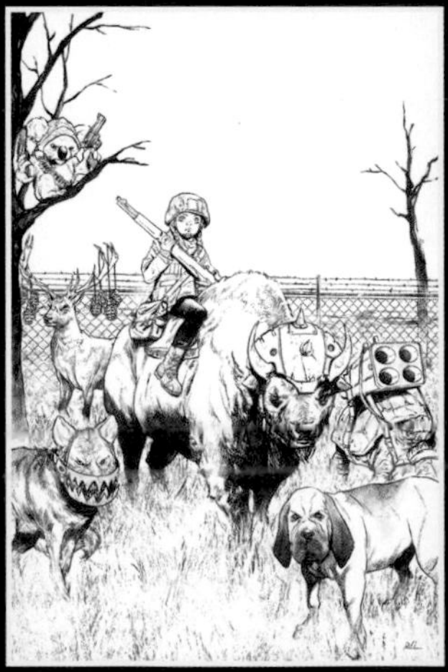

issue #3 cover inks

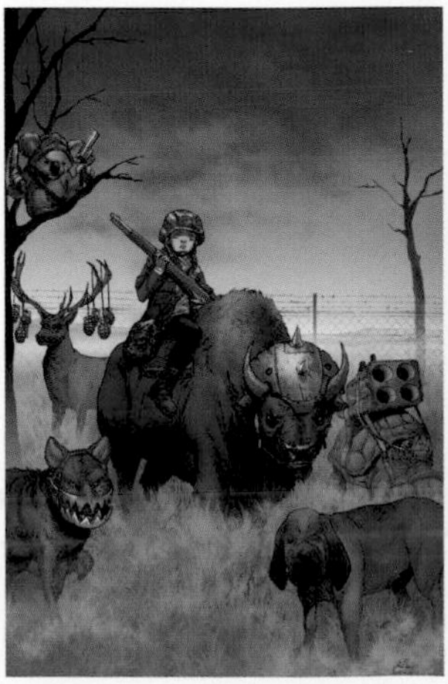

issue #3 cover color

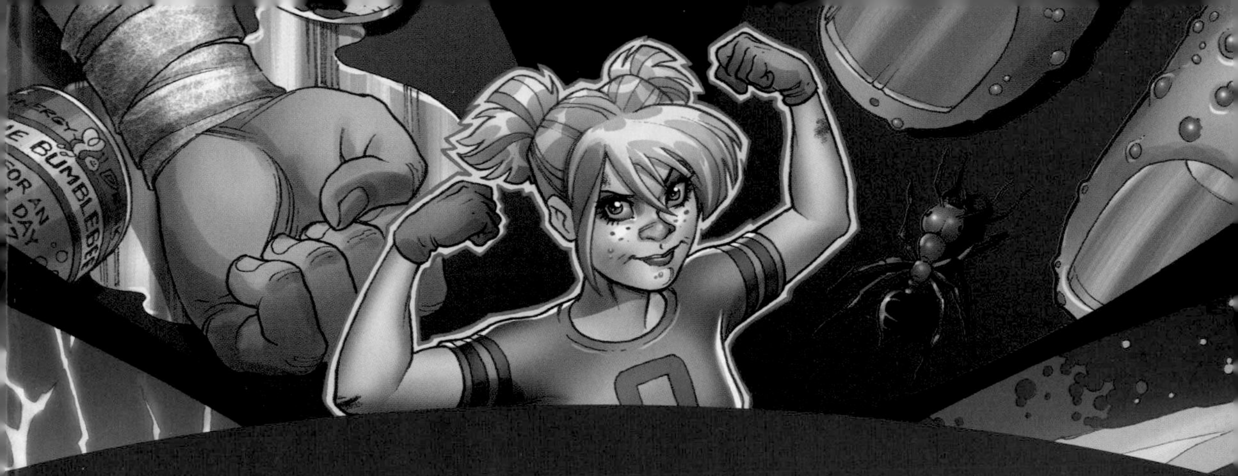

THE BUMBLEBEE
FOR AN
DAY

ABOUT THE CREATORS OF

ANIMOSITY™

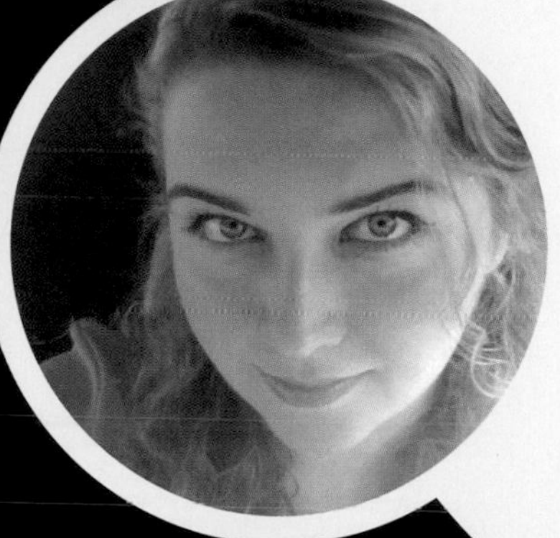

MARGUERITE BENNETT writer

@EvilMarguerite

Marguerite Bennett is a comic book writer from Richmond, Virginia, who currently splits her time between Los Angeles and New York City. She received her MFA in Creative Writing from Sarah Lawrence College in 2013 and quickly went on to work for DC Comics, Marvel, BOOM! Studios, Dynamite, and IDW on projects ranging from *Batman, Bombshells,* and *A-Force* to *Angela: Asgard's Assassin, Red Sonja,* and FOX TV's *Sleepy Hollow.*

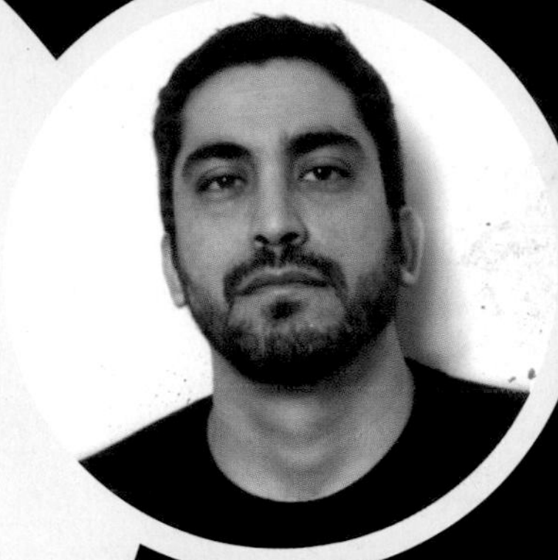

RAFAEL DE LATORRE artist

@De_Latorre

Rafael De Latorre is a Brazilian artist who has worked in illustration and advertising since 2006. His first comic book was *Fade Out: Painless Suicide,* which was nominated to the HQMix award in Brazil. He also worked on *Lost Kids: Seeking Samarkand* and *321: Fast Comics.*

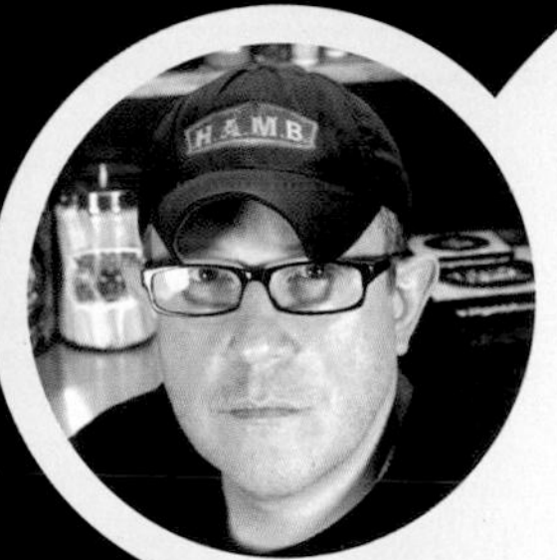

ROB SCHWAGER colorist

@robschwager

Rob Schwager is a self taught artist with over twenty-five years experience as a colorist in the comic book industry. He's worked on such iconic titles as *Batman, Superman, Green Lantern, Jonah Hex, Ghost Rider, Deadpool, Spider-Man, X-Men* and many others. He currently resides in the Tampa Bay area with his wife and three children and is extremely excited to be part of the AfterShock family of creators.

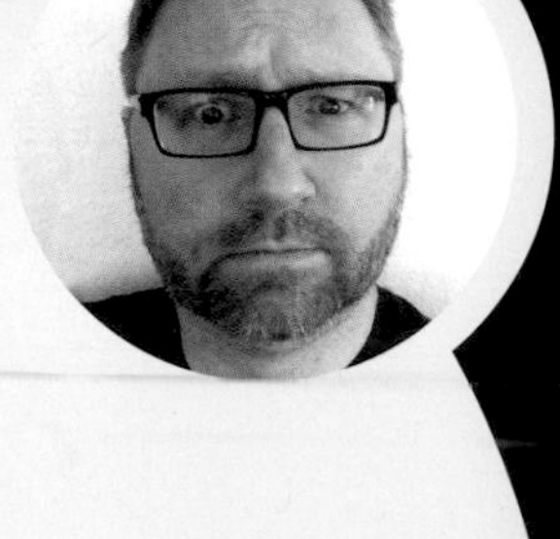

MARSHALL DILLON letterer

@MarshallDillon

A comic book industry veteran, Marshall got his start in 1994, in the midst of the indy comic boom. Over the years, he's been everything from an independent self-published writer to an associate publisher working on properties like *G.I.Joe, Voltron,* and *Street Fighter.* He's done just about everything except draw a comic book, and worked for just about every publisher except the "big two." Primarily a father and letterer these days, he also dabbles in old-school paper and dice RPG game design. You can catch up with Marshall at firstdraftpress.net.